CAMBRIDGE TEXTS IN THE
HISTORY OF PHILOSOPHY

HERDER
Philosophical Writings

Test Question
Herder thinks tha'

Howtoapplyto
Graduate School
w/out really
lying

22
megan's
b-day

CAMBRIDGE TEXTS IN THE HISTORY OF PHILOSOPHY

Series editors

KARL AMERIKS
Professor of Philosophy at the University of Notre Dame

DESMOND M. CLARKE
Professor of Philosophy at University College Cork

The main objective of Cambridge Texts in the History of Philosophy is to expand the range, variety and quality of texts in the history of philosophy which are available in English. The series includes texts by familiar names (such as Descartes and Kant) and also by less well-known authors. Wherever possible, texts are published in complete and unabridged form, and translations are specially commissioned for the series. Each volume contains a critical introduction together with a guide to further reading and any necessary glossaries and textual apparatus. The volumes are designed for student use at undergraduate and postgraduate level and will be of interest not only to students of philosophy, but also to a wider audience of readers in the history of science, the history of theology and the history of ideas.

For a list of titles published in the series, please see end of book.

JOHANN GOTTFRIED VON HERDER

Philosophical Writings

TRANSLATED AND EDITED BY

MICHAEL N. FORSTER

University of Chicago

CAMBRIDGE
UNIVERSITY PRESS

PUBLISHED BY THE PRESS SYNDICATE OF THE UNIVERSITY OF CAMBRIDGE
The Pitt Building, Trumpington Street, Cambridge, United Kingdom

CAMBRIDGE UNIVERSITY PRESS
The Edinburgh Building, Cambridge CB2 2RU, UK
40 West 20th Street, New York, NY 10011-4211, USA
477 Williamstown Road, Port Melbourne, VIC 3207 Australia
Ruiz de Alarcón 13, 28014 Madrid, Spain
Dock House, The Waterfront, Cape Town 8001, South Africa

http://www.cambridge.org

First published 2002

Typeface Ehrhardt 11/13   *System* LaTeX 2$_\varepsilon$ [TB]

A catalogue record for this book is available from the British Library

Library of Congress Cataloguing in Publication data

Herder, Johann Gottfried, 1744–1803
[Selections. English. 2002]
Johann Gottfried von Herder: Philosophical Writings / translated and edited by
Michael N. Forster.
p.   cm. – (Cambridge Texts in the History of Philosophy)
Includes bibliographical references and index.
ISBN 0 521 79088 3 – ISBN 0 521 79409 9 (pbk.)
1. Philosophy, German – 18th century.   I. Title: Philosophical Writings.
II. Forster, Michael N.   III. Title.   IV. Series.
B3051.A35 F6713   2002
193 – dc21   2001052973

ISBN 0 521 79088 3 hardback
ISBN 0 521 79409 9 paperback

Transferred to digital printing 2003

Sources of light
= time in Greece The Neoplatoians? Plato + Socrates
= German Idealism
Kant Hegel Herder Schelling

Kant thinks that all people think the same way, ethics are universal. what counts is good reason. Language has no connection with thought...

Herder v.s. Kant

→ Herder is Kant's student
Herder later disagrees with Kant...

thought vs the ability to express thought. can't really measure thought

Kant just assumes all of this...

Milton

Contents

When things are just wonderful

different languages have different limitations

Herder challenges all of this by saying that language is connected with thought. The language one has conditions how + what people think... Language sets the limits to what we can think...

same non-linguistic thought...

Hegel very hard

language is what makes us think, what makes us human...

language is a product of a people... and the language creates the people.

v

Arthon community w/o individual w/o "I" thought

coherent

thought is only thought to the extent that it could be put into language...

thought is still evolving because language is still evolving.

Contents

Introduction

Herder is a philosopher of the very first rank. Such a claim depends mainly on the intrinsic quality of his ideas, and I shall attempt to give a sense of that in what follows. But another aspect of it is his intellectual influence. This has been immense both within philosophy and beyond (far greater than is generally realized). For example, Hegel's philosophy turns out to be an elaborate systematic extension of Herderian ideas (especially concerning God, the mind, and history); so too does Schleiermacher's (concerning God, the mind, interpretation, translation, and art); Nietzsche is strongly influenced by Herder (concerning the mind, history, and morals); so too is Dilthey (in his theory of the human sciences); J. S. Mill has important debts to Herder (in political philosophy); Goethe not only received his philosophical outlook from Herder but was also transformed from being merely a clever but conventional poet into a great artist mainly through the early impact on him of Herder's ideas; and this list could go on.

Indeed, Herder can claim to have virtually established whole disciplines which we nowadays take for granted. For example, it was mainly Herder (not, as is often claimed, Hamann) who established certain fundamental principles concerning an intimate dependence of thought on language which underpin modern philosophy of language. Through those ideas, his broad empirical approach to languages, his recognition of deep variations in language and thought across historical periods and cultures, and in other ways, Herder inspired Wilhelm von Humboldt to found modern linguistics. Herder developed modern hermeneutics, or interpretation theory, into a form that would subsequently be taken over by Schleiermacher and then more systematically articulated by Schleiermacher's pupil Böckh. In doing that, he also established the methodological foundations of

[handwritten margin notes: "intrinsic qualities of ideas", "has much influence in the field", "dependence of thought on language"]

nineteenth-century German classical scholarship (which rested on the Schleiermacher-Böckh methodology), and hence of modern classical scholarship generally. Herder arguably did more than anyone else to establish the general conception and the interpretative methodology of our modern discipline of anthropology. Finally, Herder also made vital contributions to the progress of modern biblical scholarship (not only developing general hermeneutics, but also, for example, defining the genres of Old Testament poetry more adequately than had been done before, eliminating the bane of allegorical interpretations of Old Testament texts such as the Song of Solomon, and establishing the correct chronology of the four gospels of the New Testament).

The aim of the present volume is to make texts by Herder[1] in core areas of philosophy available to Anglophone readers so that his quality and influence as a philosopher can be studied.[2] To this end, the volume focuses mainly on earlier works. Herder writes in an essay here that "the first, uninhibited work of an author is . . . usually his best; his bloom is unfolding, his soul still dawn."[3] Whether or not that is *generally* true, it certainly applies to Herder himself, whose earlier writings do indeed tend to be his best. This fact, together with their other notable virtue of brevity, motivated this volume's concentration on them.

Reading Herder: some preliminaries

In certain ways Herder's philosophical texts are easier to read than others from the period. For example, he avoids technical jargon, his writing is lively and rich in examples rather than dry and abstract, and he has no large, complex system for the reader to keep track of. But his texts also have certain compensating peculiarities which can cause misunderstanding and misgiving, and which require explanation.

---

[1] Two editions of Herder's works have been used for this volume: U. Gaier et al. (eds.), *Johann Gottfried Herder Werke* (Frankfurt am Main, 1985–); B. Suphan et al. (eds.), *Johann Gottfried Herder Sämtliche Werke* (Berlin, 1887–). References to these editions take the form of the primary editor's surname initial followed by volume number and page number (e.g. G2:321 or S5:261).

[2] Two areas have been omitted (except insofar as they are touched on in passing) in order to keep the scale of the volume reasonable: Herder's philosophy of religion (very important for questions of influence, but less intrinsically relevant given modern philosophy's secular sensibilities) and his aesthetics (philosophically fascinating, but perhaps less fundamental, and also unmanageably extensive).

[3] *On the Cognition and Sensation of the Human Soul* (1778). After a first occurrence most titles will be abbreviated in this introduction.

First of all, Herder's writing often seems emotional and grammatically undisciplined in a way that might perhaps be expected in casual speech but not in philosophical texts. This is intentional. Indeed, Herder sometimes deliberately "roughed up" material in this direction between drafts (e.g. between the 1775 and 1778 drafts of *On the Cognition*). Also, when writing in this way he is often using grammatical-rhetorical figures which, though they can strike an untutored eye as mere carelessness, receive high literary sanction from classical sources and are employed artfully (e.g. anacoluthon, aposiopesis, brachylogy, chiasmus, hendiadys, oxymoron, and hysteron proteron).[4] Moreover, he has several serious philosophical reasons for writing in this way rather than in the manner of conventional academic prose. First, this promises to make his writing more broadly accessible and interesting to people – a decidedly nontrivial goal for him, since he believes it to be an essential part of philosophy's vocation to have a broad social impact. Second, one of his central theses in the philosophy of mind holds that thought is not and should not be separate from volition, or affect; that types of thinking which aspire to exclude affect are inherently distorting and inferior. Standard academic writing has this vice, but spontaneous speech, and writing which approximates it, do not. Third, Herder is opposed to any grammatical or lexical strait-jacketing of language, any slavish obedience to grammar books and dictionaries (he would be critical of such institutions as Duden in Germany and the *Chicago Manual of Style* in the USA). In his view, such strait-jacketing is inimical, not only to linguistic creativity and inventiveness, but also (much worse), because thought is essentially dependent on and confined in its scope by language, thereby to creativity and inventiveness in thought itself.

Another peculiarity of Herder's philosophical writing is its unsystematic nature. This is again deliberate, for Herder is largely hostile towards systematicity in philosophy (a fact reflected both in explicit remarks and in many of his titles: *Fragments . . .*, *Ideas . . .*, etc.). He is in particular hostile to the very ambitious type of systematicity aspired to in the tradition of Spinoza, Wolff, Kant, Fichte, Schelling, and Hegel: a theory whose parts form and exhaust some sort of strict overall pattern of derivation. Moreover, he has compelling reasons for this hostility. First, he is very skeptical that such systematic designs can be made to work (as opposed

---

[4] I have indicated some examples of such figures as they occur in the translation.

to creating, through illicit means, an illusion that they do). Second, he believes that such system-building leads to a premature closure of inquiry, and in particular to a disregarding or distorting of new empirical evidence. Scrutiny of such systems amply bears out these misgivings. Herder's well-grounded hostility to this type of systematicity established an important countertradition in German philosophy (which subsequently included, for example, Friedrich Schlegel, Nietzsche, and Wittgenstein).

On the other hand, Herder is in *favor* of "systematicity" in a more modest sense: a theory which is self-consistent and maximally supported by argument.[5] He does not always achieve this ideal (so that interpreting him calls for more selectivity and reconstruction than is the case with some philosophers).[6] But his failures are often only apparent: First, in many cases where he seems to be guilty of inconsistency he really is not, for he is often developing philosophical dialogues between two or more opposing viewpoints, in which cases it would clearly be a mistake to accuse him of inconsistency in any usual or pejorative sense; and (less obviously) in other cases he is in effect still working in this dialogue mode, only without bothering to distribute the positions among different interlocutors explicitly, and so is again really innocent of inconsistency (examples of this occur in *How Philosophy Can Become More Universal and Useful for the Benefit of the People* [1765] and *This Too a Philosophy of History for the Formation of Humanity* [1774]). Moreover, he has serious motives for this method of (implicit) dialogue. Sometimes his motive is simply that when dealing with religiously or politically delicate matters it permits him to state his views but without quite stating them as his own and therefore without inviting trouble. But there are also philosophically deeper motives: He takes over from the precritical Kant an idea (inspired by ancient skepticism) that the best way for a philosopher to pursue the truth is by setting contrary views on a subject into opposition with one another and advancing towards the truth through their mutual testing and modification. Also, he develops an original variant of that idea on the sociohistorical plane: analogously, the way for humankind as a whole to attain the elusive goal of truth is through an ongoing contest between opposing positions,

---

[5] This marks an important point of methodological contrast with Hamann, whom Herder already criticizes for failing to provide arguments in an essay from early 1765 (G1:38–9).

[6] In this connection, Charles Taylor wisely comments that "deeply innovative thinkers don't have to be rigorous to be the originators of important ideas" ("The Importance of Herder," in E. and A. Margalit [eds.], *Isaiah Berlin: A Celebration* [Chicago, 1991]). The converse holds as well: thinkers can be very rigorous without originating any important ideas.

in the course of which the best ones will eventually win out (this idea anticipates, and inspired, a central thesis of J. S. Mill's *On Liberty*). This yields a further motive for the dialogue method (even where it does not lead Herder himself to any definite conclusion), in effect warranting the rhetorical question: And what does it matter to the cause of humankind and its discovery of the truth whether those opposing positions are advanced by different people or by the *same* person? Second, Herder's appearance of neglecting to give arguments is often, rather, a principled rejection of arguments *of certain sorts*. For example (as we are about to see), he has a general commitment to empiricism and against apriorism in philosophy which leads him to avoid familiar sorts of apriorist arguments in philosophy; and a commitment to noncognitivism in ethics which leads him to refrain from familiar sorts of cognitivist arguments in ethics.

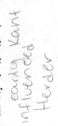

(margin annotations: does it matter that the discovery of truth (& its opposing sides) are advanced by different people or the same person? — want why does he not given certain arguments — early Kant influenced Herder)*

Herder's general program in philosophy

Hamann's influence on Herder's best thought has often been greatly exaggerated, but Kant's was early, fundamental, and enduring. However, the Kant who influenced Herder in this way was the precritical Kant of the early and middle 1760s, not the critical Kant (against whom Herder later engaged in distracting and rather ineffective public polemics). Some of Kant's key positions in the 1760s, sharply contrasting with those he would later adopt in the critical period, were a (Pyrrhonist-influenced) skepticism about metaphysics, a form of empiricism, and a (Hume-influenced) noncognitivism in ethics. Herder took over these positions in the 1760s and retained them throughout his career.[7]

Herder's 1765 essay *How Philosophy Can Become*, rough and fragmentary as it is, is a key for understanding the broad foundations of his philosophy, and the debts these owe to the precritical Kant of the early and middle 1760s. The essay was written under strong influence from Kant, and especially, it seems, Kant's 1766 essay *Dreams of a Spirit Seer*, which, Herder reports, Kant sent him before publication "a sheet at a time."

---

[7] It should by no means be inferred that Herder's debt to the *precritical* Kant is a debt to an *inferior* Kant. On the contrary, for all their greater novelty, systematicity, and fascination for professional philosophers, Kant's contrary later positions in the critical period – for example, that a noumenal freedom of the will, afterlife of the soul, and God must be believed in as presuppositions of morality; that much in natural science and philosophy can be known completely a priori; and that morality rests on a single principle analogous in character to the logical law of contradiction, the "categorical imperative" – are ultimately far less philosophically defensible than the precritical positions just mentioned.

[handwritten margin notes: answers how truths of philo. be more useful]

Herder's essay answers a prize question set by a society in Berne: "How can the truths of philosophy become more universal and useful for the benefit of the people?" This question is in the spirit of the *Popularphilosophie* that was competing with school philosophy at the time. Kant himself tended to identify with *Popularphilosophie* at this period, albeit only transiently, and Herder's selection of this question shows him doing so as well, though in his case the identification would last a lifetime. Philosophy should become relevant and useful for people as a whole – this is a basic ideal of Herder's philosophy.

[handwritten margin note: philosophy should be relevant]

Largely in the service of this ideal, Herder argues in the essay for two sharp turns in philosophy, turns which would again remain fundamental throughout his career. The first involves a rejection of traditional metaphysics, and closely follows an argument of Kant's in *Dreams of a Spirit Seer*. Herder's case is roughly this: First, traditional metaphysics, by undertaking to transcend experience (or strictly, and a little more broadly, "healthy understanding," which includes, besides empirical knowledge, also ordinary morality, intuitive logic, and mathematics), succumbs to unresolvable contradictions between its claims, and hence to the Pyrrhonian skeptical problem of an equal plausibility on both sides requiring suspension of judgment ("I am writing for Pyrrhonists"). Also (Herder adds in the *Fragments on Recent German Literature* [1767–8]), given the truth of a broadly empiricist theory of concepts, much terminology of traditional metaphysics turns out to lack the basis in experience that it would need in order even to be meaningful, and hence is meaningless (the illusion of meaningfulness arising largely through the role of *language*, which spins on, creating illusions of meaning, even after the empirical conditions of meaning have been left behind).[8] Second, traditional metaphysics is not only, for these reasons, useless; it is also *harmful*, because it distracts its adherents from the matters which should be their focus: empirical nature and human society. Third, by contrast, empirical knowledge (or strictly, and a bit more broadly, "healthy understanding") is free of these problems. Philosophy ought therefore to be based on and continuous with this.

[handwritten margin notes: 1. rejection of traditional metaphysics 2. metaphysics is also harmful 3. empirical knowledge is better than metaphysics]

Herder's second sharp turn concerns moral philosophy. He remains indebted to Kant here, but also goes further beyond him. Herder's basic claims are these: (1) Morality is fundamentally more a matter of sentiments

---

[8] This diagnosis in terms of language seems to go beyond the precritical Kant. However, it has deep precedents and roots in the empiricist tradition – especially Bacon and Locke.

than of cognitions.[9] (Herder's sentimentalism is not crude, however; in the *Critical Forests* [1769] and *On the Cognition* he acknowledges that cognition plays a large role in morality as well.) (2) Cognitivist theories of morality – espoused in this period especially by Rationalists such as Wolff, but also by many other philosophers before and since (e.g. Plato and the critical Kant) – are therefore based on a mistake, and hence useless as means of moral enlightenment or improvement. (3) But (and here Herder's theory moves beyond Kant's), worse than that, they are actually *harmful* to morality, because they weaken the moral sentiments on which it really rests. In *This Too* and *On the Cognition* Herder suggests several reasons why. First, abstract theorizing weakens the sentiments generally, and hence moral ones in particular. Second, the cognitivists' theories turn out to be so *strikingly* implausible that they bring morality itself into disrepute, people reacting to them roughly along the lines: "If this is the best that even the experts can say in explanation and justification of morality, morality must certainly be a sham, and I may as well ignore it and do as I please." Third, such theories distract people from recognizing and working to reinforce the *real* foundations of morality: not an imaginary theoretical insight of some sort, but a set of causal means for inculcating moral sentiments. (4) More positively, Herder accordingly turns instead to determining in theory and promoting in practice just such a set of causal means. In *How Philosophy Can Become* he stresses forms of education and an emotive type of preaching (two lifelong preoccupations of his in both theory and practice). Elsewhere he adds exposure to morally exemplary individuals, morally relevant laws, and literature (along with other art forms). Literature is a special focus of Herder's theory and practice. He sees it as exerting moral influence in several ways – not only through relatively direct moral instruction, but also through the literary perpetuation or creation of morally exemplary individuals (e.g. Jesus in the New Testament) and the exposure of readers to other people's inner lives and a consequent enhancement of their sympathies for them (a motive behind his publication of the *Popular Songs* [1778–9] from peoples around the world). Herder's

---

[9] Hume had provided a compelling (though not uncontested) argument for this position in terms of morality's intrinsic motivating force and cognition's motivational inertness. The precritical Kant was evidently influenced by this argument, and there are indications in *This Too* that Herder was as well.

development of this theory and practice of moral pedagogy was lifelong and tireless.

Herder's philosophy of language

The materials in the present volume relevant to this topic include not only those in the philosophy of language section but also those in the philosophy of mind and history sections.

The *Treatise on the Origin of Language* (1772) is Herder's best-known work on language. It is mainly concerned with the question whether the origin of language must be accounted for in terms of a divine source (as Süßmilch had recently argued) or in purely natural, human terms. Herder argues against the former view and for the latter. His motives are not strictly secular. Rather, he is assuming a position from Kant's *Universal Natural History and Theory of the Heavens* (1755) that explanations in terms of natural laws are not only explanatorily superior to, but also *ultimately better testimony to God's role in nature* than, ones in terms of particular divine interventions in nature. Still, he probably felt the attractiveness of his case to a secular standpoint to be an advantage – and it is from such a standpoint that it will interest a modern philosopher. Herder's *positive* argument for a human origin is perhaps made best, not in *On the Origin* itself (where it gets entangled with the polemics against Süßmilch), but in the *Fragments* (as excerpted here). The argument is especially impressive for its methodology: its adducing of a number of independent empirical considerations that seem to converge on the conclusion of a human origin, and the admirably tentative, fallibilist spirit in which it does this.

However, for all its broad plausibility, this whole case is unlikely to be a modern philosopher's main reason for interest in Herder's ideas about language – deriving its zest, as it does, from a religious background that is no longer ours. Of much greater modern relevance is Herder's theory of interpretation, including his theory of the relation between thought, concepts, and language. This theory is scattered through many works (several included here). The following are its main features.

Herder's theory rests on, but also in turn supports, an epoch-making insight: (1) Such eminent Enlightenment philosopher-historians as Hume and Voltaire still believed that, as Hume puts it, "mankind are so much the same in all times and places that history informs us of nothing new or strange." What Herder discovered, or at least saw more clearly and fully than anyone before, was that this was false, that peoples from different historical periods and cultures vary *tremendously* in their concepts, beliefs, and other propositional attitudes, perceptual and affective sensations, etc. He also saw that similar, if usually less dramatic, variations occur even between individuals in a single culture and period.[10]

(2) Because of these radical differences, and the gulf that consequently often divides an interpreter's own thought from that of the person he wants to interpret, interpretation is often an extremely difficult task, requiring extraordinary efforts.[11]

(3) In particular, the interpreter often faces, and must resist, a temptation falsely to assimilate the thought which he is interpreting to someone else's, especially his own.[12]

How is the interpreter to meet the challenge? Herder advances three fundamental theses concerning thought, concepts, and language which underpin the rest of his theory of interpretation. The first two of these made a revolutionary break with a predominant Enlightenment model of thought and concepts as separable from and prior to language, thereby establishing not only modern interpretation theory but also modern linguistics and philosophy of language.

(4) Thought is essentially dependent on, and bounded in scope by, language – i.e. one can only think if one has a language, and one can only think what one can express linguistically.[13] An important consequence of this principle for interpretation is that an interpreted subject's language is a reliable indicator of the scope of his thought.

(5) Meanings or concepts are not to be equated with the sorts of items, in principle autonomous of language, with which much of the philosophical tradition has equated them – for example, the referents involved, Platonic forms, or the "ideas" favored by the British empiricists and others. Instead,

---

[10] These positions are prominent in many works, e.g. *On the Change of Taste* (1766) and *On the Cognition*.

[11] See e.g. *On the Origin*. To his credit, Herder does not draw the more extreme – and misguided – conclusion to which some more recent philosophers, such as the Davidsonians, have been tempted that the task would be *impossible*.

[12] This theme is prominent in *This Too*.

[13] This principle is already prominent in the *Fragments*. Indeed it can be found even earlier in Herder's *On Diligence in Several Learned Languages* (1764).

To his credit, Herder normally refrains from more extreme, but philosophically untenable, versions of this principle, later favored by Hamann and Schleiermacher, which *identify* thought with language, or with inner language.

they consist in *usages of words*.[14] Consequently, interpretation will essentially involve pinning down word usages.

(6) Conceptualization is intimately bound up with (perceptual and affective) sensation. More specifically, Herder develops a quasi-empiricist theory of concepts according to which sensation is the source and basis of all our concepts, though we are able to achieve nonempirical concepts by means of a sort of metaphorical extension from the empirical ones – so that all our concepts ultimately depend on sensation in one way or another.[15] This position carries the important consequence for interpretation that any understanding of a concept must somehow recapture its basis in sensation.

Herder also has two further basic principles in interpretation theory:

(7) A principle of *secularism* in interpretation: religious assumptions must not influence the interpretation of texts, even sacred texts. In particular, the interpreter of a sacred text such as the bible may neither rely on receiving divine inspiration himself when interpreting nor on the original authors having received it, and having therefore produced a text that was true and self-consistent throughout.[16]

(8) A principle of *methodological empiricism* in interpretation: interpretation must not be conducted in an a priori fashion but must always be based on, and strictly faithful to, exact observations of linguistic and other relevant evidence. This applies when determining word usages in order to determine meanings;[17] when conjecturing an author's psychology;[18] and when defining literary genres, or the purposes and rules that constitute them.[19]

---

[14] The positive side of this doctrine and its rejection of the "way of ideas" are already prominent in the *Fragments*. For Herder's rejection of Platonic forms, see *Johann Gottfried Herder Briefe*, ed. W. Dobbek and G. Arnold (Weimar, 1977–), 1:179–80 (a letter from 1769). The *Fragments* and *On the Origin* already develop several points which speak against equating concepts with referents (e.g. that language is originally and fundamentally *expressive* rather than designative or descriptive in nature), and Herder goes on to reject this explicitly in the *Ideas*.

Note that this doctrine promises a much more satisfactory justification and explanation of doctrine (4) than the one that Herder explicitly gives in *On the Origin* (which in effect just amounts to an illicit stipulative redefinition of "language" to include a certain fundamental aspect of thought, namely the recognition of "characteristic marks [*Merkmale*]"). Herder already gives the superior justification and explanation in question in the *Fragments* and *On Diligence*.

[15] For this doctrine, see e.g. *On the Origin* and *On the Cognition*. This doctrine might seem at odds with the preceding one, but it need not be. For a *usage* of words implicitly requires a *context*, and the context in question might very well essentially include certain sensations.

[16] This principle is already prominent in writings by Herder on biblical interpretation from the 1760s not included in this volume.

[17] This point is prominent in the *Fragments*.   [18] See e.g. *On Thomas Abbt's Writings* (1768).

[19] For a classic expression of this position on genres, see Herder's essay *Shakespeare* (1773).

Beyond this, Herder also advances a further set of interpretative principles which can sound more "touchy-feely" at first hearing (the first of them rather literally so!), but which are in fact on the contrary deeply motivated:

(9) Especially in *This Too*, Herder famously proposes that the way to bridge radical difference when interpreting is through *Einfühlung*, "feeling one's way in." This proposal has often been thought (e.g. by Meinecke) to mean that the interpreter should perform some sort of psychological self-projection onto texts. But, as the context in which it is introduced in *This Too* shows, that is emphatically not Herder's idea – for that would amount to exactly the sort of assimilation of the thought in a text to one's own which he is above all concerned to *avoid*. The same context makes clear that what he has in mind is instead an arduous process of historical-philological inquiry – so *Einfühlung* is really a metaphor here. What, though, more specifically, is the cash value of the metaphor? It has at least five components: First, it implies (once again) that there typically exists a radical difference, a gulf, between an interpreter's mentality and that of the subject whom he interprets, making interpretation a difficult, laborious task (it implies that there is an "in" there which one must carefully and laboriously "feel one's way into"). Second, it implies (*This Too* shows) that this process must include thorough research not only into a text's use of language but also into its historical, geographical, and social context. Third, it implies a claim – deriving from Herder's quasi-empiricist theory of concepts – that in order to interpret a subject's language one must achieve an imaginative reproduction of his perceptual and affective sensations.[20] Fourth, it implies that hostility in an interpreter towards the people he interprets will generally distort his interpretation and must therefore be avoided.[21] (Herder is also opposed to excessive identification with them for the same reason.) Fifth, it also implies that the interpreter should strive to develop his grasp of linguistic

[20] In writings on the Old Testament Herder astutely forestalls some obvious objections here, noting that this reproduction need not involve actually *sharing* the sensations. So his idea is that a sort of imaginative reproduction of an interpreted subject's sensations is possible which, while more than a mere propositional grasp of them, is also less than an actual sharing of them, and that only this is required for interpretation. This is an important idea: for example, it suggests an effective response to Gadamer's concern that discrepancies in "pre-understanding" preclude unprejudiced interpretation.

[21] Some of Herder's own successes as an interpreter came from following precisely this principle – e.g. his recognition, in contradiction of antisemitic interpreters such as Kant, that the viewpoints of the Old and New Testaments were far more continuous than discontinuous.

usage, contextual facts, and relevant sensations to the point where this achieves something of the same immediate, automatic character that it had for a text's original audience when *they* understood the text in light of such things (so that it acquires for him, as it had for them, the phenomenology more of a feeling than a cognition).

(10) In addition, Herder insists on a principle of *holism* in interpretation.[22] This principle rests on several motives, including the following. First, in order to begin interpreting a piece of text an interpreter needs to know ranges of linguistic meanings which its words can bear. But, especially when texts are separated from the interpreter by radical difference, such knowledge presents a problem. How is he to pin down the range of possible meanings, i.e. possible usages, for a word? This requires that he collate the word's known actual uses and infer from these the rules which govern them, i.e. usages, a collation which in turn requires that he look to remoter contexts in which the same word occurs (other parts of the text, other works in the author's corpus, works by other contemporaries, etc.), or in short: holism. Second, even when that is done, a piece of text considered in isolation will usually be ambiguous in relation to such ranges, and in order to resolve the ambiguities the interpreter will need to seek the guidance provided by surrounding text. Third, an author typically writes a work *as* a whole, conveying ideas not only in its particular parts but also through the manner in which these are fitted together to make up a whole (either in instantiation of a general genre or in ways more specific to the particular work). Consequently, readings which fail to interpret the work as a whole will miss essential aspects of its meaning – both the ideas in question themselves and meanings of particular parts on which they shed vital light.

(11) In *On Thomas Abbt's Writings* and *On the Cognition* Herder makes one of his most important innovations: interpretation must supplement its focus on word usage with attention to authorial *psychology*. Herder implies several reasons for this. A first has already been mentioned: Herder's quasi-empiricist theory of concepts with its implication that in order to understand an author's concepts the interpreter must recapture his relevant sensations. Second, as Quentin Skinner has stressed (in some of the most important work on interpretation theory since Herder), understanding the linguistic meaning of an utterance or text is only a

---

[22] This insistence is especially prominent in the *Critical Forests* (not included in this volume).

necessary, not a sufficient, condition for understanding it *tout court* – in addition, one needs to establish the author's illocutionary *intentions*. For example, a stranger tells me, "The ice is thin over there"; I understand his linguistic meaning perfectly; but is he simply informing me? warning me? threatening me? joking? ... Third, Skinner implies that one can determine linguistic meanings prior to establishing authorial intentions. That may perhaps *sometimes* be so (e.g. in the example just given), but is it *generally*? Herder implies not. And this seems right, because commonly a linguistic formula's meaning is ambiguous in terms of the background linguistic possibilities, and in order to identify the relevant meaning one must turn, not only (as was mentioned) to larger bodies of text, but also to hypotheses, largely derived therefrom, about the author's intentions (e.g. about the subject matter that he intends to treat). A fourth reason consists in the already-mentioned fact that authors typically express some ideas in a work not explicitly in its parts but holistically, and that these need to be determined both for their own sakes and for the light they shed on the meanings of parts. Fifth, Herder also sees a source of the need for psychological interpretation in the second limb of his doctrine of radical difference: *individual* variations in mode of thought even within a single culture and period. Why does any special need arise here? Part of the answer seems to be that when one is interpreting a concept that is distinctive of a particular author rather than common to a whole culture, one typically faces a problem of relative paucity and lack of contextual variety in the actual uses of the word available as empirical evidence from which to infer the rule for use, or usage, constitutive of its meaning. Hence one needs extra help in this case, and knowledge of authorial psychology may supply this.

(12) In the same two works Herder also argues that interpretation, especially in its psychological aspect, requires the use of *divination*. This is another principle which can sound disturbingly "touchy-feely" at first hearing; in particular, it can sound as though Herder means some sort of prophetic process enjoying a religious basis and perhaps even infallibility. However, what he really has in mind is (far more sensibly) a process of hypothesis, based on meager empirical evidence, but also going well beyond it, and therefore vulnerable to subsequent falsification, and abandonment or revision if falsified.

(13) Finally, a point concerning the general nature of interpretation and its subject matter. After Herder, the question arose whether interpretation

was a science or an art. Herder does not really address this question, but his considered inclination would clearly be to say that it is *like* rather than unlike natural science. There are several reasons for this. First, he assumes, as did virtually everyone at this period, that the meaning of an author's text is as much an objective matter as the subjects addressed by the natural scientist.[23] Second, the *difficulty* of interpretation that results from radical difference, and the consequent need for a *methodologically subtle and laborious* approach to it in many cases, constitute further points of similarity with natural science. Third, the essential role of "divination" qua *hypothesis* in interpretation constitutes another important point of similarity with natural science. Fourth, even the subject matter of interpretation is not, in Herder's view, sharply different from that dealt with by natural science: the latter investigates physical processes in nature in order to determine the forces that underlie them, but similarly interpretation investigates human verbal (and nonverbal) physical behavior in order to determine the forces that underlie *it* (Herder explicitly identifying mental conditions, including conceptual understanding, as "forces").

Herder's theory owes many debts to predecessors. Hamann has commonly been credited with introducing the revolutionary doctrines concerning thought, concepts, and language (4) and (5). But that seems to be a mistake; Herder was already committed to them in the 1760s, Hamann only later. Instead, Herder is indebted for (4) to a group of authors, including Abbt and Süßmilch, who were influenced by Wolff, and for (1), (2), (5), (7), (8), and (10) to Ernesti. However, Herder's borrowings incorporate important refinements, and his overall contribution is enormous.[24]

Herder's theory was taken over virtually in its entirety by Schleiermacher in his hermeneutics. Certainly, Schleiermacher's theory is also directly influenced by sources which he shares with Herder, especially Ernesti, but such fundamental and famous positions in it as the supplementing of "linguistic" with "psychological" interpretation and the identification of "divination" as the method especially of the latter are

[23] This assumption has been stigmatized as "positivist" by Gadamer, but on the basis of very dubious philosophical arguments. H. D. Irmischer in "Grundzüge der Hermeneutik Herders," in *Bückeburger Gespräche über J. G. Herder 1971* (Bückeburg, 1973), questions the sort of characterization of Herder's position given here, arguing that Herder anticipates Gadamer's own conception of meaning as something relative to a developing interpretative context. There are some things in Herder which can suggest such a view. But it is clearly not his considered position. This can be seen, for example, from the excerpts included in this volume from *On Thomas Abbt's Writings*.

[24] Concerning some of these issues, see my "Herder's Philosophy of Language, Interpretation, and Translation: Three Fundamental Principles" (forthcoming in *The Review of Metaphysics*).

due entirely to Herder. Moreover, where Herder and Schleiermacher *do* occasionally disagree, Herder's position is almost always philosophically superior. For example, unlike Herder, Schleiermacher standardly inclines to inferior versions of doctrine (4) which *identify* thought with language, or inner language (such versions are easily refutable by counterexamples). He attempts to establish the deep individuality of interpreted subjects, not like Herder in an empirical way and as a rule of thumb, but in an a priori way as a universal truth, and with the extremely counterintuitive consequence that exact understanding never occurs. He worsens Herder's theory of psychological interpretation by introducing the unhelpful idea that this should consist in identifying, and tracing the necessary development of, a single authorial "seminal decision [*Keimentschluß*]" (for how many texts are written and properly interpretable in that way?). He worsens it again by restricting the evidence for authorial psychology to textual evidence only, instead of also including nonlinguistic behavior as Herder does. Finally, he mistakenly sees the role in interpretation of "divination," which like Herder he understands as a method of fallible and revisable hypothesis from meager empirical evidence, as a ground for sharply *distinguishing* interpretation from natural science, and hence for classifying it as an art rather than a science, instead of as a ground for *assimilating* them (a mistake caused by a false assumption that natural science works by plain induction).

Herder's philosophy of mind

Herder also develops an extremely interesting and influential position in the philosophy of mind. His position is thoroughly naturalistic and anti-dualistic in intent. In *On the Cognition* he tries to efface the division between the mental and the physical in two specific ways. First, he advances the theory that minds consist in forces (*Kräfte*) which manifest themselves in people's bodily behavior – just as physical nature contains forces which manifest themselves in the behavior of bodies.[25] He is officially agnostic about what force is, except for conceiving it as something apt to produce a type of bodily behavior, and as a real source thereof (not just something reducible to it). This strictly speaking absolves his theory from some common characterizations and objections (e.g. vitalism),

[25] Note that the general notion of mental forces (*Kräfte*) was common before Herder among Rationalists such as Wolff and Süßmilch.

but also leaves it with enough content to have great virtues over rival theories: On the one hand, it ties types of mental states conceptually to corresponding types of bodily behavior – which seems correct (e.g. desiring an apple does seem conceptually tied to apple-eating behavior), and therefore marks a point of superiority over dualistic theories, and over mind-brain identity theories as well. On the other hand, it also avoids *reducing* mental states to bodily behavior – which again seems correct, in view of such obvious facts as that we can be, and indeed often are, in particular mental states which receive no behavioral manifestation, and hence marks a point of superiority over outright behaviorist theories.

Second, he also tries to explain the mind in terms of the phenomenon of irritation (*Reiz*), a phenomenon recently identified by Haller and exemplified by muscle fibers contracting in response to direct physical stimuli and relaxing upon their removal – in other words, a phenomenon which, while basically physiological, also seems to exhibit a transition to mental characteristics. There is an ambiguity in Herder's position here: usually he wants to resist physicalist reductionism, and so avoids saying that irritation is purely physiological and fully constitutes mental states; but in the 1775 draft of *On the Cognition* and even in parts of the published version, that *is* his position. And from a modern standpoint, this is another virtue of his account (though we would certainly today want to recast it in terms of different, and more complex, physiological processes than irritation).[26]

A further important thesis in Herder's philosophy of mind affirms that the mind is a unity, that there is no real division between its faculties. This position contradicts theorists such as Sulzer and Kant. However, it is not in itself new with Herder, having already been central to Rationalism, especially Wolff.[27] Where Herder is more original is in rejecting the Rationalists' reduction of sensation and volition to cognition, establishing the unity thesis in an empirical rather than apriorist way, and adding a normative dimension to the thesis – this is not only how the mind *is* but also how it *ought* to be. This last idea can sound incoherent, since if the

---

[26] This second line of thought might seem at odds with his first one (forces), but it need not be, for, given his official agnosticism about what forces are, it could, so to speak, fill in the "black box" of the hypothesized real forces, namely in physicalist terms. In other words, it turns out (not as a conceptual matter, but as a contingent one) that the real forces in question consist in physiological processes.

[27] Herder's introduction to his 1775 draft (included here) shows that he is fully aware of this debt. Hamann can therefore claim little credit as an influence here (though he can claim somewhat more for the further doctrines indicated in the next sentence).

mind is this way by its very nature, what sense is there in prescribing to people that it should be so rather than otherwise? But Herder's idea is in fact the coherent one that, while the mind is indeed this way by its very nature, people sometimes behave as though one faculty could be abstracted from another, and try to effect that, and this then leads to various malfunctions, and should therefore be avoided.

Herder's whole position on the mind's unity rests on three more specific doctrines of intimate mutual involvements between mental faculties, and malfunctions that arise from striving against them, doctrines which are in large part empirically motivated and hence lend the overall position a sort of empirical basis.

The first concerns the relation between thought and language: not only does language of its very nature express thought (an uncontroversial point), but also, as we saw, according to Herder thought is dependent on and bounded by language. Herder bases this further claim largely on empirical grounds (e.g. concerning how children's thought develops with language acquisition). The normative aspect of his position here is that attempts (in the manner of some metaphysics) to cut language free from the constraints of thought or (a more original point) vice versa lead to nonsense.

A second area of intimate mutual involvement concerns cognition and volition, or affects. The claim that volition is and should be based on cognition is not particularly controversial. But Herder also argues the converse, that all cognition is and should be based on volition, on affects (and not only on such relatively anemic ones as the impulse to know the truth, but also on less anemic ones). Herder is especially concerned to combat the idea that *theoretical* work is or should be detached from volition, from affects. In his view, it never really is even when it purports to be, and attempts to make it so merely impoverish and weaken it. His grounds for this position are again mainly empirical.

A third area of intimate mutual involvement concerns thought and sensation. Conceptualization and belief, on the one hand, and sensation (both perceptual and affective), on the other, are intimately connected according to Herder. Thus he advances the quasi-empiricist theory of concepts mentioned earlier, which entails that all our concepts, and hence also all our beliefs, ultimately depend in one way or another on sensation. And conversely, he argues – anticipating much recent work in philosophy (e.g. Hansen and Kuhn) – that there is a dependence in the other direction as well, that the character of our sensations depends on our concepts and beliefs. Normatively, he sees attempts to violate this interdependence as inevitably leading to intellectual malfunction – for example, as was mentioned, metaphysicians' attempts to cut entirely free from the empirical origin of concepts lead to meaninglessness. His grounds for this position are again largely empirical.

Herder also has further important doctrines in the philosophy of mind. One of these is a doctrine that linguistic meaning is fundamentally social, so that thought and other aspects of human mental life (as essentially articulated in terms of meanings), and therefore also the very self (as essentially dependent on thought and other aspects of human mental life, and defined in its specific identity by theirs), are so too. Herder's version of this position seems meant only as an empirically based causal generalization. It has since fathered attempts to generate more ambitious arguments for stronger versions of the claim that meaning – and hence also thought and the very self – is socially constituted (e.g. by Hegel, Wittgenstein, Kripke, and Burge). However, it may very well be that these more ambitious arguments do not work, and that Herder's version is exactly what should be accepted.

Herder also insists that, even within a single culture and period, human minds are deeply individual, deeply different from each other – so that in addition to a generalizing psychology we also need a psychology orientated to individuality. This is an important idea which has had a strong influence on subsequent thinkers (e.g. Schleiermacher, Nietzsche, Proust, Sartre, and Manfred Frank). Herder advances it only as an empirical rule of thumb. By contrast, a prominent strand in Schleiermacher and Frank purports to make it an a priori universal truth. But Herder's position is again the more plausible one.[28]

Finally, like predecessors in the Rationalist tradition and like Kant, Herder sharply rejects the Cartesian notion of the mind's self-transparency, instead insisting that much of what occurs in the mind is unconscious, so that self-knowledge is often deeply problematic. This is

---

[28] The previous doctrine of the sociality of meaning, thought, and self might seem inconsistent with this doctrine of individuality. However, even when the doctrine of individuality is pushed down as far as the level of meanings, there need be no inconsistency here, provided that the doctrine of sociality is asserted only as an empirically grounded causal rule, as Herder asserts it, rather than as a stronger doctrine about social practice constituting the very essence of meanings. Society, so to speak, provides a common semantic clay, which, however, then often gets molded in individual ways.

another compelling position which has had a strong influence on subsequent thinkers.

This whole Herderian philosophy of mind owes much to predecessors in the Rationalist tradition, but it is also in many ways original. The theory is important in its own right, and it exercised an enormous influence on successors – for example, on Hegel in connection with anti-dualism, the role of physical behavior in mental conditions, faculty unity, and the sociality of meaning, thought, and self; on Schleiermacher in connection with anti-dualism and faculty unity; and on Nietzsche in connection with the interdependence of cognition and volition, or affects, the individuality of the mind and the need for a corresponding sort of psychology, and the mind's lack of self-transparency.

Herder's philosophy of history

Herder's philosophy of history appears mainly in two works, *This Too* and the later *Ideas for the Philosophy of History of Humanity* (1784–91). His fundamental achievement in this area lies in his development of the thesis mentioned earlier, contradicting such Enlightenment philosopher-historians as Hume and Voltaire, that there are radical mental differences between historical periods, that people's concepts, beliefs, and other propositional attitudes, perceptual and affective sensations, etc., differ in major ways from one period to another. This thesis is already prominent in *On the Change of Taste* (1766). It exercised an enormous influence on such successors as Hegel and Nietzsche.

Herder makes the empirical exploration of the realm of mental diversity posited by this thesis the very core of the discipline of history. For, as has often been noted, he takes relatively little interest in the "great" political and military deeds and events of history, focusing instead on the "innerness" of history's participants. This choice is quite deliberate and self-conscious. Because of it, *psychology and interpretation* inevitably take center-stage in the discipline of history for Herder.

It is less often noticed that Herder has deep philosophical reasons for this choice, and hence for assigning psychology and interpretation a central role in history. To begin with, he has *negative* reasons directed against traditional political-military history. Why, one might ask, *should* history focus on the "great" political and military deeds and events of the past? There are several possible answers. A first would be that these deeds and events are fascinating or morally edifying. But Herder will not accept this. For one thing, he denies that mere fascination or curiosity is a sufficiently serious motive for doing history. For another, his anti-authoritarianism, anti-militarism, and borderless humanitarianism cause him to find the acts of political domination, war, and empire which make up the vast bulk of these "great" deeds and events not morally edifying but morally repugnant.[29]

This leaves two other types of motivation that might be appealed to for doing the sort of history in question: because examination of the course of such deeds and events reveals some sort of overall meaning in history, or because it leads to efficient-causal insights which enable us to explain the past and perhaps also predict or control the future. Herder is again skeptical about these rationales, however. This skepticism is clearest in the material included here from the *Older Critical Forestlet* (1767–8), where, in criticism of the former rationale, he consigns the task of "the whole ordering together of many occurrences into a plan" not to the historian but to the "creator . . . painter, and artist," and in criticism of the latter rationale, he goes as far as to assert (on the basis of a Hume- and Kant-influenced general skepticism about causal knowledge) that with the search for efficient causes in history "historical seeing stops and prophecy begins." His later writings depart from this early position in some obvious ways, but in less obvious ways remain faithful to it. They by no means *officially* stay loyal to the view that history has no discernible meaning; famously, *This Too* insists that history does have an overall purpose, and that this fact (though not the nature of the purpose) is discernible from the cumulative way in which cultures have built upon one another, and the *Ideas* then tells a long story to the effect that history's purpose consists in its steady realization of "humanity" and "reason." However, Herder clearly still harbors grave doubts just below the surface. That is visible in *This Too* from the work's ironically self-deprecating title; Pyrrhonian-spirited motto; vacillations between several incompatible models of history's direction (progressive? progressive and cyclical? merely cyclical? even regressive?); and morbid dwelling on, and unpersuasive attempt to rebut, the "skeptical" view of history as meaningless "Penelope-work." (A few years later Herder would write that history is "a textbook of the nullity of all human things.") It is

---

[29] Here Herder's position is *continuous* with that of his arch opponent in the philosophy of history, Voltaire, who also anticipates him by turning away from political-military history towards a history of culture.

also visible in the *Ideas* from the fact that Herder's official account there of the purposiveness of history is contradicted by passages which insist on the *inappropriateness* of teleological (as contrasted with efficient-causal) explanations in history. Herder's official position certainly had a powerful influence on some successors (especially Hegel), but it is this quieter counterstrand of skepticism that represents his better philosophical judgment. Concerning the prospect of finding in history's "great" deeds and events efficient-causal insights that will enable us to explain the past and perhaps also predict or control the future, Herder's later works again in a sense stay faithful to his skeptical position in the *Older Critical Forestlet* – but they also modify it, and this time for the better, philosophically speaking. The mature Herder does not, like the Herder of that work, rest his case on a *general* skepticism about the role or the discernibility of efficient causation in history. On the contrary, he insists that history *is* governed by efficient causation and that we should try to discover as far as possible the specific ways in which it is so. But he remains highly skeptical about the *extent* to which such an undertaking can be successful, and hence about how far it can take us towards real explanations of the past, or towards predicting or controlling the future. His main reason for this skepticism is that major historical deeds and events are not the products of some one or few readily identifiable causal factors (as political and military historians tend to assume), but rather of chance confluences of huge numbers of different causal factors, many of which, moreover, are individually unknown and unknowable by the historian (e.g. because in themselves too trivial to have been recorded, or because, in the case of psychological causes, the historical agent failed to make them public, deliberately misrepresented them, or was himself unaware of them due to the hidden depths of his mind).[30]

Complementing this negative case against the claims of traditional political-military history to be of overriding importance, Herder also has positive reasons for focusing instead on the "innerness" of human life in history. One reason is certainly just the sheer interest of this subject matter for Herder and others of his sensibility – but, as was mentioned, that would not be a sufficient motive in his eyes. Another reason is that his discovery of radical diversity in human mentality has shown there to be a

---

[30] Herder's arguments against these three rationales, though more fully stated individually elsewhere, are all in a way briefly summarized in the Tenth Collection of the *Letters for the Advancement of Humanity* (1793–7), Letters 121–2 (included in this volume).

much broader, less explored, and more intellectually challenging field for investigation here than previous generations of historians have realized. Two further reasons are moral in nature. First, Herder believes, plausibly, that studying people's minds through their literature, visual art, etc. generally exposes us to them at their moral best (in sharp contrast to studying their political-military history), so that there are benefits of moral edification to be gleaned here. Second, he has cosmopolitan and egalitarian moral motives for such study: because literature, visual art, etc. make us acquainted with different peoples, at different social levels, including lower ones, and at their most sympathetic, it promises to enhance our sympathies for different peoples at different social levels, including lower ones (unlike elite-focused and morally unedifying political-military history). Finally, doing "inner" history is also an important instrument for our *non*moral self-improvement. First, it serves to enhance our self-understanding. One reason for this is that it is by, and only by, contrasting one's own outlook with the outlooks of other peoples that one recognizes what is universal and invariant in it and what by contrast distinctive and variable. Another important reason is that in order fully to understand one's own outlook one needs to identify its origins and how they developed into it (this is Herder's rightly famous "genetic method," which subsequently became fundamental to the work of Hegel, Nietzsche, and Foucault). Second, Herder believes that an accurate investigation of the (nonmoral) ideals of past ages can serve to enrich our own (nonmoral) ideals and happiness. This motive finds broad application in his work. An example is his exploration of past literatures in the *Fragments* largely with a view to drawing from them lessons about how better to develop modern German literature.[31]

Herder's decision to focus on the "innerness" of history's participants, and his consequent emphasis on psychology and interpretation as historical methods, strikingly anticipated and influenced Dilthey. So too did Herder's rationale for this, as described above, which is indeed arguably superior to Dilthey's, especially on its positive side.

Finally, Herder is also impressive for having recognized, and, though not solved, at least grappled with, a problem that flows from his picture of history (and intercultural comparisons) as an arena of deep variations in human mentality. This is the problem of skepticism. He tends to run

---

[31] As often in this introduction, the reasons listed in this paragraph are culled from a large number of writings only some of which are included in this volume.

together two problems here: first, that of whether there is any meaning to the seemingly endless, bewildering series of changes from epoch to epoch (or culture to culture); and, second, the problem that the multiplication of conflicting viewpoints on virtually all subjects that is found in history (or in intercultural comparisons) produces, or at least exacerbates, the ancient skeptic's difficulty of unresolvable disputes forcing one to suspend belief on virtually all subjects. The first problem has been discussed. Here it is the second that concerns us. This is a problem that Troeltsch would make much of in the twentieth century, but Herder had already seen it.

Herder is determined to avoid this sort of skepticism. He has two main strategies for doing so, which are inconsistent with each other. His first is to try to defuse the problem at source by arguing that, on closer inspection, there is much more common ground between different periods and cultures than it recognizes. This strategy plays a central role in the *Ideas*, where in particular "humanity" is presented as a shared human value. Herder's second strategy is rather to acknowledge the problem fully and to respond with relativism: especially in *This Too* he argues that – at least where questions of aesthetic, moral, and prudential value are concerned – the different positions taken by different periods and cultures are equally valid, namely for the periods and cultures to which they belong, and that there can therefore be no question of any preferential ranking between them. The later *Letters* vacillates between these two strategies.

Neither of these strategies is satisfactory. The first, that of asserting deep commonalities, is hopeless (notwithstanding its eternal appeal to empirically underinformed Anglophone philosophers). For one thing, it flies in the face of the empirical evidence. For example, Herder in this mode sentimentally praises Homer for his "humanity," and thereby lays himself open to Nietzsche's just retort that what is striking about Homer and his culture is rather their *cruelty*.[32] For another thing, it flies in the face of Herder's own better interpretative judgments about the empirical evidence – for example, his observation in *On the Change of Taste* that basic values have not only changed through history but in certain cases actually been inverted (an observation which strikingly anticipates Nietzsche's brilliant insight that an inversion of ethical values occurred in later antiquity).

---

[32] Nietzsche, *Homer's Contest*. The historical issue here is of course very complicated.

Herder's alternative, relativist, strategy, while more promising, is not in the end satisfactory either (even concerning values, where its prospects seem best). There are several potential problems with it. One which is of historical interest but probably not in the end fatal is this: Hegel in the *Phenomenology of Spirit* and then Nietzsche in his treatment of Christian moral values saw the possibility of accepting Herder's insight that there were basic differences in values but nonetheless avoiding his relativism by subjecting others' values to an internal critique, a demonstration that they were internally inconsistent. For example, Nietzsche (whose version of this idea is the more plausible) traced back such Christian values as forgiveness to a contrary underlying motive of resentment (*ressentiment*). However, in order to work, such a response would need to show that the inconsistency was *essential* to the values in question, not merely something contingent that could disappear leaving the values consistently held – and this it probably cannot do. A more serious problem is rather a double one which Nietzsche again saw. First, we cannot in fact sustain such a relativist indifference vis-à-vis others' values. (Do we, for example, *really* think that a moral rule requiring the forcible burning of dead men's wives is no better and no worse than one forbidding it?) Second, nor does the phenomenon of fundamental value variations require us to adopt such an indifference. For, while it may indeed show there to be no universal values, it still leaves us with a better alternative to indifference: continuing to hold our values and to judge others' values in light of them, only now in a self-consciously nonuniversal way. (As Nietzsche put it, "My judgment is *my* judgment." Or if we reject Nietzsche's extreme individualism, "Our judgment is *our* judgment," for some less-than-universal *us*.)

Herder's political philosophy

Herder is not usually thought of as a political philosopher. But he was one, and moreover one whose political ideals are more admirable, thematic foci of more enduring relevance, and theoretical stances more defensible than those of any other German philosopher of the period. He was interested in political philosophy throughout his career, but his most developed treatment of it occurs late, in a work prompted by the French Revolution of 1789: the *Letters* (including the early draft of 1792, important for its frank statement of his views about domestic politics).

What are the main features of Herder's political philosophy? Let us begin with his political *ideals*, first in domestic and then in international politics. In domestic politics, the mature Herder is a liberal, a republican and democrat, and an egalitarian (this in circumstances where such positions were not commonplaces, and were embraced at a personal cost). His liberalism is especially radical in demanding virtually unrestricted freedom of thought and expression, including freedom of worship. He has several reasons for this position. First, he feels that such freedom belongs to people's moral dignity. Second, he believes that it is essential for individuals' self-realization. Third, as was mentioned earlier, he believes that people's capacities for discerning the truth are limited and that it is through, and only through, an ongoing contest between opposing viewpoints that the cause of truth gets advanced. (J. S. Mill later borrowed these considerations – partly via intermediaries such as von Humboldt – to form the core of his case for freedom of thought and expression in *On Liberty*.) Herder is also committed to republicanism and democracy (advocating a much broader franchise than Kant, for example). He has several reasons for this position, each deriving from an egalitarian concern for the interests of all members of society. First, he thinks it intrinsically right that the mass of people should share in their government, rather than having it imposed upon them. Second, he believes that this will better serve their *other* interests as well, since government *by* also tends to be government *for*. Third, he in particular believes that it will diminish the warfare that is pervasive under the prevailing autocratic political systems of Europe, where it benefits the few rulers who decide on it but costs the mass of people dearly. Finally, Herder's egalitarianism also extends further. He does not reject class differences, property, or inequalities of property outright, but he opposes all hierarchical oppression, argues that all people in society have capacities for self-realization and must receive the opportunity to realize them, and in particular insists that government must intervene to ensure that they do (e.g. by guaranteeing education and a minimum standard of living for the poor).

Concerning international politics, Herder is often classified as a "nationalist" or (even worse) a "German nationalist,"[33] but this is deeply

[33] For example, by R. Ergang, in *Herder and the Foundations of German Nationalism* (New York, 1931), and K. R. Popper, in *The Open Society and its Enemies* (London, 1945), who includes Herder in a sort of Hall of Shame recapitulating the rise of German nationalism.

misleading and unjust. On the contrary, his fundamental position in international politics is a committed cosmopolitanism, in the sense of an impartial concern for *all* human beings. This is a large part of the force of his ideal of "humanity." Hence in the *Letters* his slogan is "No one for himself only, each for all!" and he approvingly quotes Fénelon's remark, "I love my family more than myself; more than my family my fatherland; more than my fatherland humankind."

Herder does indeed *also* insist on respecting, preserving, and advancing national groupings. But this insistence is unalarming, for the following reasons. First, for Herder, this is emphatically something that must be done for *all* national groupings *equally* (not just or especially Germany!).[34] Second, the "nation" in question is not racial but linguistic and cultural (Herder rejects the very concept of race). Third, nor does it involve a centralized or militaristic state (Herder is an advocate of such a state's disappearance and replacement by loosely federated local governments with minimal instruments of force). Fourth, Herder's insistence on respecting national groupings is accompanied by the strongest denunciations of military conflict, colonial exploitation, and all other forms of harm between nations; a demand that nations instead peacefully cooperate and compete in trade and intellectual endeavors for their mutual benefit; and a plea, indeed, that they actively work to help each other.

Moreover, Herder has compelling reasons for his insistence on respecting national groupings. He believes that the deep diversity of values between nations entails that homogenization is ultimately impracticable, only a fantasy; that it also entails that, to the extent that homogenization *is* practicable, it cannot occur voluntarily but only through external coercion; that in practice attempts to achieve it, for example by European colonialism, are moreover coercive from, and subserve, ulterior motives of domination and exploitation; and, furthermore, that real national variety is positively valuable, both as affording individuals a vital sense of local belonging and in itself.

Herder's fundamental principle of cosmopolitanism was not new, of course. In particular, it was shared by, and no doubt partly due to, his

---

[34] Herder certainly worked especially hard in Germany's interests. However, this was from a version of what we would today call the principle "Think globally, act locally" (hence when he lived in Riga, a Russian possession, during the 1760s his efforts instead focused on the interests of *Russia*) and from a (realistic) sense of Germany's present inferiority in comparison with neighbors such as France and Britain. Unlike Fichte for example, Herder never claimed or sought Germany's *superiority*, instead emphatically rejecting all such ideas of a "Favoritvolk."

former teacher Kant, who published his own version of it in his essay *Idea for a Universal History from a Cosmopolitan Point of View* (1784). However, Herder's version of the position is more attractive than Kant's. First and foremost, it is a "nasty little secret" about Kant that, alongside his official cosmopolitan concern for all human beings (or, more accurately, and significantly differently, for the "rationality" in all human beings), he harbored some very intellectually irresponsible (i.e. empirically counterevidenced, unevidenced, or at best underevidenced) and morally objectionable prejudices about human beings of various sorts. In particular, he was a misogynist, an antisemite (a passage in his *Lectures on Ethics* in effect says that all Jews are liars because all Jews are cowards), and a racist (he published a seminal essay on racial taxonomy, and makes wholesale negative remarks about such races as African negroes in his *Anthropology*). In sharp contrast, and to his eternal credit, Herder emphatically rejected such prejudices, and worked tirelessly to combat them. Thus, as can already be seen in *How Philosophy Can Become*, far from being a misogynist, he is a proto-feminist who recognizes women's potentials and seeks to make possible their realization; far from being an antisemite, he wrote works on the Old and New Testaments which give extremely favorable interpretations of ancient Judaism and stress its continuity with Christianity, and in several places he expresses disgust at modern persecutions of Jews by European Christians; and far from being a racist, he rejects the very concept of race, instead preferring the linguistic-cultural concept of a nation or people, and he argues for equal respect for all peoples, and in particular denounces colonialism and slavery in the strongest terms. Second, Herder's insistence on, and arguments for, combining cosmopolitanism with respect for different national groupings (discussed above) are a further point of superiority. The critical Kant's implausible assumption of the implicit universal acceptance of a single moral standpoint (the "categorical imperative") prevented him from seeing a real issue here, let alone feeling the weight of Herder's arguments. A third and final point of superiority is the foundation of Herder's position on a plausible noncognitivism in ethics, instead of on the critical Kant's implausible cognitivist ethical theory.

Some readers may have nodded in assent up to this point, but still feel inclined to object that all this does not yet really amount to a political *theory* – such as other philosophers have given, including some of Herder's contemporaries in Germany. In a sense that is true, but philosophically defensible; in another sense it is false. It is true in this sense: There is certainly no grand metaphysical theory underpinning Herder's position – no Platonic theory of forms, no correlation of political institutions with "moments" in a Hegelian Logic, no "deduction" of political institutions from the very nature of the self or the will à la Fichte and Hegel, etc. But that is deliberate, given Herder's skepticism about such metaphysics. And is it not indeed philosophically a *good* thing? Nor does Herder have any elaborate account purporting to justify the moral intuitions at work in his political position as a sort of theoretical insight – in the manner of Kant's theory of the "categorical imperative" or Rawls's theory of the "original position," for example. But that is again quite deliberate, given his noncognitivism in ethics, and his rejection of such theories as both false and harmful. And is he not right about this, and the absence of such an account therefore again a *good* thing? Nor is Herder sympathetic with such further tired staples of political theory as the state of nature, the social contract, natural rights, the general will, and utopias for the future. But, again, he has good reasons for skepticism about these ideas.[35] This, then, is the sense in which the objection is correct; Herder does indeed lack a "political theory" of *these* sorts. But he lacks it on principle, and is arguably quite right to do so.

On the other hand, he does have a "political theory" of another, and arguably more valuable, sort. For one thing, consistently with his general empiricism, his position in political philosophy is deeply empirically informed. For instance, as can be seen from his *Dissertation on the Reciprocal Influence of Government and the Sciences* (1780), his thesis about the importance of freedom of thought and expression, and the competition between views which it makes possible, for producing intellectual progress is largely based on the historical example of ancient Greece and in particular Athens (as contrasted with societies which have lacked the freedom and competition in question). And in the 1792 draft of the *Letters* he even describes the French Revolution and its attempts to establish a modern democracy as a sort of "experiment" from which we can learn (e.g. whether democracy can be successfully extended to nations much larger than ancient Athens). For another thing, conformably with his general noncognitivism about morals, he is acutely aware that his political position ultimately rests on moral sentiments – his own and, for its

[35] For some helpful pointers about this, see F. M. Barnard, *Herder's Social and Political Thought: From Enlightenment to Nationalism* (Oxford, 1965), pp. 54–5, 64–6, 105–6, 141.

success, other people's as well. Hence, for example, the Tenth Collection of the *Letters* stresses the fundamental role of moral "dispositions" or "feelings" as required supports for his political position's realization. This standpoint absolves him of the need to do certain sorts of theorizing – not only precluding cognitivist groundings of the moral intuitions in question, but also promising short, effective answers to some problems that would probably look like real brain-teasers to a cognitivist.[36] However, it also leads him to engage in another sort of theorizing, namely theorizing about how, and by what means, people's moral sentiments should be molded in order to realize the ideals of his political position. His discussion of moral "dispositions" in the Tenth Collection is an example of such theorizing (in this case concerning the how rather than the means; some of his theorizing about means was sketched earlier). *These* two sorts of theorizing *are* deeply developed in Herder, and they are arguably much more pointful than the sorts which are not.

In short, to the extent that Herder's political philosophy really is theoretically superficial, it is arguably, to borrow a phrase of Nietzsche's, "superficial – *out of profundity*" (whereas more familiar forms of political philosophy are profound out of superficiality). And in another, more important, sense it is not theoretically superficial at all.

These, then, are some features of Herder's positions in the several areas of philosophy covered by the present volume which seem to me noteworthy. A number of years ago Isaiah Berlin and Charles Taylor attempted to bring Herder's philosophical importance to the attention of Anglophone philosophy. Anglophone philosophy was quick to recognize the quality of the messengers, but has been paradoxically slow to heed their message. It is my hope that the present volume may help to rectify this unfortunate situation.

---

[36] For example: How do you reconcile your cosmopolitanism with your respect for different nations when these nations turn out to have really inhumane practices? This problem would probably strike a cognitivist as the discovery of an embarrassing contradiction in Herder's position. But to a noncognitivist like Herder it instead just looks like the sort of practically challenging but theoretically unpuzzling conflict that can *always* in principle arise when one has multiple sentiments, or commitments. How do you reconcile your devotion to Mary with your commitment to your job when your job requires you to neglect her?

Chronology

Karoline Flachsland in Darmstadt; then to Strasbourg, where he
meets, and has a powerful impact on, the young Goethe.

1771 Herder wins a prize from the Berlin Academy for his best-known
work in the philosophy of language, the *Treatise on the Origin of
Language* (published 1772). He takes up a position as court
preacher to the ruling house in Bückeburg which he will hold until
1776.

1773 He publishes a seminal essay, *Shakespeare*, which contrasts ancient
and Shakespearean tragedy as distinct genres and defends the
latter against critics.

1774 He publishes his first major essay on the philosophy of history, *This
Too a Philosophy of History for the Formation of Humanity*.

1776 He is appointed General Superintendent of the Lutheran clergy in
Weimar, partly through Goethe's influence, a post in which he will
remain for the rest of his life.

1778 He publishes the important essay in the philosophy of mind, *On
the Cognition and Sensation of the Human Soul*. He begins
publishing an influential collection of translations of popular
poetry from around the world, *Popular Songs* (1778–9).

1781 Kant publishes his *Critique of Pure Reason*.

1782 Herder begins publishing his most important work on the Old
Testament, *On the Spirit of Hebrew Poetry* (1782–3).

1784 He begins publishing his well-known longer work on the
philosophy of history, the *Ideas for the Philosophy of History of
Humanity* (1784–91). Hamann finishes his *Metacritique on the
Purism of Pure Reason*, an attack on Kant's *Critique of Pure Reason*.

1785 Kant publishes two condescending reviews of Herder's *Ideas for the
Philosophy of History of Humanity*. Jacobi publishes letters in which
he reveals and rejects Lessing's Spinozism, thereby opening a
famous controversy on this subject.

1787 Herder publishes an influential work in the philosophy of religion,
God. Some Conversations, in which he defends a modified version
of Spinoza's monism.

1788 Hamann dies. Kant publishes his *Critique of Practical Reason*.

1789 The French Revolution begins. Herder welcomes it
enthusiastically.

1790 Kant publishes the last of his three *Critiques*, the *Critique of
Judgment*.

1793 Herder begins publishing a work largely on political philosophy,
written in reaction to the French Revolution, the *Letters for the
Advancement of Humanity* (1793–7).

1794   He begins publishing a series of essays concerned mainly with the origins, character, relations between, and proper principles for interpreting the parts of the New Testament, the *Christian Writings* (1794–8).

1799   He publishes the first of two works criticizing aspects of Kant's critical philosophy, *A Metacritique on the Critique of Pure Reason*, directed against the theoretical philosophy of Kant's *Critique of Pure Reason*.

1800   He publishes the second of his works criticizing Kant's critical philosophy, the *Calligone*, directed against the aesthetic theory of Kant's *Critique of Judgment*.

1803   Herder dies.

1804   Kant dies.

Further reading

Translations

Herder has not been very extensively translated into English. Indeed, many important works have not yet been translated at all. H. Adler, E. A. Menze, *On World History* (Armonk, 1996) contains short excerpts on history from a variety of works, prominently including the *Ideas*. F. M. Barnard, *J. G. Herder on Social and Political Culture* (Cambridge, 1969) is especially helpful, including good (partial) translations of Herder's *Journal of My Journey in the Year 1769*, the *Dissertation on the Reciprocal Influence of Government and the Sciences*, and the *Ideas*, as well as a very good introduction. F. H. Burkhardt, *God. Some Conversations* (New York, 1940) is a translation of Herder's most important work in the philosophy of religion. T. Churchill, *Outlines of a Philosophy of the History of Man* (London, 1800) is a translation of the *Ideas*. J. Marsh, *The Spirit of Hebrew Poetry* (Burlington, VT, 1833) is a translation of Herder's most important work on the Old Testament. E. A. Menze, K. Menges, M. Palma, *Johann Gottfried Herder: Selected Early Works, 1764–7* (University Park, Pennsylvania, 1992) contains some early essays and excerpts from the *Fragments*. J. H. Moran, A. Gode, *On the Origin of Language* (Chicago, 1986) contains a partial translation of *On the Origin*. H. B. Nisbet, *German Aesthetic and Literary Criticism: Winckelmann, Lessing, Hamann, Herder, Schiller, Goethe* (Cambridge, 1985) contains two pieces of Herder's on aesthetics, including his important essay *Shakespeare*.

Secondary literature in English

Concerning general treatments, I. Berlin, *Vico and Herder* (New York, 1976) is concise and excellent. R. T. Clark Jr., *Herder: His Life and Thought* (Berkeley, 1955) is fairly detailed and useful though unimaginative. F. C. Beiser, *The Fate of*

Reason (Cambridge, MA, 1987), ch. 5, covers several topics helpfully, including Herder's philosophies of language, mind, and religion. Concerning Herder's general program and his debts to the precritical Kant, J. H. Zammito, *Kant, Herder, and the Birth of Anthropology* (Chicago, 2001) is helpful. Concerning Herder's philosophy of language, two essays by C. Taylor are especially useful: "The Importance of Herder," in E. and A. Margalit (eds.), *Isaiah Berlin: A Celebration* (Chicago, 1991), and "Language and Human Nature," in C. Taylor, *Human Agency and Language: Philosophical Papers 1* (Cambridge, 1996). Concerning Herder's philosophy of history, A. O. Lovejoy, "Herder and the Enlightenment Philosophy of History," in his *Essays on the History of Ideas* (Baltimore, 1948), is a helpful short treatment which explains Herder's position in the context of Enlightenment thought. F. Meinecke, *Historism: The Rise of a New Historical Outlook* (London, 1972), ch. 9, is especially helpful. Concerning political philosophy, R. Ergang, *Herder and the Foundations of German Nationalism* (New York, 1931) is informative both on Herder's political thought and on his general intellectual influence (though marred by an assimilation of Herder's form of nationalism to later German, state-centered nationalism, and by an unduly warm assessment of such a position – for both of which flaws Barnard, Berlin, and Beiser are good correctives). F. M. Barnard, *Herder's Social and Political Thought: From Enlightenment to Nationalism* (Oxford, 1965) is helpful, esp. chs. 3–5 on Herder's political thought. F. C. Beiser, *Enlightenment, Revolution, and Romanticism* (Cambridge, MA, 1992), esp. ch. 8, is outstanding, among other things decisively refuting the lingering myth that Herder and other German philosophers of his age were apolitical. Concerning other subjects, H. B. Nisbet, *Herder and the Philosophy and History of Science* (Cambridge, MA, 1970) provides an excellent account of Herder's stance towards science. R. E. Norton, *Herder's Aesthetics and the European Enlightenment* (Ithaca, 1991) is helpful both on aspects of Herder's aesthetic theory and on Herder's general relation to the Enlightenment (though the Herderian theory correlating different art forms one-to-one with different senses on which Norton largely focuses is far from the most philosophically interesting aspect of Herder's aesthetics).

Secondary literature in German

This is extensive. By far the most helpful single item remains R. Haym, *Herder nach seinem Leben und seinen Werken* (Berlin, 1880) – a classic, detailed intellectual biography whose treatment is outstanding (despite a Kantian bias and an occasional unwarranted note of condescension). Also extremely helpful are the specific textual commentaries in U. Gaier et al. (eds.), *Johann Gottfried Herder Werke* (Frankfurt am Main, 1985–). H. D. Irmischer has written several important articles relevant to the subjects covered in this volume, including "Grundzüge der Hermeneutik Herders," in *Bückeburger Gespräche über J. G. Herder 1971* (Bückeburg, 1973), and "Grundfragen der Geschichtsphilosophie Herders bis 1774," in *Bückeburger Gespräche über J. G. Herder 1983* (Bückeburg, 1984). A. F. Kelletat, *Herder und die Weltliteratur* (Frankfurt am Main, 1984) is an excellent, unpretentious treatment of Herder's interest in world literature, and in particular his theory and practice of translation. T. Willi, *Herders Beitrag zum Verstehen des Alten Testaments* (Tübingen, 1971) is a very good treatment of Herder's work on the Old Testament. Two fairly useful recent collections of essays which cover a broad range of topics are G. Sauder (ed.), *Johann Gottfried Herder 1744–1803* (Hamburg, 1987) and M. Bollacher (ed.), *Johann Gottfried Herder: Geschichte und Kultur* (Würzburg, 1994).

Note on the texts and translation

The texts are based on two excellent German editions: U. Gaier et al. (eds.), *Johann Gottfried Herder Werke* (Frankfurt am Main, 1985–) and B. Suphan et al. (eds.), *Johann Gottfried Herder Sämtliche Werke* (Berlin, 1887–). References to these editions take the form of the primary editor's surname initial followed by volume number and page number (e.g. G2:321 or S5:261). The former edition is the main source, with the latter serving for the 1775 draft of *On the Cognition*, supplements to other texts, and certain emendations. I have occasionally also made emendations myself, but conservatively and always with an explanatory footnote.

The translator of Herder works in the shadow of Herder's own formidable theory and practice of translation. His theory of translation is represented in this volume by the selections from the *Fragments*. Two principles of the theory, both deeply grounded in his philosophy of language, are particularly noteworthy: First, translation proper (*Übersetzung*) (which he distinguishes sharply from mere imitation [*Nachbildung*], a genre which, however, he also tolerates and sometimes practices) can and should cope with the discrepancies that frequently occur between concepts, or word usages, in the original language and concepts, or word usages, in the language into which the translation is to be done by "bending" the (closest) latter word usages over the course of the translation.[1] This in particular entails preferring to give uniform translations of a given word/concept in the original rather than varying translations, despite (and indeed in a way for the sake of) the greater impression of strangeness to which this will give rise in certain contexts. The alternative

---

[1] On this see, besides the *Fragments*, also *Popular Songs*, G3:26.

way of proceeding can make for smoother reading, but only at the un-
acceptable cost of a sacrifice in the exactness with which readers of the
translation can grasp the author's meaning. Second, translation should
also attempt to reproduce the more musical and stylistic features of the
text translated. This is not, for Herder, merely a desirable luxury over
and above the more fundamental goal of faithfully reproducing meaning; it is also a requirement for the latter. One reason for this is that the
musical and stylistic aspects of a text provide readers with indispensable
clues to the exact character of the authorial sensations which, according to
Herder's quasi-empiricist theory of concepts, are internal to the author's
meanings.[2]

The present volume aims at translation proper, a faithful reproduction
of meaning (rather than mere imitation). The texts involved here do not
pose the challenges that Herder's two principles are designed to address in
as high a degree as some (e.g. conceptual discrepancy is a bigger problem
with ancient texts, and musical-stylistic features are more important in
poetry than in prose). Nonetheless, they do pose them to a degree, and
I have generally attempted to conform to Herder's two principles as far
as possible where they are relevant – not because they are Herder's, but
because they seem to me broadly correct.

Accordingly, I have attempted to translate important terms in a uniform way as far as possible (e.g. *Menschheit*, which Herder sometimes uses
in a more or less descriptive, morally neutral way and sometimes in a way
which connotes a moral ideal, is always translated as *humanity* rather than
sometimes as the morally neutral *humankind* and at other times as the
more morally suggestive *humanity* – a choice made easy in this case by the
fact that even in standard English *humanity* is sometimes used in a descriptive, morally neutral way). However, a few important terms resisted uniform translation for various reasons (prime examples are *bilden/
Bildung*, which, depending on the context, appear here as *form/formation*,
educate/education, *civilize/civilization*, *cultivate/cultivation* or *culture*; a
less extreme example is *Geist*, which, depending on the context, becomes
either *mind* or *spirit*).[3] In such cases, I have compensated by indicating the
single German word involved in square brackets or footnotes.

---

[2] See e.g. G2:1159: it is essential to preserve Shakespeare's rhymes in translation because of the
semantically relevant nuances of feeling which only they convey exactly.

[3] Such cases illustrate an important point about Herder's injunction to "bend" usages in translation:
this cannot well be sustained as an absolute requirement, only as a presumption.

I have also attempted to preserve the musical and stylistic features of the texts as far as possible. This in particular meant preserving, rather than smoothing out, the deliberate roughness of Herder's writing – including his use of such artfully rough rhetorical devices as anacoluthon, chiasmus, and hysteron proteron.[4]

With regard to punctuation, the translation is much freer. Some of Herder's idiosyncrasies have been kept for various reasons (e.g. his use of quotation marks not only for quotations but also for emphasizing statements of his own), but otherwise punctuation has been freely modernized in the interest of conveying his meaning as effectively as possible.

Some more detailed observations concerning these and other matters relating to the translation can be found in footnotes at relevant points in the texts.

Lettered footnotes are Herder's own; numbered footnotes mine. Square brackets, [ ], indicate an editorial supplement to Herder's texts, or the original German wording; curved brackets, ( ), are Herder's own.

---

[4] In this spirit, Herder praised Abbt's translations of Latin authors for preserving the distinctive roughness of the originals rather than smoothing it out into easier-to-read "Frenchified German."

Part I General Philosophical Program

constrasts

philosophy + healthy understanding
↓   ↓ (rooted in beliefs of a people)
can be harmful   good
if not useful

(at best it's useless
at worst it's
 harmful)

Kant - reason is universal

morality is based on sentiment

cognitivism ——————— emotivism   Herder
-reason   -sentiment
-formulated   limitations -passion
 explicitedly   -thought   - feeling
-can be written   isn't   - predujice
down   involved in   (prejudgments)
(deontology)   this, there
        ↳obligations needs to be   virtue theorists
                    a cognitive Sen's consequentialism
(utilitarianism)   element.   - common sense

Philosophy   Herder would say that healthy
_____   understanding is acquired by proper
so universal   rarsing
or general
it's vague
and therefore
useless.

↱The philosopher can redeem philosophy by
↳ reforming it

Morals are like language, not born w/ but learn it, but
for the most part one can just talk, we know what
we should be doing... and we do it

Hegel- reason changes over time

Herder- life requires examination when you run into
        problems but he wouldn't say the unexamined
        life isn't worth living
Socrates looks for the form of the thing

[Handwritten marginalia, top of page:]

-diff methods of philosophizing
1. dialogues
2. essay

Herder - morality ≠ mathematics
morality rooted in the practices of a people... you don't need to articulate
- not universal reason = reflexive - still judgment on others

Psychoanalysis - is the illness of which it takes itself to be the cure.

and ethical intervention

How Philosophy[1] Can Become More Universal and Useful for the Benefit of the People[2] (1765)

[Introduction][3]

If any science has been an object of contradictions, and yet amid these stones and earthen clods that have been cast at it an object of reverence, then it is exalted philosophy [*Weltweisheit*].[4] Since its beginning it had constantly been a source of annoyance to the one party, a corner-stone of truth to the other; and this so peculiar phenomenon of contradiction has not merely been a mark of distinction and a shibboleth, so to speak, among whole ages, peoples, and sects, but philosophy has had to survive this metamorphosis of judgment at one time and among one people, indeed often in different phases of one and the same person. This is indeed as remarkable a phenomenon of the human understanding for a person who is not a scholar as it is a remarkable thing for a person who is not a politician when people conflict with people. Philosophy has become a Proteus among the nations. Where it was victorious, behold, it generally built its throne on the ruins of mathematics and experiences from physics; but commonly it remained an ally of philology, with which it also commonly associated

[Handwritten marginalia, right side:]
philosophy annoying or truth had to survive this judgment phenom of human understanding is based off of math + physics

[Handwritten, bottom:] Philosophy is changing...

---

[1] *Philosophie.* In this essay Herder also uses the more colorful word *Weltweisheit* more or less interchangeably with this word.

[2] This title is taken by Herder's German editor from a letter that Herder wrote to Hamann about this essay on 23 April 1765. An earlier draft of the essay actually bore the similar but not identical title *How Can the Truths of Philosophy Become More Universal and Useful for the Benefit of the People?* There would be a good argument for retaining the latter title.

[3] Headings in square brackets are supplied by Herder's German editor in light of an essay plan for this essay which Herder wrote.

[4] Herder uses this word more or less interchangeably with *Philosophie* in this essay. Literally it means *world-wisdom,* but I have translated both terms as *philosophy* throughout.

too intimately; whereas one can say that *mathematics* and *philology* hardly ever took root together.

Since in the *defenses*, the offensive wars, and the defensive wars over metaphysics [*Metaphysik*] the most patent *sectarianisms*, partisanships, have certainly been the banner, one ought not to be surprised that the raging heat of the battle and the fog of which each person accused the other left no party's eyes free but only their hands, and that no one lost the blindfold of the fact that he was fighting with specters, and perhaps with his own shadow. But since this battle was so longlasting, switched *between such different* fortunes, since in it the circle of military stratagems, fighter's tricks, and real bravery had almost been exhausted, it is surprising that no *idle* spectator with cool passion made bold enough to turn himself into a *pragmatic* Thucydides or Polybius from it, surveyed the whole in the large with an alert eye, the possibility of explaining the drives, the connection of the motives, and the secret effects. I say a Polybius, for we have no shortage of newspaper reporters.

It is still worse that people have fought over mere abstractions, without seeing the real benefit. The defenders thought their benefit too holy and great and obvious even to want to make trials of it. And even had they been unwilling to do this for the sake of their translators – which trial would have been very necessary, however – they should at least have presented it to the weak as a demonstration of undeniability. The despisers, on the other hand, mostly thought the abstractions so completely useless that it was a new foolishness to think of applying them in other sciences. At least economics had posed the problem: What must I do with a good-for-nothing [metaphysics] which unfortunately exists, which has for so long spread harm? What must I do with it in order to reap from it, instead of harm, some benefit at last?

All enemies of metaphysics fight in two great hordes, each of which has a different side of the enemy, different weapons and rules of warfare, its own manner of attack and defense. One attacks the truths of philosophy [*Philosophie*], the other their use and application. The former is the sect of the mathematicians who often concede to their enemy no truth, never certainty, very rarely clarity; and when they finally add complete uselessness to the result of their calculation, the condemnation is complete.[5] These two sciences have been constant enemies: if the one won, etc. In the

---

[5] The translation here follows Gaier's clearly correct hypothesis about Herder's intentions (G1:973), rather than Gaier's printed text.

4

end, since neither could eliminate the other, they proceeded like the Turks and Saracens: philosophy, the weaker, borrowed from mathematics its manner, its procedure, its expressions, and in the process really lost its spirit. Even in individual men these disciplines' spirits have never been able to coexist: in Spinoza and Descartes philosophy turned into a tissue of unfortunate hypotheses; Leibniz was a more fortunate poet; and Wolff, the great spokesman of his inventor [Leibniz], gave philosophy its mathematical regimentation and slogans with what success? It would be a digression from my purpose to pass judgment on this; I merely point to a theme which has perhaps not yet received an answer.

Whence comes the inner quarrel between philosophy and mathematics? How can it be settled? Should one science be compared with the other, in order to demand mathematical certainty, clarity, and usefulness in philosophy? How can one science flow into the other without doing it the damage which we have experienced from the unification of both? One will see in what respect.

The second species of those who contradict philosophy is merely an offshoot of the former one: the *physicists* (but unfortunately there have been too few of them). They dared to investigate the phenomena of abstraction like the noteworthy features of nature etc., to judge them from experiences not from hypotheses, to transfer the spirit of physical analysis into philosophy instead of mathematical synthesis, in short, to attempt a *dissection* of the products of our spirit, be they errors or truths. In physics Descartes' hypotheses were followed by a Newton. In philosophy, may the mathematical aeons be followed by the physical ones – stat palma in medio, qui poterit, rapiat![6]

Those who have made a posteriori observations about philosophy also constitute two armies of quite different people: they are the theologians and the political thinkers, or if one prefers, the friends of God and men. The former have in a very premature manner transplanted philosophical truth into the realm of religious truth, and thereby distorted both. What are all the scholastic methods of our dogmatics but sad remains from the Aristotelian leaven, which unfortunately protect themselves by means of the prejudice of holy old age, and which scarcely two or three of our theologico–philosophers have begun to root out with fearful boldness? On the other hand, one will also be able to call to mind the newest

[6] The palm stands in the middle, whoever can, let him seize it.

5

fashion-philosophy in Germany, which brings postulates from theology into the first principles of metaphysics, considers the whole of philosophy from a trembling theological point of view as though it were an enemy, so to speak, and hence is[7] the idol of young theologians, who are to be metaphysicians at others' expense. To discover the whole enormous difference in viewpoint, manner of inference, and manner of proof, indeed in the original sources of knowledge of the two sciences (which scarcely bear the name 'science' in a single sense), to eliminate so many useless philosophical doctrines from the method of our theologians, and, on the other hand, to discover new paths and plans for spreading a *philosophical spirit* about the most biblical truths so that one is not believing a holy nullity – this is a labor for which the English and a few German theologians have already bequeathed us fragments, or at least good examples of application.

The fourth *viewpoint* is the most useful and the most appropriate for our economico-political age. It is, with a slight modification, the question of a patriotic society, "How can the truths etc.?"[8] How can philosophy be reconciled with humanity and politics so that it also really serves the latter? A question which [has had] more than one career-philosopher as answerer, and which least of all needs such a person to decide it. The question over which *Plato, Rousseau, Hume,* and *Shaftesbury* pondered very deeply and plunged into doubt.[9]

England is full of deep observers of nature, full of natural philosophers, politicians, mathematicians. France is full of literary types [*Schöngeister*], full of *men*, experts in statecraft, full of geometers. Germany – hardworking Germany – has only the national virtue of *being philosophical* [*weltweise zu sein*]. The former cannot reach up to us, and so they belittle us. Oh, is it not therefore a task for everyone who has German blood in his veins and a German philosophical spirit to develop this patriotic theme, to show how philosophy stands in relation to political science, mathematics, the literary arts [*den schönen Wissenschaften*], so that he cedes nothing belonging to philosophy and to its standing?[10]

---

[7] Reading *ist* for *sind*.

[8] The "patriotic society" was one in Berne, Switzerland which had set the prize question: "How can the truths of philosophy become more universal and useful for the benefit of the people?"

[9] As Gaier points out (G1:974), in a deleted passage of the introduction Herder associates these names with that of *Pyrrho* as well. Cf. Herder's remark in the first section below, "I am writing for Pyrrhonists."

[10] Question mark added. Henceforth I shall not specifically note such revisions in punctuation, which are frequent.

The people – as one society[11] takes the question – is the greatest, the most venerable, part of the public, in contrast to which philosophy is a troglodyte-people living in caves with Minerva's night-owls! If the latter have treasures, well then, they must become common property. If they do not have them, if they are themselves useless to the state, then let their caves be destroyed and let the night-owls of Minerva be taught to look at the sun.

people / everyone but philosopher

I take the word 'people' in the general sense of each citizen of the state insofar as he merely obeys the laws of healthy reason without choosing higher philosophy as his guide. And although it is so difficult to determine exactly the borders between wealth [*Reichtum*] and being comfortably off [*Wohlhabenheit*], between rhetorical eloquence [*Beredsamkeit*] and good style [*Wohlredenheit*], between healthy thought and learned thought,[12] nevertheless we are secure from confusion if we will take note of the meaning of the word 'philosophy' and understand by 'people' all those who are not such philosophers.

If I were a president of an academy comprising four or more academic trades who unfortunately fits into none of these, then this problem would require a different solution from the theologian, from the geometer, from the natural scientist and the political scientist, and I would judge the matter as a human being, without preference for philosophy (which is in the process of getting condemned), for one of my own pet inclinations, or for one of my academic categories. And in this way the truth would become clear, if one did not aim[13] to refute, to express novelties, to become famous, but wrote as a human being who is learning and trying to make up his mind.

) ?

I have laid out all these various *viewpoints* in advance in order to make clear the necessity which properly belongs to my question, and to show all the various viewpoints and sides from which it can be considered. So I am undertaking to write about this question: ["How can the truths etc.?"], and have had to present justifications for thinking that one must write about it. If the question were one of those set topics of the academies about which one has to shrug one's shoulders, then it would effect its own punishment by virtue of the fact that in general a miserable riddle attracts the company

---

[11] I.e. the "patriotic society" mentioned above.
[12] Note that Herder is here employing the rhetorical figure of chiasmus (i.e. inverting the order) between the first two pairs of examples and the last.
[13] Reading *wollte* instead of *will*.

of a miserable Oedipus. But I wish for this question more attention, better fortune, and more application. I am speaking about a German theme, I am speaking before Germans, who are the deepest and, after the English, the least biased philosophers [*Weltweise*] of Europe. I am speaking as a German. Instead of sowing words, I am planting thoughts and prospects. I leave it to others to raise these seeds, and to make them trees, and perhaps also to gather fruit. And I request for myself only the attention which one applies in order to find a seed that may perhaps be noble.

I will divide up my question, and say about each part of philosophy what sort of fruits it does not bear and how it can bear fruits for the state. I know that my thread, my viewpoint, and often also my thoughts will not seem orthodox. But I also hope that it will in the end become clear why I did not choose the viewpoint which was perhaps easiest and which everyone else would have chosen.

[First section:] Truths in philosophy

If I showed that there are truths in philosophy, I [would] seem to be like that advocate who, in order to defend the innocence of a virgin, laid bare her most private parts merely in order to show that he was not talking about a male person. (But, just as this would not exactly have been the strictest proof of her innocence for the judges, likewise it must merely constitute the possibility of an advocate that philosophy have truths, that they can be applied.) Since I am writing for Pyrrhonists, it follows etc.[14]

[Logic in its first part,] since it is opposed to the natural order of our soul, merely contains the order of verbal presentation. And here is a matter of a small though indispensable triviality to which one can never give all those much-promising names.[15]

The second part of Logic is merely a word-register which can entertain a distracted attention and somewhat fill out thoughts. And these definitions are mostly quite superfluous in philosophy as instrumental concepts. One learns them merely for the logicians. And *learning*? Yes, that is a real corruption for the *philosophoumenos*:[16] if in the art which teaches him to use his soul he is at most trained to retain, he also comes to think that

[14] There is a gap in the manuscript at this point – probably a fairly substantial one.
[15] The first lines of the section up to this point contain, besides a gap, also various other problems in Herder's manuscript. My translation of them is therefore somewhat conjectural.
[16] *philosophoumenos*: philosophizer.

all philosophical thinking is *retaining*. He learns to define, he swears by the words of his teacher. Why do we have so few independent thinkers? Because already in school they were hemmed in with Logic. O you his machine-like teacher, well do you need to suppress his healthy understanding with your school Logic; otherwise he would take your measure, repeat the gobbledygook you took an hour to trot out afterwards *naturally* but without school-cleverness in three words. He would despise you! But woe unto you; from a thousand heads who would have become men only ten will be bold enough to be wise; the rest are choked with school-dust – like the Egyptian midwife.[17]

So our Logic contains comfortless, far-too-universal rules, besides these[18] a philosophical register, and then a scholastic method of ancient disputation. Consequently, its truths cannot be made universal for the benefit of the people. Even for scholars it is no instrumental science, even the philosophical use of this method, since this use mostly turns philosophical thinking into disputation, and since our times no longer arm themselves with Sorites paradoxes and enthymemes. [Because of this] it is just as fruitless a task to concern oneself with the tying and untying of such knots as it is to toss lentils through the eye of a needle.

But can they not become more useful? I will answer this question differently for scholars and for the people, which knows nothing about the law of a Logic. When I consider what is good in our Logic precisely, our Logic seems to me to be merely a quite wrongly separated part of psychology [*Psychologie*] that must be treated as metaphysics and not at all presupposed as instrumental knowledge. Our Logic presupposes the greater part of psychology, unless one wants to consider it as mutilated limbs of our soul and as a field full of corpses. For who will speak of the abilities of something whose forces I do not yet know? But our Logic must also be united with the marrow of the science of the soul [*Seelenlehre*] if it is to be useful. In short, I have attempted to plant its limbs back into the body, and I have seen how then everything lives, a spirit enters these bones, they are full of life.

[17] Gaier (G1:976) conjectures that there is an allusion here to the practice among Egyptian peasant women of giving birth while squatting on the ground, a practice presumably leading to the newborn infant sometimes choking in the dust, and to related problems for the midwife. The midwife is presumably the philosophical teacher whom Herder is discussing – in virtue of an allusion to Socrates' use of the metaphor of the midwife to describe himself and his philosophical activity in Plato's *Theaetetus*.

[18] Reading *ihnen* for *ihr*.

9

But is this not *at most* a mistake in ordering [the disciplines]? It would be a big enough one etc. But it is also a mistake in the *matter itself.* If Logic ought to be treated as metaphysics, then I must *dissect* the subjective concept of thought and the objective concept of truth, not explain and name them in an arbitrary fashion, but unfold them, and by means of an extensive analysis of the concept so to speak seek the origin of all truth and science in my soul. In this way this part of psychology becomes an art of invention,[19] an art of judgment and verbal presentation, when it shows these capacities within me, when it, so to speak, impresses on me a philosophical history of good and bad use, when it reveals my soul to me as, so to speak, the spirit from which a science has flowed with all its mistakes, riches, etc. In this way, it cannot fail to happen that if I have a motive within me it will hereby be awakened, that I so to speak make myself into God and philosopher in respect of my own soul, like Peter[20] etc. – The proof lies in the inventions.[21]

This much presupposed in order to determine how Logic in itself – but without my giving this name to another science – can become useful. And for the people's use? If there existed a Logic which was arrayed in all the *ideal perfections of our idol,* which banished errors, etc., should it become more universal for the use of the people? As long as one passes judgment on the perfection or imperfection in an ideal science of thought without showing this goddess in the plain clothes of humanity, one acknowledges much to be good which itself shows its flaws in its application. Certainly philosophical thinking is a perfection. But whether this perfection is one for human beings like us whose slogan was spoken by nature, "Live, reproduce, and die!" and whether thinking philosophically is for citizens to whom the state spoke the slogan "*Act!*" is a question which is *very relevant* for our problem.

All philosophizing (in the strict sense) to which the best Logic can raise us is dispensable to the state. Let someone ask the project-man Beaumelle[22] and name for me that greatest action, that finest project, which grew in the lap of abstraction and not in the bosom of healthy reason. The greatest deeds of war, the finest establishments of the state [are] pure fruits of the Logic which our nurses implanted in us, not of the Logic which our schoolteachers wanted to stamp us with. And if no philosophy may be

---

[19] Or: discovery.   [20] I.e. Peter the Great.   [21] Or: discoveries.
[22] L. A. de la Beaumelle (1726–73), an author who wrote on his contemporaries' passion for projects.

permitted to raise itself up to these rungs, then the people is even more free of these ordinances. *of Logic* .. [*we're not thinking for self*]

The highest degree of *philosophical ability* cannot at all coexist with the highest level of the healthy understanding; and so the dissemination of the former becomes *harmful* for the people. As soon as our soul transcends the bounds of need, it is insatiable in the desire for excess, and if philosophy determines nothing essential in what is necessary, then it is among those sciences which never allow an end of curiosity. If philosophy raised us *to thought* we would unlearn action; for if any Muse loves tranquillity it is the goddess of philosophy. Clinging to creations of our own reason – something which we philosophers learn thoroughly – we give up the habit of lively regard for the creations of nature and society. We lose the honorable name of a patriotic people if we want to be scholars. Opinions hold sway here just as much as there. But does not a higher thinking alone remove a thousand mistakes, prejudices, errors of the healthy understanding? Let someone name for me instead of a thousand just one. All the shortcomings of the healthy understanding must be capable of being removed by itself. Thus does nature everywhere cure itself. And it is not angels that are sent as doctors for human beings. Our philosophical reason only, like Daedalus, creates for itself labyrinths, in order to make itself a guiding thread; it ties knots in order to be able to untie them; it throws itself into battles where swords and arrows wound in order to play the part of a holy art. O doctor, aid yourself. Lucky is the people that does not need your aid. [?]

So either [do] nothing or, philosopher, you who teach me to think truths, improve my abilities which I need, the healthy understanding. This needs an improvement, but not a guidance. One sees quite naturally that there must be a Logic of intelligence which merits general dissemination by our people, a Logic which, *not yet invented*, must in part however be more difficult than our rules of reason, since it should[23] order the imagination and sensation, a Logic which never consists in rules but requires much philosophical spirit for its application. In short, it is the method of "preserving for the human spirit its natural strength in full vivacity, and of being able to apply it to each case."[24]

---

[23] Reading *soll* for *sollen*.

[24] Herder often, as here, uses quotation marks not for quotation but in order to emphasize a statement of his own. This practice takes a little getting used to, but I have retained it in these translations (rather than substituting italics, for example) for several reasons, including (1) the fact that this preserves a potential for double emphasis – italics within emphatic quotation marks – which

Where else is this Logic than in the writings of our patriotic friend of humanity Rousseau?[25] His great theme is all too closely related with mine: he has proved to everyone who has human eyes which have not been weakened by the philosophical telescope "that for the benefit of the human people no development of the higher powers of the soul is desirable," and I have had to prove that for the benefit of the people in the state, of these creatures who are still nearer to nature than scholars, no development of the philosophical powers of the soul is desirable. However, he needed a great philosophical spirit in order to, so to speak, show all these shortcomings of humanity and of those miserable consolers, the philosophers, and equally great philosophers are required in order to set such a negative Logic into operation, to direct the people back to the healthy understanding's well after long experiments at logical springs which, it turns out, are full of holes, etc. Then the truth will become universal for the benefit of the people and our science of thought will become useful for the people.

Recapitulation: Our Logic does not teach us to think more or better (scholarly thought is merely for the scholar, and even that Logic cannot accomplish unless it is treated as a part of metaphysics). The people ought not to become a philosopher, for in that case it ceases to be the people. It is harmful to the people, and the people needs guidance – through philosophy – in other words, the Logic of the healthy understanding.

Are there philosophical truths which should be made universal in order to destroy principles which are practical prejudices and to make people morally good?

Our moral theory [*Moral*] is a science of our obligations. It shows us our duties in a new light. Since it depicts for us reasons in clear colors, it destroys, though, prejudices and bad principles. It educates the philosophically virtuous man, the sublime wise man, who is not clothed in false illusion, who raises himself above the crowd. – Oh, too many praises for even one perhaps to be true.

Herder often exploits, and (2) the fact that it makes possible a faithful reproduction of hybrid cases in which quotation marks both emphasize and quote (such as occur near the start of the *Treatise on the Origin of Language*, for example).

[25] Rousseau's ideas play an important role in this essay. For helpful details, see Gaier's notes.

Has the people real practical bad *principles* contrary to morality [*Moralité*]? I think not. For the majority of them does not in fact act in accordance with any principles in the strict sense. *In accordance with what?* The bridle that guides him. Thanks to nature, which created us, there are not cognitions but sensations, and these are all good. They are voices of *conscience*, our leader, sent by God. They can be made weaker, but not obscured. I draw further inferences. Everything that the *principles* and maxims of moral theory [*Moral*] say each person knows, implicitly and obscurely. Let someone show me a rule of moral theory which I as a human being do not know – that is the best indication that it does not pertain to me. But *obscurely*? Yes to be sure, obscurely. But this obscurity is a shadow of the rule's dignity, it is inseparable from what is moving. All the light that the philosopher gives the rule makes a thing distinct that was already certain for me beforehand. He teaches it to my *understanding*. And my heart, not the understanding, must feel it. If rules make people virtuous, then clothes make men, then the philosophers are gods, they are creators. What one will also want to object to me: the most learned in moral theory sees the truth in the greatest light, he knows reason and rule, he absolutely has to be the most virtuous.

Let my whole preceding section[26] be applied: moral theory does not teach new rules, nor the old rules better; the light that moral theory gives them is for the understanding. (But *are there not prejudices?* How much influence has not the understanding on the heart? But perhaps not philosophical reason.) But are there then only purely virtuous people if conscience is sufficient for moral goodness? No! But ignorance is not what is capable of producing vice. Otherwise nature would have been a step-mother who left such an important function to the very deceptive work of the human being himself. Rather it is ruling prejudices, corruptions, bad dispositions. "Good! And that is what philosophy is supposed to eliminate!" Oh, this is where philosophy is fully disgraced. Overthrowing idols, like false honor, insincere modesty, which are dependent on others'

---

[26] Or possibly just: paragraph. But presumably Herder in the missing opening part of the preceding section on Logic made points about the rules of Logic which were parallel to those which he here goes on to make about moral theory. Hence note that he evidently goes on below to make the parallelism of his preceding treatment of Logic and his present treatment of moral theory complete with the words "And therefore the second part [of philosophy] too is merely a lexicon of terms of art which turn moral theory into an art of disputation."

judgment, which rule tyrannically over the peoples, which have lodged themselves in the finest nerves, which have so to speak molded[27] themselves together with the strings of our hearts, and which cause such infinite evil – can our moral philosophy do this? Oh, on the contrary, it is a new impediment. As soon as sensation turns into principle it ceases to be sensation. I think, I consider, I grasp moral duty – my viewpoint is quite different, I unlearn its opposite: to act, to apply the principle. Each skill is opposed to the other. The greatest teacher of moral theory in the deepest demonstration must as much avoid every pious moan as a listener to a sermon who wants to be moved must avoid the development of a proposition he hears. The scholar who looks at his beauty's cheek through a magnifying glass will discover lumps and holes, sheer proportions, but he will not be moved by beauty.

And what is moral philosophy? A collection of rules which are mostly too general to be applied in individual cases, and yet always remain too flaccid to oppose a whole stream of bad dispositions and form a people's whole manner of thought. Nothing is more ridiculous than hearing a thin philosopher – ex grege communi[28] – go on about the supreme strength of moral theory. Unless another science helps him – be it metaphysics or politics or often even a miserable economics – he is a mere talker. If you take away from him his philosophical barrel which he stands in, if you take away from him the venerable barbarism of his words, then he gets booed off.

And therefore the second part [of philosophy] too is merely a lexicon of terms of art which turn moral theory into an art of disputation. And anyone who asked a teacher who has written twelve disputations about the highest good whether he possessed it more than all those whom he wanted to teach would earn the answer: this is as irrelevant to the matter as etc.

But I know that some teachers of practical philosophy lay claim to the great merit of wanting to edify. I do not want to investigate whether this does not usually happen at the expense of philosophy, since it is far easier to moralize than to penetrate into the fundamental grounds of moral theory. So I only point out that in this it is no longer the philosopher but the human being who speaks – and the human being will also understand it and profit from it, but for everything else I need to be a *philosopher*. And

[27] Reading *bildeten* for *bildete*.   [28] From the common herd.

14

here one sees that the question resolves itself into our previous position: the people must be a philosopher in order to understand moral theory. But at what cost! It no longer remains the people; tanti poenitere non emo![29]

In brief, it turns out: Moral theory, in order to remain philosophy, must remain nothing more than a metaphysics of the will which scouts out my sensations, my strength, my moral feelings, and my basic drives – the animal, the spirit, great depths of divinity, and infinite elucidations, etc.[30] Then it must erect our obligations from these drives, up to the highest first concept of morality [*Moralität*], of a law. It must bring this to the sharpness of metaphysical demonstration. It must not only cite the vices but explain them etc. Although I could say much about this – the extent to which our moral theory has become demonstrable or not etc., to what extent it has confused the boundaries etc. – I merely indicate the viewpoint and leave it at that etc. I am not working on the question "How can philosophy be made useful for the benefit of philosophers?"

The people need philosophy neither in order to think nor in order to have better sensations. Philosophy is therefore very dispensable as a means to purposes. Its path is too laborious to be my path. So, you philosopher, who want to make philosophy universal, behold its shortcomings etc. If you do not see them, all right, you are still blinded by its false illusion etc. Strip it, see it with the human being's eyes, and it will appear to you a Venus, but not that heavenly Venus, the sister of wisdom etc., but the earthly Venus, the sister of learning etc., the deformed offspring of human beings who fornicates with her fathers.[31] But if you know her, good!, I implore you by the holiest thing that I can name, by yourself: be a human being and have sympathy with your brothers who are better than you, who think healthily on the path of nature without getting lost in the labyrinth of endless doubts and errors, who are honest without having a hundred reasons and as many doubts and among the hundred doubts a thousand errors. Behold!, you are already a philosopher; oh, be a human being, and think for human beings, that they may act and be happy. In this way you sacrifice yourself for a world. Philosophy is not universal but, fortunately, *narrower*, and precisely thereby more useful.

---

[29] I do not buy at such great cost in order to repent.
[30] The thought behind this string of topics and its connection to the context are obscure.
[31] For the two Venuses, cf. Plato's *Symposium*, 180d.

The truths of abstract philosophy viewed as purposes.
Should they be made universal?

From this point of view they merely satisfy our curiosity, and stand in opposition to a happy ignorance.

Yet curiosity is a very effective drive in the soul, since it is this that has changed the sphere of the human being into the broad orbit of the scholar, the needs of the animal into the needs of a human being. Since curiosity has become a mother of philosophy, her sons habitually show her great favor in return. They call her the first, simplest, most effective impetus, indeed even the basis of all pleasure. Speaking loosely, they are right, but in reality she is not the first basic drive, but the instinct for self-preservation is her father; she is a drive composed from self-preservation and self-defense, and within the bounds of nature merely defensive, never offensive. The Hottentot is also curious when it is a matter of investigating terrible ships which are arriving, but dead to every finer curiosity. The latter is an artificial drive which aims at pleasure, and hence the last and most superficial of all impetuses of the soul. It runs through nature and creates for itself – when one allows it free rein – new worlds, realms of ideas. Here it becomes insatiable, infinite. It transcends our abilities and either dreams up for itself imaginary clouds of errors and hypotheses, or if it has run through the whole course of things becomes dull, and we cry out "All is vanity!" Since even in the midst of its pleasure's passion only color constitutes light and shade [for it], [since it] stays clinging to the surfaces of things without excavating their viscera, since its essence is inconstancy and its fetish change, it is not the main pleasure but the last pleasure. To be sure, it is found wherever anything delights, but it is the last thing that makes them delightful.

Our curiosity is therefore not at all unqualifiedly good, and if one accepts as the first main law of a soul the drive to extend our ideas, then even a perverse idea still has a claim on my cognition, and the people, in order to become human beings, must stretch itself to the very limit of the abstract. A sad fate, which entangles me in eternal errors and tears me away from myself. Indeed this is the first principle of the philosopher, but is curiosity your happiness? [If you follow it,] you are an insatiable dropsy, and even if you were to drink pure nectar, you are unhappy.

So why do we want to waken the ear of those unphilosophical people to a siren song which draws them further and further from their way and plunges them into ruin? Why do we want to make them thirsty in order to be able to slake them? Why do we want to take them, who already taste the bitterness of curiosity, away from their happy ignorance? O you who wish to tear away with a bold hand the veil that nature wove before things, may your hand tremble back. You schoolteacher, who force your pupils to abstract philosophy, you work contrary to nature – feverishly and yet uselessly, indeed as a destroyer of nature.

In reality, it is also the case that the whole of metaphysics has nothing worthy of mention, since it merely *says* what the healthy understanding thinks. The second circle is a tissue of words, the third hypotheses. Our history of philosophy is fable: at most I hear something that concerns the human being and could be allowed to pass; I hear the fool in apophthegms and deeds; or if I get to see the philosopher, then it is his bust, mutilated like Dagon,[32] and the hands and head have been added by the charity of moderns, as with most Roman statues. These [statues] deceive many, but not Winckelmann, whom the former do not indeed know, but then what does the healthy understanding think about this etc.? Did the philosophers not almost always form a sect, never the same one, never the *right* one – perhaps still now not, and perhaps also still now more the work of three great men whom the rest piously echo as the cause of all learned nature than the actual cause of all learned nature?[33] These days we piously echo three men, and each of us has his head. The first was a mathematician, everything that the healthy understanding thinks naturally and healthily he flooded with etc. Another is a theologian etc. The third is a mystic and poet etc.[34] What truth of ontology can claim etc.? It is fitting that the ancients called it 'terminology';[35] it is still now a box of words too. Whoever will [enter] the fray etc.? Is the whole of cosmology, except for a little which belongs to natural theology, not a particular tissue of words which explains chance in terms of the world and the world in terms

---

[32] Dagon, God of the Philistines who was knocked down and mutilated (1 Samuel 5:2–6).

[33] The text is messy here. I am reading the words *als der Sache ganz gelehrter Natur* as a conflation of two constructions: (1) *als die Sache ganz[er] gelehrter Natur* (i.e. the second half of the comparison introduced by *mehr*); (2) *als der Sache ganz[er] gelehrter Natur* (i.e. specifying how the rest *nachbeten* the three great men).

[34] Gaier conjectures that the three men in question here are Descartes, Leibniz, and Shaftesbury, respectively.

[35] This was a scholastic name for ontology.

17

of chances etc.? Who will dare to enter the Humean quarrel about the commerce of bodies[36] (natural theology)? Few attractions [in this] for the human understanding, unless it is very degenerated. It is fortunate that nature gave human beings no inclination for it. They are human beings, not philosophers.

Philosophy is in general useless for human beings, useless for each human being, but also harmful for society. The people loses its honorable name of 'people' when it etc. It unlearns attentiveness to small things when it concerns itself with grounds etc. Which Hume also [says] about businessmen etc. At least they are not [inattentive] when they work.

These days politics has incorporated his[37] opinions and errors. Either a revolution must proceed, which is impossible given our present luxurious weakness, or discordant etc. It is some benefit to remove the opportunity for worse. [This] requires application to our schools, female education. The benefit of the people.

Second section[38]

So push forth, O people, into the holy places of philosophy. Tear down all the idols, and construct there state buildings, assemblies where instead of philosophical nonsense the healthy understanding counsels the state, humanity. Tear from the philosophers their Diogenes-capes and teach them pillars of the state.

No, O republic!, by means of this devastation you plunge yourself into the jaws of barbarism; to avoid a small harm, you drown yourself in the Euripus.[39] A thousand others lurk around you who, even if they always think the same way you do, would now think in opposition to you.

Only philosophy can be an antidote for all the evil into which philosophical curiosity has plunged us.

Certainly the transplantation of a state into finer circumstances has, like Pandora's box, spread misfortune. But it is also the case that only

---

[36] Gaier plausibly interprets this as an allusion to Hume's concern with the problem of the interaction of bodies *with souls* – a problem which was also central to German philosophy in the eighteenth century, e.g. in M. Knutzen and the precritical Kant, where it involved a large theological dimension (hence the "natural theology" which here follows in parentheses).

[37] Or possibly: its (i.e. the people's). The meaning of this whole paragraph is rather unclear.

[38] Note that this section takes the form of a (semi-explicit) dialogue between (initially) opposed viewpoints. See the editor's introduction for some discussion of this Herderian technique.

[39] Euripus, a Greek sea-strait.

philosophy is the antidote. Philosophy thinks for a million others so that these act; it does not teach them so that they should improve themselves but itself improves them – on the streets, as it strayed, it learned to give others right directions; it forms [*bildet*] the human being, the citizen, in accordance with better principles. In this way it becomes useful, for the benefit of the people. The patriotic philosopher becomes an honorable bard among his brothers; peoples listen to his every word; he proclaims philosophy.

To be sure our philosophy must descend from the stars to human beings. The abstract component must for its part remain unattacked, un-mutilated. But is there not in addition to it a philosophy which is imme-diately useful for the people: a philosophy of the healthy understanding? I must talk to the people in its language, in its manner of thought, in its sphere. Its language is things and not words; its manner of thought lively, not clear – certain, not proving; its sphere real advantage in daily affairs, foundations for advantage, or lively pleasure. Behold!, that is what philosophy must do in order to be a philosophy of the common people. Who recognizes our philosophy in this picture?

Instead of Logic and moral theory, this philosophy with a philosoph-ical spirit forms the human being in independent thought, and in the feeling of virtue. Instead of politics, it forms the patriot, the citizen who actually acts. Instead of a useless science of metaphysics, it presents him with a really delightful one, which immediately . . . Behold what I have to accomplish in order to have said what I want! And fortunately most of it is prospects which have already for a long time been favorite plans of mine.

No, O people, you remain honorable without putting on fancy airs through philosophy. But the philosopher too remains more honorable for one, equipped with the unction of the sciences. He, who attained perhaps the highest level to which the human spirit raises itself, who in order to develop his soul renounced so much pleasure, who in order to enjoy a pleasure of the understanding withdrew from the enjoyment of life, he is honorable for you.

However, not only [as] a prodigy of the unusual should he [receive] admiration, but make prayer to his shade as a martyr for the truth. Since he ran such difficult courses in order to guide you on an easy path; since he thought learnedly on the streets which he found before him in such a bad state in order to free you from them; since he made it more difficult for his own heart to be moved through a web of speculation in order to justify your cause; since he mined the first principles of politics so that you could apply the mined gold for the decoration of your townhalls; since he strayed through the field of metaphysics in order to make more exact distinctions in the experiences of natural science – kiss the sweat from his brow, he is for you a martyr. One does not fell a cedar; even if it falls, it needs the space of colossi and fells many small bushes.

Who can determine the border between philosophy and the other sciences? As soon as philosophy is banished, barbarism comes unavoidably. The human understanding is deprived of its highest level, it is limited and lets its wings sink. Barbarism is a leaven. In order to see the truth of my point, let the present condition of the sciences and the governing tone of philosophy in all the sciences be considered. The theologian as much as the jurist, the doctor and the mathematician, all want to make abstract philosophy their foundation, but virtually all have mixed up its[40] borders. Now although most of this is based on a false appearance and on a remnant of scholastic philosophy, nevertheless such a revolution would have to occur first in order that not everyone wanted to become a philosopher when he had no right to become one. Something that will be enduring . . .

Certainly I concede that the theologians etc. can build their heaviest principles on the healthy understanding. But when their enemies receive weapons against them from a half-understood philosophy, creep into the dark, [cover] themselves with fig-leaves etc., then a philosopher must know their tricks of combat in order to use these in defense. Then even if they fought with all their might, he would always defeat them.

You the philosopher and you the plebeian, make a common alliance in order to become useful. That much [this alliance][41] can expect of every citizen, and likewise from you [the philosopher], who are supposed to be a good example, who have eaten the marrow of the state for so long and have always produced ambiguous benefit.

[Third section]

However, the benefit of the philosophers for the people has so far overall been small. Even if these philosophers had the mines etc., they are usually specters in social intercourse, and cannot put all their finds in a favorable

---

[40] Or possibly: their.   [41] Or possibly: the plebeian.

light. Schoolteachers to the common part of the people, and academics to the galant shadow-spirits . . . Their language, method, manner of thought, perhaps also really their activities, have formed a fence, and it is a problem which must concern every philosopher's head and every friend of humanity's heart, How can I . . . ?[42] Those savages[43] demanded of the academic who had clambered onto the cordilleras[44] to be told where his cow was, and very often the benefit that one expects from a philosopher is just as etc. If we are right that it belongs within a philosopher's domain, then woe to philosophy if usability should decide it. In order to become useful, learn to write and calculate, to think nothing and say much. However, it is still not good that the philosopher should exist merely for himself.

No!, the philosopher himself must determine his benefit (he is his[45] highest tribunal). Let him ask the human being, the patriot, the philosopher within himself. The people is only a human being and patriot, nothing of philosophy belongs under its jurisdiction. You [the philosopher], and not the people, know whether you have been a poison. Be you, and not the people, an antidote as well.

I here divide the people and the philosophers into two parts: one part philosophy must merely form to become acting machines; for the others the philosopher can indeed strike a note so that they start thought themselves, but without taking them up into his guild. The former is accomplished by a philosophy in the form of an art, the latter by a philosophy in the form of a technical science.

The human being who merely acts knows no other categories than man and woman, and if philosophers can form souls why should it not be possible for there to be among them men-philosophers and women-philosophers?[46]

If philosophy [*Philosophie*] is to become useful for human beings, then let it make the human being its center. Philosophy, which has weakened itself by far too huge overextensions, will become *strong* when it restricts itself to its center. Let a philosopher [*Weltweiser*] who is a human being,

---

[42] I.e.: How can I make the truths of philosophy more universal and useful for the benefit of the people?

[43] Herder frequently uses this demonstrative form of reference in order to introduce a familiar story or proverb.

[44] Mountain ridges, especially in South America.   [45] Or possibly: its.

[46] "Men-philosophers and women-philosophers" preserves an ambiguity in Herder's German which would permit either a less or a more radical interpretation: are the "women-philosophers" merely (male) philosophers *for* women, or are they philosophers who (also) *are* women?

a citizen, and a wise man [*Weiser*] go through the retail store of our philosophical specialties – much-promising titles which would often be useless even if they lived up to all their promises. Seneca said about all finery, "How much I can do without!" – and let us throw three-quarters of our learnedness overboard in order to reach the harbor safely with that little amount. The art of squandering is a necessary part of the household regime of a rich man who does not wish to be too full or too poor.

I shall bury ninety-nine pounds and make the most of the hundredth. And who should say this more than the man who wants to make himself useful to the people, which does not know what [is] right etc. and also does not need to know it? Happy if philosophy showed him the path on which he teaches the people to act without thinking, to be virtuous without knowing it, to be citizens without pondering about the fundamental principles of the state, to be Christians without understanding a theological metaphysics.

[Logical education [Bildung][47]]

A philosophy that wants to be useful must begin by removing harm, and this first of all in a human being's education [*Erziehung*]. As long as the child is still merely an animal, the philosopher merely leaves it in the hands of human beings, but of human beings whom he has already himself improved by means of his principles – very rarely the doctor and not at all the teacher of religion. Here he molds the child's body without compulsion, and its senses with all the freedom of the animal. In order to achieve this one must make the higher faculties ripen as late as possible, and in more than one respect keep in mind the principle: do not educate [*bilde*] the philosopher until you have educated [*gebildet*] the human being.

When the *embryo* is developed then philosophy gives the second great counsel through a thousand experiences: let him taste the marrow of philosophy without ever recognizing it, and let him merely digest it as nutritive juice. Set before him instead of words a large number of actions, let him see instead of reading, instead of wishing to educate [*bilden*] his head let him educate [*bilden*] himself and merely protect him from miseducating

---

[47] The basic meaning of the verb *bilden* is *to form, to mold*. But it frequently shades over into meaning things more like *to educate, to cultivate,* or *to civilize*. I have preferred the former translations wherever they are not too misleading – as hitherto in this essay – but have resorted to translations from the latter group where they would be – as here.

[*mißbilden*] himself. All the great preparations of method, the profession-
ally philosophical aspect of the understanding, merely achieves illusion,
it gives the people a quite mistaken concept of this holy name.

Try to imprint in him a philosophical spirit, so that he[48] never desires
to become a professional philosopher. May your main law be freedom and
dependence on oneself, uncompelled self-observation, and independence
from others' judgment. Everything that the philosophers teach and cannot do, those do who are closest to nature, the simple country-dwellers.
These are the greatest observers of nature, in their serfdom the freest
people, who despise the tyrant honor, who never let others' judgment
take precedence over their own. In short, O philosopher, go to the country and learn the way of the farmers, refine this picture into an ideal,
and overthrow the unphilosophical manner of living, overthrow the idol
which shows you philosophy as corruption of the world, but not through
philosophy. He who inspects the people with a philosophical eye, how
many uncomprehended concepts... When it is taught nothing foreign
etc. We learn merely what we do not need. Let this be said to the private
tutors, they can improve a whole house if they are philosophers; to the
country people; to the teachers of religion, from whom we unfortunately
also learn to think; to the teachers of the humbler part of the people.

[*Moral education* [Bildung]][49]

Philosophy becomes useful if it shows the ways to make him virtuous
without science. Perhaps they are these:

If one does *not make him virtuous too early*.[50] Among all conditions of
the soul it is morality [*Moralité*] which develops latest. If ever abstract
concepts are at all necessary even for the people which should merely act,
then they are the moral ones, and even these, I should like to say, because of
the misuse which has already been introduced. But go through all the ranks
of the people: in no subject are there as many uncomprehended names

---

[48] Reading *er* for *er es*.

[49] A sentence from Herder's essay plan relating to this section is worth quoting: "*Moral theory*: Let
one not educate [*bilde*] through speculation but through public fora the feeling for the noble."

[50] The exact force of this "If..." sentence and of those that follow at the beginnings of subsequent paragraphs is not entirely clear. The force could be simply that of a conditional with an
aposiopesis implying "then philosophy becomes useful" (cf. a moment ago "Philosophy becomes
useful if..."). Alternatively it could be that of a tentative proposal, modeled on the French "si on
(+ imperfect)." Or perhaps it hovers between the two.

as here. Oh, and our holy religion itself becomes in the people's mouth a collection of barbaric words which they do not understand (words which belong in the Orient). I am too modest to say that their teacher himself did not understand them, too modest to say that they mean nothing *for us* except through accommodations. I say only: perhaps they were taught to them as prejudices. There really is an age without morality [*Moralité*], and to want to implant virtue in it is to impress on the heart an attitude which retains its quirks for ever. What explains the fact that virtue is almost an ideal picture which each paints specially for himself, often a Dulcinea of Toboso?[51] What explains the fact that virtue almost suffers the same fortune as our sensations of beauty when they were planted on sensations and not on reason? It sprouted too early. I think, I embrace *virtue*, and it turns out to be an attitude of strict or sweet sensation adopted invito genio meo.[52]

If one does not teach him virtue but imprints it in him. The moral concepts are, among all concepts, very subtle, and yet they are perhaps the *only* abstract concepts which given the present condition of the world are least avoidable. But go [through] all the ranks . . . Even our religion etc. On the other hand, if I make an enclosure around these abstractions, then let my philosophy make itself as useful as possible. If I do not preach virtue to his understanding, but preach to his conscience the virtue which he understands, then I merely lend a hand to nature. On the ground of his conscience the whole field already sleeps etc. I wake it up etc. I impress in him an image which never dies out, and without any help from art. No sophistry can confuse him, because he learned this image without sophistry. If I only here had voice enough to awaken our venerable teachers of virtue to be philosophers as well when they preach virtue, and to be such ones as lay aside philosophy! When I here hear one who leads a simple flock into a labyrinth full of distinctions – either the sheep become intimidated and remain ignorant or they get lost in the thorns, they get wounds. O teachers of religion!, how many young souls you have laid waste through words which they did not understand and which developed in them into prejudices that can never be rooted out! Oh, lay aside methods, become children. Otherwise it would be better if you had kept silent. The majority are not sufficiently philosophers in order that to others they . . . You who preach to me in half an hour a pile of uncomprehended

---

[51] An apparent ideal beauty worshiped by Don Quixote who was in reality merely a farm maid.
[52] Contrary to the will of my nature.

moral words which are torn from their context, which are for us Oriental nonsense, take a day's time in order to explain yourself. I bet you will extend the time at least to a year. Are not all these words etc. etc.?

If one does not preach to him duties which are too strict, foreign obligations which his heart does not prescribe to him, but one presents to him true duties in a native light. Our time is not a time of strictness but of luxury, and what was appropriate for other times is perhaps contrary to our manner of thought. Times of rough simplicity have virtues and vices of strength, we have virtues and vices of weakness. They had Alcibiadeses, *and Themistocleses*, and Davids, whereas we are too weak even for the errors in motivation of which they were guilty. If I now attack those crude excesses, I am attacking a foreign castle, and on the side that matters the enemy remains safe and hidden. Oh, let us, in order to become useful, learn morals [*Moral*] from human beings' hearts, not from foreign times. But of course instead of philosophers I am speaking with etc. . . . Whoever becomes my teacher of virtue is my philosopher etc. And where are there gatherings of the people for virtue but [through] preachers etc.? These philosophers one cannot escape etc. From them the most benefit etc. But [they must] also be philosophers. They preach for *men* and *women* etc. So why do they preach like monks who know no women etc.? They preach for people, for society. So why like monks in another language etc.? Why not virtue etc.? Oh, how many great opportunities etc. Confessionals etc. Gatherings etc. Why did you busy yourselves with philosophy etc.? Armed with the prestige of God . . . That is the *interest* of the people – *useful* for ever.

[Political education [Bildung]:] How philosophy can be useful
for the benefit of the people as citizens

Here philosophy must work miracles etc., the time when philosophers were statesmen must come, the state must be improved from below:

If the philosopher educates [*bildet*] citizens, if they are human beings. – Each human being is free and independent from others. All societies are contracts, and if these are destroyed on one side, then they also cease to hold on the other side etc. I must indeed exist in society etc. But one must keep faith etc. Should a monarch [subject] his etc., then the people must force him. Does this not lead to the discontentment of the people etc.? No! Even the farmer will live content in the manner allowed by his

25

unrefined traits etc. I have not the brilliant misery etc. You have what you need.

If one educates [*bildet*] citizens as a patriot. – This fire spreads, reproduces itself etc. Complaint that there is no place for it. But development. In republics it is etc. And society. Education [*Erziehung*] too early. Books. Abbt.[53] Also sermons. Family spirit etc. As soon as I understand that I am connected etc. *Farmer cold* etc. Somewhat more refined family spirit etc. Hence the nobles etc. In schools of war warrior etc., in mercantile cities merchant etc., in republics citizen. There society is not too cold. Deeds ignite deeds etc. Here philosophers are not excluded from deeds. Encouragement when they lend a hand.

If one educates [*bildet*] citizens, not rationalizers. – Preachers as husbandmen – philosophers.

The difference between our republics and ancient republics. Disadvantages when the crowd thinks for us.

A people more refined by books[54]

Women are [part of the] people.[55] A philosopher really ought to think of their upbringing. This is important. Difference between a learned man and woman. They have no means, not academies, not schools, not society, not writings. They can first be improved . . . As the greatest [task] of the schools . . . May they not become philosophers. Not learned. Some sciences omitted. May they not learn by heart. May they learn nothing *masculine*, foreign: wars, politics. May they learn to think beautifully [*schön denken*].[56] Plan of women's studies etc. Of an aesthetic etc. May they learn to feel virtue – very easy. Plan of a morals [*Moral*] for them. May they learn *society and taste*. Means for that: better household tutors; more socializing between both [sexes]; one must get more books into women's hands; suitable organization of the books; of women's occupations; from the side of mothers; from the side of young men; then in society.

---

[53] Herder actually wrote *Abt* here, but means, I take it, to refer to Thomas Abbt, the German patriotic author who was a great favorite of Herder's and the subject of a eulogy excerpted later in this volume. If this is right, he has slightly misspelled the name. As he spells the word it would usually mean an "abbot."

[54] A sentence from the part of Herder's essay plan relating to this section is worth quoting: "Philosophy is reduced to anthropology, modified according to the [different] types of the people."

[55] The part of Herder's essay plan relating to the present section contains a more radical version of this point: "[Women] are the people par excellence [*am meisten*]."

[56] A key concept in Baumgarten's aesthetics.

Nobler males in schools and academies. The changing of them. Nothing should be learned by heart. There should be no disputation. Books should be organized differently. Socializing more open. They are the easiest to improve, closest to the philosopher. Here philosophy is a very good part of luxury. Boredom. Curiosity.

[Fourth section.] Overview

Our philosophy has for so long still lacked a *plan of education* [*Bildung*]. Let the human being be taken out of philosophy, and applied to everything else.

History of humanity – not of human beings (politics, history, fragments); not of humanity's rules; not of humanity's works; but nature itself; the core is psychology and ... the great stage

Diversity of bodies, and of minds [*Gemüter*] etc., of opinions and of tastes, of sensations etc. Great exceptions.

Then the works of humanity, and everything as human being. Fruits of this which he enjoys as a human being.

In duties. Subjective ethical doctrine etc. Variety and unity in everything etc. Lack ...

In religion

In thinking – history of scholarship from the human being; core the history of philosophy

In the political constitution – such a book as Montesquieu – restriction of philosophy to anthropology – luxury should be introduced ... [List breaks off.]

For this plan, great gifts are needed at each point in order to hide the *teacher*, and to make all the impressions into anything but labors. For this plan, equally favorable circumstances are needed on the side of the parents and the pupils, equally favorable connections in society and outside society, much experience and taste and love of humankind on the part of the teacher. In short!, a philosophy which is the finest because it seeks to become useful to the finest part of the people.

And in order to set up this philosophy, is not an introduction of the philosopher into women's quarters and parties required here? A conversation with this fair sex which draws from them, and displays, their finest ideas and enriches philosophy with such a valuable portion, the knowledge of the *fair* [part of the] people, which knowledge must be the foundation

27

for its education [*Bildung*]: education for the human being, the man, society, and children![57]

Fifth section: How can philosophy refine the people's taste for the people's benefit?

The people, which besides the games of the circus needs philosophers to entertain itself as well, has weighty claims that their writings should accord with its[58] time and manner of thought. As soon as it were recognized as a basic rule that one's book must be written not [only] for the inhabitants of scholarship but also for one's neighbors, it becomes a duty to pay attention to every entryway into the taste of the people.

In the oldest time of the Greek and Roman republics the language of the writer and of the common people was identical. Even the divine Homer spoke words which were in his time prose, as *Blackwell* shows,[59] or the people of his time spoke poetry just as each *aoidos* [60] sang it. Something which is paradoxical for us, but which *Longinus* asserts, and *Blackwell* justifies: poetry is older in common life than prose. This is also why the first writers are poets, the first *nomoi* [61] songs, and the oldest religions mythologies, all of which speak the language of the sensuous people, a language which is as unintelligible for us as it would be difficult for our eye to understand their hieroglyphics, or for our ear to put up with their music.

In times of finer culture [*Bildung*] prose developed out of poetry, and Strabo has preserved for us the names of those who became these inventors of the style which accorded with the new *plebeian* taste. Here ever gradually step by step poetry and prose separated[62] over the course of history, until they finally parted ways completely in the times of Ptolemy Philadelphus and here in the times of Augustus, and prose alone remained to the people along with a few minor genres of poetry. Perhaps this is also the reason

---

[57] The translation again here preserves some ambiguities in Herder's German which make possible less and more radical interpretations: Is the "knowledge of the *fair* [part of the] people" merely knowledge *about* it or rather (also) knowledge *belonging to* it? Is the "it" in "its" merely "the *fair* [part of the] people" or rather "the people" *tout court*?

[58] Reading *seiner* for *ihrer*.

[59] T. Blackwell (1701–57), *An Enquiry into the Life and Writings of Homer* (1735).

[60] *aoidos*: singer, bard.   [61] *nomoi*: laws, songs.

[62] This verb is here in the singular, whereas the "parted ways" that follows is in the plural. This singular verb with two nouns is an example of the rhetorical figure of hendiadys ("one through two") – used with striking aptness given the context of thought involved here.

why the later Greeks and later Romans remained inferior in high tragedies and finer comedies.

We have already for ages past counting lost the public: the people [*Volk*] of citizens and the people of scholarship. As long as our ancestors were warriors their bards sang the history of past times; these became legislators when they developed themselves more into cities, and who can count, from this metamorphosis on, all the invasions and transformations which have torn from us the word 'people'? It has been torn from the theater-poets, and *Holberg's* comedy on the bad side and *Diderot's* and *Gellert's* by contrast on the good side show the condescension towards the commoner part of our theater audience that has been attempted. Still more, though, does our *bourgeois* and weepy tragedy bring home how very little we share in the *pathos* of the ancient people. The word 'people' has died out for the philosophers since the moment these had to construct an anthill of their own, and since the moment the distinction came into force that the intellectual world is heaven, the people's republic earth – so to speak two sides of one and the same coin.

All philosophy which is supposed to belong to the people must make the people its central focus, and if philosophy's viewpoint gets changed in the manner in which out of the Ptolemaic system the Copernican system developed, what new fruitful developments must not occur here, if our whole philosophy becomes anthropology.[63] Perhaps there will be some people who expected in answer to the problem I am writing about merely things that I want to include in this section, and so I must try to do justice to these.

[63] This is a rather striking anticipation of the critical Kant's metaphor of a Copernican revolution in philosophy. Presumably, Kant was already using the metaphor prior to the critical period – though, of course, not yet with the full idealist meaning that it would eventually acquire for him – and Herder is here borrowing it from him.

Part II Philosophy of Language

Fragments on Recent German Literature (1767–8)
[excerpts on language]

It remains generally true: "The exactitude of a language diminishes its richness."[a] And in order to make this obvious we may compare the *oldest* language, the Hebraic or Arabic language, with our language in respect to richness; the richness is as different as the domestic economies of those regions and ours. They collected livestock and slaves, we collect gold and household equipment; it is the same with the richness of the two languages.

Their language is rich in *livestock*. In it *names of natural things* are frequent. In the small book of the Hebrews, which is all that we still have remaining, there are already 250 botanical words, names which our language can indeed express but does not *know* how to express,[b] because the *kaloi k'agathoi*[1] of our *bourgeois* world devote themselves to anything rather than gathering shepherds' knowledge, because our natural philosophers live among books and are again turning to Latin books. Our bucolic poets and singers of nature therefore cannot pluck the flowers of these plants; even if we had German names, they would not be familiar enough, they would not have enough poetic dignity, for our poems are no longer written for shepherds but for city-dwelling Muses, our language is limited to the language of books. – On the other hand, *Leibniz* already noted that our language is a language of *hunting* and *mining*. I think though

---

[a] *Literaturbriefe* [i.e. *Briefe die neueste Literatur betreffend* (Berlin, 1759–65)], vol. 15, p. 179.

[b] See Michaelis, *Réflexions sur l'influence des opinions* etc. [I.e. J. D. Michaelis (1717–91), *De l'influence des opinions sur le langage et du langage sur les opinions* (1760).]

[1] Literally: fair/beautiful and good men. But better translated: gentlemen. See, however, Herder's own extended discussion of the term below.

in part *was*, because many of these words are either *obsolete* or serve as terms of art and craft, since our manner of life is no longer the hunt and mines.

We are therefore more concerned with household equipment. Terms of art, bourgeois expressions, social sayings are the commonest small change in oral and written commerce. The ancients, by contrast, exchanged gold pieces; they spoke through images, whereas we at most speak *with* images, and the image-rich language of our depicting poets relates to the oldest poets like an example to an allegory, like an allegory to an image done with one stroke. Read Homer and then read Klopstock. Homer paints when he speaks, he paints living nature and the political world; Klopstock speaks in order to paint, he depicts – and in order to be new – a quite different world, the world of the soul and of thoughts, whereas Homer by contrast clothes these in bodies and says "Let them speak for themselves!"

The economy of the Easterners was rich in *slaves*; and their language is so too. The inventors of languages, who were certainly anything but philosophers, naturally expressed by means of a new word what they were not yet able to classify under another concept. In this way there arose *synonyms*, which were as advantageous for the poet as they are annoying for the grammatical philosopher. The Arab poet who has 500 words for the lion which signify different conditions of it, for example, young lion, hungry lion, etc., can paint with one word and can speak more *many-sidedly* through these images sketched with one stroke when he sets them into contrast with one another than we can who only make this distinction clear through added determinations. The choruses of the Easterners can *almost* repeat themselves in their two contrasting phrases, but the image or the moral receives novelty through an expression or a word. The coloring changes and this change pleases the Easterners' ears, whereas our language which is chained to these *almost-synonyms* must either express the repetitions *without this nuance*, and then they are for our ears *irritating* tautologies, or expresses them with a sheer *glance to the side* and strays from the main idea of the picture, as very often happens in the German translation of the bible. The mistake really lies in the difference between our languages and is difficult to avoid.

This, I believe, provides the explanation of the remark of our philological *prophet* in the Oriental languages "that these tautologies which pleased the ears of the Easterners are intolerable to our ears."[c] *They were not tautologies* for them, for tautologies are always revolting and can at least never please, but when one chorus explained or determined the other, or made the presented picture new with nuances, this satisfied eye and ear. I believe that Michaelis will find that they are in the native language rarely *complete* repetitions. But to be sure, in the German translation, and above all in Cramer's psalms,[2] there we do find perpetuae tautologiae, Europae invisae, aures laedentes, prudentioribus stomachaturis, dormitaturis reliquis.[3]

Cramer seems both in his sermons and in his so-called *odes*, in his cantatas and in his flowing prose, to have got so used to these repetitions and periphrases that he forgets the question whether the German ear, which demands brevity, and the German understanding, which loves emphasis, is satisfied with them. His uncommonly fortunate ease in versification leads him so far astray that he forgets the question whether his repetitions are also appropriate for the German language. His odes – and before *Klopstock* and *Ramler* they were the paradigm of German odes – are often, it must be said, a jingle of rhymes, and I doubt whether a *David* or *Assaph* would in our time and in our language have written psalms in Cramer's manner. "But then didn't he intend to *translate* them, not to *transform* them?" Good, then let him translate them as Oriental psalms with all their light and shade. Only he must not transform anything, for in that case it is much more natural for our genius and language to abbreviate them. I judge frankly, because I believe that I can and may so judge: if *Michaelis* had *Cramer's* talent for versification, or *Cramer* had *Michaelis's* sense of the Orient, then for the first time we would be able to preserve the Eastern poems in accordance with the genius of our language as a German treasure; as things are now, both of them lack something.

But my remark strays too far from the theme that grammar and reasoning about language has weakened its richness. The stewardly philosopher asked "Why are there so many useless *slaves*? They get in each other's way!" and he got rid of them, but prescribed to the others their precise

---

[c] Michael. praef. in Lowth. lectiones P. I. [I.e. J. D. Michaelis, preface to R. Lowth, *De sacra poesi hebraeorum praelectiones academicae* (originally 1753, ed. Michaelis 1758).]

[2] J. A. Cramer (1723–88), *Poetische Übersetzung der Psalmen* (1755–64).

[3] Perpetual repetitions, hateful and jarring for Europe, making the wiser irritated and the rest fall asleep. (This is a free rendering by Herder of a free rendering by Hamann of a comment in Michaelis's preface to Lowth.)

function so as not to be idle. I shall speak without metaphors! When people learned to classify concepts under one another more, then they expressed with a determination (adjective, participle, adverb) that for which they initially introduced a new word. There still remained synonyms, though! But the philosopher sought to bring fine distinctions into them, and hence to use them as new, valid words. In proof I cite for German *Wolff* and *Baumgarten*. Through Wolff's German writings the words which stand under philosophical jurisdiction have been greatly reduced in synonyms, since he attempted to determine them precisely. And even more Baumgarten; go through his metaphysics and take note of the German words cited below; philosophy gives most idle synonyms work and determinate posts. But that is the language of philosophy. Let *Sulzer*, the still living *Baumgarten*, determine the words *angenehm, schön, lieblich, reizend, gefällig*[4] in his aesthetics – the world will be very grateful to him. Let others continue on Baumgarten's path and a *Kant* in his *Observations on the Beautiful and the Sublime* note fine distinctions between words that are almost the same – they work for German philosophy and German philosophical language, but not for language mastery in general.

You cannot determine them all, philological philosopher! You will presumably want to throw those ones away? But does everyday language also throw them away? No! Your jurisdiction does not yet extend that far, and still less into the land of the poets. The poet will inevitably become furious if you rob him of synonyms; he lives from *superfluity*. And if you determine them? But aside from the fact that you cannot, then *beautiful* prose and *beautiful* poetry disappears[5] completely, everything becomes a rosary of counted-out terms of art. It is ever a stroke of luck for the poet and a stroke of bad luck for the philosopher that the first inventors of language were not philosophers and its first developers were mostly poets.

So our language has limited synonyms and strives to collect, instead of slaves, gold and coins. Let me be allowed to compare the words for abstract ideas with these.[6] Both are struck by wilful decision and enter general circulation through a value fixed by wilful decision. The most valuable among both of them get hoarded up as treasures, what is more

---

[4] Roughly: *pleasing, beautiful, lovely, charming, pleasant.*

[5] Herder quite often uses a singular verb for a plural subject in this way. This is an ancient rhetorical figure sometimes known as "the Pindaric construction" (and is distinct from hendiadys, in which the subject is only verbally but not conceptually plural).

[6] "With these," *damit*, is vague in its reference. The sentences which follow show that, while it refers in the first instance to (gold and) *coins*, it also refers to the *limiting of synonyms*.

trivial becomes small change. On this side too there is loss to our poetry, in which the imagined value evaporates and only the natural value counts, where therefore abstract words only count insofar as one can represent them sensually. – The art of poetry can hence gain nothing through our philosophers, and has gained nothing; just as little as the ancients could translate our book- and academic-language in all its nuances can we speak like the ancients.

And now what follows from all this? Perhaps much, but for now one thing may suffice! German could certainly use a *Girard*,[7] very much so, but he must not become a legislator *throughout*. To want to do away with all synonyms in a language which is not an ideal philosophical language is the attitude of a second *Claudius* or *Chilperich*, who wanted to introduce new letters and made grammarians into ABC-martyrs.[8]

*

On the other side, people have to such an extent recommended translations in order to develop our language that I quote a noteworthy passage from the *Literaturbriefe* on this subject:

"The true translator has a higher intention than that of making foreign books intelligible to his readers, an intention which raises him to the rank of an author and refashions the small trader into a merchant who really enriches the state.

Now this intention is none other than that of fitting to his mother-language excellent thoughts according to the example of a more complete and perfect language. In this way did Apollo contrive that Achilles' armor fitted Hector as well as if it had been made for his body.[9] In the absence of experiments which are connected with this intention, no primitive language can become complete and perfect, no prose writer in it can become complete and perfect.

Only public speakers receive enough encouragement to make their own experiments in the formation of the language, and the greatest part of these experiments is in vain. But let one do it by means of experiments on the model of a better language. Such a language already represents to us in a clear way many concepts for which we have to look for words, and

---

[7] G. Girard (1677–1748), French philologist who wrote on French synonyms.
[8] Claudius the Roman emperor and Chilperich the king of the Franks both reportedly had projects of linguistic reform involving the introduction of new letters.
[9] *Iliad*, bk. 17, ll. 209–15. Actually, it was Zeus who did this.

presents these concepts in such juxtapositions that we develop a need for new connections. Not to mention here musical harmony, which can be better measured whenever the ear has immediately beforehand been filled by a sentence very correctly.

What great advantages would not inevitably accrue to our language if it learned to mold itself to the Greek and Latin languages as far as possible, and showed its flexibility to the public's eyes! These translations could become our classical authors. There could be no objection to the thoughts, because the seal of excellence has already long since been set on these; and care in preserving the harmony of their expression would also transfer as much musical harmony into our language as our language's genius permitted. If our translators add to these ancients also some modern foreigners whose genius is proven and whose language is related with ours, what would we not have to be grateful to our translators for! And they would also be satisfied with our gratitude, something that they can receive assurance of from Ebert, whom as an excellent translator we rightly number among our best authors. Are we, then, lacking in the virtue quae serit arbores, ut alteri seculo prosint?"[d][10]

Thus the true translator is supposed to fit words, expressions, and connections to his mother-language from a more developed language, from the Greek and Latin languages especially, and then also from modern languages. Now let us talk about this in accordance with our presupposed premises:

All ancient languages have, like the ancient nations and their works in general, more that is distinctive than what is newer. Hence our language can inevitably learn more from them than from those languages with which it is more closely related; or at least the difference between the two sides supplies philosophers of language with a mass of data for observations. Let us try something of the latter.

Just as the best deeds of heroism which we did as youths disappear from our memories, likewise the best poets are always lost to us from the youth-age of language, because they precede writing. In Greek we have from this time actually only Homer alone, whose rhapsodies by a lucky chance survived for many Olympiads after his death until they

[d] *Literaturbriefe*, vol. 13, p. 98.

[10] The author of this whole passage is Abbt. Its last sentence is here read as a question with Suphan rather than as an exclamation with Gaier. The Latin means: which plants trees so that they may benefit the next century.

were collected, whereas all the other poets before him and many after him are lost. *Aeschylus* and *Sophocles* and *Euripides* concluded the poetic era; in their age *Pherecydes* invented prose; *Herodotus* still wrote his history without refined sentences [*Perioden*];[11] soon Gorgias gave oratory the form of a science, philosophy began to be taught publicly, and grammar was determined.[12] What are we supposed to steal from this time through translations for our language?

Only let it not be *meters*! For it is immediately apparent that these must be difficult to imitate.[13] At that time, when the *aoidoi* and *rapsôdoi* still sang, when people even *in daily life* expressed words in such a *high* pitch that they made clearly heard not only long and short syllables but also *high* and *low* accents, that *every* ear could be the judge of prosody – at that time the rhythm of the language was still *so clear* that the cadence in which the verses were recited or, as the ancients expressed it, *sung* could *tolerate the pace of a hexameter*. And this was therefore the *most preferred* meter, which incorporated the most harmony in itself, which lay as *exactly* in their language as iambics prove natural for our song, and which was most suitable for their ears and throats, because their *melody* in *song* and in the *recitation* of *common life* ascended and descended a higher scale of pitches than ours does. But *we* speak with *fewer* accents *more monotonously*, whether one calls it flowing or creeping; we are therefore not used to the measure of a hexameter. Give a good healthy understanding without school-wisdom iambics, dactylics, and trochaics to read, and if they are good he will scan them immediately; but give him a *mixed* hexameter, and he will get nowhere with it. Listen to the *cadences* in the songs of children and fools;

[11] *Periode* here and in what follows generally signifies not merely any old sentence but a sentence constructed in a careful, roundabout way (cf. the original Greek meaning of *periodos*), in order to meet subtle aesthetic-rhetorical requirements. For fuller discussion, see Gaier, G1:1055–6.

[12] In the second edition Herder adds here: "Hence only Homer stands on the shore of this great, dark sea, like a Pharos, so that it is at least possible to see ahead in one's voyage back in time [*hinan sehen*] for a long distance. And this singer of Greece occurs, I believe, precisely at the point, which is as thin as a hair and as sharp as a sword's sharpness, where nature and art united in poetry, or rather where nature set the completed work of her hands on the border of her realm so that from here on art might begin, but that the work itself might be a monument to her greatness and an embodiment of her perfections. With Homer everything is still nature: song and ethics, gods and heroes, vices and virtues, content and language. Song is rough and magnificent, ethics primitive and at the summit of human strength, the gods mean and sublime, the heroes vulgar and great, vices and virtues between morals and inhumanity, language full of poverty and superfluity – everything a witness to the nature that sang through him, but that set him up as a model whom all art should emulate, though without ever surpassing him."

[13] In the second edition Herder modifies the preceding two sentences as follows: "Meter with great difficulty. At least meter will never become for us what it was for Homer, singing nature."

they are never *polymetrical*. Or if you laugh at that, then go among the farmers, pay attention to the oldest hymns; their falling pitches are shorter and their rhythm *uniform*. By contrast, the Greek rhapsodes sang their *long* poems in *perpetual* hexameters – doubtless *because for their ears the hexameter* was not too long, even for street songs, and for their language was not too polymetric; and because their prosody and manner of singing determined every syllable and pitch properly. But now! If you want to read Greek hexameters, then first learn prosody in order to be able to bring the syllables to their correct pitches! You want to make German hexameters? Make them as well as you can, and then nevertheless have the verse form printed over them, as *Klopstock* was advised to do, or request, like *Kleist*, that this meter be read as prose. Can you recite hexameters? Good! Then you will also know that the best recitation is the one that most hides its feet and only lets them be heard when they support the substance. See! The hexameter and the polymetric meters are so little natural to our language; with the Greeks their *singing* recitation, their ear *used to song*, and their *variously paced* language demanded it, but with us language and ear and recitation forbid it.

What are we supposed to imitate from this time then? The *guiding of the refined sentence* [*des Perioden*]? Not this either! Homer sang and was collected late! The tragedies of Aeschylus and Sophocles were sung throughout on the stage, as the ancients collectively bear witness. The language therefore in those days rested mightily on a recitation which has completely died out for us and which in those days gave it spirit and life. We therefore lose with this recitation also the use of many particles, connectives, and expletives which belong to the recitation of those days. The *All' hotan* with which the oracles always began, the *alla*, *de*, and *autar* of Homer with which he connects the limbs of his sentences, would, since we are used to prose sentences, sound very odd in translation – just as ridiculous as if the honest, blind bard stood up to sing his twenty-four letters to us.[14]

We can therefore imitate nothing of this. But it *does* belong to a poetic reading of the ancients of this era. When I read Homer, I in my mind's eye stand in Greece on an assembled market-place and imagine how the

---

[14] I.e. the twenty-four books of the *Iliad* or the *Odyssey*, which later Greeks distinguished by designating them with the twenty-four letters of the Greek alphabet. In the second edition Herder adds here: "He tears apart and dismembers his sentence, but with the holy rhythm with which – in Theocritus's phrase – the Bacchants dismembered Pentheus."

singer Ion in Plato sings to me the rhapsodies of his divine poet, how he, "full of divine inspiration, amazes his audience; how, when he, beside himself, tells of Ulysses as he reveals himself to his enemies, or of the time that Achilles attacks Hector, he makes each timid person's hair stand upright and heart pound; how he brings tears into everyone's eyes when he sings of the misfortunes of Andromache, of Hecuba, of Priam. Just as the Corybantes, delighted by the melody of the god who inspires them, show their drunken joy in words and gestures, so likewise Homer inspires him and makes him into the divine messenger of the gods."[15] In this delight, my ear and soul are filled with the whole harmony of the hexameter and the whole splendor of Homer's sentence; every connection and every epithet comes alive and contributes to the pomp of the whole. And when I find my way back to my native land again, then I feel sorry for those who want to read Homer in a translation, even if it were as correct as possible. You are no longer reading Homer, but something which *approximately* repeats what *Homer* said inimitably in his poetic language.

Are we supposed to enrich our language with the *inversions* which in those days in their flexible language yielded to every hint of passion and emphasis?[16] Try it! Shackles of grammatical construction have been put on our language, even on the most free and confused Klopstockian hexameter, which will generally destroy the harmony of the Greek sentence. Or are we supposed to train our language in forming *vivid words* [*Machtwörter*][17] in imitation of the Greek? Try it! Even if you are a Swiss, you will often enough have to paraphrase the *epithets* in *Homer, Aeschylus*, and *Sophocles*.

I do not consider the hymns of Orpheus so old that they would in their present form reach back as far as Orpheus. But just as our church language and church poetry constantly remain centuries in the past, those hymns do best show, in my opinion, how the oldest language of poetry in the time of the high style was. Now good! Try to transplant these hymns into German the way Skaliger translated them into old Latin. Despite all the strength, you will nonetheless often miss the old German, which may

[15] *Ion*, 535b–536c, abbreviated. Here translated from the German.
[16] In Herder's second edition this sentence instead reads: "And almost the same thing happens to us with the inversions which in those days in that flexible, unlimited language yielded to every hint of passion and emphasis."
[17] *Machtwörter* are defined as follows by Breitinger in his *Kritische Dichtkunst* (1740): "By *Machtwörter* one means . . . those which signify a concept which is broad and in all aspects precisely determined, which hence make one think of much, and convey a thing with special emphasis," for example, "*to break off* [*abreißen*] the conversation . . . I am on the *threshold* [*Antritt*] of my joys . . . I was ashamed and *cast down* [*betreten*] by this" (pp. 50, 55).

have sounded Orphic with the old Druids in their holy oakwoods! May a young, spirited genius make such bold experiments for our language, but let him also allow old, unbiased philologists to pass judgment on them.

Homer, Aeschylus, Sophocles created the beauties in a language which still had no developed prose; may their translator transplant these beauties into a language which remains prose even in meter and – as we think to have proved – even in the hexameter, so that they lose as little as possible. Those poets clothed their thoughts in words and their sensations in images; the translator must himself be a creative genius if he wants to do justice to his original and to his language here. A German Homer, Aeschylus, Sophocles who is as classical in German as they in their language erects a monument which strikes the eye of neither a fop nor a schoolmaster but which captivates the eye of the wise man through its still greatness and simple splendor and deserves the inscription: HOLY FOR POSTERITY AND ETERNITY! Such a translator is undoubtedly many heads taller than another who translates, from a *nearer* age, from a *related* language, from a people which shares *the same* manner of thought and genius with us, a work which is written in the easiest poetic style, namely *didactically*, and which despite that *still* loses *its best coloring* in the translation – even if this translator should be *Ebert* himself. His Young could still have written his *Night Thoughts* in German, in our time, in accordance with our ethics [*Sitten*][18] and religion. But could those poets have written their works in our language? In our time? With our ethics? Never! As little as we Germans will ever receive a *Homer* who is in all respects for us that which Homer was for the Greeks.

*

I am hence in such great despair about the translation of the oldest Greek poets. But let one try all the more to exploit selectively the Greek prose of a *Plato* or a *Xenophon*, a *Thucydides* or a *Polybius*, and to exploit the later Greek poets. At this period lived the *kaloi k'agathoi* of the sciences, who are more closely related to the genius of our time; the refined sentence [*Periode*] was in its highest splendor; and idioms were becoming milder.

[18] I have used *ethics* as the translation for *Sitten* throughout this volume. But it is important to stress that Herder means by *Sitten* something pre-theoretical (morals or moral customs), not the theoretical discipline of ethics. For the theoretical discipline of ethics he instead usually uses the term *Moral*, which I have normally translated *moral theory*. It was mainly the presence in the texts of this word *Moral*, along with that of another word, *Moralität*, that dissuaded me from translating *Sitten* as *morals* or *moral customs*, as might otherwise have been most apt.

42

From these authors the German language can unquestionably learn much, because it can adapt itself more readily and more flexibly to the Greek language than to Latin, because the Greek language also unquestionably deserves it more, and because for the Germans a developed *poetry and prose of the good understanding* is unquestionably the *best* language.

Heilmann, the translator of *Thucydides*, who certainly knew his author and the art of translation, seems not to have had the flexibility of the German language sufficiently under his control in order to make the German language fit together with the Greek language. However, it must be admitted that this *Baumgartian* philologist still chose his author pretty felicitously, for he does give us the pithy Thucydides, whose manner of writing he has depicted for us with masterful strokes:

"One sees everywhere the attitude of the great, the noble, man who writes as a statesman but who also wishes to write only for statesmen, who has in mind no thought at all of becoming a classical author from whom at some point in the future orators would gather examples for their rules. He thus everywhere looks only to the dignity in the thoughts and the nobility in the expression. He comprehends the thoughts concisely, and in expression he is constantly at pains to keep away from what is common. In his youth he had unerringly grasped the fundamental principles of oratory, but he retained them afterwards in order to use them, not to bind himself to them. He is an author who makes the thoughts everything, and the expression only as much as is required for the thoughts; who comprehends his ideas precisely and concisely, and wants to express them throughout as he has grasped them – and expression, sentences [*Sätze*] and their connections, refined sentences [*Perioden*] and their relations, and everything must tailor themselves to this. His manner of writing and thinking is lofty in the highest degree. He has perfect knowledge of his language, so that he is able to achieve that blossoming which he could have achieved through the richness of expression which he quite lacks through the choice of the most emphatic words and through their energetic bending and combination. And he is bold enough to make this sort of thing when he does not find it already at hand. From these features taken together arises a manner of writing which is difficult, dense, and complex in respect of whole statements, strange and often irregular in respect of syntax, very fruitful but also new and unusual in respect of expression. He is the creator of his whole manner of writing. This is made clear above all by the fact that what is special in his manner of writing nowhere shows itself more than in those places where he is merely thinking for himself, in his speeches and interspersed observations. Here the refined sentences are often of unusual length, for he does not conclude until his series of thoughts has reached its end. Here the syntax is very obscure and interrupted by frequent parentheses, for he wants to express every concept precisely at that point, in that relation, where it occurs in the composite image of his ideas. Here the individual expressions are distant from their usual meaning and use because the usual would not exactly express the balance of his concepts and a paraphrase seemed to him too boring."[e] This is how Heilmann characterizes Thucydides' manner of writing – and perhaps his own as well, as he had formed it through this translation and the reading of Baumgarten's writings. How sharply this depiction contrasts with that which *Geddes* gives of Thucydides – Geddes as a schoolmaster and *Heilmann* as a man of taste. What a shame for German literature that it was robbed of *Heilmann* so early.

One seldom finds Greek-translators of such good taste, and yet one *should* find them, because the German *historical* style can most be formed through the Greeks. And this style is especially in need of forming, "for a language which indicates little distinction in times, which can do little without auxiliary words, which cannot easily replace one mood with another, and which can employ little change in word order – such a language is not especially suited for history, and one must therefore here give it the greatest aid."[f] And that is how the German language is.[19]

But what was Homer in regard to *religion*, to the *artists*, to the *poets*, to the *orators*, to the *wise men*, to the *language*, to *ethics*, to *education* for the *kalous k'agathous* of the Greeks?

This nasty Greek word persecutes me, as much as I flee from it, and my knot is not untied until it is defined. For the critic poses the question: "Is it true that the ancient Greeks taught their youth wisdom from *Homer*? And was Homer even understood by all those who[20] received the epithet *kaloi k'agathoi*?"[g] His question means No! But my answer is Yes! *Aemilius Scaurus* denies it, *Valerius* affirms it – which of the two do you Romans believe?

---

[e] See *Literaturbriefe*, vol. 3, p. 202.   [f] *Literaturbriefe*, vol. 17, p. 187.
[g] *Literaturbriefe*, vol. 1, p. 46.

[19] This first excerpt was from G1:194 ff.   [20] Reading *welchen* with Suphan.

Besides the evidence that I have already cited, I can validate my initial Yes with the following passage from the *Symposium* of *Xenophon*: "'My father,' says *Niceratus*, 'who wanted to make me an effective, honest man (*agathos*) insisted that I learn all the poems of Homer by heart, so that I can still now recite the whole of the *Iliad* and the *Odyssey*.'"[21] Here was a good, fair [*hübscher*] man who also wanted to make his son one and therefore had him learn Homer. So Homer was taught to the youth in this way. So he was certainly understood by those who were *good, fair* people, for they were educated to be so through Homer.

But does *kalos k'agathos* mean a good, fair man or is it a Swiss virtuoso?[22] Both parties can preserve their claim to be right, if they are willing to listen to each other – and if they *throw dust in each other's eyes*,[h] perhaps neither of them is right. More than a good, fair man and far less than a Shaftesburian *virtuoso* in the high taste of our time. I remember having seen the essay of a grammarian about this word, and since I do not like to do what another has done before me, I do not want to make a register of the passages where this word appears. I write from memory.

In every language all words which express the distinctive character of the age must change, and precisely this seems to me true of *kalos k'agathos*. I do not recall having read it in the oldest Greeks; it is a word from the age of beautiful prose and fine political ethics. In the times when *areté*, virtue, still meant only braveness of body and spirit, only a *brave* man counted as *agathos*. Thus in Homer the heroes know no better word for their dignity than when his Agamemnon says, often enough, *agathos gar eimi*.[23] Just as little as the word *agathos* means a *moral goodness* here, at a time when bravery counted above everything else, equally little would this age put up with *kalous k'agathous* in Shaftesbury's refined sense. The word *kalos* had this origin as well, and was applied to the *andrasin agathois*[24] who fought *eu*[25] and *kalôs* (*bravely*) in battle. But with time the spirit of ethics became more refined: the word *areté* meant utility; the words *agathos* and *kalos* meant a man effective in affairs, and even the name of honor *anêr*[26] lost something of its manliness. Because in that age *wisdom*

---

[h] *Literaturbriefe*, vol. 1, p. 52.

[21] Here translated from the German.

[22] Wieland, who lived for a time in Switzerland, had interpreted the Greek expression as meaning a *virtuoso*, following Shaftesbury in this interpretation.

[23] For I am *agathos*.   [24] *andrasin agathois*: *agathoi* men/heroes (dat. pl.).

[25] *eu*: well, mightily.   [26] *anêr*: man, hero.

too was still only a servant of the state, the wise men therefore undertook to educate [*bilden*] such useful men who were *honest human beings* and *effective citizens.* Hence *Xenophon* asks *Socrates* in *Diogenes Laertius*, "Tell me, how can one become a *kalos k'agathos*?" and Socrates introduces him to his own mode of instruction. Hence *Niceratus* says in the cited passage: "My father, who wanted to make me an *effective* man (*agathos*), made me learn Homer." Hence the Athenians, who were foremost in striving for this political culture, were constantly speaking of it (*kalos k'agathos*), and it was for them, as a scholiast says, summa omnis laudationis![27] And therefore certainly perforce more than a good, fair man is for us.

The reviewer says he wants even just a single proof that *kalos k'agathos* means something more than this? Fine! Let it be precisely the passage in which he claims to find nothing more than the good, fair man; unfortunately I find more there, and precisely the description of the *kalou k'agathou*. Socrates asks the young *Theages* in *Plato*: "*ti oun; ouk edidaxato se ho patêr kai epaideusen, haper enthade hoi alloi paideuontai, hoi tôn kalôn k'agathôn paterôn huiees; hoion grammata te kai kitharizein kai palaiein kai tên allên agônian.*"[28] Can *kaloi k'agathoi* here appropriately mean *good, fair people*, as we use this term? No! In order to make their sons into *kalois k'agathois* as well, they made them learn *sciences* (not to read and write the ABC), *music* – which in the Greek way of thinking was far more a fine art [*schöne Kunst*] than it is for us, and inseparable from the art of poetry – and fine [*schöne*] *physical training.* Thus the man who had developed his *understanding*, his *fine taste*, and his *body* was an Attic *kalos k'agathos.* He was neither a wise man nor a poet nor a fighter, but he had the wherewithal to become a wise man, a poet, and an Olympic victor. Whoever wants to see a Greek *kalos k'agathos* in all his glory, let him read – although the word itself does not stand over them as a heading – some of Pindar's odes for his Greek youths, who were certainly more than good, fair boys.

But to be sure not virtuosi in Wieland's exalted taste either! Or rather, directly, in the taste of *Shaftesbury*, from whom Wieland borrows not only the concept of the virtuoso but also the analogy with *kalos k'agathos.* This philosopher, who dresses up Platonism according to the taste fashionable in his day, and who in the end finds this favored taste in Greece as well,

---

[27] The epitome of all praise.

[28] *Theages*, 122e: "What? Did your father not teach and educate you in that in which the other sons of *kalloi k'agathoi* fathers are here educated? For example, writing and lyre-playing and wrestling and other competitive sport."

defines his virtuosi as follows: "The real fine gentlemen, the lovers of art and ingenuity; such as have seen the world, and informed themselves of the manners and customs of the several nations of Europe, searched into their antiquities and records; considered their police,[29] laws, and constitutions, observed the situation, strength, and ornaments of their cities, their principal arts, studies, and amusements; their architecture, sculpture, painting, music, and their taste in poetry, learning, language, and conversation." He afterwards compares with this concept the honestum, pulcrum, *kalon*[30] of the ancients, and philosophizes on in his endearing manner for pages. Now although there was admittedly also an age in Athens when love of the arts, taste in poetry and literature, refined tone in society, and the spirit of passing judgments on police and antiquities were the ruling fashion, I am nevertheless quite unable to persuade myself that the *kaloi k'agathoi* bloomed in those days in Shaftesbury's broad sense. This philosopher rather seems to depict himself, and to raise and refine the taste which in his day held sway at the court of Charles the Second into a certain ideal which can indeed in modern times be a model of a useful, skillful, pleasant man, but which must always transform the concept of the Greek word, even as it is used by *Plutarch* and the more recent Greeks. Admittedly, *Shaftesbury* demands for his virtuoso, if he existed in Greece, the reading of Homer, and that indeed as his first ABC. But a *moral* reading of Homer? An enormous difference!

Why, though, so much about a word? About a word which was ever the expression of their character and the summit of their praises one can never say too much. The explanation of such words unlocks for us manner of thought and police, *character* and ethics, in short, the secret of the nation – without which we always make distorted judgments about a people, learn distortedly from it, and imitate it intolerably. I would recommend it to a man of *philology*, historical knowledge, and taste, as a contribution to the history of Greek and Roman literature, that he track precisely the metamorphosis which in Greek the words *anêr, anthrôpos, agathos, kalos, philokalos, kalok'agathos, kakos, epicheirêtês*,[31] and in Latin the words vir, homo, bonus and melior and optimus, honestus, pulcher

---

[29] "Police" here and in Herder's remarks below in the old broad sense of *civil administration*.

[30] Roughly: honorable, beautiful, beautiful.

[31] Roughly: *man, human being, good, beautiful, tasteful, good and fair, bad, enterprising*. The last word in the list, *epicheirêtês*, is my conjecture in place of Herder's *epicheiragathos*, a word which does not exist in Greek.

and liberalis, strenuus,[32] and such national names have undergone, names which were the honor or shame of their age and which changed with it. That is how one becomes acquainted with peoples, and learns to profit from them.[33]

Perhaps many readers are surprised that I have such high expectations of an empty language-matter. But I have more right to be surprised that people have still drawn so few advantages from the fact that they could have regarded "language as a vehicle of human thoughts and the content of all wisdom and cognitions."

*

Language is even more than that: the form of the sciences, not only in which, but also in accordance with which, thoughts take shape; where in all parts of literature thought sticks to the expression, and forms itself according to the latter. I say in all parts of literature, because if one believes that only in the criticism of artistic literature, in poetry and oratory, much depends on the expression, then one defines the borders of this connection too narrowly. In education we learn thoughts through words, and the nurses who form [*bilden*] our tongues are therefore our first teachers of Logic. In the case of all sensuous concepts in the whole language of common life the thought sticks to the expression. In the language of the poet, whether he articulates sensations or images, the thought enlivens the language, as the soul enlivens the body. All perceptual cognition connects the thing with the name. All of philosophy's word-explanations satisfy themselves least of all, and in all sciences it has had good or bad consequences that people have thought with words and often according to words. Since I give a fragmentary essay on the question of how the thought sticks to the expression in the third part of my book, I continue here merely in a general manner.[34]

---

[32] Roughly: man, human being, good and better and best, honorable, beautiful and free-minded, vigorous.

[33] This second excerpt was from G1:318 ff.

[34] This paragraph is very important but also a bit confused. In order to understand it, it helps to note that, having started out stressing the dependence of thought on language, the paragraph in its last four sentences – beginning at "In the language of the poet, ..." – switches to two other favorite themes of Herder's: (1) the converse dependence, of language on thought, and (2) the dependence of both on sensation.

If it is true that we cannot think without thoughts, and learn to think through words, then language sets limits and outline for the whole of human cognition. Therefore, even merely considering the symbolic aspect of the manner of thought, there must be a great difference between us and higher beings, if one wishes to use of the two sides Homer's saying: "This is what it is called in the language of human beings, but the blessed gods name it differently." This general consideration of human cognition [as occurring] through and by means of language inevitably yields a negative philosophy [which asks] how far human nature should really ascend in its ideas since it cannot ascend higher, and to what extent one should express and explain oneself since one cannot express and explain oneself any further. How much one would be able to sweep away here which we say without in the process thinking anything, which we think falsely because we said it falsely, which we want to say without being able to think it! A man who thought this negative philosophy into existence would stand at the sphere of human cognition as though on a globe, and if he could not raise his head above these limits and look around into open air, at least he would dare to thrust forth his hand and would cry, "Here is emptiness and nothing!" And this man would have in a novel sense the highest Socratic science: of knowing nothing! If I am not mistaken, in that case ideas would creep away out of our whole metaphysics, from ontology to natural theology, to which merely the words have given admission and a false citizenship – and they are precisely the ideas about which there has been most conflict. Nothing is more prone to be quarreled about than what none of the parties understands, and unfortunately there is nothing that humanity is more inclined to than wanting to explain [to others] what it cannot explain to itself.

We think in language, whether we are explaining what is present or seeking what is not yet present. In the first case we transform perceptible sounds into intelligible words and intelligible words into clear concepts. Hence a matter can be dissected for as long as there are words for its component concepts, and an idea can be explained for as long as new connections of words set it in a clearer light. In the second case, which concerns the discovery of new truths, the discovery is often as much an unexpected consequence of various word connections as can be the product of various combinations of signs in algebra. And so what remarkable impressions can language not bury even into the deepest ground of the abstract sciences!

In every type of sensuous and beautiful expression these impressions are certainly more visible and recognizable. And in common life it is indeed obvious that thinking is almost nothing but speaking.

Hence each nation speaks in accordance with its thought and thinks in accordance with its speech. However different was the viewpoint from which the nation took cognizance of a matter, the nation named the matter. And since this was never the viewpoint of the Creator – who not only saw the becoming of this matter in its inner nature but also commanded it – but was instead an external, one-sided viewpoint, this viewpoint got imported into the language at the same time too. Precisely thanks to this, it was therefore possible for the eyes of all later people to be, so to speak, accustomed, tied, limited, or at least brought close, to this viewpoint. In this way truths and errors were preserved and passed on, as advantageous or disadvantageous prejudices; advantageously or disadvantageously, side ideas attached themselves which often have a stronger effect than the main concept; advantageously or disadvantageously, contingent ideas were confused with essential ones; areas filled or left empty; fields cultivated or turned into wastelands. The three goddesses of human cognition – truth, beauty, and virtue – became as national as language was.

If then each original language which is the native growth of a country develops in accordance with its climate and region, if each national language forms itself in accordance with the ethics and manner of thought of its people, then conversely, a country's literature which is original and national must form itself in accordance with such a nation's original native language in such a way that the two run together. The literature grew up in the language, and the language in the literature; unfortunate is the hand that wants to tear the two apart, deceptive the eye that wants to see the one without the other. He is the greatest philologist of the Orient who understands the nature of the Eastern sciences, the character of the native language, like an Easterner. He is an original and national Greek whose sense and tongue have been, so to speak, formed under the Greek sky; whoever sees with foreign eyes and wants to talk about Greek holy places with a barbarian tongue, him Pallas does not regard, he is an unconsecrated person in the temple of Apollo.

The literature of foreign peoples and languages is often imported among other nations as a foreign colony; and because of this mixing together of ideas, of ethics, of manners of thinking and seeing, of languages, and of sciences, everything has necessarily had to take on such a different form that literature seems to be a true Proteus when one pursues it through peoples and times and languages. Borrowed viewpoints got shifted to a new manner [of thinking and seeing], inherited truths got restruck to the point of unrecognizability, half-understood concepts became ghosts, incorrectly perceived objects became bizarre forms, and a language which has received its literature from various climates and regions, from many sorts of languages and peoples, must naturally be a mixture of equally many foreign manners of representation which have won a place in one science or the other. To the extent that this language has taken colonies from various dialects for the cultivation of its learning, to the same extent it will also approximate the Babylonian mixing of languages, and will often be a Cerberus which barks out nine different sorts of language from nine mouths, albeit in words which are pure and its own. If every language leaves behind impressions in those sciences which dwell in it, then it must unquestionably be possible to see in the literature how many hands and forms it has been in, in how many different sorts of languages people have thought about it.

Each head who thinks for himself will also speak for himself, and so his manner of expression gets formed in his own way too: he will impress on his language characteristic features of his manner of seeing and characteristic features of the weaknesses and virtues of his manner of thought, or in short, a distinctive form of his own, into which his ideas have cast themselves. Now I have noticed from experiences that thought and expression do not seem to interdepend in an equally firm way with everyone who thinks and speaks, that not merely is the manner of expression looser and more flexible in one person's case than in another's (for this is too familiar and easy to explain), but in the latter's case the thought itself sticks more to the word and the whole manner of thought is, so to speak, more symbolic and sign-interpreting than in the former's case. Much could be said about this point, and perhaps much that is useful – but this does not belong here. For here let it suffice that even if we only posit a few authors of rank and respect who accommodate their thoughts to their language or their language to their thoughts in such a distinctive way of their own, then necessarily there are, both on the small and on the large scale, phenomena worthy of consideration.

The matter about which I am writing – that language is the tool, the content, and, so to speak, the cut, of the sciences – is so immeasurable, even in a plan that aims to do no more than sketch viewpoints, that it seems to me that, with all that I have said, I have still said nothing of what I wanted to say. So I shall break off.[35]

But to begin with, a word of refreshment for this dark way towards the origin of language – for me and my readers. It is always one of the most pleasant fields that human curiosity can stray onto to philosophize about the origin of that which is. If we can even half flatter ourselves with the sweet dream of knowing *what* something is, unsatisfied, our yearning for knowledge immediately climbs up higher: Was it always that way? How did it become? In the end therefore this yearning has strayed in its ascent up to that bold summit on which it appears like a cloud-creature: that of wanting to know the origin itself, of either experiencing it historically or explaining it philosophically or guessing it poetically.

The last of these is indeed only satisfying for the imagination; for the understanding it is at most a track of footsteps to help it reach the cave where the giant himself is asleep, though also in this respect full of appeal. The oldest reports of the childhood of the world – the beginnings of noteworthy constitutions; early discoveries in sciences and arts; the cosmogonies which each people dreamed up for itself; the poetic fictions in which all wisdom and art clothed themselves at their birth like swaddling clothes – all these survivals from the origin of things would, if collected as remains of an ancient aeon, constitute building material for a temple which, built up from ruins, would be impressive to the eye. With what pleasure we dream through poetic narratives about this or that origin: here *the first sailor*, there the first kiss, here the first garden, there the first dead man, here the first camel, there the first woman – poetic inventions in which the poets of our language are still so sparing. Ovid's *Metamorphoses* are on the one hand as tasteless as fairy tales can ever be; but on the other hand, when they explain to us from mythology how now this, now that, came to be, they can be read as entertaining anecdotes from the archive of divine and human discoverers, as poetic inventions to which a rich poetic imagination gave birth. Homer stands as a vanguard before all others in this too, Homer who knows how to clothe a whole story in an image and the whole creation of a thing in a mythological tale. In Homer one can slumber as pleasantly and enthusiastically over the philosophy of the earliest time as in the temple of poetic Apollo who sent divine dreams.

---

[35] This third excerpt was from G1:556 ff.

Now if one could combine the poet with the philosopher and turn what they both supply into history – a plan which the miserable Polydorus Vergilius[36] so ruined, a plan for which Goguet[37] collected materials with great industry, a plan over which Iselin[38] and others have worked illustriously – what would become of this plan in the hands of one wise about the childhood of the ages? Certainly more than a convoluted play of the imagination and a diversion for idle readers. With the origin of a thing we lose a part of its history – which history must, though, explain so much in the thing – and usually the most important part. Like the tree from its root, art, language, and science grow up from their origin. In the seed lies the plant with its parts, in the spermatozoon the creature with all its limbs, and in the origin of a phenomenon the whole treasure of elucidation through which the explanation of the phenomenon becomes *genetic*. Whence have so many confusions arisen as from the fact that one took the later condition of a thing, a language, an art for its first condition, and forgot the origin? Whence so many errors as from the fact that *a single* condition in which one considered everything inevitably yielded nothing but *single-sided* observations, divided and incomplete judgments? Whence so much disagreement as from the fact that each person considered *these his* concepts and rules, one-sided as they were, the only ones, made them into pet thoughts, decided everything *according to* them, and declared everything *besides* them to be nothing, to be deviation? Whence lastly so much self-confusion, that one could in the end make nothing of a thing which did not always remain the same but always appeared altered – whence all this, but because one did not have the *first* point from which the web of confusion unspun itself, did not have the beginning from which the whole tangle can afterwards be so easily unwound, and did not know the origin on which the whole history and explanation rests as on a foundation.[39]

Now to be sure we are groping in dark fields when we creep off in pursuit of the voice sounding to us from afar, "How did this arise?" And with few arisings does as much night surround us as with the question,

---

[36] Polydorus Vergilius (approx. 1470–1555), Italian historian, author of *De inventoribus rerum* (1499).

[37] A. Y. Goguet (1716–58), French scholar, author of *De l'origine des lois, des arts, et des sciences; et de leurs progrès chez les anciens peuples* (1758).

[38] I. Iselin (1728–82), Swiss historian, author of *Über die Geschichte der Menschheit* (1764).

[39] Herder changes his construction in the course of this last sentence, thereby shifting ground from the weaker claim that ignorance of origins is the cause *most* responsible for various bad consequences to the stronger claim that it is *solely* responsible for them.

"How did language arise?" The causes which weave this darkness can be more easily indicated than dispelled. I shall attempt to indicate them, for a cloud can perhaps more easily be dissolved when one knows whence it arose, and at least many a person who supposes this path so clear will learn to advance more cautiously.

The securest path to knowledge about the childhood of language would be historical reports. But in order for these reports to be possible, to be secure, to reach as far as us – for this one of the most difficult and latest inventions is itself required: the art . . . I do not want to say the *art of thinking*, otherwise I would get into the labyrinth, "To what extent has the art of thinking formed and developed the art of speaking, and vice versa?"[40] So I leave it at the art *of writing* – of writing what one wants, writing for eternity. And how much later is [not] this invention than the art *of speaking* and of speaking what one wants? And how many revolutions had [not] language survived before this point was reached and before a written report was thought of? And for how many centuries does [not] this latter art, in the form it then had, count for nothing?[41] Even tradition, in those days the sole preserver of historical reports, had long since shouted itself hoarse, got mixed up with lies and fables, before the remains of its legend were recorded in writing. Tradition was only ever able like Echo to awaken another Echo, to pass on to the latter a weak, abbreviated, and whispered sound; this sound became more and more abbreviated, dark, and weak; it almost fell silent, and was imperceptible, until it finally found a human ear which was able to spell little or nothing from it. The Greek language had already reached its highest peak in Homer, before anyone had heard of the art of writing books. And so whence *reports* of the origin of language which were not themselves *guesses*?

In addition, no human invention exists immediately, and least of all the first and greatest of all inventions, language! It was not straightaway what it became and is. For behold! this majestic river: it arose – from a source which would in itself have remained unknown had it not given birth to this son. And the source itself? That is more difficult! It sprang forth from hiddenness, arose bit by bit; no one *wanted* to take note of its origin, and it is enough of a task to explain how it *could* have arisen.

---

[40] The subject of an essay by Michaelis cited in an earlier footnote (note b).
[41] The preceding three sentences are all examples of a common Herderian idiom: the rhetorical question, equivalent to a positive statement, which would normally be formulated negatively but which Herder formulates without any negation (here supplied in square brackets).

That is how it is with the greatest things; they were miserable experiments, they became games – knacks – arts – instituted arts – and late enough a science. Likewise with language too: read the great Homer, the essence of all language of the gods, and pursue this divine language back to its origin; you will find it in the husks of human need, in a cradle of childhood, in swaddling clothes, of which you would have to be ashamed.

And even if we do not take on such a towering height, even if we rather go back in search of the beginning when the creature is born, when it sees the light, after it is already completely formed: it was formed in hiddenness, and how it was *begotten* cannot be seen from it. All human productions in this way have a begetting and a birth; from the latter begins form, season of life, and chronology; but how much noteworthy alteration, indeed the whole process of formation itself, is forgotten in contemplating this! Likewise in the case of language: Who can take note of it before it exists, how it comes into being? It must exist, and fully so, before it even becomes capable of being noted, and the investigator wants to know the first step!

Most things in the world are brought forth, further, high, and low through chance, and not through purposeful efforts. And so where am I to go with my conjectures in a magic land of the accidental, where nothing happens according to principles, where everything escapes the laws of the will and of the purposive in the most abrupt way, where everything, including what is greatest and most valuable, falls into the hands of the god of chance? If we had a history of human inventions, how we would find products which arose in accordance with the cosmogony of Epicurus, through a confluence of the atoms! Series of causes worked together, against each other, and after each other; cog caught cog; one motive against the other; without plan or rule one thing harried another; hot and fast the throws changed; chance had almost exhausted its bad lots before better ones fell. Now let someone sketch plans according to a philosophical heuristic concerning how a thing could have arisen, should have arisen – he turns out with all his a priori principles to be a fool! Not how language should have arisen or could have arisen, but how it arose – that is the question!

*

Well then? If people had thought about such a state of affairs when they wanted to make judgments about the origin and childhood of language, what would have happened to many philological hypotheses which were merely tailored according to the modernized yardstick of our times? What to many confused judgments which saw everything in distorted, halved, disfigured shapes because they took their armchair as a viewing point and did not know how to transpose themselves into the times and circumstances in which language came into being and then existed? What to the dictatorial stubbornness which presumed to contradict reports of the ancients without refuting them, to twist them to its own liking, and when they could not be twisted, to throw them away, to ridicule them? And what to the whole hypothesis of the *divine origin* of language *demonstrated from its very nature?*

From its very *nature*? If this had happened, and had happened recently through Süßmilch,[i] then how could he have taken a late, a completed, condition of language for the origin, and how could he have taken a cultivated [*gebildete*] language, on which even with the most primitive people centuries have labored, to which millions of human beings have contributed, which has survived so many ages, for a language in its becoming? Behold this tree with its strong stem, with its magnificent crown, with branches and foliage, blooms and fruits, on its roots as on a throne – behold it *as it is*, and you will admire, marvel, and cry out "Divine! Divine!" But now behold this small seed, behold it, buried in the earth, raise itself up in a delicate shoot, grow buds, win leaves, grow; you will still cry out "Divine!" but in a more dignified and reasonable manner. Let me not be forced to make the application; it is too obvious. Perfection, order, and beauty are in language. But how and when did they enter it? This is the crucial question! If the former tree had *had to* rise from the earth, to press through the lap of its bearing mother [the earth] with its fair top, to break its mother with all its thousand arms, and to raise itself into the breezes with its strong stem, just as it is – if it had *had* to do this – if I had seen it – then to be sure its origin would be unintelligible, inexplicable, divine! If language had appeared to the earth arrayed in all its perfection, order, and beauty, like a Pallas who stepped forth from the head of Jupiter, then I

---

[i] *Süßmilch*, Über den Ursprung der Sprache. [I.e. J. P. Süßmilch, *Versuch eines Beweises, daß die erste Sprache ihren Ursprung nicht vom Menschen, sondern allein vom Schöpfer erhalten habe* [Attempt at a Proof that the First Language Received its Origin not from Man but Solely from the Creator] (1766). Note that Herder often italicizes authors' names both in main text and in footnotes, in the latter case leaving the titles of their texts unitalicized for contrast. I reproduce this footnoting practice when it occurs, as here – otherwise using italics in the more conventional, opposite way.]

would without hesitation, blinded by its splendor, step back, cover myself, fall down, and pray to it as a divine apparition from Olympus . . .

But is this the case? And why must it be? Are there not a thousand indications in one language, and millions of traces in the variety of languages, precisely that peoples have learned gradually to think through using language, and to use language through thinking? Is it really the case that the beauty, order, and perfection of language – of so many, indeed of all, languages – is formed according to *one* plan? What a monstrous hypothesis to introduce into this great mass and variety a single ideal! What monstrous imagination to find this one ideal in all of them, and evidently to be able to see that the spirit of idiomaticness in every main language, in every national language, is nothing but anomaly, merely deviation from the rule, which we have chosen arbitrarily! And then even if this model of *one* language *for all* were accepted, what cleverness to see that this model *has to* be formed straightaway, to see that it *has to* be formed in the *divine* understanding and in no other, to see, and be able to say with precision, that it was possible for this much perfection, beauty, and order to be introduced into the language *of human beings* through the combined efforts of whole ages, centuries, races, but that *this* order, *that* perfection, *that* beauty[42] simply transcend the power of the human understanding, even if I regard the human understanding as a composition of millions of heads, as a product of whole millennia, and as a creation to whose formation an endless confluence of accidents and trivialities, an intervention of countless missteps and situations, had to contribute!

In short, the whole hypothesis of the divine origin of language is contrary to the analogy of all human inventions, contrary to the history of all world events, and contrary to all philosophy of language. It presupposes a language which is developed [*ausgebildet*] through thinking and thought out [*ausgedacht*] as an ideal of perfection (a picture which, notwithstanding all its infirmity, we still often imagine beautiful and healthy) and clothes this child of stubborn idiosyncrasy [*des Eigensinnes*], which was obviously a rather late creation and a work of whole centuries, with the rays of Olympus, so that it may cover up its nakedness and shame. And in the way that Süßmilch in particular has presented this hypothesis, he has achieved nothing – except shown that he lacks

---

[42] I have added the emphatic italics in "*this . . . that . . . that . . .*" in order to make Herder's meaning clearer.

the philosophical spirit to value the true ideal of a language, the historical spirit to examine its various chronological phases and seasons of life, and above all the philosophical genius to be able to explain it as a *development* [Entwicklung][43] *of reason* and as a *production of human mental forces.*[44] He imagines for himself a language as he wishes it, and can hence also prove what he wishes. He is right in details all over the place, and has overall said nothing!

I may therefore always presuppose a human origin. Every other origin is beyond our sphere; it does not allow us to unravel the knot of the investigation but, in the manner of Alexander's bright idea in the Gordian temple, makes us cut it off. One cannot judge at all about divine productions, and all philosophizing about them *kat' anthrôpon*[45] becomes awkward and useless; for of course we always have to consider them as human productions, to presuppose secretly a human originator all the time, only a human originator who stands on a higher level and operates with higher powers. So let me be allowed to presuppose a human origin of language, even if only for my poor philosophy's sake, and for the sake of my better participation – in short, out of consideration for my delicate stomach! What is more worthy and important for human beings than to investigate productions of human forces, the history of human efforts, and the births of our understanding?[46] And how interesting the philosophy about the childhood of language becomes when I simultaneously see the human soul develop in it, form language according to itself, and form itself according to language. The greatest work of the human spirit! So on this occasion I follow two blind heathen, Diodorus of Sicily and Vitruvius; two Catholic Christians, the holy Gregory and the for me still holier Richard Simon; and in modern times an academic

[43] This paragraph has now given two examples of Herder's use of a rhetorical figure especially favored by Aeschylus in the ancient world and sometimes aptly called "re-etymologizing," i.e. restoring or creating for a word a meaning suggested by its etymology but not preserved in its normal current usage. Thus *Eigensinn*, which normally means "stubbornness," was above re-etymologized to include the meaning "own sense," or "idiosyncrasy." And here *Entwicklung*, which normally means "development," is being re-etymologized to include the meaning "untwining."

[44] Note that the two genitives here ("of reason," "of human mental forces") could be either objective (reason and human mental forces are *being* developed/produced by language) or subjective (they are *doing* the developing/producing of language). The former meaning seems uppermost, but the latter is probably intended as well – since the process is understood by Herder to be reciprocal.

[45] Literally: according to man. I.e. by a human measure.

[46] The phrase *die Geburten unseres Verstandes* could mean either (1) our understanding's stages of being born or (2) our understanding's givings-of-birth (or more concretely, offspring). The former sense seems uppermost for Herder – but, again because of his conception that language and understanding develop interdependently, the latter sense is probably intended as well.

and a Jewish metaphysician, Maupertius and Moses Mendelssohn; and I presuppose, if not for more, then at least for amusement: "Human races [*Menschengeschlechter*][47] have themselves formed their language for themselves." And if not for more, then at least for amusement, I continue with my parallel: a human race [*Menschengeschlecht*][48] and a human being in its childhood are similar to each other. Only I am talking, not about the conception, nor even about the birth, but merely about the childhood of their language.

*

A language in its childhood? However one wants to call this historical age, it remains a condition of *primitive nature*. Nature was then still everything – *art, science*, writers, philosophers, grammarians did not yet exist; everything was the people which formed its language for itself, from necessity and then gradually for comfort. The beginning of language was in a simple shape, as a tool for the sake of use; the nature of the use dictated the form of the tool. Hence right down to stubborn idiosyncrasy, ignorance, errors, and poverty the oldest language must be a mirror of the nation and of the historical age; let one investigate the nature of the latter, then one has the nature of the former, of the language in its childhood.

Now without fancifully making up a Rousseauian condition of nature or exaggerating the picture of a people in a process of becoming, I must however still pay attention to the voices of the whole of antiquity saying that the first condition of a people was a situation of poverty and strength. Whoever has not heard these thousand voices in the halls of antiquity himself, let him hear their echo in the useful work of Goguet, who has collected the passages about this, let him go among the savages in all travel descriptions and learn their manner. Then he will no longer doubt that a British observer is correct: "In the infancy of states, the men . . . are ignorant and undesigning, governed by fear, and superstition its companion . . . Every new object finds them unprepared; they gaze and stare, like infants taking in their first ideas of light."[49]

I do not want to paint out in detail my comparison between children and these animal-humans. One must deny all the reports of the ancients and be quite unable to transplant oneself out of one's present condition of a cultivated [*gebildeten*] nature, of a civilized, comfortable, and luxurious

---

[47] Or just possibly: human generations.   [48] Or just possibly: human generation.
[49] T. Blackwell, *An Enquiry into the Life and Writings of Homer*, p. 42.

Philosophy of Language

life, if one finds all this unintelligible. And if one does not, then how can one find the influence on *language* foreign?

A society which, exposed to a thousand dangers, wanders about in unfamiliar regions amidst the teeth and claws of the animals and the animal-humans, of the robbers and the murderers; in which each person secures his own life through a friend, as through a guardian angel, from whom he expects help in a moment; which stares transfixed before every new object out of fear, is amazed before every thing not yet seen as before a miracle, and falls down before it out of ignorance and superstition; a people for whom therefore horror, fear, amazement, and marveling must be the most frequent emotions, as with children – such a people will also communicate this spirit to its language, will announce great passions with violent gestures and mighty sounds, will register rapid needs through short and powerful accents of shouting. Unarticulated noises will transform themselves into rough and monosyllabic words; strong and unpolished organs will utter forth inflexible sounds; the breath will not take its time to expand lungs and sentences, but will come and come again in short and frequent intervals. That will be the language which, according to Horace, made human beings, for human beings were animals until they found words, quibus voces sensusque notarent.[50]

I have had to stretch the string taughtly in order to give the note clearly and distinctly. The string slackens by itself, and hence the sharpness of the sound will leave the note. There is as little remembrance of the first periods of a people as of our years of tutelage. The recollection of our last age of boyhood when we received discipline is the dawn in our memory; likewise the first reports from the historical age of language when it began to receive youth's discipline. This lateness will of itself tone down our too highly pitched note.

The oldest languages have a sort of sensuous formation, as is still shown by the languages of peoples who live in the youth of their cultivation [*Bildung*]. Climate and region are not yet relevant, for both the hot Easterners and the savage Americans[51] confirm what I say. Everything reminds us of the morning of the world, when a nation formed its language for itself according to tongue, ear, and eye, and spoke for ear and eye.

Just as it is the oldest manner of writing to paint one's objects in pictures, likewise the first language painted too: things which struck the senses

[50] With which to mark sounds and meanings.   [51] I.e. native Americans.

through motion, for the ear; things which became intelligible through visual observation, for the eye. One can therefore say of the first language what Plutarch said[52] of the Delphic Apollo: *oute legei, oute kruptei, alla sêmainei.*[53]

The oldest languages had much *living expression*, as the remains of ancient and original languages, though each according to its country, bear witness. These languages, formed immediately according to living nature, and not like more modern languages according to arbitrary, dead ideas, not only had an emphatic stride for the ear, but were also capable, with the easiest application, of rushing with the whirlwind, of resounding in the battle, of raging with the sea, of roaring with the river, of cracking with the collapsing rock, and of speaking with the animals. From our closer acquaintance with the animals at that time, which we no longer have the honor of enjoying, stems also presumably the old poetic legend that men and animals understood each other in the Golden Age. For me this tale in Plato[54] and others has much appeal and dignity, and it could possibly also yield some enlightenment about the childhood of the art of poetry. Here I only cite the fact that if it is reported of several of their oldest wise men to their honor that they – for example, Melampus, Tiresias, and others – were able to converse with animals, still now the Easterners have not entirely left behind bird language. An Arab living in the desert can easily learn to distinguish several kinds of animal cry, and since a poetic, enthusiastic imagination can make from any impression whatever it wants, this first animal language seems to me to carry within it the seed for many poetic fictions. Homer's heroes may therefore speak with their horses, and Aesop turn the whole of nature into action – I have no objection.

For a long time with the ancients *singing* and *speaking* (*audaein*[55] and the imitating word *canere*[56]) were one thing: oracles sang and the voices which the god sang were called sayings (*phata*),[57] the laws sang and were

---

[52] The saying was originally Heraclitus's.
[53] He neither speaks [Herder means in a *rational* way, a way involving *logos*] nor conceals but indicates.
[54] *Statesman*, 272b–c.
[55] *audaein* (corrected from Herder's misspelling *audaiein*): to speak. But Herder supposes a connection with *aeidein/aoidiaein*: to sing. Blackwell was the source of this idea, *An Enquiry into the Life and Writings of Homer*, p. 38.
[56] *canere*: to sing. But in certain cases also: to utter, to signal.
[57] *phata*: things said. Herder probably meant *phêmai*: sayings, oracles, songs. Both nouns are cognate with the verb *phêmi*, to say.

called songs (*nomoi*),[58] the prophets and poets sang and what they sang were called speeches (*epea*),[59] Homer's heroes speak throughout winged words (*epea pteroenta*) and his heralds are "like crickets which sit on the trees in the forest and make a pleasant sound."[60] In common life (and there was not yet any other) people spoke words in a higher pitch, so that they made more clearly heard not only long and short accents but also high and low syllables; the rhythm of language was clearer; and in such rhythmic falling pitches the language naturally fell into articulation; not bound in connections, it acquired uniform cadences. Still now in common life the chained style of books becomes repellent and an orator's refined sentence unbearable. And in that age, when people had not yet thought of books, what was language then? Nothing but singing and speaking nature.

Flying fragments would ill help themselves with a heavy armor of scholarship. So the reader is safe from terrible testimonies and citations from the ancients – which Vossius,[61] Meibom,[62] and Du Bos[63] have partly collected. One always judges wrongly if one insists on taking the expression *to sing* as inauthentically as we use it: one speaks as though in a dream if one demotes the theater-singing of the ancients to a fashionable recitation in the taste of the French ear, perhaps merely in order to pay a compliment to the music and the stage of one's own time. In that case, it is better if, like Vossius, one does not undertake to explain this singing of the ancients at all, or that, like most, one speaks indefinitely and confusedly about it, or best of all . . . let one say with Dacier[64] that if the Greeks sang where we speak then they were fools, simply that!

It is completely necessary that one be able to leave one's own time and one's own people in order to judge about remote times and peoples. That nation which preserves its ethics and customs without alteration, in good Egyptian style, the Chinese, has kept, along with its sign-writing and thing-language, also its singing. Many savage nations with old languages and ethics still sing, they have even in their prose the high and heavy accent of which we know so little. Thus the ear of the ancients took pleasure in

---

[58] The word *nomos* can mean either law or song.　　[59] The basic meaning of *epos* is: word.
[60] *Iliad*, bk. 3, ll. 149–53. Actually it was the elders of Troy.
[61] G. J. Vossius (1577–1649), Dutch theologian and philologist, author of several works on poetry.
[62] M. Meibom (1626–1711), music historian and theorist, author of *Antiquae musicae auctores septem* (1652).
[63] J.-B. Du Bos (1670–1742), French writer, author of *Réflexions critiques sur la poésie, la peinture, et la musique* (1719).
[64] A. Dacier (1651–1722), *Poétique d'Aristote* (1692).

singing as our ear in childhood could be quieted and put to sleep with uniform cadences; song was natural to them.

And chiming in with this song for the ear there in addition spoke with a hundred voices *gestures* and *signs* for the eye, so that in consequence this speech is to be called *painting* in a new sense.[65] If I wanted to begin the matter ab ovo[66] I could go on here at length about the fact that signs occupied the place of writing, that symbolic actions made everything impressive, venerable, and solemn; that people chose sign language in question and answer – but all this does not belong here. I only point out that the savage and free nations, who remain more human beings and less citizens, speak far more through bodily gestures than our imported properness, our sense of decency, allows us to; just as the ancients spoke and recited speech much more with gestures than we do. I cite Homer, who even in his smallest descriptions knows how to depict how mightily passion speaks through a single gesture and the free soul through a free body. How often one will cry out at small and mighty traits: "No, divine old man, only you saw spirits and could depict passions corporeally; we no longer see them; we juggle or stand like statues; now the spirit no longer speaks as it spoke before your eyes, it has fled from mighty gestures into quiet facial-expressions and -traits, where instead of speaking in fullness it stammers and falls silent." Gesturing ever had to help out when the still undeveloped language was unable to adapt itself, and since passion anyway gave rise to gestures of itself, how this lively interpunctuation must have given incisiveness, modulation, and emphasis to language!

The parallel between children and a newly born people runs still more exactly when we investigate the inner nature of their languages in both cases. *Names* are the vocabulary of a child, whether one calls these names nouns or verbs; and likewise in language as well these two things are the first. In the Greek language even noun and verb were only distinguished late *grammatically*, and the remaining parts of speech belong either to the family or to the accompaniment of this pair, and the simple forms of the Eastern languages show sufficiently that conjugations and declensions were an addition of later times. Still now the languages of the Hurons, the Iroquois, and other original nations consist mostly of verbs, and even in our language too the *living noise* which resounds in the verbs shows

[65] I.e. new in addition to the sense, expressed more than once earlier in these excerpts, that primitive language "paints" aspects of sensuous experience because it is still sensuous in nature.
[66] Literally: from the egg on. I.e. from the very beginning.

that they are the oldest part of the language – just as every doing and undergoing, every action and motion, which is cast in verbs makes more of an impression than the active or passive being itself which nouns express.

With time synonyms and pleonasms naturally had to enter the oldest languages. The world of objects which surrounded people was the content of their language. And where was the philosopher who would have ordered what he saw into classes and washed away the excess? New subject matters, new objects, conditions, circumstances, yielded new names – and in this way language became only all too rich. Sensuous objects were referred to sensuously – and from how many sides, from how many viewpoints they can be referred to! In this way language became full of crazy and untamed word transformations, full of irregularity and stubborn idiosyncrasy. Images were introduced as images as far as possible, and in this way there arose a stock of metaphors, of idioms, of sensuous names. Rough strength in passions and deeds, in virtues and vices, was the stamp of the age – and inevitably of the language as well, which with each people in a thousand contingent circumstances was just as good and as bad as it had to be in order to be a language *of the sensuous people.*

*

I collect my scattered fragments together and see what can be made of them. Anything but a philosophical language, and the youth of language knows of no philosophical grammar – which compared with that youth is an old man with grey hair. I repeat once more: let one collect the preceding fragments, a language full of images and passions, idioms and pleonasms, word transformations and stubborn idiosyncrasy, which sang and gestured, painted for eye and ear. What is this language, when a little art comes on top? Nothing other and nothing better than *a poetic language.* Language did not produce poets alone, but the age which produced language created *poets* who were at that time everything to the age, whom it supported with everything, and among these supports language was, if not more, then the final one.[67]

[67] This long final excerpt is from G1:600 ff.

Treatise on the Origin of Language (1772)

Vocabula sunt notae rerum.[1] *Cicero*

First part: Were *human beings*, left to their natural abilities, able to invent *language* for themselves?[2]

First section

Already as an animal, the human being has language. All violent sensations of his body, and the most violent of the violent, the painful ones, and all strong passions of his soul immediately express themselves in cries, in sounds, in wild, unarticulated noises. A suffering animal, as much as the hero Philoctetes,[3] when overcome with pain, will whine!, will groan!, even if it were abandoned, on a desolate island, without the sight, the trace, or the hope of a helpful fellow creature. It is as though it breathed more freely by giving vent to its burning, frightened breath; it is as though it moaned away a part of its pain, and at least drew into itself from the empty atmosphere new forces for getting over its pain, by filling the deaf winds with groaning. This is how little nature has created us as isolated rocks, as egoistic[4] monads! Even the finest instrument strings of animal feeling (I have to use this metaphor because I know no better for the mechanism of feeling bodies!) – even these strings, whose sound and straining does

---

[1] Words are signs of things.
[2] The question of the Berlin Academy which Herder is answering in this essay asked in the first of its two parts: "Supposing men abandoned to their natural faculties, are they in a position to invent language?"
[3] In Sophocles' play of the same name.
[4] "Egoistic" mainly in the sense *solipsistic*, as frequently in Kant.

not come from volition and slow deliberation at all, indeed whose nature all of investigating reason has not yet been able to bring to light through investigation, even these are directed in their whole play, even without the consciousness of foreign sympathy, at an expression to other creatures. The struck string performs its natural duty: it sounds!, it calls to a similarly feeling Echo – even when none is there, even when it does not hope or expect to be answered by one.

If physiology should ever get to the point where it demonstrated the science of the soul – which I very much doubt that it will, however – then it would cast many a ray of light on this phenomenon from the dissection of the nerve structure, but would perhaps also distribute it over bonds[5] which were individual, too small, and too coarse. Let us accept the phenomenon for now in the whole, as a clear law of nature: "*Here is a sensitive being which can enclose none of its lively sensations within itself, which in the first moment of surprise, even without volition and intention, has to express each of them in sound.*" This was, so to speak, the final, maternal imprint of nature's forming hand, that she sent all into the world accompanied by the law: "*Do not have sensation for yourself alone, but may your feeling resound!*" And since this final creating imprint was of a single sort on all beings of a single species, that law became a blessing: "*May your sensation resound for your species in a single way, and therefore be perceived by all, as by a single one, with sympathy!*" Now let it not be touched, this weak, sensitive being! As alone and individual and exposed to every hostile storm of the universe as it seems, it is not alone; it stands allied with the whole of nature!, delicately strung, but nature has hidden in these strings sounds which, stimulated and encouraged, awaken other equally delicately built creatures in turn, and can communicate sparks to a remote heart, as though through an invisible chain, so that it feels for this unseen creature. *These groans, these sounds, are language. Hence there is a language of sensation which is an immediate law of nature.*

That the human being originally shares this language of sensation with the animals is, to be sure, evidenced more now by certain remains than by full eruptions. But even these remains are irrefutable. Our artificial language may have displaced the language of nature, our civilized manner of life and our social polite behavior have dammed, dried out, and drained off the flood and sea of the passions, as much as one wants, but the most

5 B edition (1789): parts.

violent moment of sensation, wherever and however seldom it occurs, still reassumes its right, and immediately resounds in its mother tongue through emphases. The impetuous storm of a passion, the sudden accession of joy or happiness, pain and misery when they dig deep furrows into the soul, an overpowering feeling of revenge, despair, fury, fright, horror, etc. – all announce themselves, and each one differently according to its kind. However many species of feeling slumber in our nature, just as many kinds of sounds slumber there too. – So I note that *the less human nature is related to an animal kind, the less similar it is to the latter in nerve structure, then the less the latter's natural language is intelligible to us*. As land creatures we understand the land creature better than the water creature, and on land the herd animal better than the forest creature, and among the herd animals those most which are closest to us. Only admittedly with the qualification that even in the last cases intercourse and familiarity determines the degree.[6] It is natural that the Arab who constitutes just a single unit with his horse understands it more than the man who sits astride a horse for the first time – almost as well as Hector in the *Iliad*[7] could speak with his horses.[8] The Arab in the desert who has around him nothing living except his camel and perhaps the flight of wandering birds can more easily understand the camel's nature and think that he understands the birds' cries than we in our abodes. The son of the forest, the hunter, understands the voice of the stag, and the Laplander that of his reindeer. – But this all follows or is an exception. Actually, *this natural language is a language-of-a-people for each species among itself, and hence the human being has his as well*.

Now, to be sure, *these sounds are very simple*; and when they get articulated and get spelled out on paper as interjections, then the most opposed sensations have almost a single expression. The dull "Ah!" is both a sound of melting love and a sound of sinking despair; the fiery "Oh!" is both an eruption of sudden joy and an eruption of impetuous fury, both of rising admiration and of welling lamentation. But do these sounds exist in order to be depicted on paper as interjections, then? The tear that swims in this clouded, extinguished eye pining for consolation – how touching it is in the whole picture of the face of sadness. But take it by itself and it is a cold drop of water!, bring it under the microscope and – I do not want to

---

[6] B: are necessary for achieving the optimal.
[7] *Iliad*, bk. 8, ll. 184–97. Cf. Achilles at bk. 19, ll. 400–24.
[8] B: – he speaks with it almost as well as Hector in the *Iliad* could speak with his horses.

know what it may be there! This tiring breath, the semi-groan, which dies so movingly on the lip distorted by pain – separate it from all its living helpers and it is an empty blast of air. Can it be otherwise with the sounds of sensation? In their living context, in the whole image of effective nature, accompanied by so many other manifestations, they are moving and self-sufficient. But separated, torn away, from them all, robbed of their life, they are, to be sure, nothing but ciphers. The voice of nature is [then] a painted, voluntarized letter. – *There are few of these linguistic sounds*, indeed. But sensitive nature, as far as it is merely mechanically affected, also has fewer main kinds of sensation than our psychologies ascribe or fictively attribute to the soul as passions. Only, each feeling is, in such a condition, the less that it is split up into threads, a that much more mightily attracting bond; the sounds do not speak much, but they do so strongly. Whether that moaning sound is whining[9] over wounds of the soul or of the body, whether this cry is forced forth by fear or by pain, whether this soft "Ah" presses itself to the breast of the beloved woman with a kiss or with a tear – this language did not exist in order to determine all these sorts of distinctions. It was supposed to draw attention to the picture; this picture will certainly already speak for itself! It was supposed to sound, but not to depict! – Speaking generally, in accordance with that Socratic fable,[10] pain and pleasure border on one another; nature has joined their ends together in sensation. And so how can the language of sensation do otherwise than show such points of contact? – Now I may apply this.

In all original languages remains of these natural sounds still resound – only, to be sure, they are not the main threads of human language. They are not the actual roots, but the juices which enliven the roots of language.

In a refined, late-invented metaphysical language, which is a degeneration, perhaps at the fourth degree, from the original savage mother [tongue] of the human species, and which after long millennia of degeneration has itself in turn for centuries of its life been refined, civilized, and humanized – such a language, the child of reason and society, can know little or nothing any more about the childhood of its first mother.[11] But the old, the savage, languages, the nearer they are to the origin, the more of it they contain. I cannot here yet speak of the slightest *human* formation

---

[9] Reading with Suphan *wimmere* for *wimmern*.   [10] *Phaedo*, 60c.
[11] This sentence is a good example of Herder's – frequent – use of the rhetorical figure of anacoluthon, or the deliberate failure to carry a grammatical construction through consistently to the end of the sentence.

[*Bildung*] of language, but can only consider raw materials. There does not yet exist for me any word, but only sounds towards the word for a sensation. But behold!, how many preserved remains of these sounds there are in the languages mentioned, in their interjections, in the roots of their nouns and verbs! The oldest Eastern languages are full of ex-clamations, for which we later-cultivated [-*gebildeten*] peoples often have nothing but gaps or dull, deaf misunderstanding. In their elegies there resound, as with the savages at their graves, those sounds of howling and lamentation, a continual interjection of the language of nature; in their praising psalms the cry of joy and the repeated Hallelujahs which *Shaw* explains as coming from the mouths of female mourners and which are with us so often solemn nonsense.[12] In the pace, in the rhythm, of their poems and of other ancient people's songs resounds the sound which still enlivens the dances of war and religion, the songs of mourning and hap-piness, of all savages, whether they live at the foot of the *Cordilleras* or in the snow of the *Iroquois*, in *Brazil* or on the *Caribbean Islands*. Finally, the roots of their simplest, most effective, earliest verbs are those first exclamations of nature, which only later got molded, and the languages of all ancient and savage peoples are therefore in this inner, living sound eternally unpronounceable for foreigners!

I can explain most of these phenomena in connection only later. Let just one thing be said here. One of the defenders of the divine origin of language[a] finds divine order to admire in the fact *"that the sounds of all languages known to us can be reduced to some twenty letters."* But the fact is false, and the inference still more incorrect. Not a single livingly resounding language can be completely captured in letters, and still less in twenty letters. Each and every language bears witness to this. The ar-ticulations of our linguistic instruments are so numerous, each sound is pronounced in such a diversity of ways, that for example Mr. *Lambert* has rightly been able to show in the second part of his *Organon* "how many fewer letters we have than sounds," and "how inexactly therefore the latter can be expressed by the former."[13] And mind you, that is merely

---

[a] *Süßmilch's* Beweis, daß der Ursprung der menschlichen Sprache göttlich sei [i.e. *Versuch eines Beweises, daß die erste Sprache ihren Ursprung nicht vom Menschen, sondern allein vom Schöpfer erhalten habe*] (Berlin, 1766), p. 21.

[12] T. Shaw (1694?–1751), English author of a book on travels in North Africa known to Herder in the German translation *Reisen oder Anmerkungen verschiedene Teile der Barbarey und der Levante betreffend* (tr. 1765).

[13] J. H. Lambert (1728–77), *Neues Organon* (1764).

shown from the case of the German language, which has not yet even taken up the many-soundedness and the diversity of its dialects into a written language. Much less [are the sounds expressed exactly] when the whole language is nothing but such a living dialect! Whence come all the peculiarities and idiosyncrasies of orthography but from the awkwardness of writing as one speaks? What living language can be learned, in its sounds, from book letters? And so what dead language be awoken? – Now the more living a language is, the less people have thought of capturing it in letters, the more originally it rises to the full and not selectively analyzed sound of nature, then the less it can be written as well, the less written with twenty letters; indeed [the more it is] often quite unpronounceable for foreigners. *Father Rasles*, who stayed for ten years among the *Abenaki* in North America, complains so much about the fact that despite all his attentiveness he still often only repeated half of a word and made himself ridiculous. How much more ridiculously he would have done the calculation with his French letters![14] *Father Chaumonot*,[15] who spent fifty years among the Hurons, and ventured to write a grammar of their language, nevertheless complains about their gutteral letters and their unpronounceable accents: "Often two words which would consist of completely identical letters would have the most different meanings." *Garcilaso de la Vega* complains about the Spaniards how much they distorted, mutilated, falsified the Peruvian language in the sound of its words and because of mere falsifications wrongly attributed to the Peruvians the most awful nonsense. *De la Condamine* says about a small nation on the Amazon river: "A part of their words could not be written, not even very incompletely. One would have to use at least nine or ten syllables for this where they seem in their pronunciation to pronounce barely three." *La Loubere* concerning the Siamese language: "Among ten words which the European pronounces a native Siamese understands perhaps not a single one – however much effort one makes to express their language with our letters." And what need have we of peoples from such remote ends of the earth? Our small residue of savages in Europe, Estonians and Lapps etc., often have sounds that are just as half-articulated and unwritable as Hurons and Peruvians. Russians and Poles, long as their languages have been written and formed by writing, still aspirate in such

[14] In manuscript a it is "such an expression" that Rasles would have had even more difficulty calculating with French letters; in edition B it is "the language."
[15] Corrected from *Chaumont*, following Irmischer.

a way that the true sound of their languages' organizations[16] cannot be depicted by means of letters. How much does the Englishman torture himself to write his sounds, and how far is he who [only] understands written English still from being a speaking Englishman! The Frenchman, who draws breath up from his throat to a lesser extent, and that half-Greek, the Italian, who, so to speak, talks in a higher region of the mouth, in a finer ether, still retain a living sound. Their tones have to remain within the organs where they were formed; however comfortable and distinctive the long use of writing has made them, as depicted letters they are forever only shadows!

So the fact is false, and the inference even more false; it does not lead to a divine origin but, quite the opposite, to an animal origin. Take the so-called divine first language, Hebrew, from which the greatest part of the world has inherited its letters: that it was in its beginning so livingly sounding, so unwritable,[17] that it could only be written very incompletely, this is shown clearly by the whole structure of its grammar, by its so common confusions of similar letters, and of course most of all by the complete absence of its vowels. Whence comes the idiosyncrasy that its letters are only consonants, and that precisely those elements of words on which everything depends, the vowels, were originally not written at all? This way of writing, writing the inessential and omitting the essential, is so opposed to the course of sound reason that it would have to be unintelligible to grammarians, if grammarians were in the habit of understanding. With us the vowels are the first and most lively thing and the door hinges of language; with the Hebrews they are not written. Why? Because they could not be written. Their pronunciation was so lively and finely organized, their breath was so spiritual and ethereal, that it evaporated and could not be captured in letters. Only for the first time with the Greeks were these living aspirations unraveled into proper vowels, which, however, still needed the help of breathing [*Spiritus*],[18] etc. – whereas with the Easterners speech was, so to say, entirely breathing, continuous breath [*Hauch*] and spirit [*Geist*] of the mouth, as they also so often name it in their painting poems. It was the life-breath [*Othem*][19] of God, wafting air,

---

[16] B: of their utterances. [17] B omits "so unwritable."

[18] *Spiritus* is *breathing* in the technical sense in which this term is used in Greek grammar, but it is also of course Latin for *spirit*.

[19] *Othem* is a word for breath which has stronger religious-biblical overtones than the word for breath used up to this point, *Hauch*.

which the ear snatched up, and the dead letters which they painted down were merely the corpse which in reading had to be ensouled with the spirit of life [*Lebensgeist*]. This is not the place to say what sort of mighty influence that has on the understanding of their language. But that this wafting something reveals the origin of their language is obvious. What is less writable than the unarticulated sounds of nature? And if language is more unarticulated the closer it is to its origin – then what follows but that it is surely not the case that language was invented by a higher being for the twenty-four letters and these letters were invented straightaway with language, that these letters were a much later and only imperfect attempt to set up for oneself a few markers for memory, and that language arose not from letters of God's grammar but from savage sounds belonging to free organs?[b] Otherwise it would be a fine thing that precisely those letters from and for which God had invented language, and with whose help he had taught language to the first human beings, should be exactly the most imperfect ones of all in the world, which said nothing at all[20] about the spirit of the language and clearly confess in their whole manner of construction that they mean to say nothing about it.

This letter-hypothesis admittedly merited only a single hint according to its worth. But because of its universality and its manifold ornamentation I needed to lay bare its groundlessness, and at the same time to explain it in this groundlessness, as, to me at least, no explanation is [yet] familiar. Back to our course:

Since our natural sounds are destined for the expression of passion, it is natural *that they also become the elements of all moving [of another person]!* Who is there who, faced with a shaking, whining tortured person, with a moaning dying person, and even with a groaning farm animal when its whole machine is suffering, is not touched to his heart by this "Ah!"? Who is such a feelingless barbarian? The more harmoniously the sensitive string-play is woven even in the case of animals with other animals, the more even these feel with one another; their nerves come to a similar tension, their souls to a similar pitch, they really share each other's pain mechanically. And what a steeling of his fibers!, what a power to block up

---

[b] The best text for this material, which has in part still not been worked out, is Wachter's *Naturae et scripturae concordia* [*Concordance of Nature and Scripture*] (Hafn., [Leipzig and Halle,] 1752), which is as different from Kircher's and so many others' dreams as ancient history is from fairy stories.

[20] B: little.

all the entryways of his sensitivity, is required for a human being to become deaf and hard against this! – *Diderot*[c] expresses the opinion that a person born blind should be less sensitive than a sighted person to the moans of a suffering animal. But I believe that in certain cases the opposite is true. To be sure, the whole moving visual drama of this miserable, shaking creature is masked from him. But all examples testify that precisely through this masking the sense of hearing becomes less distracted, more attentive, and greatly more penetrating. There he listens in darkness, consequently, in the stillness of his eternal night, and each moan penetrates his heart that much more deeply and sharply, like an arrow! Now let him in addition take in aid the touching, slowly embracing sense of feeling, let him touch the shakings, feel the breaking, of the suffering machine for himself in their entirety – horror and pain shoots through his limbs, his inner nerve structure feels the breaking and destruction in sympathy; the death rattle sounds. That is *the bond of this natural language*!

Everywhere Europeans – despite their cultivation [*Bildung*], and miscultivation! – have been strongly moved by the primitive moans of savages. *Leri* recounts from Brazil how much his people were softened to the point of tears by these Americans' heartfelt, spontaneous cry of love and sociability. *Charlevoix* and others cannot say enough about the horrifying impression made by the war- and magic-songs of the North Americans. When we have an opportunity later to remark how much ancient poetry and music was enlivened by these natural sounds, then we will also be able to explain more philosophically the effect that, for example, the oldest Greek song and dance, the ancient Greek stage, [made on the Greeks,] and in general music, dance, and poetry still make on all savages. And even in our case too, where, to be sure, reason often puts an end to the role of feeling and the artificial language of society to that of natural sounds, do not the loftiest thunders of oratory, the mightiest strikes of poetry, and the magical moments of accompanying gesture still often come close to this language of nature, through imitation? What is it that there among the gathered people works miracles, penetrates hearts, and bowls over souls? Spiritual talk and metaphysics? Metaphors and rhetorical figures? Art and cold persuasion? To the extent that the rapture is not blind, much must happen through these things, but everything? And precisely this highest

[c] *Lettre sur les aveugles à l'usage de ceux qui voient* etc. [*Letter on the Blind, for the Use of Those who See* (1749)].

element of blind rapture, what brought this about? A quite different force! These sounds, these gestures, those simple courses of melody, this sudden turning point, this twilight voice – and who knows what else. With children, and the sensuous people, with women, with people of delicate sensibility, with sick people, lonely people, depressed people, they are a thousand times more effective than the truth itself would be if its soft, fine voice resounded from heaven. These words, this sound, the turning point of this horrifying ballad, etc. penetrated our souls in our childhood when we heard them for the first time together with who knows what army of associations of horror, of festivity, of fright, of fear, of joy. The word resounds, and like a throng of ghosts they suddenly all rise from the grave of the soul in their obscure majesty; they obscure the pure, clear concept of the word which could only be grasped without them. The word is gone and the sound of sensation resounds. Obscure feeling overwhelms us; [even] the careless person is horrified and trembles – not about thoughts, but about syllables, about sounds of childhood, and it was the magical power of the orator, of the poet, to make us children once again. No careful thought, no pondering, but this mere law of nature was the fundamental cause: "*The pitch of sensation should transpose the sympathetic creature into the same pitch!*"[21]

So if we wish to call these immediate sounds of sensation 'language,' then I certainly do find their origin very natural. It is not only not superhuman, but clearly animal: *the natural law of a sensitive machine.*

*

But I cannot conceal my astonishment that philosophers, that is, people who seek distinct concepts, were ever able to arrive at the idea of explaining the origin of human language from this cry of the sensations. For is human language not obviously something completely different? All animals, down as far as the dumb fish, sound forth their sensation. But it still is not the case that just because of that any animal, even the most perfect, has the slightest real beginning towards a human language. Let one form and refine and organize this cry however one wants, unless an understanding is added, so as to use this sound with intention, then I do

---

[21] "Pitch" in this last sentence translates *Ton*, the word that has been translated "sound" up to this point in the paragraph. The reason for switching the translation here is that in its two occurrences in this last sentence *Ton* has – in the first occurrence partly, and in the second exclusively – a metaphorical force which the word "sound" cannot well express in English but the word "pitch" can.

not see how from the preceding natural law human, voluntary language ever comes about. Children utter noises of sensation like the animals, but is not the language that they learn from human beings a quite different language?

The Abbé *Condillac*[d] is among these people. Either he has from the first page of his book presupposed the whole thing, language, as already invented, or I find on each page things that could not have happened at all in the ordering of a formative [*bildenden*] language. He posits as the basis of his hypothesis "two children in a desert before they know the use of any sign whatever." Now why he posits all this: "two children," who hence must die or become animals, "in a desert," where the difficulty of their livelihood and of their invention increases still further, "before the use of any natural sign, and indeed before any knowledge of one," without which, however, no infant still exists a few weeks after its birth – why, I say, in a hypothesis which is supposed to trace the natural course of human knowledge, such unnatural, self-contradictory data have to be assumed as the basis, its author may know, but that no explanation of the origin of language is built upon them I am confident of being able to prove. His two children come together without the knowledge of any sign, and – behold!, in the first moment "they are already in reciprocal intercourse" (#2). And yet merely through this reciprocal intercourse do they first learn "to associate with the cries of sensations the thoughts whose natural signs those cries are." Learn natural signs of sensation through intercourse? Learn what sorts of thoughts should be associated with them? And yet immediately in the first moment of coming together, still before knowing what the most stupid animal knows, have intercourse? Be able to learn what sorts of thoughts should be linked with certain signs? I understand nothing of this. "Through the repetition of similar circumstances" (#3) "they get used to associating thoughts with the sounds of sensations and the various signs of the body. Already their memory receives training. Already they can have control over their imagination, and already – they have reached the point of doing with reflection what they previously did merely through instinct" (but which, as we just saw, they were allegedly unable to do before their intercourse). I understand nothing of this. "The use of these signs expands the effects of the soul" (#4) "and these effects perfect the signs: it

---

[d] *Essai sur l'origine des connaissances humaines* [*Essay on the Origin of Human Knowledge* (1746)], vol. 2. [The translations from this and other works which follow are from Herder's German rather than from the French.]

was hence the cry of sensations" (#5) "which developed the forces of the soul: cry of sensations which gave them the habit of associating ideas with voluntary signs," (#6) "cry of sensations which served them as a model to make a new language for themselves, to articulate new sounds, to get used to designating things with names." I repeat all these repetitions and understand nothing of them. Finally, after the author has built up the meter, recitation, music, dance, and poetry of the ancient languages on this childish origin of language, and here and there presented good observations, which, however, are irrelevant for our purpose, he then takes up the thread again: "In order to understand" (#80) "how human beings came to agree among themselves about the meaning of the first words which they wanted to use, it suffices to note that they pronounced them in circumstances in which each person was obliged to associate them with the same ideas, etc." In short, words arose because words existed before they existed. I do not think that it is worth pursuing our explainer's thread any further, since it is – tied to nothing.

Condillac, it is known, provided the occasion through his hollow explanation of the origination of language for *Rousseau*[e] in our century to afford currency to the question in his own manner, that is, to call it into doubt. In order to come up with doubts against *Condillac's* explanation there was certainly no need of a *Rousseau*. But immediately to deny any possibility of a human invention of language simply because of that – for this some Rousseauian *élan* or leaping, however one wants to call it, was indeed necessary. Just because *Condillac* had explained the matter badly, does it therefore follow that it cannot be explained at all? Just because a human language can never arise from sounds of sensation, does it follow from this that it was unable to arise from any other source?

That it really is only this implicit fallacy that leads *Rousseau* astray is shown clearly by his own conception of[f] "how, if on the other hand by some remote chance language *should* have arisen from a human source, it would have had to arise." Like his predecessor, he begins with the cry of nature, from which human language allegedly arises. I shall never see how it could have arisen from that source, and I am astonished that the intelligence of a *Rousseau* was for a moment able to make it arise from that source.

[e] *Sur l'inégalité parmi les hommes* etc. [i.e. *Discours sur l'origine et les fondements de l'inégalité parmi les hommes* [*Discourse on the Origin and Foundations of Inequality among Mankind*] (1754)], part 1.
[f] Ibid.

Maupertius's little book[22] is not available to me; but if I may trust the epitome of a man[g] of whom faithfulness and precision was not the smallest merit, then Maupertius too failed to separate the origin of language sufficiently from these animal sounds, and hence takes the same path as the preceding people.

Finally, *Diodorus*[23] and *Vitruvius*,[24] people who moreover rather believed in than derived the human origin of language, corrupted matters most obviously, since they make men first of all roam for ages as animals with cries in forests, and then afterwards – God knows whence and God knows for what purpose! – invent language for themselves.

Since, then, most representatives of the human origination of language fought their case from such insecure territory, which others, for example *Süßmilch*, attacked with such good reason, the *Academy* wanted to see this question, which is hence still entirely unanswered, and over which even several of the Academy's former members have been at variance, at last settled.

And since this great theme promises so many prospects into the psychology and natural order of the human species, into the philosophy of languages and of all cognitions which are discovered with language – who would not want to make an attempt at it?

And since human beings are the only linguistic creatures that we know, and are distinguished from all the animals precisely by language, where would the path of investigation begin more securely than with experiences concerning the difference between animals and human beings? *Condillac* and *Rousseau* inevitably erred concerning the origin of language because they were so famously and variously mistaken about this difference – since the former[h] made animals into human beings, and the latter[i] made human beings into animals. I therefore need to begin from rather far back.

*

That the human being is far inferior to the animals in strength and sureness of instinct, indeed that he quite lacks what in the case of so many animal

---

[g] Süßmilch, *Beweis für die Göttlichkeit*, etc. [i.e. *Versuch eines Beweises . . .*], appendix 3, p. 110.
[h] *Traité sur les animaux [Treatise on Animals (1755)].*
[i] *Sur l'origine de l'inégalité etc. [i.e. Discours sur . . .].*

[22] P. L. M. de Maupertius (1698–1759), *Réflexions philosophiques sur l'origine des langues et la signification des mots* (1747).
[23] Diodorus Sicilus (first century BC), Greek historian.
[24] Vitruvius (first century BC), Roman architect and theorist of architecture.

species we call innate abilities for and drives to art, is certain. Only, just as the explanation of these drives to art has so far gone wrong for most philosophers, and lastly again for a thorough philosopher from Germany,[j] likewise the true cause of the lack of these drives to art in human nature has also so far resisted elucidation. It seems to me that a central perspective has been missed from which one can give, if not complete explanations, then at least observations about the nature of animals which – as I hope to show in another place – can throw much light on the doctrine of the human soul. This perspective is *"the sphere* [Sphäre] *of animals."*

Each animal has its circle [*Kreis*][25] to which it belongs from birth, into which it immediately enters, in which it remains all its life, and in which it dies. But now it is strange *"that the sharper animals' senses are and the more marvelous the products of their art, then the smaller their circle is, the more limited in kind the product of their art."* I have pursued this relationship and I find everywhere a marvelous, observed[26] *"inverse proportion between the lesser extension of their movements, elements,[27] nutrition, preservation, reproduction, upbringing, society* and their *drives and arts."* The bee in its hive builds with the wisdom that *Egeria* could not teach her *Numa;*[28] but beyond these cells and beyond its destined occupation in these cells the bee is also nothing. The spider weaves with the art of Minerva; but all its art is also woven out in this narrow spinning-space; that is its world! How marvelous is the insect, and how narrow the circle of its effect!

On the other hand, *"the more numerous the functions and the destiny of animals are, the more dispersed their attention is over several objects, the less constant their manner of life is, in short, the larger and more diverse their sphere is, then the more we see their sensuousness distribute itself and weaken."* It cannot be my intention here to secure this great relationship, which runs through the chain of living beings, with examples. I leave the test to each person or refer him to another occasion and continue my inferences:

---

[j] *Reimarus,* Über die Kunsttriebe der Tiere [i.e. *Allgemeine Betrachtungen über die Triebe der Tiere, hauptsächlich über ihre Kunsttriebe* (1760)]. See reflections on this in the *Briefe, die neueste Literatur betreffend,* etc. [*Letters concerning the Most Recent Literature*].

[25] Note that there is no implication in the German of a *social* circle. For this reason "sphere" would in a way be a better English translation here, except that the geometrical meaning is different and "sphere" is needed to translate *Sphäre.*

[26] B: marvelously observed.   [27] "Elements" is omitted in B.

[28] Egeria was a nymph who was said to have taught Romulus's successor as king of Rome, Numa Pompilius, about how to organize society.

According to all probability and analogy, then, it is possible *"to explain all drives to and abilities for art from animals' forces of representation,"* without it being appropriate to assume blind determinations (as even Reimarus still assumed, and which destroy all philosophy). When infinitely fine senses are confined to a small circle, to uniformity, and the whole remaining world is nothing for them, how they must penetrate! When forces of representation are confined to a small circle and endowed with an analogous sensuality, what effect they must have! And finally, when senses and representations are directed at a single point, what else can become of this but instinct? Hence these explain the sensitivity, the abilities, and the drives of the animals according to their kinds and levels.

And hence I may assume the proposition: *"The sensitivity, abilities, and drives to art of the animals increase in strength and intensity in inverse proportion to the size and diversity of their circle of efficacy."* But now –

The human being has no such uniform and narrow sphere where only a single sort of work awaits him; a world of occupations and destinies surrounds him.

His senses and organization are not sharpened for a single thing; he has senses for everything and hence naturally for each particular thing weaker and duller senses.

His forces of soul are distributed over the world; [there is] no direction of his representations on a single thing; hence *no drive to art, no skill for art* – and, one thing which is more especially relevant here, *no animal language.*

But what is that which, besides the previously cited sounding forth of the sensitive machine, we in the case of several species call *animal language* other than a result of the remarked-on features that I have marshaled together – *an animal species' obscure, sensuous common-understanding* [Einverständnis]*among its members about its destiny in the circle of its efficacy?*

Hence the smaller the sphere of animals is, the less they need language. The sharper their senses are, the more their representations are directed at a single thing, the more pull their drives have, then the narrower is the common-understanding in whatever sounds, signs, expressions they may make. It is living mechanism, ruling instinct, that speaks and hears there. How little it must[29] speak in order to be heard!

[29] Or possibly: may.

Hence animals of the narrowest domain are even without hearing, they are for their world entirely feeling, or smell, or sight – entirely uniform image, uniform impulse, uniform occupation. Hence they have little or no language.

But the larger animals' circles, and the more differentiated their senses . . . But why should I repeat? *For with the human being the scene changes completely*. What is the language of even the most talkative, most diversely sounding, animal supposed to achieve for the human being's circle of efficacy, even when he is in the most needy condition? What is even the obscure language of all the animals supposed to achieve for his dispersed desires, for his divided attention, for his more dully detecting senses? That language is for him neither rich nor distinct, sufficient neither in its objects nor for his organs – hence thoroughly not *his language*. For what, when we decline to play with words, is the *peculiar language of a creature* but the language which is appropriate for its sphere of needs and types of work, for the organization of its senses, for the direction of its representations, and for the strength of its desires? And what animal language is like this for the human being?

However, we can also dispense with the question, *What language* (besides the earlier mechanical one) *does the human being possess as instinctively as each animal species possesses its language in, and in accordance with, its own sphere?* The answer is short: none! And precisely this short answer is decisive.

With each animal, as we have seen, its language is an expression of such strong sensuous representations that these become drives. Hence language is, along with senses and representations and drives, *innate* and *immediately natural* for the animal. The bee hums just as it sucks, the bird sings just as it makes a nest . . . But *how does the human being speak by nature? Not at all!* – just as he does little or nothing through sheer instinct as an animal. I make an exception in the case of a newborn child of the cry of its sensitive machine; otherwise *this child is dumb*; it expresses neither representations nor drives through sounds, as by contrast every animal does according to its kind; merely set among animals, therefore, it is the most orphaned child of nature. Naked and bare, weak and needy, timid and unarmed – and, what constitutes the culmination of its miserable state, deprived of all nurturing guides in life. Born with such a dispersed, weakened sensuality, with such indeterminate, dormant abilities, with such divided and weakened drives, obviously dependent on and directed to a thousand needs, destined for a large sphere – and yet so orphaned and abandoned that it does not even enjoy the gift of a language with which to express its shortcomings . . . No! Such a contradiction is not nature's way of organizing her household. There must, instead of instincts, be other hidden powers sleeping in the human child! *Born dumb, but . . .*[30]

Second section

But I shall make no leap. I shall not straightaway suddenly give the human being new forces, "*no language-creating ability,*" like an arbitrary qualitas occulta.[31] I shall merely search further among the previously noted gaps and shortcomings.

Gaps and shortcomings cannot, however, be the character of his species – or nature was the hardest step-mother to him, whereas she was the most loving mother to each insect. She gave to each insect what, and as much as, it needed: senses for representations, and representations developed into drives;[32] organs for language, as many as were necessary, and organs for understanding this language. With the human being everything stands in the greatest disproportion – senses and needs, forces and the circle of efficacy that awaits him, his organs and his language. We must therefore "*lack a certain middle term for calculating the so disparate terms of the equation.*"

If we were to find this middle term, then by the whole analogy of nature "*this compensation would be the human being's distinctive feature, the character of his species,*" and all reason and justice would demand that this discovered trait be treated as what it is, as a *natural gift*, as essential to him as instinct is to the animals.

Were we, moreover, to find "*precisely in this character the cause of those shortcomings, and precisely in the midst of these shortcomings,*" in the hollow of that great bereftness of drives to art, the *germ of a substitute*, then this attunement would be a genetic proof that "*the true orientation of humanity*" lies here, and that the human species does not stand above the animals in *levels* of more or less, but in *kind*.

---

[30] This is a good example of Herder's – fairly frequent – use of the rhetorical figure of aposiopesis. In manuscript a he at first completed the sentence, in a way which helps one to interpret the aposiopesis, as follows: Born dumb, but it will perhaps itself create a language for itself!

[31] Hidden quality.

[32] Cf. in the last paragraph of the preceding section: "[representations] become drives."

And if we were to find in this newly discovered character of humanity even "*the necessary genetic basis for the arising of a language for this new kind of creatures,*" as we found in the instincts of the animals the immediate basis of language for each species, then we have quite reached our goal. In this case "*language would become as essential to the human being as – he is a human being.*" You can see that I develop [all this] not from voluntary or societal forces, but from the general economy of animal life.

*

And now it follows that if the human being has *senses* which, for a small patch of the earth, for the work and the enjoyment of a stretch of the world, *are inferior in sharpness* to the senses of the animal that lives in this stretch, then precisely because of this they receive an *advantage in freedom*; "precisely because they are not for one point, they are more universal senses of the world."

If the human being has *forces of representation* which are not restricted to the construction of a honey cell and a cobweb, and hence also *are inferior to the abilities for art of the animals in this circle*, then precisely thereby these forces receive "*a larger prospect.*" The human being has no single work, in which he would therefore also act in a manner subject to no improvement; but he has free space to practice in many things, and hence to improve himself constantly. Each thought is not an immediate work of nature, but precisely because of this it can become his own work.

If, then, in this way the *instinct* which followed merely from the organization of the senses and the restricted realm of the representations and which was no blind determination must disappear, then precisely thereby the human being receives "*more clarity.*" Since he does not fall blindly on one point and remain lying there blindly, he becomes free-standing, can seek for himself a sphere for self-mirroring, can mirror himself within himself. No longer an infallible machine in the hands of nature, he becomes his own end and goal of refinement.

Let one name this whole disposition of the human being's forces however one wishes: understanding, reason, taking-awareness [*Besinnung*],[33]

---

[33] I translate the two key terms *Besinnung* and *Besonnenheit* as *taking-awareness* and *awareness* respectively. One main reason for this translation is that, as will become clear later in the present essay (see especially the beginning of the second part), and rather contrary to what one might have inferred from the normal linguistic value of these terms, for Herder *Besonnenheit* is a precondition of *Besinnung* but not conversely (*pace* normal usage, which would if anything have suggested the converse dependence).

etc. It is indifferent to me, as long as one does not assume these names to be separate forces or mere higher levels of the animal forces. It is the "*whole organization of all human forces; the whole domestic economy of his sensuous and cognizing, of his cognizing and willing, nature.*" Or rather, it is "*the single positive force of thought,* which, bound up with a certain *organization of the body*, is called *reason* in the case of human beings, just as it becomes *ability for art* in the case of animals, which is called *freedom* in the case of the human being, and in the case of animals becomes *instinct.*" The difference is not in *levels* or the *addition* of *forces*, but in a *quite different sort of orientation* and *unfolding of all forces.* Whether one is Leibnizian or Lockean, Search or Knowall,[k] idealist or materialist, one must in accordance with the preceding, if one is in agreement about the words, concede the matter, "*a distinctive character of humanity*" which consists in this and nothing else.

All those who have raised difficulties against this are deluded by false representations and confused concepts. Human reason has been imagined as a new, quite separate force added into the soul which became the property of the human being in preference to all animals as an additional gift, and which must hence also be considered alone, like the fourth rung of a ladder after the three lowest ones. And that is indeed philosophical nonsense, however great the philosophers may be who say it. All the forces of our souls and of animals' souls are nothing but metaphysical abstractions, effects! They get separated off because our weak spirit was unable to consider them all at once. They stand in chapters, not because they took effect thus chapter by chapter in nature, but because a pupil perhaps best unfolds them for himself in this way. The fact that we have brought certain of their functions under certain main titles, for example, cleverness, intelligence, imagination, reason, does not mean that a single act of spirit would ever be possible in which cleverness or reason takes effect alone, but only that in this act we discover a preponderance of the abstraction which we call cleverness or reason, e.g. the comparison or the rendering distinct of ideas – though in every case the whole, undivided soul takes effect. If a human being was ever able to perform a single act in which he thought entirely like an animal, then he is also through and through no longer a human being, no longer

---

[k] A favorite dichotomy in a new metaphysical work: Search, *Light of Nature Pursued* (London, 1768). [This was a book by A. Tucker published under the pseudonym Search in which Search and Knowall were fictive interlocutors.]

capable of any human act at all. If he was without reason for a single moment, then I cannot see how he could ever in his life think with reason, or [in other words,] his whole soul, the whole economy of his nature, was changed.[34]

According to more correct ideas, the *rationality* of the human being, the character of his species, is something different, namely, "*the total determination of his thinking force in relation to his sensuality and drives.*" And taking all the previous analogies in aid, it could not have been otherwise here than that:

If the human being had *animal drives*, he could not have that which we now call *reason* in him; for precisely these drives would naturally tear his forces so obscurely towards a single point that no free circle of taking-awareness arose for him. It was inevitably the case that:

If the human being had animal *senses*, then he would have no *reason*; for precisely his senses' strong susceptibility to stimulation, precisely the representations mightily pressing on him through them, would inevitably choke all cold awareness [*Besonnenheit*]. But conversely, in accordance with precisely these laws of combination belonging to domestically managing nature, it was also inevitably the case that:

If animal sensuality and restriction to a single point *fell away*, then a different creature came into being, *whose positive force expressed itself in a larger space, in accordance with finer organization, more clearly*, and which, separated and free, not only cognizes, wills, and effects, but also knows that it cognizes, wills, and effects. This creature is the human being, and we wish – in order to escape the confusions with specific forces of reason, etc. – to call this whole disposition of his nature "*awareness.*" Hence it follows from precisely these rules of combination, since all those words – sensuality and instinct, imagination and reason – are after all only

---

[34] The last two sentences illustrate Herder's common practice of combining verbal tenses and moods in unusual ways. For example, in the first sentence, after the past tense "was ever able" one would have expected the past tense again but instead gets the present tense "he is . . . no longer." It would be absurd to suppose that this is just the result of ineptness on Herder's part (one need only look at samples of his more conventional prose in order to see that). Rather, he is deliberately aiming at certain effects by writing in this way. Most obviously, he has an aesthetic goal of breaking the monotony of more conventional prose that uses verbs in more conventional ways (in a manner that is in fact already characteristic of much oral discourse). But also, he hopes to achieve further goals of various sorts – for example, in the case of the first sentence, the switch to the present conveys, both by its own abruptness and by its character as a sort of historic present (which is typically used for dramatic narration), the *immediacy* of the consequence that is being described (i.e. the person's no longer being a human being).

determinations of a single force in which oppositions cancel each other, that:

If the human being *was supposed to be no instinctive animal*, he *had to be a creature with awareness* in virtue of the freely effective positive force of his soul. – If I draw out the chain of these inferences yet a few steps further, then I thereby get a leap ahead of future objections which shortens the path greatly.

If, that is to say, reason is no compartmentalized, separately effective force but an orientation of all forces that is distinctive to his species, *then the human being must have it in the first condition in which he is a human being*. This awareness must reveal itself in the first thought of the child, just as in the case of the insect [it had to be evident] that it was an insect. – Now that is something that more than one author has been unable to grasp, and hence the material about which I am writing is full of the most primitive, most revolting objections. But they were unable to grasp it because they misunderstood it. Does, then, thinking rationally mean thinking with *developed* reason? Does the claim that the infant thinks with awareness mean that he rationalizes like a sophist on his rostrum or the statesman in his cabinet? It is fortunate and thrice fortunate that he should not yet know anything of this fatiguing jumble of rationalizings! But do they not, then, see that this objection merely denies a *thus and not otherwise*, a *more or less cultivated* [gebildeten] *use* of the forces of the soul, and not at all the positive fact of a force of the soul itself? And what fool will claim that the human being in the first moment of life thinks *in the same way as* after many years' practice – unless one simultaneously denies the growth of all forces of the soul and precisely thereby confesses oneself to be a child-without-any-say [*einen Unmündigen*]? But since, on the contrary, this growth can mean nothing at all but an easier, stronger, more diverse *use*, must not, then, that which *is to be used* already *exist*? Must not that which is to *grow* already be a *germ*? And is not the whole tree hence contained in the germ? As little as the child has claws like a condor and a lion's mane can it think like a condor or lion; but if it thinks in a human way, then *awareness*, that is, *the accommodation of all its forces in this central direction*, is already *in the first moment* its fate, just as it will be so in the *last*. Reason already expresses itself amid the child's sensuality so actually that the all-knowing one who created this soul already saw in its first condition the whole network of life's actions – as, for example, the geometer, according to a given class, from one term of the progression finds the progression's whole condition.[35]

"But in that case, this reason was after all at that time more an ability for reason (*réflexion en puissance*) than a real force?" The exception means nothing. Mere, bare ability which even without a present obstacle is no force, nothing but ability, is as empty a sound as plastic forms which form but are themselves no forms. If not the slightest positive contribution to a tendency is present with the ability, then nothing is present – then the word is merely a school abstraction. The recent French philosopher[1] who made this *réflexion en puissance*, this spurious concept, so deceptively dazzling still, as we shall see, only made deceptively dazzling a bubble which he drives along before him for a time but which to his own surprise bursts on his way. And if there is nothing in the ability, through what means is it supposed ever to enter the soul? If in its first condition the soul has nothing positive of reason in it, how will this become real even in millions of succeeding conditions? It is sophistry that the *use* can transform an ability into force, something merely possible into something actual; if force is not already present, then of course it cannot be used and applied. In addition, lastly, what are these two things, a separate ability for reason and force of reason in the soul? One is as unintelligible as the other. Posit the human being as the being that he is, with that degree of sensuality and that organization, in the universe: from all sides, through all senses, this universe streams upon him in sensations. [Not] through human senses? [Not] in a human way? Does this thinking being [not], therefore, in comparison with the animals, get less flooded?[36] This being has the space to express its force more freely, and this state of affairs is called rationality. Where is the mere ability here? Where the separate force of reason? It is the positive, single force of the soul which is effective in such a disposition – where more sensuously, then less rationally; where more rationally, then in a less

---

[1] Rousseau, *On Inequality* etc. [i.e. *Discours sur l'origine* . . .].

[35] Herder's thought here seems to be roughly this: In mathematics, if one knows a function defining a progression ("a given class") and also the first term of the progression ("one term of the progression"), then one can work out the whole progression – e.g. if one knows the function "+1" and the first term of the progression of the positive integers which it defines, namely 1, then one can work out the whole progression of the positive integers. Similarly, if one knows that an infant has awareness, and also knows the initial condition of its soul, then one can work out the whole (subsequent) progression of its soul's conditions.

[36] These three questions are further examples of a Herderian idiom noted earlier: the negative rhetorical question – equivalent to a strong affirmation – expressed without a negation (here supplied).

lively way; where more clearly, then less obscurely – that is all obvious, is it not! But the most sensuous condition of the human being was still human, and hence awareness was still effective in that condition, only in a less marked degree; and the least sensuous condition of the animals was still animalistic, and hence despite any amount of clarity of their thoughts awareness of a human concept was never operative. And let us not play with words any further!

I am sorry to have lost so much time merely in order to define and order bare concepts. But the loss was necessary because in modern times this whole part of psychology lies before us so pathetically devastated, since French philosophers have confused everything so much in their preoccupation with a few apparent peculiarities in animal and human nature, and German philosophers order most concepts of this sort more for their own system and according to their own perspective than with a view to avoiding confusions in the perspective of the usual way of thinking. I have also in this clearing up of concepts made no digression, but we are suddenly at our goal! Namely:

*

The human being, put in the condition of awareness which is his very own, with this awareness (reflection) operating freely for the first time, invented language. For what is reflection? What is language?

This awareness is characteristically his own, and essential to his species. Likewise language and his own invention of language.

The invention of language is hence as natural for him as is his being a human being! Only let us unfold both concepts! – reflection and language.

The human being demonstrates reflection when the force of his soul operates so freely that in the whole ocean of sensations which floods the soul through all the senses it can, so to speak, separate off, stop, and pay attention to a single wave, and be conscious of its own attentiveness. The human being demonstrates reflection when, out of the whole hovering dream of images which proceed before his senses, he can collect himself into a moment of alertness, freely dwell on a single image, pay it clear, more leisurely heed, and separate off characteristic marks for the fact that this is that object and no other. Thus he demonstrates reflection when he can not only recognize all the properties in a vivid or clear way, but can in his own mind *acknowledge* one or several as distinguishing properties.

The first act of this acknowledgment[m] provides a distinct concept; it is the first judgment of the soul – and . . .

What brought about this acknowledgment? A characteristic mark which he had to separate off and which as a characteristic mark of taking-awareness fell distinctly within him.[37] Good! Let us shout to him the *heurêka!*[38] This *first characteristic mark of taking-awareness was a word of the soul! With it human language is invented.*

Let that lamb pass before his eye as an image – [something that happens] to him as to no other animal. Not as to the hungry, scenting wolf!, not as to the blood-licking lion – they already scent and savor in their minds!, sensuality has overcome them!, instinct impels them to attack it! Not as to the aroused ram, which feels the [she-]lamb only as the object of its pleasure, and which is hence again overcome by sensuality and impelled by instinct to attack it. Not as to every other animal to which the sheep is indifferent, and which[39] consequently allows it to proceed past in light and shade because its instinct directs it[40] to something else. Not so to the human being! As soon as he develops a need to become acquainted with the sheep, no instinct disturbs him, no sense tears him too close to the sheep or away from it; it stands there exactly as it expresses itself to his senses. White, soft, woolly – his soul, operating with awareness, seeks a characteristic mark – *the sheep bleats!* – his soul has found a characteristic mark. The inner sense takes effect. This bleating, which makes the strongest impression on the soul, which tore itself away from all the other properties of viewing and feeling, jumped forth, penetrated most deeply, remains for the soul. The sheep comes again. White, soft, woolly – the soul sees, feels, takes awareness, seeks a characteristic mark – it bleats, and now the soul recognizes it again! "Aha! You are the bleating one!" the soul feels inwardly. The soul has recognized it in a human way, for it recognizes and names it distinctly, that is, with a characteristic mark. More obscurely? In that case the sheep would not be perceived at all for the soul because no sensuality, no instinct directed at the sheep, would compensate the soul for its lack of something distinct with something that

---

[m] One of the finest essays to throw light on the essence of *apperception from physical experiments* – which so rarely get to clarify the metaphysics of the soul! – is the essay *in the publications of the Berlin Academy of 1764.* [This refers to J. G. Sulzer, *Sur l'apperception et son influence sur nos jugements* [*On Apperception and Its Influence on our Judgments*].]

[37] B: remained distinctly within him.   [38] I have found it.   [39] Reading *das* with Suphan.
[40] Herder's *ihn* should strictly be an *es*, but gets attracted into the gender of the following word, "human being."

was clear in a more lively way. Distinctly in an immediate way, without a characteristic mark? No sensuous creature can have outer sensation in this way, since it must always suppress, so to speak destroy, other feelings, and must always recognize the difference between two things through a third thing. *With a characteristic mark therefore?* And what else was that but *an inward characteristic word?* "The *sound* of bleating, perceived by a human soul as the distinguishing sign of the sheep, became, thanks to this determination to which it was destined,[41] the *name* of the sheep, even if the human being's tongue had never tried to stammer it." The human being recognized the sheep by its bleating; this was a *grasped sign* on the occasion of *which the soul distinctly recalled to awareness an idea*. What else is that but a word? And what is the *whole of human language* but a *collection of such words?* So even if the human being never reached the situation of conveying this idea to another creature, and hence of wanting or being able to bleat forth this characteristic mark of taking-awareness to it with his lips, still his soul has, so to speak, bleated internally when it chose this sound as a sign for remembering, and bleated again when it recognized the sheep[42] by it. Language is invented! Invented just as naturally, and as necessarily for the human being, as the human being was a human being.

Most people who have written about the origin of language have not sought it in the sole place where it could be found, and consequently many have had numerous obscure doubts floating before their minds about whether it was to be found anywhere in the human soul. People have sought it in the *better articulation* of the instruments of language – as though an orangutan with precisely those instruments would ever have invented language! People have sought it in *the sounds of passion* – as though all animals did not possess these sounds, and any animal had invented language from them! People have assumed a principle of the *imitation* of nature and hence also of nature's sounds – as though anything could be meant by such a blind inclination, and as though the ape with precisely this inclination, or the blackbird which is so good at aping sounds, had invented a language! Finally, the greatest number have assumed a *mere convention*, an agreement – and *Rousseau* is the one who has spoken against this most strongly; for indeed, what sort of obscure, tangled expression

[41] The phrase "determination to which it was destined" translates the single word *Bestimmung* which could here mean any or all of the following: (1) destiny, (2) determining (of the sound as a "distinguishing sign"), (3) determination/property. A simpler solution might be to read *Besinnung* from a with Suphan: "thanks to this taking-awareness."

[42] Reading *es* for *ihn*.

is this, a natural agreement concerning language? These so numerous, unbearable falsehoods which have been stated about the human origin of language have in the end made the opposite opinion almost universal. But I hope that it will not remain so. Here it is no *organization* of the mouth which produces language, for even the person who was dumb all his life, if he was a human being, if he took awareness, had language in his soul! Here it is no *cry of sensation*, for no breathing machine but a creature taking awareness invented language! *No principle of imitation* in the soul; the imitation of nature, if it occurs, is merely a means to the one and only purpose which is supposed to be explained here. Least of all is it *common-understanding*, arbitrary societal convention; the savage, the solitary in the forest, would necessarily have invented language for himself even if he had never spoken it. Language was the common-understanding of his soul with itself, and a common-understanding as necessary as the human being was human being.[43] If others found it unintelligible how a human soul was *able* to invent language, then it is unintelligible to me how a human soul was able to be what it is without precisely thereby, already even in the absence of a mouth and society, *inevitably* inventing language for itself.

Nothing will unfold this origin more distinctly than the objections of the opponents. The most thorough,[n] the most detailed, defender of the divine origin of language becomes, precisely because he penetrated beneath the surface which the others only touch, almost a defender of the true human origin. He stopped immediately at the edge of the proof, and his main objection, merely explained a bit more correctly, becomes an objection against himself and a proof of his [opinion's] antithesis, the human potential for language. He claims to have proved "that the use of language is necessary for the use of reason!" If he had done so, then I do not know what else would thereby be proved "than that since the use of reason is natural to the human being, the use of language would have to be so equally!" Unfortunately though, he has not proved his proposition. He has merely demonstrated very laboriously that such many fine, interwoven actions as attention, reflection, abstraction, etc. can *not properly* happen without signs on which the soul relies; but this *not properly, not easily,*

---

[n] Süßmilch, op. cit., sec. 2.

[43] This sentence is an example of Herder's use of the rhetorical figure of brachylogy, or "shortening." Without brachylogy the sentence would end something like this: "as necessary as it was necessary that the human being was a human being."

not probably does not yet exhaust anything. Just as we with few forces of abstraction can think only a little abstraction without sensuous signs, so other beings can think more without them. At the least it does not yet follow at all that *in itself* no abstraction is possible without a sensuous sign. I have proved that the use of reason is not merely not properly possible without a characteristic mark, but that not the least use of reason, not the simplest distinct acknowledgment, not the simplest judgment of a human awareness is possible without a characteristic mark; for the difference between two things can only ever be recognized through a third thing. Precisely this third thing, this characteristic mark, consequently becomes an inner characteristic word; hence language follows quite naturally from the first act of reason. – Mr. Süßmilch claims to demonstrate[o] that the *higher* applications of reason could not occur without language, and for this cites the words of *Wolff*, who, though, even of this case only speaks in terms of probabilities. The case is actually irrelevant to the question, for the higher applications of reason, as they take place in the speculative sciences, were of course not necessary for the first foundation stone of language construction. – And yet even this easily proved proposition is only *explained* by Mr. S., whereas I believe that I have *proved* that even the first, lowest application of reason was not able to occur without language. But when he now infers that no human being can have invented language for himself because reason is already required for the invention of language, so that language would have already had to be present before it was present, then I stop the eternal circle, consider it rightly, and now it says something completely different: ratio et oratio![44] If no reason was possible for the human being without language, good!, then the invention of the latter is as natural, as old, as original, as characteristic for the human being as the use of the former.

I have called *Süßmilch's* manner of inference an eternal circle because I can of course just as well turn it against him as he can against me – and the thing revolves on and on. Without language the human being has no reason, and without reason no language. Without language and reason he is incapable of any divine instruction, and yet without divine instruction he has no reason and language – where do we ever get to here? How can the human being learn language through divine instruction if

[o] Ibid., p. 52. [Suphan corrects this to: p. 49.]

[44] Reason and speech.

he has no reason? And of course he has not the slightest use of reason
without language. So he is supposed to have language before he has it
and before he is able to have it? Or to be capable of becoming rational without the slightest use of reason on his own part? In order to be
capable of the first syllable in the[45] divine instruction, he of course had,
as Mr. Süßmilch himself concedes, to be a human being, that is, to be
able to think distinctly, and with the first distinct thought language was
already present in his soul; hence it was invented from his own means and
not through[46] divine instruction. – I know of course what people usually
have in mind with this divine instruction, namely, parents' instruction
of their children in language. But let it be recalled that this is not the
case here at all. Parents never teach their children language without the
children constantly themselves inventing it as well; parents only draw
their children's attention to distinctions in things by means of certain
verbal signs, and hence they do not, as might be supposed, *substitute* for
them language for the use of reason, but only *facilitate* and *promote* for
them the use of reason by means of language. If someone wants to assume such a supernatural facilitation for other reasons, then that is quite
irrelevant to my purpose; only in that case God has not at all *invented*
language for human beings, but these still had to *find* their language for
themselves through the effect of their own forces, only under a higher
management. In order to be able to receive the first word as a word, that
is, as a characteristic sign of reason, even from God's mouth, reason was
necessary; and the human being had to apply the same taking-awareness
in order to understand this word as a word as if he had originally thought
it up. So all the weapons of my opponent fight against himself; the human
being needed to have a real use of reason in order to learn divine language;
that is something a learning child always has too unless it should, like a
parrot, merely utter words without thoughts. But what sort of worthy
pupils of God would those be who learned in such a way? And if they
had always learned in such a way, whence would we have got our rational
language, then?

I flatter myself that if my worthy opponent still lived[47] he would understand that his objection, made somewhat more determinate, itself becomes
the strongest proof against him, and that he has hence in his book un-
wittingly himself gathered together materials for his own refutation. He

[45] Reading *im* for *in* with Suphan.   [46] B: and not mechanically through.
[47] Süßmilch died in 1767.

92

would not hide behind the expression "ability for reason, which, though, is not yet in the least reason." For whichever way one chooses to turn, contradictions arise! A rational creature without the least use of reason, or a reason-using creature without language! A reasonless creature to which instruction can give reason, or a creature capable of being instructed which is however without reason! A being which is without the slightest use of reason – and yet a human being! A being which could not use its reason from natural forces and yet learned to use it naturally through supernatural instruction! A human language which was not human at all, i.e. which was unable to arise through any human force, and a language which is rather so human that without it none of the human being's actual forces can express itself! A thing without which he was not a human being, and yet a condition in which he was a human being and did not have the thing, which thing was therefore present before it was present, had to express itself before it could express itself, etc. All these contradictions are obvious when human being, reason, and language are taken as the real things that they are, and the ghost of a word 'ability' ('human ability,' 'ability for reason,' 'linguistic ability') is unmasked in its nonsensicality.

"But those savage human children among the bears, did they have language? And were they not human beings?"[P] Certainly! Only, *first of all*, human beings in an unnatural condition! Human beings in degeneration! Put the stone on this plant; will it not grow crooked? And is it not nevertheless in its nature an upwards-growing plant? And did this force for straight growth not express itself even in the case where the plant entwined itself crookedly around the stone? Hence, *second*, even the possibility of this degeneration reveals human nature. Precisely because the human being has no such compelling instincts as the animals, because he is capable of so many kinds of things and is more weakly capable of everything – in short, because he is a human being, was he able to degenerate. Would he, then, have learned to roar in such a bearlike way, and to creep in such a bearlike way if he had not had flexible organs, if he had not had flexible limbs? Would any other animal, an ape or a donkey, have got so far? So did his human nature not really contribute to the fact that he was able to become so unnatural? But *third*, given such a situation,[48] this human nature still remained human nature. For did

[P] Süßmilch, p. 47.

[48] The phrase "given such a situation" tries to capture two senses between which *deswegen* hovers here: (1) therefore, (2) despite this.

he roar, creep, feed, scent *completely* like a bear? Or would he not have eternally remained a stumbling, stammering human-bear, and hence an imperfect double-creature? Actually, as little as his skin and his face, his feet and his tongue, were able to change and turn into a complete bear form, just as little – let us never doubt it! – was the nature of his soul able to do so. His reason lay buried under the pressure of sensuality, of *bearlike* instincts, but it was still human reason, because those instincts were never completely *bearish*. And that this is how things were is indeed shown, *finally*, by the development of the whole scene. When the obstacles were rolled away, when these bear-humans had returned to their species, did they not learn to walk upright and to speak *more naturally* than they had – ever *unnaturally* – formerly learned to creep and to roar? The latter they were only ever able to do in a *bearlike* way; the former they learned in less time *quite humanly*. Which of their former fraternal companions in the forest learned this with them? And because no bear was able to learn it, because none possessed the disposition of body and soul for this, must it not have been the case that the human–bear had still preserved this disposition in the condition of his degeneration into savagery? If mere instruction and habituation had given this disposition to him, why not to the bear? And then what would it mean to give reason and humanity to someone through instruction when he does not already have them? Presumably in that case this needle has given the power of sight to the eye from which it removes cataracts . . . Whatever, then, would we want to infer about nature from the most unnatural of cases? But if we confess that it is an unnatural case – fine!, then it confirms nature![49]

The whole *Rousseauian* hypothesis of the inequality of human beings is, famously, built on such cases of degeneration, and his doubts against the human character of language concern[50] either false sorts of origins or the difficulty earlier touched on that the invention of language would already have required reason. In the first case his doubts are right; in the second they are refuted, and indeed can be refuted out of *Rousseau's* own mouth. His phantom, the natural human being – this degenerate creature which he on the one hand fobs off with the ability for reason, on the other hand gets invested with perfectibility, and indeed with perfectibility as a distinctive character trait, and indeed with perfectibility in such a high

---

[49] B continues the sentence: nature, and through its deviation points to the human possibility of language in a better condition.

[50] B: hence concern.

degree that thanks to it this natural human being can learn from all the species of animals. And now what has *Rousseau* not[51] conceded to this natural human being! [He has conceded] more than we want and need! The first thought – "Behold! That is something peculiar to the animal! The wolf howls! The bear roars!" – this is already (thought in such a light that it could combine with the second thought, "That is something I do not have!") actual reflection. And now the third and fourth thoughts – "Fine! That would also accord with my nature! I could imitate that! I want to imitate that! Thereby my species will become more perfect!" – what a mass of fine, inferentially connected reflections!, since the creature that was able to consider only the first of these necessarily already had a language of the soul!, already[52] possessed the art of thinking which created the art of speaking. The ape always apes, but it has never imitated: never said to itself with awareness, "I want to imitate that in order to make my species more perfect!" For if it had ever done that, if it had made a single imitation its own, made it eternal in its species by choice and intention, if it had been able to think even just a single time a single such reflection . . . then at that very moment it was no longer an ape! For all its ape form, even without a sound of its tongue, it was an inwardly speaking human being,[53] who was bound to invent his outward language for himself sooner or later. But what orangutan has ever, with all its human language instruments, spoken a single human word?[54]

To be sure, there are still negro-brothers in Europe who simply say, "Perhaps so – if only the orangutan wanted to speak! – or found itself in the right circumstances![55] – or could!" *Could*! – that would no doubt be the best formulation; for the two preceding *if*s are sufficiently refuted by the history of animals, and, as mentioned, the ability is not impeded in this animal's case by the instruments.[56] It has a head which is like ours both outside and inside, but has it ever spoken? Parrot and starling have learned enough human sounds, but have they also thought a human word? Quite generally, the outer sounds of words are not yet of any concern to us here; we are talking about the inner, necessary *genesis* of a word, as the characteristic mark of a distinct taking-awareness. But when has an animal

---

[51] B: not hereby. [52] B: in that it already. [53] B: inwardly a speaking human being.

[54] B substitutes "human-like" for "human" both times in this sentence.

[55] Reading *Umstände* with Suphan.

[56] Footnote added by Herder in the B edition of 1789: "It is clear from Camper's dissection of the orangutan (see his translated short writings [i.e. *Sämmtliche kleine Schriften*, 1785]) that this claim is too bold; however, formerly, when I wrote this, it was the common opinion of anatomists."

species ever, in whatever way, expressed that? This thread of thoughts, this discourse of the soul, would still have to be capable of being followed, however it might express itself. But who has ever done that? The fox has acted a thousand times in the way that Aesop makes it act, but it has never acted with the meaning attributed to it by Aesop, and the first time that it is capable of doing so, Master Fox will invent his own language for himself and be able to make up fables about Aesop just as Aesop now makes them up about him. The dog has learned to understand many words and commands, however not as words but as signs associated with gestures, with actions; if it were ever to understand a single word in the human sense, then it no longer serves, it creates for itself art and republic and language. One can see that if one once misses the exact point of genesis, then the field for error on both sides is immeasurably large! – then language becomes now so superhuman that God has to invent it, now so inhuman that any animal could invent it if it gave itself the trouble. The goal of truth is only a point! But, set down on it, we see on all sides: why no animal can invent language, why no God must[57] invent language, and why the human being as a human being can and must invent language.

I do not want to pursue the hypothesis of the divine origin of language any further on a metaphysical basis, for its groundlessness is clear psychologically from the fact that in order to understand the language of the gods on Olympus the human being must already have reason and consequently must already have language. Still less can I indulge in a pleasant detailing of the animal languages, for, as we have seen, it turns out that they all stand completely and incommensurably apart from human language. What I renounce least happily here are the many sorts of prospects which would lead from this point of the genesis of language in the human soul into the broad fields of Logic, Aesthetics, and Psychology, especially concerning the question, *How far can one think without language, what must one think with language?*, a question which subsequently spreads itself in its applications over almost all the sciences. Let it suffice here to note that language is the real differentia of our species from without, as reason is from within.

In more than one language *word* and *reason*, *concept* and *word*, *language* and *originating cause* [*Ursache*], consequently also share one name,[58] and this synonymy contains its whole genetic origin. With the Easterners it

[57] Or possibly: may.　[58] E.g. Greek, in which the word *logos* can bear all these meanings.

became the most everyday idiom to call the *acknowledgment* of a thing *name-giving*, for in the bottom of the soul both actions are one. They call the human being the *speaking* animal, and the nonrational animals the *dumb* – the expression characterizes them sensuously, and the Greek word *alogos*[59] comprises both things.[60] In this way language becomes a *natural organ of the understanding*, a *sense of the human soul*, just as the force of vision of that sensitive soul of the ancients builds for itself the eye, and the instinct of the bee builds for itself its cell.

[It is] excellent that this new, self-made sense belonging to the mind is immediately in its origin a means of connection in its turn.[61] I cannot think the first human thought, cannot set up the first aware judgment in a sequence, without engaging in dialogue, or striving to engage in dialogue, in my soul.[62] Hence the first human thought by its very nature prepares one to be able to engage in dialogue with others! The first *characteristic mark* that I grasp is a *characteristic word* for me and a *communication word* for others!

– Sic verba, quibus voces sensusque notarent
Nominaque invenere –[63]   *Horace*

Third section

The focal point at which Prometheus's heavenly spark catches fire in the human soul has been determined. With the first characteristic mark language arose. But which were the first characteristic marks to serve as elements of language?

I. Sounds

Cheselden's blind man[q] shows how slowly sight develops; with what difficulty the soul arrives at the concepts of space, shape, and color; how

---

[q] *Philosophical Transactions [of the Royal Society of London,* no. 402, 1728] – Abridgement. Also in Cheselden's Anatomy, in *Smith-Kästner's* Optics, in *Buffon's* Natural History, the Encyclopedia, and ten small French dictionaries under *aveugle*.

[59] *alogos*: without speech, without reason.
[60] B substitutes for "and ... *alogos* ..." "the ... *alogos* too ..."
[61] B: is and must be in its origin a means of connection in its turn!
[62] A Platonic doctrine. See *Theaetetus,* 189e ff.
[63] Thus did they invent words and names with which to mark sounds and meanings.

many attempts must be made, how much geometry must be acquired, in order to use these characteristic marks distinctly. This was not therefore the most suitable sense for language. In addition, its phenomena were so cold and dumb, and the sensations of the cruder senses in their turn so indistinct and mixed up, that according to all nature either nothing or *the ear became the first teacher of language.*

There, for example, is the sheep. As an image it hovers before the eye with all objects, images, and colors on a single great nature picture. How much to distinguish, and with what effort! All characteristic marks are finely interwoven, beside each other – all still inexpressible! Who can speak shapes? Who can sound colors? He[64] takes the sheep under his groping hand. Feeling is surer and fuller – but so full, so obscurely mixed up. Who can say what he feels? But listen! The sheep bleats! There a characteristic mark of itself tears itself free from the canvas of the color picture in which so little could be distinguished – has penetrated deeply and distinctly into the soul. "Aha!" says the learning child-without-any-say [*Unmündige*], like that formerly blind man of *Cheselden's*, "Now I will know you again. You bleat!" The turtle-dove coos! The dog barks! There are three words, because he tried out three distinct ideas – these ideas for his logic, those words for his vocabulary! Reason and language took a timid step together, and nature came to meet them half-way *through hearing*. Nature sounded the characteristic mark not only forth but deep into the soul! It rang out! The soul laid hold – and there it has a *resounding word*!

The human being is therefore, as a listening, noting creature, naturally formed for language, and even a blind and dumb man, one sees, would inevitably[65] invent language, if only he is not without feeling and deaf. Put him comfortably and contentedly on a lonely island; nature will reveal itself to him through his ear, a thousand creatures which he cannot see will nonetheless seem to speak with him, and even if his mouth and his eye remained forever closed, his soul does not remain entirely without language. When the leaves of the tree rustle down coolness for the poor lonely one, when the stream that murmurs past rocks him to sleep, and the west wind whistling in fans his cheeks – the bleating sheep gives him milk, the trickling spring water, the rustling tree fruit – interest enough to know these beneficent beings, urgent cause enough, without eyes and

[64] B: The human being.   [65] Reading with Suphan *müßte*.

tongue, to *name* them in his soul. The tree will be called the rustler, the west wind the whistler, the spring the trickler. A small vocabulary lies ready there, and awaits the speech organs' minting. How impoverished and strange, though, would have to be the representations which this mutilated person associates with such sounds!ʳ

Now set all of the human being's senses free, let him simultaneously see and touch and feel all the beings which speak into his ear. Heaven! What a classroom of ideas and language! Bring no Mercury or Apollo down from the clouds as operatic dei ex machina; all of many-sounded, divine nature is language mistress and Muse! There she leads all creatures past him; each bears its name on its tongue, and names itself to this enshrouded, visible god! as his vassal and servant. It delivers unto him its characteristic word into the book of his governance like a tribute, that he may remember it by this name, call it in future, and enjoy it. I ask whether this truth – "Precisely the understanding, through which the human being rules over nature, was the father of a living language, which it abstracted for itself from the sounds of resounding beings as characteristic marks for distinguishing!" – whether this dry truth[66] can ever be expressed more nobly and beautifully in an Eastern way than [in the words]: "God led the animals to him that he might see how he should name them! And however he would name them, thus were they to be called!"[67] Where can it be said more definitely in an Eastern, poetic way: the human being invented language for himself! – from the sounds of living nature! – to be characteristic marks of his governing understanding! And that is what I prove.

If an angel or heavenly spirit had invented language, how could it be otherwise than that language's whole structure would have to be an offprint of this spirit's manner of thought? For by what else could I recognize a picture that an angel had painted than by the angelic quality, the supernatural quality of its traits? But where does that happen in the case of our language? Structure and layout, yes, even the first foundation stone of this palace, betrays humanity!

ʳ *Diderot* hardly came to this central material in his whole letter *Sur les sourds et muets* [i.e. *Lettre sur les sourds et muets à l'usage de ceux qui entendent et qui parlent* [*Letter on the Deaf and Dumb for the Use of Those who Hear and Speak*], 1751], since he only stops to discuss inversions and a hundred other minor matters. [The B edition is more complimentary here: Diderot's letter is "instructive" and instead of "minor matters" he discusses "subtleties."]

[66] " . . . whether this truth . . . whether this . . . truth" is an example of the rhetorical figure of anadiplosis, or "doubling," which Herder uses fairly often.

[67] Genesis 2:19.

In what language are heavenly, spiritual concepts the first ones? Those concepts which would also have[68] to be the first according to the order of our thinking spirit – subjects, notiones communes,[69] the seeds of our cognition, the points about which everything turns and [to which] everything leads back – are these living points not elements of language? After all, the subjects would naturally have[70] to have come before the predicate, and the simplest subjects before the compound ones, that which does and acts before what it does, the essential and certain before the uncertain contingent . . . Yes, what all could one not infer, and – in our original languages the clear opposite happens throughout. A hearing, listening creature is recognizable but no heavenly spirit, for *resounding verbs are the first ruling elements.*[71] Resounding verbs? Actions, and still nothing which acts there? Predicates, and still no subject? The heavenly genius may need to be ashamed of that, but not the sensuous, human creature, for what moved the latter – as we have seen – more deeply than these resounding actions? And hence what else is language's whole manner of construction than a mode of development of this creature's spirit, a history of its discoveries? The divine origin explains nothing and lets nothing be explained from it; it is, as *Bacon* says of another subject, a holy Vestal Virgin – consecrated to God but barren, pious but useless![72]

The first vocabulary was therefore collected from the sounds of the whole world. From each resounding being its name rang out, the human soul impressed its image on them, thought of them as characteristic signs. How could it be otherwise than that these resounding interjections became the first?[73] And so it is that, for example, the Eastern languages are full of verbs as basic roots of language. The thought of the thing itself still hovered between the agent and the action. The sound had to designate the thing, just as the thing gave the sound. Hence from the verbs arose nouns, and not from the nouns verbs.[74] The child names the sheep not as a sheep but as a bleating creature, and hence makes the interjection into a verb. This matter becomes explicable in the context of the steps of development of human sensuality, but not in the context of the logic of the higher spirit.

[68] Reading with Suphan *müßten.*   [69] Common concepts.   [70] Reading with Suphan *müßten.*
[71] B: ruling elements of the oldest languages.
[72] B adds here: The human origin explains everything and hence very much.
[73] B: the first vivid words [*Machtworte*] of language.
[74] Reading with Suphan for *und Nomina aus den Verbis* instead *und nicht Verba aus den Nominibus.* Suphan gives a compelling explanation from the manuscripts of how the corruption arose.

All old, savage languages are full of this origin, and in a *"philosophical dictionary of the Easterners"* each stem-word with its family, properly presented and soundly developed, would be a map of the course of the human spirit, a history of its development, and a whole such dictionary would be the most excellent proof of the human soul's art of invention. But also of God's linguistic and pedagogical method? I doubt it!

Since the whole of nature resounds, there is nothing more natural for a sensuous human being than that *it lives, it speaks, it acts*. That savage saw the high tree with its splendid crown and admired.[75] The crown rustled! That is the work of divinity! The savage falls down and prays to it![76] Behold there the history of the sensuous human being, the obscure link, *how nouns arise from the verbs – and*[77] *the easiest step to abstraction!* With the savages of North America, for example, everything is still alive: each thing has its genius, its spirit. And that it was just the same with the Greeks and the Easterners is shown by[78] their oldest vocabulary and grammar – they are, as the whole of nature was to the inventor, a pantheon!, a realm of living, acting beings!

But because the human being related everything to himself, because everything seemed to speak with him, and really acted for or against him, because he consequently took sides with or against it, loved or hated it, and imagined everything to be human, all these traces of humanity impressed[79] themselves into the first names as well! They too expressed *love or hate, curse or blessing, softness or opposition*, and especially there arose from this feeling in so many languages *the articles*! Here everything became human, personified into woman or man – everywhere gods; goddesses; acting, wicked or good, beings!; the roaring storm and the sweet zephyr; the clear spring and the mighty ocean – their whole mythology lies in the mines, the verbs and nouns, of the ancient languages, and the oldest vocabulary was as much a resounding pantheon, a meeting hall of both genders, as nature was to the senses of the first inventor. Here the language of those ancient savages is a study in the strayings of human imagination and passions, like their mythology. Each family of words is an overgrown bush around a sensuous main idea, around a holy oak on which there are still traces of the impression that the inventor had of this Dryad. The feelings are woven together for him; what moves lives; what resounds

---

[75] B: admired it.   [76] B: "That," he said, "is the work of divinity!" He fell down and prayed to it.
[77] B: *and simultaneously.*   [78] Reading *zeigt* for *zeugt.*   [79] Reading with Suphan *drückten.*

speaks – and since it resounds for you or against you, it is friend or enemy; god or goddess; it acts from passions, like you!

A human, sensuous creature is what I love when I reflect on this manner of thought: I see everywhere the weak and timid sensitive person who must love or hate, trust or fear, and would like to spread these sensations from his own breast over all beings. I see everywhere the weak and yet mighty creature which needs the whole universe and entangles everything into war or peace with itself, which depends on everything and yet rules over everything. – The poetry and the gender-creation of language are hence humanity's interest, and the genitals of speech, so to speak, the means of its reproduction.[80] But now, if a higher genius brought language down out of the stars, how is this? Did this genius out of the stars become entangled on our earth under the moon in such passions of love and weakness, of hate and fear, that he wove everything into liking and hate, that he marked all words with fear and joy, that he, finally, constructed everything on the basis of gender pairings? Did he see and feel as a human being sees, so that the nouns had to pair off into genders and articles for him, so that he put the verbs together in the active and the passive, accorded them so many legitimate and illegitimate children – in short, so that he constructed the whole language on the basis of the feeling of human weaknesses? Did he see and feel in this way?

To a defender of the supernatural origin [of language] it is divine ordering of language "that most stem-words have one syllable, verbs are mostly of two syllables, and hence language is arranged in accordance with the measure of memory."[81] The fact is inexact and the inference unsure. In the remains of the language which is accepted as being most ancient the roots are all[82] verbs of two syllables, which fact, now, I can explain very well from what I said above, whereas the opposite hypothesis finds no support. These verbs, namely, are immediately *built* on the sounds and interjections of resounding nature – which often still resound in them, and are here and there even still preserved in them as interjections; but for the most part, *as semi–unarticulated sounds, they were inevitably lost* when the language *developed*. Hence in the Eastern languages these first attempts of the stammering tongue are absent; but the fact that they are absent, and that only their regular remains resound in the verbs, precisely this testifies[83] to the originality and . . . the humanity of language. Are these

---

[80] B: of its arising.   [81] Süßmilch, *Versuch eines Beweises*, p. 22.
[82] B replaces "all" with "usually."   [83] Reading *zeugt von* for *zeigt von*.

stems treasures and abstractions from God's understanding, or rather the first sounds of the listening ear, the first noises of the stammering tongue? For of course the human species in its childhood formed for itself precisely the language which a child-without-any-say stammers; it is the babbling vocabulary of the wet-nurse's quarters – but where does that remain in the mouths of adults?

The thing that so many ancients say, and so many moderns have repeated without sense, wins from this its sensuous life, namely, "that *poetry was older than prose!*" For what was this first language but a collection of elements of poetry? Imitation of resounding, acting, stirring nature! Taken from the interjections of all beings and enlivened by the interjection of human sensation! The natural language of all creatures poetized by the understanding into sounds, into[84] images of action, of passion, and of living effect! A vocabulary of the soul which is simultaneously a mythology and a wonderful epic of the actions and speakings of all beings! Hence a constant poetic creation of fable with passion and interest! What else is poetry?

In addition. The tradition of antiquity says: *the first language of the human species was song.* And many good, musical people have believed that human beings could well have learned this song from the birds. That is, it must be admitted, a lot to swallow! A great, heavy clock with all its sharp wheels and newly stretched springs and hundredweight weights can to be sure produce a carillon of tones. But to set forth the newly created human being, with his driving motives, with his needs, with his strong sensations, with his almost blindly preoccupied attention, and finally with his primitive throat, so that he might ape the nightingale, and from the nightingale sing himself a language, is – however many histories of music and poetry it may be asserted in – unintelligible to me. To be sure, a language through musical tones would be possible (however *Leibniz*[s] arrived at this idea!). But for the first natural human beings this language was not possible, so artificial and fine is it. In the chain of beings each thing has its voice and a language in accordance with its voice. The language of love is sweet song in the nest of the nightingale, as it is roaring in the cave of the lion; in the deer's forest it is troating lust, and in the cat's den a caterwaul. Each species speaks its own language of love, not

[s] *Oeuvres philosophiques*, publiées par Raspe [*Philosophical Works*, edited by Raspe], p. 282.

[84] B: personified into.

for the human being but for itself, and for itself as pleasantly as Petrarch's song to his Laura! Hence as little as the nightingale sings in order to sing as an example for human beings, the way people imagine, just as little will the human being ever want to invent language for himself by trilling in imitation of the nightingale. And then really, what sort of monster is this: a human nightingale in a cave or in the game forest?

So if the first human language was song, it was song which was as natural to the human being, as appropriate to his organs and natural drives, as the nightingale's song was natural to the nightingale, a creature which is, so to speak, a hovering lung – and that was ... precisely our resounding language. *Condillac, Rousseau,* and others were half[85] on the right track here in that they derive the meter and song of the oldest languages from the cry of sensation – and without doubt sensation did indeed enliven the first sounds and elevate them. But since from the mere sounds of sensation human language could never have arisen, though this song certainly was such a language, something more is still needed in order to produce this song – and that was precisely the naming of each creature in accordance with its own language. So there sang and resounded the whole of nature as an example, and the human being's song was a concerto of all these voices, to the extent that his understanding needed them, his sensation grasped them, his organs were able to express them. Song was born, but neither a nightingale's song nor *Leibniz's* musical language nor a mere animals' cry of sensation: an expression of the language of all creatures within the natural scale of the human voice!

Even when language later became more regular, monotonous, and regimented [*gereiht*], it still remained *a species of song,* as the accents of so many savages bear witness; and that the oldest poetry and music arose from this song, subsequently made nobler and finer, has now already been proved by more than one person. The philosophical *Englishman*[t] who in our century tackled this *origin of poetry and music* could have got furthest if he had not excluded the spirit of language from his investigation and had aimed less at his system of confining poetry and music to a single point of unification – in which neither of them can show itself in its true light – than at the origination of both from the whole nature of the human

[t] Brown. [J. Brown (1715–66), author of *A Dissertation on the Rise, Union, Power, the Progressions, Separations, and Corruptions, of Poetry and Music* (1763).]

[85] B: very much.

being. In general, because the best pieces of ancient poetry are remains
from these language-singing times, the misconceptions, misappropria-
tions, and misguided errors of taste that have been spelled forth[86] from
the course of the most ancient poems, of the Greek tragedies, and of the
Greek orations are quite countless. How much could still be said here by
a philosopher who had learned among the savages, where this age still
lives, the tone in which to read these pieces! Otherwise, and usually, people only ever see the weave of the back of the carpet!, disjecti membra
poetae![87] But I would lose myself in an immeasurable field if I were to go
into individual observations about language – so back to the first path of
the invention of language!

*

How words arose from sounds minted into characteristic marks by the understanding was very intelligible, but *not all objects make sounds*. Whence,
then, characteristic words for these [other] objects for the soul to name
them with? Whence the human being's art of turning something that is
not noise into noise? What does color, roundness have in common with
the name which arises from it just as[88] the name 'bleating' arises from the
sheep? The defenders of the supernatural origin [of language] immediately have a solution here: "[This happens] by arbitrary volition! Who can
comprehend, and investigate in God's understanding, why green is called
'green' and not 'blue'? Clearly, that is the way he wanted it!" And thus the
thread [of inquiry] is cut off! All philosophy about the art of inventing
language thus hovers arbitrarily-voluntarily in the clouds, and for us each
word is a qualitas occulta,[89] something arbitrarily willed! Only it may not
be taken ill that in this case I do not understand the term 'arbitrarily
willed.' To invent a language out of one's brain by arbitrary volition and
without any ground of choice is, at least for a human soul, which wants
to have a ground, even if only a single ground, for everything, as much
a torture as it is for the body to have itself tickled to death. Moreover,
in the case of a primitive, sensuous natural human being whose forces
are not yet fine enough to play aiming at what is useless, who, in his lack
of practice and his strength, does nothing without a pressing cause, and
wants to do nothing in vain, the invention of a language out of insipid,
empty arbitrary volition is opposed to the whole analogy of his nature.

[86] B: the misconceptions that have been spelled forth under the name of errors of taste . . .
[87] Limbs of the mutilated poet.   [88] B: just as naturally as.   [89] Hidden quality.

And in general, it is opposed to the whole analogy of all human forces of soul, a language thought out from pure arbitrary volition.

So, to the matter. How was the human being, left to his own forces, also able even to invent for himself

II. a language when no sound resounded for him as an example?

How are sight and hearing, color and word, scent and sound, connected?

Not among themselves in the objects. But what, then, are these properties in the objects? They are merely sensuous sensations in us, and as such do they not all flow into one? We are a single thinking sensorium commune,[90] only touched from various sides. There lies the explanation.

Feeling forms the basis of all the senses, and this already gives to the most diverse sensations such an inward, strong, inexpressible bond that the strangest phenomena arise from this connection. I am familiar with more than one example in which people, perhaps due to an impression from childhood, by nature could not but through a sudden onset immediately associate with this sound that color, with this phenomenon that quite different, obscure feeling, which in the light of leisurely reason's comparison has no relation with it at all – for who can compare sound and color, phenomenon and feeling? We are full of such connections of the most different senses, only we do not notice them except in onsets which make us beside ourselves, in sicknesses of the imagination, or on occasions when they become unusually noticeable. The normal course of our thoughts proceeds so quickly, the waves of our sensations rush so obscurely into each other, there is so much in our soul at once, that in regard to most ideas we are as though asleep by a spring where to be sure we still hear the rush of each wave, but so obscurely that in the end sleep takes away from us all noticeable feeling. If it were possible for us to arrest the chain of our thoughts and look at each link for its connection, what strange phenomena!, what foreign analogies among the most different senses – in accordance with which, however, the soul habitually acts! In the eyes of a merely rational being, we would all be similar to that type of madmen who think cleverly but combine very unintelligibly and foolishly!

[90] Collective organ of sensation ("inner sense").

In the case of sensuous creatures who have sensation through many different senses simultaneously this collecting together of ideas is unavoidable, for what are all the senses but mere modes of representation of a single positive force of the soul? We distinguish them, but once again only through senses; hence modes of representation through modes of representation. With much effort we learn to separate them in use – but in a certain basis they still function together. All dissections of sensation in the case of *Buffon's, Condillac's,* and *Bonnet's* sensing human being are abstractions; the philosopher has to neglect one thread of sensation in pursuing the other, but in nature all these threads are a single web! Now, the more obscure the senses are, the more they flow into each other; and the more untrained they are, the less a person has yet learned to use one without the other, to use it with skill and distinctness, then the more obscure they are! – Let us apply this to the beginning of language! The childhood and inexperience of the human species made language easier!

The human being stepped into the world. What an ocean immediately fell upon him! With what difficulty did he learn to distinguish!, to recognize senses!, to use recognized senses alone! Vision is the coldest sense, and if it had always been as cold, as remote, as distinct as it has become for us through an effort and training lasting many years, then indeed I would not see[91] how one can make audible what one sees. But nature has taken care of this and has shortened the path, for even this vision was, as children and formerly blind people testify, to begin with only feeling. Most visible things move, many make a sound when they move, and where not, then they, so to speak, lie closer to the eye in its initial condition, immediately upon it, and can hence be felt. Feeling lies so close to hearing; its descriptive terms, for example, *hart, rauh, weich, wollig, sammt, haarig, starr, glatt, schlicht, borstig,*[92] etc., which of course all concern only surfaces and do not even penetrate deeply, all make a sound as though one felt the thing. The soul, which stood in the throng of such a confluence of sensations, and in need of forming a word, reached out and got hold perhaps of the word of a neighboring sense whose feeling flowed together with this one. In this way words arose for all the senses, and even for the coldest of them. Lightning does not make a noise, but if it is to be expressed, this messenger of midnight!,

[91] Reading *sehe* as *sähe*.
[92] Hard, rough, soft, woolly, velvety, hairy, stiff, smooth, sleek, bristly.

> That, in a spleen, unfolds both heaven and earth,
> And ere a man hath power to say, "Behold!"
> The jaws of darkness do devour it up[93]

then naturally this will be done by a word which through the help of an intermediary feeling gives the ear the sensation of what is most suddenly quick which the eye had: *Blitz!*[94] The words *Duft, Ton, süß, bitter, sauer,*[95] etc. all make a sound as though one felt – for what else are all the senses originally but feeling? But how feeling can express itself in sound – this we have already in the first section accepted as an immediate natural law of the sensing machine which we may explain no further!

And hence all the difficulties lead back to the following two proven, distinct propositions: 1) *Since all the senses are nothing but modes of representation belonging to the soul,* let the soul only have *distinct representation,* and consequently a *characteristic mark,* and with the characteristic mark it has *inner language.*

2) Since all the senses, especially in the condition of human childhood, are nothing but *ways of feeling belonging to a soul,* but *all feeling* according to a law of sensation pertaining to animal nature *immediately has* its *sound,* let this feeling only be elevated to the *distinctness of a* characteristic mark, then the *word for external language* is present. Here we come to a mass of special observations concerning "how nature's wisdom has thoroughly organized the human being so that he might invent language for himself." Here is the main observation:

"Since the human being only receives the language of teaching nature through the sense of hearing, and without this cannot invent language, hearing in a certain way became the middle one of his senses, the actual door to the soul, and the bond connecting the other senses." I want to explain myself!

1) Hearing is the middle one of the human senses *in regard to sphere of sensitivity from outside.* Feeling senses everything only in itself and in its organ; vision throws us far outside ourselves; hearing stands in its degree of communicativity in the middle. What does that do for language? Suppose a creature, even a rational creature, for whom feeling were the main sense (if this is possible!). How small its world is! And

---

[93] Shakespeare, *A Midsummer Night's Dream*, act 1, scene 1, ll. 146–8.   [94] Lightning!
[95] Scent, sound, sweet, bitter, sour.

since it does not sense this through hearing, it will no doubt perhaps like the insect construct a web for itself, but it will not construct for itself a language through sounds! Again, a creature that is all eye. How inexhaustible the world of its visual observations is! How immeasurably far it is thrown outside itself! Dispersed into what infinite manifoldness! Its spoken language (we have no idea of it!) would become a sort of infinitely fine pantomime, its writing an algebra by means of colors and strokes – but resounding language never! We creatures who hear stand in the middle: we see, we feel, but seen, felt nature resounds! It becomes a teacher of language through sounds! We become, so to speak, hearing through all our senses!

Let us feel the comfortableness of our position – through it *each sense becomes capable of language.* To be sure, only *hearing* actually gives sounds, and the human being cannot invent but only find, only imitate. But on the one side *feeling* lies next door, and on the other side *vision* is the neighboring sense. The sensations unite together and hence all approach the region where characteristic marks turn into sounds. In this way, what one sees, what one feels, becomes soundable as well. The sense for language has become our middle and unifying sense; we are linguistic creatures.

2) Hearing is the middle one among the senses *in respect of distinctness* and *clarity*, and hence again the sense for language. How obscure is *feeling*! It gets stunned [*übertäubt*]! It senses everything *mixed up*. There it is difficult to separate off a characteristic mark for acknowledgment; it proves inexpressible!

Again, vision is so *bright and blinding* [*überglänzend*], it supplies such a mass of characteristic marks, that the soul succumbs under the manifoldness, and can for example separate one of them off only so weakly that recognition by means of it becomes weak.[96] *Hearing* is in the middle. It leaves aside all feeling's mixed-up, obscure characteristic marks. All vision's excessively fine characteristic marks as well! But does a sound tear itself free there from the felt, observed object? Into this sound the characteristic marks of those two senses gather themselves – this becomes a characteristic word! So hearing reaches out on both sides; it makes clear what was too obscure, it makes pleasanter what was too bright; it introduces more unity into the *obscure manifold* of feeling, and also into the

[96] a: becomes difficult.

excessively bright manifold of vision; and since this acknowledgment of the manifold through one, through a characteristic mark, becomes language, hearing is language.[97]

3) Hearing is the middle sense with *respect to liveliness* and hence the sense for language. Feeling overpowers [*überwältigt*]; vision is too cold and indifferent. The former penetrates too deeply into us to be able to become language; the latter remains too much at rest before us. Hearing's sound penetrates so intimately into our souls that it inevitably becomes a characteristic mark, but still not so stunningly [*übertäubend*] that it could not become a clear characteristic mark. That is the sense for language.

How brief, tiring, and unbearable the language of any cruder sense would be for us! How confusing and mind-emptying the language of excessively fine vision! Who can always taste, feel, and smell without soon, as *Pope* says, dying an aromatic death? And who always attentively gape at a color-piano without soon going blind? But we can for longer and almost for ever hear, think words with hearing, so to speak; hearing is for the soul what green, the middle color, is for sight. The human being is formed to be a linguistic creature.

4) Hearing is the middle sense in *relation to the time in which it operates*, and hence the sense for language. Feeling casts *everything into us at once*, it stirs our strings strongly but briefly and in jumps. Vision presents everything to us *at once*, and hence intimidates the pupil through the immeasurable canvas of its *side-by-side*. Behold how [nature] the teacher of language spares us through hearing! She counts sounds into our souls only one after another, gives and never tires, gives and always has more to give. She thus practices the whole knack of method: she *teaches progressively!* Who in these circumstances could not grasp language, invent language for himself?

5) Hearing is the middle sense *in relation to the need to express oneself,* and hence the sense for language. Feeling operates too obscurely to be expressed; but so much the less *may* it be expressed – it concerns our *self* so much!, it is so selfish and self-engrossed! Vision is inexpressible for the inventor of language; but why does *it need* to be expressed immediately? The objects remain! They can be shown by means of gestures! But the objects of hearing are bound up with movement; they proceed past; but precisely thereby they also resound. They become expressible because they must be

---

[97] a: is the organ of language.

expressed, and through the fact that they must be expressed, through their movement, do they become expressible.[98] What an ability for language!

6) Hearing is the middle sense *in relation to its development*, and hence the sense for language. The human being is feeling through and through: the embryo in its first moment of life feels as does the infant; that is the natural stem out of which the more delicate branches of sensuality grow, and the tangled ball out of which all finer forces of the soul unfold. How do these unfold? As we have seen, *through hearing*, since nature awakens the soul to its first distinct sensation through sounds. Hence, so to speak, awakens it out of the obscure sleep of *feeling* and ripens it to still finer sensuality. If, for example, vision was already there unfolded before hearing, or if it were possible that it should be awakened out of feeling otherwise than through the middle sense of hearing – what wise poverty!, what clairvoyant stupidity! How difficult it would become for such a creature – all eye!, when it should instead be a human being – to name what it saw!, to unite cold vision with warmer feeling, with the whole stem of humanity! However, the very governing assumption [*Instanz*] turns out to be self-contradictory; the way to the unfolding of human nature – is better and single! Since all the senses function cooperatively, through the sense of hearing we are, so to speak, always in nature's school, learning to abstract and simultaneously to speak; vision refines itself with reason – reason and the talent of referring.[99] And so when the human being comes to the most subtle characterization of visual phenomena – what a store of language and linguistic similarities already lies ready! He took the path from feeling into the sense of his visual images [*Phantasmen*] no otherwise than via the sense of language, and has hence learned to sound forth what he sees as much as what he felt.

If I could now bring all the ends together here and make visible simultaneously that web called human nature: through and through a web for language. For this, we saw, were space and sphere granted to this positive force of thought; for this were its content and matter measured out; for this were shape and form created; finally, for this were the senses organized and ordered – for language! This is why the human being does not think more clearly or more obscurely; this is why he does not see and feel more

---

[98] Herder's thought here is evidently that hearing's objects (unlike feeling's or vision's) become expressible because (a) there is a need for them to be so, and (b) they can be so. "Because" expresses need or purpose; "through" expresses enabling condition or means.

[99] B: reason becomes the talent of referring.

sharply, at greater length, more vividly; this is why he has these senses, not more and not different ones – everything counterbalances!, is spared and substituted for!, is disposed and distributed intentionally! – unity and connection!, proportion and order!, a whole!, a system!, *a creature of awareness and language, of taking-awareness and creating language*! If someone after all [our] observations still wanted to deny this destiny [of the human being] as a linguistic creature, he would have to begin by turning from being nature's observer into being its destroyer! He would have to tear apart all the indicated harmonies into discords, strike the whole magnificent structure of human forces into ruins, lay waste its sensuality, and in place of nature's masterpiece feel a creature full of shortcomings and gaps, full of weaknesses and convulsions! And if then now, on the other hand, *"language also precisely is as it had to become according to the basic outline and momentum of the preceding creature?"*

I shall proceed to the proof of this latter position, although a very pleasant stroll would still lie before me here calculating in accordance with the rules of *Sulzer's theory of pleasure*[100] "what sorts of advantages and comforts a language through hearing might have for us over the language of other senses." That stroll would lead too far, though; and one must forgo it when the main road still stretches far ahead in need of securing and rectifying. – So, first of all:

I. "The older and more original languages are, the more noticeable becomes this analogy of the senses in their roots!"[101]

Although in later languages we characterize *anger* in its roots as a phenomenon of the visible face or as an abstraction – for example, through the flashing of the eyes, the glowing of the cheeks, etc. – and hence only see it or think it, the Easterner hears it! He hears it snort!, hears it spray burning smoke and storming sparks! That became the stem[102] of the word; the nose the seat of anger; the whole family of anger words and anger metaphors snort their origin.

If for us *life* expresses itself through the pulse, through undulation and fine characteristic marks, in language too, it revealed itself to the Easterner respiring aloud[103] – the human being lived when he breathed, died when

---

[100] J. G. Sulzer (1720–79), *Über den Ursprung der angenehmen und unangenehmen Empfindungen* (1762).
[101] The examples which follow are borrowed from A. Schultens, *Origines hebraeae* (1724–38).
[102] Reading *Stamm* with manuscript a. Editions A and B say "name."
[103] Reading, with Suphan, *laut* instead of *Laut*.

he breathed out his last, and one hears the root of the word breathe like the first living Adam.

If we characterize *giving birth* in our way, the Easterner hears even in the names for it the cry of the mother's fear, or in the case of animals the shaking out of an afterbirth. This is the central idea around which his images revolve!

If we in the word *dawn* [*Morgenröte*] obscurely hear such things as the beauty, the shining, the freshness, the enduring nomad in the Orient feels even in the root of the word the first, rapid, delightful ray of light which one of us has perhaps never seen, or at least never felt with the sense of feeling.[104] – The examples from ancient and savage languages of how heartily and with what strong sensation they characterize on the basis of hearing and feeling become countless, and "a work of this sort that really sought out the basic feeling of such ideas in various peoples" would be a complete demonstration of my thesis and of the human invention of language.

II. "The older and more original languages are, the more feelings also intersect in the roots of the words."

Let one open any available Eastern dictionary and one will see the impetus of the desire to achieve self-expression! How the inventor tore ideas out of one type of feeling and borrowed them for another!; how he borrowed most in the case of the heaviest, coldest, distinctest senses!; how everything had to become feeling and sound in order to become expression! Hence the strong, bold metaphors in the roots of the words! Hence the metaphorical transferences from one type of feeling to another, so that the meanings of a stem-word, and still more those of its derivatives, set in contrast with one another, turn into the most motley picture. The genetic cause lies in the poverty of the human soul and in the confluence of the sensations of a primitive human being. One sees his need to express himself so distinctly; one sees it to an ever greater extent the further away in sensation the idea lay from feeling and sound – so that one may no longer doubt the human character of the origin of language. For how do the champions of another origination claim to explain this *interweaving of ideas* in the roots of words? Was God so poor in ideas and words that he had to resort to such confusing word usage? Or was he such a lover

---

[104] B: with the mind.

of hyperboles, of outlandish metaphors, that he imprinted this spirit into the very basic-roots of his language?

The so-called divine language, the Hebrew language, is entirely imprinted with these examples of daring, so that the Orient even has the honor of designating them with its name. Only, let this spirit of metaphor please not, though, be called 'Asiatic' as if it were not to be found anywhere else![105] It lives in all savage languages – only, to be sure, in each one in proportion to the nation's level of civilization [*Bildung*] and in accordance with the peculiar character of the nation's manner of thought. A people which did not distinguish its feelings much and did not distinguish them sharply, a people which did not have enough heart to express itself and to steal expressions mightily, will also be less at a loss because of nuances in feeling, or will make do with slothful semi-expressions. A fiery nation reveals its courage in such metaphors, whether it lives in the Orient or in North America. But the nation which in its deepest ground reveals the most such transplantations has the language which was the poorest, the oldest, the most original ahead of others, and this nation was certainly in the Orient.

One sees how difficult "*a true etymological dictionary*" must be in the case of such a language. The so very diverse meanings of a root which are supposed to be deduced and traced back to their origin in a genealogical chart are only related through such obscure feelings, through fleeting side ideas, through coinciding sensations [*Mitempfindungen*], which rise up from the bottom of the soul and can be but little grasped in rules! *Moreover*, their relationships are so national, so much according to the peculiar manner of thinking and seeing of that people, of that inventor, in that land, in that time, in those circumstances, that they are infinitely difficult for a Northerner and Westerner to get right, and must suffer infinitely in long, cold paraphrases. *Moreover*, since they were forced into existence by necessity, and were invented in affect, in feeling, in the need for expression – what a stroke of fortune is necessary to hit on the same feeling! And *finally*, since in a dictionary of this kind the words and the meanings of a word are supposed to be gathered together from such diverse times, occasions, and manners of thinking, and these momentary determinations hence increase in number ad infinitum, how

---

[105] There existed in Herder's day a tradition, reaching back into antiquity, of distinguishing between an Attic and an Asiatic tendency in rhetoric, and seeing the latter tendency as characterized especially by its bold use of metaphors.

the labor multiplies here!, what insightfulness [is necessary] to penetrate into these circumstances and needs, and what moderation to keep within reasonable bounds in this in one's interpretations of various times!, what knowledge and flexibility of soul is required to give oneself so completely this primitive wit, this bold imagination, this national feeling of foreign times, and not[106] to modernize it according to ours! But precisely thereby there would[107] also "be borne a torch not merely into *the history, manner of thinking*, and *literature of the land*, but quite generally into the *obscure region of the human soul*, where *concepts intersect* and *get entangled*!, where the *most diverse feelings produce* one another, where a *pressing occasion summons forth all the forces of the soul* and *reveals the whole art of invention of which the soul is capable*." Every step in such a work would be discovery! And every new observation would be the fullest proof of the human character of the origin of language.

Schultens has earned himself renown in the development of several such origins *of the Hebrew language.*[108] Each of these developments is a proof of my rule. But for many reasons I do not believe that the origins of the first human language, even if it were the Hebrew language, can ever be developed *fully*.

I infer a further remark which is too universal and important to be omitted. The basis of the bold verbal metaphors lay in the first invention. But what is going on when late afterwards, when all need has already disappeared, such species of words and images remain out of mere addiction to imitation or love for antiquity? And even get extended and elevated further? Then, oh then, it turns into the sublime nonsense, the turgid wordplay which in the beginning it actually was not. In the beginning it was bold, manly wit which perhaps meant to play least at the times when it seemed to play most! It was primitive sublimity of imagination that worked out such a feeling in such a word. But now in the hands of insipid imitators, without such a feeling, without such an occasion ... ah!, ampullae of words without spirit! And that has *"been the fate in later times of all those languages whose first forms were so bold."* The later French poets cannot stray in peaks because the first[109] inventors of their language did not stray in peaks; their whole language is sound reason's prose and

---

[106] Adding *nicht*. This seems to accord best with the rest of the paragraph, and with the rest of this section II as a whole (e.g. its final paragraph).

[107] Reading with Suphan *würde* instead of *wurde*.

[108] A. Schultens, *Origines hebraeae.*   [109] B: the late.

originally has virtually no poetic word that might belong to the poet. But the Easterners? The Greeks? The English? And we Germans?

From this it follows that the older a language is, the more such bits of boldness there are in its roots, if it has lived for a long time, has developed for a long time, then so much the less must one *automatically head for every original bit of boldness* as though *every one of these* intersecting concepts had also *on every occasion* in *every* late use been *thought of as a component*. The original metaphor was [a result of] the impulse to speak. If later, in every case when the word had already gained currency and had worn down its sharpness, it is taken to be fruitfulness and energy to combine all such peculiarities – what miserable examples abound before us in whole schools of the Eastern languages!

One more thing. If, pushing things further, *certain fine concepts of a dogma, of a system, adhere to,* or *get fixed to,* or *are supposed to be investigated from,* such bold word struggles, such transpositions of feelings into an expression, such intersections of ideas without rule or plumb-line – heaven!, how little were these word experiments of an emerging or early emerged language the definitions of a system, and how often people end up creating word idols of which the inventor or later usage had no thought! – But such remarks would go on for ever. I proceed to a new canon:

III. "The more original a language is, the more frequently such feelings intersect in it, then the less these can be exactly and logically subordinated to each other. The language is rich in synonyms; for all its essential poverty, it has the greatest unnecessary excess."

The defenders of the divine origin, who know how to find divine order in everything, can hardly find it here, and *deny*[u] the synonyms. Deny them? Fine then, let it be the case that among the 50 words that the *Arab* has for the lion, among the 200 that he has for the snake, among the 80 that he has for honey, and among the more than 1,000 that he has for the sword fine distinctions are present, or would have been present but have been lost. Why were they there if they were bound to be lost? Why did God invent an unnecessary vocabulary which, as the Arabs say, only a divine prophet was able to grasp in its entire scope? Did He invent for the emptiness of oblivion? *Comparatively speaking,* though, these words *are* still synonyms, *considering the many other ideas for which words are quite*

[u] Süßmilch, #9.

lacking. Now let someone, then, unfold divine order in the fact that He who enjoyed oversight of the plan of language invented 70 words for the stone, and none for all the so essential ideas, inner feelings, and abstractions, that He in the former case smothered with unnecessary excess, but in the latter case abandoned in the greatest poverty, so that people had to steal, to usurp metaphors, to talk semi-nonsense, etc.

Humanly, the matter explains itself. As improperly as difficult, *rare* ideas had to be expressed could the *available* and *easy* ideas be expressed *frequently. The less familiar* one was with nature, *the more* sides one could *look at* it from and hardly recognize it because of inexperience, *the less* one invented a priori but *in accordance with sensuous circumstances*, then the more synonyms! *The more people* invented, *the more nomadic* and *separated* they were when they invented, and yet for the most part invented only *in a single circle* for *a single kind* of things, then, when they afterwards came together, when their languages flowed into an ocean of vocabulary, the more synonyms! They could not be thrown away, all of them. For which should be thrown away? They were current with this tribe, with this family, with this poet. And so it became, as that Arab dictionary writer said when he had counted up 400 words for misery, the four hundredth misery to have to count up the words for misery. Such a language is rich because it is poor, because its inventors did not yet have enough of a plan to become poor. And *that* futile inventor of precisely the most imperfect language would be God?

The analogies of all savage languages confirm my thesis: each of them is in its way prodigal and needy – only each in its own manner. If the Arab has so many words for stone, camel, sword, snake (things among which he lives!), then the language of *Ceylon* is, in accordance with its people's inclinations, rich in flatteries, titles, and verbal ornamentation. For the word 'woman' it has twelve sorts of names according to class and rank, whereas we impolite Germans, for example, have to borrow in this area from our neighbors. *Thou* and *you* are articulated in eight sorts of ways according to class and rank, and this as much by the daylaborer as by the courtier. This jumble is the form of the language. In *Siam* there are eight ways of saying *I* and *we*, depending on whether the lord is speaking with the slave or the slave with the lord. The language of the savage *Caribs* is almost divided into two languages belonging to the women and the men, and the most common things – bed, moon, sun, bow – the two sexes name differently. What an excess of synonyms! And yet precisely these Caribs have only four words for the colors, to which they must refer all others. What poverty! The *Hurons* have in each case a double verb for something that has a soul and something that lacks a soul, so that *seeing* in 'seeing a stone' and *seeing* in 'seeing a human being' are always two different expressions. Let one pursue that principle through the whole of nature. What a richness! 'To use one's own property' or 'the property of the person with whom one is speaking' always has two different words. What a richness! In the main language of *Peru* the genders are named in such a peculiarly distinct way that the sister of a brother and the sister of a sister, the child of a father and the child of a mother, are called something quite different. And yet precisely this language has no real plural! – Each of these cases of synonymy is so interconnected with the custom, character, and origin of the people – but everywhere the inventing human spirit reveals its stamp. – A new canon:

IV. "Just as the human soul can recollect no abstraction from the realm of spirits that it did not arrive at through occasions and awakenings of the senses, likewise also no language has an abstractum that it did not arrive at through sound and feeling. And the more original the language, then the fewer abstractions, the more feelings." In this immeasurable field I can again only pick flowers:

The whole construction of the *Eastern* languages bears witness that all their abstracta were previously sensualities: *Spirit* was *wind, breath, nocturnal storm! Holy* meant *separate, alone. Soul* meant *breath. Anger* meant the *snorting* of the nose. Etc. The more universal concepts were hence only accreted to language[110] later through abstraction, wit, imagination, simile, analogy, etc. – in the deepest abyss of language there lies not a single one of them![111]

With all *savages* the same thing happens, according to the level of the culture. In the language of *Barantola*[112] the word *holy*, and with the Hottentots the word *spirit*, could[113] not be found. All missionaries in all parts of the world complain about the difficulty of communicating Christian concepts to savages in their own languages, and yet of course these communications are never supposed to be a scholastic dogmatics but

[110] I leave *ihr*, "to it," i.e. to language, but it may be a slip for *ihnen*, "to them," i.e. to the Eastern languages.
[111] The text has *keine einzige* where, strictly, only *kein einziger* would be grammatically correct. Herder is probably thinking of *Abstraktionen*.
[112] Barantola, capital of Tibet.   [113] Reading with Suphan *mußte* instead of *müßte*.

only the common concepts of the common understanding. If one reads here and there samples of this presentation among the savages, or even only among the uncivilized languages *of Europe*, for example the Lapp, Finnish, or Estonian languages, in translation and looks at the grammars and dictionaries of these peoples, the difficulties become obvious.

If one is not willing to believe the missionaries, then let one read the philosophers: de la *Condamine* in *Peru* and on the *Amazon river*, *Maupertius* in *Lapland*, etc. *Time, duration, space, essence, matter, body, virtue, justice, freedom, gratitude* do not exist in the tongue of the Peruvians, even though they often show with their reason that they infer in accordance with these concepts, and show with their deeds that they have these virtues. As long as they have not made the idea clear to themselves as a characteristic mark, they have no word for it.

"Where, therefore, such words have *entered* the language, one clearly recognizes in them their origin." The church language of the *Russian* nation is for the most part Greek. The Christian concepts of the *Latvians* are German words or German concepts transposed into Latvian. The *Mexican* who wants to express his *poor sinner* paints him as someone kneeling who is making auricular confession, and his *triunity* as three faces with halos. It is known by what routes most abstractions have entered *"into our scientific language,"* into *theology* and *law*, into *philosophy* and other subjects. It is known how often scholastics and polemicists could not even fight with words of their own language and hence had to import arms (hypostasis and substance, *homoousios* and *homoiousios*[114]) from those languages in which the concepts were abstracted, in which the arms were whetted! Our whole *psychology*, as refined and precise as it is, has no word of its own.

This is so true that it is not even possible for mystic fanatics and the enraptured to characterize their new secrets from nature, from heaven and hell, otherwise than through images and sensuous representations. *Swedenborg* could not do otherwise than intuit-together his angels and spirits out of all the senses, and the sublime *Klopstock* – the greatest antithesis to him! – could not do otherwise than construct his heaven and hell from sensuous materials. The *Negro* intuits his gods down from the treetops for himself, and the *Chinghailese*[115] hears his devil into existence for himself from the noise of the forests. I have crept in pursuit of several

---

[114] These Greek words mean "identical in essence" and "similar in essence" respectively.
[115] Native inhabitants on a river near the Amazon.

of these abstractions among various peoples, in various languages, and have perceived "*the strangest tricks of invention of the human spirit.*" The subject is much too large, but the basis is always the same. "*When the savage thinks that this thing has a spirit, then there must be a sensuous thing present from which he abstracts the spirit for himself.*" Only the abstraction has its very diverse species, levels, and methods. – The *easiest* example of the fact that no nation has in its language more or other words than it has learned to abstract is those doubtless very easy abstractions, the *numbers.* How few do most savages have, however rich, excellent, and developed their languages may be! Never more than they needed. The trading Phoenician was the first to invent arithmetic; the shepherd who counts his flock also learns to count; the hunting nations, which never have work involving large numbers, only know to describe an army as like hairs on a head! Who can count them? Who, if he has never counted up so high, has words for this?

Is it possible to disregard all these traces of the changing, language-creating mind, and to seek an origin in the clouds? What sort of proof does anyone have of a "*single word which only God could have invented?*" Does there exist in any language even a single pure universal concept which came to man from heaven? Where is it even merely possible?[v] – "And what 100,000 *grounds* and *analogies* and *proofs* there are of the *genesis* of *language* in the *human soul* in accordance with the *human senses* and *manners of seeing*! What proofs there are of the *progress of language with reason*, and of its *development* out of reason, among all *peoples, latitudes,* and *circumstances!* " What ear is there that does not hear this universal voice of the nations?

And yet I see with astonishment that Mr. *Süßmilch* again confronts me and on the path where I discover the most human order imaginable finds divine order.[w] "That no language has at present yet been discovered which was entirely unsuited to arts and sciences" – what else does that show,[116] then, than that no language is brutish, that they are all human? Where, then, has anyone discovered a human being who was entirely unsuited to arts and sciences? And was that a miracle? Or not precisely

---

[v] The best treatise on this matter that I know is by an Englishman: *Things Divine and Supernatural Conceived by Analogy with Things Natural and Human* (London, 1733), by the author of *The Procedure, Extent, and Limits of Human Understanding* [i.e. P. Browne].

[w] Süßmilch, #11.

[116] Reading, with a and B, *zeigt* for *zeugt*.

the most common thing, because he was a human being? "All missionaries have been able to talk with the most savage peoples and to convince them. That could not have happened without inferences and grounds. Their languages therefore must have contained abstract terms, etc." And if that was so, was it divine order? Or was it not precisely the most human thing, to abstract words for oneself where one needed them? And what people has ever had even a single abstraction in its language which it did not acquire for itself? And then, were there an equal number in the case of all peoples? Were the missionaries able to express themselves equally easily everywhere, or has one not read the opposite from all parts of the world? And how, then, did they express themselves but by molding their new concepts onto the language according to analogy with it? And did this everywhere happen in the same manner? About the *fact* so much, so much[117] could be said! The *inference* says entirely the opposite: "Precisely because *human reason* cannot exist *without abstraction*, and *each abstraction* does not come to be *without language*, it must also be the case that in *every* people language contains *abstractions*, that is, is an *offprint* of *reason*, of which it was a *tool*." "But as *each language* contains only *as many* abstractions as the people was able to make, and *not a single one* that *was made without the senses*, as is shown by its[118] originally sensuous expression, it follows that divine order is nowhere to be seen except *insofar as language is through and through human*."

V. Finally, "since every grammar is only a philosophy about language and a method for language's use, the more original the language, the less grammar there must be in it, and the oldest language is just the previously indicated vocabulary of nature!" I shall sketch a few amplifications.

1) *Declensions* and *conjugations* are nothing but abbreviations and determinations of the use of nouns and verbs according to number, tense and mood, and person. Hence, the more primitive a language is, the more irregular it is in these determinations, and it shows in each step forward the course of human reason. Initially, in the absence of art in use, language is mere vocabulary.

2) Just as the verbs of a language are earlier than the nouns roundly abstracted from them, likewise also *at the beginning, the less people have*

---

[117] This is another example of Herder using the rhetorical figure of anadiplosis, "doubling."
[118] The reference of "its" is ambiguous in the German – Herder could either mean the *language*'s or an *abstraction*'s.

learned to subordinate concepts to one another, the more conjugations there are. How many the Easterners have! And yet there are really none – for what transplantations and violent transpositions of verbs from conjugation into conjugation still occur! The matter is quite natural. Since nothing concerns the human being as much, or at least touches him as much linguistically, as *what he is supposed to narrate, deeds,* actions, events, it is inevitable that such a mass of *deeds* and *events* accumulates originally that there comes to be a new verb for almost every condition. "In the Huron language everything gets conjugated. An art that cannot be explained allows the nouns, pronouns, and adverbs to be distinguished in it from the verbs. The simple verbs have a double conjugation, one for themselves and one which refers to other things. The forms of the third person have both genders. Concerning tenses, one finds the fine distinctions which one observes, for example, in Greek; indeed, if one wants to give the account of a journey, one expresses oneself differently depending on whether one has made it by land or by water. The active forms multiply as many times as there are things that fall under the action; the word 'eat' changes with every edible thing. The action of an ensouled thing is expressed differently from that of a thing without a soul. To use one's own property and that of the person with whom one is speaking has two forms of expression. Etc."[119] Let one imagine all this multiplicity of verbs, moods, tenses, persons, conditions, genders, etc. – what effort and art [it would take] to set this in hierarchical order to some extent! To turn what was entirely vocabulary into grammar to some extent! *Father Leri's* grammar of the *Topinambuans* in Brazil shows exactly the same thing! For "just as the first *vocabulary* of the human soul was a living *epic* of *resounding, acting nature,* so the *first grammar* was virtually nothing but a *philosophical attempt* to turn this *epic into more regular history.*"[120] It therefore works itself to exhaustion with very verbs, and works in a chaos which is inexhaustible for the art of poetry, when more ordered very rich for the determining of history, but last of all usable for axioms and demonstrations.

3) The word which immediately followed the sound of nature, imitating it, already followed something *past:* "*past tenses are hence the roots of verbs,* but past tenses which still almost hold for the *present.*"[121] A priori the fact

---

[119] This information about the Huron language seems to derive from P. G. M. Chaumonot, a Jesuit missionary in Quebec who wrote a grammar of the Huron language.

[120] The closing (emphatic) quotation mark is omitted in Gaier's text. Its location here is therefore conjectural.

[121] Ditto.

is strange and inexplicable, since the present time ought to be the *first*, as indeed it has come to be in all languages which were formed later. But according to the history of the invention of language it could not have been otherwise. "One *shows* the present, but one has to *narrate* what is past." And since one could narrate what was past in *so many ways*, and to begin with, in the need to find words, had to do this so diversely, there arose "in all ancient languages many past tenses but only one or no present tense." In more civilized [*gebildeteren*] ages, now, *the art of poetry* and *history* inevitably found much to rejoice at in this, but philosophy very little, because philosophy does not like a confusing stock. – Here *Hurons, Brazilians, Easterners*, and *Greeks* are again alike: everywhere traces of the course of the human spirit!

4) All modern philosophical languages have modified the noun *more finely*, the verb *less* but *more regularly*. For language grew more "for cold observation of what exists and what existed rather than still remaining an irregularly stammering mixture of what *perhaps* existed." People got used to expressing the former *one thing after another*, and hence to determining it through numbers and articles and cases, etc. "*The ancient inventors wanted to say everything at once*,[x] not merely what had been done but who had done it, when, how, and where it had happened. So they immediately introduced into nouns the *condition*; into each *person* of the verb the gender; they immediately distinguished through preformatives and adformatives, through affixes and suffixes; verb and adverb, verb and noun, and everything flowed together." The later, the more distinguishing and counting out took place; breaths turned into articles, word endings [*Ansätzen*] turned into persons, word beginnings [*Vorsätzen*] turned into moods or adverbs;[122] the parts of speech flowed apart; now *grammar* gradually came into being. Thus this *art of speaking*, this philosophy about

---

[x] Rousseau divined this thesis, which I here define [more closely] and prove, in his *hypothesis*. [Rousseau had written in his *Discours sur l'origine et les fondements de l'inégalité parmi les hommes*: "One must judge that the first words of which men made use had in their minds a much broader significance than have those which are employed in the already developed languages, and that, not knowing the division of speech into its constitutive parts, they initially gave each word the meaning of an entire proposition."]

[122] This sentence is difficult. I interpret *Ansätze* as word endings and *Vorsätze* as word beginnings – cf. above "preformatives and adformatives,...affixes and suffixes." Some of the things that Herder may perhaps have in mind here: (1) "Breaths turned into articles": the transition from the absence of definite articles in Homeric Greek to their presence in Attic Greek. (2) "Word endings turned into persons": the transition from the normal omission of personal pronouns ('I,' 'you,' 'he,' etc.) in Greek and Latin to their normal inclusion in related modern languages such as French and English. (3) "Word beginnings turned into ... adverbs": the transition from ancient

language, was only formed [*gebildet*] slowly and step by step, down through centuries and ages, and the first mind who contemplates "a *true philosophy of grammar,* the *art of speaking!*" must certainly first have thought over "the *history of the same down through peoples and levels."* But if we only had such a history! With all its progressions and deviations it would be a map of the humanity of language.

5) But how was it possible for a language to exist entirely without grammar? A mere confluence of images and sensations without interconnection and determination? Both were provided for; it was living language. There the great attuning participation of *gestures* so to speak set the rhythm and the sphere to which what was said[123] belonged; and the great *wealth* of determinations which lay in the vocabulary itself substituted for the art of grammar. Observe the old writing of the Mexicans! They paint sheer individual images; where no image enters the senses, they have agreed on strokes and the *interconnection for everything* must be given by the world, to which it belongs, from which it gets *prophesied.*[124] This *"prophetic art of guessing interconnection from individual signs"* -- how far only[125] individual *dumb and deaf people* can still exercise it![126] And if this art itself belongs to the language as a part of it, itself gets learned from childhood on as a part of it, if this art becomes ever easier and more perfect with the tradition [*Tradition*][127] of generations, then I see nothing unintelligible [in it].[128] -- But the more this art is made easier, then the more it diminishes, the more *grammar* comes into being -- and that is the progressive course of the human spirit!

Proofs of this are, for example, *La Loubere's* reports about the Siamese language. How similar it still is to the interconnection of [the language of] the Easterners -- especially before more interconnection yet entered through later cultivation [*Bildung*]. The *Siamese* wants to say "If I were in

---

Greek's frequent inclusion of an adverbial precisification of a verbal idea in the form of a prefix in the verb (*kata-, hupo-,* etc.) to the common reliance of modern languages such as English on a separate adverb to express the same precisification.

[123] Edition A just has *es,* "it," here, but B specifies more precisely "what was said."

[124] Grammatically, the *its* in this sentence both refer to *everything.* But at least in the case of the second one, the intended reference really seems rather to be to *the interconnection* (cf. the next sentence).

[125] "Only" seems to function ambiguously here, both restricting the scope of the claim and emphasizing the whole exclamation.

[126] Reading with Suphan *sie* for *ihn.*

[127] Here, as often in Herder, "tradition" is meant mainly in the etymologically derived sense of the *handing over* (of the art in question by successive generations).

[128] B: unintelligible in it.

Siam, then I would be happy!" and says "If I being city Siam, I happy heart much!" He wants to pray the *Lord's Prayer* and has to say "Father us being heaven! God's name wanting hallowing everywhere, etc." How Eastern and original that is! Just as interconnecting as a Mexican image-writing!, or the stammerings of those who are ineducable in foreign languages!

6) I must explain here one further strange phenomenon which I again see misunderstood in Mr. Süßmilch's divine ordering: "namely, the diversity of the meanings of a word according to the difference between minor articulations!"[129] I find this knack among almost all savages – as, for example, *Garcilaso de la Vega* cites it of the *Peruvians*, *Condamine* of the *Brazilians*, *La Loubere* of the *Siamese*, *Resnel*[130] of the *North Americans*. I find it likewise in the case of the ancient languages, for example, the *Chinese* language and the *Eastern* languages, especially *Hebrew*, where a minor sound, accent, breath changes the whole meaning. And yet, I find in it nothing but a very human thing: *poverty* and *comfort* of the *inventors*! They needed a new word, and since unnecessary invention out of nothing is so difficult, they took *a similar word with the alteration of perhaps only a single breath.* That was a law of *economy*, initially very *natural* for them with their *interwoven feelings* and still fairly *comfortable* for them with their *more forceful pronunciation of words.* But for a foreigner, who has not habituated his ear to this from childhood, and to whom the language is now hissed forth with phlegm, the sound half remaining in the mouth, this law of economy and neediness makes speech inaudible and inexpressible. The more a sound *grammar* has imported *domestic management* into languages, the less necessary this parsimony becomes. So [it is] precisely the opposite of an indication of divine invention – in which case the inventor would certainly have been very inept at coping if he had to resort to *such a thing.*

7) Finally, the *progress of language through reason* and of *reason* through *language* becomes most obvious "when language *has already taken a few steps*, when *pieces of art already exist* in it, for example, poems, when *writing is invented*, when one *genre of writing* develops after the other." Then no step can be taken, no new word invented, no new happy form given currency in which there is not *an offprint of the human soul.* Then through

---

[129] The phrase "the difference between minor articulations" is an example of the rhetorical figure of hypallage, or making an adjective agree grammatically with a noun other than the one it is really meant to qualify. Thus the phrase is virtually equivalent to "the minor difference between articulations." On the other hand, the situation is not clear-cut, for cf. below "a minor sound, accent, breath."

[130] Identity unknown. Herder may mean Rasles, whom he discussed earlier.

poems meters, choice of the strongest words and colors, and ordering and zest in images enter language; then through *history* distinction between tenses and precision of expression enter language; then, finally, through the *orators* the full rounding-out of the refined sentence enters language. Now just as *before* each such addition nothing of the sort yet existed in the language, but everything was *introduced by the human soul* and *could* be introduced by the human soul, where would one want to set limits to this creativity, this fruitfulness? Where would one want to say "Here the human soul began to operate, but not earlier"? If the human soul was able to invent what is finest, what is most difficult, then why not what is easiest? If it was able to institute, why not to experiment, why not to begin? For after all, what else was the beginning but the production of a single word as a sign of reason? And this the soul had to do, blindly and dumbly in its depths, as truly as it possessed reason.

*

I am vain enough to suppose that the *possibility* of the human invention of language is so proven by what I have said, from *within* in terms of the *human soul*, and from *without* in terms of the *organization* of the *human being* and in terms of the *analogy* of all *languages* and *peoples*, *partly* in the *components* of all *speech*, *partly* in the *whole great progress* of language with *reason*, that whoever does not deny reason to the human being, or what amounts to the same, whoever merely knows what reason is, whoever in addition has ever concerned himself with the elements of language in a *philosophical* way, whoever moreover has taken into consideration with the eye of an observer the constitution and history of the languages on the earth, cannot doubt for a single moment, even if I were to add[131] not one word more. [The case for] the genesis [of language] in the human soul is as *demonstrative* as any philosophical proof,[132] and the external analogy of all times, languages, and peoples [possesses] as high a degree of *probability* as is possible in the most certain historical matter.[133] However, in order to forestall all objections for good, and also to make the thesis as externally

---

[131] Reading with Suphan *hinzusetzte*.
[132] As Herder wrote this first part of the sentence, i.e. without the additions in parentheses, it is a striking example of his use of brachylogy, or "shortening."
[133] As Herder wrote this whole sentence, i.e. without the additions in parentheses and in particular the word "possesses," it is a good example of his use of the rhetorical figure of zeugma, i.e. using a verb with two nouns when it really only applies to one of them (and leaving the reader to infer the verbal idea that really applies in the other case, here "possesses").

certain as a philosophical truth can be, so to speak, let us in addition prove from all external circumstances and from the whole analogy of human nature "that the human being *had to* invent his language for himself, and under *which circumstances he was able to invent it for himself most suitably.*"

Second part: In what way the human being was most suitably able and obliged to invent language for himself[134]

Nature gives no forces in vain. So when nature not only gave the human being abilities to invent language, but also made this ability the distinguishing trait of his essence and the impulse behind his special direction [in life], this force came from nature's hand no otherwise than *living*, and hence it could not but be set in a sphere where it had to be effective. Let us consider more closely a few of these circumstances and concerns which straightaway occasioned the human being to develop language when he entered the world with the immediate disposition to form language for himself. And since there are many of these concerns, I collect them under certain main laws of the human being's nature and of his species:

First natural law

"The human being is a freely thinking, active being, whose forces operate forth progressively. Therefore let him be a creature of language!"[135]

Considered as a naked, instinctless animal, the human being is the most miserable of beings. Here there is no obscure, innate drive which pulls him into his element and into his circle of efficacy, to his means of subsistence and to his work. No sense of smell or power to scent which pulls him towards plants so that he may sate his hunger! No blind, mechanical master craftsman who would build his nest for him! Weak and succumbing, abandoned to the contention of the elements, to hunger, to all dangers, to the claws of all stronger animals, to a thousandfold death,

---

[134] The second part of the Berlin Academy's question, which Herder is now going on to address, asked: "And by what means will they [i.e. men abandoned to their natural faculties] arrive at this invention [i.e. the invention of language]?"

[135] I have added emphasizing quotation marks to Herder's statements of his first three natural laws, which lack them in Gaier's text. This addition is suggested both by the obvious importance of these statements and by the fact that Herder does use emphasizing quotation marks around his fourth natural law in Gaier's text.

he stands there!, lonely and alone!, without the immediate instruction of his creatress [nature] and without the sure guidance of her hand – thus, lost on all sides.

But as vividly as this picture may be painted out, it is not the picture of the human being – it is only a single side of his surface, and even that stands in a false light. If *understanding* and *awareness* [*Besonnenheit*] is the *natural gift of his kind*,[136] this had to[137] express itself immediately when the weaker sensuality and all the poverty of his lacks expressed itself. The *instinctless, miserable* creature which came from nature's hands so abandoned was also from the first moment on the *freely active, rational* creature which was destined to help itself, and inevitably had the ability to do so. All his shortcomings and needs as an animal were pressing reasons to prove himself with all his forces as a human being – just as these human forces were not, say, merely weak compensations for the greater animal perfections denied to him, as our modern philosophy, the great patroness of animals!, claims, but were, without comparison or actual balancing of one against another, *his nature*. His center of gravity, the main direction of his soul's efficacies, fell as much on this *understanding*, on *human awareness* [*Besonnenheit*], as with the bee it falls immediately on sucking and building.

If now it has been proved that not even the slightest action of his understanding could occur without a characteristic word, then *the first moment of taking-awareness* [*Besinnung*] was also *the moment for the inward emergence of language*.

Let one allow the human being as much time as one wants for this first distinct taking-awareness [*Besinnung*]. Let one – in the manner of *Buffon* (only more philosophically than he) – make this creature that has come into being *achieve conscious control gradually*. But let one not forget that immediately from the very first moment on it is no animal but a human being, to be sure not yet a creature which *takes awareness* [*von Besinnung*] but one which already *has awareness* [*von Besonnenheit*], that awakens into the universe. Not as a great, clumsy, helpless machine which is supposed to move, but with its stiff limbs cannot move; which is supposed to see, hear, taste, but with thick fluids in its eye, with a hardened ear, and with a petrified tongue, can do none of this – people who raise doubts of this sort really ought to keep in mind that this human being did not come from

[136] This is another example of Herder using the rhetorical figure of hendiadys, "one through two."
[137] Reading with Suphan *mußte*.

Plato's cave,[138] from a dark jail where, from the first moment of his life on through a series of years, without light or movement, he had sat with open eyes until he was blind, and with healthy limbs until he was stiff, but that he came from the hands of nature, with his forces and fluids in the freshest of conditions, and with the best immediate disposition *to develop himself from the first moment.* To be sure, creating Providence must have presided over the first moments of coming to conscious control – but it is not the job of philosophy to explain the miraculous aspect in these moments, as little as philosophy can explain the human being's creation. Philosophy takes up the human being in his first condition of *free activity*, in his first *full feeling of his sound existence*, and hence explains these moments only *in human terms.*

Now I can refer back to what was said before. Since no metaphysical separation of the senses occurs here, since the whole machine senses and immediately works up from obscure feeling to taking-awareness [*Besinnung*], since this point, the sensation of the *first distinct characteristic mark*, precisely concerns *hearing*, the middle sense between seeing and feeling – therefore the genesis of language is *as much an inner imperative* as is the impulse of the embryo to be born at the moment when it reaches maturity. The whole of nature storms at the human being in order to develop his senses[139] until he is a human being. And since language begins from this condition, "*the whole chain of conditions in the human soul is of such a kind that each of them forms language further [fortbildet].*" I want to cast light on this great law of the natural order.

Animals connect their thoughts obscurely or clearly but not *distinctly*. Just as, to be sure, the kinds which are closest to the human being in manner of life and nerve structure, the animals of the field, often display much *memory*, much *recollection*, and in some cases a *stronger* recollection than the human being, but it is still always only *sensuous* recollection, and none of them has ever demonstrated through an action a memory that[140] it had *improved its condition for its whole species*, or had *generalized experiences in order to make use of them subsequently.* To be sure, the dog can recognize the bodily gesture which has hit him, and the fox can flee the unsafe place where he was ambushed, but neither of them can illuminate for itself a *general reflection* concerning how it could ever escape this

---

[138] Herder is here alluding to Plato's famous cave allegory in the *Republic*.
[139] a: in order to develop his forces, in order to develop his senses . . .
[140] B: through which . . .

blow-threatening bodily gesture or this hunters' ruse for good. So the animal still always only remained *stuck at the individual sensuous case*, and its *recollection* became *a series of these sensuous cases, which produce and reproduce themselves* – but never *connected "through reflection"*; a manifold without distinct unity, a dream of very sensuous, clear, vivid representations without an overarching law of clear wakefulness to order this dream.

To be sure, there is still a great difference among these species and kinds. The narrower the circle is, the stronger the sensuality and the drive is, the more uniform the ability for art and the work in life is, then the less is even the slightest progress through experience observable, at least for us. The bee builds in its childhood as it does in advanced age, and will build the same way at the end of the world as in the beginning of creation. They are individual points, shining sparks from the light of God's perfection, which, however, always shine individually. An experienced fox, on the other hand, is indeed very different from the first apprentice of the chase; he already knows many tricks ahead of time, and attempts to escape them. But whence does he know them? And how does he attempt to escape them? Because the law of this action follows immediately from such experience.[141] In no case is *distinct* reflection operative, for are not the cleverest foxes still now tricked in the same way as by the first hunter in the world? In the case of the human being a different law of nature obviously governs the succession of his ideas: *awareness*. Awareness still governs even in the most sensuous condition, only less noticeably. [The human being is] the most ignorant creature when he comes into the world, but immediately he becomes nature's apprentice in a way that no animal does; not only does each day teach the next, but each minute of the day teaches the next, each thought the next. It is an essential knack of his soul to learn nothing for this moment, but to marshal everything either along with what it already knew or in readiness for what it intends to link with it in the future. His soul hence takes into account the store which it has already collected or still intends to collect. And in this way the soul becomes *a force of steadily collecting*. Such a chain continues on until death. [He is,] so to speak, never the *whole human being*; always in development, in progression, in process of perfection. One mode of efficacy is transcended through the other, one builds on the other, one develops out of the other.

[141] a: Because he has had immediate experience of them ahead of time, and because the law of his action follows immediately from such experience. B: Because the law of this and no other action follows immediately from such and such experience.

There arise periods of life, epochs, which we only name according to the noticeable steps, but which – since the human being never feels how he is growing but always only how he grew – can be divided infinitely finely. We are always growing out of a childhood, however old we may be, are ever in motion, restless, unsatisfied. The essential feature of our life is never enjoyment but always progression, and we have never been human beings until we – have lived out our lives. By contrast, the bee was a bee when it built its first cell. To be sure, this law of perfecting, of progress through awareness, does not operate with equal noticeability at all times. But is what is less noticeable therefore nonexistent? In a dream, in a thought-dream, the human being does not think as orderly and distinctly as when awake, but nonetheless he still thinks as a human being – as a human being in a middle state, never as a complete animal. In the case of a healthy human being his dreams must have a rule of connection as much as his waking thoughts, only it cannot be *the same* rule, or operate as uniformly. Hence even these exceptions would bear witness to the validity of the overarching law. And the obvious illnesses and unnatural conditions – swoons, madnesses, etc. – do so even more. Not every action of the soul is immediately a *consequence of taking-awareness* [*Besinnung*], but every one is a *consequence of awareness* [*Besonnenheit*]. None of them, in the form in which it occurs in a human being, could express itself if the human being were not a human being and did not think in accordance with such a law of nature.

"Now if the human being's *first* condition of taking-awareness was not able to become actual without the *word* of the soul, then *all conditions of awareness in him become linguistic; his chain of thoughts becomes a chain of words.*"[142]

Do I mean to say by this that the human being can make every sensation of his most obscure sense of feeling into a word, or cannot sense it except by means of a word? It would be nonsense to say this, since precisely to the contrary it is proven that "a sensation which can only be had through the obscure sense of feeling is susceptible of no word for us, because it is susceptible of no distinct characteristic mark." Hence the foundation of humanity is, if we are talking about voluntary language, linguistically

---

[142] Or perhaps: ... *prove to be linguistic* ... *proves to be a chain of words* (taking the verb *werden* in an epistemic rather than a developmental sense). Were it not for the need to keep verbal faith with the unequivocally developmental "become" of "become actual" which precedes, the translation would here preserve the ambiguity between an epistemic and a developmental sense (as is done below) by translating: ... *turn out to be linguistic* ... *turns out to be a chain of words*.

inexpressible. But then, is the foundation the whole form? Plinth the whole statue? Is the human being in his whole nature a *merely obscurely feeling oyster*, then? So let us take the *whole thread* of his thoughts: since this thread is woven from *awareness* [*Besonnenheit*], since there is no condition in it which, taken as a whole, is not itself *a taking of awareness* [*Besinnung*] or at least capable of being illuminated in a *taking of awareness*, since in it the sense of feeling does not *rule* but the whole center of its[143] nature falls on *finer* senses, vision and hearing, and these constantly give it[144] *language*, it follows that, taken as a whole, *"there is also no condition in the human soul which does not turn out to be* [werde][145] *susceptible of words or actually determined by words of the soul."* To think entirely without words one would have to be the most obscure mystic or an animal, the most abstract religious visionary or a dreaming monad. And in the human soul, as we see even in dreams and in the case of madmen, no such condition is possible. As bold as it may sound, it is true: *the human being senses with the understanding and speaks in thinking.* And now, due to the fact that he always thinks on in this way and, as we have seen, implicitly puts each thought together with the preceding one and with the future, it must be the case that:

　"Each condition which is linked up in this way through reflection thinks better and hence also speaks better." Allow him the free use of his senses; since the mid-point of this use falls on vision and hearing, where the former gives him the characteristic mark and the latter the sound for the characteristic mark, it follows that with each easier, more formed [*gebildeteren*] use of these senses language gets *formed further* [*fortgebildet*] for him.[146] Allow him the free use of his *forces of soul*; since the mid-point of their use falls on *awareness*, and hence does not occur without language, it follows that with each easier, more formed use of awareness language gets *more formed* for him.[147] Consequently, *"the progressive formation of language turns out to be* [wird][148] *as natural for the human being as his nature itself."*

[143] Or possibly: his.　　[144] Or possibly: him.

[145] "Turn out to be" translates *werde* which seems to hover between a merely *epistemic* sense (which, note, would leave a real contradiction between the present principle and the preceding one in quotation marks) and a *developmental* sense (which, note, would promise an escape from that contradiction). The translation tries to preserve this ambiguity. B inserts a *sei*, and thereby opts for yet a third sense which could have been expressed by the original wording in A (though somewhat less naturally from a linguistic standpoint, and again leaving a contradiction with the preceding principle): *"there is also no condition in the human soul which neither is* [sei] *susceptible of words nor actually gets determined by words of the soul."*

[146] B: his language gets *formed further* too.　　[147] B: his language gets *more formed* too.

[148] Again, *wird* here hovers between a merely *epistemic* and a *developmental* sense, an ambiguity which the translation "turns out to be" tries to preserve.

Who is there, then, who would know the scope of the forces of a human soul, especially when they express themselves with full effort against difficulties and dangers? Who is there who would assess the degree of perfection at which, through a constant, inwardly complicated, and so diverse progressive formation, the soul can arrive? And since everything comes down to language, how great is that which an individual human being must collect towards language! If even the blind and dumb person on his lonely island had to create a meager language for himself, then the human being, the apprentice of all the senses!, the apprentice of the whole world! – how much richer he must become! What should he eat? Senses, sense of smell, ability to scent, for the plants that are healthy for him, disliking for those that are harmful for him, nature has not given him; so he must experiment, taste, and, like the Europeans in America, learn from watching the animals what is edible. Hence collect for himself characteristic marks of plants, and therefore language! He is not strong enough to confront the lion; so let him flee far from it, know it from afar by its sound, and in order to be able to flee it in a human way and with forethought, let him learn to recognize it and a hundred other harmful animals *distinctly*, and therefore *to name* them! Now the *more* he collects experiences, becomes acquainted with *various* things and from *various sides*, the *richer* his language becomes! The *more often* he sees these experiences and repeats the characteristic marks to himself, the *firmer* and *more fluent* his language becomes. The *more* he *distinguishes* and *subordinates one thing to another*, the more *orderly* his language becomes! This, continued through years, in an active life, in continual changes, in constant struggle with difficulties and necessity, with constant novelty in objects, is the beginning of language. Unimpressive? And observe!, it is only *the life of a single human being!*

A human being who was dumb in the sense in which the animals are, who could not even in his soul think *words*, would be the saddest, most senseless, most abandoned creature of creation – and *the greatest self-contradiction!* Alone, as it were, in the whole universe, attached to nothing and there for everything, secured by nothing, and still less by himself, the human being must either succumb or else rule over everything, with the plan of a wisdom of which no animal is capable, either take distinct possession of everything or else die![149] Be thou nothing or else the monarch

---

[149] This sentence is another example of Herder's use of the rhetorical figure of chiasmus.

of creation through understanding! Fall in ruins or else create language for thyself! And if, now, in this pressing circle of needs all forces of the soul bring themselves to conscious control, if the whole of humanity struggles to be human – *how much can be invented, done, ordered!*

We human beings of society can only ever imaginatively project ourselves into such a condition with trembling: "Oh! If the human being is only destined to save himself from everything in such a slow, weak, inadequate manner . . . Through reason? Through reflection? How slowly this reflects! And how fast, how pressing his needs are! His dangers!" – This objection can indeed be richly decked out with examples. But it is always fighting against a quite different position [from the one in question].[150] Our society, which has brought many human beings together so that with their abilities and functions they should be one, must consequently distribute abilities and afford opportunities [to people] from childhood on in such a way that one ability gets developed in preference to another. In this way, the one human being becomes for society entirely algebra, entirely reason, so to speak, just as in another human being society needs only heart, courage, and physical force. This one is of use to society by having no genius and much industry; the former by having genius in one thing and nothing in anything else. Each cog must have its relationship and position, otherwise they do not constitute a whole machine. But let this distribution of the forces of the soul, in which people noticeably suffocate all the other forces in order to excel beyond other people in a single one of them, not be transferred to the condition of a natural human being. Set a philosopher, born and raised in society, who has only trained his head for thinking and his hand for writing, set him suddenly outside all the protection and reciprocal comforts that society affords him for his one-sided services – he is supposed to seek his own means of subsistence in an unfamiliar land, and fight against the animals, and be his own protecting deity in everything. How helpless! He has for this neither the senses nor the forces nor the training in either! In the strayings of his abstraction he has perhaps lost the sense of smell and sight and hearing and the gift of quick invention – and certainly that courage, that quick decisiveness, which only develops and expresses itself in dangers, which needs to be in constant, new efficacy or else it dies. If, now, he is of an age when the life-source of his mental abilities has already ceased to flow, or is beginning

[150] a: position than the one we are defending.

to dry up, then indeed it will be forever too late to want to educate him into [*hineinbilden*] this circle. But then, is this the case in question? All the attempts at language that I am citing are not at all made in order to be philosophical attempts. The characteristic marks of plants that I am citing are not discovered as *Linnaeus* classified them. The first experiences are not cold, slowly reasoned, carefully abstracting experiments like the leisurely, lone philosopher makes when he creeps in pursuit of nature in its hidden course and no longer wants to know *that* but *how* it works. This was precisely what concerned nature's first dweller least. Did he need to have it demonstrated to him that this or that plant is poisonous? Was he, then, so much more than brutish that even in this he did not imitate the brutes? And did he need to be attacked by the lion in order to be afraid of it? Is not his timidity combined with his weakness, and his awareness combined with all the subtlety of his forces of soul, enough by itself to provide him with a comfortable condition, since nature herself acknowledged that it was adequate for this? Since, therefore, we have no need at all of a timid, abstract study-philosopher as the inventor of language, since the primitive natural human being who still feels his soul, like his body, so entirely of a single piece is more to us than any number of language-creating academies, and yet is anything but a scholar . . . why on earth, then, would we want to take this scholar as a model? Do we want to cast dust in each other's eyes in order to have proved that the human being cannot see?

Süßmilch is again here the opponent with whom I am fighting. He has devoted a whole section[y] to showing "how impossible it is that the human being should have *formed* a language *further* [*fortbilden*] for himself, even if he had invented it through imitation!" That the invention of language through mere imitation without a human soul is nonsense is proven, and if the defender of the divine origin of language had been *demonstratively* certain of this cause, that it is nonsense, then I trust that he would not have gathered together a mass of half-true reasons against this nonsense which, as things are, all prove nothing against a human invention of language through *understanding*. I cannot possibly explain the whole section in its totality here, woven through with arbitrarily assumed postulates and false axioms about the nature of language as it is, because the author would always appear in a certain light in which he should not appear here. So

[y] Section 3.

I select only as much as is necessary, namely,[151] *"that in his objections the nature of a human language that forms itself further* [sich fortbildenden] *and of a human soul that forms itself further is entirely misperceived."*

"If one assumes that the inhabitants of the first world consisted only of a few thousand families, since the light of the understanding already shone so brightly through the use of language that they understood what language is and hence were able to begin thinking of the improvement of this splendid instrument, it follows . . ."[z] But no one assumes anything of all these antecedent propositions. Did people need a thousand generations to understand for the first time what language is? The first human being understood it when he thought the first thought. Did people need a thousand generations to reach the point of understanding for the first time that it is good to improve language? The first human being understood it when he learned to order better, correct, distinguish, and combine his first characteristic marks, and he immediately improved language each time that he learned such a thing for the first time. And then, how, though, could the light of the understanding have become so brightly enlightened over the course of a thousand generations *through* language if in the course of these generations *language* had not already become *enlightened*? So *enlightenment* without *improvement*?, and after an improvement lasting through a thousand families the *beginning* of an improvement still *impossible*? That is simply contradictory.

"But would not writing have to be assumed as[152] a quite indispensable aid in this philosophical and philological course of instruction?" No! For it was not at all a philosophical and philological course of instruction, this first, natural, living, human progressive formation of language. And then, what can the philosopher and philologist in his dead museum improve in a language which *lives* in all its efficacy?

"Are all peoples supposed, then, to have proceeded with the improvement in the same way?" In exactly the same way, for they all proceeded in a human way – so that we can be confident here, in the rudiments of language, about taking one person for all. When, however, it is supposed to be the greatest miracle[aa] *that all languages have eight parts of speech*, then once again the fact is false and the inference incorrect. Not all languages have from all times on had eight, but [even] the *first* philosophical look

---

[z] Pp. 80–1.   [aa] #31, 34.

[151] B: as is necessary to show . . .   [152] Correcting with Suphan *also* to *als*.

at the manner of construction of a language shows that these eight have developed out of each other. In the oldest languages verbs were earlier than nouns, and perhaps interjections earlier than even regular verbs. In the later languages nouns are immediately derived together with verbs – but even[153] of the Greek language *Aristotle* says that even in it these were initially all the parts of speech, and the others only developed out of them later through the grammarians. I have read precisely the same of the language of the *Hurons*, and it is obvious of the Eastern languages. Indeed, what sort of trick, then, is it in the end, this arbitrary and in part unphilosophical abstraction by the grammarians into eight parts of speech? Is this as regular and divine as the form of a bee's cell? And if it were, is it not entirely explicable and shown necessary in terms of the human soul?

"And what is supposed to have attracted human beings to this most bitter labor of improvement?" Oh, [it was] not at all a bitter speculative study-labor! Not at all an abstract improvement a priori! And hence [there were] also certainly no attractants to do it, which only occur in our condition of refined society. I have to part company with my opponent completely here. He assumes that "the first improvers would have to have been really good philosophical minds who would certainly have seen further and deeper than most scholars are now wont to do in regard to language and its inner constitution." He assumes that "these scholars would have to have recognized everywhere that their language was imperfect and that it was not only capable but also in need of an improvement." He assumes that "they had to judge the purpose of language properly, etc., that the representation of this good which was to be achieved needs to have been adequate, strong, and vivid enough to become a motive for taking on this difficult labor." In short, the philosopher of our age was not willing to venture even one step outside of all our age's accidental features. And how, then, could he from such a point of view write about the *origination* of a language? To be sure, in our century language *could have originated* as little as it *needs to originate*.[154]

But do we not, then, already now know human beings in such various ages, regions, and levels of civilization [*Bildung*] that this so transformed great drama would teach us to infer with greater sureness back to its first scene? Do we not, then, know that precisely in the corners of the earth

---

[153] B omits this redundant "even."
[154] Or possibly, giving *darf* its more common and modern meaning: *may originate*.

where reason is still least cast into the fine, societal, many-sided, scholarly form, sensuality and primitive cleverness and cunning and courageous efficacy and passion and spirit of invention – the whole undivided human soul – still operates in the most lively way? Still operates in the most lively way – because, not yet brought to any longwinded rules, this soul still ever lives whole in a circle of needs, of dangers, of pressing demands, and hence ever feels new and whole. There, only there, does the soul reveal forces to form [*bilden*] language for itself and to form it further [*fortzubilden*]! There the soul has enough sensuality and, so to speak, instinct in order to *sense* the whole sound and all the self-expressing characteristic marks of living nature as wholly as we are no longer able to, and, when the taking of awareness then isolates one of these characteristic marks, in order to *name* it as strongly and inwardly as we would not name it. The less the forces of the soul are yet unfolded and each one adjusted for a sphere of its own, then the more strongly *all* operate *together*, the *deeper* the mid-point of their *intensity* is. But separate out this great, unbreakable sheaf of arrows and you can break them all, and then certainly the miracle cannot be performed with a single wand, then certainly language can never be invented with the *philosophers' single cold gift of abstraction*. But was that our question? Did not that other sense for the world penetrate more deeply? And, with the constant confluence of all the senses, in whose mid-point the inner sense was always alert, were not ever new characteristic marks, orderings, viewpoints, rapid modes of inference present, and hence ever new enrichments of language? And did the human soul not therefore receive its best inspirations for language (if one does not want to count on eight parts of speech) for as long as, still without any of the stimulations of *society*, it only stimulated itself all the more mightily, gave itself all the activity of sensation and thought which it had to give itself in view of inner impulse and external demands? There *language was born with the whole unfolding of the human forces.*

It is unintelligible to me how our century can lose itself so deeply in the shadows, in the obscure workshops, of that which relates to art without even wanting to recognize the broad, bright light of unimprisoned nature. The greatest heroic deeds of the human spirit which it could only do and express in impact with the living world have turned into school exercises in the dust of our school-prisons, the masterpieces of human poetic art and oratory into childish tricks from which aged children and young children learn empty phrases and cull rules. We grasp their formalities and have lost their spirit, we learn their language and do not feel the living world of their thoughts. It is the same with our judgments concerning the masterpiece of the human spirit, the formation of language in general. Here dead reflection is supposed to teach us things which were only able to ensoul the human being, to summon him, and form him further, from the living breath of the world, from the spirit of great, active nature. Here the dull, late laws of the grammarians are supposed to be the most divine thing, which we revere while forgetting the true divine linguistic nature which formed itself in its core with the human spirit – however irregular this true divine linguistic nature may seem. The formation of language has retreated to the shadows of the schools, whence it no longer achieves anything for the living world – consequently it is said that there never even was a bright world in which the first formers of language had to live, feel, create, and poetize. I appeal to the sensitivity of those who do not fail to recognize the human being in the root of his forces, and what is forceful, powerful, and great in the languages of the savages, and the essential nature of language in general. So I continue:

Second natural law

"The human being is in his destiny a creature of the herd, of society. Hence the progressive formation of a language becomes natural, essential, necessary for him."

The human female has no season for being in heat like animal females. And the man's power of procreation is not so unrestrained but enduring. If, now, storks and doves have *marriages*, I cannot see why the human being should not have them, for several reasons.

The human being, compared to the rough bear and the bristly hedge-hog, is a weaker, needier, more naked animal. It needs caves, and these very naturally become, due to the preceding reasons, *communal* caves.

The human being is a weaker animal which in many zones would be very badly exposed to the seasons. The human female therefore in her pregnancy, as a birth-giver, has greater need of *societal help* than the ostrich which lays its eggs in the desert.

Finally, especially the human *young*, the *infant* put into the world – how much he is a vassal of human help and societal pity. From a condition in which he depended as a plant on his mother's heart, he is thrown onto the earth – the weakest, most helpless creature among all the animals, were

139

not maternal breasts there to nourish him, and did not paternal knees come towards him to take him up as a son. To whom does not "*nature's household-management in the interest of humanity's socialization*" become obvious from these facts? And indeed a natural household-management that is as *immediate*, as *close to instinct*, as could be the case with a creature possessed of *awareness*!

I must develop the last point further, for nature's work shows itself most clearly in this, and my inference proceeds from it that much more quickly. If, like our crude Epicureans, one wants to explain everything from blind pleasure or immediate self-interest – who can explain the feeling of parents towards their children? And the strong bonds that this produces? Behold! This poor earth-dweller comes wretched into the world without knowing that he is wretched; he needs pity without being able to make himself in the least deserving of it; he cries, but even this crying ought to[155] become as burdensome as was the howling of Philoctetes, even though he had so many meritorious accomplishments, to the Greeks, who abandoned him to the desolate island. Thus according to our cold philosophy the bonds of nature precisely ought to[156] *break* earliest here, where they are [in fact] most strongly *efficacious*! The mother has finally delivered herself with pains of the fruit that has caused her so much trouble – if the matter depends merely on enjoyment and new pleasure, then she throws it away. The father has cooled his burning lust in a few minutes – why should he concern himself further with mother and child as objects of his *effort*? Like *Rousseau's* man-animal, he runs into the forest and seeks for himself another object of his animal *enjoyment*. How quite opposite is the order of nature here, with animals and with human beings, and how much more wise. Precisely the pains and troubles increase maternal love! Precisely the infant's lamentableness and unamiableness, the weak, frail quality of his nature, the troublesome, vexing effort of his upbringing, doubles the strivings of his parents! The mother regards with warmer emotion the son who has cost her the most pains, who has threatened her with his departure most often, on whom she shed most tears of care. The father regards with warmer emotion the son whom he saved from a danger early on, whom he raised with the greatest effort, who cost him the most in instruction and education [*Bildung*]. And likewise nature also knows "how to make *strength* out of *weakness* in *the whole of the species*." The human being comes

---

[155] Reading with Suphan *müßte*.　　[156] Reading with Suphan *müßten*.

into the world weaker, needier, more abandoned by nature's instruction, more completely without skills and talents, than any animal, precisely in order that, like no animal, he "may enjoy an *upbringing*, and the human species may, like no animal species, become an *inwardly united whole!*"

The young ducks slip away from the hen which hatched them out and, happily splashing in the element into which the call of maternal nature drew them, they do not hear the warning, calling voice of their step-mother who laments on the shore. The human child would do the same as well if it came into the world with the instinct of the duck. Each bird brings the skill of building nests with it from its egg and also takes it with it, without transferring it to others, into its grave; nature instructs for it. Thus everything remains individual, the immediate work of nature, and so there arises "*no progression of the soul of the species*," no *whole*, of the sort that nature wanted in the case of the human being. Nature consequently bonded together the human being [with other human beings] through necessity and a caring parental drive for which the Greeks had the word *storgê*,[157] and in this way "a bond of *instruction* and *upbringing*" became essential to him. In this case parents had not collected the circle of their ideas *for themselves*; at the same time it was there in order to be *communicated*, and the son has the advantage of already inheriting the wealth of their spirit early, as though in epitome. The former pay off nature's debt by teaching; the latter fill up the idea-less need of their own nature by learning, just as they will later in turn pay off their natural debt of increasing this wealth with their own contribution and transferring it again to others. No individual human being exists *for himself*; "he is *inserted into the whole of the species*, he is *only one for the continuing series.*"

What sort of effect this has on the whole chain we will see later. Here we will restrict ourselves to the connection between the first two rings only!, to "*the formation of a familial manner of thinking through the instruction of upbringing*" and –

Since the *instruction of the single soul* is *the parental language's circle of ideas*, "the *further formation of human instruction* through the *spirit of the family*, through which spirit nature has united the whole species, becomes also the *further formation of language*."

Why does this child-without-any-say [*Unmündiger*] cling so weakly and ignorantly to the breasts of his mother, to the knees of his father? That

---

[157] Parental love.

he may desire to be taught and may learn language. He is weak so that his species may become strong. Now the whole soul, the whole manner of thinking, of his begetters gets communicated to him with the language; but[158] they communicate it to him gladly precisely because it is what they have thought for themselves, felt for themselves, invented for themselves that they are communicating. The infant who stammers[159] his first words, stammers a repetition of the feelings of his parents, and swears with each early stammering, in accordance with which[160] his tongue and soul forms itself,[161] that he will make these feelings endure eternally, as truly as he calls them father- or mother-tongue. For his whole life these first impressions from his childhood, these images from the soul and the heart of his parents, will live and take effect within him: with the word will come back the whole feeling that then, early on, flowed over his soul; with the word's idea all the side ideas that then presented themselves to him when he made this new, early dawn-survey into the realm of creation – they will return and take effect more mightily than the pure, clear main idea itself. This therefore becomes *familial manner of thinking* and hence *familial language*. Here, then, stands the cold philosopher[bb] and asks "through what law, then, indeed, human beings could have forced their arbitrarily invented language on one another, and caused the other part to accept the law." This question, about which *Rousseau* preaches so loftily and another author[162] so long, answers itself immediately when we take a look at "the *economy of the nature of the human species*" – and who can then endure the aforementioned sermons?

Is it not, then, law and making-eternal enough, this familial further formation of language? The *woman*, in nature so much the weaker party – must she not accept law from the experienced, providing, language-forming man? Indeed, is that properly even called law which is merely the gentle good deed of instruction? The weak *child*, who is so aptly called a child-without-any-say [*Unmündiger*],[163] does it not have to accept language, since it consumes the milk of its mother and the spirit of its father with language? And must not this language be made eternal if anything is made eternal? Oh, the laws of nature are mightier than all the conventions

[bb] Rousseau.

[158] B: and.   [159] Reading with Suphan *stammelt*.   [160] Reading with Suphan *nach dem*.
[161] This is another example of Herder's use of hendiadys.   [162] Probably Süßmilch.
[163] *Unmündiger*, a minor, i.e. one underage or not yet legally responsible, but literally "one without a mouth."

that cunning politics agrees to and the wise philosopher wants to enumerate! The words of childhood – these our early playmates in the dawn of life!, together with whom our whole soul formed itself jointly – when will we fail to recognize them? When will we forget them? For our mother-tongue was simultaneously the first world that we saw, the first sensations that we felt, the first efficacy and joy that we tasted! The side ideas of place and time, of love and hate, of joy and activity, and whatever the fiery, turbulent soul of youth thought to itself in the process, all gets made eternal along with it. Now *language really becomes tribal core* [Stamm]![164]

And the *smaller* this tribal core is, the more *it gains in inner strength.* Our fathers, who thought nothing for themselves, who invented nothing themselves, who learned everything mechanically – what do they care about the instruction of their sons, about making eternal what they do not even possess themselves?[165] But the first father, the first needy inventors of language, who sacrificed the work of their souls on almost every word, who everywhere in the language still felt the warm sweat which it[166] had cost their activity – what informant could they call upon? The whole language of their children was *a dialect of their own thoughts, a paean to their own deeds*, like the songs of *Ossian* for his father *Fingal.*[167]

[164] *Stamm* can mean either a trunk/stem/core or a tribe. Herder is punning here. "Tribal core" approximates the semantical content of the pun.
[165] B: what they only possess as though in a dream.
[166] Reading *sie* for *er*.
[167] Manuscript a includes the following interesting continuation after "father *Fingal*": "For the philosopher there appears on precisely this path, especially at points more remote from this warm family feeling, a source of the most harmful errors of the human species, namely because through the tradition of language errors do not merely get transmitted and eternalized, but also get made and newly produced, so that the human spirit eternally fights for breath under a load of them. If every person invented his language for himself or brought it with him into the world as the animals bring their drives to art, then nature would have taken care of them or at least they would have gone wrong in a way that was peculiar to themselves and original and, so to speak, at their own expense. But as things are, what a great heap of errors and prejudices exists at the expense of their fathers. Children learn language, and children have learned it from the beginning – who were therefore not in the least able to think over, to test, who accepted all truths and prejudices of the inventors on the basis of their teachers' prestige, and swore them eternal loyalty. Here, as has been shown, along with words viewpoints got established as shrines for youthful adoration at the same time, so that the world should be regarded from these viewpoints and no others for a whole lifetime! [These were] the pillars of Hercules marked with the holy oracle: Let no one venture further! Here, with the words of tradition, the most popular truths and prejudices flowed down on the river of time like light chaff; what was heavy perished and perhaps only reveals itself by having clouded speech and left behind strange word combinations, paradoxes beyond human understanding, which, however, only became such monsters through the transmitter and the receiver, like some old philosophical systems! Here it was especially the idols of bold liars about the truth, the phantoms of hot-headed fanatics, and the prejudices which

Rousseau and others have raised so many paradoxes about the origin
of and right to the first property. And if the former had only asked the
nature of his beloved animal–human, then this animal–human would have
answered him. Why does this flower belong to the bee that sucks on
it? The bee will answer: Because nature made me for this sucking! My
instinct, which lands on this flower and no other, is dictator enough for
me – let it assign me this flower and its garden as my property! And if
now we ask the first human being, Who has given you the right to these
plants?, then what can he answer but: Nature, which gave me *the taking
of awareness [Besinnung]*! I have come to know these plants with effort!
With effort I have taught my wife and my son to know them! We all live
from them! I have more right to them than the bee that hums on them
and the cattle that grazes on them, for these have not had all the effort[168]
of coming to know and teaching to know! Thus every thought that I have
designed on them is a seal of my property, and whoever drives me away

were mightiest in their effect and hence the most harmful for the human understanding that
forced their way on down! Before we were able to think we were taught to fall down before
linguistic concepts as before statues, instead of observing and studying them moving about in
nature like living bodies. And here we get, as Bacon, the leader in sensitivity to this weakness
of humanity, calls them: trade idols, idols from a dark cave, idols which are the seduction of the
market, idols which are the drama of the stage, all of which are made eternal by nothing as much
as by language. Here lie rules and laws [commanding people] to think in accordance with the
analogy of their fathers and not in accordance with the analogy of nature, to read the images of
the universe in the distorting mirror of tradition and not in nature. Here lie the forms of that
cave in which the inventors of language and all their followers thought: the plastic shapes of those
small worlds from out of which they looked into the great world, the puppets which through the
usage of the centuries have become images of gods, linguistic fables and mere hollow vessels of
expressions which through the loud noise of our dear habit from youth up have become forms in
our heads. Whoever can, let him think his way beyond them, or rather right through them – for
if one means to destroy all these images and prejudices (praeiudicata) as prejudices (praeiudicia)
and empty idols, then indeed one has the easy work of the Goths in Italy or the Persians in Egypt,
but one also leaves oneself with nothing more than a desert. Precisely thereby one has stripped
oneself of the aid of all the centuries of one's fathers, and stands there naked, in order to build
from the small heap of materials that one has oneself gathered and of arbitrary words that one
has perhaps oneself explored a little system which is as similar to that work of the centuries as
the little temples which the worshipers of Diana had made for themselves to the great building
of wonder at Ephesus. So, unless we want to follow the warning example of all those who make
systems out of their own heads, there is nothing for us to do in such a case but to throw ourselves
into the great ocean of truths and errors, and, with the help of all those who have lived before us,
to see how far we get, then, in beholding and observing nature and in naming it through distinct
linguistic ideas! There is nothing for us to do but to become children again in the footsteps of
great people before us, and to learn to recognize and examine the great treasure that has come
down to us with the language and the mass of thoughts belonging to all nations. What could
be attempted here, but has been little attempted, from and concerning several languages for the
benefit of the general philosophy of humanity is almost inexpressible."
[168] B: for all these have not had the effort . . .

from them takes away from me not only my life, if I do not find this means of subsistence again, but really also the *value of my lived years*, my sweat, my effort, my thoughts, my language. I have earned them for myself! And should not such a signature of the soul on something through coming to know, through characteristic mark, through language, constitute for the first among humanity more of a right of property than a stamp on a coin?

"How much *ordering* and *development* [*Ausbildung*] language therefore already receives precisely by becoming *paternal teaching*!" Who does not learn in the process of teaching? Who does not reassure himself of his ideas, who does not examine his words, in the process of communicating them to others and so often hearing them stammered by the lips of the child-without-any-say [*des Unmündigen*]? Language therefore already here wins an *artistic form, a methodical form*! Here the first grammar, which was an offprint of the human soul and of its natural logic, already got[169] corrected by a sharply examining censorship.

Rousseau, who here exclaims in his usual manner, "What great amount did the mother have to say to her child, then? Did the child not have more to say to its mother? Whence, then, did the child already learn language in order to teach it to its mother?" also, though, in his usual manner, here makes a panicky battle clamor. Certainly the mother had more to teach the child than the child the mother – because the former *was able* to teach it more, and because the *maternal instinct*, love and sympathy, which Rousseau from compassion concedes to the animals but from pride denies to his own species, *compelled* her to this instruction, as the excess of milk compelled her to suckle. Do we not, then, see even in some animals that the older ones habituate their young to their manner of life? And now, when a father habituated his son to hunting from early youth on, did this happen without instruction and language, then? "Yes!, such a dictation of words certainly indicates a formed language which one is teaching, [but] not a language which is just being formed!"[170] And again, is this a difference that constitutes an exception? To be sure, *that* language *which* they taught their children was already *formed* in the father and mother, but does this imply that the language already had to be *completely* formed, including even that language which they did not teach their children? And could the children in a newer, broader, more refined world not, then, invent anything more in addition? And is, then, a partly *formed* language

---

[169] Reading with Suphan *wurde* for *würde*.
[170] B: "But such a dictation of words would already indicate . . . , not a language . . ."

which is still undergoing *further formation* a contradiction? When, then, is the French language, which has been so much formed through academies and authors and dictionaries, so *finally formed* that it would not have to *form*, or deform, itself anew with each new original author, indeed with each mind who introduces a new tone into society? It is with such fallacies that the champions of the opposite opinion are adorned. Let it be judged whether it is worthwhile to go into every trivial detail of their objections.

Another,[171] for example, asks "but how, then, human beings could ever have wanted to form their language further due to necessity if they had been Lucretius's mutum et turpe pecus,"[172] and goes into a pile of half-true evidentiary examples of savages. I merely answer: *Never!* They could never have wanted to, or been able to, do it if they had been a mutum pecus.[173] For in that case did they not, of course, lack all language? But are savages like this? Is, then, even the most barbarous human nation without language? And has the human being ever been so, then, except in philosophers' abstractions and hence in their heads?

He asks "whether, then, really, since all animals eschew constraint, and all human beings love laziness, it can ever be expected of *Condamine's Orenocks* that they should change and improve their longwinded, eight-syllabled, difficult, and most cumbersome language." And I answer: First, the *fact* is again incorrect, like almost all that he cites.[cc] "Their long-winded, eight-syllabled language" it is not. Condamine merely says that it is so unpronounceable and distinctively organized that where they pronounce three or four syllables we would have to write seven or eight, and yet we would still not have written them completely. Does that mean that it *is* longwinded, eight-syllabled? And "difficult, most cumbersome"? For whom is it so except for foreigners? And they are supposed to make improvements in it for foreigners? To improve it for an arriving Frenchman who hardly ever learns any language except his own without mutilating it, and hence to Frenchify it? But is it the case that the Orenocks have *not yet* formed *anything* in their language, indeed not yet *formed* for themselves any language, just because they do not choose to exchange the genius which is so peculiarly theirs for a foreigner who comes sailing along? Indeed, even assuming that they were to form *nothing more* in their

[cc] Süßmilch [*Versuch eines Beweises*, p. 92].

[171] I.e. Süßmilch.   [172] Dumb and ugly/shameful cattle.   [173] Dumb cattle.

language, not even for themselves – has a person, then, never grown if he no longer grows? And have the savages, then, done nothing because they do not like to do anything without need?

And what a *treasure familial language is* for a developing race! In almost all small nations of all parts of the world, however little cultivated [*gebildet*] they may be, ballads of their fathers, songs of the deeds of their ancestors, are the treasure of their language and history and poetic art, [they are] their wisdom and their encouragement, their instruction and their games and dances. The Greeks sang of their Argonauts, of Hercules and Bacchus, of heroes and conquerors of Troy, and the Celts of the fathers of their tribes, of Fingal and Ossian! Among Peruvians and North Americans, on the Caribbean and Mariana Islands, this origin of the tribal language in the ballads of their tribes and fathers still holds sway – just as in almost all parts of the world father and mother have similar names. And it is only precisely here that it can be indicated why among many peoples, of which we have cited examples, the *male* and *female* genders have almost two different languages, namely, because in accordance with the customs of the nation the two, as the noble and the base genders, almost constitute two quite separate peoples, who do not even eat together. According, then, to whether the upbringing was paternal or maternal, the language too inevitably became either *father-* or *mother-tongue* – as, in accordance with the customs of the Romans, it even became lingua vernacula.[174]

Third natural law

"Just as[175] the whole human species could not possibly remain a single herd, likewise it could not retain a single language either. So there arises a formation of different national languages."

In the real metaphysical sense, it is already never possible for there to be a single language between man and wife, father and son, child and old man. Let one, for example, go through, in the case of the Easterners, the long and short vowels, the many different kinds of breathings and gutteral letters, the easy and so manifold exchanging of letters by one kind of organ,[176] the pause and the linguistic signs, with all the variations which are so difficult to express in writing: pitch and emphasis, increase and diminution of this, and a hundred other contingent small things in the

---

[174] The language of homeborn slaves.   [175] B: Since...   [176] B: by all kinds of organs.

elements of language. And let one, on the other hand, note the diversity of the linguistic organs in both genders, in youth and in old age, even simply in the case of two similar people – in accordance with many contingencies and individual circumstances which alter the structure of these organs, given many habits which become second nature, etc. "As little as there can be two human beings who share exactly the same form and facial traits, just as little can there be two languages in the mouths of two human beings which would in fact still be only one language, even merely *in terms of pronunciation*."

Each race will bring into its language *the sound belonging to its house and family*; this becomes, in terms of pronunciation, a different dialect.[177]

Climate [*Klima*],[178] air and water, food and drink, will have an influence on the linguistic organs and naturally also on language.

Society's ethics and the mighty goddess Habit will soon introduce these peculiarities and those differences[179] in accordance with behavior and decency – a dialect. – "*A philosophical essay on the Easterners' related languages*" would be the pleasantest proof of these theses.

That was only *pronunciation*. But *words* themselves, *sense*, the *soul* of language – what an endless field of differences. We have seen how the oldest languages necessarily came to be full of synonyms. And now, when, of these synonyms, this one became more familiar to the one person, that one to the other person, more appropriate to his viewpoint, more original for his circle of sensation, more frequently occurring in the course of his life, in short, of greater influence on him – then there arose *favorite words, words of one's own, idioms, linguistic idiom.*

For the former person that word became extinguished, this word remained.[180] That word got bent away from the main subject through a secondary viewpoint; here the spirit of the main concept itself changed

[177] B: a different dialect already.
[178] The word *Klima* in Herder sometimes means *climate*, as here, but at other times it instead means *clime* or *region*, in which cases I have translated it *clime*. At yet other times it is hard to tell which meaning Herder has in mind, either because he himself hovers between the two meanings or because inadequate guidance from the context leaves the reader doing so – and in these cases too I have used the translation *clime*, since this word can bear either meaning or both together in English.
[179] Reading with Suphan *jene Verschiedenheiten.*
[180] In this sentence "that" and "this" evidently do not mean, as they often do in German, *former* and *latter* but in effect just the opposite, i.e. the words referred to as "that" and "this" in the preceding remark "this one became more familiar to the one person, that one to the other person."

with the passage of time.[181] There hence arose here distinctive *bendings, diversions, changes, promotions* and *additions* and *transpositions* and *removals,* of whole and half *meanings* – a new idiom! And all this as naturally as language is for the human being the sense of his soul.

The *livelier* a language is, the nearer it is to its origin, and hence [the more] it is still in the periods of youth and growth, then the more changeable it is. If the language exists only in books, where it is learned according to rules, where it is used only in sciences and not in living intercourse, where it has its set number of objects and applications, where therefore its vocabulary is closed, its grammar regulated, its sphere fixed – such a language can the more easily remain unchanged in what is noticeable, and yet even here only in what is noticeable. But a language in savage, free life, in the realm of great, broad creation, still without formally minted rules, still without books and letters and accepted masterpieces, poor and imperfect enough still to need daily enrichment, and youthfully supple enough still to be capable of it at the first hint from attentiveness, the first command from passion and sensation – this language inevitably changes with each new world that is seen, with each method in accordance with which people think and progress in thinking. Egyptian laws of uniformity cannot effect the opposite here.

Now it is obvious that the whole face of the earth is made for the human species, and the human species for the whole face of the earth. (I do not say that every inhabitant of the earth, every people is immediately, through the most sudden leap, for the most opposite clime [*Klima*] and hence for all zones of the world, but the whole species for the whole circle of the earth.) Wherever we look about us, there the human being is as much at home as the land animals which are originally destined for this region. He endures in Greenland amid the ice and roasts in Guinea under the vertical sun; he is on home turf when he glides over the snow with his reindeer in Lapland, and when he trots through the Arab desert with his thirsty camel. The cave of the troglodytes and the mountaintops of the Kabyles,[182] the smoking fireplace of the Ostyaks[183] and the golden palace

---

[181] This sentence seems to loosen the connection with the preceding paragraph that was sustained in the sentence before, "That word . . . here . . ." in effect just meaning "In the case of one word . . . in the case of another . . ."

[182] Kabyles: members of a group of Berber tribes in Algeria and Tunisia.

[183] Ostyaks: members of a Finno-Ugric people living in Western Siberia.

of the Mogul, contain – *human beings*. For them is the earth flattened at its pole and raised at its equator, for them does the earth revolve around the sun as it does and not otherwise, for them are the earth's zones and seasons and changes – and they in their turn are for the zones, for the seasons, and for the changes of the earth. This natural law is hence apparent here too: "Human beings should live everywhere on the earth, while every animal species merely has its land and its narrower sphere"; *the earth-dweller* becomes apparent. And if that is so, then his language becomes *language of the earth* as well. A *new* language in every *new world, national language* in every *nation* – I cannot repeat all the aforementioned determining causes of the change – *language becomes a Proteus on the round surface of the earth*.

Some recent fashionable philosophers[184] have been so unable to bind this Proteus and see him in his true form that it has seemed to them more probable that nature was as able to create for each large region of the earth a pair of human beings to found tribes as it was to create special animals for each clime. These human beings then – it is alleged – invented for themselves such a regional and national language of their own as had a whole construction that was made only for this region. On this account, the little Lapp, with his language and his thin beard, with his skills and his spirit, is as much a human animal original to Lapland as his reindeer [is an animal original to Lapland];[185] and the Negro, with his skin, with his ink-bubble blackness, with his lips, and hair, and turkey language, and stupidity, and laziness, is a natural brother of the apes of the same clime. One should – it is alleged – as little dream up similarity[186] between the languages of the earth as between the [physical] formations of the [different] races of human beings. And it would have been a very unwise plan of God's – the account proceeds – to have put forth, so weak and timid, a prey for the elements and animals, only one pair of human beings into one corner of the earth as tribal parents for the whole earth, and to have abandoned them to a thousandfold hazard of dangers.

At least – an opinion which asserts less continues – language is a natural product of the human spirit which only gradually moved to foreign climes with the human species; hence it must also have changed only gradually. One would need to observe the subtle alteration, the movement forth, and

[184] Gaier identifies especially Voltaire in his *Essai sur les moeurs et l'esprit des nations* [*Essay on the Ethics and Mind of the Nations*] (1769).
[185] This is another example of Herder's use of brachylogy, or "shortening."
[186] B: an identity of origin.

the relatedness of peoples progressing in connection with one another, and to be able to give oneself an exact account everywhere of manner of thought, manner of speech or dialect, and manner of life in terms of small nuances. But who can do that? Does one not find in the same clime, indeed right next to each other, in all parts of the world little peoples who in the same sort of circle have such different and opposite languages that everything becomes a confusing thicket? Whoever has read travel descriptions from North and South America, from Africa and Asia, does not need to have the tribes of this thicket counted out to him. So here, these doubters conclude, all human investigation comes to an end.

And because these people merely doubt, I want to attempt to show that the investigation does not come to an end here, but that this "*difference [between peoples] right next to each other* can be explained just as naturally as the *unity* of the *familial language* in one nation."

The division of the families into separated nations certainly does not proceed in accordance with the slow and boring connections between distance, migration, new relationship, and that sort of thing, as the idle, cold philosopher, compasses in hand, measures [them] on the map, and as, in terms of this measurement, large books have been written "on *relatednesses of the peoples*," wherein everything is true except the rule in accordance with which everything was calculated. If we take a look at the living, active world, there are motives there which must very naturally give rise to the difference of language among peoples near to each other – only let one not want to force the human being to change in accordance with some pet system. He is no *Rousseauian* forest man; he has *language*. He is no *Hobbesian* wolf; he has a *familial language*. But in other connections he is also no *premature lamb*. So he can form for himself an opposed nature, habit, and language. In short, "the basis of this difference between such near little peoples in language, manner of thought, and manner of life is – *reciprocal familial and national hatred*."

Without any blackening of human nature or stigmatizing of it as heretical, [we can say,] if we transpose ourselves into their familial manner of thought, [that] two or more near tribes cannot do otherwise than soon find things to quarrel over. It is not merely that similar needs soon entangle them in a struggle of – if I may put it this way – hunger and thirst, as for example two bands of shepherds quarrel over well and pasture, and in view of the [physical] constitution of their regions of the world may often very naturally quarrel. A much hotter spark kindles their fire: *jealousy*, *feeling of honor, pride in their race* and their *superiority*. The same liking for family which, turned *inward on itself*, gave strength to the *harmony of a single* tribe, turned *outward from itself*, against another race, produces strength of *dissension, familial hatred*! In the former case it drew many all the more firmly together into a single whole; in the latter case it makes two parties immediately into enemies. The basis of this enmity and these eternal wars is in such a case more noble human weakness than base vice.

Since humanity on this level of civilization [*Bildung*] has more *forces of efficacy* than goods of possession, it is also the case that pride in the former is more the point of honor than miserable possessing of the latter, as in later, fiberless ages. But in that age to be a brave man and to belong to a brave family were almost the same thing, since the son in many ways even more truly than is the case with us inherited and learned his virtue and bravery from his father, and the whole tribe in general supported a brave man on all occasions. Hence the slogan soon became natural: *Whoever is not with and of us is beneath us*! The foreigner is *worse* than us, is a *barbarian*. In this sense 'barbarian' was the watchword of contempt: a foreigner and simultaneously a more ignoble person who is not our equal in wisdom or bravery, or whatever the age's point of honor might be.

Now, indeed, as an *Englishman* correctly notes,[187] if what is at stake is merely selfishness and security of possession, then this fact, that our neighbor is not as brave as we are, is no reason for hatred, but we should quietly rejoice about it. But precisely because this opinion is only an opinion, and is the same opinion of both parties, who have the same feeling for their tribe – precisely hereby the trumpet of war is blown! This touches the honor, this awakens the pride and courage, of the whole tribe! Heroes and patriots [come forth] from both sides! And because the cause of the war affected each person, and each person could understand and feel this cause, the *national hatred* was made eternal in perpetual, bitter wars. And there the second synonym was ready: *Whoever is not with me is against me. Barbarian* and *spiteful one*! *Foreigner, enemy*! As the word *hostis*[188] originally [illustrates] in the case of the Romans![dd]

The third thing followed immediately: complete *division* and *separation*. Who wanted to have anything in common with such an enemy, the

---

[dd] Vossius, *Etymologicon* [i.e. *Etymologicon linguae latinae* [*Etymological Dictionary of the Latin Language*] (1662)].

[187] Gaier conjectures that Herder means Hume in the *Treatise of Human Nature*.

[188] *hostis*: foreigner, enemy.

contemptible barbarian? No familial customs, no remembrance of a single origin, and least of all *language*. For language was actually *"characteristic word of the race, bond of the family, tool of instruction, hero song of the fathers' deeds,* and the *voice of these fathers from their graves."* Language could not possibly, therefore, remain *of one kind,* and so the same *familial feeling* that had formed a single language, when it became national hatred, often created *difference, complete difference* in language. He is a *barbarian,* he speaks *a foreign language* – the third, so usual synonym.

As inverted as the etymology of these words may seem, the history of all little peoples and languages, which are at issue in this question, on the contrary fully proves its truth. And the layers of etymology are only abstractions, not divisions in history. All such near polyglots are simultaneously the fiercest, most irreconcilable enemies – and indeed, not all[189] from desire to rob and greed, since for the most part they do not plunder, but only kill and lay waste, and *sacrifice to the shades of their fathers.* Shades of their fathers are the divinities, and the sole invisible dei ex machina, of the whole bloody epic – as in the songs of *Ossian.* It is they who stir and stimulate the leader in dreams, and for whom he spends his nights awake; it is they whose names his companions name in vows and songs; it is to them that the captured are consecrated in all tortures; and it is also they, on the other side, who strengthen the tortured one in his songs and dirges. *"Family hatred made eternal"* is hence the cause of their wars, of their so jealous separations into peoples, which are often scarcely even like families, and in all probability also of the *"complete differences between their customs and languages."*

An Eastern document *about the division of the languages*[ee] – which I consider here only as a poetic fragment for the archaeology of the history of peoples – confirms through a very poetic *narrative* what so many nations from all parts of the world confirm through their *example.* "The languages did not change gradually," as the philosopher multiplies them through migrations; "the peoples united, the poem says, for a great work; then the frenzy of confusion and of the multiplicity of languages flowed over them, so that they desisted and separated." What was this but a rapid embitterment and quarrel, for which precisely such a great work provided the richest stimulus? There the spirit of family awakened, insulted on

---

[ee] Moses, bk. 1, ch. 11. [I.e. Genesis 11.]

[189] This is clearly the sense in B. In A the meaning could alternatively be: and indeed, all not . . .

what was perhaps a trivial occasion. Alliance and purpose fought themselves to pieces. The spark of disunity shot into flames. They sped apart, and achieved "*now all the more violently* what they *had wanted to forestall through their work: they confused the unitary constituent of their origin, their language*. In this way there arose different peoples, and there, the later report says,[190] the ruins are still called: confusion of the peoples!" – Whoever knows the spirit of the Easterners in their often so far-fetched clothings [of their ideas] and their epic, miraculous histories (I do not mean here to exclude for theology a higher Providence), will perhaps not fail to recognize the main thought that is made sensuous [here]: that "division over a great common purpose," and not only the migration of peoples, became a contributing cause of so many languages.

Setting aside this Eastern testimony (which, moreover, I only in fact meant to cite here as a poem), one sees that the *multiplicity of languages can constitute no objection to the natural and human character of the further formation of a language*. To be sure, mountains can be raised up here and there *by earthquakes*, but does it, then, follow from this that the earth as a whole, with its mountain ranges and rivers and seas, cannot have won its form *from water*? – Only, indeed, just the same consideration also imposes on etymologists and ethnographers a useful constraint to caution, "*not to infer too despotically from dissimilarities in languages to their genealogy.*" Families can be very closely related and yet have had cause to suppress the relatedness of their coats of arms. The spirit of such little peoples gives sufficient cause for this.

Fourth natural law

"Just as in all probability the human species [*Geschlecht*] constitutes a single progressive whole with a single origin in a single great household-economy, likewise all languages too, and with them the whole chain of civilization [*Bildung*]."[191]

---

[190] Genesis 11:9.

[191] I have had to vary the translations of the words *Geschlecht*, *Bildung*, and their compounds/cognates over the course of the next few paragraphs to an unusual extent in order to make clear what I take to be Herder's sense. The reader can if need be see how this has been done by following the German in square brackets.

The distinctive characteristic plan which governs a human being has been pointed out: his soul has the habit of always ranking what it sees with what it has seen, and there thus arises through awareness "*a progressive unity of all conditions of life.*" Hence, *further formation* [Fortbildung] *of language*.

The distinctive characteristic plan which governs a human race [*Menschengeschlecht*] has been pointed out: that through the chain of instruction parents and children become one, and hence each link only gets shoved by nature between two others in order to receive and to communicate. Thereby arises "*further formation of language.*"

Finally, this distinctive plan also continues *to the whole human species* [*Menschengeschlecht*], and thereby arises "a *further formation* in the highest meaning of the expression" which follows immediately from the two preceding.

Each individual is a human being; consequently, he continues to think for the whole chain of his life. Each individual is a son or daughter, was educated [*gebildet*] through instruction; consequently, he always inherited a share of the thought-treasures of his ancestors early on, and will pass them down in his own way to others. Hence in a certain way there is "*no thought, no invention, no perfection which does not reach further, almost ad infinitum.*" Just as I can perform no action, think no thought, that does not have a natural effect on the whole immeasurable sphere of *my* existence, likewise neither I nor any creature of my kind [*Gattung*] can do so without also having an effect with each [action or thought] for *the whole kind* and for the *continuing totality of the whole kind*. Each [action or thought] always produces a large or small wave: each changes the condition of the *individual* soul, and hence the *totality* of these conditions; always has an effect *on others*, changes *something in these* as well – the first thought in the first human soul is connected with the last thought in the last human soul.

If language were as innate to the human being as producing honey is to bees, then this greatest and most splendid of buildings would immediately fall apart in ruins! Each person would bring *his little bit of* language into the world for himself, or rather, since "bringing into the world" for a [faculty of] reason means nothing but inventing language for itself immediately – what a sad isolated thing each human being becomes! Each one invents his own rudiments, dies at work on them, and takes them into his grave, like the bee its skilled producing; the successor comes, tortures himself working on *the same* beginnings, gets exactly as far, or exactly as little distance, dies – and so it goes on ad infinitum. One sees that "the plan that holds for the animals, who invent nothing, cannot hold for creatures who must invent" – otherwise it becomes a planless plan![192] If each creature invents by and for itself alone, then useless effort gets increased ad infinitum and the inventing understanding gets robbed of its best prize, that of *growing*. What[193] sort of reason could I have for stopping somewhere in the chain, instead of, as long as I perceive the same plan, also *inferring back in time* about language? If *I* came into the world in order to need to enter immediately into my family's instruction, then likewise *my father*, likewise *the first son of the first father of the tribe*; and just as I spread my thoughts about me and among my successors, likewise my father, likewise the father of his tribe, likewise the first of all fathers. The chain goes on and only stops "with *one, the first*"; in this way, we are all his sons, from him begin species, instruction, language. He began the process of invention; we have all invented, formed, and deformed in his wake.[194] No thought in a human soul was lost, but nor was a single skill of this species ever present in its entirety straightaway, as in the case of the animals: "*in accordance with the whole economy*" it was always *in progress*, in *motion* – nothing invented like the [bee's] production of a cell, but everything in process of invention, in process of producing further effects, *striving*. From this point of view how great a thing language turns out to be! "*A treasure room of human thoughts to which each person contributed something in his own way! An epitome of the efficacy of all human souls.*"

"At most," – intervenes here the preceding philosophy which would like to consider the human being as a property of land and domain – "at most,[195] though, surely, this chain may reach only as far as each in-dividual first tribal father of a land from whom its race, like its native language, was born."[ff] I cannot see why it should only reach *that far* and *not further*, why these fathers of lands could not in turn have had among

---

[ff] *Philosophie de l'histoire* etc. etc. [This is an allusion to Voltaire, *La philosophie de l'histoire* [*The Philosophy of History*] (1765).]

[192] The expression "a planless plan" is an example of the rhetorical figure of deliberate oxymoron – especially favored in the ancient world by Aeschylus.

[193] a: Now, what . . . (This is probably what Herder intended in A as well, *nun* getting changed to *um* by error.)

[194] This sentence provides a striking example of Herder's readiness to depart from normal grammar when it seems to him desirable to do so – in this case mainly for reasons of euphony. He writes *wir alle haben ihm nacherfunden, bilden und mißbilden* whereas normal grammar would require something like *wir alle haben ihm nacherfunden, -gebildet und -mißbildet*.

[195] This is another example of anadiplosis.

them a father of the earth, since "the whole *continuing similarity of the household-economy of this species* demands that this be so." Of course, we heard the objection: "As if it would have been *wise* to expose one weak, wretched human pair in a corner of the earth as a prey for danger!" And as if it would have been *wiser* to set many such weak human pairs separately in different corners of the earth as prey for tenfold worse dangers! The circumstance of reckless lack of forethought is not merely everywhere *the same*, but also gets *endlessly increased* with every increase in numbers. A human pair anywhere in the best, most comfortable clime of the earth, where the climate is least rigorous on their nakedness, where the fruitful soil of itself benefits the needs of their inexperience, where everything is, so to speak, set out round about like a workshop in order to come to the aid of the childhood of their arts – is this pair not more wisely provided for than any other human land animal that, under the unfriendliest sky in *Lapland* or *Greenland*, surrounded by the whole poverty of naked, frozen nature, is exposed to the claws of equally poor, hungry, and all-the-more-cruel animals, and hence to infinitely more difficulties? The certainty of preservation hence diminishes the more the original human beings of the earth get increased by pairs. And then, how long does the pair in the more favorable clime remain one pair? It soon becomes a family, then soon a small people, and when now it spreads as a people – it enters another land – it already enters *as a people* – how much wiser!, how much more certain! Many in number, with hardened bodies, with tried and tested souls, indeed with the inheritance of their ancestors' whole treasure of experiences – how multiply strengthened and increased thus their souls! Now they are capable of perfecting themselves soon into land creatures of this region! In a short time they become as native as the animals of the clime with their manner of life, manner of thought, and language. But does not precisely this prove "the *natural progress of the human spirit, which starting from a certain mid-point can form itself for everything*"? It never turns on a mass of mere numbers but on the validity and progression of their meaning, never on a mass of weak subjects but on forces with which they operate. These operate most strongly precisely in the simplest context; and so only *those* bonds encompass the whole species which proceed from a single point of attachment.

I shall go into no further arguments for this origin in a single stem-tribe – for example, that no true evidential data have yet been found of new human kinds which would deserve this name like the animal kinds;

that the obviously gradual and progressive population of the earth shows exactly the opposite of native land animals; that the chain of culture and of similar habits shows it as well, only more obscurely, etc. I shall remain with *language*. If human beings were national animals so that each such animal had invented its own language for itself quite independently and separately from others, then this language would certainly have to display "a *difference in type*," such as the inhabitants of Saturn and of the earth may perhaps have vis-à-vis each other. And yet it is obvious that with us *everything develops on a single basis*. On a single basis concerning not only the *form* but also the actual *course of the human spirit*, for among all peoples of the earth *grammar is constructed in almost a single manner*. As far as I know, only the Chinese language constitutes an essential exception – which I am very confident of explaining as an exception, however. "How many *Chinese grammars*, and how *many types* of them, there would have to be if *the earth had been full of language-inventing land animals!*"

What explains the fact that so many peoples have an *alphabet* and yet there is almost only one alphabet on the face of the earth? The strange and difficult thought of forming *arbitrary signs* for oneself from the components of arbitrary words, from sounds, is such a leap, so complicated, so strange, that it would certainly be inexplicable how many and so many would have hit upon the *same* so *remote* thought, and how all of them would have done so exactly *in the same way*. That they all *ignored* the much more natural signs, the *pictures of things*, and *depicted breaths*, among all possible breaths depicted *the same twenty*, and *resorted to poor expedients* vis-à-vis the other missing ones, that so many used *the same arbitrary signs* for these *twenty* – does not *tradition*[196] become apparent here? The Eastern alphabets are at bottom one; the Greek, the Latin, the Runic, the German, etc. are derivatives; hence the German still has letters in common with the Coptic, and Irishmen have been bold enough to declare Homer to be a translation from their language. Who, however much or little he counts on it, can entirely fail to perceive *relatedness* in the basis of the languages? "Just as there lives only a single human people on earth, likewise only a single human language; but just as this great kind has nationalized itself into so many little types specific to a land, likewise their languages no differently."[197]

[196] "Tradition" again with its etymological meaning of *handing over, handing down*.
[197] Only the opening (emphatic) quotation marks are printed in Gaier's text; the location of the closing ones is therefore conjectural.

Many have made attempts at *"genealogies of these language species."* I shall not attempt it – for how many, many incidental causes could have produced changes in this descent and in the recognizability of this descent which the etymologizing philosopher cannot anticipate and which deceive his genealogy. In addition, there have been so few true philosophers of language among the travel describers and even the missionaries who could have given us or would have wanted to give us information about the genius and the characteristic basis of their native peoples' languages that one in general still goes astray here. They give lists of words – and from this jumble of sounds one is supposed to infer! Also, the rules of a true deduction of language are so subtle that few . . . But all this is not my task! Overall, the natural law remains clear: *"Language reproduces itself and forms itself further with the human species."* Under this law I shall enumerate only *main types which add a different dimension.*

I. Each human being has, to be sure, all the abilities that his whole species has, and each nation the abilities that all nations have. However, it is nevertheless true that *a society invents more than a human being*, and *the whole human species invents more than a single people* – and this indeed not merely *as a result of the quantity of heads* but *as a result of the manyfold and intensive increase of relational circumstances.* One should think that a lonely human being, without pressing needs, with all comfort in his manner of life, would for example[198] invent much more language, that his leisure would stimulate him to exercise his forces of soul, and hence constantly to think up something new, etc. But the opposite is clear. Without society he will always in a certain manner go to seed and soon languish in inactivity once he has only first put himself in the strategic, middling position for satisfying his most essential needs. He is always a flower which, torn from its roots, broken from its stem, lies there and withers. Set him into society and more needs, let him have to take care of himself and others. One should think that these new burdens would rob him of the freedom to raise himself up, that this increase of inconveniences would rob him of the leisure to invent. But precisely the contrary. Need makes him stretch, inconvenience awakens him, restlessness keeps his soul in motion; he will do more, the more amazing it becomes that he does it. In this way, therefore, the *further formation of a language already increases from a [solitary] individual to a*

---

[198] B omits "for example."

human being who belongs to a family in a very high ratio. Setting everything else aside, how little the lonely person – even the lonely philosopher of language – on a desolate island would in fact invent! How much more and more strongly the tribal father, the man who belongs to a family. Nature has hence *chosen this further formation.*

II. An individual, separated family, one would think, will be able to develop its language more in comfort and leisure than in distractions, war against another tribe, etc. But nothing could be further from the truth. The more it is turned against others, then the more strongly it is compressed within itself, the more it centers itself on its root, makes its ancestors' deeds into songs, into calls to action, into eternal monuments, preserves this linguistic remembrance that much more purely and patriotically – *the further formation of language, as the dialect of the [familial] fathers, progresses that much more strongly.* That is why nature has *chosen this further formation.*

III. But with time this tribe, when it has grown into a little nation, also *"gets stuck in its circle."* It has its measured circle of needs, and language for these too – further it does not go, as we can see from the case of all little, so-called barbarous nations. Separated with their necessities, they can remain in the strangest ignorance for centuries, like those islands without fire and so many other peoples without the easiest of mechanical arts. It is as though they did not have eyes to see what lies before them. Hence, then, the outcry of other peoples about such peoples as stupid, inhuman barbarians; whereas in fact we were all just the same barbarians a short time ago and only received these pieces of knowledge from other peoples! Hence also the outcry of many philosophers about this stupidity as the most incomprehensible thing; whereas in fact in accordance with the analogy of the whole household-management [of nature] with our species nothing is more comprehensible than this! – Here nature has linked a new chain: tradition from people to people! *"In this way arts, sciences, culture, and language have refined themselves in a great progression over the course of nations"* – the finest *bond of further formation that nature has chosen.*

We Germans would still, like the Americans,[199] live quietly in our forests, or rather still roughly war and be heroes in them, if the chain of

---

[199] I.e. native Americans.

foreign culture had not pressed so near to us and compelled us with the force of whole centuries to participate in it. The *Roman* got his culture [*Bildung*] from *Greece* in this way, the *Greek* received it from *Asia* and *Egypt*, *Egypt* from *Asia*, *China* perhaps from *Egypt* – thus the chain proceeds on from a first ring and will perhaps some day stretch over the earth. The art that built a Greek palace already shows itself with the savage in the building of a forest hut; just as the painting of *Mengs*[200] and *Dietrich*[201] already in its most primitive basis shone on the red-painted shield of *Hermann*.[202] The *Eskimo* in front of his army already has all the seeds for a future *Demosthenes*, and that nation of sculptors on the *Amazon* river[gg] perhaps a thousand future Phidiases. Only let other nations move ahead and those ones turn back – then everything, at least in the temperate zones, is as in the ancient world. *Egyptians* and *Greeks* and *Romans* and moderns did nothing but build ahead; *Persians*, *Tatars*, *Goths*, and *priests* interfere and produce ruins; all the more freshly does building proceed further from and after and on such old ruins. The chain of a certain perfection of art progresses over everything (although other natural properties by contrast on the contrary suffer) and likewise over language as well.[203] The Arabic language is certainly a hundred times finer than its mother in the first, primitive beginning; our *German* certainly finer than the old *Celtic*; the grammar of the *Greeks* was able to be and become[204] better than the Eastern grammar, for it was the latter's daughter; the *Roman* grammar more philosophical than the *Greek*, the *French* more than the *Roman*. Is the dwarf on the shoulders of the giant not always taller than the giant himself?

Now one sees immediately how deceptive the proof[205] of the divinity of language from its order and beauty turns out to be. Order and beauty are there. But when, how, and whence did they come? Is this so admired language the original language, then? Or not already the child of whole

---

[gg] De la Condamine.

[200] A. R. Mengs (1728–79), painter and author.
[201] C. W. E. Dietrich (1712–74), painter. B: *Dürer*.
[202] Klopstock, *Hermanns Schlacht* [*Hermann's Battle*], scene 12.
[203] The text is problematic here. It looks as though Herder initially wrote *über alles*, "over everything," meaning "through everything," "whatever the obstacles," but then paused in his writing and when he resumed misread himself as having meant it rather in the sense "about everything," "concerning every subject" – a sense which he then presupposed in the phrase translated here "and likewise over language as well."
[204] The phrase "to be and become" is an example of the rhetorical figure of hysteron proteron, or "later earlier."
[205] a footnotes here: Süßmilch, section 1.

centuries and many nations? Behold! Nations and regions of the world and ages have built at this great building. And because of it that poor hut could not have been the origin of the art of architecture? Because of it a god immediately had to teach human beings to build such a palace? Because human beings could not have built such a palace *straightaway*? What an inference! And what an inference it is in general to say: I do not completely understand this great bridge between two mountains, how it is built – consequently, the devil built it! It takes a high degree of daring or ignorance to deny that language formed itself progressively with the human species in all levels and changes. That is shown by history and poetry, oratory and grammar – and, if nothing else, reason. Did language, then, eternally form itself progressively in this way and never begin to form itself? Or did it always form itself humanly, so that reason could not function without it and it could not function without reason, and then suddenly its beginning is different? And moreover, different as sense-lessly and groundlessly as we showed at the beginning? In any case the hypothesis of a divine origin in language turns out to be – implicit, subtle nonsense!

I repeat the deliberately spoken hard word: *nonsense*! And I want, in con-clusion, to explain myself. What does a divine origin of language mean but either:[206] "I cannot explain language from human nature, consequently it is divine." – Does this inference make sense? The opponent says: "I can explain it from human nature, and fully so." Who has said more? The former hides behind a screen and calls forth "God is here!"; the latter stands visible on the stage, acts – "Behold! I am a human being!"

Or a higher origin says: "Because I cannot explain human language from human nature, no one at all can explain it – it is entirely inexplicable." – Does this inference follow? The opponent says: "No element of language in its beginning or in each of its steps of progress[207] is incomprehensible to me in terms of the human soul; indeed, the whole human soul becomes inexplicable to me if I do not posit language in it; the whole human species no longer remains the natural species [that it is] if it does not progressively form language." Who has said more? Who talks sense?

---

[206] The *ors* correlative with this *either* come in the next two paragraphs.

[207] The printed text, *in jeder ihrer Progreßion*, is just possible, taking *ihrer* as a feminine singular personal pronoun in the genitive, but it seems more likely that we should read *Progreßionen*. The resulting sense is almost the same either way, however.

Or finally, the higher hypothesis even says: "Not only can no one understand language in terms of the human soul, but I also see distinctly the reason why, according to its nature and the analogy of their species, it was completely uninventable for human beings. Indeed, I see distinctly in language and in the essence of the deity the reason why no one but God was able to invent it." – Now the inference would become logical, certainly; but it also now becomes the most horrible nonsense. It becomes as probative as that proof of the Turks for the divinity of the Koran: "Who other than the prophet of God could have written in this way?" And also who other than a prophet of God can know that only the prophet of God could have written in this way? No one except God could have invented language! But also no one except God can grasp that no one except God could have invented it! And what hand can be so bold as to measure against each other not only perhaps language and the human soul but also language and deity?

A higher origin has nothing speaking for it, not even the testimony of the Eastern text to which it appeals, for this text clearly gives language a human beginning through the naming of the animals. Human invention has everything speaking for it and nothing at all against it: *essence of the human soul* and *element of language*; *analogy of the human species* and *analogy of the advances of language – the great example of all peoples, times, and parts of the world*!

The higher origin, as pious as it may seem, is entirely irreligious; with each step it diminishes God through the lowest, most imperfect anthropomorphisms. The human origin shows God in the greatest light: *His work, a human soul, creating and continuing to create a language through itself because it is His work, a human soul.* The human soul builds for itself this *sense of reason* as a creator, as an image of His nature. The origin of language hence only becomes divine in a worthy manner insofar as it is human.

The higher origin is useless and extremely harmful. It destroys all efficacy of the human soul, explains nothing, and makes everything, all psychology and all sciences, inexplicable. For have human beings, then, with language received all the seeds of forms of knowledge from God? So *nothing* comes from the human soul? So the *beginning of every art, science*, and form of *knowledge* is always *unintelligible*? The human origin lets no step be taken without prospects, and the most fruitful explanations in all parts of philosophy, and in all types and genres of language. The author has supplied a few here and can supply a lot of them.

*

How happy he would be if with this treatise he were to displace a hypothesis that, considered from all sides, causes the human soul only fog and dishonor, and moreover has done so for too long! For just this reason he has transgressed the command of the Academy and *supplied no hypothesis*. For what would be the use of having one hypothesis outweigh or counterbalance the other? And how do people usually regard whatever has the form of a hypothesis but as a philosophical novel – *Rousseau's, Condillac's,* and others'? He preferred to work "at *collecting firm data from the human soul, human organization, the structure of all ancient and savage languages,* and *the whole household-economy of the human species,*" and at *proving* his thesis in the way that the firmest *philosophical truth* can be proved. He therefore believes that with his disobedience he has achieved the will of the Academy more than it could otherwise have been achieved.

Part III Philosophy of Mind

On Thomas Abbt's Writings (1768)
[selections concerning psychology]

A human soul is an individual in the realm of minds [*Geister*]:[1] it senses in accordance with an individual formation [*Bildung*], and thinks in accordance with the strength of its mental organs. Through education these have received a certain, either good or negative, direction of their own according to the situation of circumstances which formed or deformed in the case in question. So in this way our manner of thought gets formed, becomes a whole body in which the natural forces are, so to speak, the specific mass which the education of human beings shapes. After a certain number of years of formation a later learning is seldom able, as I believe, to cause a new creation, seldom able to transform shape and mass, but all the more recognizably can it take effect on the surface through manifold phenomena, lend and take and emphasize coating, vestment, and bearing and propriety. My long allegory has succeeded if it achieves the representation of the mind of a human being as an individual phenomenon, as a rarity which deserves to occupy our eyes. But it would be even better if, through this allegory, as through a magical spell, I were also able to open our eyes to see, to observe, minds like corporeal phenomena.

Our psychology is still not yet far beyond childhood when it continues on its way through inferences and conjectures merely in accordance with the most familiar element which all human souls have in common, without paying attention to the peculiarities of individual subjects with the precision which the natural scientist applies in dissecting the bodies of animals in order to steal into the inner workshop of nature. Monsters, congenital

[1] *Geist* could alternatively be, and in what follows sometimes is, translated "spirit."

167

deformities, rarities are for the natural scientist welcome, instructive, and useful; and so should be for the philosopher all extraordinary minds who flare up and disappear like comets. If our systematic philosophers in the theory of the mind are *Linnaeuses* who stubbornly stratify and classify, then there should be made to accompany them an unsystematic head who, like *Buffon*, stubbornly disrupts their classes and dissects individuals.

But here I must say: Which human being knows what is in the human being except it be the human mind in him? And even this only knows itself, as we know our face, intuitively but not distinctly. With a lively but confused consciousness of ourselves we proceed forth as though in a dream of which one piece and another occurs to us only as occasion allows, torn off, inadequate, without connection. We ourselves often pay no attention to our thoughts; but – as in Platonic recollection from the realm of minds[2] – we recognize ourselves at the moment when another person exhibits thoughts which seem taken from our own soul. We ourselves cannot fully answer the question of how our visage is shaped, but we will no doubt give a great start if an image of ourselves, a second I, were to confront us. Thus did *Socrates* find himself pinned down when the physiognomist read in his soul; but he shook his head when he saw what *Plato* claimed to find in him.[3] I pass over the whole *dark foundation* of our soul, in whose unfathomable depths unknown forces sleep like unborn kings, in which, as in an earthen realm covered with snow and ice, the germ molders for a springtime of paradisiacal thoughts, in which, as in dark ashes, the spark glows for great passions and drives. How there suddenly arises here the idea wherein I think to myself the image of the deity: He who summons the morning stars and the spirits [*Geister*] by their names, who knows the thought from afar before it is born – only He, the Creator, knows a soul created by Him!

If, then, our philosophers do not yet so frequently attempt this cognition of individual minds [*Geister*], another person has more opportunity and duty for this: the *historian*. And he who knows how to see, to sketch, to represent a human soul in its whole manner of thought has done more than that painter of the soul, *Parrhasius* or *Aristides*.[4] But on the other hand, you can be sure that I mean something different here from what our

---

[2] See the *Meno*, 81c ff., the famous slave-boy passage; also *Phaedo*, 73a ff.
[3] Cicero reports that the physiognomist Zopyros read vices in Socrates' facial traits which Socrates confirmed as his natural flaws but claimed to have suppressed through rational knowledge.
[4] Famous painters in the ancient world.

clever neighbors[5] call *character-sketches* and *portraits* – vignettes which have scarcely ever been drawn by truth but rather by artifice, which are sketched from the imagination and not according to nature, and which are painted out by a childish mind that often only aims to give itself pleasure by means of alternating shadow pictures on the wall and to overwhelm the viewer's eye by means of furious contrasts. It annoys me when I hear a recent German author[6] get called so bold, a pragmatic historian of our century, merely because he has stuck a few such French vignettes onto his dry and broken-backed skeleton, in quite the wrong place.

A *biographer*, if he wants to deserve this name, must above all know how to draw [*reißen*][7] the form of his hero from his visage, so to speak. And since, as was indicated previously, we do not even know ourselves from within, and we could therefore hardly become perfect biographers of ourselves even if we were all like *Montaigne*, it follows that the historian must all the more study his author *from without* in order to scout out his soul in *words and deeds*. In this way he sketches the image of the sun not from its shining visage but after its reflection in water.[8]

This is the great distinguishing mark that separates the biographers of ancient and modern times miles apart from each other: the former show us their subject in actions and deeds which, right down to the smallest nuances, betray his soul, whereas the modern biographers themselves depict for us his character, which is often a fiction of theirs and more often a fiction of their author's. I know very well the reasons why the ancients were better able than we to be biographers of the soul; but if I were to write a life, then I would either emulate them and, instead of talking myself, make deeds do the talking, or, if after all I fell short of them, I would readily write in preface to my work: "Some events from the life . . . as I know them, and his character as it appears to the form and weakness of my eyes."

What all is not required for a biographer who wants to set the true image of his author, neither beautified, nor distorted, nor unresembling, in its true place in the order of minds? As *Rousseau* knew the son of his imagination, the wonderful Emile, before his birth and in the marriage bed, likewise the biographer would have to have accompanied his friend

5 I.e. the French.　6 I.e. K. R. Hausen (1740–1805), German historian.
7 Herder is punning on two different senses of *reißen* in a way that is approximately reproduced by *to draw*.
8 Cf. *Phaedo*, 99d–e.

through all the scenes of his life, and to have become the intimate of his secrets; and yet he would have to be able constantly to observe him foreignly like a leisurely observer in order to follow every moment with attention. He would have to judge without bias like a judge of the dead; and yet – does it not almost require a small degree of love-struck enthusiasm to imprint one's subject sufficiently into one's imagination that one can afterwards sketch his image as though out of one's head? And if this image is supposed to be sketched out of one's head, how easy is it [not] then for saps to flow up from the heart's chamber to touch it up and paint it out? It gets minted in our mind, and behold! our own stamp makes its mark on it from below and interferes with the other's traits. I am citing a few absolute difficulties; the possible ones will already be felt by every person who has ever only so much as had the thought of writing a life.

I would perhaps have begun things too far back with my long, heavy preface if I were not taking precisely this strange path in order to say that much more distinctly how much I ought to supply and how little I can supply.

Abbt has *portrayed* himself, but only as an *author*; so I am considering only one side of his mind, the *scholarly* thinking, without undertaking to sketch his *human* thinking. I know that both sides explain each other, as in the case of coins obverse image and reverse image; I also feel as strongly as anyone the mighty traits of integrity, loyalty, and truth with which *Abbt* writes from his mind and from his heart – and I will make great use of these traits. But overall, I am not so much on the side of those people who want to look into the writings as a mirror of the heart and the human dispositions; I am modestly content to write about an author. – And this modesty will save me from many an embarrassment. I shall to be sure not put *Abbt* in the first rank of the meritorious just because he has written about merit;[9] for he himself shows us the great gulf that stands between the *thought* and the deed. I shall to be sure not put him among the heroes who have died a death for their fatherland just because he has praised death for one's fatherland;[10] for certainly a hero who writes before the battle about death for one's fatherland would not have written as *Abbt* did. But on the other hand, I will also be spared from having to scold him as a careless man and damn him to an *auto da fé* just because he wrote

[9] Herder is referring here to Abbt's essay, *Vom Verdienst* [*On Merit*] (1765).
[10] Herder is referring here to Abbt's essay, *Der Tod fürs Vaterland* [*Death for One's Fatherland*] (1761).

this popular pamphlet;[11] for what an immeasurable space may separate writing piously as a scholar and thinking piously as a human being; may this space be measured out by those people who want to cast *Abbt* into hell because he could write an *auto da fé* and to put themselves into heaven because they are able to write sermons.

Where, however, I need to present *Abbt* as a human being, I shall cast a passing glance at the account of his life.[12] I recommend it to my readers as an introduction and foundation for my essay, for just as I could not have written without it, likewise I also cannot be read without it. Moreover, it so reveals the masterful technique of a biographer precisely by virtue of the fact that it infers from *Abbt's* works to his mind and from his mind to his works, explains one in terms of the other, and knows how to set *Abbt* the *human being* and *friend* alongside *Abbt* the *author*. However, I repeat that my glances at this area will remain merely passing glances.

I limit myself still further: I draw the lines for my image merely according to the *reduced scale of his few, uncompleted* writings. To be sure, these are living offprints of their author's mind, since he put on no disguise, but they never exhaust his facial traits. If one has known one's author as a friend, heard him in real life as his pupil, then one studies him deeper in a little time than can ever happen in the dead reading of his writings. In the latter case I have only the contents list of his manner of thought, in the former case the chapter itself; and one knows how mightily those people stumble who have their learning merely from indexes and titles. Still less can these few, uncompleted writings be a measure of his mind. That honor remains peculiar to those who so jail their minds in their books – as that Spaniard shut up the lame devil in the bottle,[13] or Ariosto his hero's understanding in the flask from the moon[14] – that they had nothing left. These consequently have the pleasure of writing themselves out in a double sense, of outliving themselves in a double sense, and of bequeathing their whole mind to the world faithfully without any

---

[11] Herder is referring here to Abbt's satire against the intolerance of some Protestant clergy, *Erfreuliche Nachricht von einem hoffentlich als zu errichtenden protestantischen Inquisitionsgerichte, und dem inzwischen in Effigie zu haltenden erwünschten Evangelischen Lutherischen Auto da Fe* [*Happy Report of a Protestant Court of Inquisition Hopefully to be Set Up, and the Desired Evangelical Lutheran Auto da Fé which is to be Held in Effigy in the Meantime*] (1766).

[12] F. Nicolai, *Ehrengedächtniß Herrn Thomas Abbt* [*A Memorial to Herr Thomas Abbt*] (1767). Nicolai wrote this work at Herder's instigation.

[13] Allusion to A. Guevara (1480–1545), *El diablo cojuto* [*The Lame Devil*] (first published 1641).

[14] Allusion to Ariosto (1474–1533), *Orlando furioso* (1516), where the hero receives back his lost understanding out of a bottle brought from the moon.

withholding or deception. *Abbt* was not enough the professor to provide in this way for his pupils, and death was not slow enough to provide in this way for his biographer; his writings are a small fragment, a small but that much more valuable relic, of his mind. And if now I want to erect for *Abbt* a memorial statue out of these writings of his, how can I call it anything but a mutilated torso?

Most of all it is necessary to abstract from an author what belongs to *his time* or to the *past world*, and what he leaves over for *the world of posterity*. He bears the chains of his age, to which he offers his book as a gift; he stands in his century like a tree in the realm of earth into which it has driven its roots, from which it draws nourishing juices, with which it covers its originating members. The more he wants to do meritorious service to *his* world, the more he must accommodate himself to it, and penetrate into its manner of thought in order to mold it. Indeed, since he is himself formed in accordance with this taste, and the first form can never be entirely deconstructed, each great author *must* bear on himself the birthmarks of his time. You are a critical fool!, you who want to rob him of them; you are taking from him traits of his individuality, aspects of his beauty, scars of his merits.

But one can and should *take note* of them, for they are instructive, and *that* commentator on an author is for me the greatest who does not *modify* him to accord with his own century, but explains him in all the nuances of his time, and then complements him. Let the commentator not attempt to clean him of his dross; for even if there should remain no gold in this dross, still he who knows how to use it always loses much with it. Rather, let him just patiently undertake the chemical operation of dissolving everything into its components, so that we can see the manner of origination. I am not so interested in having someone know how to extract from the spirit [*Geist*] of an author his spirit in its turn,[15] and approach me with a signifying expression [saying] "Behold! I have obtained for you potable gold."[16] For far too much deception has taken place with

---

[15] Herder is here playing on two slightly different senses of *Geist*: on the one hand, simply *mind*, on the other hand, something more like *significant essence* (as in St. Paul's distinction between the letter and the spirit). So Herder is in effect referring to, and distancing himself from, a presumption to extract the *significant essence* of an author's *mind*.

[16] Herder is thinking here of selective popular editions published in the eighteenth century such as W. Dodd, *Beauties of Shakespeare* – the counterparts of modern horrors like "Bach's greatest hits."

this *spirit* and *potable gold*. Instead, the man I want is the *explainer* who defines the borders of an author's past world, own time, and world of posterity – what the first supplied to him, how the second helped or harmed him, how the third developed his work. A history of authors that was executed in accordance with this conception – what a work it would be! The foundation for a history of the sciences and of the human understanding. Even if we only had a single *Bacon* explained from ancient times, justified from his own, improved and complemented from ours in this way, then we would have a great aid that would advance us; and there could arise by it a second *Bacon*, as Alexander did by the grave of *Achilles*, and *Caesar* by the statue of *Alexander*. Would *Aristotle* in all probability ever have become so harmful if even only a single such glance had been cast at him? But if an author's birthmarks, which are for his time, survive this age and get anachronistically imitated, then I see standing before me the servant of *Alexander* who mimics his lord's crooked neck, which as far as I am concerned can suit his lord, or must, but looks pathetic on *him*. In this way what can be the honor of an author becomes a shame for us – and what could benefit us harms.

I have thus indicated some main lines of Abbt's character[17] – perhaps lines like those drawn by that Corinthian girl around the shadow of her sleeping lover, lines in which she thought she saw his image because her imagination filled up the outline, but an alien observer saw nothing. *Abbt was a philosopher of the human being, of the citizen, of the common man, not a scholar*; he was *educated* through *history*, and *among deeds*; in love with *Tacitus's* brevity, which, however, he mixed with *French expressions* and *British images*; educated for theology, from which he also retained some biblical language; and for the rest, not in favor of *strict systematic presentation*.

Now I should turn his image around, as Anacreon did to the image of his Bathyllus, and say, "Art is envious that it cannot express the best thing, his soul." I should, now that I have observed him from outside, reach into the inner mechanism that effected such great things – stop its motion with a strong hand, and dissect the wheels and springs that moved everything. Or, to bend to the tone of the *times*: I should practice

---

[17] This final excerpt follows the main body of Herder's account of Abbt (here omitted), and forms the conclusion of Herder's essay.

in *psychometrics*[18] and *take his measure* like a Prussian recruiter – a court to which poets and painters have had to suffer subjection after their death, and for which just recently our *Kleist* had to take off his shoes.[19] But since I have no skill in this art, and would not like to make Abbt more *lengthy* than *great*, as that *Hylas* represented *Agamemnon*,[20] I refer for this matter to his *Memorial*,[21] whose author knew him personally.

When I read Abbt's writings *into his soul*, how I see so many of its forces in motion! Sensuous *attentiveness* fixes itself on each point of the object, flies from side to side, and throws rays of light on each point; his idea becomes lively, cumulative, luminous, and his speech scintillates. The light is not sharp, not strict, but dispersed, ever coming in new waves. He becomes comprehensible through the *number* of his characterizing marks; he illuminates even if he did not *prove*; he casts light [on the matter] even if he did not *develop* [it]; he makes sure, certain, strong; even if he did not *convince* [*überzeugte*], he *persuades* [*überredet*] to the point of obviousness.[22] His whole book *On Merit* is a single great example here.

Often he speaks as though through an *inner sense* – as, for example, when he depicts the *greatness*,[a] *strength*,[b] and *goodness* of the heart as no one depicted them before him. He comes upon concepts which he *feels* deeply, thinks with effort, but expresses with difficulty. Since he sensed them as though through a divination [*Divination*] and beheld them as though in a vision, he consequently also goes on to express them like a messenger of secrets and resorts to images which often seem to us an *illusion* of the senses, but perhaps were not so for him. This side of Abbt's mind is for me the *holiest* and each discovery in it a disclosure in the science of the soul, despite the fact that our soulless critics charge Abbt with obscurity and lack of precision just because of it.

His *imagination* is rich, fecund, rhapsodic, and, in a noble way, unrestrained: not always an architect who erects well-structured buildings, but a witch who strikes on the ground and behold! suddenly we are in

[a] Pp. 44–51.   [b] Pp. 56–145.

[18] A discipline devoted to the mathematical measurement of mental processes, first proposed by the Rationalist philosopher Wolff.

[19] This is probably an allusion to F. Nicolai, *Ehrengedächtniß Herrn Ewald Christian von Kleist* [*A Memorial to Herr Ewald Christian von Kleist*] (1760).

[20] This story can be found in Macrobius, *Saturnalia*, bk. 2, ch. 7.

[21] I.e. Nicolai, *Ehrengedächtniß Herrn Thomas Abbt*.

[22] The distinction between *convincing* and *persuading* assumed here is drawn sharply in Kant's Logic lectures.

the midst of magnificent materials. She touches them and behold! they move themselves, rise up, combine, structure themselves, and, oh miracle!, there arises before our eyes, as though autonomously, or rather through an invisible force, a palace – magnificent, great, bewitching, only not in the manner of *Vitruvius's* or *Vincentius's* art.[23] We step nearer in order to learn whether it is a mere mirage for our eyes; we touch it, and behold!, it *is* real; we feel for solidity, it *stands*; finally, we dare to enter it, convince ourselves of its permanence, and make it our abode. It is rare that the *imagination* always remains a sister of *truth*, as is usually the case with Abbt. That is due to the fact that she everywhere mates with the *good, healthy understanding*, leaves to this the governance of the man, and becomes for him only a mother of fecundity and a stewardess of his wealth. Everywhere with Abbt we hear judgment, and his judgment is *fiery, sharp* and *correct, complete*.

Fiery: He has a strong sense of feeling for the *beautiful*, the *human* and *ethical*. Hence his aesthetic taste, his human and moral judgment, is founded on sensation, not on rules as with feelingless teachers of ethics or art. One sees that he judges with pleasure or displeasure, not in the insipid tone of indifference in which castrated word-merchants go on. The subjects that he considers soon become his intimates and native to his soul; he holds them close to his eyes and to his heart; he cannot see the beautiful without being *charmed*, or the good without being *moved*; each trait of his face, each motion of his hands, shows that in him a something speaks that is not made of cold earth or pure air but is related to flame and speaks as though to people who can be warmed. This is why his *aesthetic judgments* are full of good taste, as many examples in the *Literaturbriefe* show; his psychological investigations not without sensitivity, as is proved by the opening of his article on *greatness of mind*,[24] many remarks on *strength of soul*,[25] and especially his insertion on *Empfindnis* and *Empfindung*;[26] and in human situations it is his whole heart that speaks. It is very rare that this threefold feeling for the *beautiful*, for the *human*, and for the *good*

---

[23] Roman and Italian architects, respectively.

[24] A chapter of *Vom Verdienst* [*On Merit*] bears this title.

[25] A chapter of *Vom Verdienst* [*On Merit*] bears this title.

[26] Roughly, *sentiment* and *sensation*. Abbt explains the distinction as follows in *Vom Verdienst*, himself using these English equivalents: "*Empfindung* may serve for sensation and *Empfindnis* for sentiment . . . *Empfindung* relates a thing to us in a lively way but confusedly by means of the senses; *Empfindnis* relates it in a similar way by means of imagination. In the former case the thing occupies us as though present; in the latter case, even if it should be present, it is more its image that occupies us."

is combined, and where they are combined they inevitably produce that *enthusiasm* which *Nicolai* indeed observes in the case of our Abbt. If the mere feeling of *beauty* can raise the virtuoso, and the mere feeling for *humanity* and *virtue* the man of merit, to the point of rapture, then, where these three goddesses combine, rapture will be able to become a sort of enthusiasm even for truth, and just such a likable fanatic was Abbt.

I do not say that his feeling for all three kinds was equally strong. That is rare, or even half impossible – for when one kind becomes too strong, it weakens the others. His feeling for poets did not reach the point of poetry; his inclination for the fine arts did not reach the point of a main occupation; he stayed on the middle string of *human* sensation, whence he is generally wont to touch the strings of aesthetic taste and of moral feeling – as I have stolen after this course of his soul at various points with pleasure. Since his feeling is also more *forceful* than *delicate*, in these judgments it has often seemed to me as though there stood before my eyes that hero of Homer's who almost equalled *Jupiter* in wisdom: "as he with strong voice sends forth from his breast words that resemble drives of snowflakes."[27]

His judgment is *sharp* and *correct*, for it is formed by the healthy under-standing, which here reflects, compares, quickly summarizes, and speaks. It has not been dulled, hardened, and made stubbornly idiosyncratic among books, but only more whetted and corrected. It has not been initiated into being sensitive through the scholarly scents of a cattle shed – which shed was recommended to that French duchess as a cure and gets recommended to us as education – for, as *Petronius* says rightly of the degenerated scholarliness of his time, whoever has been brought up in the midst of such a thing can as little think cleverly as those who live in the kitchen can smell well; but since Abbt judges with *sensitivity* and strength like the common man, and with intelligence like a thinker, he is – unless a playful wit deceives his sharpness, and hasty imagination chases a sort of storm of images through his quiet reflection – a paragon.

Indeed, in the *completeness* of his spirit of judgment (I deliberately do not say: the *deepness*) still more so – since he, "as soon as he merely formed a wish to explore in this or that province of the realm of the sciences, went through it in rapid flight with incredible industry and gave proofs that it

---

[27] *Iliad*, bk. 3, ll. 221 ff. Here translated from Herder's German. The passage describes Odysseus, who is the Homeric hero to whom Herder is referring.

was already familiar to him, according to a general map so to speak!";^c since he did not bury himself beneath a pile of ancient ruins, or jail himself in a narrow structure of professional literature; and especially since his rich *memory* supplied him from *experience* and *history* with as much as was necessary in order to make his judgment *complete*.

When I dissect Abbt's mind in his writings in such a way as this, then I first of all come to the thought, "How much a human soul contains!" and then after I have jumped across a great gulf I sigh, "How much we have lost with Abbt!"

> Claudite iam Parcae nimium reserata sepulcra
> Claudite plus iusto iam domus ista patet.[28] – *Ovid*

---

^c See Miller's preface [to Abbt, *Fragment der ältesten Begebenheiten des menschlichen Geschlechts* (1767)].

[28] Close now, ye Fates, these too gaping tombs, / Close them, this house has now lain open too long.

[Handwritten notes at top of page:]

P 178 – P 186

• Herder rejects the idea of 2 faculties of the mind that are completely different. Herder - all sensations are conceptualized and all concepts are based on sense experience - they're both connected

• Descartes - distinction between mind + matter (how is the mind related to the body?). ↳ pineal gland... [extended in space →]

• Spinoza - complements. mind + body 2 aspects of the same thing (substance)

• Leibniz - what's happened, has already happened... mind + matter in sync

On Cognition and Sensation, the Two Main Forces of the Human Soul (1775) [preface][1]

Est Deus in nobis, agitante calescimus illo.[2] – *Virgil*

[Handwritten margin notes: c + s intertwined can't have one w/o the other; attempted to unity in all sciences]

Cognition and *sensation* are with us mixed creatures intertwined; we have cognition only through sensation, our sensation is always accompanied with a sort of cognition. Since philosophy abandoned the fragmenting, useless cleverness of the scholastics and attempted to find unity in all sciences, in the science of the soul too it has made great advances on this royal path. Since philosophy found common characteristic marks in thought and sensation; because the nature of the one could not be fully illuminated without the properties of the other; most of all, because [philosophy] the thinker was at heart a friend to and related to thinking, [philosophy] the seer to seeing, it inevitably proved comfortable for philosophy to posit a single force of the soul, *thought*, and to want to derive from it simply everything right down to the obscurest, most arbitrary sensation.

---

[1] This is a short excerpt from Herder's 1775 draft of the essay *On the Cognition and Sensation of the Human Soul* published in 1778 and fully translated next in this volume. The excerpt consists of the preface, a statement by Herder of the Berlin Academy's prize essay task, and the first paragraph or so of the first section of the essay – all material that was dropped from the published version of 1778 but is of great interest and significance, especially for its critical discussion of the Rationalist theory of the mind and explanation of the relation in which Herder's own theory stands to it. At the point where this excerpt from the 1775 draft stops, the 1775 draft continues with a version of the material with which the published version of 1778 begins (from "In everything . . ." in the translation that follows). However, the two drafts contain significant differences beyond the 1775 draft's inclusion of and the 1778 version's exclusion of the introductory materials translated here. Some of the most important of these differences, especially passages in which the 1775 draft develops a more consistently and elaborately *physiological* theory of the mind than is found in the version of 1778, are indicated in footnotes to the translation of the 1778 version which follows. However, the 1775 draft would certainly repay more attention than can be given to it in this volume.

[2] God is within us, when he stirs us we are inflamed.

"No cognition," philosophy says, "is without sensation, i.e. without some feeling of good or bad, of pleasure or pain, of being or nonbeing, in oneself or in the object. If the soul feels that it cognizes, then it enjoys itself, strives forth, develops its forces; the less impeded, the more lively. That is why a person is irritated by *curiosity*, i.e. the drive of *wanting* to know.

Assume that the soul does not cognize. Cognition is its essence. Hence it has lost its existence, its enjoyment with it; there is darkness, death here, paralysis.

Assume that the soul considers a nothing as something. It can do so only as long as the deception that presents to it nothing as something endures. But even in the nothing it sought only *something*, application of its positive force on a given world-facet of the Creator. If it came to its senses, i.e. if it arrived at the application of this force, then it penetrated into the object, cognized, distinguished, illuminated; the delusion has disappeared, the soul no longer sees a cloud of fog but stars.

Assume," it is inferred finally, "that the soul cognizes, advances, but ungently, without any commensurateness between what it is supposed to grasp and its grasping forces – then how bitter the work turns out to be for it; it thirsts, like a tired hiker, until it sinks down where it can no longer break through, at the place of the greatest strain, or if it still has forces goes back. It has lost its desire for cognition with this object, it goes another path. Behold, thus is *cognition never without sensation*. The word *curiosity* [Neugierde],[3] *yearning* for cognitions, says it; *experience*, the nature of things, which always posits sensation for a drive and rewards the drive with enjoyment, confirms it. Is the whole mountain of our cognition supposed to be accumulated without feeling? Is the most godlike force of our soul supposed to build with less reward than a bee, and to fly to the goal of cognition like a shot arrow, like a ray of light, quickly and also just as without feeling? No! In cognition there lives sensation, the deepest, most spiritual, godlike sensation! Error and ignorance are night and fog; truth is brightness and sun, bound up with the feeling 'This is the right place to be!' like on the mountain of transfiguration. The quickest judgment of the soul is affirmation or denial, i.e. in cruder terms, only expression of good or bad, of harmony or discord, of pain or pleasure.

[3] Note that *Gier* = eagerness, greed.

On the other side," ordering metaphysics continues, "no sensation can be imagined entirely without *cognition*, i.e. without an obscure representation of perfection or of unsuitability. Once again, even the word *sensation* [*Empfindung*][4] says it. Is one not in sensation *occupied* with oneself and one's condition along with the object that becomes one with it? Does one not therefore *cognize* one's condition and the influencing object at least obscurely? Does one not feel decrease or increase, rising or falling, in the enjoyment of perfection, continuation or destruction? Even the plant if it has sensation must have sensation *in this way*; it must slumber as though in the deepest dream of self-cognition with an intuition of what is influencing this self. Even the stone, if it fell through an inner drive, would have to cognize, i.e. to feel, its drive towards the mid-point in the obscurest way.

If, in addition, a sensation should awaken activity, should abbreviate or lengthen the conditions, what a force, what a plan in cognition – albeit in the most obscure cognition – does not precisely thereby lie at the basis! Hence in sensation lies hidden great, deep, effective cognition, receiving motion from the highest angel of the worlds down to – if it feels – the falling stone."

Thus does metaphysics order – truly a sunny plan full of manifoldness and unity! First and last is thinking nature, inner intuition of perfection, and stretching of our forces to come closer to this perfection, to turn it more and more into our selves. Metaphysics reveals the unity in everything splendidly, but does it also reveal as distinguishingly the eachness in each thing? The harmony of our forces splendidly, but also as thoroughly their disharmonies, contradictions, and shortcomings?

In all the forces of our soul there is activity, representation, perception; but can representation and (as we often impute it) clear, even distinct, representation explain, measure, fathom, each of our activities? If every cognition is sensation, what then in that case does that clear, luminous, encompassing cognition lack so that it is not and does not become sensation? Not every sensation is at the command of thought, so what does this sensation lack so that it does not mate with thought and produce with it common fruit? What I cognize so luminously as good, I do not as often love so as also to cognize it truly, i.e. actively, as good, to sense, live, and

---

[4] Note that *finden* = to find, to consider.

act in it. What I sense, want, and do is as deeply buried in my heart and viscera, as far from my thought, as the heart is remote from the head. It gets formed in the obscure center of my being; when the pondering thought digs down that far and illuminates it with its torch, then it is no longer what it was. There seems to be such an immeasurable gulf fixed between thought and sensation that neither of them often gets over to the other – the cold thought luminous but cold like the northern lights; sensation shot through with pondering no longer sensation but thought. Two modes of our existence that seem to be hemispheres and antipodes, that only touch a common earth with their feet; two poles one of which attracts what the other repels.

Natural science was unable to arrive at forces as long as people failed to regard each individual thing as what it is, as unique, as long as they always only imputed to it what it could be or should be in general. The science of the soul must become entirely natural science in regard to each individual force, as though there was no other force but it. There is always time to classify, to unite, when we have first cognized individually; but we will never cognize what something is if we only begin by measuring it according to what it is *not*, i.e. if we only grasp it as a deviation, negatively. Do not the lovers of the science of the soul themselves say that the field of the higher, the thinking, forces is much more cultivated than the broad region of sensations, drives, affects, of action? And are these not the heart of our being? Are these not what everything rests on, what everything proceeds from, what the soul feels deeply bound up with, even in its most abstract functions? Hence if they get disregarded or treated with a foreign spirit, with the spirit of the higher forces, as speculation, then what stirring will stand before us as it is? A garden full of the most diverse plants, flowers, and fruits, the human soul which senses a thousandfold and a thousandfold differently becomes on top the dew of a universal vapor cloud; it gets called *body, obscure ideas, feelings.*

May I give a few examples of the shortcomings of the aforementioned one-sidedness? Since *Descartes* made thinking into his entire doubting I, what systems have arisen, each one more unnatural than the other. He hung up the soul in the pineal gland and made it think; but how then move the body? It cannot, even if it had to be a matter of the purest mechanism; it has for that neither force nor location nor leisure. It consequently got proved, in accordance with its thinking nature, that it could not do this. What then? God had to come and move the body; thinking madam soul[5] on her restful carpet only indicates to her slave the occasion. Thus Descartes. Spinoza, a more penetrating mind, the theologian of Cartesianism, brought both to the point whither Descartes brought [only] one; why should not thought be as much an immediate effect and property of God as motion? All individuals were therefore extinguished for the thinking like the moving God. Both are properties of a single being which Spinoza forgot or despaired of bringing closer together since he had pushed them so far away from himself. He had deceived himself so high up into the empyrean of infinity that all individualities faded deep beneath his eye; this is his atheism and truly no other. Leibniz came, feared the abyss, but stood on Descartes' bank. It remained [for him] that the soul cannot move the body, and God not in every moment either; but what if the body moved itself, if its Creator had taken care of that from the beginning, although no human being could say how? Just as long as the body always comes right away for thinking madam soul. And thus there arose from this the beautiful system of preestablished harmony with its splendid simile of the two clocks – the cleverest system and the most fitting simile that was ever thought up.

What a dead, wooden clock the soul and the science of the soul has now become. In all the mutual perceptions of thought and sensation it lacks deep derivation, fruitfulness, and truth.

The soul with all its forces feels itself *living* in its diverse, thousandfold organized body; even its forces of cognition and volition are only results, aggregates, of this connection; it is only *present* in the universe through action and reaction on this body full of sensations, full of irritations; it otherwise lacks even self-consciousness. Will I, therefore, ever be able to feel apart and together, i.e. to explain, the harmony of our being, the mutually attuned and yet so diverse concert of our thoughts and sensations, in its whole art, with its wonderful contrasts and counterpoints, weakenings and strengthenings, if I lack immediate insight into the influence? Two machines attuned in the most artificial way so that for eternity they should not touch each other! – The science of the soul has been robbed of all spirit of immediate observation, all guidance by the most secret,

---

[5] The word "soul," *Seele*, is feminine in German.

science + soul = 2 different things

what's the influence? – God

soul living in body even though cognitions are results of the connection between the soul + the body. this is explained thru actions/reactions of the body, which are based on sensations

miraculous, deep experience. If my soul is supposed to unfold from out of itself what it does not have from out of itself at all, then things turn into a tower up to the clouds without basis, an eternal petitio principii. If I fail to recognize the bond between cause and effect where I feel it through marrow and bone at every moment, where will I perceive it in its invisible, spiritual, heavenly nature when it does not lie nearly as close to my rogue's eye, my doubting deceptive senses? Finally, if it may for certain heads be all the same to take apart a clock or to unfold and educate a living, fruitful seed, for every living, sensing being it should not be all the same. It is a thousandfold deeper joy to see how the beautiful flower of thought sprouts from sensation and produces new sensation than to gape at a dead marionette-play that the great dramatist played from the beginning of the creation.

The cold, sensationlessly thinking science of the soul has perpetrated its deception as far as into life and action. What romantic systems of freedom and perfection of the human soul, which occur where else but in textbooks! The force of thinking, of acting according to an ideal of perfection, is the essence of the soul; sensations and drives, in accordance with which it in fact acts, have been considered only as additions, even as disorders in accordance with which it should not act. Thus there arose a hypocritical figment of the imagination which the metaphysician calls the human soul, clothes in the gloomy rays of his abstractions, but which only appears in the presence of his magical lamp. The human being of healthy senses, the poet, the historian, the politician, the philosopher of life do not know it and have never seen it, and therefore often hate all psychology (very unjustly!) for representing to us a vaporous skeleton as a true, whole, living human being. Hence the great enmity between metaphysics and experience, between the abstract and the concrete, between thought and sensation. Hence the great illusion with which all abstractionists consider the living human being, and themselves act as shades of living human beings. Toss around general words and formulas in the midst of which all forceful distinctions and individual beings disappear; bind contradictions with general words and daub over with loose whitewash. Know so much about the human soul in general that they know nothing about each individual human soul and no longer have any vision for seeing it as what it is. How does this leave the idea that the science of the soul should be the mirror of human nature, the universal key to the education of human souls, and philosopher of the truly wise, their friend and educator? Each note would have to find its distinguished sound and proper place itself, the contradictions would have to become only differences and regularities, and there would have to be in heaven and earth, in the high region of thought and in the low but fruitful area of sensation, no phenomenon that did not belong to a single universe ...[6]

Behold a task, like the human soul, great and broad and deep. It alerts us to distinctions which were formerly disregarded beneath general formulas; it wants to see illuminated laws, relationships, and characters which make the human soul count as part of the universe and are themselves a certain universe; it dares to confront the great quarrel according to which the human being is without and within himself animal and angel, plant and god.

The angel in the human being – how does he condescend to the animal? The human plant – how does God bloom in it?

Contradictions in the human being, heart and mind!, which laws do you serve? How are you to be cognized, to be reconciled, to be used? What nourishes and strengthens your divergence? Is it a work of nature or a work of art and of corruption?

Contradictions in the human being, apparent enemies, to what extent do you mutually support each other?, where do you eliminate each other? How do you relate to the happiness of each human being and of all human beings? You great string-play of all manners of thought and sensation, human nature, who tuned you? Who strung you? Who plays on you? Who listens to you?

> Sie war die Laute seiner Hand
> die er zu unsrer Lust erfand
> er gab ihr Millionen Saiten
> und jede klingt und jeder Klang
> tönt zum harmonischen Gesang
> zur Lehre seiner Heimlichkeiten![7]

[6] There is a subtle shift in this sentence from the presentation of an objection to according the current science of the soul the exalted status described in the preceding sentence ("Each note would ... ") to an indication of ways in which the discipline would have to be improved in order to deserve that status ("the contradictions would ... and there would have to be ... ").

[7] It was the lute of His hand / which He invented for our pleasure, / He gave it millions of strings / and each one sounds, and each sound / rings to a harmonious song, / to the teaching of His secrets! (J. P. L. Withof, 1725–89).

Task[8]

The soul possesses two original abilities (the foundation of all its properties and efficacies): the ability to cognize and the ability to sense.

   If it exercises the first, it is occupied with an object which it considers
as a thing outside itself in which it has curiosity; in this case its entire
efficacy seems to be only to see well. If it exercises the other, it is occupied
with itself and its condition,[9] and feels well or ill. Its efficacy in this case
seems to be solely to want to change the condition if it feels discomfort,
or to enjoy the condition if it feels well. Assuming this, we wish:

1. An exact development of the original determinations of both abilities
   and of the universal laws which they follow.
2. A thorough investigation of the reciprocal dependence of both faculties
   on each other and of the manner of their influence on each other.
3. Basic principles which make clear how the genius and the character
   of a human being depends on the degree, strength, and liveliness [of
   the one or the other of these abilities],[10] and on the steps of progress
   that the one or the other of these abilities has achieved, and on the
   proportion that holds between them both.

   In regard to the first question, the Academy wishes to see illuminated
the conditions under which a representation only affects the faculty of
sensation, and on the other hand to what order those representations
belong which only rouse curiosity and occupy the faculty of cognition. In
both cases it will be perceived that these conditions depend partly on the
representation or on the object itself, partly on the condition of the soul
at the time when the representation affects it.

   Concerning the second question, the Academy wishes a luminous, satisfying explanation of the psychological observation that the heart so often
apes the mind, and of the further phenomenon that certain speculative
heads[11] sense only weakly.

---

[8] This section simply contains Herder's translation into German of the Berlin Academy's prize
essay task and elucidatory remarks about this task, which were originally in French. The English
translation is done from Herder's German.

[9] Reading *Zustande* for *Gegenstande* ("object"). The French said *son état*: its condition.

[10] The French actually said here *du degré de force et de vivacité* ...: on the degree of strength and
liveliness ...

[11] I.e. minds, people.

In the case of the third question it is a matter of the requisite conditions for a human being having a greater aptitude for exercising the forces of cognition than the faculty of sensation or vice versa.

First section

Development of the original determinations of the two abilities of the human soul, of the faculties of cognition and sensation, together with the universal laws that they follow.

> Qui vers la verité sent son ame élancée
> Animal par les sens est Dieu par la pensée. – *Poésie diverse*[12]

1. *Development of the original determinations of the faculty of sensation in the human soul, together with the universal laws that it follows.*

We possess concerning the two faculties of the soul which are named in the task the development by a philosopher for whom the science of the soul has long been the field of his victory.[a] He has opened for us the temple of cognition with its hundred doorways of sensations that lead to it, partly in individual treatments, partly in the great work concerning the fine arts and sciences whose title should be "Ozymandias's Monument."[13] I could set his treatise here as the foundation and goal of my work were it not that the lover prefers to evade the eye of his beloved in order to encounter it more fully, and that the bold steersman has to turn his back to the bank towards which he is steering.

[At this point the 1775 draft continues with a version of the material in the published version of 1778 that follows below, beginning at "In everything . . . "]

---

[a] *Sulzer,* Über den verschiedenen Zustand, darin sich die Seele bei Ausübung ihrer Hauptvermögen befindet [*On the Different Conditions in which the Soul Finds Itself in the Exercise of its Main Faculties*] – see Histoire de l'Académie Royale des Sciences, vol. 19, Berlin 1770, pp. 407–20. *Sulzer's* Vermischte philosophische Schriften, Leipzig 1773, part 7. [Two facts about Sulzer are worth noting in this connection: (1) He was transparently the author of the Berlin Academy's task – so Herder is indulging in some bootlicking here. (2) Contrary to Rationalism, and also to Herder's own deepest philosophical convictions, Sulzer believed in a sharp separation of mental faculties, in particular the faculties of representation and sensation.]

[12] Whoever feels his soul thrust towards truth/[Though] an animal by his senses is a god by his thought (*Miscellaneous Poetry*).

[13] This refers to Sulzer, *Allgemeine Theorie der schönen Künste* [*General Theory of the Fine Arts*] (1771–8).

On the Cognition and Sensation of the Human Soul (1778)

Observations and dreams

To pneuma hopou thelei pnei kai tên phônên autou akoueis, all' ouk oidas pothen erchetai kai pou hupagei.[1]

First essay
On cognition and sensation in their human origin and the laws of their efficacy

In everything that we call dead nature we know no inner condition. We daily express the words *mass, impact, fall, motion, rest, force*, even *force* of *inertia*, and who knows what they mean within the thing itself?

But the more we thoughtfully observe the great drama of effective forces in nature, the less we can avoid everywhere feeling *similarity with ourselves*, enlivening everything with our sensation. We speak of efficacy and rest, of own or received, of remaining or communicating, dead or living, force, completely from the case of our souls. *Mass* seems to us a yearning for the mid-point, for the goal and place of rest; *inertia* the little partial rest on a thing's own mid-point through its connection with itself; *motion* a foreign drive, a communicated and onwardly effective striving which overcomes rest, disturbs the rest of foreign things, until it finds its own rest again. What a wonderful phenomenon *elasticity* is – already a sort of automaton, which can indeed not give itself motion, but can restore motion to itself; the first apparent spark towards activity in noble natures. That Greek

---

[1] John 3:8: "The wind blows where it wishes, and you hear its voice; but you do not know whence it comes or whither it goes."

wise man[2] who had an intimation of Newton's system in a dream spoke of bodies' *love* and *hate*; the great magnetism in nature which attracts and repels has long been considered as *soul of the world*. Likewise *warmth* and *coldness*, and the finest, noblest warmth, *electrical current*, this strange phenomenon of the great, all-present spirit of life. Likewise the great secret of the *progressive formation, renewal, refinement* of all beings, this abyss of hate and love, attraction and transformation into and from self. – The sensing human being feels his way into everything, feels everything from out of himself, and imprints it with his image, his impress. Hence *Newton* in his system of the world became a poet contrary to his wishes, as did *Buffon* in his cosmogony, and *Leibniz* in his preestablished harmony and doctrine of monads. Just as our whole psychology consists of figurative terms, for the most part it was *a single* new image, *a single* analogy, *a single* striking metaphor that gave birth to the greatest and boldest theories. The philosophers who declaim against figurative language and themselves serve nothing but old, often uncomprehended, figurative idols are at least in great contradiction with themselves. They do not want new gold to be minted, while on the other hand they do nothing but ever and ever spin the same threads out of precisely such, often much worse, gold.

But how so? Is there in this "*analogy to the human being*" also truth? Human truth, certainly, and as long as I am a human being I have no information about any higher. I am very little concerned about the superterrestrial abstraction which places itself beyond everything that is called "*circle of our thinking and sensing*" onto I know not what throne of divinity, creates there worlds of words, and passes judgment on everything possible and actual. What we know we know only through analogy, from the creation to us and from us to the Creator. So if I should not trust Him who put me into this circle of sensations and similarity, who gave me no other key for penetrating into the inside of things than my own impress or rather the reflected image of His mind in my mind, then whom should I trust and believe? Syllogisms cannot teach me anything where it is a matter of the *first conception* of the truth, which truth syllogisms naturally only develop after it has been conceived; hence the talk of verbal definitions and proofs is for the most part only a board game which rests on assumed rules and hypotheses. The quiet similarity which I sense and intuit in the whole of my creation, my soul, and my life; the great spirit

[2] I.e. Empedocles.

[*Geist*] that breathes upon me and shows me a single course, a single sort of laws, in what is small and what is large, in the visible world and the invisible world – this is my seal of truth. [It were] fortunate if this work had that seal on it as well, and quiet, modest readers (since I do not write for others) sensed just the same *analogy*, the feeling of the One who rules in all manifoldness! I am not ashamed to suck at the breasts of this great mother nature as a mere child, I run after images, after similarities, after laws of harmony into One, because I know no other play of my thinking forces (if indeed one must think), and moreover believe that *Homer* and *Sophocles*, *Dante*, *Shakespeare* and *Klopstock* have supplied psychology and knowledge of humankind with more material than even the *Aristotles* and *Leibnizes* of all peoples and times.

1. Of Irritation [Reiz]

We probably cannot accompany sensation in its origination further down than to the strange phenomenon that *Haller* has called 'irritation.'[3] The irritated little fiber contracts and expands again – perhaps a stamen, the first little glimmering spark, towards sensation, to which dead matter has purified itself up through many courses and levels of mechanism and organization. – As small and obscure as this beginning of the noble capacity that we call sensing may seem, it must be equally important – so much gets achieved through it. Without seeds there is no harvest, no plant without delicate roots and filaments, and perhaps without this sowing of obscure stirrings and irritations our most divine forces would not exist.

Already in animal nature, what burdens are loaded on the force and efficacy of a muscle! How much more these tiny, thin fibers pull than crude strings would do according to the laws of mechanism! Whence, then, this so much greater force unless perhaps precisely through mainsprings of inner *irritation*? Nature has woven together a thousand little, living strings into a thousandfold fight, into such a manifold touching and resisting; they make themselves shorter and longer with inner force, participate in the play of the muscle, each in its own way – that is what makes the muscle carry and pull. Has anything more wonderful ever been seen than a beating heart with its inexhaustible irritation? An abyss of inner, obscure forces, the true image of the organic almighty which is perhaps deeper

---

[3] A. von Haller (1708–77), Swiss scientist and poet, author of *Elementa physiologiae corporis humani* (1766).

than the motion of the suns and earths. – And now irritation spreads out from this inexhaustible fount and abyss through our whole I, enlivens each little playing fiber – all according to a single-formed, simple law. If we are in good health, our chest is broad, the heart beats healthily, each fiber performs its official role in the play. Then *fright* storms upon us, and behold, as our first movement, without yet any thought of fear or resistance, our irritable I retreats to its mid-point, our blood to our heart, our fiber, even our hair, stands on end – so to speak, an organic messenger for defense, the guard stands ready. *Anger* in its first attack, an army of war stirring itself for resistance, how it shakes the heart, drives the blood to the extremities, to the cheeks, into the arteries, flame into the eyes –

> meneos de mega phrenes amphimelainai
> Pimplant', osse de hoi puri lampetoônti eiktên.[4]

The hands strive, are more powerful and stronger. Courage elevates the chest, life-breath the breathing nose, the creature knows no danger. Pure phenomena of the *stirring up* of our irritations in fright, of the violent *impulse forth* in anger. By contrast, *love*, how it softens and calms! The heart wells up, but not to destroy, fire flows, but only in order to well over towards [its object] and blow out its soft glow. The creature seeks *unification, dissolution, melting-away*; the structure of its fibers expands, is as though embracing another, and only returns when the creature welling towards [another] again feels itself alone, a separated, isolated One. Hence still in the most complexly woven sensations and passions of our so composite machine the *single* law which stirred the little fiber with its little glimmering spark of irritation makes itself visible, namely: *Pain*, the touching of something foreign, *contracts*; here force concentrates, increases for resistance, and restores itself. Wellbeing and loving warmth *expands*, causes rest, gentle enjoyment, and dissolution. What in dead nature expansion and contraction, warmth and coldness, are – that do these obscure stamens of irritation towards sensation seem to be here: an ebb and flow in which, like the universe, similarly the whole sensing nature of human beings, animals, and however much further down it may extend, moves and stirs.

As to everything, there belongs to this too *modulation, measure*, gentle *mixing*, and *progress*. Fear and joy, fright and anger – what strikes suddenly like a thunderbolt can also kill like a thunderbolt. The fiber that (to speak

[4] *Iliad*, bk. 1, ll. 103–4: "And his wits, black all about, filled mightily with anger, and his two eyes resembled blazing fire."

mechanically) expanded cannot come back; the one that contracted cannot lengthen itself again; a death blow put a stop to their play. Every affect that strikes, even gentle shame, can suddenly kill.

Gentle sensations are, to be sure, not so violent, but uninterrupted they destroy likewise. They wear out, make dull and forceless. How many sybarites have, among tickles and rose scents, passed away with a living body, and certainly by no gentle death.

If we are entirely without irritation – a cruel illness; it is called desert, boredom, monastery. The fiber so to speak consumes itself, rust eats the idle sword. Thence that checked *hate* which cannot become *anger*; the miserable *envy* which cannot become *act*; *regret, sadness, despair* which neither undo nor improve – cruel serpents which gnaw at the human being's heart. Silent fury, disgust, vexation with impotence is the hell's wolf that eats at itself.

The human being is created for receiving and giving, for efficacy and joy, for acting and undergoing. In health his body draws in and exudes, receives easily and proves easy for him to give; nature does him gentle violence, and he nature. In this attraction and expansion, activity and rest, lies health and happiness in life.

I am interested in the prize question, "What sort of effects does inhaling actually produce in the living body?" For my purpose I consider it here just evenly as the harmonious rhythm with which nature planned to move our machine and breathe life-spirit into it. Thus our machine is in perpetual effort and recuperation, right down to the subtlest instruments of sensations and thoughts; everything works, like those stones, to the lyre of Amphion.[5] Through inhaling, the child, which had been a plant, becomes an animal. In the case of a sick person, in the case of a groaning person, how inhaling gives courage, whereas each sigh so to speak breathes away forces. "Praise be to the Almighty," says the Persian poet *Sadi*, "for each life-breath. A breath that one draws into oneself strengthens, a breath that one releases from oneself gives joy to life; in each breathing there are two sorts of mercies." – Just as each artery beats, just as it is only through contraction that the heart receives force to propel forth in its expansion the life-stream, likewise too the air's breath must come from outside to invigorate and enliven the heart in modulations. Everything seems ordered according to one sort of laws. – But I would never finish pursuing

---

[5] According to legend, Amphion, in founding Thebes, made the stones move by playing his lyre.

this great phenomenon of efficacy and rest, contraction and expansion, through all its ways; let us hurry further.

*

A mechanical or supermechanical play of expansion and contraction means little or nothing if its cause from within and without were not already presupposed: *"irritation, life."* The Creator must have linked a spiritual bond that certain things are similar to this sensing part, and others contrary to it – a bond which depends on no mechanism, which cannot be further explained, but must be *believed* because it *exists*, because it *reveals* itself in a hundred thousand phenomena. Observe that plant, that beautiful structure of organic fibers! How it twists, how it turns, its leaves to drink the dew that refreshes it! It lowers and revolves its root until it stands. Each bush, each little tree inclines towards fresh air as much as it can. The flower opens to the arrival of her bridegroom, the sun. How some roots flee their enemy beneath the earth, how they spy out and seek space and nourishment for themselves! With what wonderful diligence a plant purifies alien juice into parts of its more subtle self, grows, loves, gives and receives seeds on the wings of the zephyr, produces living off-prints of itself, leaves, germs, blooms, fruits. Meanwhile, it ages, gradually loses its irritations for receiving and its force for giving anew, dies. A true miracle of the power of life and of life's efficacy in an organic plant body.

If we were to see through the infinitely subtler and more complexly woven animal body, would we not likewise find each fiber, each muscle, each irritable part in the same function and in the same force, of seeking life-juice in its own way? Blood and chyle – do they not get stolen by all strands and glands? Each seeks what it needs, certainly not without a corresponding inner satisfaction. Hunger and thirst in the whole machine of an animal body – what mighty spurs and drives! And why are they so powerful but because they are an aggregate of all the obscure wishes, the longing yearning, with which each little thicket of life in our body thirsts for satisfaction and its own preservation. It is the voice of a sea of waves whose sounds get lost in each other more obscurely or more loudly, a flower garden thirsting for juice and life.[6] Each flower wants to do its work, to

---

[6] The images of a "sea of waves" and a "flower garden" are borrowed from Leibniz, who had used them for, respectively, the individually subconscious but collectively conscious "petites perceptions [little perceptions]" (in the *New Essays on Human Understanding*) and the fullness with life of even the smallest piece of matter (in the *Monadology*). Herder is about to turn to a criticism of Leibniz's theory of preestablished harmony.

receive, to enjoy, to purify forth, to give. The plant consumes water and earth and purifies them up into parts of itself; the animal makes less noble plants into nobler animal-juice; the human being transforms plants and animals into organic parts of his life, introduces them into the processing of higher, subtler irritations. Thus does everything purify itself up; higher life must *come to be* from inferior life through sacrifice and destruction.

Finally, the deepest irritation, as it is the mightiest hunger and thirst: *love!* That two beings mate, feel themselves one in their need and yearning, that their shared stirring, the whole fount of organic forces, is reciprocally one and becomes a third in their shared image – what an effect of irritation in the whole living I of animal beings! Animals have still been able to mate without a head, just as a torn-out heart still beats on irritably for a long time. The deep abyss of all organic irritations and forces seems to be in reciprocal overflow; the spark of creation kindles and there comes into being a new I, the mainspring of new sensations and irritations, a third heart beats.

*

People have had such strangely mechanical dreams "about the origin of human souls" as though they were truly made from clay and dirt. They lay formed in the moon, in limbo, and waited, doubtless naked and cold, for their preestablished sheaths, or clocks, or clothes, the not-yet-formed bodies; now the housing, garment, clock is ready and the poor, so-long-idle inhabitant gets added to it mechanically, that he may – by the body [*bei Leibe*]!,[7] not affect it, but only in preestablished harmony with it spin thoughts out of himself, just as he spun them there in limbo too, and that it, the clock of the body, may strike in agreement with him. There is probably nothing to be said about the unnatural poverty of this system; but what was able to give rise to it is difficult for me to imagine. If a force exists in nature which merely through organic irritation forms from two bodies a third which has the whole spiritual nature of its parents, as we see happen with each flower and plant; if a force exists in nature so that two irritable fibers, woven together in a certain way, produce an irritation which was unable to arise from a single one of them and is now of a new sort, as, it seems to me, every sense, indeed every muscle, shows us analogically;

---

7 Herder is making a sort of pun here which cannot be well preserved in English: *bei Leibe!* is an idiomatic exclamation commonly used to emphasize a negation, and roughly equivalent to the English "by Jove!" or some such, but taken more literally it can also mean "with a body."

finally, if a force exists to produce from two bodies which seem to us dead, from the mixing of two elements, if nature does it, a third body which is similar to the preceding ones but is a new thing and if dissolved into them by art loses all its force – if all this, however unintelligible it may be, *exists* and cannot be denied, then who is there who would suddenly here cut off the course of analogy, the great course of creation, with his pocket knife and say that the revealed deep abyss of the irritation of two through-and-through organic, living beings, without which both would of course be nothing but dead clods of earth, cannot now in the greatest fervor of onward striving and unification produce an offprint of itself in which all its forces live? If the heart has the power of so uniting sensations which lie around it that a single drive, a single desire *comes into being*; if the head has the power to bring sensations which flow through the body into a single representation, and to *guide* the former through the latter, which seems to be of such a different nature – how [can one insist] that a single life-spark does not, so to speak, well up from out of the flame of all united irritations and life in swift flight and hence far above and beyond the crawlingly slow course of mechanical floors and mechanisms to a new, higher level of its purification, and as the distillation of all the forces of two beings created for each other *become* the first principle of a life of a higher order? Does not all life sprout further? Does not each spark of creation purify itself upward through channels to a subtler flame? And in this case, moreover, it was the most ensouled spark of the irritation and the creative force of two through-and-through ensouled beings that leapt.

  I do not say that I hereby *explain* anything; I have not yet known any philosophy that explained what *force is*, whether force stirs in a single being or in two beings. What philosophy does is to *observe, order* together, *elucidate* after it always already *presupposes* force, irritation, efficacy. Now I do not understand why, if nothing can be explained in each *individual*, one should *deny* the efficacy of one thing on another and deride in the unification of two things phenomena of nature which one *accepts* unexplained in the case of each thing individually. Whoever will tell me what force is in the soul and how it takes effect for the soul, to him am I willing to explain immediately how it takes effect outside itself, also on other souls, also on bodies, which are perhaps not in nature separated from the soul (*psychê*) by such strong walls as the rooms of our metaphysics separate them.[8]

---

[8] This is another example of Herder's use of brachylogy.

Quite generally, nothing in nature is separated, everything flows onto and into everything else through imperceptible transitions; and certainly, what life is in the creation is in all its shapes, forms, and channels only a single spirit, a single flame.

Especially, I think, the system of preestablished harmony ought to have been alien to the great inventor of the monad-poem, for, it seems to me, the two do not hold well together. No one said it better than Leibniz that body as such is only an appearance of substances, as the milky way is of stars, and the cloud of droplets. Indeed, *Leibniz* tried to explain even motion as an appearance of an *inner condition* which we do not know but which could be representation because no other inner condition is familiar to us. What? And the soul as such could not have effect on this inner condition of the forces and substances of its body? – this soul which after all shares their nature, and is itself innermost, most effective force. So the soul would govern only in the domain of its sisters, of beings entirely similar to itself; and it could not govern there?

*

But it is too early to give room to individual inferences; we remain still with phenomena of the whole machine. The inner human being with all his obscure forces, irritations, and drives is only *single*. All passions, lying about the heart, and stirring many sorts of tools, are connected together by invisible bonds and plant roots in the subtlest structure of our ensouled fibers. Each little strand, if only we could have insight into it, undoubtedly belongs to this as well, each narrower and wider vessel, each more strongly and more weakly welling drop of blood. The courage of the lion, like the fearfulness of the hare, lies in its ensouled inner structure. Through the narrower arteries of the lion his warmer blood presses forth violently; the stag has a heart with wide, open vessels, a timid king of the forest despite his crown. In the mating season, however, even the timid stag is bold; it is the period of his aroused irritations and increased inner warmth.

In the deep abyss of irritation and of such obscure forces lies in human beings and animals the seed of all passion and enterprise. More or less irritation of the heart and of its servants makes heroes or cowards, heroes in love or in anger. The heart of Achilles was shaken in its plexus by black anger, it required irritability to become an Achilles. The sated lion has lost his courage, a woman can hunt him; but a hungry wolf, vulture, lion – what mighty creatures!

The bravest were usually the happiest human beings, men of open, broad chest – often heroes in love as in life. A eunuch is, in action as in voice, one arrested in youth, without force or deep expression. – The fervor, depth, and dispersion with which we receive, process, and communicate passion makes of us the shallow or deep vessels that we are. Often there lie under the diaphragm causes which we very incorrectly and laboriously seek in the head; the thought cannot reach there unless the sensation was in its place beforehand. The extent to which we participate in what surrounds us, how deeply love and hate, disgust and revulsion, vexation and pleasure, plant their roots in us – this tunes the string-play of our thoughts, this makes us into the human beings that we are.

Now it is in the face of this sort of deep abyss of obscure sensations, forces, and irritations that our bright and clear philosophy is horrified most of all; it crosses itself before it as before the hell of the soul's *basest* forces and prefers to play on the Leibnizian chess-board with a few empty words and classifications about *obscure* and *clear, distinct* and *confused* ideas, about *cognition in* and *outside oneself, with oneself* and *without oneself*, and so forth. This method is so lovely and easy that it has already been chosen as a basic principle to introduce into philosophy nothing but *empty* words, with which, it is held, one is as little required to think as the calculator with his numbers: this, it is held, will enable philosophy to attain the perfection of mathematics, that one can keep on inferring without thinking[9] – a philosophy from which may all the Muses save us! What else is the reason why even good, true philosophy has sunk so low but precisely that in it for whole chapters and doctrines nothing has been thought in connection with entirely general words? Every healthy head necessarily casts these aside and says, "I *want* to *have* something *determinate* to think with each word, even in each new place where it is newly used." And my!, how inadequate our metaphysical concepts and words are!, what care one therefore needs to take to keep a firm grip on the concept at each moment, to pay close attention whether it is still the same concept in this case or is now only its empty phantom. In my modest opinion, no *psychology* is possible which is not in each step determinate *physiology*. *Haller's* physiological work raised to psychology, and enlivened with mind

[9] Herder is here mainly alluding to a proposal of this sort that had been made by J. A. Eberhard in his *Allgemeine Theorie des Denkens und Empfindens* [*General Theory of Thinking and Sensation*] (1776). Cf. Leibniz's ideal of a "universal characteristic."

like Pygmalion's statue[10] – then we can say something about thinking and sensation.[11]

I only know of three paths that might lead to this. Biographies, observations of doctors and friends, prophecies of poets – these alone can provide us with material for the true science of the soul. Biographies, above all autobiographies, if they are faithful and intelligent – what deep idiosyncrasies they would supply! If no two things in the world are the same, if no dissector has ever yet found two identical arteries, glands, muscles, or canals, then let this difference be pursued through a whole human structure right down to each little cog, each irritation and vapor of the mental life-stream – what an infinity, what an abyss! A sea of depths where wave upon wave stirs and where all the abstractions of similarity, category, general order are only boarded walls of neediness or colorful houses of cards to play with.

If, now, an individual human being had the integrity and faithfulness to sketch *himself*, fully, as he knows and feels himself, if he had enough courage to look into the deep abyss of Platonic recollection and to suppress nothing to himself, enough courage to pursue himself through his whole living structure, through his whole life, with everything that each index finger points out to him in his inner I, what a living physiognomy would emerge from that, certainly deeper than from the outline of forehead and nose. No part, I think, no limb would be without its contribution and indication. It would be able to say to us: "Here the heart beats weakly; here the chest is flat and unarched; there the arm forceless; here the lung wheezes, there the sense of smell is dull; here living breath is lacking, sight, hearing are in twilight – the body dictates to me weakly and confusedly here; therefore my soul must write here and there as well. This is lacking to me; whereas I have that other thing, and for such a reason." – If the faithful historian of himself then pursued this through all its consequences, showed that no shortcoming and no force remains in *one* place but has broader effect, and that the soul unsuspectedly draws

---

[10] According to myth, Pygmalion, a king of Cyprus, fell in love with an ivory statue of a woman, asked Aphrodite to give him a woman resembling it, returned home to find that the statue had come alive, and married her.

[11] Herder's 1775 draft contains the following interesting variant on these last remarks: "Sensation is only the aggregate of all obscure irritations, just as thought is the luminous aggregate of sensation. Physiology is the shrine of the soul. *Haller's* work is Pygmalion's statue warming up under the hands of the lover of the human soul."

broader inferences in accordance with such given formulas, showed how each error and coldness, each false combination and absent stirring, *must* of necessity arise in every case, and how one *must* supply in each effect the offprint of one's whole I with its force and shortcoming – what instructive examples descriptions of that sort would be! Those will be philosophical times, when people write such descriptions – not when they veil themselves and all human history in general formulas and word-fog. If the Stoic Lipsius[12] and others of his party had been willing to sketch themselves in this way, how differently they would appear from the way they now appear out of the twilit word-products of their upper floor!

I know of no biographies of individual human beings by themselves which did not in each case, however one-sided and superficial their viewpoints sometimes were, have much that was worthy of attention. Besides what *Augustine, Petrarch,* and *Montaigne* have strewn into their writings about themselves, I shall only name *Cardano*[13] and a weak self-tormentor[a] before whose extreme weakness, eternal trembling towards and away from suicide, one shudders. A number of strange phenomena, concerning how a creature can run so blindly into danger, or can perpetually flee from its own shadow so dizzily, timidly, and cowardly, have not been able to be presented more horrifyingly than thus, from the soft marrow of his own sensation. It is strange how an autobiography also shows the whole man from sides from which he precisely does not want to show himself, and one sees from cases of this sort that everything in nature is a whole, that, just precisely in obscure indications and examples, one can disown oneself before oneself least of all.

However, since we will still have to wait a long time for biographies of that sort, and it would perhaps not even be good or useful to betray the deepest sanctuary within us, which only God and we should know, to every fool, other people take our place, and in the case of remarkable people their friend should become what the doctor is in the case of sick people. There is no doubt at all but that among the many observations

[a] M. *Bernd's* own Lebensbeschreibung samt einer aufrichtigen Entdeckung einer der größten, obwohl großenteils noch unbekannten Leibes- und Gemütsplage [*Biography together with an Honest Revelation of one of the Greatest, although for the Most Part still Unknown, Bodily and Mental Diseases*], Leipzig 1738, especially pp. 257–372. [Bernd's initial was not M. but A., so the M. here may stand for "Monsieur," in which case, since Bernd was German, not French, Herder would be making a rather mean insinuation that his sort of weakness is typically French.]

[12] J. Lipsius (1547–1606), Dutch philologist and neo-Stoic philosopher.
[13] H. Cardano (1501–76), Italian philosopher, mathematician, and doctor.

of the doctors of ancient and modern times there must also be a lot that cast light on these obscure irritations and forces; the most complex pathology of the soul and of the passions depends on these, and not on speculation; but to my knowledge they are unordered, uncollected, and not everyone has the desire or the leisure for this. With them the strangest anomalies and analogies of human fancifulness would certainly come to light, and the director of a hospital for the incurably insane would make the most striking contributions towards the history of the *geniuses* of all times and lands. – When I count the friends along with the doctors I am not wrong to do so; they have exactly the same perspective that the doctors have, and moreover in the circumstances of greater intimacy and action. It is beyond comprehension the sort of obscure effect, intuition, and influence that one human soul often exercises on another, as can often be seen in the strangest examples of harmonious dispositions, desires, and forces. Sympathy and love, pleasure and ambition, envy and jealousy solve, through looks, through secret hints, the riddle of what lies so well hidden beneath the breast, scent out, so to speak, from nothing but small, visible signs the deeply hidden secret. – These are small distorted examples of the power that, with diligence, love, and tending, a pure human soul has over another person, and how far it can penetrate into him! – a depth of which no one has as yet either attained the bottom or knows a plummet for getting to the bottom. The purest human being on earth *knew them all, needed no testimony from outside, for he well knew what was in the human being*, and it is ascribed to the human mind in an especially splendid analogy with the mind of the deity that only *the mind of the human being knows what is in the human being*, so to speak, rests on itself and explores in its own depths.

If no one else, then the *poets' prophecies and secret intuitions* have proved this. A character created, conducted, maintained by *Shakespeare* is often a whole human life in its hidden springs; without knowing it, he depicts the passion right down to the deepest abysses and fibers from which it sprouted. When someone recently claimed that Shakespeare is no physiognomist on the basis of the nose's profile, then I gladly concede that to him, for Shakespeare has little time for a detail of that sort, except when, as in the case of Richard the Third, the most obvious necessity demands it. But that he is no *physiologist*, with everything in which physiology even reveals itself outwardly – that no one could say who had seen *Hamlet* and *Lear, Ophelia* or *Othello* so much as in a dream; quietly, he depicts Hamlet right down to his hair. Since everything external is only the reflection of the inner soul, how deeply has the barbaric, Gothic Shakespeare not everywhere reached through strata and layers of earth to the basic traits from which a human being grows, as *Klopstock* to the most secret waves and oscillations of a pure, heavenly soul! The study of the poets for this purpose is something that has for the most part only been attempted by the English (only with their poets, of course; for what will an Englishman find good outside of England?); for us Germans there still remains here a great field of times and peoples, instead of [our usual] useless eulogies and childish reviews.

And until these three tasks are exhausted the answer [to the question] "Under what conditions does something irritate?" may be postponed. I could give ten formulas for a solution in empty and uncertain expressions, say that something irritates us when we cannot *avoid* its irritating us, when the object lies so close to us that it rubs against us and stirs us. Or I could say that the object irritates when it is so similar, so analogous, to us . . . But what would this all mean? Basically, still just that it irritates when it irritates, and that everyone believes. And it must be *believed*, that is, experienced, sensed, and flees every general word-mongery and abstract prediction. If an object of which we did not dream, from which we hoped for nothing, suddenly appears so close to our I that the most secret drives of our heart willingly follow it, just as the wind stirs the tips of the grass blades and the magnet stirs the iron filings, then what is there to ponder, to argue about, here? It is new *experience*, which may no doubt follow from the system of the best world, but does not exactly follow from our system now. It is a new, prophetic drive which promises us enjoyment, makes us intuit this obscurely, jumps over space and time, and gives us a foretaste of the future. Perhaps that is how it is with the instincts of the animals. They are like instrument strings which a certain sound of the universe stirs, on which the world-spirit plays with a single one of his fingers. They are connected with the element, with the creature, with the young, with the unknown region of the world whither they speed; invisible bonds pull them in that direction, whether they arrive there or not, whether it is an egg or chalk that the hen broods on. The sides of creation are so many in kind, and since every side was supposed to be felt, intuited, sensed up, therefore the instincts, irritations, and roots of sensation had to be so various that often no other being except the one that itself sensed them comprehends or intuits them.

And it is splendid that things are so, and that the deepest depth of our soul is covered with night! Our poor lady thinker [the soul] certainly did not have the ability to grasp each irritation, the seed of each sensation, in its first components; she did not have the ability to hear a rushing world-sea of such obscure waves aloud[14] without embracing it with horror and worry, with the anxiety of all fear and timidity, and having the rudder fall from her hand. Maternal nature hence removed from her what *could* not depend on her clear consciousness, weighed out each impression that she received from it, and spared every channel that might lead to her. Now she does not separate out roots but enjoys the bloom. Scents waft to her from obscure bushes which she did not plant, did not tend; she stands on an abyss of infinity and does not know that she stands on it; through this happy ignorance she stands firm and secure. It is no less good for the obscure forces and irritations which must cooperate on such a subordinate post; they do not know *why*; they cannot and should not know it; the degree of their obscurity is kindness and wisdom. A clump of earth breathed through by the life-breath of the Creator is our clay housing.

2. Senses

If our soul was subject to a sea of advancing waves of irritation and feeling from *outside*, the deity gave us *senses*; if from *inside*, the deity wove for us a nerve structure.[15]

The nerve proves more subtly what has been said concerning the fibers of irritation generally; it contracts or advances according to the type of object that comes to it. In one case it floats towards [the object] and the points of its extremest thickets[16] stand on end. The tongue tastes in advance; the little smelling-thickets open up for the approaching scent; even ear and eye open up to the sound and the light, and especially in the case of the coarser senses the life-spirits hasten mightily to receive their

---

[14] Herder is here again borrowing an image used by Leibniz in a similar way in the *New Essays on Human Understanding*.

[15] Herder's 1775 draft continues at this point: "Let no one demand here the physiology of these parts; it suffices for us to know that the pith of the nerves is nothing but a finer web of fibers, the string-play of an irritation which is now called *sensation* and now communicates itself and takes effect in an infinitely more mentalistic, higher way. Do we, then, encounter the preceding laws and properties of irritation here too? Certainly! Only in a higher equation."

[16] I.e. the nerve endings.

new guest. – On the other hand, when pain approaches the nerve flees and shudders. We contract with a shiver in the presence of an extremely disharmonious noise; our tongue is repelled in the presence of a bad taste, as our sense of smell in the presence of an unpleasant scent. The ear, says the speaker of Latin, is repelled to hear, the eye to see;[17] if it could, the feeling-bud would close up, like the flower in the face of the cold evening breeze. Shuddering, shivering, vomiting, and in the case of the sense of smell sneezing, are through and through such phenomena of *retreat*, of *resistance*, of *opposition*, as a gentle *floating towards* and *melting away* shows *transition* and *yielding* in the case of pleasant objects. At bottom, therefore, we still have here those laws and phenomena which we noticed in the case of every irritable fiber, and that additionally that law holds in the case of the mental sensations of the *beautiful* and the *sublime*, that, namely, each feeling of the sublime is bound up with a *retreat* into oneself, with *feeling for oneself*, and each sensation of the beautiful with *floating towards* from out of oneself, with *sympathy* and *communication*, has been well explained by the excellent author of a very well-known treatise[b] – a theory which, even though among noble affairs and dispositions it was only play, only recreation for him, almost causes me to envy him.

Perhaps I will soon receive favorable leisure to collect together essays that I have thrown on paper about the manner of sensation of a few individual senses; here my purpose aims only at what is general. And observe – what I said formerly in the case of irritation and its object – that here in the case of the senses too there is a *medium*, a certain mental *bond*, without which the sense could neither intimately reach the object nor the object the sense, and which we therefore *must* trust, believe in, in the case of all sensuous cognitions. Without light our eye and the seeing force in our soul would be idle, without noise our ear would be empty; hence a special sea had to be created that would flow into both senses and bring the objects into them, or in other words, "*that abstracts from created beings* [Geschöpfe] *as much as this portal can receive, but leaves to them everything else, their whole infinite abyss.*" Wonderful organ of the being in

---

[b] *Burke*, Untersuchung über den Ursprung unserer Begriffe vom Erhabenen und Schönen [*Philosophical Enquiry into the Origin of Our Ideas of the Sublime and the Beautiful*], Riga, 1773. [Herder's 1775 draft refers to Burke at this point as "the author of the splendid, truly Newtonian system concerning the causes of the *beautiful and sublime*."]

[17] Herder here uses the German verb *entsetzt sich*, which means "is appalled" but etymologically "moves itself away." He is evidently alluding to the Latin verb *horrere* which similarly combines an original physical sense, "to stand on end, to shudder," with a psychological sense, "to dread."

whom all live and sense! The ray of light is His indication, His finger or [pointing-]stick, for our soul; noise is His breath, the miraculous word of His creatures [*Geschöpfe*] and servants.

How mightily the Creator has hereby *broadened* His world for us! All coarse senses, fibers, and irritations can only sense *in themselves*; the object must come in addition, touch them, and in a certain sense itself become one with them. Here a way is already opened up for cognition *outside us*.[c] Our ear hears across miles; the ray of light becomes a stick with which we reach up as far as Sirius. Immediately before my eye the great eye of the world has spread out a general organ which brings a thousand creatures into me, which clothes a thousand beings with one robe *for me*. About my ear flows a sea of waves which His hand poured out in order that a world of objects might penetrate into me which would otherwise have to remain for me eternally an obscure, silent grave of the dead. There does my sense use all the tricks and subtleties that a blind man with his stick uses to grope, to feel, to learn distance, difference, size, and in the end without this medium we know nothing, we must *believe* it. If the noise, the light, the scent, the spice deceives me, if my sense is false, or if I have only got in the habit of using it falsely, then with all my cognition and speculation I am lost. Also, for a thousand other senses in a thousand other media the object can be something completely different, in itself completely an abyss, of which I scent out and intuit nothing; for me it is only what the sense and its medium – the former the portal, the latter the deity's index finger for our soul – presents to me. *Internally* we know nothing beyond ourselves; without senses the world-structure would be for us an interwoven tangle of obscure irritations; the Creator had to part, separate, spell out *for us* and *in us*.

Now I must again remark that to investigate exactly the *contribution* which each sense supplies to the soul would inevitably be a pleasant and extremely noteworthy pleasure-course which we save up for ourselves for another time. But that this contribution of the senses cannot with two human beings be identical in kind and strength, depth and extent, is shown by many examples. Sight and hearing, which provide the most material for thought, seldom exist in the same degree of development

---

[c] See *Sulzer's* excellent essay on thinking and sensation [*Anmerkungen über den verschiedenen Zustand, worin sich die Seele bei Ausübung ihrer Hauptvermögen, nämlich des Vermögens, sich etwas vorzustellen, und des Vermögens zu empfinden, befindet* (first edition, in French, 1763)], in his miscellaneous philosophical writings, treatise 7, and Histoire de l'Académie Royale de Berlin [History of the Royal Academy of Berlin], vol. 19, pp. 407–20.

and natural strength in a human being. Clarity of the eye often hates deep receptiveness of the ear (to put it in mental terms), hence the two steeds that pull first on the soul's car are unequal.[18] The three greatest epic poets in the whole world, *Homer, Ossian*, and *Milton*, were blind, as though this quiet obscurity was required in order for all the images that they had seen and grasped now *to be able* to become *sound, word, sweet melody*. A congenitally blind poet and a congenitally deaf philosopher would inevitably show strange peculiarities, just as the blind *Saunderson* along with hearing loved smell and feeling.[19] If a universal philosophical language were ever invented, it would perhaps be by someone congenitally deaf and dumb who was, so to speak, entirely sight, entirely signs of abstraction. No two poets have ever used one meter in the same way, or probably felt it in the same way either. A Sapphic ode from the Greek woman, from Catullus, and from Horace is hardly the same thing. What mediocre ear will not distinguish a hexameter by *Klopstock, Kleist, Bodmer* or by *Lucretius, Virgil, Ovid* almost at the first sound? For the one poet his Muse is *sight, image*, for the other *voice*, for the third *action*. One prophet was awakened through the play of strings, the other through visions. No two painters or poets have seen, grasped, depicted a single object, even if only a single metaphor, in the same way.

If one could pursue this difference in the contributions of different senses through lands, times, and peoples, the matter would inevitably become an infinity. [One would ask,] for example, what the cause is of the fact that Frenchmen and Italians in music, Italians and Dutchmen in painting, understand something so different. For obviously at this parting of the ways the arts get sensed by [different] nations with different mental senses, perfected with different mental senses. But here we continue on, [noting] that, however different this contribution of different senses to thought and sensation may be, in our inner selves everything flows together and becomes one. We usually call the depth of this confluence *imagination [Einbildung]*, but it does not consist only of images *[Bildern]* but also of sounds, words, signs, and feelings, for which language would often have no name. Sight borrows from feeling and believes that it sees what it only felt. Sight and hearing decode each other reciprocally. Smell seems to be the spirit of taste, or is at least a close brother of taste. From

---

[18] Herder is here alluding to Plato's famous metaphor for the soul at *Phaedrus*, 246a ff.: a charioteer steering two steeds.

[19] Diderot, *Lettre sur les aveugles*.

all this, now, the soul weaves and makes for itself its robe, its sensuous universe.

Here too illusions and visions, illnesses and dreams, are often the strangest betrayers of what sleeps within us. That giant *Pascal* whose soul ever tears down cliffs and reveals flaming abysses beside them reached the point that in the end he always saw the dark, burning abyss next to him. More than one fanatic of a gentler sort believed himself always surrounded by bright light. And even the great thinker *Tsirnhausen*,[d] whose manner of studying was at least romantic enough, did not find himself in the true flow of thought until he saw sparks and rays around him. I know of the example of another philosopher[20] who at the beginning of his illness in a sort of strange swoon heard words, the last words of what he had read. *One* human being possesses the art of *seeing* far more than the art of *hearing*; whether he be a poet or a philosopher, his cognition, his presentation, his style, his composition will certainly shape itself accordingly. How many are called poets and are only wits and men of understanding because they are entirely lacking in poetic imagination with respect to sight and hearing, and how many who like *Plato* only paint out a few metaphors and the metaphors last eternally. But I am straying too far.

*

If in this way everything flows together out of our senses into the imagination, or however we want to call this sea of inner sensuality, and our thoughts, sensations, and drives swim and float upon it, has nature not woven anything further that unites them, that guides them? Certainly, and this is the *nerve structure*. Delicate silver bonds through which the Creator links the inner and outer worlds, and within us heart and head, thought and volition, senses and all limbs. Truly such a medium of sensation for the minded human being as outwardly light was able to be for the eye, sound for the ear.

We have sensations only of what our nerves give us; also, only according to and from this can we think. Now, whether one calls this living mind that undulates through us flame or ether – enough, it is the incomprehensible heavenly being that brings everything to me, and unites everything in me. What does the object that I see have in common with my brain, the brain

[d] See the Eloge de Tsirnhausen par M. Fontenelle [Eulogy of Tsirnhausen by Mr. Fontenelle].

[20] Probably M. Mendelssohn (1729–86).

with my undulating heart, that the former becomes an *image*, the latter a *passion*? Behold, there exists here a something that must have a strange nature because it serves such strange differences. Light was able to do only one thing, namely turn the whole obscure abyss of the world into an image, make everything *eyeable* for the eye [*dem Auge alles veräugen*]; sound was able to do only one thing, namely make audible that which would otherwise only exist for other senses. And so forth. This inner ether need not[21] be light, sound, scent, but it must be able to receive and transform everything into itself. It can become light for the head, irritation for the heart; hence it must be of their nature or immediately border thereon. A thought, and a flaming stream pours from the head to the heart. An irritation, a sensation, and a thought flashes like lightning, there arises volition, plan, deed, action – everything through one and the same messenger. Truly, if this is not to be called string-play of the deity, then what should be called that?

Now, if I had enough power and knowledge to represent this noble string-play in its structure, in its conducting and knotting, entwining and subtilizing, to show that no branch, no bond, no little knot is in vain, and that in proportion as it binds and guides itself our sensations, limbs, and drives bind, stimulate, and strengthen each other too (though, to be sure, not mechanically through blows and impacts!) – oh, what a work of strangely fine developments and observations from the foundation of our soul it would have to become! I do not know whether it already exists, whether a thinking and feeling physiologist has written it especially for the purpose for which I wish it. It seems to me that it would have to contain the Creator's most beautiful writing in letters, [expressing] how He bound and divided limbs, ensouled them more or less, derived, suppressed, knotted, strengthened feelings, so that the eye need only see and the viscera undulate, the ear hears and our arm strikes, the mouth kisses and fire flows through all the limbs – miracle upon miracle! a true, subtle writing in flames by the Creator.

But we again remain merely with general phenomena, for example, the so-called "effects of the imagination in the womb." Many people have flatly denied them because their system did not tolerate them, whereas in fact striking examples of them can be familiar to almost everyone. What good would it do, therefore, to deny experiences for the sun? If it were

---

[21] Or possibly: must not.

a question of clumsy mechanism, wooden pressure and impact, in our body, and especially in the delicate body of the mother at the time when she carries the unborn child, if the soul with its imagination resided in the pineal gland and should now have to reach the child with poles and ladders, certainly in that case one could shake one's wise head. But as things stand, since according to all experiences everything is full of irritation and life, since these lives are in such a miraculous manner a unity in us, a *soul-human* (*anthrôpos psychikos*) whom all mechanical mechanisms and limbs willingly serve, and since now precisely this confluent, ensouled unity in us is what is called *imagination* when we understand the word in its true scope, what is incoherent in the idea that this soul-world in whose midst the child floats, so to speak, this whole psychological human being who holds the child in her arms, should also communicate to it all impressions, all irritations from herself? In a context of mental forces space and time, which seem to exist only for the coarse world of bodies, disappear. We get formed, says the old Eastern piece of wisdom,[22] in the lap of the mother who gives us life, as in the mid-point of the earth, whither all influences and impressions flow together. In this matter women are our philosophers, not we theirs.

Just the same applies to the so-called "influence of the soul on the body and of the body on the soul." If something here were supposed to be explained through pineal gland, elastically tensed nerves, blows and impacts, then let a person still scruple and deny. But as things are, since our structure knows nothing of such a wooden weaver's loom, since everything swims in irritation and scent and force and ethereal stream, since our whole body, so manifoldly ensouled in its diverse parts, seems to be only *a single realm of invisible, inner,* but *less bright* and *obscure forces* which is in the strictest bond with the lady monarch who thinks and wills within us, so that everything is at her command and in this inwardly linked realm space and time disappear – what could be more natural than that she rules over those *without which she would not be what she is?* For only through this realm, in this connection, did she become and is she a *human soul.* Her thought only arises from sensation; her servants and angels, messengers of air and flame, stream to her her food, just as they only live in her will. She rules, to speak with Leibniz, in a realm of slumbering, but that much more deeply effective, beings.

---

[22] Psalm 139, vs. 13–16.

I cannot at all imagine how my soul should spin something *out of itself* and dream a world *out of itself*, indeed I cannot even imagine how it should sense something outside itself of which there exists no analogon in it and its body. If there were in this body no light, no sound, then we would have no sensation in the whole wide world of anything that was sound and light; and if there were nothing analogous to sound, to light, in the soul itself, or around it, then any concept of this would still be impossible. But as things stand, all the steps that we have taken so far show that the deity achieved all of this for us through ways and channels which always receive, purify, wash forth, unify more, make more similar to the soul, that which at a distance was still so dissimilar to it. I therefore am not at all fearful of the old expression that the human being is a little world, that our body *must* be an epitome of the whole realm of bodies, as our soul a realm of all mental forces which reach us, and that what we are simply not we also *can* not know and sense. The philosophy-of-preprinted-forms [*Formular-Philosophie*][23] which unwinds everything from out of itself, from out of the monad's inner force of representation, admittedly has no need of all this, since it has everything in itself; but I do not know how it got there, and this philosophy itself does not know.

"But then naturally the soul would be material?, or we would even have many immaterial souls?" We have not yet reached that point, my reader; I do not yet know what 'material' or 'immaterial' is, but I do not believe that nature has fixed iron sheets between the two because I do not see the iron sheets in nature *anywhere*, and can certainly suspect them least of all where nature united so intimately. Enough, we now turn first of all to

3. Cognition and volition

All sensations which rise to a certain clarity (the inner condition in the case is unnameable) become *apperception, thought*; the soul *cognizes* that it *senses*.

Now whatever *thought* is, there is observable in it the most intimate force for making out of many which stream to us a *luminous One*, and, if I may put it this way, a sort of *reaction* which feels most clearly that it is a *One*, a *self*. A figurative language of this sort indeed seems mystical, but in mysteries, and in the deepest mystery of the creation of our soul, one

[23] The hyphenated expression approximately captures a pun that is in the German.

can scarcely explain oneself otherwise. Enough, what we saw in the case of each irritation, each sensation, each sense, namely that nature "unites a many," that happens here in the clearest, most intimate way.

If, now, we are willing to follow experience, then we see that the soul spins, knows, cognizes nothing *out of itself*, but what its universe streams towards it from within and without and God's finger indicates to it. It gets back nothing from the Platonic realm of the previous world; it has also not put itself in the place where it now stands; it does not even know how it got there. But this it does know, or should know, that it only cognizes what this place shows it, that there is nothing to the idea of a mirror of the universe drawing *from out of itself*, of an infinite ascent of its positive force in omnipotent autonomy. It is in a school of the deity which it has not given itself; it must use the irritations, the senses, the forces and opportunities which became its own through a fortunate, unearned inheritance, or it retreats into a desert where its divine force goes lame and blind. Abstract egoism,[24] therefore, even if it were only language of the schools, seems to me contrary to the truth and the open course of nature.

I cannot here go into individual detail in order to show in the case of each sense how wisely and kindly the father of our nature everywhere trains us in *formulas of His wisdom and kindness*, but that he constantly trains us in this way, that our soul actually can do nothing and does nothing but solve formulas of this sort, with a shot of *divine energy* produce light, not indeed from darkness, but from twilight, bright, warm sparks from a damp flame – this, it seems to me, is shown and said by all the actions of our cognizing, willing soul. This soul is the image of the deity and seeks to imprint this image on everything that surrounds itself, makes the manifold one, seeks from lies truth, from vacillating rest clear activity and effect. And it is constantly as though it in the process looks into itself and with the lofty feeling "I am the daughter of God, am His image" says to itself "Let us!" and wills and rules. We have no conception of a more intimate activity than that of which a human soul is capable; it retreats into itself, rests on itself, so to speak, and can turn and overcome a universe. Every higher degree of *power*, of *attention* and *abstraction*, of *voluntary choice* and *freedom*, lies in this obscure foundation of the most intimate *irritation* and *consciousness* [that the soul has] of itself, of its *force*, of its inner *life*.

---

[24] "Egoism" in the sense that it often bears in Kant: solipsism.

People are in the habit of according to the soul a mass of subordinate forces, *imagination* and *foresight*, *poetic talent* and *memory*, but many experiences show that what in them is not *apperception, consciousness* of *self-feeling* and of *self-activity*, belongs only to the sea of inflowing sensuality which stirs the soul, which supplies it with materials, but not to the soul itself. One will never get deeply to the bottom of these forces if one merely treats them superficially as ideas that dwell in the soul, or, worse still, separates them from one another as walled compartments and considers them individually in independence. In *imagination* and *memory*, *recollection* and *foresight*, too the *single* divine force of our soul, "*inner activity that looks within itself, consciousness, apperception,*" must reveal itself. In proportion to the latter does a human being have *understanding, conscience, will, freedom*; the rest are inflowing waves of the great world-sea.

People say the word *imagination* and are wont to credit it to the poet as his patrimony; but it is very ill if the *imagining* is without consciousness and understanding, the poet is only a raving dreamer. So-called philosophers have decried *wit* and *memory*, assigned the former only to buffoons, the latter to word-merchants – which is a shame for these noble forces. *Wit* and *memory*, *imagination* and *poetic talent*, have been used with such understanding by good souls that their great understanding could certainly not have grown to maturity without those broadly gripping roots. *Homer* and *Shakespeare* were certainly great philosophers, as *Leibniz* was a thinker with much wit in whom it was usually a metaphor, an image, a casually written simile that produced the theories which he casually wrote on a quarto sheet and from which[25] the weaving-guilds after him spun thick volumes. *Rabelais* and *Swift*, *Butler* and even the great *Bacon*, were thinkers of wit; the last also belongs among those

> – Whose ring through one thought-pair
> In trust and chastity wed oft thousands did bear.[26]

But it would not be my enemy on whom I wished *their* wit and *their* figurative language. *Bacon* was hostile to scholastic cleverness, but only to *scholastic* cleverness, which turns every living creature of God into mold. True cleverness he himself loved and showed. *Locke's* philosophy was the trimming knife for *Descartes'* weavings, and *Leibniz' wit* was required to unfold *Bayle's* dialectical cleverness in its exaggeratedness. The verbal

---

[25] Reading *denen* for *der*.
[26] Lines adapted by Herder from a poem by J. P. L. Withof.

memory of the school pedants is a miserable thing and dries up the soul into a sorry list of names; but for a *Caesar* or *Mithridates* was not in these cases their *memory for names* essential too? In short, all these forces are at bottom only a single force if they should be human, good, and useful – and that is *understanding, intuition* with inner *consciousness*. Let one remove this from them, and then the imagination is illusion, the wit childish, the memory empty, the cleverness a cobweb; but in proportion as they have it, these forces that would otherwise seem to be enemies unite and become merely roots or sensuous representations of one and the same *energy of the soul.* Memory and imagination become the extended and deep image of truth; cleverness separates and wit combines so that precisely a clear, weighty *One* arises; fantasy flies up, self-consciousness folds the wings – through and through expressions of one and the same energy and elasticity of the soul.

What though? Does this inner elasticity have no helper, no staff, on which it supports and holds itself, no *medium,* if I may put it that way, which awakens it and guides its effect, as we found in the case of each irritation, each sense? I believe so! – and this medium of our self-feeling and mental consciousness is – *language.* People congenitally deaf and dumb show through strange examples how deeply reason, self-consciousness, slumbers when they cannot imitate, and I believe (rather contrary to my previous opinion)[27] that really such a staff of awakening had to come to the aid of our *inner consciousness,* as light to the aid of the eye, that it might see, sound to the aid of the ear, that it might hear. Just as these external media are really for their senses [forms of] language which spell out for them certain properties and sides of things, similarly, I believe, *word, language* had to come to aid in order likewise to awaken and guide our *innermost* seeing and hearing. Thus, we see, does the child achieve mental focus, it *learns* to speak just as it learns to see, and precisely in accordance to think. Whoever has noticed children, how they learn to speak and think, the strange anomalies and analogies that get expressed in the process, will hardly doubt any longer. In the deepest languages too *reason* and *word* are only *a single* concept, *a single* thing: *logos.*[28] The human being gapes at images and colors until he *speaks,* until he, internally in his soul, *names.* Those human beings who, if I may put it this way, have much of this inner

---

[27] I.e. in the *Treatise on the Origin of Language.* This revision by Herder of his earlier view is very important.

[28] *logos:* word, reason.

word, of this intuiting, divine *gift of designation*, also have much *under-standing*, much *judgment*. Those who do not have it, even if a whole sea of images were to swim around them, only gape when they see, can not grasp, not transform into themselves, not use. The more one strengthens, guides, enriches, forms this inner language of a human being, then the more one guides his *reason* and makes alive the divine in him, which needs staffs of truth, and raises itself up with them as from slumber. – We will see in another place the great world of consequences that this yields.

Our cognition is therefore, although admittedly it *is* the deepest self *in us*, not as autonomous, voluntarily choosing, and unbound as is believed. Setting all that aside (what has been shown so far), one can see that in order for our cognition even to arise from sensation, the object still has to come to us through *secret bonds*, through an *indication* which *teaches* us to cognize. This teaching, this sense of an alien which imprints itself in us, gives our thinking its whole shape and direction. Regardless of all seeing and hearing and inflow from outside, we would grope about in deep night and blindness if instruction had not early on thought *for us* and, so to speak, imprinted in us ready-made thought-formulas. There did our force raise itself up, learn to feel and use itself. For a long time, and often our whole lives long, we walk with the support of the staffs that were reached to us in earliest childhood, ourselves think but only in forms in which others thought, cognize what the finger of such methods indicates to us; the rest is for us as though it did not exist at all.

For the most part this "*birth of our reason*" is so indecent to the wise men of our world that they quite fail to recognize it and revere their reason as a congenital, eternal, utterly independent, infallible oracle. Doubtless these wise men never walked in children's smocks, never learned to speak as their nursemaids spoke, or perhaps have no limited "circle of sensation," no *mother- and human-tongue*, at all. They speak like the gods, that is, they *think purely* and cognize ethereally – wherefore, then, also nothing but sayings of the gods and of reason are able to come from their lips. Everything is for them innate, implanted, the spark of infallible reason stolen from heaven without a Prometheus. Let them talk and pray to their idol-words [*Bildwörter*]; they know not what they do. The more deeply someone has climbed down into himself, into the structure and origin of his noblest thoughts, then the more he will cover his eyes and feet and say: "What I am, I have become. I have grown like a tree; the seed was there, but air, earth, and all the elements, which I did not deposit about myself, had to contribute in order to form the seed, the fruit, the tree."

*

Cognition without *volition* is nothing as well, a false, imperfect cognition. If cognition is only *apperception*, deep feeling of the truth, who will see truth and *not* see? Who cognize goodness and not *will* and *love*? Precisely these divisions show how much the tree of our inner self is pulled apart and shredded, so that speculation can count for us as cognition and play as activity. Speculation is only striving for cognition; only a fool forgets the *having* over the process of striving. Speculation is dividing up; whoever perpetually divides will never possess and use entirely. But if one possesses and feels that one possesses, then in the case of a healthy person use and enjoyment is natural.

Hence also, *no* passion, *no* sensation is excluded that would not become volition through such cognition; precisely in the best cognition all can and must be effective, because the best cognition arose from all of them and only lives in all of them. [Those are] liars or enervated people who boast of having nothing but pure fundamental principles and curse inclinations, from which alone true fundamental principles arise! That would amount to sailing without wind, and fighting without weapons. Irritation is the mainspring of our existence and it must also remain so in the noblest cognition. What inclination and passion [is there] that could not be enlivened with cognition and love, of God and one's neighbor, so that it takes effect only that much more purely, certainly, and mightily? The dross gets burned off but the true gold should remain. Every force and every irritation that sleeps in my breast should awaken and take effect only *in the spirit of my Creator*.

But who teaches me this? Is there a conscience, a moral feeling, that, separated from all cognition, might show me the right path? The words themselves seem nonsense when one presents them in that way – but I hardly believe that such a thing has ever been a human being's opinion. If no thorough cognition exists without volition, then also no volition can exist without cognition; they are only *a single energy* of the soul. But just as our cognition is only *human* and must be that way if it is to be *right*, likewise our volition can only be *human* as well, hence from and full of *human* sensation. Humanity is the noble measure according to which we cognize and act; hence *self-* and *other-feeling* (once again expansion and contraction) are the two expressions of the elasticity of our will; *love* is the noblest cognition, as it is the noblest sensation. To love the great Creator in oneself, to love one's way into others, and then to follow this sure pull – that is moral feeling, that is conscience. It stands opposed only to empty speculation, but not to cognition, for true cognition is *loving*, is *feeling* in a human way.

Behold the whole of nature, observe the great analogy of creation. Everything feels itself and creatures of its kind, life flows to life. Each string reverberates to its sound, each fiber interweaves itself with its playmate, animal feels with animal – why should not human being feel with human being? Only he is *God's image*, an epitome and administrator of the creation; hence there sleep within him a *thousand* forces, irritations, and feelings; hence *order* must rule in them, so that *all* awaken and can be applied, so that he may become the sensorium of his God *in everything living* in creation *in proportion as* it is related to him. This noble *universal* feeling hence becomes precisely through what it is *cognition*, the noblest knowledge of God and his fellow creatures through *efficacy* and *love*. Self-feeling should remain only the conditio sine qua non, the clod that holds us firmly in our place, not end but means. But a necessary means, for it is and remains true that we love our neighbor only as ourselves. If we are disloyal to ourselves, how will we be loyal to others? In the degree of the depth of our self-feeling lies also the degree of our other-feeling for others, for it is only ourselves that we can, so to speak, feel into others.

It seems to me that those are therefore empty quarrels [which ask] where the principle of our morality lies, whether in volition or cognition, whether in our own or in alien perfection. All volition indeed begins from cognition, but also in its turn all cognition only arises through sensation. I can only attain my own perfection through the perfection of others, as the latter [can only do so] through the former. *Hippocrates* already called human nature a living circle, and that it is. A chariot of God, eye all round, full of wind and living wheels. Hence there is nothing that one must guard against as much as one-sided mutilation and dissection. Water alone is not enough, and dear, cold, speculating reason will sooner cripple your will for you than give you will, motives, feeling. Whence is it supposed to enter your reason if not through sensation? Would the head think if your heart did not beat? But on the other hand, if you mean to heed every insistent knocking and welling of your heart, every echo of an irritated fiber, as though it were the voice of God, and follow it blindly, where can you [not] end up? – since in that case your understanding arrives too late. In short, follow nature! Be no polyp without a head and no stone bust without a heart; let the stream of your life beat freshly in your breast, but let it also be purified up into the subtle marrow of your understanding and there become *life-spirit*.

Hence the question whether this volition of ours is something inherited or acquired, something free or dependent, would resolve itself here too. It resolves itself entirely on the basis of this reason: that true cognition and good volition are just one sort of thing, *a single force* and *efficacy of the soul*. If, now, our cognition did not exist through itself, voluntarily choosing and unbound, if, in order to feel itself most deeply as a self, it needed staffs for raising itself, inner *language*, then certainly things will not be able to be otherwise for the will. *Agamemnon* had his scepter from *Thyestes*, he from *Atreus*, the latter from *Pelops*, finally the latter from *Zeus*, and *Hephaistos* had wrought it;[29] that is how it is with the noblest kingly scepter as well, "the *freedom of our soul*."

To go on about freedom is very easy if one serves every irritation, every seeming good as a cause sufficient *for us*. For the most part this talk of sufficient grounds is a miserable deception in which the universal always seems true and the particular individual aspect of the specific case is a lie. One is a slave of the mechanism (this, though, disguised as bright heavenly reason) and imagines oneself free, a slave in chains and dreams to oneself that these are wreaths of flowers. As soon as one enters upon speculation one can make anything from anything, one fancies oneself flown up to the empyrean, and [in reality] the poor maggot still lies in its casing without wings or springtime. – Here it is truly the first seed of freedom to feel that one is *not* free, and with *which* bonds one is bound. The strongest, freest human beings feel this most deeply and strive further; insane slaves born for the prison mock them and remain lying in the mire full of high dreaming. *Luther* with his book *De servo arbitrio*[30] was

---

[29] Herder's 1775 draft continues at this point: "What late members we are in the human species, and what a composite medium purified through millennia it is that awakens, strengthens, spreads, directs our forces of cognition and of sensation from our first entry into the world!"

[30] *The Bondage of the Will* (1525).

and still is understood by the fewest people; people objected pathetically or whimper in agreement. Why? Because they do not feel and struggle upwards like Luther.

Where the Lord's spirit is, there is freedom. The deeper, purer, and diviner our cognition is, then the purer, diviner, and more universal our efficacy is too, hence the freer our freedom. If from everything only *God's light* shines upon us, if everywhere only *the flame of the Creator* flows to us, then in His image we turn from being slaves to being kings, and we receive – what that philosopher sought[31] – a point within us in order to overcome the world about us, a point outside the world in order to move the world with everything that it contains. We stand on higher ground, and with each thing on *its* ground, move in the great sensorium of God's creation, the flame of all thought and sensation, *love*. Love is the highest reason, as it is the purest, divinest volition. If we are unwilling to believe Saint John on this point, then we may believe on it the doubtless still more divine *Spinoza*, whose philosophy and morality entirely revolves around this axle.

> Prima creatura Dei fuit lux sensus: postrema, lux rationis. Et hoc ipsum est, coelo in terris frui, quando mens humana in caritate movetur, in providentia quiescit et supra polos veritatis circumfertur.[32] – *Bacon, De Veritate*

> Luce intellettual piena d'amore
> Amor di vero, ben pien de letizia
> Letizia che trascende ogni dolzore.[33] – *Dante*

> Sie war die Laute seiner Hand
> die er zu seiner Lust erfand
> er gab ihr Millionen Saiten
> und jede klingt und jeder Klang
> tönt zum harmonischen Gesang
> der Lehre seiner Heimlichkeiten.[34] – *Withof*

---

[31] I.e. Archimedes.

[32] God's first creation was the light of sense, His last the light of reason. And to enjoy heaven on earth is just this, when the human mind moves in love, rests in providence, and revolves over the poles of truth.

[33] It is a spiritual light and full of love, / Love of the true good, full of joy, / And it is joy beyond all delights.

[34] It was the lute of His hand / which He invented for His pleasure / He gave it millions of strings / and each one sounds, and each sound / rings to a harmonious song, / to the teaching of His secrets.

Second essay
The influence of the two forces on one another and on the human being's character and genius
(Of which last matter more another time.)

We have had to dwell almost too long on commonplaces after which many a person who is not used to dear abstraction is perhaps just as wise as he was. Let us, in order to become in some measure useful, call down philosophy from its heaven in the clouds onto the earth, and consider our proposition in determinate individual cases and classes:

1. Our thought depends on sensation

1. *In the case of each individual human being.* Whoever goes into a madhouse finds all the fools raving in a different way, each in his world; thus do we all rave, very rationally, each according to his fluids and tempers. The deepest basis of our existence is individual, both in sensations and in thoughts. Only observe in individual cases from what strange germs and seeds the harvest of this or that person's passions grows. What leaves the one person cold causes the other to glow; all the animal species are perhaps less different among themselves than human being from human being.

If a human being could sketch the deepest, most individual basis of his enthusiasms and feelings, of his dreams and trains of thought, what a novel! As things stand, it is only perhaps illnesses and moments of passion that do this – and what monsters and amazing sea-miracles one often perceives!

One ought to be able to regard every book as the offprint of a living human soul; the more lively and true the offprint is, the less the author flattered and gave a miserable commonplace drivel between the four corners of the margin, how strange and individual the book often seems to us! It is often a riddle without a solution, a coin without a marginal inscription.[35] The shallowest readers, and usually the hollowest, hence

---

[35] Herder's 1775 draft continues after the word "inscription": "– one knows the author and he becomes the key. Perhaps we now praise what we initially hardly forgave, recognize when we perceive it what we gaped at; but perhaps also find, [viewed] against the abyss of life in him, that which initially delighted us base. And likewise the converse of all this.

"Every living work of a human soul – what a mirror it is of the soul itself! Read in the spirit of the author and you see which senses ruled and which were subordinate in him, according to what

also the loudest of all, the respectful critics, measure according to their unauthoritative, slight self, cry out, and damn.[36] The more modest wise man judges as Socrates judged Heraclitus's writings,[37] seeks to read more in the spirit of the author than in the book; the more he penetrates into it, the clearer and more coherent everything becomes. The life of an author is the best commentary on his writings – that is, if he is faithful and one with himself, does not bleat after a flock at forks and highways.

Every poem, especially a whole, great poem, a work of [its author's] soul and life, is a dangerous betrayer of its author, often where he least believed that he was betraying himself. One sees in the poem not only, for instance, as the masses proclaim, the man's poetic talents; one also sees which senses and inclinations governed in him, by what paths and how he received images, how he ordered and adjusted them and the chaos of his impressions, the favorite sides of his heart, and likewise often the fates of his life, his manly or childish understanding, the staffs of his thinking and of his memory . . . But for our critics, who have never in their lives dreamed of such a thing, I may already have said much too much. To be sure, not every soul from the gutter is worthy of such a study; but of a soul from the gutter one would also need no offprints, neither in writings nor in deeds. Where it is worth the effort, this *living reading*, this divination into the author's soul, is the *only* reading, and the deepest means of education [*Bildung*]. It becomes a sort of enthusiasm, intimacy, and friendship which is often most instructive and pleasant for us where we do not think and feel in the same way, and which really indicates what the name *favorite author* refers to. Such reading is competition, *heuristic*; we climb up with the author to creative peaks or discover the error and the deviation in its birthplace. The more one knows the author from life and has lived with him, the livelier this intercourse becomes.

---

rules he ordered and adjusted the chaos of his impressions, what images and sounds he clung to and made into guiding staffs of his thinking. The study of the human soul in this manner is the deepest means of education. We no longer consider the head, the dead bust, but the person, the whole living being. Through a sort of inspiration and sympathy, we think, sense with him, climb on creative peaks or discover the error in its birthplace. This is living criticism, deep heuristics. Now for the first time do we understand what we are reading, feel it from its root up to the shoot. Such a reading is competition; it teaches much when the fellow competitor is worthy of the competition."

[36] With the words "respectful" and "unauthoritative, slight" Herder is mimicking critics' formulaic false politeness and false modesty.

[37] According to Diogenes Laertius, Socrates was asked by Euripides what he thought of Heraclitus's writings and replied: "What I understood of them is excellent; I believe the same of what I did not understand as well."

A human being at different times of his life is not the same, thinks differently according as he has different sensations. Everyone knows how often, especially in the case of sudden passions, our *first* judgment deceives us, and how on the other hand there is nothing to equal the *first impression* for freshness and novelty. The first, uninhibited work of an author is therefore usually his best; his bloom is unfolding, his soul still dawn. Much with him is still full, unmeasured sensation that later becomes pondering or mature thought which has already lost its youthful rosiness. We always love the half more than the whole, the promising morning more than the midday with the sun at its zenith. We prefer to have sensation rather than to know; to guess for ourselves, and perhaps too much, rather than to receive slowly enumerated. However, for the world's best interest all times of life and times of day are necessary.

The ancient Germans made decisions in drunkenness and executed them sober, others will make them soberly and execute them drunk. Meanwhile, it is true: our sphere always moves about these two foci of our ellipse and is seldom equally near to both. Perhaps it cannot and should not be so either; only let it beware of each extreme case from which it cannot return again. It grows exhausted in pure understanding and sinks in burning passion.

Perhaps no one has more richly and naturally observed the weakness of human beings and their dependence on the smallest trivialities of sensation than *Montaigne* and *Yorik*.[38] They have worked on the *hygrometry* of humanity; others must provide the *photometry*[39] and the *dynamics* of human souls. *Shakespeare*, I believe, gives examples of everything.[40]

2. Like *individual human beings*, similarly *families* and *peoples* are different from each other, and still more so; according to the circle of their manner of sensation, their manner of thought orients itself as well. Sons of a single tribal father who share a more identical organization[41] in one

---

[38] Yorik is the fictional narrator of Sterne's *Sentimental Journey*.

[39] Herder's 1775 draft explains the *hygrometry* in question as concerned with "the wet fire of our diverse little irritations and aversions" and the *photometry* in question as concerned with "how clear, how bright, how strong, how abiding the light could become."

[40] In Herder's 1775 draft we find a version of this paragraph (minus the reference to Shakespeare) set in the context of an avowal of a form of determinism. Thus immediately after the paragraph, Herder writes: "The deeper a human being has come in cognition of himself, then the more he sees little bonds, the psychological and moral servitude of his cognitions and executions . . . Free, i.e. lawless, blindly choosing, we can never become; but we become serfs of purer sensations, of a higher order – creatures of a purer, more encompassing universe. Here the soul swung itself on high with inner elasticity; the closer and more similar to God, then the freer."

[41] By "organization" Herder often means *physiological* organization.

sort of world and climate inevitably think more similarly to each other than antipodes in ethics and sensation. People have always found savage, terrible, and astonishing the religion and morals of peoples who live in rough territories, between mountains and rocky ravines, on a fire-spitting, oft quaking earth, or by terrible seas, and often nations which obviously share a single origin, close by each other, exhibit the strangest differences in this respect. Laws, government, manner of life count for still more, and in this way a people's manner of thought, a daughter of the whole, becomes also the witness of the whole. I prefer not to cite any examples because the whole sphere of the earth is a witness to this fact, and we already have several good collections about the different *minds* of the peoples based on their *circles of sensation* and *of life*. I wish we had one without any hypotheses, and as far as possible full of tested truth.[42]

To want to foist a *new doctrine* and *manner of thought* upon the quite unaltered stem of a nation's sensations without the nation mixing with this new doctrine and manner of thought in the slightest is for the most part useless and often also harmful. A people's manner of thought is the bloom of its manner of sensation; one must influence the latter or the former wilts. Suddenly loading upon a savage people the result of the subtlest abstractions, for which it has neither head nor heart, neither an analogy in mode of life nor language, always turns into a marvelous mishmash. What became of Aristotle in the hands of the Arabs? What did papacy become in China? The former a Muslim, the latter a living Confucianism.

When missionaries go to India and smell of animal blood which causes the Brahmin to shudder with horror, how much the poor Indian has to overcome before he can *hear* what is wanted of him! And when simple,

---

[42] This paragraph is in certain ways clearer in Herder's 1775 draft (a contrast which can also serve to illustrate the way in which Herder throughout intentionally "roughed up" his writing between the 1775 draft and the published version of 1778). In the 1775 draft the first part of the paragraph reads as follows: "2. Our species falls into heaps: peoples, cities, families, which all certainly live closer in a single circle of sensation, a single region, a single mode of life. Sons of a single tribal father of more identical organizations, hence also of more similar manners of thought. How different is the world in which the Arab and the Greenlander, the soft Indian and the rock-hard Eskimo, live! How different their civilization, food, education, the first impressions that they receive, their inner structure of sensation! And on this structure rests the structure of their thoughts, and the offprint of both, their language. People have always found savage and astonishing the religion and morals of peoples who live in rough territories between rocks, ravines, earthquakes, by terrible seas and volcanoes – offprint of their sensations and of the thoughts corresponding to them. What a mode of life and sensation in Japan compared to neighboring China! The former people's manner of thought is as really the daughter and witness of their sky and their earth, their mode of life and their government, their mountains and their sea, as the Chinese language and wisdom is the daughter of strict reins and rules." (Herder at this point goes on to give further empirical examples.)

noble Christianity (certainly the religion for all peoples of the earth!) even appears to them in the haze of a narrow sect and scholar's study, how is that supposed to reconcile itself with their poor brains?

Providence itself is the best converter of peoples; it changes times, manners of thought, ethics, just as it changes heaven and earth, circles of sensations and circumstances. Let Germany be compared with what it was in Charlemagne's or Hermann's times. Would they recognize it if they were to reappear? The greatest change in the world is "this *progress and cycle in the realm of minds* in accordance with *changed sensations, needs, and situations.*" The history of peoples researches into it, but who knows, given the complicated courses of fate, the *purpose* and *goal*?

Since, though, Providence never acts without means, human beings are precisely the noblest tools for this *"transformation of cognitions through sensations"* also. Those men who achieved the most in the world never stopped short at the bloom of such and such opinions but ventured to the root of sensation, the heart, the mode of life. Poets or wise men, lawgivers or generals, founders of religions or demagogues, they impacted the heart and thereby did they take effect on ideas. *Bacon* set aside divisions and scholastic speculations and went for first concepts, things, nature. Like those brothers,[43] he dug for the treasure and the rich harvest on the turned field grew of itself.

The greatest truths, like the worst lies, the most sublime cognitions and the most awful errors, of a people usually grow from seeds that are not recognized as such, they get enlivened by influences that are often taken to be the exact opposite of what they are. So let the doctor who wants to cure ills seek them in the basis; but precisely when he seeks there will the child or the sick century give him poor thanks. If he condescends to its dear infirmity and seeks to weave a fabric of health over it, who is greater and more welcome than he! – the pillar of all science and all renown. But now he lunges for our heart, for our pet sensations and weaknesses, with which we felt so comfortable – away with him, the betrayer of humanity, the murderer of our best cognitions and joys! We were willing to form an alliance with him to remain up in the tree and were willing to serve him well for that, but now he digs at the root and slits open the smooth bark – the ingrate!

---

[43] In Aesop's fable "The Farmer and His Children" (Aesop, *The Complete Fables*, Penguin, 1998, no. 83).

Socrates before his judges compared the wise city of Athens with a community of children from whom he wanted to take away their sweets and who were consequently all his enemies.[44] Socrates died, not as the thief of Athenian sweets, but as a corrupter of youth and atheist. The sophists of his time, those faithless doctors who mixed sweet poison, all worked on the flourishing of their citizens' science and happiness.

The best blessing that a father can leave behind for his philosophizing, administering (and however one wants to continue this *-ing* further) son is this: "Dear little son, caress the cheeks of your business, and let the ulcer eat and consume within. Take care of the tree at its crown and cut it according to the latest shape for example; but don't worry about the root and stem." This is precisely the father's blessing in *Gellert's* fable,[45] only with finer words.

It is an old, eternal observation that the worthiest enlighteners and improvers of the world did not take effect immediately, often went unrecognized their whole lives, and only after centuries did their renown bloom forth. Why? The sphere of their thoughts or sensations was too distant from, and too high for, their century. "What does this lump of stone mean to say?" they said at the foot of the statue (for their view did not reach higher up) and threw filth on the poor pedestal (not the statue, to which their hands full of dung did not reach). After centuries, when the day was brighter, nature emerged from the mist, and now it became clear that already at that earlier time in the dark as well many a thing had taken effect and made room for a better age. In general, a *true* thought or a *good* sensation was never lost. What is true and good is bound up with the sensorium of the creation, the great spirit on whose robe nothing comes to grief. The aloe plant blooms late but splendidly: a whole garden in a single tree!

3. Just as there is a universal *human sensation*, there must also be a universal *human manner of thought* (sensus communis) – but with no term do the moral-philosophical philistines trade in worse contraband than with this. When each person immediately appeals to universal human understanding and human sensation wherever the shoe presses his corn, then truly he does not honor the genius of humanity, which he changes into his corn, and he shows every smart person nothing more than that

---

[44] See Plato, *Gorgias*, 434a, 521e–522a.

[45] C. F. Gellert (1715–69), "Der sterbende Vater" ["The Dying Father"]. In his 1775 draft Herder sums up the dying father's message in the fable as follows: "Son, be stupid! Thus are you the cleverest!"

the suffering gentleman can think of nothing *better* to console himself with. All respect for human reason and universal human understanding and human sensation – but, dear friend, these things are something other than your lordship's [*eure*][46] nightcap.

I could tell many a fairy tale here about the universal human understanding, for example of that clever man who believed all the ships in the harbor at Athens his and felt very good about it. Or of that Arab who always calls upon all his brothers of the desert to be his guests although he has nothing for them and well knows that for miles around there is no living soul. Or of that Moorish king who allows all the potentates of the earth to eat now that he has eaten. Or – or – I am afraid, though, that universal human reason and human love and human tolerance and human ***[47] might turn against me, the inhuman one, first; so, satis superque![48]

To be sure there must be a universal human understanding, just as [there is a universal] angels' understanding, lions' understanding, and beasts' understanding; but I fear that an individual member of the species, especially an *ailing* and *infirm* one, could hardly give information about it, and sketch its height, depth, breadth, and length. As much as we go on about universal reason, just as little have we yet explained what this actually is, and where it resides, whence our reason has unfolded itself, where peoples diverge and where all come together. Universal human reason, as we would like to understand the term, is a cover for our favorite whims, idolatry, blindness, and laziness. And what true human reason, human sensation, and human need is and will be eternally – we shut our eyes and ears to that. – But again enough, and onwards to the other bright splendid question:

2. What effect does our thinking have on sensation?

And if I should also here write my first sensation as my answer, then I must say: Presently very little! What does our century not know! How does it not practice in thinking, cognizing, yes even ex professo[49] in sensation! And if the tree is only known from its fruits, where is the fruit from this thinking and sentimentalizing?

---

[46] I am taking *eure* here as an (ironically) ultra-polite singular, hence the translation "your lordship's." Alternatively, it might simply be a plural "your."

[47] Presumably the omitted word is *Scheiße*: crap.

[48] Enough and more than enough.   [49] Declaredly.

"Doubtless it must therefore not be the *right* thinking, the *right* sensation!" – and that I too believe. Mere speculating and sentimentalizing does no good; the former dulls the soul as the latter the heart. The head turns into a buried granary floor where nothing sprouts, the heart into a washed-out, shredded rag that in the end is good for nothing but becoming compost.

The evil begins early, often already in the womb. As we are, so are our children; no one can give anything better to posterity than *himself*. Life-spirits exhausted too early, fibers withered by softness, luxury, and idleness reproduce themselves – for no descended stream leaps higher than its source. The most famous speculators and sentimentalizers are hence already *born* that way. What can be impressed on this tough marrow, on this melting wax, that would remain there, that would continue to have effect? The creature slips away from the hands that would mold it like slime or jelly.

As it is raised, so does it grow up. The teachers all act as though *what they say to it were not true*; and usually it is not true for them, for they have learned it in just the same way and have not detected or sensed anything of it in their lives. This is how parents and teachers, pulpits and academic rostrums, are; the child and boy everywhere hears *talk, lies*, where it almost reaches the point that a person stops in the middle of speaking and says what that man[50] said about the punishments of hell: "Don't be afraid, dear child, I merely *have to* say that to you. Believe nothing of it, for I myself believe nothing, as you see." The great voice of example says this to them loudly and constantly.

Raised in this way among pure *word-mongery* and *active lies*, the boy learns to *recognize* only a single truth, which he also *believes* with all his heart, namely: "Creep through life like those who are before you, enjoy and talk a lot, but do little, everything only for yourself, so that you deprive yourself of nothing, and be a slave to your desires." This doctrine scents and wafts towards him out of each soft, bad habit, out of each spicy, sweet cup and warm bowl, from each heaving breast and flirting, pleasant face; he practices it early and he will practice it his whole life long.

Now how does that yield *subtle* sensations and speculations? You warm rooms, you soft pillows, you pleasant parties, and you lovely ease of silent and loud sins, what wild passions you have destroyed, to what fair novels of

[50] The source of the story is unclear. J. O. Thieß (1762–1810) recounts a similar story of himself in his *Geschichte seines Lebens und seiner Schriften*, but this was only published 1801/2.

sensations and speculations you have given birth! The eye is extinguished, the body withered, the view unsteady, the brain self-devouring. It wells up and sinks down; no impressions stick, neither beloved nor friend. No taste for the real, no longer any hope or any force for enjoyment; all the more romantic dreams and plans in the clouds. Sensations, systems, speculations with a charming transience and subtlety, in which no human being *believes* less than their author. And how should he? He can no longer believe in *anything*, thoroughly cognize *anything*, have full sensation of *anything*.

May you fare well, innocent youth, on a chaste stem, from a noble seed, you a healthy, firmly shut bud. Not blooming and unfolded too early, so as soon to wither, not rocking luxuriously in the breath of mild zephyrs; preferably, shaken by rough winds, grown up in distress, danger, and poverty, that your cognitions might become deed, your stupid, chaste, shut-up sensations truth, truth for your whole life –

> multa tulit fecitque puer, sudavit et alsit
> abstinuit Venere et vino – cui ex meliori
> – luto – finxit praecordia Titan.[51]

How well the father of humankind has provided for the *greatest* part of his race, in that he let it be born far from these overfilling cognitions and spoiling sensations. The common man and countryman cognizes and senses much more healthily than the toff and scholar, the moral savage much more healthily than the immoral European, the man of observation and activity better than the idle, half-insane genius. Irritation and salt are required for life; but like all spices, they must be used in moderation, otherwise they eat away instead of nourishing. When one beholds the *faithful* human kind which knows little but senses and practices that little fully, and then perceives the other part of humanity where cognition *destroys* sensation and vice versa, so that nothing comes of either of them, ought one not to think that speculation and sentimentalizing have been given us as the most bitter of curses? Who remained more faithful to his calling? Whose forces are more in balance and order? Who enjoys more bliss and tranquillity? Neither cognition nor sensation *alone* can provide them, without both supporting, raising, and strengthening each other.

---

[51] Much did he bear and do as a boy, sweated and froze, abstained from love and wine – whose heart the Titan made from superior stuff (Horace).

The healthiest human beings of all time had nothing exclusive about them: in them cognition and sensation flowed *together* for human life, for action, for happiness. Even the most abstract science has its observation, and for the most part even in it the happiest insight was only born in daily business, action, deed. Thus *Bacon, Sarpi*,[52] *Grotius*, and almost always *every best man* in his kind. He came to science as a friend, as a favorite, not as a serf and slave; that is why he found favor and approval. If *Homer* and *Sophocles, Ossian* and *Shakespeare, Milton* and *Dante*, had been professors of poetry, or if they had been paid by princes for their song, they would hardly have become what they are.

Cognition and sensation live only *in action*, in *truth*. Religion has died out in a circle where it does not live in *paragons*; dead confession, customs, formula-learning, and quibbling, even if it did its work in the original languages and on the lips of the [religion's] founders, can neither represent nor substitute for that daughter of heaven, who must live in human beings – or she exists no longer, she has turned back to her fatherland like Astraea.[53]

Hence in times when everything was still closer together and the threads of human destiny, gifts, and forces had not yet been so unwound and tugged out of their complex ball, in times when a single human being was more than single and each was everything that he could be – history shows clearly that great, active, good human beings were less rare then than in ages when everything is separated, each is supposed to serve with only a single force or a single forcelet of his soul, and for the rest groans under a miserable mechanism. I take the Greeks in their fairest times as an example. What might a man then be!, and what was he! *Aeschylus, Sophocles, Xenophon, Plato*: here one force supported the other, and everything remained in a forceful natural play. Since, with classes, rank, and modes of life, alas!, the abilities have separated as well; since there stands written on our chairs "what *he who sits there is supposed to be*," and he therefore, like the Pythia, doubtless learns it from beneath;[54] since diplomas, appointments, and exclusive charters make of each person

---

[52] P. Sarpi (1552–1623), Italian scholar.

[53] According to myth, Astraea, daughter of Zeus and Themis, spread the sense for justice and virtue among humankind in the Golden Age, but when humankind lost its ideals and succumbed to wickedness she returned to heaven and became a star in the constellation Virgo.

[54] The Pythia, or priestess of the Delphic oracle, was said to receive her inspiration from fumes emitted through a fissure in the rocks beneath her tripod. Herder is making a rude joke.

everything that an ape would want – since then, *one person* only[55] *thinks*, he does not see, investigate, sense, act, only calls all the time, like that locked-up bird that did not know how to say anything, "*I think!*"; another person is supposed to *act* and *direct* without using his head; no individual member any longer shares in the whole, which, by contrast, in the dear human body, the first exemplar of the republic of many forces, even the hair and the toe do.[56] And so this is why there exists that mass of dry or rotten protuberances, excrescences, and nails, accumulated piles of oyster-shells which, nailed up in rows or ground to powder, are very decorative and ornamental. Speculators without hands or eyes, talkers without feeling, rule-givers without any art or practice, parrots, ravens and critics, miserable half-thinkers and half-sensers. Hardly then does a new boil or a tiny pock shoot up on the skin anywhere on the sick, dried-out, worn-out body, but everyone runs and pilgrimages to it, is astonished, and wonders at how much force and sap the *blessed* body still has.

"Poor, sorry lady, *Philosophy*," says Shaftesbury, "she is locked up behind obscure walls, faculties, and school-prisons, and ponders and thinks"[57] – dissects what she does not have, does not enjoy, and thinks that of and about which she has no sensation. What was the scholastic speculation of the middle ages, limited to dead Aristotle, whom people did not understand and that much more dissected? And what are the empty concepts, word wreaths, and abstractions, that legion of moral-political systems, that board game of philosophical language in which everything is desecrated, in which no one any longer thinks or has any purpose, neither author nor reader? Word idols. And they get that much more worshiped because they are *supposed* to effect nothing and *effect* nothing.

No murder is more destructive than that of God's three noble gifts: *reason, sensation, language*. The youth is supposed to learn to abstract and speculate. If he learns to do so, he becomes miserable – a young

---

55 Reading *nur* for *nun*.
56 The counterpart to this sentence in Herder's 1775 draft is less wholly negative in its assessment of modern conditions: "How afterwards with classes and modes of life abilities divided too, and the one person received the calling to think, while the other was supposed to sense and act, and the body of state hence separated into limbs that were called eye and ear, head and breast, hand and foot! How thereby science and the life of the whole won, after the forces and the offices of the individuals had divided; but thereby also simultaneously all those flaws were produced which oppress our world when the individual limb is separated off and does not deeply participate in its way in the life of the whole!"
57 This is a free rendition of lines from Shaftesbury, *The Moralists* (1709). It is here translated from Herder's German.

ancient, a hollow vessel, which, however, resounds all the *more loudly*. If he does not learn to do so, and kicks the cobweb with his feet, how much that is good gets kicked to bits along with it! Who has caused the great Diana of German Ephesians, Philosophy, to be now so decried and ignobly despised but, of old!, her dear worshipers, the builders, not of gold and silver shrines, but of wooden compendia, theories, and systems.[58]

In opposition to them, the sect of the sentimentalizers has become large – the sect of small giants with high chests, strong passion, and force for action. "Has not the former great *Helvétius* proved that genius and virtue belong together like cat and dog, and are moral human beings not the weakest, most pitiful under the sun? Great will, strong independence and autonomy, a perpetual struggle with gods and demons – that is what produces heroes, nephilim,[59] lions."

If there were people who seriously thought like that, then, I believe, little happiness would lie in heroism; for Milton's devil, who built the Pandemonium and even a bridge over Chaos, always remained an unhappy devil. *Wallenstein*[60] and *Cromwell* were in the end unhappy human beings, and the lion that they had to deal with probably had its claws most deeply in their own faces. Like monsters and wild animals, human beings of that sort too can be of use to a corrupted time and political constitution; often they are rat poison and brooms to sweep the hall clean. Just as often, though, the best, most ethical, and really greatest human beings also get decried under images of that sort because, for example, they associated too closely with an oppressor and abuser of men, or because rats and frogs revolted against them. No one at all can add either a dram or a yard to his strength and stature; and the shouting of the boys on stilts behind the giant who goes ahead of them, or the braying of the little donkeys in lions'

[58] Herder's 1775 draft contains a somewhat longer and different attack on speculative, abstract philosophy. Particularly interesting, perhaps, is its description of such philosophy as something *pathological*: "[Speculators] are weaklings either through nature or through practice. If they received from nature weak organs, weak irritations, as everything weak is simultaneously subtle, they were precisely thereby determined to serve holy abstraction . . . Or they mutilated themselves, in that through abstraction they constantly weakened sensations until in the end they were no longer capable of any whole sensation . . . In both cases, one can see that one is dealing with sick people . . . A weak brain that can no longer observe due to pure speculation, no longer believe and act due to pure abstraction, weaves cobwebs instead of the silk of truth."

[59] A race of giants referred to in the Old Testament.

[60] A. W. E. von Wallenstein (1583–1634), general and statesman.

skins,[61] soon gets betrayed. This much is certain: every great and strong soul also has the capacity to become the most virtuous. Where *this* passion was possible, another that counterbalanced it was possible as well. And in general, what passion and sensation must be applied to bad, then, in order to prevent a person from being able to do otherwise? Perhaps human beings with strong souls have more *difficulty* in overcoming themselves, but they also have more *force*, and only when they have completed the victory should one call them *great* human beings – that is, when they have become *good* human beings. And then it is surely really beyond doubt that a ship that travels with great winds and well-set sails gets further than the lazy, leaking bark there at the flat, shallow bank.

Deep sensations must always be able to permit deep cognitions as well which rule over them, and hence the strongest passions and drives, well ordered, are only the sensuous schema of the strong reason that is effective in them. Even every botched great soul proves this in its *better* happy hours. When it comes to its senses after excesses and insanities, when regret and the good nature within it return, how much *more deeply* it then feels the good and bad that it has done than those loquacious talkers, those shallow heads and hearts! It would like to cry tears of blood, and the, even late, *better* cognition will certainly subsequently dig *deeper* in it, take effect more quietly and more, than the bubbling talk of all sophists has taken effect in their own dear selves, let alone in others. I know in history no fallen great man in whose case one would not still even in the debris have to admire the temple and sigh: Noble palace, how did you become a murderer's den?

*

I think that I probably need not continue these observations further since, of course, it is not the strong sensations but the weak, subtle, and delicate ones which are the favorite strings of our instrument, and we consider the former only fanciful. The stream of the ages flows strangely between its banks; it meanders, like all streams and even the great sea of the world, this way and that in opposing corners. Now the earth is favorable to cognition, now to sensation, and hence always *those* plants bloom best which sprout from the natural earth of this people, of this age. In one

---

[61] This is an allusion to Aesop's fable "The Ass Clothed in the Skin of a Lion and the Fox" (Aesop, *The Complete Fables*, no. 267).

age all the wise men gape upwards, look towards the sky and count the stars, and are for the rest nowhere less at home than in their fatherland, in their city. At another time people conduct crusades after the golden fleece of tolerance, universal religion, and love of humankind – perhaps just as fancifully as the crusaders seeking the holy grave and the system of foreign worlds.[62] This person works to make the human species into that image with a golden head, which rests on feet of clay however;[63] for another person the human species should become a monster, griffin and sphinx. The deity lets them work, and knows how to steer *one* scale of the balance through the other: sensation through better cognitions, cognition through sensation.[64]

How many prejudices we have really got beyond before which another age bent its knees! A few gentle rays of light from the nobler souls of divine human beings showed themselves,[65] initially shimmering, in a dawn. Darkness armed itself and fought long; but then the splendid sun rose and the dark night had to roll away. – Lose not heart, dear morning star, or you fair, individual rays of rosy dawn; you do not yet constitute midday, but behind you is the torch of the Almighty; irresistibly it will begin and end its course.

Light was the beginning of creation, and there is no nobler fate in the world than to illuminate, if the light is of the right sort. Even the Son of God could do nothing better here on earth than teach truth; but his light was warmth, his truth eternal life. The saying is recorded[66] that *human beings only hate truth* and *love darkness more than light because their works are inadequate*, but that in this secret and often very prettified hate there also lies the *greatest court of judgment*. The Son of God did not grow tired of *teaching truth* and even of dying as a *king of truth*. He *returned whence he had come* and left behind his footstep the blessing that *light* must *eternally remain light*, must according to its nature always *conquer darkness*, and that *everything done in it will come to God*.

---

[62] The phrase "crusaders seeking . . . the system of foreign worlds" refers to a tradition that began with Bruno and was paradigmatically exemplified by Fontenelle, *Entretiens sur la pluralité des mondes* [*Conversations on the Plurality of Worlds*] (1686).

[63] Daniel 2:31–5.

[64] Herder's optimistic picture here is amplified and made a little clearer in his 1775 draft where he concludes his historical points with the remark: "until finally – *on what level, in what favorite mixture of cognitions and sensations*, we might stand."

[65] Reading *sich* for *sie*.   [66] John 3:19–21.

It seems to me that this flight will seem so high to many readers that it is probably best to break off and treat a question which is more within the field of vision, and in accordance with the pleasure, of our age.

3. What effect does the diverse cognition and sensation have on the diverse geniuses, characters, *or whatever these magical names are?* [67]

But here I am completely dry, because I know nothing less in the world than what *genius* is – whether its gender be masculine, feminine, or neuter. [68] No one has known more about it than the genius-rich French, especially

---

[67] The corresponding section in Herder's 1775 draft is both longer and considerably less dismissive of the notion of genius than what follows here. Especially interesting are some of its opening remarks in which Herder attempts to explain the phenomenon of individual genius in accordance with the physiological theory of the mind that is more stressed and developed in the 1775 draft than in the published version of the essay:

"No two things in the world are identical to each other, let alone such an artful, infinitely manifold structure as the human being is, let alone each living wheel of this structure with its product, the irritation, the vapor of sensation, the mental water of life, let alone the eternal confluence and the mixing of these vapors in all their portals, paths, and drives, let alone, finally, the omnipresent, inwardly living I, the image of the Creator that takes effect back [on these] from out of itself. If no dissector has yet found two identical arteries, glands, muscles, canals in two bodies, then multiply and pursue the products of this difference through each play of each irritation and each sensation up to the innermost workshop of consciousness – a mass for which all numbers are too small! Infinity! Abyss!

Similarities, classes, orders, and levels are therefore only boarded walls of necessity or card-houses of play. The Creator of all things does not see as a human being sees; He knows of no classes, each thing is only identical to itself ...

The vapor of the irritation can be different in strength and weakness; and with a single degree of strength, in inner ardor and extension. The fiber can be easily stirred, and even by the light-ray; but the subtler the stirring is (may I be permitted these crude elastic expressions), then the quicker the vibrations, the more they press on and displace each other, the more lively and transient the sensation is. Or the fiber is stirred with difficulty, but strongly and deeply; then the longer does the impression last, it moves and resounds in the marrow. All phenomena of inner ardor and extension, of quick liveliness and slow strength, that are true in the levels of temperament flow from this source; only its streaming forth, mixing, and crossing is infinite.

Each ray of light contains all colors, each sound all pitches, in itself; but how differently colored are the things of the world, how differently do bodies sound! Likewise, the human being is a world of all colors, pitches, vapors, from the lowest seed of life of which he was capable up to the highest; and all are ordered by the nature in them and for the great whole to which the human being belongs into a single image, into a single string-play. He is a string-play, but in another regard only a string, the pitch of one string – though simultaneously the free player of his own string-play.

If we saw into the secret of a human conception, if we saw in the moment of becoming the confluence of all irritations, forces, life, the victory and domination of this or that pitch in the struggle – behold there the impress of this creature from the hand of its Creator!, the pitch which it is destined to sound forth for the string-play of its species and universe, in the real sense of the word, its *genius*, its *character*. It is God's seal on the brow of a conceived being; the string will sound this pitch its whole life long."

[68] This is an allusion to the still unsettled gender of the word in Herder's day.

the deep speculator, the late *Helvétius*.[69] He has, it seems to me, very subtly and wisely distinguished *having genius, being a genius*, being a man of genius and not being a man of genius; and he has also incontrovertibly proved that there really exists *no genius* (congenital natural manner) at all, but that we all appear in the world as equal flatheads, and that everything depends on how we get *trained*, and what fodder we get hold of for *becoming* geniuses. *Vaucanson* got his genius from a clock in the anteroom where he had to wait one time,[70] etc.

We Germans too have then in the most recent times followed this fair and deep track. Our philosophy and language lacked so much when neither yet knew anything about "*Schenie*";[71] suddenly there was treatise upon treatise, essay after essay, about it and we probably still have a task "about genius" to look forward to from one or another metaphysical academy in Denmark, Holland, Germany, or Italy: "What is genius? What components does it consist of, and can it naturally be decomposed into again? How does one arrive at it and lose it? And so forth."

The modest German, says *Klopstock*, thankfully calls it *giftedness*, and I have no further concept or explanation of it. *Genius* and *character* are – "the individual *human nature*[e] that God has given to someone," neither more nor less.

Now there are as many *giftednesses* as there are human beings on earth, and in all human beings there is to an extent also only a single giftedness, *cognition* and *sensation*, that is, inner *life* of *apperception* and *elasticity* of the soul. Where this *is present there is* genius, and there is *more* genius where it is *more* and *less* where it is *less*, etc. Only this inner life of the soul gives to imagination, memory, wit, intelligence, and however one counts further, *extension, depth, energy, truth*. Let one genius take on brighter colors than the peacock with its tail, let that [other] genius be more imaginative than Bellerophon's nag, let this one distinguish things finer than a cobweb – but separate from their works and undertakings *understanding, feeling* for *truth*, inner *human life*, then these are only animal forces in which a farm

---

[e] *Genius, ingenium, indoles, vis animae, character* have this meaning in all languages.

[69] C.-A. Helvétius (1715–71), *De l'esprit* [*On the Mind*] (1758) and *De l'homme, de ses facultés intellectuelles, et de son éducation, ouvrage posthume* [*On Man, on His Intellectual Faculties, and on His Education, Posthumous Work*] (1772).
[70] The example of Vaucanson is discussed by Helvétius in the second of the two works cited in the preceding note.
[71] Herder is here mocking this spelling, preferred over Abbt's, and the modern, spelling *Genie* by J. M. Heinze.

animal defeats them in each case. The orator becomes a syllable-counter, the poet a versifier or madman, the grammarian a word-merchant, as soon as heaven has denied him *that living source* or the latter dries up for him.

In this sense nature is therefore not as unfecund in geniuses as we imagine when we merely consider as such book-geniuses and paper-moths. Every human being of noble, living forces is a genius in his place, in his work, for his vocation, and truly, the best geniuses are outside the study. It is simple-minded when the educated *Gray* in his *Elegy* [*Written*] *in a* [*Country*] *Church-Yard* there pities the young farmer fellow for not having become a genius like he; he would probably have become a greater one than *Gray*, but in neither his own nor the world's best interest. Also, the eternal questions as to why nature produces fewer great *poets* than great *legislators, generals,* and so forth are deeply onesided and simple-minded, and also, as that lion said[72] when he saw his slaughtered brother on the tapestry, usually get answered, proudly or very piously, not by lions but human beings, by witnesses in their own cause.[73] As long as nature has no shortage of healthy seeds and blooming trees, it will have no shortage of human geniuses either – as the repellent idolatrous flatterers and followers of great people always fear. Mr. Thomas[74] in his eulogies to great men is especially rich in this sort of affected wit and bombast, doubtless because he is himself a great man.

Nature has no shortage of noble seeds, only we fail to recognize them and tread them to bits with our feet because we usually estimate *genius* according to *deformity,* according to premature ripeness or exaggerated growth. A well-formed, healthy, forceful human being, living in his place and functioning very intensely there, does not draw our attention to himself as much as that other person with *a single* exaggerated, trained trait that nature bestowed on him (in grace or in anger?) and that thither-flowing, superfluous saps nourished from youth up. Just as when one eye is missing the other sees somewhat more sharply, just as in the woodcutter and burden-carrier his working muscles grow strongest, and finally, just as there are diseases in which a member, the head for example, swells up and grows monstrous while the other members wither, so it is with what the language of the riff-raff calls *genius.* Here an exaggerated wit without

---

72 Reading *sagte* for *sagt.*
73 Herder is here alluding to a fable that ultimately goes back to Aesop, "The Man and the Lion Traveling Together" (Aesop, *The Complete Fables,* no. 59).
74 A.-L. Thomas (1732–85), French scholar and author who won prizes for his eulogies.

healthy understanding or faithfulness of heart; there a flying sun–steed who scorches the earth; here a speculator without the slightest observation or action, who plays with the most important things as though with meaningless numbers; a hero with passion reaching close to madness; finally, a *good head*, as people call it, that is, a bubbler and talker about things of which he understands not a word, but about which he plays with the fashionable formulas. – If *that* is genius, then how you have fallen from heaven, you fair morning star, and weave and dance like a will-o'-the-wisp on marshy meadows, or roll on as a harmful comet, before you horror and after you plague and corpses. If *that* is genius, who would want it? Who would not rather wish that nature formed such humps and monsters extraordinarily rarely! And nature does form them more rarely than our human society. When in our human society all classes, offices, professional occupations, and reasons to function are so divided and are mostly just little numerators for a single denominator that no human being dares to express, then each ruined proud *Liliputian* desires to become a giant in *his* place, to be distinguished ahead of a thousand others in his sphere. He forces the stream of his cognitions and sensations towards a single point that it may roar splendidly there, seeks to become an individual in his kind through the greatest exaggeration – he is called a *genius*! Thanks be to nature that such weeds do not grow on all fences. Before every flock, says *Huarte*,[75] there should be only a single billy-goat, otherwise they would all run astray.

Let one only read the lives of such people and they are a proof in strokes of flame of the unhappiness of their fate. Where does more unrest, envy, misanthropy, jealousy, and thirst for revenge, or, in cases when they had still baser purposes, more greed, vanity, or lust, rage than with such afterbirths and bastards of humanity? Hence with this person that godless industry that dries all the oil out of his life-lamp, with that person a gnawing hunger for science and dominating power such that he stands there like a ghostly skeleton with glowing eyes or like a living night-lamp. This person is an abstraction put together from bones, that person a flapping stork on the top of a tower in a nest full of stolen snakes and toads. The first genius who stole the spark from heaven[76] got gnawed on by the vulture, and those geniuses who wanted to go as far as to storm heaven[77] lie beneath Etna and other mountains. They even in part had a

[75] Huarte de San Juan (approx. 1529–88), Spanish doctor and philosopher.
[76] I.e. Prometheus.   [77] I.e. the Giants.

hundred hands and snakes' tails, like the heaven-storming geniuses and new religion-creators of our times, but father Zeus was strong enough for them.

Happy he whom nature early on preserved from such genius-madness!, whom the angel confronted in good time and for whom also, where necessary, when he hit his beast, the angel opened its mouth to oppose his journey, so that he did not prophesy *according to his desires*, but preserved his heart and his ways in innocence.[78] Let us – since I cannot bring myself to praise this race of hostile geniuses of the human species according to all the predicaments and attributes of inspiration; creative force; originality; heaven-aspiring, independently self-developing original power; and so forth – rather fold our wings and praise the "true genius who distinguishes himself only through his modesty," also doing so, in accordance with his modesty, more on account of what he does not know about than on account of what the world resounds with. I wish for nothing but that these strokes that I have written down may find readers who do not cheer truth at them but with a gently beating heart feel after them and ahead of them.

*

Every *noble human nature* sleeps, like all good seed, in the quiet germ – is present and does not recognize itself. What is called *genius* in regard to forces of the soul is in regard to will and sensation *character*. Whence does the poor germ know, and whence should it know, what irritations, forces, vapors of life flowed upon it in the moment of its becoming?[f] God's seal, the cover of creation, rests upon it; it was formed at the center of the earth.

This much we can see, that a child, just as it brings with it the form of its body and face, also brings with it the traits of its manner of thinking and sensing; it is a formed, entire human being, although in microcosm. You cannot add a limb that it lacks, remove a passion, a main trait that is present. Whoever knows how to eavesdrop on the delicate string-play of young children and boys, whoever only knows how to read their faces – what observations of genius and character, that is, *of individual human nature*, he will make! There sound soft notes that seem to come from another world,

---

[f] Ella si sedea/umile in tanta gloria/coverta dell' amoroso nembo:/qual fior cadea sul lembo/qual su le trecce bionde/qual si posava in terra e qual su l'onde. – *Petrarch*. [She sat humble in such glory, wrapped in a lovely cloud; a flower fell on her seam, one on her blond braids, one fell down to the ground and another onto the waves.]

[78] The allusion here is to the story of Balaam's ass, Numbers 22:21 ff.

so to speak; here and there stirs a trait of reflection, passion, sensation that prophesies a whole world of sleeping forces, an entire living human being, and it is, I think, the most flat-footed opinion that ever entered a superficial head that all human souls are alike, that they all come into the world as flat, empty tablets. No two grains of sand are like each other, let alone such rich germs and abysses of forces as two human souls – or I have no grasp at all of the term 'human soul.' Even Leibniz' simile of blocks of marble in which the outline for the future statue already lies present still seems to me insufficient, at least too dead. In the child there is a fount of diverse life, only still covered with vapor and fog. A bud in which the whole tree, the whole flower, blooms enclosed.

Do not tear it open too early, this bud pregnant with life, let it hide itself in the foliage of modesty and often dullness (as we call it). It is an irremediable harm if one opens the dear virginal flower so that it withers its whole life long. Do you not feel the joys of rosy dawn, its dear first twilight ray? Wait!, the great sun will certainly step forth.

In our age, when everything ripens early, people cannot hasten enough with the raising of young human plants either. There they stand, these young men, these hundred-year-old children, so that one beholds and shudders. The confused emotion that, as *Winckelmann* says,[79] first betrays itself through a passing irritation must be defined immediately, experiences and cognitions that should only be the fruits of adult years must be forced in with violence, so that in a short time youths even lose the desire to live, the genuine joys of young years become ever rarer, and arrogance, forwardness, rashness, and excess alternate with miserable weakness and exhaustion or end with them. If a man before the flood, a patriarch, or even just (to speak very unidealistically) an old honest farmer had the idea of judging the clamor and the shameless shrieking of our young geniuses – poor humanity, how he would pity you!

If genius and character are only *living human nature*, nothing more and nothing less, then observe this, nourish the inner source, train the activity and elasticity of the soul, but only as *it wants* to be trained. Word-memory, shells without nuts, and bodies without souls are useless, for even the smallest child is a *living* human being and had all human forces of the soul, not merely, as you imagine, the noble gift of memorizing. But just as nature makes everything grow, its noblest plant too, the human creature,

---

[79] J. J. Winckelmann (1717–68), *Abhandlung von der Fähigkeit der Empfindung des Schönen in der Kunst* [*Treatise on the Capacity for the Sensation of the Beautiful in Art*] (1763).

must grow in coverings; woe unto him who destroys and corrupts, perhaps for ever, one of the innocent through his precocity and orderless ethical wisdom!

The awakening youth finds himself at the fork of his life when boyhood and youth part ways. Often his genius appears to him there and shows him the path and heights of his future, but only – in an obscure dream. Meanwhile, for an old man too, on the last day of his life, the dream of youth, the first pulse of his whole future life, is prophetic rapture.

Whoever needs only a little development for his future work and manner of being also finds his developer easily. Some were awakened by a *Euclid*, a clock, a painting, a page of unknown figures, as though it were Apollo himself with his lyre; for others much danger, experience, often a *Rubicon*, is necessary. – *Caesar* crying at Alexander's statue, *Alexander* crying at Achilles' grave – what a prophetic, moving sight! There it sleeps in the soul, or rather it no longer sleeps but can now only come out in tears; some time in the future it will stream out otherwise.

Here too only a soul discovers the soul; only a person's own good human nature can understand, console, and intuit an alien human nature. Often it is an experience-rich, quiet, envyless old man who notices the youth lost in himself and says to him a word that resounds in his soul his whole life long. Or the same old man casts a mere glance, sign, ember down casually beside him; the youth picked it up, it was long since dead and forgotten, and then it glows again, precisely now, in the period of this demoralization, gloom, and cold; he warms his heart with it as if it just now came from the altar of love and wisdom.

Often for the young sailor, already beneath rosy dawn's visage, storms are ordained. He goes astray, comes into the land of monsters and giants, or finds his way into the gardens of *Armida*.[80] Fortunately, if the goddess with the mirror of truth appeared to him soon, that he might see himself and take courage again! Then, if he gets away early enough, the storms and pilgrimages that trained his untried ship were very useful to him. Every noble resistance, every deep and quiet suffering, imprints excellent traits on our faces and souls; the first triumphs of our youth become the punctum saliens[81] of our whole suffering life. Lamentations, though, if the youth succumbs, if he dwells too close to depressing or seducing objects! He becomes deformed, becomes hard and dry, or soft and lecherous, and

---

[80] An enchantress in Tasso's *Gerusalemme liberata*.   [81] Literally: jumping point.

lightly breathes away his life in the prime of his years. Spoiled too early, he spoils in his turn, and knows no better. Exposed to enmity too early and too long, he covers everything with misanthropy and bile – many good human beings are entirely or half lost in this way.

It is well known that an oak grows long and slowly, whereas the toadstool shoots up in a single night. This often happens with those human beings who are most special and destined for the greatest things as well. *Brutus* the younger long remained brutus;[82] *Ximenes*[83] long went round with his beggar's bag, which did not well suit him; and *Correggio* was no longer young when he cried out his *io son pittore*.[84] The noble human being has within him the heaven's ladder which he must first surmount before a single word escapes him; the everyday talker, that is, the *good head*, the talkative human being with the easy lip, is always at the end, even before he has started. He has, as people say, *an immediate answer for everything*. He can swill the ocean dry with an opened nutshell for dessert.

O you holy, dear quietness of delicate, modest hearts, how beneficial you are! You are beneficial for him who enjoys you; he spares himself a hundred reproaches, illusions, astonishments, questions, and doubts; he spares others the sight of effort, and affords action. *Newton* the youth had all the theories that immortalized his life ready, and did not know that he had them. The fall of an apple under the tree taught him the system of the worlds, and for his whole life he remained the modest, quiet, chaste man, the true worshiper of God. Look at *Shakespeare's* face, [and say] whether there on its gentle, quiet surface in which all objects, actions, and characters in the world were able to be reflected the ape-wit, the grinning malice, the *Yahoo* that distinguishes other geniuses governed. He was and remained an actor who never even raised himself to the first roles. *Bacon's* bright soul had much similarity with the heavenly body at whose darkening he always fell into a swoon;[85] he does not burn, but he shines gently and illuminates. What a loving singer of human beings *Homer* must have been, when one glides down the ever level and gentle stream of his songs! What quiet, envyless men *Virgil* and *Horace*, *Petrarch* and *La Fontaine*,[86] *Copernicus* and *Kepler*, *Montaigne* and *Sarpi*. The mystic

---

[82] *brutus*: clumsy, stupid.
[83] F. J. de C. Ximenes (1436–1517) became archbishop of Toledo and was of poor origin.
[84] "I am a painter [too]."   [85] I.e. the moon.
[86] J. de La Fontaine (1621–95), French poet.

Malebranche allowed himself to be tortured with criticism by R. *Simon* for a long time before he found his *Descartes*. *Luther* struggled for a long time with himself before he began to struggle with the world, and, despite iron hardness and strength in the work of his calling, always remained in private life the gentlest and most honest man, who wrestled more with himself than some believe of him.

Generally, what people theorize on and on concerning congenital *inspiration*, the clear, ever streaming, and self-rewarding source of *genius*, is puerile hysteria. The true man of God rather feels his weaknesses and limitations than that he bathes with moon and sun in the deep abyss of his "positive force." He *strives* and hence must not yet *have*; often knocks himself sore on the cover that surrounds him, on the shell that encloses him, so far from feeling himself always in the empyrean of his perfect blessedness. The ray that from time to time penetrates deep inside him [saying] what he is and what no one else *should* be for him is for the most part only a consoling sight, only a cup of fortification for new striving ahead. The more infinite is the medium, the side of the world, for which he has a sense immediately behind his own clod of earth, the more he will feel powerlessness, desert, exile, and thirst for new sap, for a higher flight, and the completion of his work.

I could continue for a long time sketching strokes of this sort – which, to be sure, only stand here for the person with understanding, and should seem nonsense to the great mass of people – but what good would it do? To the man who has *genius* and *character*, that is, a good individual nature, as God gave it to him and he believes himself not to have received in vain, such lines say infinitely less than he himself knows. And since they without doubt mean *nothing* to the mass of crows, sparrows, and magpies, therefore rest, dear feather!, rather give them a definition of *Schenie*[87] and its diverse kinds, the *universal* and *particular, philosophical* and *aesthetic, historical* and *psittaco-critical*[88] genius, etc.

*

But unfortunately! I cannot receive that from my goose-feather. It cackles to me that of course those are no distinctions *of nature* but of human *guilds* and *books*, but that nature does not make its divisions according to the

---

[87] Herder is again mocking this spelling preferred by some of his contemporaries.
[88] The Greek word *psittakos* means a parrot.

compartments of our bookshelves and the doctoral caps of our academic faculties. It has the goose-genius and the goose-character to say aloud that in these cells and districts the healthy human understanding and human character which are the sole true genius often stops;[89] indeed, it would almost prefer to cackle through the streets of the cobblers and tailors, rag-and-bone-men and linen-weavers, page-boys [*Jäger*][90] and hackney-cab drivers, and to cluck at their diverse *Schenie's*. – You are right, dear feather!, for no gardener has ever yet named his plants according to the blue or red pot into which he happened to put them, let alone has a botanist regarded merely those plants that grow on dung-beds and in greenhouses as all the living flora. One would therefore have either to characterize *from out of the soul* or to go through *all* the positions, forms, and vocations in and for which nature ever molds its human beings. But who can do that? And who therefore can make a division of, and characterize, *geniuses*? – However, let us at least attempt a single division!

In everything that is force, *intensity* [*Innigkeit*] and *extension* can be distinguished. It must also be that way in the case of *human nature*, and *that* would perhaps be a division. A human being who is strong in himself feels himself into only little, but very deeply, and can almost live his life in a single thing. These are human beings of strong sense, of deep cognition and sensation, and mother nature has already herself marked out this species of her children. One sees no unsteady look; no small transient fire; no confused, semi-sketched traits – what their formation says it says entirely, simply, and with deep effect. A human being who felt thus strong, healthy, and well through all members and passions, how faithfully he must receive and give everything!, how many distractions, prejudices, and semi-judgments he must be free of! – a mortal image of divine strength and simplicity. Armed against ten small vices, despising *many small* motives, he prefers to act from a single great motive, pays no heed to others because he feels his own self, etc. – Another species of force compensates through extension, through liveliness and speed, for what it lacks in deep intensity. These are the *esprits*,[91] spirits, all colors in play. Nature has *ensouled* their formation, given them inclinations that are not

---

[89] This is a rather striking example of hendiadys or the Pindaric construction.

[90] *Jäger*, literally "hunters," but here evidently used, as its French equivalent, *chasseurs*, often is, to refer to page-boys and the like.

[91] *esprits*: minds, spirits, wits.

a glowing but a shimmering of rays far around them. Full of imagination, flight, talent, ease in planning, in announcing, in showing, but little of persistence, action, endurance. – I could make a division in this way and make much play of how, then, Mr. *Understanding* and Mrs. *Sensation* relate to each other in this connection; how these two classes of thinkers and sensers are necessary complements to each other, in order to limit, strengthen, and raise each other; that intensity is the center and extension the radius, etc. – But behind all this play what determinate would have been said, then? And would not the levels of *intensity* and *extension* still endlessly break into and apart from each other?

Now I could go through the forces of the soul alphabetically and show:

> that in the soul, while *memory* prevails
> the solid pow'r of *understanding* fails,
> where beams of bright *imagination* play
> the *memory's* soft figures melt away –

as the wise *Pope* chose to put it. Or I could with *Bacon* divide the dry, cold makers of *distinctions* from the warm, sublime *pairers* of new thoughts and images – a division which certainly contains more deep and modest truth than that jingle of Pope's. Or with *Pascal* the deux sortes d'esprits, l'un de pénétrer vivement et profondément les conséquences des principes – l'esprit de justesse; l'autre de comprendre un grand nombre des principes sans les confondre, l'esprit de géométrie[92] – which for the most part boils down to my first division between the intensity and the extension of the mental gift. – I could pursue these two sortes d'esprits[93] and even with *Huarte* order the four compartments of the brain in accordance with them – but enough!, drop everything until we get the task set by some European society or other that would like to know what genius is and how many types of genius there are.

The body of universal human nature is mightily large, and who knows who is a fiber of its eye or a part of its heart muscle, a nail on its foot or a piece of skin belonging to its fingertip "that one smooths off in order to have subtler sensations," as the most recent theorist of all

[92] The two sorts of spirits, the one of penetrating in a lively and profound way the consequences of principles, the spirit of justice; the other of understanding a large number of principles without confusing them, the spirit of geometry.
[93] Sorts of spirits.

learned geniuses – the sentimentalizers and mystics not excepted – has remarked?[94]

*

I prefer to conclude the whole of my long treatise with a few general notes:

1. If anything in it is true, how fine is the *marriage* that God has made in our nature between *sensation* and *thinking*! A fine web, only separable into the two through verbal formulas. The highest creature seems to share with us a single fate, to have to *sense* if it does not call forth the whole from out of itself and [yet] *thinks*. And what creature can do that? None except our philosophers, the teachers and apprentices on the high tree of wisdom.

2. All so-called *pure thinking* into the deity is deception and game, the worst mysticism, which only fails to recognize itself as such. All our thinking arose from and through sensation, and also still bears, despite all distillation, rich traces of it. The so-called *pure* concepts are for the most part numerals [*Ziffern*] and zeros from the mathematical table, and, applied flat-footedly and clumsily to natural things of our so composite humanity, also have the value of ciphers [*Ziffernwert*].[95] For that man who seeks out and gets rid of these little ghosts in the whole of modern metaphysics, for him wait more than for the ghost-hero *Thomasius* wreaths of honor.[96] Only he must also not be frightened by many an empty scare, and by lunges that these little ghosts make at his face.

3. To want to escape a few oppressive *sensations* by shaking off the burden of this life is a dangerous step, for *dreams*, as Hamlet says,[97] or as we said, *sensations* and *thoughts*, must come again. And now, *which* sensations? *Which* thoughts? Let one approach a suicide, and ask why he did it, how small the causes were, how easy to deal with if only someone had paid heed to his inner state – and as things are, he closed himself up,

---

[94] J. A. Eberhard had remarked in his *Allgemeine Theorie des Denkens und Empfindens* (1776) concerning subtlety of feeling: "Those who file off the upper skin on their fingertips want to provide themselves with a more exact sense of feeling, and to perceive the otherwise imperceptible unevenness of a surface" (p. 105).

[95] Herder is punning here, in a way impossible to reproduce in English, on two different meanings of the word *Ziffer*: (1) a numeral, (2) a cipher, i.e. an arithmetical symbol possessing no intrinsic value (though multiplying whatever number it is placed after). His point is evidently that, when given the sort of inept application which he mentions, the so-called pure concepts have no value.

[96] This is presumably an allusion to the campaign by C. Thomasius (1655–1728) against the persecution of witches.

[97] *Hamlet*, act 3, sc. 1, ll. 65 ff.

the tree gathered all its violence in order to uproot itself – there it lies. Withered, but the roots and twigs are on it. And where is the Dryad that gave life to this whole tree? Where is she?

4. The immortality of a metaphysical monad is nothing but *meta-physical* immortality, whose physical side does not convince me. If *soul* is what we feel, what all peoples and human beings know about, what its name says too, namely, that *which ensouls us*, original source and epitome of our thoughts, sensations, and forces, then no demonstration of its im-mortality *from out of itself* is possible. We enfold in words what we want to unfold, presuppose what no human being can prove or even just com-prehends or understands, and one can hence infer whatever one wants. The *transition* of our *life* into a *higher life*, the *remaining and waiting* of our *inner human being* for the *day of judgment*, the *resurrection* of our *body* to a *new heaven* and a *new earth*, cannot be demonstrated from out of our monad.

5. It is an inner characteristic mark of the truth of religion that it is entirely *human*, that it neither sentimentalizes nor theoretically ponders, but thinks and acts, lends force and resources for thinking and acting. Its cognition is *living*, the epitome of all cognition and sensations, *eternal life*. If there is a universal *human reason* and *sensation*, it is in religion, and precisely this is its most unrecognized side.

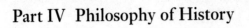

Part IV Philosophy of History

On the Change of Taste[1] (1766)

On the diversity of taste and of manner of thought among human beings

As soon as I find something true or beautiful, as soon as I can convince myself by means of reasons that something is true or beautiful, then nothing is more natural than the expectation that every human being will have the same feeling, the same opinion, with me. Otherwise, of course, there would be no basic rule of truth and no firm basis for taste. As soon as it is shown that what I on the basis of reasons take to be true, beautiful, good, pleasant can likewise on the basis of reasons be regarded by another as false, ugly, bad, unpleasant, then truth, beauty, and moral value is a phantom that appears to each person in another way, in another shape: a true *Proteus* who by means of a magic mirror ever changes, and never shows himself as the same.

That this contradiction has real weight and not merely superficial sparkle: Let us observe how annoyed and dismayed those people become to whom it suddenly presents itself in an unusual light. A good, honest man who only knows the world from the market-place, from the coffeehouse, and at most out of the *Hamburg Correspondent* is as amazed when he comes upon a story and discovers that manner of thought and taste change with climate, with regions of the earth, and with countries – I say, he is as amazed as Paris can ever be astonished at the arrival of an Indian prince. His astonishment in the end dissolves into laughter:

---

[1] I retain this title used by Herder's German editors. However, as will be seen from the essay's contents, it is misleadingly narrow; Herder is by no means exclusively concerned with aesthetic judgments.

247

"But what sort of fanciful stuff" he exclaims "is there not in books! Who will ever believe this?" Or he takes all these nations to be fools, each in its own way. Why? Because they have another manner of thought and taste than his lady mother, his dear nurse, and his wise schoolmates implanted in him. – Do we not often make ourselves participants in this error when we immediately declare the manner of thought and taste of savages to be fanciful or foolish because it deviates from ours? – And yet we laugh at the Chinese who took their country to be the rectangle of the world and painted us poor inhabitants of the entire rest of the world as gargoyles and monsters into the four corners of this rectangle. Why? They did not know us, and they took themselves to be the monopolists of insight and taste!

How often one must think one is in China when in common life one daily hears such Chinese judgments which out of ignorance and pride (two dear sisters who never leave each other's side) reject everything that contradicts their manner of thought and comprehension. They are so stubborn in support of their opinions and sensations that they are as ready with the names *dumb* and *foolish* as the Greeks and Romans [were] with the title *barbarian*, which with sovereign majesty they conferred on all peoples who were not – Greeks and Romans. – Now since the words *dumb* and *foolish* occur in no Logic among the reasons apt for convincing, the other party supports his opinion and his taste with still firmer stubbornness – and thus do we see among nations and private individuals a contention of viewpoints which perplexes a wise man and makes him uncertain whether, then, all these fanatical people know what they are contending about.

Many of the doubting [sort of] philosophers have therefore tied all these scruples together into a knot which they have taken to be beyond untying: "If one were to consider the great diversity that holds sway between opinion and opinion, taste and taste, viewpoint and viewpoint among nations and individual people, then one would almost have to doubt oneself." Is, then, even what I take to be true true, since hundreds who have an equally good human understanding take it to be false? Is, then, even that beautiful which I imagine so? Can I trust myself? – Among the ancients, the *Pyrrhonists* and the *Academic* sect are known for these doubts. Among the moderns, *La Mothe le Vayer, Montaigne,* and *Hume* have especially occupied themselves with the *aforementioned* type of scruple.

I do not believe that I am writing this page for doubters; so I shall let all the aforementioned men rest in peace. I merely want to gather historical examples of how far the diversity of human beings can extend, to bring it into categories, and then to try to explain it. I shall lead my readers onto a knoll and show them how in the valley and on the plain creatures stray about that are so diverse that they hardly have a common name left; however, they are our fellow brothers, and their history is the history of our nature. – I therefore hope that this view will be entertaining and instructive; instructive because it advises us to gain for ourselves firmness in opinions and taste, and pleasant because it summons past our eyes a very various train of images and play-acts – a drama which Lucretius draws with the following magnificent colors:

> Suave, mari magno turbantibus aequora ventis,
> E terra magnum alterius spectare laborem – –
> Suave etiam belli certamina magna tueri
> Per campos instructa – –
> Sed nihil dulcius est, bene quam munita tenere
> Edita doctrina sapientum templa serena:
> Despicere unde queas alios, passimque videre
> Errare, atque viam palantes quaerere vitae,
> Certare ingenio, contendere nobilitate. – –[2]

First section: Are human beings diverse in relation to the judgments of the senses?

It is indeed true that in modern times the great differences in body that were invented about whole nations in the old cosmographies and travel descriptions have disappeared; there are no longer people who have their heads on their chests, their mouths in the region of their navels, who have a foot with whose blade they provide themselves with shade against the heat of the sun; the nations of *Pygmies* and *Patagonians*, of dwarfs and giants, have become more or less imperceptible; the men with apes' tails on *Borneo* have not been confirmed, although *Maupertius* still ventures a treatise on account of their tails, devoted to justifying them as an extended

---

[2] It is sweet, when on the high sea the winds stir up the waves, to observe from land the great toil of another . . . It is sweet too to behold the great struggles of war arrayed through the plains . . . But nothing is pleasanter than to occupy a serene temple well fortified by the established doctrine of the wise, whence to look down on others, and to see them stray in every direction, and wandering seek life's way, compete for genius and contend for nobility. (Lucretius, *De Rerum Natura* [*On the Nature of Things*], bk. 2, ll. 1–11.)

vertebra; all these nations belong with the *Cacklogallinians, Liliputians,* and *Houyhnhnms* in the world that *Swift* created.

But despite that, there are still great diversities in relation to the structure of the human body: in size and shape, in color and lineaments, in the proportion and the varying firmness of the parts. *Buffon* has a treatise in the third part of his natural history about the diverse types of human beings in relation to the formation of the body which collects together what is most noteworthy, albeit very incompletely, and to which I refer [the reader]. Thus one knows that the negroes (who are distinguished from the actual Moors or Mauritanians) get their coal-black color not from the surface of a sunburned skin, but from glands which lie beneath their spongy, fatty skin and are full of a black, ink-colored fluid. Since this structure of the body cannot simply be derived from the heat of the sun, some have been compelled to assume a divine punishment on the sons of Ham, and yet others even a black Adam, because the diversity between them and the whites was too extensive; others, by contrast, have wanted to explain it from the overflowed bile of the tribal father of this nation; meanwhile, the difference certainly still remains a noteworthy phenomenon. – Likewise it is amazing that certain peoples have a curly wool on their whole body instead of hair, as in the case of all genuine negro nations in Africa, and that in great regions of the earth, for example *North America* and *Lapland,* beards are as much foreign to the men as [it is the case that] we for our part give ourselves the greatest trouble twice or thrice weekly to get rid of this burden and to become elegant under the hands of a barber, i.e. to get a femininely smooth chin.

But I do not want to talk about this formation of the body in general, but only insofar as it has an influence on the manner of thought, and here I am talking about the *senses,* which, after all, are so to speak the door for all our concepts, or the *optical medium* though which the idea comes in like a ray of sunlight. Now if these instruments are constituted in a special way, then the manner of thought arising therefrom must be formed in a special way as well. And this can therefore be the first source of the diversity in *concepts* and in *sensation.*

Virtually all animals and most savages excel us infinitely in the strength of their senses because in the case of our more subtle constitution the soul gets developed for thought and the inner sense can only be effective to the extent that we abstract from outer sensations; our body becomes that much duller the more we become, especially during the years of growth in which the nerves are supposed to develop themselves for sensation, so to speak betrothed to abstraction. By contrast, the savage, whose senses get trained from youth up by hunting and fear, receives from the companions with whom he stands in such a relation of equality something of their sharp sensuality as well: from the bird of prey its hawk- and eagle-eye, from the pursued deer its fine hearing, and from beasts of prey their sharp sense of smell. – All travel descriptions confirm that a Kaffir excels the European in the strength of the senses to such an extent that it often seems incredible to us.

But human beings are very diverse not only in respect of the strength and weakness but in respect of the very constitution of their sensation. I begin with the crudest sense, that of feeling – in which case, to go by the few traces that one can discover, there must be the greatest diversity, except that it proves impossible to express this diversity of sensation verbally. What softness or hardness, coldness or warmth, smoothness or roughness is we only know through feeling; a person who was born without feeling has no conception of all these ideas, and nor can he (let one attempt it some time in relation to oneself), nor can he[3] be given any. Thus although all human beings are more or less in agreement in what they call *soft* or *hard*, *smooth* or *rough*, still I can never say whether they are in full agreement because I have no way of testing it. Since the whole sensation depends on the constitution of the nerves pertaining to feeling, no human being is quite exactly in agreement in feeling with another, because it cannot easily be the case that in two human beings the whole structure of the nerves is *entirely* tuned in a single way.

This is why so many people have a *stubbornly idiosyncratic* [*eigensinniges*] sense of feeling which noticeably deviates now in this matter and now in that from the sensation of another person. This person can never lightly touch velvet, whereas that person by contrast feels a voluptuous thrill in doing so. I have known a man who made a festive hour of rooting through all sorts of fine blond hair, for which his commercial office was a storage depot, with gently shut eyes – a pleasure which certainly presupposes a special structure of his sensory fibers. How many people there are who feel a shudder run over their whole body when they hear an iron stylus scratch over stone, for whom the cry of a *single* animal is unpleasant, as for the lion the cock's crowing, and for the camel the yelping of dogs;

---

[3] This is another example of Herder using anadiplosis.

how many who faint when they encounter a smell which is neither too strong nor in itself unpleasant merely because it is unpleasant for them; how many who experience a nausea when they encounter a certain taste, even if they only see the food in the dish; how many who at the sight of a color or of something else want to, so to speak, jump out of their skins due to a natural, instinctive shudder. I would have to cite many more illustrations here, except that this matter is too obvious, so that example upon example must occur to each of my readers. – If, therefore, feeling displays so many deviations and differences as soon as it expresses itself in senses in relation to which we are more able to explain ourselves, then what is more probable than that it can be just as diverse in its coarser consistency, except that this diversity does not express itself. I would need to take on another body if I wanted to experience whether two different human beings have a completely similar sense of feeling.

Would it perhaps be possible to prevent such a *stubbornly idiosyncratic* sort of sensation? Since in most cases it depends on the structure of the nerves – hardly! – That is why in most such cases there is also a cause which affected them, either during the mother's pregnancy or in the earliest period of their lives – except that very often the cause remains unknown. Their fiber-web has so to speak received a pitch that is peculiar to it through a contingent event, and every sensation that fights against this pitch through a complete discord causes a shuddering that is as unnatural as that which occurs in the parts of a glass that gets shattered by a cry. – And in this case all disputing against what the other person feels is useless, "I will not allow myself to be talked out of what I feel!"

However, it is also possible for an early aping of others and a long habituation to bring us to the fancy that we cannot bear this or that sensation, whereas in fact the aversion is not natural to us. In this way does the weakly child who was raised behind the oven become cowardly; he falls into a swoon when he smells gunpowder and is thunderstruck when he sees the dagger flash; and finally the pitiable creature forms the fancy that he cannot bear to see a drawn dagger because he was neglected in his mother's womb. In this way do spoiled children very often fancy themselves to have a natural disgust for foods, an aversion innate to them against this or that, an insurmountable fear of vaults and coffins which they have merely adopted through a bad education in their youth, through the little ghost stories of their nurses, and through bad contingent events. Those parents earn their children's eternal gratitude who watch over them in this regard so that they do not in older years, when habit has turned into second nature for them, when they are sick in their imaginations, become a burden to themselves among others. How often in the years when we still take in all impressions like soft wax could that be driven out of us, through a small reprimand, through two words of better instruction, through a bit of serious effort, or at most through a little prescription of birch twigs, which afterwards turns into deeply rooted *stubborn idiosyncrasy* in *sensation*. Then one would not so often hear the words, [delivered] with a superior wrinkling of the nose, "I cannot do that, I was not brought up for that!" Then many would not need to arm themselves against the scent of the masses with much solemn dignity through a prise de contenance.[4] We would have the same sensations as others. Why? Because we *want* to have the same sensations as others.

However, I make here with a deep respectful bow a small exception: that there can be a certain *artificial stubborn idiosyncrasy* of sensation which in the case of the fair sex also appears *fair*. When a fair woman starts back, here from a frog, there from a spider, and here from a little mouse (even if it runs about attached to a thread), then in one woman this shows a fine delicacy of feeling, and in another it is supposed to show that, and she imitates this fair fright, this delicate shudder. In the case of the latter woman it still proves a fair trait; in the case of another woman it does perhaps indeed already appear artificial because she lacks the grace to confer on it value and effectiveness. But if there occurs, to top it all, an effeminate dandy who affects this peculiarity of sensation as a *hermaphrodite*, then he proves a puppet of self-indulgent imagination [*Einbildung*] and an unbearable male woman. – [Text breaks off.]

On the change in nations' taste through the sequence of the ages (a fragment)

When that man saw trees being planted for descendants he cried out: "We always have to be doing something for our descendants; I really wish that our descendants would do something for us too!"[5] This foolish man, who did not remember that he was himself a descendant, that he owed everything to his ancestors, and that posterity would be a part of him,

4 Adoption of a superior attitude.
5 This story seems to be based on a saying of the Roman poet Statius about the virtue "quae serit arbores, ut alteri seculo prosint [which sows trees that they might benefit another century]."

should have moved ahead several centuries in his imagination and put himself in the position of the descendants who would enjoy these trees. What were these now able to do for him as their ancestor? Think of him! But what were they able to do for their descendants? Work for them!

Every human being in every age thus stands in a middle, so to speak. He can gather about him the extinguished images of his ancestors, he can call forth their shades and, so to speak, make a feast for his eyes when he makes them rustle past before his eyes. But can he also cast a prophetic look into the later times beyond his own grave and, so to speak, see his children and grandchildren walking upon his ashes? History makes the look into the past certain; the prospect into the future is more obscure – but even this shadowy darkness causes pleasure.

When from this philosophical height one casts a look before one and behind one, when one calls the spirit of a dead century from its ashes, so to speak, when one compares various succeeding ages with one another and believes that one glimpses a continuous thread, a connected whole, then what sort of conjecture is more natural than this: Is this chain of changes that has run around many centuries in such a regular manner destined to break off with us? Is it not destined to continue running on after us? How so? When one takes together many alterations of the past, when one sees what a force for change the arm of time has, and how it has used it hitherto, is not the bold view then somewhat forgivable: these will perhaps be the consequences of change behind our backs; everything before us has changed in this way, everything after us will change in this way?

However, even if this prophetic view were illusory, still the prospect upon the world of the past remains all the more useful. The spirit of changes is the kernel of history, and whoever does not make it his main focus to separate out this spirit, so to speak, to put together in imagination the taste and the character of each age, and to travel through the various periods of world events with the penetrating look of a traveler hungry to learn, he, like that blind man,[6] sees human beings as trees, and consumes in history a dish of husks without a kernel, in order to ruin his stomach. – The greatest historians have therefore reached their peak by taking note of this change over the course of time, by when narrating also keeping in mind that they are leading their reader about not merely in order

---

[6] Mark 8:23–5.

to make him see but also in order to make him learn. If *Voltaire* has some merit as a historian, then it is in the viewpoint of his often telling remarks about the spirit of events. But the greatest man in this regard, in my opinion, is the *historian* of *Britain, Hume*, an author who knows the difficult art of applying the pragmatic techniques of a *Tacitus* and a *Polybius* in accordance with the taste of our own age.

My preface is admittedly too long for this one little treatise. But if this treatise were to be well received by the public, then it might be merely the precursor of similar observations *about the spirit of the changes in various ages*. When philosophy is led by history and history is enlivened by philosophy, then it becomes doubly entertaining and useful.

*

People who, ignorant about history, know only their own age believe that the current taste is the only one and so necessary that nothing but it can be imagined. They believe that everything that they find indispensable because of habituation and education has been indispensable for all ages, and they do not know that the more comfortable something is for us then the more novel it must probably be. Generally, pride accompanies this ignorance as well (two siblings who are as inseparable as envy and stupidity); their times are the best because they live in them and other ages lack the honor of their acquaintance. These people are similar to the Chinese who, because they knew no one but themselves, considered their country to be the rectangle of the earth and painted gargoyles and monsters in the corners of this rectangle – a space which was supposed to give portraits of us poor inhabitants of the rest of the world. We laugh about these Chinese, but how often does one not think one is in China when one hears judgments from people who know the world only according to the corner in which they find themselves, and according to the *Hamburg Correspondent*.

Two looks at history dissolve this prejudice. Time has changed everything so much that one often needs a magic mirror in order to recognize the same creature beneath such diverse forms. The *form* of the earth, its *surface*, its *condition*, has changed. Changed are the *race*, the manner of *life*, the manner of *thought*, the form of government, the taste of nations – just as families and individual human beings change. And if our original ancestor Adam, if Noah, if the tribal fathers of each people were to rise from the dead – heaven!, what a sight this would be for them!

None of these changes is as difficult to explain as the alteration of *taste* and *manner of thought*. Could it be that what a nation at one time considers good, fair, useful, pleasant, true it considers at another time bad, ugly, useless, unpleasant, false? – And yet this happens! Is not truth, fairness, moral goodness the same at all times? Yes, and yet one observes that propositions for which at certain times each person would have sacrificed his last drop of blood at other times get damned to the fire by precisely the same nation; that fashions which a few years ago each person found fair soon afterwards get hissed off; that ruling customs, that favorite concepts of honor, of merit, of what is useful can blind an age with a magical light, that a taste in these and those sciences can constitute the tone of a century, and yet all this dies with the century. – This skepticism should almost put us off trusting our own taste and sensation. – [Text breaks off.]

3:30

Older Critical Forestlet (1767/8) [excerpt on history]

The plan in accordance with which Herr Winckelmann wanted to execute his excellent history [*Geschichte*] of art is by his own advertisement this, and I confess that in a modern book such an advertisement has seldom been so greatly executed: "The history of the art of antiquity is no mere narration of the chronological sequence and of the changes in it, but I understand the word *history* [*Geschichte*] in the broader meaning that it has in the Greek language,[1] and my intention is to supply an attempt at a doctrinal structure [*Lehrgebäude*]."

I shall leave it to certain philologists of my nation to collect together the loci for many meanings from several lists and dictionaries. To keep it nice and short!, the word *history* [*Historie*] can according to its Greek origin mean "observation, knowledge, science," and a history is of course also a correct narration of things that have happened.

But a doctrinal structure? Did the Greeks want to construct such a thing in their history [*Geschichte*]? Can such a thing be constructed so that the work still remains history? – For my purpose it does not yet matter whether history be a narration of complicated occurrences [*Begebenheiten*][2] or of simple productions, whether of data or of facta.[3] Even a history of the thoughts, the science, the art of a people, or of many peoples, is, however simple the subject matter may be, still a history of occurrences, deeds, changes. And so if a single historian must be able to supply a doctrinal

[1] Although Winckelmann uses the Germanic word *Geschichte* here, he is thinking of the Greek word *historia*, for which German has the cognate *Historie*, a word which Herder goes on to use more or less interchangeably alongside *Geschichte* in this material.
[2] Literally: things given (cf. *data* in the continuation of the sentence).
[3] Literally: whether of things given or of things done/made.

257

structure, then consequently every historian must be able to do so in his manner as well.

And why should he not be able to supply it? Every occurrence, every factum[4] in the world is in its manner *a whole*, a whole that can be represented for instruction. So what is such a clear representation, a complete description concerning it for the instruction of other people, but a historical [*historisches*] doctrinal structure? Every occurrence, every factum, in the world has its grounds and causes which, so to speak, produced its nature; it also has consequences of its nature – and what else is a description of this but a historical doctrinal structure? Finally, every occurrence is merely a link in a chain, it is woven into the connection with others, it is effective in the coming together of worldly things through attraction and repulsion – and a plan of this connection, of this world-system of effects, is this not a historical doctrinal structure? Is a historian of this scope not a philosopher? Not a pragmatic systematizer?

All too gladly! And among all philosophers, architects of doctrine, and systematizers such a philosopher of the world would for me be the first, the greatest, if he existed. But precisely his greatness makes it the case that I am unable to reach his face; so I cast down my eyes, and prefer to think.

If history [*Geschichte*] in its simplest sense were nothing but a description of an occurrence, of a production, then the first requirement is that the description be *whole*, exhaust the subject, show it to us from all sides. Even the annalist, the writer of memoirs, is obligated to this completeness, and hence consequently duty bound to give a "doctrinal structure" in an individual sense. To be sure: in an individual sense. Here a merely one-sided viewpoint is erroneous, a one-sided sketch of it useless. Let his historical datum be for him a structure that he goes around on all sides, that he sketches from all sides. But I would like to see the historian who even merely in this *could* achieve all completeness. Just as it is impossible for a whole body to be perceived, represented on a surface, as it is without projection from a viewpoint, it is equally impossible for the annalist and the writer of memoirs to make a historical doctrinal structure out of a subject, even if it were the most important of subjects, and even if his account of the detail were nothing less than [*nichts minder als*][5] rambling

---

[4] Literally: thing done/made.

[5] The German phrase *nichts minder als* would more commonly mean almost the opposite of this: anything but. But for Herder's use of it, as here, in the same sense as its English look-alike, cf. *This Too a Philosophy of History for the Formation of Humanity*, G4:42.

excess. Only ever, even just individually, even just in external appearance, the *attempt* at a doctrinal structure, and that is already enough!

Enough for us one-sidedly seeing human beings, but not enough for its many-sided subject matter; and how much less enough for this subject matter's *inner aspect*, for the causes of its origination, for the condition of its nature! Here historical seeing stops and prophecy begins. Since I [can] never see cause as cause and effect as effect, but must always infer, conjecture, guess; since in this art of inference nothing but the similarity between cases is my witness, and hence my intelligence or my wit for finding this similarity between cases, this consequence of one case through another, is my sole guarantor of truth; since, however, this guarantor can be nothing but *my* intelligence, *my* wit, and hence can be a deceptive witness, and perhaps a prophet of truth only *for me* and a few of my brothers – one therefore sees that the historian and the philosopher of history do not fully stand on common ground. Set two observers with the same kind of telescope in one spot and they will see more or less similarly; but judge, infer, conjecture about what they have seen – no longer so completely similarly. The one of them seeks the causes of the occurrence who knows where, and how differently – and there and thus differently does he find them as well. The one of them and the other – each according to the state of his head, according to the domestic constitution of his intelligence and wit. Finally, it is completely the case that no human being can see the efficacy of the discovered cause, the more or less of its efficacy; this each person has to infer, suspect, guess. It is not, therefore, the actual historian, not the witness of what has been seen, who indicates and weighs the causes – why something has come about and to what extent it has done so because of this – but none other than the rationalizer about history, who – more or less truly, more or less certainly, more or less probably – seeks grounds, and measures off and continues forth the bond between ground and consequence.

So the historian should therefore be no rationalizer or – why put it so contemptuously? – no philosopher of history? Not so fast, my reader – we have not yet reached that point. I do not mean to be a historical doubter, and I leave to our new historical society[6] the important investigation: "To what extent in matters of history is the sensus communis[7] of judgment still one in kind in the case of human beings of different classes and modes

---

[6] Herder is referring to a historical society in Göttingen.
[7] Common sense.

of life, but even more with different compositions of their souls' forces, and above all with different educations and modifications of those forces? How far can a mind's whim go in seeking its favorite prospects and favorite causes even in history? To what extent can this whim contribute to my also finding in what I sought what I wanted to find, and finding it the better the more I wanted to find it? To what point can self-persuasion contribute to confusing experience and judgment, to having faith as though one saw, and to rationalizing as though one had sensation of what is really opinion? How much can the distinctive character of our thinking bind us to these or those prospects and make a certain state of the historical soul into the most comfortable one, then into the necessary one, and finally into the sole one for us? From this [follows] the determination of historical certainty and probability in its psychological measure and weight! From this the difference between – and this last *from this* is really for me – from this *the difference between history* and *judgment, history* and *doctrinal structure.* History one must believe, but whatever in it should be only doctrinal structure, investigate."

But what in a history can be doctrinal structure is not merely the connection between *one* cause and effect, the weighing up of each individual cause and effect, but finally, thirdly, the whole ordering together of many occurrences into a plan, into a vision [*Absicht*] – that is doctrinal structure. But how so? Without this plan, without this ordering together of occurrences into a vision, can there even really exist here, according to our theory of history, a true historian par excellence? The mere narrator is an annalist, a writer of memoirs, of newspapers; the reasoner about the individual narration is a historical rationalizer; but the man who orders together many occurrences into a plan, into a vision – he is, our historical art says, he is[8] the true historical artist, the painter of a great painting of the most excellent composition; he is the historical genius, he is the true creator of a *history*! And if that is right, then history and doctrinal structure are one and the same thing!

By all means! *Creator, genius, painter*, and *artist* of history. But my simple understanding, which has learned from Socrates to take its time for [arriving at] the concept of a thing, is still so far behind that the first question occurs to it again: the historical creator who imagined a world of occurrences, wove together their connection, and created a history

---

[8] This is another example of Herder using anadiplosis.

according to this plan – to what extent is he still a historian? It can be seen, I am thus again at the great A.[9]

And since I do not have enough of a memory to bring to my mind all the historical rules from Lucian[10] to Abbt and Gatterer,[11] since, moreover, there were really paragons of history earlier than rules of history, how would it be if I were to take a stroll out to a few of the oldest paragons, and to investigate the extent to which their history was a doctrinal structure. Thus there [do we find] the father of all, at least of all Greek and Roman, history: Herodotus. — *Greek historian* — *history hold differently*

Herodotus's history, as confused as it may seem, is yet with its episodes and transitions a unitedly ordered structure – as artful as ever in Egypt the hand of Daedalus could lay out a labyrinth that was certainly no labyrinth in the artist's idea. *Gatterer* has recently shown this to an extent,[12] and in his dissection (I am not talking about the application to our times) has very well pinned down the standpoint from which Herodotus wrote and must be read. Still a son of his age who was used to songs and Homeriads, he also worked out his history like a complexly interrelated song, lays down as a foundation in the manner of epics a theme which he executes with episodes and digressions almost as a historical rhapsode: "I want to celebrate in song Greece freed from the Persians!"[13] For this theme he takes along as much from his past and contemporary worlds as might be needed for its execution. Did he not therefore work up his history half as a historical epic and half as a historical doctrinal structure?

No otherwise! But what if he only had to do this to accord with his age? If such a structure merely stemmed from the poverty of his age? If just because of that he had no imitator in this among his successors? If just because of it he became the target of historical objections? Should the episodic structure that is his history in that case still be as much a paragon for our time as the aforementioned renowned teacher of history [*Gatterer*] believes? – Herodotus had no historians before him. Hence, as the first one, he had to take a longer leap backwards and always reach back to

---

[9] Presumably "A" here means, on the model of such idioms as *von A bis Z*: my original question. (Surely not as Grimm suggests: A[ristotle].)

[10] Lucian (second century AD), Greek satirist who authored a treatise about how to write history.

[11] T. Abbt (1738–66) and J. C. Gatterer (1727–99) were contemporary Germans who wrote about history (the former is the Abbt eulogized by Herder in this volume).

[12] In an essay *Vom historischen Plan und der darauf sich gründenden Zusammenfügung der Erzählungen* (1767).

[13] This is not literally a quotation from Herodotus, but is in his spirit.

primordial times in each part of his history – that was the foundation for *his* historical structure; but it is not in general a paragon of a plan for those who no longer need to write as aboriginals. *Herodotus* wrote for a public that had been neither in Persia nor in Egypt and also did not yet half or wholly know these lands from a Hübner.[14] So he had to become such a *Hübner* and insert travel descriptions, not because they belonged there, but because without them his history would have been unintelligible for *his* Greece, and because – why should we not say it? – he would otherwise also have traveled for nothing, and who wants that? In this way he became with these patched-in rags of geography and foreign history so useful, so indispensable, to his own and all subsequent ages; but in the composition of his *digressive* plan still precisely no paragon in this. Finally, *Herodotus* was an Asian, but an Asiatic Greek; hence especially his setting of his nine Muses *around his* fatherland;[15] hence the national tone that rules throughout, and which someone should investigate exactly; hence the construction of his history on the basis of Greek concepts, with which it is clothed in religion and politics and mode of life; hence the fact that his work became a historical *doctrinal structure* for his Greeks – but not, indeed, the paragon of a plan for the whole world.

Not even for the Greek ages after him. *Thucydides*, precisely that *Thucydides* whom no one else but *Herodotus* awakened as a historian, that *Thucydides* who as a boy cried tears of emulation when he heard Herodotus's history read out, did not, as a man, as a historian, imitate it, but wrote according to a plan that seemed not to know about it. All the worse for him, it will be said. "That is why he also has a less important subject than Herodotus; that is why he also weaves in such dreadfully long speeches of which Herodotus has no exact knowledge; that is why he also lacks the gentle bond between his periods of history; that is why, we are sorry to say, that is why we also find him not beside historians but among annalists." Perhaps it will not exactly pain Thucydides very much to be found there, because he put himself there of his own free will. His history does not reach out round about it in such a broad sphere of scope as Herodotus's and his introduction is not such a magnificent gateway as Herodotus's courtyard of Asiatic extent. But that is fine!, for his introduction was written by a statesman who took up from ancient history only

---

[14] J. Hübner (1668–1731) had written widely known works on the bible, history, and geography.
[15] Herder is alluding to the (in fact Hellenistic) division of Herodotus's work into nine books, each one bearing the name of a Muse.

as much as he – not as much as he needed, for Herodotus was there, but as he – wanted to correct or to explain in the ruling preconceptions about the antiquity of Greece. He wrote in terms of winters and summers – a natural division of the course of war in his time, and as appropriate for a general conducting wars as it is for a shepherdess to calculate her life in terms of springs. He inserted speeches – the documents and motivations of that age, whose collection and correction cost him so much, but which have the misfortune of being regarded by us as oratorical exercises that a great general is supposed to have given himself practice dressing up. He dwells on inessential matters for a long time and often too long a time, does not in his narration adequately measure with an eye to the inner importance for the whole, because he – why should we not say this as well? – because he still stood too close to the occurrences, could not yet observe them from the appropriate distance in order to survey them as a whole, because they were still too pressing for him, and so to speak *in*, not *before*, his eyes. Right at the start of the war he decided to write about the war, during it he collected materials and put them in order – how therefore could it have been otherwise than that he had to[16] write in such a piecemeal way, and completed his history not as a circle like Herodotus but serially and in detail, though with that much more *detailed* precision and ornamentation, completed everything not side by side like Herodotus but intertwined and sequential? But what am I saying? *Completed?* He did not complete it,[17] and even if he had completed it, still anything could have become of it sooner than "a *doctrinal structure* about the Peloponnesian War."

But now! the first of the philosophers who became a historian, the amiable pupil of Socrates who revealed to us the memorabilia[18] from the soul of his teacher, who was able to be a philosopher and a statesman, from horse breeding, hunting, the art of domestic management on to the education of a prince, to instructions and eulogies for rulers. When he came to history what will have become of it but a doctrinal structure of statecraft and philosophy? What rich opportunities to let the statesman, the general, the Socratic knower-of-men speak! If Xenophon had lived in our time, how could it well have been otherwise? But now, what a shame

---

[16] Reading *schreiben mußte* for *schreiben* – though the sentence may be a case of deliberate anacoluthon rather than simple word-omission.
[17] Thucydides' work breaks off in the middle of book 8.
[18] This is the title of Xenophon's most famous work.

that according to his ideas, as it seems, doctrinal structure and history could not exist [together]; so he separated the two completely. Where the statesman, the economist, the philosopher was supposed to speak, well, in that case he let him speak – but not in history. Whether biographer or war narrator, [he was] always anything but an architect about the history of his hero, his war; always nothing but the noblest, the gentlest, historian. The historian who seems to know of no plan, of no opinions of his own, to whom it does not occur to order things according to these opinions and prospects, with whom occurrences seem to order themselves, thoughts to flow forth out of each other, history to have written itself. I do not think that *one* pet bias[19] binds me to Xenophon, but for me he is the most classical of the Greek prose writers, and at that point at which he maintains the golden middle between the digressions of his predecessors and his successors. Thus a paragon of history. But with whom, indeed, are history and doctrinal structure more separated than with him? And with whom could they have stood together more completely than with the author of the *Cyropaedia*, the teacher of the great Scipio, Lucullus, and [gap in text.]

Thus Xenophon. But his successors scarcely any longer. The barriers of this historical moderation became too narrow for them, so they made a broader course for themselves; out of historians developed philosophers about a history. The clear onward flow of historical occurrences and, mixed in therewith, of a quiet historical wisdom tasted too watery to them; the drink got spiced with philosophy, spiced ever more strongly, and in the end so strongly that it can no longer be called history but rather philosophy on the occasion of a history, and then history was indeed doctrinal structure. The historian [was] no longer Xenophon but Polybius – I can give no more complete example.

[Deleted part.]

And so that it does not seem as though I am looking for an example for my cause in him, his most recent British translator may speak, who certainly knew him and still more certainly was more prejudiced for than against him: "Everywhere Polybius speaks in a didactic tone. Everywhere the official face of the teacher, too dark, too proud and insulting, to be able to make friends. That is the source of his excessive striving to be distinct and more distinct, which accordingly degenerates into nauseating

---

[19] *Lieblingsvorurteil*. But perhaps Herder meant to write *Lieblingsvorteil*: pet advantage.

repetitions and shames the reader as a pupil. If Polybius had merely written for his compatriots, the Arcadians, then . . . but as it is he aspires to be the teacher of all Greece and thinks his readers children. No historian of his own or of earlier times satisfies him, and he reproaches in others with the extremest strictness errors which he himself commits."[20] Hampton continues, and although he will have none of the idea that *Polybius*, besides the main intention of his history, *explicitly* had the secondary intention of *promoting* the art of war, although he afterwards praises him richly enough, he still cannot, though, fail to recognize the attitude that Polybius makes free with concerning the historians. To be sure, [he is] a statesman, a general, a philosopher who speaks quite intimately with us in his room, and through thorough and deep observations puts us in a position to learn both from the bad conduct and from the cleverness of past times; certainly, [he is] the friend, the adviser, the companion of Scipio, the teacher of Brutus, and also in our times the teacher of kings and heroes, just as he ought also to be so in more things than just the art of war if he were read from a different viewpoint than Folard's.[21] All this is true, to be sure, but still – [he is] entirely more than a historian. And whoever wants to be more than that must inevitably arrive at points where he is no longer a true historian. That is indeed true of Polybius, whose history has already been called by others a philosophy full of examples. And to be sure, that is a *doctrinal structure*.

I skip over the Romans, and where will I find the moderns? Wherever I want to find them – partly with mere, and often pedantic, narrators; partly with historical artists who love nothing so much as to paint, draw out historical sentences like avenues, and afterwards make for us such splendid character sketches, portraits, and depictions which perhaps live merely in their brains; finally, [there are] those wise in statecraft who have been able to write via history a whole doctrinal structure for a whole nation in all its political constitutions. In the first category the majority will perhaps be Germans; in the second Frenchmen; and in the third Englishmen and Scotsmen – and among the last especially a *Hume*. – *Hume*, certainly one of the greatest minds of our time, whom I always read with reverence, but if I may say so again, not as a historian but as

---

[20] This is a very free rendering by Herder of remarks by the translator in question, Hampton. The translation here is from Herder's German.

[21] J.-C. de Folard (1669–1752) was a French officer and military author who wrote a controversial commentary on Polybius.

a philosopher of British history. The person who did not admire in him
the insightful statesman, the deep thinker, the penetrating narrator, the
enlightening judge, would not be worthy of being his reader; however, as
much as there is that I want to learn from him, among this much the least
is – history. [What I want to learn from him] is what Hume thinks about it,
how the state of things appeared to him, how his judgment flows from his
representation, how he imagines the occurrences that have happened and
the people, how he situates them, but not necessarily how they happened,
how they were.

I cite a British author – because, since among the British there is the
most striking difference of minds and judgments about their national
affairs, the comparison of different and also differently thinking historians
concerning an event can show us what a gulf there is between history and
doctrinal structure, between occurrence and judgment.

Unexpectedly, therefore, I am at that point in my critical forestlet
whence I set out. And what do I bring home with me from my mental
walk? Approximately the following:

A history can be a doctrinal structure to the extent that it represented to
us *a single* occurrence, in its entirety, like a structure. But if this occurrence
is individual, then such a description cannot properly be called a doctrinal
structure.

So, second: that it seeks out the causes of the occurrence, the bond
between ground and consequence. This bond is not seen, but inferred,
and the art of inferring concerning it is no longer history but philosophy.

Emphatically, as our third point: If a great sequence of occurrences
should be linked together for *a single* vision, in *a single* plan with a certain
harmony of the parts, then there is still greater danger that this doctrinal
structure [formed] according to the criterion of a single understanding is
not in everything simple and clear history.

From these main propositions – which could be made pretty provable
if it were a matter of philosophical language – it would follow:

That if one must believe a legitimate history, one must investigate
everything in it that may be doctrinal structure.

That the degrees of historical probability and of the probability of the
systematic part of it must not be confused.

That the plainer a history is, the more it rests on obvious facta or data,
then the more probable it is; the more a history is historical art, the more

pragmatic it is, then the more instructive it is perhaps, but also the more in need of scrutiny.

That in order to give a nation history, one must never begin from the highest thing, the historical plan, the pragmatic aspect of history, etc. before we have mastered the pure, clear Herodotian manner of writing and thinking. If the former happens, as in all six – otherwise useful – volumes of the new historical academy[22] one has still hardly got any further than the plan (investigations which ought to have remained precisely for the end), then we get exactly as far as with all the theatrical rules about the three unities and the [plot-]plan, without in that case providing for the dramatic genius, or in our case for the historical genius, with a single crumb.

That historiography never degenerates more than when it begins to be a rationalizing or even a system without a historical foundation. In Germany we have already with our wealth of pragmatic instructions made a fine start towards rationalizing, almost without knowing about what – a fact to which, for example, Hausen's history of the Protestants bears witness.[23]

Finally, that that history is best in which what is history in it and what doctrinal structure are, as quite different sorts of things, indeed combined, but also recognizably distinguished, and the degree is specified [concerning] what the author has drawn up as history and what he has added in thought as doctrinal structure.

Even if our present historical boom in Germany had not guided me onto this path of thought, it might be accepted as a self-examination of the extent to which a reader has, even in the case of a history of art, the double duty to believe and to investigate. And thus I am now again at the subject of Winckelmann.[24]

---

22 This was a publication of the Göttingen historical society alluded to earlier.
23 K. R. Hausen, *Pragmatische Geschichte der Protestanten in Deutschland* (1767).
24 Herder at this point in the text turns to a more detailed discussion of Winckelmann.

This Too a Philosophy of History for the Formation of Humanity [an early introduction]

[In early drafts, Herder began his essay with a question. He initially formulated the question as follows: "What sorts of virtues or unvirtues have governed human beings at all times, and has the tendency of human beings been improved or worsened with time, or always remained the same?" In a subsequent early draft the question was reformulated to read: "Have human beings' inclinations changed from time to time, and what are the virtues and vices that have governed them here and there more or less?" Responding to this question, Herder then made the following introductory observations before giving a version of the text which he would eventually publish in 1774 and which is translated next.]

To develop this question *metaphysically* seems to me entirely beyond our purpose and out of place. The human heart has always remained the same in inclinations, just as the mind has in abilities, and, whatever sorts of angelic or devilish forms people have sometimes wished to imagine in it, has always been only human. Recalcitrant and faint-hearted, striving in need, languishing in rest and luxury, nothing without stimuli and exercises, through these with gradual progress almost everything that has been wished – a monster or the most important hieroglyph of all the good and bad of which history is full – what painter of the soul could paint it with one stroke?

Historically and *physically* too I immediately presuppose as established several observations over which the philosophical spirit of our century has perhaps already poetized and pondered only too much. That there is a certain creation and influence by the clime, hence certain national and

268

provincial vices, forces, and virtues; that in some regions and climates some inclinations, like some plants, must develop only weakly and saplessly, but in others strive upwards with whole, full nature – I may presuppose this physics of history, science of the soul, and politics as conceded on the whole, although in individual detail there will be eternal uncertainty and confusion in the offsetting and addition of these operative causes with other ones, and hence in the whole application of this geography of humanity, because there are always too many and too dissimilar forces operating in proximity.

Politically too I am presupposing that cycle [*Kreislauf*] to which individually every nation, and perhaps every human undertaking, seems to be destined, namely that of running through in a circle precisely all those numerals [*Ziffern*] which only this hand on this clock-face [*Zifferblatte*] can touch. It is an observation that has inevitably forced itself before the eyes of even the most stupid historian that every people, like every art and science, has its period of growth, bloom, and decline. And since the first of these usually coincides with the times of virtue and need, the last with those of luxury and rest, between which the middle, highest peak only occupies a short time, and perhaps the very minimum that could be conceded to it, precisely from this have arisen the pervasive questions about national poverty and luxury, industry and rest, virtues and vices, which in part belong along with the cycle of useless questions that the human understanding should run through but that no human force should solve or apply. Since a nation's inclinations always here lie in the wheel of its fate, and get jolted round and carried along by it, admittedly a political philosopher can raise himself up for a moment and get an overview of a section of the wheel and give his modest opinion about it; but regardless of that, wheel and axle-pin, along with everything that belongs thereto, himself not excluded, rolls on.

After the subtraction of all these questions which would lead onto too large or too small a plain, we pin down for ourselves the single problem whose solution would perhaps also excel all the preceding: "Is there, historically and physically, a certain progress in the inclinations of the human species? Can one observe in the bond between the diverse periods, connections, and revolutions of the peoples of this earthly sphere a thread and plan of formation [*Bildung*] for developing in the human heart little by little certain inclinations and forces for which people previously and on another path saw no clear trace? And which, then, would be the inclinations on this path which were developed at this point and that, of which people did not yet find any trace in advance or in a neighboring region, which had to arise, ferment up, decline, and bring forth others in turn precisely thus and now? In short, if there exists in the hand of fate a thread of the development of human forces through all centuries and revolutions, and if a human heart can observe it – which is it?" The question either contains the deepest, pleasantest, and most useful philosophy of all history or is beyond and above the human field of vision. Either it must ground itself on a study of the human heart in its most diverse forms, under the most manifold influence of times, needs, contingencies, ethics, habits, forms of government, etc., or it depicts a dream.

And in order not to depict the latter, let there also be permitted right at the start the separation of two side-concepts which could confuse everything, namely that "of moral virtue and of human beings' happiness in this sequence or in this cycle of their inclinations." For both of these we not only still lack a correct criterion, but it could even perhaps be that human nature had such a flexibility and mutability as to be able to form out [*ausbilden*] for itself in the most diverse situations of its efficacy also the most diverse ideals of its actions into what is called *virtue* and the most diverse ideals of its sensations into what is called *happiness*, and to be able to maintain itself therein until circumstances change and further formation occurs [*man weiter bildet*]. Who, now, would have enough flexibility and mutability to place himself always into this inner feeling without which nothing could be made out concerning the two words? So let it be enough for us to sketch the phenomenon of many sorts of forces and inclinations from outside, without investigating how much in each case each had of moral virtue in it or contributed to the happiness of the part, of the whole, and of which whole. We seek and weigh forces, not the phantom of their abstractions and consequences, which perhaps change with every ray of the sun. And how much we would already have taken on with the first job!

Certainly not merely the wretched and so often treated and mistreated question "Has the world improved or worsened?" For this question we have precisely thereby separated off, from the standpoint of ethics and happiness. But rather [the task which we have taken on is one of] seeking the sap and pith of all history, on the basis of which subsequently so much could be made out about all plans for the formation [*Bildung*] and change of human inclinations. Since all ethics are based on inclinations, and all human institutions form [*bilden*] or presuppose ethics, since the favorite notions over which our century ponders and works are to contribute to this formation or transformation [*Bildung oder Umbildung*] of human inclinations, and we really in many different respects live in such a strange crisis of the human spirit, and why not also of the human heart?, I therefore imagine the results of my investigation so great and useful that I would only wish for myself as guide and Muse of my observations that *genius* who was the genius of the human species in all its conditions and invisibly guided, still guides, and alone completely surveys the thread of the development of its forces and inclinations.

This Too a Philosophy of History[1] for the[2] Formation[3] of Humanity[4] (1774)

A contribution to many contributions of the century

Tarassei tous anthrôpous ou ta pragmata alla ta peri tôn pragmatôn dogmata.[5]

Philosophy of history for the formation of humanity

First section

The further illumination advances in the investigation of the most ancient world history, its migrations of peoples, its languages, ethics, inventions, and traditions,[a] the more probable becomes, with each new discovery, *the origination of the whole species from a single man* as well. We are getting

---

[a] Most recent historical investigations and journeys in Asia. [For examples, see G4:855.]

[1] This Too a Philosophy of History: This part of the title alludes polemically to Voltaire, *La philosophie de l'histoire* [*The Philosophy of History*] (1765).

[2] for the [*Zur*]: As becomes clear from the way the contents of the essay unfold, the *zur* here means both (1) *concerning* and (2) *in promotion of*.

[3] Formation [*Bildung*]: No single word in English captures or can well be made to capture the spectrum of meanings that the word *Bildung* bears in Herder. Its most basic meaning is *formation, molding*, but it also takes on meanings such as *development, education, culture, cultivation, civilization*. In the present essay and elsewhere in this volume, I have preferred *formation* wherever possible, but have sometimes varied the translation to other words from the group mentioned in cases where *formation* would be too forced or misleading.

[4] Humanity [*Menschheit*]: *Menschheit* most often in this essay means *humankind*, but it also at points drifts into (instead or also) meaning *humanity* in the sense of a moral ideal. The English word *humanity* can bear both these senses and has therefore been used to translate *Menschheit* throughout.

[5] It is not things that disquiet human beings but dogmas concerning things. (Epictetus, *Encheiridion*, ch. 5. But note that this view is highly characteristic of the Pyrrhonists as well – see e.g. Sextus Empiricus, *Outlines of Pyrrhonism*, bk. 1, chs. 6, 12.)

closer and closer to the *happy clime* where *a single pair of human beings*, under the gentlest influences of *creating Providence*, with the *help* of the most facilitating *dispensations* all around them, began spinning the thread that has since drawn itself out further far and wide with such entanglements; where hence also all initial *contingencies* can be regarded as the arrangements of a maternal Providence for developing a delicate double seed of the whole species with all the selectiveness and care that we must always credit to the Creator of such a noble species and to His outlook ahead over millennium[6] and eternity.

[It is] natural that these first developments were as *simple, delicate,* and *miraculous* as we see them in *all of nature's products.* The seed falls into the earth and dies; the embryo gets formed [*gebildet*] hidden away, as the philosopher's spectacles would hardly approve a priori, and comes forth fully formed; hence the history of the human species' earliest developments, as the oldest book describes it, may sound so *short* and *apocryphal* that we are embarrassed to appear with it before the philosophical spirit of our century which hates nothing more than what is *miraculous* and *hidden* – [but] exactly for that reason it is *true.* Just one point to note, then. Does it not seem even for the mole's eye of this brightest century that in fact a *longer life,*[7] a *nature operating more quietly and more interconnectedly,* in short, *a heroic period of the patriarchal age,* is required in order to mold into the tribal fathers of all posterity, and to mold onto them as a beginning for eternity, the first *forms of the human species* – whatever these may be? Now we only hurry by, and, as vagrants, through the world – shades on earth! All the good and bad that we bring with us (and we bring little with us, because we first receive everything here) we mostly also have the fate to take away with us again; our years, careers, good examples, undertakings, impressions, the sum of our efficacy beyond ourselves on earth, is the forceless dream of a single sleepless night – *talk!* – *Thou carriest them away* etc.[8] Just as now, with the *great store of forces* and *abilities* which we find *developed* before us, with the *faster course* of our *fluids and impulses, life-ages and thought-plans,* in which one of them rushes to pursue and destroy

---

[6] It is tempting here to read the plural *Jahrtausende* for the printed singular *Jahrtausend.* However, the singular is probably intentional – motivated by its aesthetic superiority over the plural in the context of the following singular noun *eternity.*

[7] See Genesis 5. Literal acceptance of the bible's age- and time-specifications was still common in Herder's day.

[8] Psalm 90, v. 5: "Thou carriest them away like a flood; they are as a sleep, just as grass that soon, though, withers." (Here translated from Luther's German.)

the other like one water bubble the other, with the often *discordant relations* between *force* and *prudence, ability* and *cleverness, talent* and *good heart,* which always distinguish a century of decline – just as with all this it seems *intention* and *balanced wisdom* to *moderate* and *secure* a *great mass of childish forces* through *a short, forceless duration of life's play,* was not also that *first, quiet, eternal life of trees and patriarchs* alone requisite in order to *root* and *ground* humanity in its first inclinations, ethics, and institutions?

What were these inclinations? What were they supposed to be? The most natural, the strongest, the simplest!, the eternal foundation for all the centuries of human formation [*Menschenbildung*]: *wisdom* instead of science, *piety* instead of wisdom, *love of parents, spouse, and children* instead of politeness and debauchery, [with] *ordering of life, rule and regency for God over a house* as the original model of all civil ordering and institution – in all this humanity's *simplest enjoyment* but also simultaneously its *deepest.* How was that all supposed to get – I do not mean to ask how was it supposed to get fully formed, but only – first formed, developed, except – through that *quiet, eternal power of the exemplary model,* and *of a sequence of exemplary models,* with their rule about them? With our measure of life, each invention[9] would have got lost a hundred times over, [would have] sprung forth as an illusion and disappeared as an illusion. What minor should accept it, what – too soon, again – minor force [others] to accept it? The first bonds of humanity would in this way fall apart at the beginning. Or rather, how could such thin, short threads at that time ever have become the strong bonds without which even after millennia of formation [*Bildung*] the human species still falls apart *through mere weakening*? No!, with a happy shudder I stand there before the holy cedar of a tribal father of the world![10] All around already a hundred young blooming trees, a beautiful forest of posterity and perpetuation! But behold!, the old cedar still blooms on, has its roots far round about and bears the whole young forest with sap and force from the root. Wherever the original father *has* his cognitions, inclinations, and ethics *from,* whatever and however few these may be, round about *a world and a world of posterity* has already formed itself, and formed itself to firmness, in these inclinations and ethics merely through the *quiet, forceful, eternal observation of his divine example*! Two millennia were only two generations.

---

[9] Or possibly: discovery.
[10] Cf. Psalm 92, v. 12: "The righteous . . . shall grow like a cedar in Lebanon."

*

However, even disregarding these heroic beginnings of the formation of the human species, judging by the mere *ruins of worldly history* and by the hastiest rationalizing about it à la Voltaire, what *conditions* can be thought up to tempt forth, form, and form to firmness *first inclinations of the human heart* except those that we already find really applied in the *traditions of our oldest history*? *The shepherd's life in the fairest clime of the world* where freely-willing nature so anticipates, or comes to the aid of, the simplest needs; *the peaceful and at the same time nomadic mode of life of the fatherly patriarchal hut* with everything that it gives and hides from the eye; *that time's circle of human needs, occupations, and pleasures* along with everything that according to fable or history came in addition *to guide* these *occupations* and *pleasures* – let one imagine everything set in its natural, living light; what a chosen *garden of God* for raising the first, most delicate *human plants*! Behold this man full of *force* and *feeling of God*, but feeling as *ardently* and *peacefully* as the sap presses in the tree here, as the instinct that, distributed there in a thousand forms among creatures – that presses so mightily in each creature individually – as this quiet, healthy natural drive collected into the man ever *can* operate![11] The whole world round about full of God's blessing – a great, courageous family of the father of all – this world his daily sight – tied to it with need and enjoyment – striving against it with work, prudence, and gentle protection – under this heaven, in this element of life-force *what a form of thought, what a heart had to form itself*! Great and bright like nature!, like nature, quiet and courageous in his whole course!, *long life, enjoyment of himself* in the most indivisible way, *division of the days* through *rest and exhaustion, learning and retaining* – behold, such was the patriarch just *by himself*. – But why this *just by himself*? God's blessing through the whole of nature – where was it more fervent than in the *image of humanity as it feels its way forward* and *forms itself forward*: in the *woman* created *for him*, in the *son* similar *to his image*, in the *divine species* that round about and after him fills the earth. There God's blessing was *his* blessing: *his* she whom he governs, *his* the son whom he raises, *his* the children and grandchildren about him down to the *third and fourth generation*, whom he guides, all of them, with religion and law, order and happiness. – This is the unforced ideal of a *patriarchal world*

---

[11] Even by the standards of this essay, this sentence is a rather extreme example of Herder's use of – here multiple – anacoluthon.

towards which everything in nature pressed; without it, no purpose of life, no moment of comfort, or application of force was thinkable – God!, what a condition for the formation of nature in the simplest, most necessary, pleasantest inclinations! – *Human being, man, woman, father, mother, son, heir, priest of God, regent,* and *paterfamilias,* he was meant to be formed there for all millennia!, and eternally, except for the thousand-year realm and the fantasies of the poets, eternally will *patriarchal region* and *patriarchal tent* remain the *Golden Age of humanity in its childhood.*

*

Now, that there belong to this world of inclinations even *conditions* which, due to a deception of our age, we often *fictionally represent* to ourselves in a much too *alien and terrible manner* might be shown by one induction after the other. – We have abstracted for ourselves an *Oriental despotism* from the most exaggerated, violent phenomena of realms mostly in a state of decay which are only putting on a struggle of resistance with it in their last terror of death (but which precisely thereby also show terror of death!) – and since, now, according to our European concepts (and perhaps feelings) one can speak of nothing more terrible than despotism, one consoles oneself that one can *divert* it from itself *into circumstances* where it was certainly *not the terrible thing* that we *on the basis of our condition dream it to have been.*[b] It may be that only *respect, exemplary model, authority* ruled in the patriarch's tent, and that hence, in the artificially strung language of our politics, *fear* was the driving motive of this constitution – however, do not, O human being, let yourself be put off by the *word of the philosophical professional,*[c] but first observe what sort of *respect,* what sort of *fear,* it is, then. Is there not in every human life an age in which we learn nothing through dry and cold reason, but through *inclination, formation,* in obedience to authority, everything? In which we have no ear, no sense, no soul for pondering and rationalizing about the good, true, and beautiful, but have everything for the so-called *prejudices* and *impressions of upbringing?* Behold!, these so-called prejudices, grasped without *barbara celarent,*[12] and accompanied

---

[b] *Boulanger,* [Recherches sur l'origine] du despotisme oriental [*Investigations on the Origin of Oriental Despotism*]; *Voltaire,* [La] philosophie de l'histoire [*The Philosophy of History*], [Traité sur] la tolérance [*Treatise on Tolerance*], etc.; *Helvétius,* De l'esprit, disc. 3 [*On the Mind,* 3rd discourse], etc. etc.

[c] Montesquieu's throngs of followers and imitatorum servum pecus [slavish herd of imitators].

[12] I.e. valid syllogistic reasoning.

by no demonstration of natural law, how *strong*, how *deep*, how *useful* and *eternal*! – *foundation pillars* of everything that is supposed to be built upon them later, or rather already through and through *seeds* out of which everything later and weaker, however glorious it may be called, *develops* (each person after all only rationalizes according to his sensation) – hence the strongest, eternal, almost divine *traits* which *bless* or *ruin* our whole life; with which, when they abandon us, everything abandons us. – And behold: what is unavoidably necessary for each *individual human being in his childhood* is certainly not less so for *the whole human species in its childhood*. What you call *despotism* in its most delicate seed, and was actually only *paternal authority* for governing house and hut – behold how it achieved things which, with all your *cold philosophy of the century*, you now surely have to leave undone!, how it, did not indeed demonstrate, but instead *cast firm in eternal forms* what *was right* and *good* or at least *seemed* so, with a radiance *of divinity and paternal love*, with a sweet *peel of early habituation*, and *everything that was living in the childhood ideas* from *its world*, with all the *first enjoyment of humanity*, magically turned it into a memorial with which nothing, nothing in the world, can be equated. How necessary!, how good!, how useful for the whole species! – there *foundation stones* were laid which could not be laid in another way, could not be laid so easily and deeply – they *lie there*! Centuries have *built* on top of them, storms of world-ages have *deluged them* with deserts of sand but not *been able to shake* them, like the bases of the pyramids – they still lie there!, and happily so, for *everything rests upon them*.

Orient, you land of God truly chosen for this! The *delicate sensitivity* of these regions, with the quick, flying imagination that so likes to clothe everything in a divine radiance; *reverence* for everything that is might, respect, wisdom, force, footstep of God, and hence immediately child-like *submission*, which for them naturally, for us Europeans incomprehensibly, mixes with the feeling of reverence; the defenseless, dispersed, tranquillity-loving *flock-like condition* of the shepherd's life which *wants to live itself out* gently and without exertion on a plain of God's – all this, more or less *supported by circumstances*, indeed it did in the later sequel supply full materials for the *despotism of conquerors* as well, such full materials that despotism will perhaps be eternal in the Orient, and no despotism in the Orient has yet been toppled through *foreign, external* forces, rather it always just had to *fall apart* through its *own weight* alone because *nothing stood in opposition to it* and it *extended its scope immeasurably.* Certainly, this despotism also often produced the most terrible effects, and, as the philosopher will say, the most terrible of all, that *no Oriental* as such is yet able hardly *to possess any deep concept of a humane, better constitution.* – But all that set aside for later, and admitted – at the beginning, under gentle *paternal government*, was not precisely the Oriental with his *sensitive child's sense* the *happiest* and *most obedient student?* Everything was tasted as mother's milk and father's wine! Everything preserved in children's hearts and sealed there with the seal of *divine authority!* The human spirit received the first forms of wisdom and virtue with a *simplicity, strength,* and *loftiness* that now – speaking frankly – in our philosophical, cold, European world surely has nothing, nothing at all, like it. And precisely because we are so incapable of *understanding!*, of *feeling!*, it any more, let alone of *enjoying* it, we *mock, deny*, and *misinterpret!* The best proof!

Without a doubt *religion* is part of this as well, or rather, *religion* was "the *element* in which all this lived and functioned." Even disregarding all *divine impression* in the *creation* and earliest *care* of the human species (necessary to the *whole* as much as parental care is to each *individual* child after its birth), even disregarding all that, when old man, father, king so naturally represented *God's place*, and just as naturally the *obedience to paternal will*, the *sticking* to *old habit*, and the *reverent submission* to the *hint of one's superior* who had the memorial respect of ancient times[d] mixed with a sort of *childlike religious feeling* – must they, then, as we imagine with such certainty on the basis of the spirit and heart of our own time,[e] have been nothing but *deceivers* and *villains* who *foisted* such ideas [on people], had cunningly *made them up*, and cruelly *misused* them? It may be that this sort of religious feeling, as an element of our actions, would be from both within and without extremely shameful and harmful for *our philosophical part of the world*, for our civilized [*gebildete*] age, for *our* constitution with its freedom of thought (I believe that this religion is – what is still more – unfortunately! – *quite impossible* for it),[13] and let it be the case that the messengers of God, if they were to appear now, would be deceivers and villains – but do you not see that things are quite different with the spirit of the age, of the land, of the level of

[d] *Montesquieu*, [De l']esprit des lois [*On the Spirit of the Laws*], bks. 24, 25.

[e] *Voltaire*, [La] philosophie de l'histoire [*The Philosophy of History*], *Helvétius, Boulanger,* etc.

[13] There are some problems with the German text in this first part of the sentence, but they do not call the general sense into question.

the human species, that prevailed there? Already the oldest philosophy
and form of government alone had so naturally in all lands to be originally *theology*! – The human being *gazes in wonder* at everything before
he *sees*, only arrives at the *clear idea* of the true and the beautiful through
amazement, only at the first possession of the good through *submission* and
obedience – and certainly likewise the *human species*. Have you ever taught
a child language from the *philosophical grammar?*,[14] taught[15] him to walk
from the most abstract *theory of motion?* Was it necessary, or required,[16]
or possible to make the easiest or most difficult duty intelligible to him
from a *demonstration* in the *science of ethics?* God precisely be praised!
that it was *not required*[17] or *possible!* This sensitive nature, *ignorant* and
consequently very curious for everything, *credulous* and hence *susceptible to* any *impression, trustingly obedient* and hence inclined to be led to
everything good, grasping everything with imagination, amazement, admiration, but precisely in consequence also *appropriating* everything *that
much more firmly* and *wonderfully* – "*faith, love*, and *hope* in his sensitive
heart, the sole *seeds* of all *cognitions, inclinations*, and *happiness*." Do you
blame God's creation, or do you not see in each of your so-called faults
a vehicle, the sole vehicle, of everything good? How foolish when you want
to stigmatize this ignorance and admiration, this imagination and reverence, this enthusiasm and child's sense, with the *blackest devil's forms of
your century, deception* and *stupidity, superstition* and *slavery*, to make up
for yourself an army of *priest-devils* and *tyrant-ghosts* which only exist in
your soul! How it would be a thousand times more foolish if you wanted
generously to favor a child with your *philosophical deism*, your *aesthetic
virtue* and *honor*, your *universal love of peoples* full of tolerant *subjugation,
exploitation*, and *enlightenment* in the high taste of your time! A *child?* O
you the worst, most foolish child!, and you would thereby rob him of his
better inclinations, the *bliss* and *foundation* of his nature; would make him,
if you were successful in this senseless plan, into the most unbearable
thing in the world – an *old man of three years*.

Our century has marked the name *Philosophy!* on its forehead with
aqua fortis, which seems to exercise its force deep into the head – hence
I have had to answer the disdainful look *of this philosophical critique of the
oldest times*, of which notoriously all *philosophies of history* and *histories of
philosophy* are now full, with a disdainful look, though one of indignation

[14] This presumably refers to the Port Royal *Grammar* (1660).
[15] Reading *gelehrt* for *gelernt*. [16] Or perhaps: allowable. [17] Or perhaps: allowable.

and disgust, without finding it necessary to concern myself about the *consequences of the one* or *of the other*.[18] Go forth, my reader, and still now after millennia feel the so long preserved *pure Oriental nature*, bring it to life for yourself from the *history of the oldest times*, and you will "meet *inclinations* as they could only be molded *onto the human species* over time *in that land, in that way*, for the *great purposes of Providence*." What a painting if I could supply it to you *as it was*!

*

Providence guided the thread of development further – down from the *Euphrates, Oxus, and Ganges* to *the Nile* and to the *coasts of Phoenicia* – great steps!

It is seldom that I step back from ancient Egypt and from the consideration of what it became *in the history of the human species* without reverence! A land where a part of humanity's *boyhood* was destined to be formed [*gebildet*] in inclinations and cognitions, like its childhood in the Orient! The metamorphosis here was just as easy and unnoticed as the genesis there.

Egypt was without *livestock pastures and shepherd's life*; hence the patriarchal spirit of the first hut was lost. But, *formed from the slime of the Nile* and *fructified* by it, there appeared, almost just as easily, the most excellent *agriculture*. Hence the shepherd's world of ethics, inclinations, cognitions became a district of *field-farming people*. The nomadic life stopped; there developed permanent residences, *land-ownership*. Lands had to be measured out, each person allotted his, each person protected on his; hence each person could also be found on his – there developed *security of land, cultivation of justice, order, civil administration*, as all this had never been possible in the nomadic life of the Orient; there developed *a new world*. Now there arose an *industry* such as the blessed, idle hut-dweller, the pilgrim and alien on earth, had not known; *arts* were invented which that hut-dweller neither used nor felt the desire to use. Given the spirit of Egyptian *precision* and *agricultural diligence*, these arts could not but attain a high degree of *mechanical perfection*; the sense for *strict diligence*, for *security and order*, permeated everything; in *knowledge of legislation* each person was duty-bound to it with need and enjoyment; hence the

[18] Note that Herder is here avowing the use of standard Pyrrhonian procedure: counterbalancing a dogmatist's argument with a counterargument, but without commitment to either.

human being also became *shackled beneath it*;[19] the inclinations which had there [in the Orient] been merely paternal, childlike, shepherdly, patriarchal became here *citizenly, village-based, citified.* The child had grown out of its child's smock; the boy sat on the school bench and learned *order, diligence, citizens' ethics.*

An exact comparison of the Oriental and Egyptian spirits would inevitably show that my analogy taken from human ages in life is no play. Obviously, everything whatever that both ages shared in common had lost its *heavenly coating* and had had mixed into it *earth-keeping* and *field-clay*; Egypt's *cognitions* were no longer *paternal oracular pronouncements of the deity* but already *laws, political rules of security*, and the remains of the former merely got painted as a *holy image*[20] on the board so that it might not perish, so that the boy should stand before it, unravel, and learn wisdom. Egypt's *inclinations* no longer had as much childlike sensitivity as those in the Orient; the feeling for family weakened, and instead became *concern* for family, *class, artist's talent*, which *was handed down with the class*, like house and field. The idle tent where the man ruled had become a *hut of work* where the woman too was *definitely already a person*, where the patriarch now sat *as an artist* and *made a meager living*. God's free pasture full of flocks, *fields full of villages and cities*; the child who ate milk and honey, a boy who in performing his duties *was rewarded with cake* – there functioned through everything a new virtue which we want to call *Egyptian diligence, citizen's faithfulness* but which was not Oriental feeling. The Oriental, how he is even now disgusted by *agriculture, city life, slavery* in *art workshops*! How few beginnings he has still made in all that after millennia. He lives and functions as a free animal of the open field. The Egyptian, by contrast, how he hated and felt disgust at the herder of livestock with everything that stuck to him!, just as subsequently the more refined Greek in his turn raised himself above the *burden-bearing* Egyptian – it was just a matter of the child in its swaddling clothes disgusting the boy, and the youth hating the boy's school-jail; but overall all three belong *on and after each other*. The Egyptian without Oriental childhood instruction would not be an *Egyptian*, the Greek without Egyptian school-diligence not a *Greek* – precisely their hate shows *development, progress, steps of the ladder*!

[19] These two *its* could refer (in the German as in the English) either to the *security and order* or to the *legislation*.
[20] I.e. a hieroglyph.

They are amazing, the easier ways of Providence; Providence, which enticed and raised the child through religion, developed the boy through nothing but *needs* and the *dear 'must' of school*. Egypt *had no pastures* – hence the inhabitant had to *well learn* agriculture; and how much Providence facilitated this difficult learning for him through the *fecund Nile*. Egypt had *no wood*, people had to learn to build with stone; *there were stone-quarries enough there*, the *Nile was comfortably there* to transport them thence – how high the art rose!, how much it developed other arts! *The Nile flooded* – people needed *measurements, drainage channels, dams, canals, cities, villages* – in what diverse ways people were *bound to the earthen clod*!, but also how much organization did the *earthen clod* develop! To me this earthen clod is on the map nothing but a *board full of figures* where each person has unraveled meaning – as original as *this land* and its *products*, a likewise distinctive *kind of human being*![21] The human understanding has learned much in this earthen clod, and there is perhaps no region of the earth where this learning was as clearly *culture of the ground*[22] as here. *China* is still its imitator; let one judge and conjecture.

Here again too, stupidity to tear a *single Egyptian virtue* out of the land, the time, and the boyhood of the human spirit and to measure it with the *criterion of another time*! If, as was shown, it was already possible for the Greek to be so mistaken about the Egyptian and for the Oriental to hate the Egyptian,[23] then, it seems to me, it really ought to be one's first thought to see him merely *in his place*, otherwise one sees, especially looking hither from Europe, the most distorted caricature. The development took place hither from the Orient and childhood – so naturally *religion, fear, authority, despotism* still had to become the *vehicle of formation* [*Bildung*], for even with the boy of seven years one cannot yet *rationalize* as with an old man or a man.[24] So naturally, also, for our taste, this vehicle of formation had to cause a *hard husk*, often *such troubles*, so many *sicknesses*,

---

[21] Herder's basic idea here seems to be to use the deciphering of meanings from hieroglyphs as a metaphor for the Egyptian people's transformation of Egypt's natural conditions into new meaningful arts, institutions, modes of thought, and hence a new type of human being.

[22] *Kultur des Bodens* – a pun that turns on two different senses of the word *Kultur* and two different uses of the genitive case: (1) cultivation of the ground, (2) culture belonging to the ground.

[23] Herder may possibly have meant to write here: and for the Egyptian to hate the Oriental.

[24] The phrase "with an old man or a man" is a good example of Herder's use of the rhetorical figure of hysteron proteron.

which one calls *boys' fights* and *canton-wars*.[25] You can pour out as much gall as you like on Egyptian *superstition* and *clericalism*, as for example that amiable Plato of Europe[f] who wants to model everything only too much on a Greek original model has done – all true!, all good, if Egyptian antiquity were supposed to be *for your land* and *your time*. The boy's coat is certainly too short for the giant!, and the school-jail disgusting for the youth with a fiancée – but behold!, your formal gown is in turn too long for the former, and do you not see, if you know a bit of the Egyptian spirit, how your *citizen's cleverness, philosophical deism, easy trifling, travel to all parts of the world, tolerance, propriety, international law*, and however this stuff's names may go on, would have in turn made the boy into a miserable old man of a boy? He had to be shut in; there had to be a certain privation of cognitions, inclinations, and virtues, in order to develop what lay within him and could now in the sequence of world events be developed only by *that land, that place*! Hence these disadvantages were for him *advantages* or *necessary evils*, as is for the child care with alien ideas, for the boy adventures and school discipline. Why do you want to shift him from his place, out of his age in life, to kill the poor boy? – What a large library of such books! – the Egyptians now made *too old*, and *what wisdom* picked out of their hieroglyphs, beginnings in art, constitutions of civil administration!,[g] now on the other hand so deeply despised in comparison with the Greeks[h] – merely because they were Egyptians and not Greeks, as for the most part the Hellenophiles [judged] when they left behind their favorite land. Clear injustice!

The best historian of the art of antiquity, *Winckelmann*, obviously only passed judgment on the artworks of the Egyptians according to a Greek criterion, hence depicted them very well *negatively*, but so little according to *their own nature and manner* that with almost every one of his sentences in this most important matter the obviously one-sided and sidewards-glancing aspect glares forth. Thus *Webb* when he contrasts their

[f] *Shaftesbury*, Charact[eristics of Men, Manners, Opinions, Times], vol. 3; Miscell[aneous Reflections].

[g] *Kircher, D'Origny, Blackwell*, etc.

[h] *Wood, Webb, Winckelmann, Newton, Voltaire* now one, now the other, according to location and occasion.

[25] Herder is here thinking of a theory propounded by A. Y. Goguet (1716–58) that the oldest forms of warfare were aimed solely at harming the opponent and ended with the return of each party to its "canton."

literature with Greek literature. Thus several others who have written about *Egyptian ethics and form of government* even with a European spirit. – And since what happens to the Egyptians is mostly that people come to them from Greece and hence with a merely Greek eye – how can worse happen to them? But dear Greek!, these statues, now, were (as you could perceive from everything) supposed to be anything but paragons of beautiful art *in accordance with your ideal!* – full of charm, action, movement, about all of which the Egyptian knew nothing, or which his purpose precisely cut off for him. They were supposed to be *mummies!, memorials to deceased parents* or *ancestors* according to all the exactness of *their facial traits, size,* according to a hundred *fixed rules* to which the boy was bound. Hence naturally, precisely without charm, without action, without movement, *precisely in this grave-pose* with hands and feet full of rest and death – eternal marble mummies! Behold, that is what they were supposed to be, *and that is what they are too!*, that is what they are in the *highest mechanical aspect* of art!, in the *ideal of their intention!* How your fair dream of fault-finding is lost now! If you were to elevate the boy tenfold through a magnifying glass into a giant and to shine a light on him, you can no longer *explain* anything in him; all his *boy's stance* has gone, and yet [he] is anything but a giant!

*

The *Phoenicians*, despite the fact that they were *so* related to the Egyptians, were or became to a certain extent their *opposite in formation [Bildung]*. The Egyptians, at least in later times, *haters of the sea* and *of foreigners*, in order "to develop *all the potentials and arts of their land*" only natively; the Phoenicians retreated behind mountain and desert to a coast in order to establish a new *world on the sea.* And on what a sea? On an *island sound*, a *bay between lands*, which seemed properly brought there, properly formed with coasts, islands, and promontories, in order to facilitate *for a nation the effort of sailing and seeking land* – how famous you are in the history of the human spirit, archipelago and Mediterranean sea! *A first trading state, based entirely on trade,* which *first really extended the world beyond Asia, planted peoples,* and *bound peoples together* – what a great *new step* in *development!* Now, to be sure, Oriental shepherd's life inevitably already became almost *incomparable* with this emerging state: family feeling, religion, and quiet enjoyment of the land in life withered; the form of government took a mighty step *towards the freedom of a republic*, of which neither Oriental nor Egyptian had actually had any idea; on a trading coast *aristocracies* of cities, houses, and families inevitably soon emerged, contrary to people's knowledge and will, so to speak – with all this, what a change *in the form of human society*! Consequently, as hatred of foreigners and shutting-off from other peoples withered, although it was *not from love of humankind* that the Phoenician visited nations, there became visible a sort of *love of peoples, familiarity with peoples, international law of peoples*, of which now of course quite naturally a shut-in tribe or a little Colchian people could know nothing. The *world* became broader, *human races became more connected* and *closer*, with trade a mass of arts got developed, an entirely new *drive to art* especially, *for advantage, comfort, luxury*, and *splendor*! Suddenly human beings' diligence climbed down from the heavy *industry of pyramid construction* and from *agricultural work* into a *"dainty play of smaller occupations."* Instead of those useless, *partless obelisks*, the art of construction turned to *composite*, and in each part *useful, ships*. From the silent, standing pyramid there emerged the *roving, speaking mast*. In the train of the Egyptians' statuary and construction-work on a grand and monstrous scale, people now played so advantageously with *glass*, with *metal* cut into pieces and etched, *purple* and *linen, utensils* from Lebanon, *jewelry, containers, ornaments* – people conveyed this to the hands of foreign nations – what a different world of *occupation*!, of *purpose, utility, inclination, application of soul*! Naturally the difficult, mysterious hieroglyphic writing had now to "become an *easy, abbreviated, usable art of calculation* and *lettering*; the inhabitant of ship and coast, the expatriate *sea rover* and *runner between peoples*, had now to seem a quite different creature to the inhabitant of tent or farmer's hut; the Oriental had to find it possible to reproach him for *weakening human feeling*, the Egyptian for *weakening feeling for fatherland*, the former for *losing love* and *life*, the latter for *losing faithfulness and diligence*, the former for knowing nothing of the *holy feeling for religion*, the latter for *putting on public display* in his trading-markets the *secret content of the sciences*, at least in remains." All true. Only on the other hand there also developed in contrast with that something quite different (which I indeed in no way mean to *compare* with that, for I do not like *comparing* at all!): *Phoenician activeness* and cleverness, a new sort of *comfort* and *good living*, the transition to Greek *taste*, and a sort of *knowledge of peoples*, the transition to Greek *freedom*. *Egyptian and Phoenician* were hence, despite all the contrast between their manners of thought, *twins from one mother*, the *Orient*, who afterwards together formed *Greece* and hence *the world beyond it*. Hence both *instruments of onward guidance* in the hands of fate, and, if I may remain with my allegory, the Phoenician the more grown-up *boy* who *ran about* and brought the remains of the primally ancient wisdom and skill to *markets and alleyways more cheaply*. What all does the formation of Europe [not] owe to the deceptive, profit-crazed Phoenicians! – And now the beautiful Greek *youth*.

*

Just as we above all remember our *youth* with pleasure and joy – forces and limbs formed to the point of *life's bloom*; our abilities developed to the point of pleasant *talkativeness* and *friendship*; all inclinations tuned to *freedom* and *love, pleasure and joy*, and all of them now in their first sweet sounding – just as we consider those years *the Golden Age* and an *Elysium of our memory* (for who remembers his undeveloped childhood?), years which *strike the eye* most brilliantly, precisely in the *opening of the bloom bearing in their lap* all our future efficacy and hopes – in the history of humanity *Greece* will forever remain the place where humanity spent her *most beautiful youth* and her *bridal bloom*. The boy has outgrown hut and school and stands there – noble *youth* with beautiful, oiled *limbs, favorite of all the Graces*, and *lover of all the Muses, victor in Olympia* and all other games, *mind and body* together just *a single blooming flower*!

The *oracular pronouncements of childhood* and the *instructive images* of the *laborious school* were now almost forgotten, but the youth developed from them for himself everything that he needed for *youthful wisdom* and *virtue*, for *song* and *joy, pleasure* and *life*. He despised *crude laborious arts* as he did merely *barbarian splendor* and the excessively simple *shepherd's life* – but he plucked from all this the *bloom of a new, beautiful nature*. – *Manual labor* became through him *beautiful art*; subservient agriculture a free *guild of citizens*; strict Egypt's heavy ladenness with meaning *light, beautiful Greek passion* of all kinds. Now what a new *beautiful* class of *inclinations* and *abilities* of which the earlier age knew nothing, but for which it gave the seed. The *form of government* – was it not necessary that it had swung its course down from Oriental *patriarchal despotism* through the Egyptian *land guilds* and Phoenician semi-*aristocracies* before there could occur *the beautiful idea of a republic in the Greek sense*, "obedience paired with freedom, and wrapped about with the name of *fatherland*"? The bloom unfolded – lovely phenomenon of nature! Its name "*Greek freedom*"! *Ethics* had to have become gentler from Oriental *father-sense*

286

and Egyptian *daylaborer-sense* through Phoenician *travel-cleverness* – and behold!, the new beautiful bloom unfolded: "*Greek lightness, gentleness, and patriotism.*" Love had to thin the veil of the *harem* through several degrees before it became the *beautiful play* of the Greek *Venus*, of *Amor*, and of the *Graces*. Thus *mythology, poetry, philosophy, fine arts* [*schöne Künste*][26] – developments of primally ancient seeds which here found *season and place* to *bloom* and to *send scent* into the whole world. Greece became the cradle of *humanity*, of *love of peoples*, of *beautiful legislation*, of *what is most pleasant in religion, ethics, manner of writing, poetry, customs, and arts.* – Everything youthful joy, grace, play, and love!

It has been in part sufficiently developed what sorts of circumstances contributed to this unique product of the human species, and I shall only set these circumstances *into the larger context of the universal connection between time periods and peoples.* Behold this beautiful Greek *climate* and within it the *well-formed human race* with its free brow and fine senses – a true *intermediate land* in *culture* in which *from two ends* everything flowed together which they so easily and nobly altered! The beautiful bride was served by two boys on the right and the left, all she did was to *idealize beautifully* – *precisely the mixture* of Phoenician and Egyptian *manners of thought*, each of which *took away* from the other its national aspect and its jagged stubborn idiosyncrasy, formed the Greek head for the *ideal*, for *freedom*. Now the *strange causes* of their *separation* and *unifications* from the earliest times on – their *division* into peoples, *republics, colonies*, and yet the *common spirit* of these; *feeling of one nation, of one fatherland, of one language!* – The special *opportunities* for the formation of this *universal spirit*, from the journey of the *Argonauts* and the *campaign against Troy* to the victories *against the Persians*; and the defeat against *the Macedonian*[27] when Greece died! – Their *institutions of common games and competitions*, always with little *differences* and *modifications* in each tiniest region and people. All this and ten times more gave Greece *a unity and manifoldness* which here too constituted the *most beautiful whole*. *Fighting* and *coming to aid, striving* and *moderating* – the forces of the human spirit attained the most beautiful *balance and imbalance* – harmony of the Greek lyre!

But now, that precisely thereby immeasurably much of the old, earlier *strength* and *nourishment* inevitably got lost – who would want to deny this? Since the Egyptian hieroglyphs had their *heavy casing* stripped from

[26] Literally: beautiful arts.   [27] I.e. Alexander the Great.

them, it can indeed be that a *certain depth, fullness of meaning, wisdom about nature* that was the *character* of this nation evaporated over sea therewith as well; the Greek kept nothing but *beautiful image, game, feast for the eyes* – however you want to call it in contrast to that heavier quality – enough, *this is all he wanted!* The religion of the Orient had its *holy veil* taken away, and naturally, since everything was *put on display* in the *theater* and the *market* and the *dancing place*, it soon became "*fable*, beautifully extended, talked about, made into poetry and remade into poetry – *youth's dream* and *girl's tale!*" Oriental wisdom, taken from behind the curtain of mysteries, a *beautiful talkativeness, doctrinal structure*, and *contention of the Greek schools* and *markets*. Egyptian art had its heavy trade apron taken away, and hence the excessively precise *mechanical aspect* and *artists' strictness*, for which the Greeks did not strive, were lost as well; the colossus diminished to a *statue*, the *giant temple* into a *stage*, Egyptian *order* and *security* slackened of itself in the multiplicity of Greece. That old priest[28] could in more than one respect say "O, you eternal children who know nothing and talk so much, have nothing and display everything so beautifully," and the old *Oriental* from his patriarchal hut would speak still more violently – be able to blame them for, instead of religion, humanity, and virtue, only *the prostitution of all this*, etc. So be it. The human container is *capable of no full perfection all at once*; it must always *leave behind* in *moving further on*. Greece moved further on – Egyptian *industry* and *civil administration* could not help them, because they had no *Egypt* and no *Nile*; *Phoenician* cleverness in trade could not help them because they had no *Lebanon* and no *India* behind them; the time was past for *Oriental* upbringing – enough!, it became what it was: *Greece!* Original and exemplary model of all beauty, grace, and simplicity! Youthful bloom of the human species – oh, if only it could have lasted forever!

I believe that the position in which I place Greece also helps to disentangle somewhat "the eternal quarrel about the *originality of the Greeks* or their *imitation of foreign nations*" – as in everything, people would have *reached agreement* here too if only they had understood each other better. That Greece *received seeds of culture, language, arts*, and *sciences from somewhere else* is, it seems to me, undeniable, and it can be clearly shown in several cases: *sculpture, architecture, mythology, literature*. But that the Greeks *as good as did not* receive all this, that they *equipped* it with a quite

---

[28] Plato, *Timaeus*, 22b ff.

new nature [*Natur*], that in each kind the "*beautiful*" in the real sense of the word is quite certainly their work – this, I believe, becomes just as certain from a little continuation of these ideas. Nothing Oriental, Phoenician, or Egyptian retained *its nature* [*Art*] any longer; it became *Greek*, and in many respects the Greeks were almost *too much* originals who *clothed* or *re-clothed* everything in accordance with their own nature. From the greatest *invention*[29] and the most important *story* down to *word and sign*. Everything is full of this; it is similarly the case from step to step with all nations – whoever still wants to build a system or quarrel about a name, let him quarrel!

*

There came the *manhood of human forces* and *strivings*: the *Romans*. *Virgil* depicted them with one stroke *in contrast to the Greeks*, with *fine arts* and *exercises of youth* left to the latter:

tu regere imperio populos, Romane, memento.[30]

And he approximately thereby also depicted their trait in contrast to the *Northerners* who perhaps excelled them in *barbaric hardness, strength in attack*, and raw *bravery*, but:

tu *regere imperio* populos –

Roman bravery idealized: *Roman virtue, Roman sense!, Roman pride!* The *great-hearted disposition* of the soul to disregard sensual gratifications, weakness, and even finer pleasure, and *to operate for the fatherland. The controlled heroic courage* never to be rash and plunge into danger but to *persist, to reflect*, to *prepare*, and *to act*. It was the unshaken course of letting oneself be deterred by nothing that is called obstacle, of being greatest precisely in disaster, and of not despairing. Finally, it was the great *eversustained plan* of being satisfied with nothing less than when their eagle covered the circle of the world. Whoever can coin a much-weighing word for all these properties, can comprehend therein simultaneously their *manly justice, cleverness*, the *fullness of their plans, decisions, executions*, and in general *of all the occupations of their world-building*, let him say it. – Enough, here stood the man who enjoyed and used[31] the youth but for

---

[29] Or: *discovery*.   [30] Remember, thou, Roman, to rule over peoples.
[31] Or possibly: needed.

his own part wanted to perform only *miracles of bravery* and *manliness –
with head, heart, and arms*!

On what a *height* the Roman people stood, what a *giant temple* they
built on this height! This people's *state- and military-structure*, its *plan*
and *means* for *execution* – colossus for the whole world! Could a childish
trick be played in Rome without blood flowing in three parts of the earth?
And the *great, worthy* people of this empire, *where* and how they had
effect beyond themselves! What parts belonged to this great machine,
almost unknowingly moved by such light forces! Whither were all their
tools *raised* and *fixed* – *senate* and *art of war* – *laws and discipline* – *Roman
purpose* and *strength* to execute it – I shudder! What with the Greeks
had been *play, youthful rehearsal* became with the Romans *serious, fixed
institution* – the Greek models on a small stage, a narrow strip of land, a
small republic, presented on *that* height and with that *strength*, became
deeds of spectacle of the world.

However one takes the matter, it was "*maturity of the fate of the ancient
world.*" The stem of the tree grown to its greater height strove to bring
peoples and nations under its shade, into twigs. The Romans never made
it their *main concern* to *compete* with Greeks, Phoenicians, Egyptians, and
Orientals, but through their *manly application* of everything *that they found
before them* – what a *Roman circle of the earth* arose! The *name linked peoples
and regions of the world together* which previously had not known each other
even by a word. *Roman provinces*!, in all of them roamed *Romans*, Roman
legions, laws, paragons of *ethics, virtues*, and *vices*. The *wall* that *separated
nation from nation* got *broken up*, the first step was taken *to destroy the
national characters of all of them, to cast* all into *one form* which was called
"*Roman people.*" Naturally, the first *step* was not yet the *work*; each nation
remained with its *rights, freedoms, ethics*, and *religion* – indeed the Romans
flattered them by themselves bringing with them a doll of this religion into
their city. But the wall lay [fallen]. *Centuries of Roman rule* – as one sees
in all parts of the world where they have been – *achieved a very great deal*:
a *storm* which *penetrated* the innermost *chambers of the national manner of
thought* of each people; with time the *bonds* became *ever tighter*; in the end
the whole *Roman empire* was destined to become only the *city of Rome*,
so to speak – all subjects *citizens* – until that empire itself sank.

Not yet to mention advantage or disadvantage at all, only *effect*. If all
peoples ceased under the Roman yoke to be the peoples they were, so to
speak, and hence an *art of statecraft, military art*, and *international law of*

peoples was introduced over the whole earth of which there had previously not yet been any example – when the machine *stood* and when the machine *fell*, and when the ruins *covered* all the nations of the Roman earth – is there in all the history of the centuries a *greater sight*! All nations *building from* or *on* these ruins! A completely new world of languages, ethics, inclinations, and peoples – there begins a new age – a sight as though of the broad, revealing [*offenbar*]³² sea of new nations. – However, let us cast from the shore one more glance on the peoples whose history we have run through.

*

I. No one in the world feels *the weakness of general characterizing* more than I. One paints *a whole* people, age, region of the earth – *whom* has one painted? One draws together peoples and periods of time *that follow one another* in an *eternal succession* like waves of the sea – *whom* has one painted?, *whom* has the depicting word captured? Finally, one after all draws them together into nothing but a *general word* in relation to which each person perhaps thinks and feels what he wants – imperfect *means of depiction*!, how one can be *misunderstood*!

Whoever has noticed what an *inexpressible thing* one is dealing with in the *distinctive individuality of a* human being – to be able to *say what distinguishes him in a distinguishing way*, how he feels and lives, how *different* and *idiosyncratic* all things become for him once *his* eye sees them, *his* soul measures them, *his* heart feels them – what *depth* lies in the character of just *a single nation* which, even if one has often enough perceived and stared at it, yet so *escapes* the *word*, and at least so rarely becomes recognizable *to everyone* in the word so that he understands and feels along – [for him] it is as though one were supposed to survey the world-sea of whole peoples, ages, and lands, comprehend it in *one view, one feeling, one word*!³³ Tired semi-*phantom* that a word is! The whole living painting of mode of life, habits, needs, peculiarities of land and climate, would have to *be added* or

---

³² The word *offenbar* involves a pun on at least three meanings that is not well capturable in English: (1) its normal meaning: *manifest, revealed*; (2) an unusual meaning made possible by an etymological construal of its components *offen* ("open") and *-bar* ("-able"): *openable* (cf. the expression *auf offener See*, "on the open sea"); (3) the further meaning: *of revealed religion* (cf. *geoffenbarte Religion*, "revealed religion").

³³ Manuscript a completes this sentence from "feels along" as follows: – he will be even more amazed and feel dizzy when he confronts what is called the spirit of inclinations in such remote peoples, ages, and lands.

to have *preceded*; one would have first to *sympathize* with the nation, in order to feel a *single one* of its *inclinations* or *actions all together*, one would have to *find* a single word, to *imagine* everything in its fullness – or one reads – *a word*!

We all believe that we still now have *paternal* and *household* and *human drives* as the Oriental had them; that we can have *faithfulness* and *diligence in art* as the Egyptian possessed them; *Phoenician activeness, Greek love of freedom, Roman strength of soul* – who does not think that he feels a *disposition* for all that, if only *time, opportunity* . . . And behold!, my reader, we are precisely there. The most cowardly villain no doubt still has a remote *disposition and potential* for being the most great-hearted hero – but between those and *"the whole feeling of being, of existence, in such a character"* – a gulf! Hence even if you lacked nothing but *time, opportunity* to change your dispositions for being an Oriental, a Greek, a Roman, into *finished skills* and *solid drives* – a gulf! Drives and finished skills are all that is in question. *The whole nature* of the soul, which *rules* through everything, which *models* all other inclinations and forces of the soul *in accordance with itself*, and in addition *colors* even the most indifferent actions – in order to share in feeling this, do not answer on the basis of the word but go into the age, into the clime, the whole history, feel yourself into everything – only now are you on the way towards understanding the word. But also only now will you lose the thought "as though you too are all that taken individually or collectively." You all taken collectively? *Quintessence of all times and peoples?* That really shows stupidity!

Character of the nations! Only *data* of their *constitution* and *history* must decide. But did not a patriarch, in addition to the inclinations which "you attribute to him, also have, and have the ability to have, *other ones*?" I say to both questions simply: *certainly*! Certainly, he had other ones, *subordinate traits* which are self-understood from what I have said or not said, which I and perhaps others with me who have his history in mind indeed already recognized in the word, and still more readily that he *had the ability* to have something very much other – in *another* place, in *this* time, with that *progress* in civilization [*Bildung*], under those *other circumstances* – why in that case should not *Leonidas, Caesar*, or *Abraham* be a *genteel man of our century*? Had the ability to be, but was not. Ask *history* about it; *that is what is in question.*

I therefore likewise prepare myself for small-scale objections based on the *great detail* of peoples and times. That no people *long* remained or could remain what it was; that *each one*, like each *art* and *science* and whatever in the world not?, *had its period of growth*, of *bloom*, and of *decline*; that each of these changing states only lasted the *very small amount of time* that could be given it on the wheel of human fate; finally, that *no two moments* in the world are *the same*, that consequently Egyptians, Romans, and Greeks were also not the same at *all times* – I tremble when I think what sorts of wise criticisms wise people, especially experts on history, can make concerning this! Greece consisted of *many lands*: *Athenians* and *Boeotians*, *Spartans* and *Corinthians*, were anything but like each other. Did not people practice *agriculture* in *Asia* too? Did not *Egyptians* at one time trade just as much as *Phoenicians*? Were not the *Macedonians* just as much conquerors as the *Romans*? [Was] not *Aristotle* just as much a speculative head as *Leibniz*? Did not our northern peoples excel the *Romans in bravery*? Were all *Egyptians, Greeks, Romans* – are all rats and mice – like each other? No! But they are still rats and mice!

How vexing it must become to speak to the public, where one always has to expect from the *noisy* part (the more nobly thinking part keeps quiet!) *such* and still *worse* criticisms, and presented in *what a tone*, and has then at the same time to expect that the *great heap* of sheep which does not know right from left immediately follows this delusion. Can there be a *general image* without an *ordering among and together*? Can there be a *distant prospect* without an *elevation*? If you hold your face close up to the image, carve at this sliver, pick at that little lump of pigment, you never see the *whole image* – you see anything but an *image*! And if your head is full of a group that you have fallen madly in love with, can your view well *embrace, order, gently follow*, a *whole* of such *changing periods*, separate out just the *main effect* in each scene, quietly *accompany* the *gradual transitions*, and now – name them? But if you can do none of all that!, history shimmers and flickers before your eyes!, a confusion of scenes, peoples, periods – first read and learn to see! Incidentally, I know as well as you do that every *general image*, every *general concept*, is only an *abstraction* – it is only the Creator who *thinks* the whole *unity of one, of all*, nations in all their *manifoldness* without having the *unity* thereby fade for him.

II. So let us leave behind these small-scale objections which miss purpose and viewpoint! Set in the perspective of the great whole of the sequence, how pathetic prove "some *fashionable judgments of our century, based on merely general concepts of the schools, concerning the advantages, virtues, happiness, of such distant, such changing, nations!*"

If human nature is no *independent divinity* in goodness – it has to *learn* everything, be *formed* through *progressions*, *step* ever further in *gradual struggle* – then naturally it is formed *most* or *only* on those *sides* where it has such *occasions* for virtue, for struggle, for progression. Therefore in a certain respect each human perfection is *national, generational* [*säkular*],[34] and, considered most exactly, *individual*. People form to greater fullness only what *time, clime, need, world, fate* gives occasion for. *Turned away* from the rest. The inclinations or capacities slumbering in the heart can never become *finished skills*. So the nation can, despite virtues of the most sublime sort on one side, on *another side* have *shortcomings*, make *exceptions*, reveal *contradictions* and *uncertainties* which astonish – but no one except he who brings with him his *ideal silhouette* of virtue from the compendium of his century and has enough philosophy to want to find the whole earth on one patch of earth, no one else! For every person who wants to recognize the human heart from the *element of its life-circumstances* such *exceptions* and *contradictions* are completely *human*: the *proportioning* of *forces* and *inclinations* for *a certain purpose* which could never be *achieved* without it[35] – hence no *exceptions* at all, but the *rule*.

Let it be, my friend, that that childlike *Oriental religion*, that *devotion* to the softest *feeling* in human life, on the other side yields *weaknesses* which you damn in accordance with the model of other times. A patriarch can be no Roman *hero*, no Greek *competitive runner*, no *merchant* of the coast, and just as little that into which the ideal of your academic rostrum or of your whim would inflate him in order *falsely to praise* or *bitterly to damn* him. Let it be that he would appear to you *fearful, afraid of death, soft, ignorant, idle, superstitious*, and if you have bile in your eye, *repellent* judged according to later exemplary models – he is what God, clime, period, and the level of the world's age could form him into: a *patriarch*! So he has in contrast to all the losses of later times *innocence, piety, humanity* – in which he will eternally be *a god* for every late age! The *Egyptian, creeping, slavish*, an *animal of the earth, superstitious* and *sad, hard* against *foreigners*, a *thoughtless creature of habit* – contrasted here with the light *Greek* who *forms* everything *beautifully*, there with a *friend of humanity* in accordance with the *high taste of our century* who carries all wisdom in his head and the whole world in his breast – what a figure! But now, also the former's

---

[34] Herder is using this word with the senses of its Latin cognate *saeculum* in mind: generation, century.

[35] Or possibly: without them (i.e. without the proportioning *and* the forces and inclinations).

patience, faithfulness, strong repose – can you compare these with Greek *pederasty* and *youthful courting* of everything *beautiful* and *pleasant?*, and again, can you fail to recognize[36] Greek *lightness, trifling* with *religion*, shortcoming in a certain *love, discipline,* and *integrity* – if you wanted to take an ideal, whoever's it might be? But was it possible for those *perfections* to be developed in that *amount* and *degree* without these *shortcomings?* *Providence* itself, you can see, did not demand it, only wanted to attain its purpose in *succession,* in *leading further* through the *awakening of new forces* and the *demise of others. Philosopher* in the northern *valley of the earth,* holding the *child's scales of your century* in your hand, do you know better than Providence?

Authoritative decisions of praise and blame which we heap, from *a discovered favorite people* in antiquity at which we stared until we fell in love with it, onto the whole world – what is your legitimacy! Those *Romans* were able to be as no other nation, to do what *no one does in imitation* – they were *Romans.* On a *summit of the world,* and everything around them *valley.* On that summit from youth on, *formed* to that *Roman sensibility, there acted* in him – what wonder? And what wonder that a *small shepherding and farming people* in a valley of the earth was not an *iron animal*[37] that could act in that way? And what wonder that this people in its turn had *virtues* which the noblest Roman did not have, and that the noblest Roman on his summit under the press of necessity was able to decide with cold blood on *cruelties* which again now the shepherd in his *small valley* did not have *on his conscience.* On the peak of that giant machine sacrifice was unfortunately! often a *triviality,* often a *necessity,* often (poor humanity, what conditions you are capable of!), often[38] a *kindness.* It was precisely the machine that made *far-reaching vices* possible which also *raised virtues* so *high, spread efficacy* so far and wide. Is humanity capable of pure *perfection* in a single present condition at all? Peak borders on valley. About noble *Spartans* there dwell inhumanly treated *Helots.* The Roman *victor* dyed with *red dye of the gods* is invisibly also *daubed* with *blood; plunder, wickedness,* and *lusts* surround his chariot; before him goes *oppression,* in his train follows *misery* and *poverty.*[39] – Hence in this sense too *shortcoming* and *virtue* always dwell together in one human hut.

36 Reading, with Steig, *verkennen* for *vergleichen* (in light of manuscript a).
37 See Daniel 7:7. The expression has traditionally been taken to refer to the Roman empire.
38 This is another example of Herder using anadiplosis.
39 This is another example of Herder using hendiadys.

Fair *art of poetry* magically to transform a *favorite people* on the earth into superhuman brilliance. The art of poetry is also *useful*, for the human being also gets ennobled through fair *prejudices*. But when the poet is a *historian*, a *philosopher*, as most of them pretend to be, and these then *model all centuries* after the *one form* of their time – and often it is very small and weak! – *Hume!*, *Voltaire!*, *Robertson!*, classical ghosts of twilight!, what are you in the *light of truth?*[40]

A *learned society*[41] of our age[i] set, doubtless with high intentions, the question "*Which was probably the happiest people in history?*" And if I understand the question correctly, if it does not lie *beyond* the horizon of a human answer, then I only know: such a point in time came to every people at a certain time and under certain circumstances or it was[42] *never a people*. For if, again, human nature is no container of an *absolute, independent, unchangeable happiness* as the philosopher defines it, but it everywhere attracts *as much happiness as it can*, is a *flexible clay* for, in the most different situations, needs, and pressures, also *forming* itself differently, [and] even the image of happiness *changes* with each condition and region (for what is this image ever but the *sum* of "*satisfactions of wishes, achievements of purposes*, and *gentle overcoming of needs*," which, though, all *shape* themselves according to *land, time,* and *place?*) – then at bottom all *comparison* proves to be *problematic*. As soon as the inner *sense* of happiness, the *inclination*, has changed, as soon as the external *occasions* and *needs form* and *fix* the *new* sense – who can compare the *different* satisfaction of *different* senses in *different* worlds? – the shepherd and father of the Orient, the farmer and artist, the sailor, competitive runner, conqueror of the world – who can compare them? Nothing turns on the *laurel wreath* or on the *sight of the blessed flock*, on the *merchant ship*

---

[i] The gentlemen must have had a terribly high ideal for as far as I know they have never found any of their philosophical tasks achieved.

[40] In manuscript a the following passage corresponds to this important paragraph: "Thus there can always be fair poetic art when someone in one or another way chooses for himself such favorite peoples and regions. Also, the poetic art can be applied very usefully because the human being can also be very ennobled through fair prejudices. Only in justice a historian or philosopher should never want to be such a poet, as however most of them, especially those of the first class, are, where almost every one of them from Herodotus to Hume has his favorite time, his favorite people, his favorite ethics in accordance with which he models everything else. Good is strewn about on the earth; because no single form or century could contain it, it got distributed among a thousand forms and roams forth slowly through all centuries. If we are unwilling to follow it on this thousand-formed Prometheus-course, then we do ourselves and the truth the greatest harm."

[41] A patriotic society in Berne, Switzerland.   [42] Reading *war* for *wars*.

or *the captured standard*, but rather on the *soul* that *needed* that, *strove* for it, has now *achieved* that, and *wanted* to achieve nothing but that. Each nation has its *center* of happiness *in itself*, like every sphere its center of gravity!

The good mother has taken care well here too. She put dispositions to *manifoldness* into the heart, but made each of them in itself so little *pressing* that if only *a few* get satisfied the soul quickly forms *a concert* for itself from these awakened notes and does not feel the unawakened ones except insofar as they *silently* and obscurely *support* the sounding song. She put dispositions of *manifoldness* into the heart, and then *a part* of the manifoldness in a circle about us, available to us; then she *reined in* the human *view* so that after a small period of habituation this circle became *horizon* for him. Not *to look beyond it*, hardly to *suspect* beyond it! – everything that is still *similar* with my nature, that can be *assimilated* to it, I covet, strive for, make my own; *beyond that*, kind nature has armed me with *feelinglessness, coldness,* and *blindness*; this can even become *contempt* and *disgust*, but only has the purpose of forcing me back *on myself*, of making me satisfied on *the center* that bears me. The Greek makes as much his own from the Egyptian, the Roman as much from the Greek, as he needs for himself; he is *sated*, the rest *falls by the wayside* and he does not strive for it! Or when in this development of distinctive national inclinations for a distinctive national happiness the *distance between people and people* has already grown too great – behold how the Egyptian *hates* the shepherd, the nomadic tramp!, how he *contemns* the superficial Greek! Thus all pairs of nations whose inclinations and circles of happiness *collide* – it is called *prejudice!, mob-thinking!*, limited *nationalism!* Prejudice is *good* in its time, for it renders *happy*. It forces peoples together into their *center*, makes them firmer on their tribal *stem*, more blooming *in their kind*, more passionate and hence also happier in their *inclinations* and *purposes*. The most ignorant, most prejudiced nation is in such a regard often the first; the age of wishful foreign migrations and journeys abroad in hope is already *sickness, bloating, unhealthy fullness, intimation of death!*

III. And the *universal, philosophical, human-friendly tone of our century* grants so gladly to each distant nation, each oldest age, in the world "our own ideal" in *virtue* and *happiness*? Is such a unique judge as[43] to *pass judgment on, condemn,* or beautifully *fictionalize* their ethics according

[43] Or possibly: Is therefore the unique judge [with authority] . . .

to its own measure alone? Is not the good on the earth *strewn about?* Because one form of humanity and one region of the earth could not grasp it, it got distributed into a thousand forms, it roams forth – an eternal Proteus! – through all parts of the world and all centuries. Also, as he roams and roams further, it is not for greater *virtue* or *happiness of the individual* that he strives – humanity ever remains only humanity – and yet a *plan of striving further* becomes visible – my great theme!

Those who have so far undertaken to unfold the *progress of the centuries* for the most part have in the process the pet idea: progress to *more virtue* and *happiness of individual human beings.* People have then for this purpose *exaggerated* or *made up* facts, *understated* or *suppressed* contrary facts, *hidden* whole sides, *taken* words for [deeds],[44] *enlightenment* for *happiness,* more and subtler *ideas* for *virtue* – and in this way people have made up novels "about the *universally progressing improvement of the world* " – novels that no one believes, at least not the true pupil of *history* and the *human heart.*

Others, who *saw the objectionableness of this dream,* and knew nothing better, saw *vices* and *virtues,* like climes, *change,* perfections *arise* and *perish* like a springtime of leaves, human ethics and inclinations fly away, turn over, like *leaves of fate – no plan!, no progress!, eternal revolution – weaving and undoing! – Penelope-work! –* They fell into a *whirlpool,* skepticism about all virtue, happiness, and vocation of humankind, into which they weave all history, religion, and ethical doctrine – the most recent fashionable tone of the most recent, in particular *French, philosophers*[i] is doubt! Doubt in a hundred *forms,* but all with the dazzling title "*based on the history of the world.*" Contradictions and ocean waves – one suffers shipwreck, or what of *morality* and *philosophy* one *saves from the shipwreck* is hardly worth talking about.

Should there not be manifest *progress* and *development* but in a higher sense than people have imagined it? Do you see this *river current [Strom]*[45]

---

[i] Good, honest *Montaigne* made the start. The dialectician *Bayle* – a rationalizer whose contradictions according to articles of his thought-form, the dictionary, *Crousaz* and *Leibniz* have certainly not been able to make up for – had further effect on the century. And then the more recent philosophers, doubters of everything with their own most bold assertions, *Voltaire, Hume,* even those of *Diderot* – it is the great century of doubting and rousing waves.

[44] Herder miswrote *Wörter für Wörter,* which makes no sense, so "deeds" is conjectural here.

[45] *Strom* can mean either *river* or *current.* The former idea is uppermost here, but the latter must be kept in view in order to make sense of "breaks off there, begins here."

swimming along – how it sprang forth from a little source, grows, breaks off there, begins here, ever meanders, and bores further and deeper – but always remains *water!, river current!*, drop always only drop, until it plunges into the ocean – what if it were like that with the human species? Or do you see that growing *tree!*, that upwards-striving human being!, having to pass through diverse *ages of life!*, all manifestly in *progress!*, a *striving* one for the other in *continuity!* Between each there are apparent *resting places, revolutions!, changes!*, and yet each has the *center* of its happiness *in itself* !; the youth is not *happier* than the innocent, satisfied child, nor the quiet old man *unhappier* than the forcefully striving man; the pendulum always swings *with the same force*, whether it swings furthest and *strives* that much more *quickly* or oscillates most slowly and *approaches rest.* However, it is still an eternal striving! No one is in his age *alone*, he builds on the *preceding one*, this becomes nothing but the foundation of the *future*, wants to be nothing but that – this is what we are told by the *analogy in nature, God's* speaking *exemplary model* in *all works!* Manifestly so in the *human species!* The Egyptian was not able to exist without the Oriental, the Greek built upon them, the Roman raised himself onto the back of the whole world – truly *progress, progressive development*, even if no individual won in the process! Its goal is on the large scale! It becomes – what husk-history boasts about so much, and what it shows so little of – *the stage of a guiding intention on earth!*, even if we should not be able to see the final intention, the stage of the deity, even if only through *openings* and *ruins of individual scenes.*

At least this view is further than that philosophy, which *mixes up*, only ever illuminates[46] here and there in the case of individual *confusions*, in order to turn everything into a *play of ants*, into a striving of individual *inclinations and forces* without a *purpose*, into a chaos in which one despairs of virtue, purpose, and deity! If I succeeded in *binding together* the most disparate scenes without *confusing* them – in showing how they *relate* to one another, *grow* out of one another, *lose* themselves in one another, all of them taken individually only moments, only through the progression *means to purposes* – what a *sight!*, what a noble *application of human history!*, what *encouragement* to *hope*, to *act*, to *believe*, even where one sees *nothing* or *not everything*. – I continue.

[46] Reading *aufhellt* with Düntzer and Brummack/Bollacher. However, the printed *aufhält* would be possible: makes [us] stop.

Second section

Even the *Roman world-constitution* reached its end, and the *greater* the
building was, the *higher* it stood, with that much greater a collapse did
it fall! Half of the world was *ruins*. Peoples and parts of the earth had lived
under the tree, and now that the voice of the holy watchers called "Cut it
down!"[47] what a great *emptiness*! Like a tear in the thread of world events!,
nothing less than a *new world* was necessary in order *to heal the tear*.

It was the *north*. And whatever origins and systems people may think
up, now, about the condition *of these peoples*, the simplest thing seems the
truest: in peace they were, so to speak, "*patriarchies as they were able to be in
the north*." Since no Oriental *shepherd's life* was possible in *such a climate*,
heavier needs weighed more on the human spirit here than where nature
worked almost exclusively for humankind, but precisely these *heavier
needs* and the *northern air hardened* human beings more than they could
be hardened in the warm, aromatic greenhouse of the east and the south,
naturally their condition remained *more primitive*, their small societies
more separated and *wilder*, but human bonds still in *strength*, human *drive*
and force in fullness. – There the land that *Tacitus* describes could arise.
And when this northern sea of peoples came into motion with all its
waves – waves pressed on waves, peoples on other peoples!, the wall and
dam around Rome was torn apart, the Romans had themselves shown
them the gaps and enticed them there to patch at these – when, finally,
everything *broke*, what a deluge of the south by the north!, and after all
the revolutions and horrors what a *new northern–southern world*!

Whoever notes the condition of the Roman lands in their last centuries
(and they were at that time the *civilized* [gebildete] *universe*!) will wonder
at and admire this path of Providence for *preparing* such a *strange sub-
stitution of human forces*. Everything was *exhausted, enervated, shattered*,
abandoned by human beings, dwelt in by enervated human beings, sinking in luxury, vices, disorder, freedom, and wild war-pride. The beautiful
Roman laws and *learning* were unable to *substitute for forces* which had disappeared, *revive* nerves which felt no life-spirit, rouse motives that just
lay there [fallen] – hence *death*!, a worn-out *corpse* lying in blood – then
in the north a *new human being* was born. Under a fresh sky, in desolate
and wild places where no one suspected it, there ripened a springtime
of strong, nourishing plants which, transplanted into the more beautiful,

---

[47] See Daniel 4:10 ff.

more southern lands – now sadly empty fields! – were destined to take on a new nature, to yield a great harvest for the fate of the world! *Goths, Vandals, Burgundians, Angles, Huns, Heruli, Franks* and *Bulgarians, Slavs* and *Lombards* came – settled, and the whole modern world from the Mediterranean to the Black Sea, from the Atlantic to the North Sea is *their work!*, *their race!, their constitution!*

Not merely *human forces*, but also what *laws* and *institutions* did they thereby bring onto the *stage of the world's formation* [*Bildung*]. To be sure, they despised arts and sciences, luxury and refinement – which had wrought havoc on humanity. But when in place of arts they brought *nature*, in place of sciences *sound northern understanding*, in place of fine ethics *strong* and *good*, although *wild, ethics*, and all that now *fermented together* – what an event! Their *laws*, how they breathe *manly courage, feeling of honor, faith in understanding, honesty*, and *reverence for gods!* Their *feudal institutions*, how they undermined the confusion of people-rich, luxurious cities, cultivated the land, occupied hands and human beings, made *sound* and precisely thereby also *happy* people. Their later *ideal beyond needs* – it aimed at *chastity* and *honor* – ennobled the best part of human inclinations – although a *novel*, nonetheless a *lofty novel* – a true *new bloom* of the human soul.

Let one consider, for example, what a *delay for recuperation* and a *training of forces* humanity received in the centuries of this fermentation through the fact that *everything* fell into *small connections, divisions*, and *orderings-together*, and so *many, many* limbs arose! Here one limb was ever *rubbing* against another, and everything sustained itself in *breath* and *forces*. Time of *fermentation* – but precisely this for so long fended off despotism (the true consuming abyss for humanity, which swallows down everything – as it says, into *peace* and *obedience*, but in truth – into *death* and uniform *pulverizing!*). Now, is it better, is it *healthier* and *more beneficial* for humanity, to produce mere lifeless cogs of a great, wooden, thoughtless machine, or *to awaken* and *rouse forces?* Even if it should be through so-called *imperfect* constitutions, *disorder, barbaric stickling about honor, savage addiction to quarreling*, and such things – if it achieves the purpose, then it is still definitely better than *while alive being dead* and *moldering*.

Meanwhile, Providence had seen fit to prepare for, and mix in with, this new *fermentation of northern-southern fluids* an additional new yeast:

the Christian religion. But, with our Christian century,[48] I do not first have to ask forgiveness for speaking of this religion as a *mainspring of the world* – for indeed considering it only as a *yeast,* as a *leaven,* for good or for bad – or for whatever else one likes.

And here the point – *misunderstood* from *two sides* – deserves some discussion.

The *religion of the ancient world,* which had come to *Greece* and *Italy* from the *Orient* via *Egypt,* had in every respect become an *evaporated, forceless* thing, the true caput mortuum[49] of what it had been and was supposed to be. If one only considers the *later mythology of the Greeks* and the *puppet* of *political peoples-religion* in the case of the *Romans,* no further word is necessary... And yet there was now also almost *"no other principle of virtue"* in the world! Roman *sacrifice for one's fatherland* had sunk from its summit and lay in the morass of carousing and warring inhumanity. Greek *youthful honor* and *love of freedom* – where was it? And the old *Egyptian spirit* – where was it when Greeks and Romans made nests in their[50] land? Whence now a *substitute? Philosophy* could not provide it – philosophy was the most degenerated *sophistical stuff, art of disputation, jumble* of *opinions without force* or *certainty,* a wooden machine hung with old rags, without efficacy on the human heart, let alone with the efficacy to improve a *fallen century,* a *fallen world!* And now the *building up* of the ruins was supposed to happen *by the agency of peoples* who in *their condition* still *needed religion,* could be guided *through religion alone,* mixed *the spirit of superstition* into everything. – And yet these peoples now found on their *new stage* nothing except what they *despised* or were unable to *understand*: Roman mythology and philosophy, along with statues and ethical forms. – And their *northern* religion, a *remnant of the Orient formed* in a *northern manner,* was insufficient – [they] needed a *fresher, more efficacious religion* – and behold!, Providence had *shortly before* made it arise *in a place* whence a substitute for the whole western world *was least hoped for.* Between the naked mountains of Judaea! *Shortly before the collapse* of the whole unrenowned people, precisely in its *final, most miserable epoch* – in *a way* which will always remain miraculous, it *arose, maintained* itself, just as strangely *beat a broad path* for itself

---

[48] Herder is being sarcastic.
[49] Literally: dead head. But the expression refers to the residue left after a chemical reaction, and hence more or less means: dross.
[50] I.e. the Egyptians'.

through ravines and caves – onto a stage which *so needed it*!, on which it has had so very, very much effect! – Certainly the strangest event in the world!

Then, however, it was certainly a great and remarkable drama how under *Julian the two most famous religions*, the *oldest heathen religion* and the *newer Christian religion*, struggled for nothing less than *rule over the world*. That was clear to him and to everyone! *Religion* in the full strength of the word was *indispensable for his fallen century*. *Greek mythology* and *Roman state ceremony* – *this was likewise clear to him*! – was *inadequate* for the purposes of the *century*. So he resorted to everything that he could, to the *most forceful* and *oldest religion* that he knew, the *religion of the Orient* – stirred up in it all the *miraculous forces, forms of magic*, and *apparitions* so that it became entirely *theurgy*; drew, as much as he could, on the aid of *philosophy, Pythagoreanism*, and *Platonism* in order to give everything the *finest coating of reason*; put everything on the *triumph-car* of the greatest *pomp*, pulled by the two most unruly beasts, *violence* and *fanaticism*, directed by the *subtlest political art*. All in vain!, the religion died!, it had lived out its life – miserable *finery* of a *dead corpse* that had been able to perform *miracles* only in another time; the *naked, new Christian religion* won!

It can be seen that the matter is observed by a foreigner who could be a Muslim and a Mameluke in order to write precisely that.[51] I continue in the same way.

But now, the same, so strangely arisen, religion was supposed – this is undeniable – *according to the meaning of its author* (I do not say whether it has become this in every age's application) – it was supposed to become *true religion of humanity, drive of love*, and *bond of all nations into one army of brothers* – its *purpose* from *beginning to end*! It is just as certain that this religion (its adherents may *later* on have made from it what they wished) – that it was the *first* that taught such *pure spiritual truths* and such *heartfelt duties, so completely without husk* and *superstition, without ornamentation* and *force*, that meant to improve the human heart so exclusively, so *universally*, so *entirely* and *without exception*. All earlier religions of the best periods and peoples were by contrast only *narrowly national*, full of *images* and *disguises*, full of *ceremonies* and *national customs*, on which the essential duties always only *hung* and were *added* – in short, religions *of one people*,

[51] In other words, Herder is claiming impartiality and objectivity on behalf of the account that he has just given.

of one region of the earth, of one legislator, of one period!, whereas this religion was obviously in everything the opposite: the *most unadulterated philosophy* of *ethical doctrine*, the *purest theory* of *truths* and *duties, independent* of all laws and little territorial constitutions, in short, if you like, the *most human-loving deism.*[52]

And hence certainly religion *of the universe.* Others, and even *its enemies*, have proved that such a religion could certainly not have sprouted or grown or stolen its way in – let one call it as one wishes – *at another time, earlier* or *later.* The human race had to be *prepared* for this deism for so many millennia, to be *gradually drawn forth* from childhood, barbarism, idolatry, and sensuality; its forces of soul had to be *developed* through so many *national formations* – Oriental, Egyptian, Greek, Roman, etc. – as *steps* and *approaches* before even merely the slightest beginnings towards perception, conception, and concession *of the ideal of religion* and *duty* and *the connecting-together of peoples* could be made. Even just considered as a *tool* it would seem that the Roman *spirit of conquest* had to *precede* in order to open paths everywhere, to establish a *political connection* between peoples which was previously unheard of, to set in motion on precisely this path *tolerance, ideas of international law among peoples* previously unheard of on that scale! In this way the *horizon* got *extended, enlightened*, and when now *ten new nations* of the earth *threw* themselves on this bright horizon, *brought with them* quite other, new *receptivities* precisely for this religion, *needed* it, collectively *alloyed* it with their own essence – yeast!, how strangely *you* are prepared!, and *everything* prepared in advance *for you*!, and *mixed in deeply* and *from far around* !, has *worked* and *fermented* long and strongly. What will it yet *ferment into*?

Thus precisely that about which people usually mock so wittily and philosophically, "Where then was this leaven called Christian religion *pure*? Where was it not *mixed* with the *dough of* [*a people's*] *own*, the *most diverse*, and often the *most awful, manner of thought*?" – precisely that seems to me to be the clear *nature of the matter.* If this religion was, as it really is, the *subtle* spirit, "a *deism of human friendship*," that was supposed to interfere in *no* individual *civil law*; if it was that *philosophy* of *heaven* that, precisely because of its loftiness and its unearthly purity, could embrace the whole earth – it seems to me that in that case it was simply impossible

---

[52] As Brummack and Bollacher point out, this paragraph is largely directed polemically against the deist Voltaire, who in his *La philosophie de l'histoire* had extolled the humanistic virtues of Roman peoples-religion over Christianity.

that this *subtle* vapor could *exist*, be *applied*, without being *mixed* with *more earthly* materials, and, so to speak, needing them as a *vehicle*. Now this was naturally *each people's manner of thought, its ethics and laws, inclinations and abilities* – cold or warm, good or bad, barbaric or civilized [*gebildet*] – everything as it was. The Christian religion was only able to and was only supposed to penetrate everything, and whoever in general has ideas of *divinely organized events* in the world and in the human realm *otherwise than* [*as occurring*] *through worldly* and *human mainsprings* is truly made more for *utopian-poetic* than for *philosophical-natural* abstractions. When *in the whole analogy of nature* has the deity acted otherwise than through nature? And is there therefore no deity, or is it not precisely deity that takes effect so entirely poured forth, uniform, and invisible *through all its works?* – On a human stage let all *human passions* play! [Let them] in each period play in a manner appropriate to the age! Thus in every part of the world, in every nation! Religion is supposed to effect nothing *but purposes through human beings* and *for human beings* – whether it is leaven or treasure, each human being carries it in his container, mixes it with his dough!, and the subtler is the vapor, the more it would evaporate by itself, then *the more it needs* to be *mixed* for use. I can see in the contrary opinion no human sense.

And thus in this case, even just speaking physically and in a human sense, precisely *this* admixture of the Christian religion was the *most choice* that one can imagine almost. It *took care of the poor* in the *necessity that was gaining ground by the day*, so that even *Julian* could not deny it this ingratiating merit. In still later times of disorder it became *the sole consolation* and *resort* in the face of the *universal affliction* (I am not speaking in the manner in which the priests have always used that [term]). Indeed, from the time when the barbarians were themselves Christians, it gradually became *real order* and *security* of the world. Since it tamed the tearing lions and conquered the conquerors – what a *comfortable leaven*[53] for *penetrating* deeply, *having effect* far and *eternally!* The *small constitutions* where it was able to *embrace* everything; the *distantly separated classes* where it became, so to speak, the *universal between-class*; the *great gaps* in the merely *warlike feudal constitution* where it *filled out* everything with *science, legality,* and *influence* on the *manner of thought*, became everywhere *indispensable* and, so to speak, the *soul* of centuries whose *body* was nothing but *warlike spirit*

[53] Herder actually writes *Teig*, "dough," but the context seems to require that we understand this as or read *Sauerteig*, "leaven."

and *slavish agriculture* – could another soul than *worship* have bonded *those* limbs, have *enlivened that* body? If the *body* had been decided on in fate's council, what foolishness to *fantasize* about this body's *spirit* outside the spirit of the age! It was, it seems to me, the sole means of progress!

To whom has it not become apparent how in each century so-called "Christianity" entirely had the *shape of* or *analogy with the constitution* with or in which it existed! How precisely the same *Gothic spirit* also penetrated the *inside* and *outside* of the church, formed *clothes* and *ceremonies, doctrines* and *temples*, sharpened the *bishop's crosier* into a *sword* when everyone wore swords, and created *priests' livings, fiefs*, and *slaves* because such were all there was everywhere. Let one imagine to oneself from century to century those *monstrous institutions* of *priestly offices of honor, monasteries, monastic orders*, finally later even *crusades* and the clear *rule over the world* – monstrous *Gothic structure!, over-freighted, oppressive, dark, tasteless* – the earth seems to sink beneath it – but how *great!, rich!, roofed over with thought* [überdacht]*!,*[54] *mighty! –* I am speaking of a *historical event!* A miracle of the *human spirit* and certainly Providence's *tool*.

If the Gothic body with its fermentations and frictions *stirred up forces* at all, then certainly *the soul*[55] that *enlivened* and *bonded it* made its own contribution. If through that body a *mixture of high concepts and inclinations* got disseminated in Europe, *never yet* effected in *that* mixture and in *that* scope, then certainly the soul[56] was *weaving its work* in this too. And without my being able to go into the various periods of the spirit of the middle ages here, we want to call it *Gothic spirit, northern chivalry* in the broadest sense – *great phenomenon* of so many centuries, lands, and situations.

In a certain sense still "*aggregate of all those inclinations* which previously *individual peoples and periods had developed.*" They can even be dissolved into these, but the *effective element* which *bonded* them all and

---

[54] The word *überdacht* is a pun; it could mean either (1) thought through, or (2) roofed over.

[55] Herder actually writes *der Geist*, "the spirit," but note (1) he had written two paragraphs ago "could another *soul* than worship have bonded those limbs, have enlivened that body?" (emphasis changed), and (2) in the very next sentence he uses the feminine singular pronoun *sie* in a way that is without any clear reference and is most naturally explained in terms of his having meant to write *die Seele* here.

[56] Herder simply writes *sie*, whose reference is quite unclear. I think the explanation is pretty clearly that he *thought* that he had just written *die Seele* in the preceding sentence rather than *der Geist*. Brummack and Bollacher instead take the reference of *sie* to be to *Providence*, but this seems less plausible.

made them all into a living *creature of God* is no longer the same in each individual one. *Paternal inclinations* and holy *revering of the female sex; inextinguishable love of freedom* and *despotism; religion* and *warlike spirit; scrupulous order* and *solemnity* and *strange partiality for adventure* – this flowed together!, *Oriental, Roman, Northern, Saracen* concepts and inclinations! – one knows *when, where,* and in *what measure* they then and there flowed together and modified themselves. – The spirit of the century wove through and bonded – the most diverse properties – *bravery* and *monkery, adventure* and *galantry, tyranny* and *nobility of mind* – bonded it into the whole which now for us – between the Romans and ourselves – *stands there* as a ghost, as romantic adventure – [but] once upon a time it was nature, it was . . . *truth.*

This spirit "of northern *knightly honor*" has been compared with the *heroic times of the Greeks*[k] – and indeed points of comparison have been found. But in itself this spirit remains, it seems to me, *unique*! in the sequence of all the centuries – *only like itself*! It has been so terribly *mocked* because it stands between the Romans and ourselves – quanti viri![57] – ourselves!; others with a somewhat fanciful brain have *raised* it so high over everything. It seems to me that it is nothing more or less than an "*individual condition of the world*!" to be compared with none of the preceding, like them with its *advantages* and *disadvantages*, grounded on them, itself in eternal alteration and striving forth – towards a *greater whole.*

The *dark* sides of this period of time are registered in all the books: every classical humanist [*Schöndenker*] who considers our century's civil administration the non plus ultra[58] of humanity has an opportunity to reduce whole centuries to *barbarism, miserable state authority, superstition* and *stupidity, lack of ethics* and *tastelessness* – in *schools*, in *country seats*, in *temples*, in *monasteries*, in *town halls*, in *artisans' guilds*, in *huts* and *houses*, and to rave about our century's *light*, that is, about its *superficiality* and *unrestraint*, about its *warmth* in *ideas* and its *coldness* in *actions*, about its *seeming strength* and *freedom*, and about its real *weakness-unto-death* and *exhaustion* under *unbelief, despotism,* and *luxury.* All the books of our *Voltaire* and *Hume, Robertson's* and *Iselin's,*[59] are full of this, and it becomes

---

[k] *Hurd*, Letters on Chivalry [and Romance (1758)].

57 What measure of men!   58 The ultimate.

59 The preceding sentence and the first part of this one provide good examples of Herder's common practice of varying the patterns of his lists, rather than sticking to some single or few conventional

such a beautiful [*schön*] picture how they derive the enlightenment and improvement of the world from the times of gloom up to the deism and despotism of souls, i.e. up to *philosophy* and *tranquillity*, that the heart of every lover of his age laughs[60] in contemplating it.

All that is true and not true. True if, like a child, one holds *color* against *color* and of course wants to have a *light, bright* little image – in our century there is, unfortunately!, so much light! Untruth if one regards that age, in its *essence* and *purposes*, *enjoyment* and *ethics*, in particular as a *tool* in the course of time. There often lay there in these seemingly *violent* episodes and connections something *firm, bonding, noble,* and *superior*[61] which we, with our – God be praised! – *refined* ethics, *dissolved* guilds and, to compensate, *bound* lands, and *innate* cleverness, and love of peoples right *to the end of the earth*, truly neither *feel* nor scarcely any longer *can* feel. Behold, you make mock of that age's *serfdom*, of the primitive *country seats of the nobility*, of the many *small islands* and *subdivisions* and what depended on them – you praise nothing so much as the *dissolution* of these bonds, and you know *no* greater good that ever happened to humanity than when Europe and with it the world became *free. Became free?* Sweet dreamer!, if it were only that, and if only that were true! But now behold also how through that condition in those times *things were achieved* over which otherwise all human cleverness would necessarily have[62] proved stupid: Europe *populated* and *cultivated;*[63] races and families, lord and serf, king and subject, pressed *more strongly* and *closer* together; the so-called primitive country seats prevented the *luxurious, unhealthy growth* of the *cities*, of these abysses for humanity's life-forces; the lack of *trade* and of *refinement* prevented *unrestraint* and preserved simple humanity – *chastity* and *fecundity* in marriages, *poverty* and *industry* and *compression together* in *houses*. The *primitive guilds* and *free baronies* produced *knight's* and *artisan's pride*, but simultaneously *reliance on oneself, firmness in one's circle, manliness* in one's *center*, fended off the worst affliction of humanity, the *yoke of land* and *soul*, under which, obviously, since all the islands have been dissolved, everyone sinks with a happy and free spirit. Then of course in somewhat later times so many *warlike republics*

---

pattern(s), such as "a, b, c, and d." His motives for this are mainly aesthetic – in particular he wants to avoid the boring predictability of doing the latter.

[60] Herder means us to ask ourselves here: In *joy* or in *ridicule?*

[61] The last two terms hover in the German as in the English between connotations of high social status and of high moral qualities.

[62] Reading *hätte* for *hatte*.   [63] Or possibly: *built*.

and *valiantly self-defending cities* were able to arise there!; once there had been *planted, nurtured,* and raised through friction the forces which, in sad remains, you still now live from. If heaven had not sent you the barbaric periods beforehand and preserved them under such manifold missiles and blows – poor, civilly administered Europe that eats or expels its children, how would you be with all your wisdom? – *a wasteland!*

"That it should be unintelligible to anyone in the world how light does not nourish human beings!, how tranquillity and luxury and so-called freedom of thought can never be universal happiness and vocation!" But *sensation, movement, action* – even if subsequently without purpose (what on the stage of humanity has an *eternal* purpose?), even if with *blows* and *revolutions*, even if with sensations which here and there become *fanatical, violent,* even *awful* – as a *tool in the hands of the course of time*, what power!, what effect! *Heart* and not *head* nourished! Everything bonded with *inclinations* and *drives,* not with *sickly thoughts! Worship* and *knightly honor, boldness in love* and *citizenly strength* – *state constitution* and *legislation, religion.* – I would rather do anything than defend the eternal peoples' migrations and devastations, vassal-wars and fights, monks' armies, pilgrimages, crusades – I would only like to explain them – how *spirit* breathes in everything, though!, fermentation of *human forces. A great cure* of the whole species through *violent movement,* and if I may speak so boldly, fate wound *up* (certainly with a great din and without the weights being able to hang there peacefully) *the great wound-down clock!* So the wheels rattled there!

How differently I see the times in this light! How much [I see] to *forgive* them, since I see them as themselves really always *fighting against shortcomings, struggling* for *improvement,* and truly them more than another time! How many *slanders* downright *false* and *exaggerated,* since abuses either get fictionally attributed to them[64] out of an alien[65] brain or are ones which were in those days far *milder* and *less avoidable, compensated* for themselves with a good on the other side, or which we already now clearly perceive as tools for *great good* in the future that *they did not themselves think of.* Who reads this history and does not often cry *"Inclinations* and *virtues* of *honor* and *freedom,* of *love* and *bravery,* of *politeness* and *word,* where are you now!" Your *depths clogged with slime!* Your *solidity a soft bed of sand*

---

[64] Herder actually writes the singular *ihr* rather than the plural *ihnen,* in a slide from the plural into the singular that already began in the preceding sentence: *sie . . . mehr als eine andere.*
[65] Reading *fremdem* for *fremden.*

full of *grains of silver* where nothing *grows!* However it may be, give us *in many respects* your *worship* and *superstition, darkness* and *ignorance, disorder* and *primitiveness* in *ethics,* and take our *light* and *unbelief,* our *enervated coldness* and *refinement,* our *philosophical exhaustedness* and *human misery!* – For the rest, though, certainly, mountain and valley must border on each other, and the *dark, solid vault* could – be nothing but a *dark, solid* vault – Gothic!

  A gigantic step in the course of human fate! Even if we merely took it that *corruptions* precede in order to produce *improvement, order* – a great step! In order to yield *that* light, such a *great* shadow was necessary; the knot needed to be tied *so firmly* in order that afterwards the *unfolding* might occur; was *fermentation* not necessary in order to yield the *yeastless, pure, divine* drink? – it seems to me that this would follow immediately from "the *pet philosophy*" of the century. You can of course prove splendidly there how so many corners had first to be violently *ground down* before the *round, smooth, nice thing* that we are could appear!, how in the church so many *outrages, errors, bits of tastelessness,* and *blasphemies* had to *precede,* all those centuries had to *struggle, cry out,* and *strive* for improvement, before your *Reformation* or *light, brightly shining deism* could arise. The *evil art of politics* had to run through the wheel of all its evils and awful deeds before our "*art of politics*" in the whole scope of the term might appear, like the morning sun from night and fog. – Still, therefore, a beautiful picture, *order* and *progress* of nature, and you shining philosopher of course on the shoulders of all!

  But not a thing in the whole of God's realm, am I able to persuade myself though!, is *only* means – everything *means* and *purpose* simultaneously, and hence certainly these centuries [are so] too. If the bloom of the spirit of the age, "*the sense of chivalry,*" was in itself already *a product* of the whole past *in the solid form of the north,* if the *mixture* of concepts *of honor* and *love* and *faithfulness* and *worship* and *bravery* and *chastity* which was now the *ideal* had previously been unheard of, then behold in this, in comparison with the ancient world, *since the strength of each individual national character had been lost,* behold precisely in this *mixture* a *substitute* and *progress* towards a *greater whole.* From the Orient to Rome it was *tribal stem;* now *branches* and *twigs* came forth from the tribal stem – none of them in itself *firm like the stem* but *more extensive, airier, higher!* Despite all the barbarism, the *cognitions* which got treated *scholastically* were *subtler* and *higher,* the *sensations* which got applied *barbarously* and *in a priestly way* were *more abstract* and *higher* – from these two things flowed the *ethics*, their image. *Such a religion*, miserable as it still looked, had nonetheless scarcely been known to any age before; even the subtler aspect of the *Turkish* religion, with which our deists credit it so highly, had only *arisen* "*through the Christian religion*," and even the *most miserable* sophistries of monkery, the *most fanciful* imaginings, show that there was enough *subtlety* and *skill* in the world to *think out*, to *grasp*, such things – that people really in earnest began to breathe in such a *subtle* element. *Popery* could after all never have existed in *Greece* or *ancient Rome*, not merely due to the causes which people usually look to but really also because of the primordial simplicity, because for such a *refined* system there was not yet any sense, any *space* – and the popery of ancient Egypt was at least certainly a much *cruder* and *more clumsy* machine. Such *forms of government* – despite all Gothic taste, they had *nonetheless scarcely yet existed before* – with the idea of *barbarous ordering* from the *element upwards* up to the *peak*, with the ever *changed attempts* to *bond* [*binden*] everything *in such a way that it would nonetheless not be in bondage* [*gebunden*]. – Contingency, or rather, primitively and freely operating force, exhausted itself *in small forms of the great form* such as a politician could hardly have thought out: chaos, in which all *strove* for a new, higher creation without knowing *how* and *in what form*. – The works of the *spirit* and of *genius* from these times are *of the same kind*, entirely full of the composite *scent* of all times – too full of *beauties*, of *subtleties*, of *invention*, of *order* to remain *beauty, order, invention* – they are like the Gothic buildings! And if the spirit reaches right down to the smallest *institutions* and *customs*, is it wrong if the crown of the old tribal stem should still appear in these centuries? (No longer tribal stem – it was not supposed to be and could not be that – but *crown*!) Precisely the aspect of *non-unity*, the aspect of *confusion*, the rich *excess of branches and twigs* – this constitutes this spirit's *nature*! There hang the blooms of *the spirit of chivalry*; there at some future time, when the storm blows off the leaves, will hang the more beautiful *fruits*.

So many *brother nations* and *no monarchy* on the earth! – *Each branch* from here, so to speak, a *whole* – and sent forth its *twigs*!; all of them sent forth [their twigs] *beside* each other, *move, tangled* together, each with its *sap*. – This multiplicity of *kings' realms*!, this *existing-alongside-each-other* of *brother communities* – all of one *German race*, all in accordance with *one ideal* of *constitution*, all in *faith in one religion*, each *fighting with itself* and with its *members*, and almost invisibly but very penetratingly *driven* and *moved* by *one holy wind, papal respect.* – How the tree is shaken! Whither, on crusades and conversions of peoples, has it not cast branches, bloom, and twigs! – If the Romans in their subjugation of the earth had had to help the peoples, not in the optimal way, to a type "of *international law of peoples* and *universal recognition of the Romans*" – the papacy with all its violence became in the hand of fate the machine for a "still *higher connection,* for the *universal recognition of people who should be Christians!, brothers!, human beings!* " The song certainly rose through discords and screeching tunings to a *higher note*: certain, several, collected, abstracted, fermented ideas, inclinations, and conditions spread themselves out over the world – how the one ancient, simple tribal stem of the human species broke out into branches and twigs!

*

Finally there followed, as we say, the dissolution, the unfolding: long, eternal night enlightened itself into *morning*, there arose *Reformation, Renaissance* of the arts, sciences, ethics! – the yeast sank and there arose – *our thought!, culture!, philosophy!* – on commençait à penser comme nous pensons aujourd'hui; on n'était plus barbare.[66]

   No temporal point in the unfolding of the human spirit has been more beautifully described than this! – since all our histories, discours préliminaires[67] to the *encyclopedia of all human knowledge*, and philosophies point to it,[1] and from east and west, from the beginning and yesterday, all the threads that are drawn out, or that wave in the head like autumnal cobwebs, know to draw towards it as the *highest peak of human civilization* [*Bildung*]. And since the system is now already so brilliant, famous, lovingly accepted, and completely evident, I dare to add[68] nothing – I merely set a few small *notes alongside.*

---

[1] *Hume,* The History of England [(1754–62)], and Vermischte Schriften [Miscellaneous Writings (German ed. 1756)]; *Robertson's* History of Scotland [During the Reigns of Queen Mary and King James VI until his Accession to the Crown of England (1759)], and [History of the Reign of the Emperor] Charles V [(1769)]; *D'Alembert,* Mélanges de littérature, [d'histoire,] et de philosophie [Miscellany of Literature, of History, and of Philosophy (1753)]; *Iselin's* [Versuch philosophischer Mutmaßungen über die Geschichte der Menschheit [Attempt at Philosophical Conjectures on the History of Humanity (1764)], vol. 2, [and] Vermischte Schriften [Miscellaneous Writings (1770)], and what limps and babbles in imitation of this.

[66] People began to think as we think today; people were no longer barbarians.
[67] Preliminary discourses. (This is an allusion to D'Alembert's *Discours préliminaire* to Diderot's *Encyclopedia.*)
[68] Reading *hinzuzusetzen* for *hinzusetzen.*

I. *First of all*, I must say concerning the excessively high renown of the *human understanding*[m] that, if I may put the matter so, *it* had less and less effect in this *universal alteration of the world* than a *blind fate* that cast and guided things. Either they were such great, so to speak, *cast-forth* events which went *beyond* all human *forces* and *prospects*, which human beings usually *resisted*, where no one [even] dreamed of the *consequences* as a *considered plan*, or they were small *accidental happenings*, more *finds* than *inventions*, applications of a thing that one had *had for a long time* and not seen, not used – or nothing at all but a *simple mechanism*, new *knack, manual skill*, that changed the world. Philosophers of the eighteenth century, if that is so, then where does that leave your *idolatry* towards the *human spirit*?

Who laid out *Venice* here in this place under the deepest pressure of necessity? And who thought through what this Venice, only in this place, could and should be *for all people of the earth* for a whole millennium? The person who cast this sound of islands into the marsh, who led these few fishermen there, was the same as he[69] who makes fall the *seed* so that[70] at this time and in this place an *oak* may grow, he who planted the *hut by the Tiber* so that *Rome*, the *eternal* capital of the world, might develop from it. It is precisely the same person who at one time brings along barbarians so that they should *destroy* the *literature of the whole world*, the *library* at *Alexandria* (so to speak, a sinking part of the world!),[71] and at another time brings along just the same barbarians so that they should *beg, preserve, a small remnant of literature* and *convey it to Europe* on a quite *different side*, on *paths* that no one had *dreamed* or *wished*.[72] Just the same person who at another time on another side makes an *imperial city*[73] be destroyed by them so that the sciences, which no one *sought* there and which had been so long *idle* there, *might flee to Europe* ... Everything is great fate!, *neither thought through, nor hoped for, nor effected* by human beings. Do you not see, you ant, that you only *crawl* on the great wheel of destiny?

---

[m] Gloire de l'esprit humain, ses progrès, révolutions, son développement, sa création, etc. [Glory of the human spirit, its steps of progress, revolutions, its development, its creation, etc.]

[69] I.e. God.   [70] Reading *daß* for *das*.

[71] Herder here follows the – no longer generally accepted – view that the decisive destruction of the Library occurred at the hands of the Arabs under the Calif Omar in 641/2.

[72] This refers to the Arabs' communication of Greek science and philosophy to Europe via Spain.

[73] Constantinople, which was conquered by the Turks in 1453, thereby leading to the flight of Greek scholars to Italy.

When we penetrate more closely into the circumstances of the origins of all so-called world illuminations, the same thing. There on a large scale, here on a small, *contingency, fate, deity*! What began *every reformation* was *small things* which never had from the start the great, monstrous plan that they won afterwards – by contrast, as often as there had been the great, really considered, human plan beforehand, it failed. All your great *church councils*, you emperors!, kings!, cardinals and lords of the world!,[74] will never change anything,[75] but this unrefined, ignorant monk, *Luther*, is destined to accomplish it! And that from *small things* in relation to which he himself anything but thinks so far ahead!, through *means* with which in the manner of our age, speaking philosophically, *such a thing could never be accomplished*!, for the most part *he himself* accomplishing the least part, only he *impelled others, awakened* reformers in all the other lands, he stood up and said "I make a move! Therefore there is movement!" – that is how what came about came about. A transformation of the world! How often such *Luthers* had earlier risen up and – sunk. Their mouths stopped up with smoke and flames, or their word did not yet find any open[76] air to resound in – but now it is *springtime*; the earth opens up, the sun incubates, and a thousand new plants emerge . . . Human being, you were only ever, almost contrary to your will, a small, *blind tool.*

"Why did not" cries out the gentle philosopher "each such reformation, rather!, happen *without a revolution? The human spirit* should just have been allowed to follow *its quiet course* instead of, as actually happened, passions in the storm of *action* giving birth to new prejudices, and evil being exchanged for evil." – Answer!: because such a *quiet course of progress* of the *human spirit* for the improvement of the world is hardly anything but a *phantom* of our heads, never *God's course* in *nature.* This seed falls into the earth!, there it lies and becomes hard; but now the *sun* comes to awaken it, then it splits open, the chambers swell apart violently, it breaks through the ground – thus bloom, thus fruit. Hardly even the horrible toadstool grows as you dream it does. The basis of every reformation was always just such a *small seed, fell quietly* into the earth, hardly worth talking about; human beings had *already* had it *for a long time, saw it* and *paid no heed to it* – but now *inclinations, ethics,* a world of *habits* are destined to be changed, *created anew,* through it – is that possible

---

[74] I.e. cardinals and *popes.*   [75] Reading *nichts* for *nicht.*
[76] Literally, and here significantly: free.

without *revolution*, without *passion* and *movement?* What *Luther* said had long been known, but now *Luther* said it! *Roger Bacon, Galileo, Descartes, Leibniz* – when *they* invented [*erfanden*],[77] things were quiet; there was a *ray of light* – but their inventions were destined to break through, to do away with opinions, to change the world – there arose *storm* and *flame.* Even if the reformer always had *passions* which the *matter*, the *science*, did not itself require, the *introduction of the matter* required them, and precisely the fact that he had them, had enough in order now to get through a nothing to whither whole centuries had not *been able to get* by institutions, machineries, and ponderings – precisely that is a *warrant for his vocation!*

"Mostly just *simple, mechanical inventions* which had in part been seen, possessed, played with, for a long time, but which now through a bright idea *applied* in this way and *not otherwise* transformed the world." Thus, for example, the application of *glass* for *optics,* of the *magnet* for the *compass,* of *gunpowder* for *war,* of the *art of book printing* for the *sciences,* of *calculus* for a completely new *mathematical world* – and everything took on a new shape. The tool had been transformed, a place had been found *outside the old world,* and thus this old world got *moved ahead.*[78]

The gun invented!, and behold, the old bravery of *Theseuses, Spartans, Romans, knights,* and *giants* is gone – war is different, and how much is different with this different war!

Book printing invented!, and to what a great extent the world of the *sciences* is changed!, facilitated and disseminated!, become light and level! Everyone can read, spell – everyone who can read gets taught.

With the *little needle* on the ocean – who can count the revolutions in all parts of the world that have been effected with this? Lands discovered, so much larger than Europe! Coasts conquered full of gold, silver, gemstones, spices, and death! Human beings made converts into, or cultivated into, mines, slave-mills, and vicious ethics! Europe depopulated, consumed in its most secret forces with diseases and luxury – who can count!, who describe! *New ethics, inclinations, virtues, vices* – who can count and describe? The wheel in which for three centuries the world has moved is

77 Or: discovered. (The preceding list of names suggests that Herder is thinking in part of discoveries as well as inventions, though the emphasis in what follows is certainly on inventions.)

78 Herder is here echoing the famous saying attributed to Archimedes, which he also cites in *On the Cognition and Sensation of the Human Soul* and elsewhere: "Give me a point outside the world and I will move the world."

endless – and what did it turn on?, what impelled it? – the *needle-point of two* or *three mechanical thoughts*!

II. Precisely for this reason it must follow that a large part of this so-called new civilization [*Bildung*] is itself real *mechanics* – more closely investigated, to what an extent this mechanics turns out to be our *modern spirit*! If for the most part *new methods* in every type and art transformed the world – new methods *made superfluous forces* which were previously nec-essary, but which now – since every unused force sleeps! – in time *got lost*. *Certain virtues* of the *science* of *war*, of *civil life*, of *shipping*, of *government* – they were no longer needed; there emerged a *machine*, and only *one man* governs the machine. With one thought!, with one sign! – and in com-pensation how many forces sleep! *The gun* invented, and thereby what sinews of *primitive, bodily* war-strength, and *soul-war-strength*, bravery, faithfulness, presence of mind in individual cases, feeling for honor that belonged to the old world exhausted! The army became a hired, thought-less, forceless, will-less machine which *one man* directs in *his head*, and which he only pays as a *puppet* of movement, a living wall, to throw bullets and catch bullets. Hence at bottom, a Roman or Spartan would perhaps say, virtues in the innermost hearth of the heart *burned off*, and a wreath of military honor withered – and what replaces them?; the soldier is the first paid servant of the state in a hero's livery – behold his honor and his vocation! He is ... and with little effort the *remains* of *individual existences exploded* – the *old Gothic forms of freedom, classes, and property*, this mis-erable building in bad taste!, shot into the ground and destroyed, gets so tightly blocked [*blockiert*][79] in its small ruins that *land, inhabitant, citizen, fatherland* is no doubt sometimes something, but *lord* and *serf*, *despot* and *liveried servant* in every office, vocation, and class – from the *farmer* to the *minister* and from the *minister* to the *priest* – is everything. It is called *sovereignty*!, refined *statecraft*!, new *philosophical form of government*! – and it really is this. The prince's hat and crown of modern centuries – on what do they rest! – as that most famous sun-eagle on all our coins shows, on *drums, flags, bullets*, and *ever-ready soldiers' caps*.[80]

---

[79] Herder seems here to be using this verb in the double sense (1) *divided into blocks* (an unusual sense) and (2) *blocked up* (a usual sense). The general overall idea is one of many little positions in society that are jammed together so that they have no freedom of movement but are under constant mechanical constraint.

[80] Herder is referring here to the coins of Frederick the Great, which from 1745 on showed on the reverse the Prussian eagle over and before war implements, including drums, flags, soldiers' caps, and cannons.

The spirit of *modern philosophy* – that it must be *mechanics* in more than one way is shown, I think, by the greater part *of its children*. Despite their philosophy and learning, often how *ignorant* and *forceless* in matters of life and of the healthy understanding! Instead of the philosophical spirit as in ancient times never existing *for itself alone*, beginning from *occupations* and *rushing* to *occupations*, and hence also only having the purpose of creating *full, healthy, effective souls*, since it stands *alone* and has become a *trade* – it is a *trade*. The however manyeth part of you considers logic, metaphysics, moral theory, physics as what they are – organs of the human soul, *tools* with which one should take effect!, *exemplary models* of *thought-forms* which are just supposed to give our soul a *more beautiful thought-form that belongs to it*. Instead, a person beats his thoughts *into these mechanically*, plays, and juggles – the strangest of pugilistic fellows! He dances with his dagger on the academic tightrope to the admiration and joy of all who sit around and cheer at the great artist that he may not break his neck and leg – this is his art. An *occupation* in the world – if you want to see it badly taken care of, then give it to the *philosopher*! On paper how pure!, how gentle!, how beautiful and great – but hopeless in *execution*!, at each step *amazed* and *staring frozen* before unseen obstacles and consequences. Meanwhile, the child was really a great philosopher, could *calculate* and play with syllogisms, figures, and *instruments* fluently, often so happily that new *syllogisms, results*, and so-called *discoveries* emerged – the *fruit*, the *honor*, the *peak* of the *human spirit*! – through *mechanical play*!

That was the more difficult philosophy – and now the *easy one*, the *beautiful one*! God be praised!, what is more mechanical than this? In sciences, arts, habits, mode of life into which it has penetrated, where it is the sap and bloom of the century, what more *mechanical* than it? Precisely *ancient tradition*, the *senseless prejudice* of *learning, slow maturation, deep penetration*, and *late judgment*, it has of course cast off like a yoke from the neck!, has brought to our *judicial bars*, instead of small, dusty, detailed knowledge in which each incident is supposed to be treated and investigated *as that which it is* – has brought into them what a *beautiful, easy, free judgment*, one of measuring and dealing with *everything* in light of *two* incidents!, of sticking – passing beyond what is *individual*, in which alone consists *species facti*[81] – to the bright, splendid *universal*, of being, instead

---

[81] This is a legal expression connoting "the representation of a controversial matter as it exists in all its circumstances" (Zedler).

of a *judge* a *philosopher* (bloom of the century!). Has brought into our *state economics* and *science of government*, instead of laboriously achieved knowledge of the needs and true condition of the land, what an *eagle's eye!*, what a *vision of the whole*, as though on a *map* and a *philosophical table!* Has developed *first principles* through the mouth of Montesquieu, from and according to which *a hundred diverse peoples* and *regions* get calculated extempore in two moments according to the *one-times-one* of *politics.* – Thus all *fine arts, manual trades,* and almost the smallest *daylabors* – who needs to clamber about, to *work*, laboriously in their depths as in a vaulted cellar? One *rationalizes! Dictionaries* and *philosophies* about all of them, without understanding a single one of them with the *tool in one's hand*. They have one and all become abrégé raisonné[82] of their former pedantry – *abstracted spirit!, philosophy* [made] out of two *thoughts* – the *most mechanical thing in the world.*[83]

Do I have to prove what a noble, *mechanical* thing *modern wit* is? Does there exist a more *formed* language and *sentential form*, that is, a *more narrow last* for *thoughts*, for *mode of life*, for *genius* and *taste*, than in the case of the people[84] from whom modern wit has spread in the world most brilliantly under a hundred shapes? What *drama* has become more the puppet of a beautiful *regularity* – what *mode of life* more the aping of a light, mechanical *politeness, gaiety,* and *verbal ornamentation* – what *philosophy* more the display of few sentiments and a treatment of everything in the world according to these sentiments, than these . . . *apes* of *humanity*, of *genius*, of *happiness*, of *virtue?* And precisely because they are nothing but this, and can be so easily aped in turn, *they are this for all of Europe.*

III. Thence it of course now becomes readily intelligible towards "*which center*" this civilization [*Bildung*] strives and ever gets guided: "*philosophy!, thought!* – easier *mechanics!, rationalizing* that reaches right down to the

---

[82] Critical summary, epitome.
[83] In manuscript a this paragraph reads, more succinctly: "The spirit of philosophy, which has penetrated into all sciences, arts, habits, houses, and trades from what small beginnings – what has it not changed and destroyed. Tradition, meaningless prejudice, paternal ethics thrown like a yoke from the neck; what beautiful, easy, free judgment, what cleverness and good sense, brought to our judicial bars instead of small, dusty, detailed knowledge! In state economics and the science of government, instead of knowledge attained with effort, what an [reading: *welcher*] eagle's eye, what a view of the needs of the land as though on a map and a philosophical table or on the one-times-one of an analysis in the most beautiful systematic manner, arisen. Thus arts, manual trades, and virtually the smallest daylabors – they are an abrégé raisonné of their former effort, precision, and order. This is how the world has made things easier for itself and improved itself."
[84] I.e. the French.

foundation pillars of society which formerly just *stood* and *carried!*" And here too I can in ten sorts of ways hardly understand how this can be so *universally* and *uniquely* rationalized as the *peak* and *purpose* of all human civilization, of all *happiness*, of all *good*. Is the whole body destined to *see*, then? And if hand and foot want to be *eye* and *brain* must not the whole body suffer? Rationalizing spread too carelessly, too uselessly – *could* it not weaken, and has it not really weakened, *inclination, drive, activity* for living?

Nevertheless now, this *exhaustion* may well be comfortable for the spirit of some lands: exhausted limbs have to go on, have no forces except . . . for example, for *counterthought*. Each cog remains in its place from *fear* or *habit* or *luxury* and philosophy, and what, then, is many a great philosophy-governed flock but a forced-together pile – livestock and wood! They think!, perhaps thinking gets *spread* abroad among them – *up to a point*, so that from day to day they *feel* themselves more than a machine,[85] but feel according to *given prejudices*, learn to grind, and *must go on*. They grind – but alas, they can do nothing but grind, and comfort themselves with *free thinking* [*Freidenken*].[86] Dear, weak, annoying, useless free thinking – substitute for everything that they perhaps needed more: *heart!, warmth!, blood!, humanity!, life!*

Now let each person calculate. *Light* infinitely increased and spread abroad, while *inclination, drive for living, is disproportionately weakened*! Ideas of *universal love of humanity, of peoples, of enemies increased*!, and the *warm feeling of father's, mother's, brother's, child's, friend's inclinations infinitely weakened*! First principles of freedom, honor, virtue spread so far and wide that every person *recognizes* them most clearly, that in certain lands everyone right down to the most insignificant has them *on his tongue and lips* – and each of them[87] at the same time bound with the *worst chains of cowardice, shame, luxury, servility*, and *miserable planlessness. Handy knacks and facilitations infinitely spread* – but all these handy knacks converge into the hand *of one person or several people*, who is the only one to think; for the machine, the desire to live, to take effect, to live in a humanly noble and beneficial way, with pleasure, has disappeared. Does the machine

---

[85] Or possibly: so that they *feel* themselves more from day to day as a machine.

[86] The sense of *Freidenken* here is mainly (1) *freedom of thought*, but Herder is also blending with this the sense (2) *freethinking* (i.e. religious agnosticism or atheism).

[87] The reference here could be either to the *first principles* or to the *people* in question.

live any longer? In the whole and in the smallest part, *the sole thought of the master.*

Is this, then, the beautiful ideal condition towards which we have been formed through everything, which *spreads* abroad further and further in *Europe*, which *sails* to all *parts of the world*, and wants to *civilly administer* everyone *to be what we are . . . Human beings* ?, *citizens* of a *fatherland* ?, *beings who are independently* something *in the world* ? – *to be* these? Perhaps! But at least and certainly, all of them in number, needs, purpose, and destiny *political calculation*; each of them in the uniform of his class machines! – There stand now those resplendent *market-places* for the formation of humanity, *pulpit* and *stage, halls* of *justice, libraries, schools*, and of course especially the crowns of them all: illustrious academies! In what splendor!, to the eternal after-renown of the princes!, to what great purposes *of the formation* and *enlightenment* of the *world, of the happiness of human beings*!, splendidly consecrated.[88] What do they do, then?, what *can they do?* – *they play*!

IV. So about several of the most famous *means* which – the honor of our century! – have the creative plan *"to form humanity"* – one word! With this we at least come to a very *practical side* of the book.

If I have not written in vain from the beginning, then it can be seen that the *formation* and *progressive formation of a nation* is never anything but a *work of fate* – the result of a thousand *cooperating causes* of the *whole element in which they live*, so to speak. And if this is so, then what *child's play* to present this formation as merely consisting in and occurring through a few *brighter ideas* towards which people have been trotting almost since the *reinstitution* of the *sciences*! This book, this author, this mass of books is said to *form*; their whole result, the philosophy of our century, is said to *form*. What would that mean but: *awaken* or *strengthen* the inclinations through which humanity is *blessed* ? And what a gulf for this to happen! *Ideas* actually yield only *ideas* – more *clarity, correctness*, and *order for thought*. But that is also all that one can count on *with certainty*. For how, then, all that might *mix* in the soul; what it *should find before it* and *change*; how *strong* and *lasting* this change might prove; and then finally, how this change might *mix* and *cast itself* into the *thousand-formed occasions* and *contexts* of *human life*, let alone of an *age*, of a *whole people*, of all Europe,

[88] In this sentence Herder is using a rhetorical device of deliberately changing the grammatical construction and thought of a sentence in midstream – a device that is particularly characteristic of Sophoclean poetry.

of the *whole universe* (as our humility imagines) – ye gods, what another world of questions!

A human being who became acquainted with *our century's artificial manner of thought* would read all the books that we read, praise, and – as it is said – *form ourselves in accordance with* from childhood up, would collect the *first principles* that we all explicitly or tacitly *concede* and also *process* with *certain forces* of our souls, etc., would want now to infer thence to the *whole, living mechanism* of the century – *pitiful fallacy!* Precisely because these *first principles* are so *commonplace*, pass as *playthings* from hand to hand and as *platitudes* from *lip* to *lip* – precisely for this reason, it proves probable that they *cannot* any longer achieve *any effect*. Does one *use* what one *plays* with? And when one has so much grain that one does not *sow*, *plant* the field but must *inundate* it as a *granary floor – barren, dry* granary floor! – can *anything take root?*, *sprout?*, does a grain even enter *the earth?*

Why should I seek examples for a truth for which almost everything, unfortunately!, would be an example – *religion* and *moral theory*, *legislation* and *common ethics*. How deluged with *beautiful first principles*, *developments*, *systems*, *expositions* – deluged to the point that hardly anyone any longer *sees the bottom* and *has a footing* – but just for this reason also simply *swims across*. The *theologian* leafs through the most stirring representations of religion, *learns*, *knows*, *proves*, and *forgets* – we are all from childhood up formed to be these theologians. The *pulpit* resounds with first principles which we all concede, know, beautifully feel, and – leave on and beside the pulpit. Likewise with *books*, *philosophy*, and *moral theory*. Who is not fed up with reading them? And what author does not already make it his main business *to dress* [*things*] *up well*, to *silver-coat* beautifully the forceless pill at all costs. Head and heart are now separated; the human being has, unfortunately!, reached the point of acting not according to what he *knows* but according to what he *likes*. What help does the ill man get from all that store of *treats* which he *cannot enjoy* with his *sick-heartedness* [*mit siechem Herzen*],[89] indeed whose excess was precisely what *made* him *sick-hearted*.

One could still allow the *disseminators* of the *medium* of this formation the language and the delusion that they form "*humanity*," and of course especially the philosophers of Paris the language and the delusion

[89] Like its strained English translation "with his sick-heartedness," the German phrase *mit siechem Herzen* can bear not only a very literal physical meaning but also a psychological one. But also important here is an intermediate meaning: "with his nausea" (cf. French *mal de coeur*: nausea).

that they form toute l'Europe and tout l'univers.[90] One knows of course what this language means – *tone!, conventional phrase!, beautiful expression*, or at most *useful delusion*. But when such letter-culture means[91] are also lighted upon by those for whom quite different tools . . . when they with those means give the century a beautiful fog, direct *eyes* to the shine of this ineffective light, precisely in order to have *hearts* and *hands* free – *error* and *loss*, you are lamentable!

There was an *age* when the art of *legislation* was seen as the sole means for forming nations, and this means, taken in hand in the strangest manner, was for the most part supposed to become only a *universal philosophy of humanity*, a *codex* of *reason*, of *humanity*, and what all more I do not know. The matter was certainly *more deceptive* than *useful*. Certainly, one was able with this "to exhaust all *common principles of what is right and good, maxims of love of humanity* and of *wisdom, prospects* from all *times* and *peoples* for all *times* and *peoples*" – for all times and peoples? – and thus, unfortunately!, precisely not *for* the people whom this legal code is supposed to fit as its suit of clothing. Such a universal ladled-off thing – is it not perhaps also *foam* that *flows to bits* in the *air* of all times and peoples? And what a different matter to *prepare nourishment* for the arteries and sinews of one's people so that this nourishment *strengthens its heart* and *invigorates its very bone and marrow*!

Between every universally stated, even the *most beautiful*, truth and its *least* application there is a gulf! And application in the *single right place?*, for the *right purposes?*, in the *single best way?* – The *Solon* of a *village* who has really eliminated only *one bad habit*, set in motion only one *stream of human sensations* and *activities* – he has done a thousand times more than all you *rationalizers* [*Raisonneurs*] about legislation, with whom everything is *true* and everything *false* – a *miserable universal shade*.

There was a time when the erecting of *academies,*[92] *libraries, halls of art* was called *formation* of the world. Splendid!, this academy is the *name* of the court, the dignified *prytaneum*[93] of meritorious men, a *support* of

---

[90] The whole of Europe and the whole of the universe.

[91] *Mittel der Letternkultur* could mean either (1) means consisting in letter-culture, or (2) means for letter-culture. Also, the word *Letternkultur* itself contains a significant pun: (1) culture of letters (i.e. of *belles-lettres*), (2) culture that is no more than alphabetical letters (cf. "*tone!, conventional phrase!, beautiful expression*").

[92] Herder has in mind the academies of both France and Frederick the Great's Prussia.

[93] The *prytaneum* was a public institution in Athens at which Olympian victors and other honored citizens were entertained at public expense (see especially Plato, *Apology*, 36d–e).

valuable sciences, a splendid *hall* at the *birthday celebration* of the monarch. But what, then, does it do for the formation of *this* land, of *this* people, of *these* subjects? And even if it did everything – to what extent does this provide happiness? Can these *statues*, even if you put them along the way and at door jambs, turn each passerby into a *Greek* so that he *looks upon* them in that way, *feels* them in that way, feels himself *in them* in that way? Hard! Can these *poems*, these beautiful recitations in the *Attic* manner create a time when these poems and speeches *worked miracles* and *had effect*? I think not! And the so-called *restorers* of the sciences, even if pope and cardinals, always still let *Apollo, the Muses*, and all the gods *play* in the modern Latin poems – they knew that it was *play*. The statue of *Apollo* was always still able to stand beside *Christ* and *Leda*[94] – all three had *one effect*: none! If theatrical performance, the stage, could produce *real Roman heroism* and create *Brutuses* and *Catos*, do you think that your stage would stand?, that your pulpit would stand? – Finally, people in the noblest sciences pile Ossa on top of Pelion[95] – a great undertaking! – people hardly know *for what purpose* they pile. The treasures *lie there* and are not used; at least it is certainly not *humanity* that now uses them.

There was a time when everyone stormed for *education* – and education was equated with beautiful *practical knowledge, instruction, enlightenment, facilitation* ad captum,[96] and of course with early *refinement* to *polite ethics*. As if all that could *change* and *form inclinations*! Without thinking about a single one of the despised means by which *good habits*, even *prejudices, trainings*, and *forces* could be restored or newly *created* and thereby a "*better world*" be formed for all. – The essay, the plan got *written, printed, forgotten!* – a *textbook* of *education* like a thousand we have! – a *codex of good rules* like a million more that we will have, and the world *will remain as it is*.

How differently ages and peoples formerly thought about this when everything was still so *narrowly national*. All formation rose out of the most particular *individual* need and returned *back to it* – pure *experience, action, life-application* in the *most defined* circle. Here in the *patriarch's hut*, there in a narrow agricultural area, there [again] in a small *republic of human beings*, where a person knows, feels, and hence was also able to

---

94 According to myth, *Leda* was wife of Tyndareus, a queen of Sparta, and the mother of Clytemnestra, Helen, Castor, and Pollux.
95 In myth the Giants tried to reach heaven by putting Pelion and then Ossa on top of Mount Olympus. The phrase "pile Ossa on top of Pelion" is hence proverbial for making great efforts.
96 ad captum [vulgus]: to entice the masses.

cause [others] to feel, everything, had control of the human heart, and surveyed what he talked about! It was consequently there a *good* reproach that our *enlightened* century makes against the less enlightened Greeks that they philosophized *nothing properly universal and purely abstracted* but always spoke in the nature of *small needs* on a *narrow* stage. There people also spoke in an *applied* way, every word found a *role* – and in the better periods when people did not yet speak through words at all, [but] through *action, habit, exemplary model, thousandfold influence* – how differently! Definedly, strongly, and eternally. We *speak about a hundred ranks*, classes, periods, human races *at once*, so as to say for each of them *nothing*. Our wisdom, so refined and immaterial, is *abstracted spirit* which without use *flies away*. There it was and remained *citizen's* wisdom, history of a human *object*, sap full of *nutrition*.

Hence if my voice had power and space, how I would call to all those who work at the formation of humanity: not *commonplaces* about *improvement!*, *paper-culture!*, or possibly institutions – [but] *act!* Let those *talk* and *form fancies* into the sky's blue who have the misfortune to be able to do nothing else. Has not the maid's *lover* a more beautiful role than the *poet* who celebrates her in song or the *suitor* who seeks her hand? Behold, he who can most beautifully *sing the praises* of human friendship, love of peoples- and faithfulness to fathers perhaps intends to inflict on it the deepest *dagger-thrust* for centuries. In appearance the noblest *legislator*, perhaps the most fervent *destroyer* of his *century*! No question of inner *improvement, humanity,* and *happiness* – he strove to follow the current of the century, became the savior of the human species *according to the delusion of the century*, hence also achieved for himself the brief *reward* of all – the withering laurel *of vanity*, tomorrow dust and ashes. – The great, divine work of *forming humanity – quietly, strongly, hiddenly, eternally –* it could not share borders with petty *vanity*!

V. Doubtless after what I have written the commonplace will be cited that people always praise what is distant and complain about the present, that it is children who fall in love with the distance of tinsel and give up for it the apple which they have in hand because they do not know the former. But perhaps I am not this child. I recognize everything *great, beautiful,* and *unique* in our century, and despite all my scolding have always at bottom kept it – "*philosophy!*, *disseminated clarity!*, *mechanical skill* and *facility* to wonder at!, *gentleness!*" How high our century has risen in this since the restoration of the sciences!, with what strangely *easy* means it has reached this height!, how strongly it has *reinforced* it and *secured* it for posterity! I believe that I have provided *observations* about this instead of the exaggerated *eulogy* that one finds in all fashionable books, especially French ones.

Truly a *great century* as *means* and *purpose* – without doubt the *highest peak* of the tree in relation to all the preceding ones on which we stand! How we have *exploited* for ourselves as much *sap* from root, stem, and branches as *ever our thin peak-twigs can take in!*, *stand high* over Oriental, Greek, Roman, especially over the Gothic barbarians who come in the middle!, hence we *see* high *over the earth!* All peoples and parts of the world under our shade, so to speak, and when a storm shakes two small twigs in Europe how the whole world quakes and bleeds! When has the whole earth ever so universally converged together *on so few united threads* as now? When have more *power* and *mechanism* been possessed for shaking whole nations to the core with one *press*, with one *movement of a finger*? Everything floats on the point of *two* or *three thoughts*!

At the same time, when has the earth been as universally *enlightened* as now? – and constantly proceeds to become more *enlightened*. If before wisdom was always still only narrowly *national*, and hence also dug deeper and drew to itself more firmly – how *far* its rays now extend!, where is what *Voltaire* writes not read!, already almost the *whole earth* shines with *Voltaire's clarity*!

And how this seems to advance further and further! *Whither* do European colonies not *reach*, and whither *will* they not reach! Everywhere the savages, the more they become fond of our brandy and luxury, become *ripe* for our *conversion* too! Everywhere approach, especially through brandy and luxury, *our culture*. Will soon, God help us!, all be human beings *like us!* – *good, strong, happy human beings*!

Trade and *papacy*, how much you have already contributed to this great business! *Spaniards*, *Jesuits*, and *Dutchmen* – you human-friendly, unselfish, noble, and virtuous nations! – how much has not the *civilization* [Bildung] *of humanity* to be grateful to you for already in all parts of the world!

If that works in the remaining parts of the world, then of course why not in Europe? Shame for *England* that *Ireland* for so long remained savage and barbarous; it is *civilly administered* and *happy*. Shame for England that the *Highland Scots* for so long went without pants; they now bear these, at least with them *on a stake*, and are happy. In our century what realm has not civilized [*gebildet*] itself to the point of *greatness* and *happiness*! A single one[97] lay there in the middle to the shame of humanity – without academies or agricultural societies, wore moustaches, and accordingly nurtured regicides. And behold!, what *noble-minded France* had already undertaken alone with savage *Corsica* – this was done by three: civilize [*bilden*] moustaches into human beings *like us*! – *good, strong, happy* human beings![98]

All the arts that we practice – risen how *high*! Can one imagine anything better than that *art of government*, that system!, that science for the *formation* [Bildung] *of humanity?*[n] – the whole single driving motive of our states: *fear* and *money*. Without in the least *needing religion* (that childish motive!) – or *honor* or *freedom of soul* or *human happiness*. How we know to *seize* the single god of all gods, *Mammon*, as a second Proteus!, and how to *change* him!, and how to *extort* everything from him that ever we want! – highest, happy art of government!

Behold an *army*!, the fairest original model of human society! All of them how colorfully and easily clothed, easily fed, harmonious in thought, free and comfortable in all limbs!, moving *nobly*! What bright, spot-on tools in their hands! *Epitome of virtues*, which they learn in every daily wielding. A *picture* of the *highest superiority* of the *human spirit* and of the *government of the world* – resignation![99]

Balance of power in Europe!, you great discovery *of which no age before had any knowledge*![100] How these great bodies of state, in which without doubt humanity can best be cared for, now rub against one another without destroying themselves or ever being able to destroy themselves, in the manner of which we have such sad examples in the miserable statecraft of the *Goths, Huns, Vandals, Greeks, Persians, Romans*, in short, of all periods before ourselves! And how they continue forth on their noble royal course to swallow up this water butt full of insects in order to create uniformity,

---

[n] *Hume*, Political Writings [i.e. Politische Versuche, in *Vermischte Schriften*, vol. 4], essays 4, 9, 25, 26, and his History.

[97] I.e. Poland.

[98] The last two sentences concern the division of Poland in 1772 by Russia, Prussia, and Austria ("this was done by three"). For some helpful details, see G4:879–82.

[99] Herder's word *Resignation* is here probably supposed to bear, in addition to the meaning of its English counterpart, also stronger connotations of *death*. In Latin the verb *resignare* can mean *to destroy*, and can also refer to the unsealing of the eyes of the dead after they die.

[100] Voltaire had praised the balance of power between states as a distinctive achievement of modern Europe.

peace, and security. Poor city? Tormented village? Salvation be ours! – for the preservation of obedience, of peace, and of security, of all *cardinal virtues* and *happinesses: mercenaries!, allies!, balance of power in Europe!* There will and must remain – salvation be ours! – eternal *tranquillity, peace, security,* and *obedience* in Europe.

Then our *political historians* and *historical epic poets* of *monarchy* only need to paint the growth of this condition from age to age!º "Formerly, sad times! when people merely, for example, acted according to *need* and their *own feeling*; *sadder times* when the power of regents was not at all yet boundless; and saddest times of all when their incomes were not yet entirely *their arbitrary choice* – when[101] – how little there is for the *philosophical epic-writing historian* to rationalize universally or to *paint onto* the whole of Europe!; no *armies* which would be able *to unsettle* distant *borders*, no *ruler of the land* who would be able to leave his land to conquer – hence everything set up merely for miserable *resistance* and *self-defense*; no *politics!*, no *regard* for *distant times* and *lands*, no *speculation* to the *moon!*, hence no unifying of lands through these human-friendly regards for one's neighbor – in short, no – and this is the word for the modernest, highest taste! – no *societal life in Europe*. God be praised! since *individual forces* and *limbs of the state* have been abolished; there has occurred such a glorious *counterweighing* and *outweighing*, and shepherding into that miraculous thing the machine, of the nobility by cities, of cities by free land, and of the nobility, cities, and free land by peoples; and no one any longer knows or may know about *autonomous justice, autonomous dignity,* and *autonomous determination* – salvation be ours!, what a *societal life* in Europe! Where the monarch has the state so entirely in *his power* that the state is no longer his *purpose* but *external action through the state* is the purpose – where he hence *sees, calculates, deliberates, acts* in this scope; everyone gets *stirred* to enthusiasm and *led* through signals of which he understands and knows nothing; no state can so much as raise a down feather without the other regarding it – without the remotest cause leading to the automatic decision of a universal bloodletting in all parts of the world! Great universality!, what concise, *humane, passionless* wars arising therefrom!, what just, *humane, fair* negotiations arising therefrom!" And

---

º *Robertson's* History [of the Reign] of [the Emperor] Charles V, the introduction, from which this is only a faithful epitome with the odd judgment on his judgment. *Tarassei tous anthrôpous ou ta pragmata alla ta peri [tôn] pragmatôn dogmata – Epictetus.*

[101] Or: since (causal).

how the highest virtue, the *resignation of each individual*, gets promoted in this – high *societal life in Europe*!

And through what glorious means[P] people have reached the point! "that the power of the monarchy has grown in equal step with the *weakening of individual* limbs and the *strength* of the *mercenary class*!, through which means the monarchy has *broadened* its privileges, *increased* its income, *subjugated* or *steered* its internal enemies, *extended* its borders – this is shown by medieval and modern, and especially – the forerunner of all Europe – *French*, history." Glorious means and how *great* the purpose: the *scales* of Europe!, Europe's *happiness*! On *these* scales and in *this* happiness *each individual* grain of sand doubtless means a lot!

"Our system of trade!" Can one imagine anything superior to the *subtlety* of this *all-embracing science*? What miserable *Spartans* they were who used their *Helots* for agriculture, and what barbaric *Romans* who shut up their slaves in prisons in the earth! In Europe slavery has been abolished[q] because it has been calculated how much more these slaves would cost and how much less they would bring in than free people. Only one thing have we still permitted ourselves: to *use as slaves*, to *trade*, to *exile* into silver mines and sugar mills, *three parts of the world* – but those are not *Europeans*, not *Christians*, and in return we receive silver and gemstones, spices, sugar, and – secret disease; thus for the sake of *trade* and for the *reciprocal brotherly help* and *community* of the lands.

"System of trade" – the greatness and uniqueness of the institution is clear! *Three parts of the world laid waste* and *civilly administered* by us, and we through them *depopulated, emasculated*, sunk in luxury, oppression, and death – that is rich and happy trading. Who is there who is not constrained to participate in the great *tornado* that is sucking Europe dry, who is not constrained to press his way into it, and, if he cannot do this to other children, to drain out his own children, as the greatest *man of trade*? The old title 'shepherd of the people' has been turned into 'monopolist' – and when, now, the whole tornado breaks loose with a hundred stormwinds – great god Mammon – whom we *all now serve* – help us!

"*Mode of life* and *ethics*!" How miserable when there were still nations and national character,[r] what reciprocal *hate*, *aversion* to foreigners,

---

[P] Still merely an epitome from *Robertson*.

[q] *Millar*, [Bemerkungen] über den Unterschied der Stände [in der bürgerlichen Gesellschaft] [*Observations concerning the Distinctions of Ranks in Society* (1771)], section 5.

[r] *Hume*, Vermischte Schriften, vol. 4, no. 24.

fixedness on one's center of gravity, ancestral *prejudices*, clinging to the *lump of earth* on which we are born and on which we are destined to rot! *Native* manner of thought!, *narrow circle* of ideas – eternal *barbarism*! With us, God be praised!, all *national characters* have been extinguished! We love *all* of us, or rather no one *needs* to love the other. We *socialize with each other*; are completely each other's *like – ethically proper, polite, blissful*!; indeed have no *fatherland*, no *our-people* for whom we live, but are *friends of humanity* and *citizens of the world*. Already now all of Europe's regents do so, and soon we will *all* speak the French language! And then – bliss! – the Golden Age begins again *"when everyone in the world had one tongue and language!,*[102] *there will arise a single flock* and *a single shepherd!"*[103] National characters, what has happened to you?

"*Europe's mode of life* and *ethics*!" *How late* the *youth* matured in the Gothic periods of Christianity; hardly attaining majority by their thirtieth year; people lost *half* of their lives in a *miserable childhood*. *Philosophy, education*, and *good ethics*, what a new *creation* you have made! We are now *mature* in our thirteenth year, and through silent and loud sins *past our bloom* in our twentieth. We enjoy life right in its *dawn* and its *fairest bloom*!

"*Europe's mode of life* and *ethics*!" What Gothic virtue, *modesty, youthful bashfulness, shame*![s] We early on get rid of the ambiguous, clumsy coat of virtue; social gatherings, women (who now are most *lacking* in respect of shame!, and who also least *need* it!), even our *parents* wipe it off our cheeks early on. Or if that does not happen, we go on journeys, those *teachers* of good ethics!, and who will bring back his outgrown garment of childhood, out of fashion and suiting [*Anstand*]?[104] We have *boldness, societal good tone, facility* in helping ourselves to everything!, beautiful philosophy!, "*delicacy of taste* and of the *passions*!"[t] How *crude* the Greeks and Romans still were in their taste!, had least of all the *good tone of social intercourse* with the fair sex! *Plato* and *Cicero* were able to write volumes of conversations about metaphysics and masculine arts and *no woman ever spoke*. Who with us should endure a play, even if it were *Philoctetes on his desolate island, without love*! *Voltaire* – but let one read how seriously

---

[s] *Hurd's* conversations on traveling [i.e. *Dialogues on the Uses of Foreign Travels considered as a Part of an English Gentleman's Education* (1764)].
[t] *Hume*, Politische Versuche [in *Vermischte Schriften*, vol. 4], nos. 1, 17, 23.

[102] Genesis 11:1.   [103] John 10:16.
[104] *Anstand* here means both (1) suiting (of a person by his clothes) and (2) suitability, decency, propriety.

he himself warned against imitating [here].[105] *Women* are our public, our *Aspasias* of taste and philosophy. We know how to dress *Cartesian* vortices and *Newtonian* attractions in a *corset*,[106] write history, sermons, and what not else, *for and as women. The subtler delicacy* of our taste is proved.

"Fine arts and sciences!"[u] To be sure, the ancients, and indeed that miserable, unstable form of constitution, *small republics*, were able to develop the cruder ones. But behold also, how *crude that oratory of Demosthenes!*, that Greek *theater! – crude* even that praised *antiquity* itself! And where their *painting* and *music* are concerned it was even just a bloated fairytale and hue-and-cry. The *subtler bloom* of the arts waited for the bliss of monarchy! At the *courts of Louis* did *Corneille* copy his heroes, *Racine* his *sensations*. An entirely new species of truth, of emotion-stirring, and of taste got invented of which the fabled, cold, splendorless ancients knew nothing: the *opera*. Salvation to you, *opera*! You collecting-place and competition of all our fine arts!

It happened in the bliss of monarchy, where there were still further inventions.[v] Instead of the old, pedantic universities, brilliant academies were invented. *Bossuet* invented a *history, entirely declamation* and *sermon* and *register of years' numbers*, which so far excelled simple *Xenophon* and *Livy*; *Bourdaloue* invented a *genre of speech* [that was] how much better than *Demosthenes!* A new *music* was invented – harmony that needed no melody;[107] a new *art of building*; what everyone had thought impossible, a new *column*;[108] and – what posterity will admire most – an *architecture on the flat* and with all the products of nature: *landscape gardening!* Full of proportions and symmetry! Full of *eternal* enjoyment and entirely *new nature* without *nature*.[109] Salvation be ours!, what we were only able to invent under monarchy!

---

[u] *Hume*, Versuche [in *Vermischte Schriften*], vol. 4, nos. 16, 17; *Voltaire*, [Le] siècle de Louis XIV, XV, and XX; and the armies of pangyrists of modern literature. [The actual title of Voltaire's book is: *Le siècle de Louis XIV*. He also wrote a book: *Précis du siècle de Louis XV*. The "and XX" is clearly humorous.]

[v] *Voltaire*, [Le] siècle de Louis XIV.

[105] Voltaire had championed a tragedy without love.

[106] This is an allusion to Fontenelle, *Entretiens sur la pluralité des mondes* (1686), which contained female-orientated popularizations of science.

[107] This is an allusion to the composer Rameau (1683–1764).

[108] I.e. a new column in addition to the traditional Ionic, Doric, etc. Herder is apparently referring to the "German" column invented by L. C. Sturm (1669–1719).

[109] This is another example of Herder using the rhetorical figure of deliberate oxymoron (the contradiction being, of course, superficial rather than fundamental).

Last of all people began to *philosophize.*[w] And how *modernly!* – without *system* or *first principles*, so that it might remain free for one always at another time to believe the opposite. Without *demonstration!*, wrapped in *wit*, for "all the strict philosophy has never improved the world."[x] Finally even – splendid invention! – in *memoirs* and *dictionaries* where everyone can read *what* and *however much* he wants – and the most splendid of splendid inventions – the *dictionary*, the *Encyclopedia of all sciences and arts.* "If at some future time all books, arts, and sciences perish through fire and water, then from and in you, *Encyclopedia!*, the *human spirit* has *everything!*" What the *art of printing* became for the sciences, the *Encyclopedia* has become for the *art of printing:*[y] the highest peak of dissemination, completeness, and eternal preservation.

Now I ought in addition to praise the best thing, our huge steps of progress in *religion* – now that we have even begun to count up the *readings* of biblical passages! In the first principles of *honor* – since we have abolished *ridiculous chivalry*, and have elevated orders' ribbons to being *leashes* for boys and *court gifts*. But above all [I ought to] praise our highest peak of *human – paternal, wifely, child's – virtues.* But who in *such* a century as ours is can praise everything? Enough, we are the "*peak of the tree!*, weaving away in *heavenly air* – the *Golden Age* is nigh!"

Third section. Additions

The heavenly air is so refreshing that one is inclined to hover above tree-top and trees for too long. Down to the sad ground in order perhaps to cast a view at the whole or the not-whole!

Great creature of God! Work of *three parts of the world* and almost *six millennia!* The delicate, sap-filled *root*; the slender, blooming *shoot*; the mighty *stem*; the strongly striving, entwined *branches*; the airy, wide-spread *twigs* – how everything rests on each other, has grown from each other. – *Great creature of God!* But *for what? For what purpose?*

That obviously this *growth*, this *progress* from each other, is not "*perfection* in the narrow sense of the schools has, it seems to me, been shown by our whole view." It is no longer *seed* when it is *shoot*, no longer

---

[w] [D'Alembert,] *Disc*[*ours*] *prélim*[*inaire*] of the Encyclopedia; *Voltaire*, Tableau encyclopédique des connaissances *humaines* [Encyclopedic Picture of the Forms of Human Knowledge]. [No work of this title by Voltaire is known. For a possible explanation of the mystery, see G4:888–90.]

[x] *Hume*, Versuche [in *Vermischte Schriften*], vol. 1, essay 1. [Herder probably meant vol. 2, essay 1.]

[y] Disc[ours] prélim[inaire] and Mélange de litt[érature] par d'Alembert, vols. 1, 4.

a delicate *shoot* when it is a *tree*. Over the stem is the *crown*; if every branch, every twig, of this wanted to be *stem* and *root*, what would happen to the *tree*? *Orientals, Greeks, Romans* were only in the world once, were destined to touch the electrical chain that fate drew out only in *a single* point, at *a single* place! – We, therefore, if we want to be Orientals, Greeks, Romans *at a single time*, we are reliably *nothing*.

"In Europe there is supposed now to be more *virtue* than there ever was in the whole world?" And why? Because it has more *enlightenment* in it. I believe that just for that reason there must be *less*.

What is it – even if one only asks the flatterers of their century – what is this [alleged] *more virtue* of Europe through *enlightenment*? *"Enlightenment!* We now *know* so much more, *hear, read* so much, that we are so *peaceful, patient, gentle-hearted, inactive*. – To be sure – to be sure – indeed – and that too as well; but for all this, the basis of our hearts still always remains so *soft* though!" Eternal *sweeties*, that is what it all amounts to – we are the *thin, airy twigs* up there, freely shaking and *whispering* with every wind. But surely, the *sun's ray* plays so beautifully through us!, we stand *so high* over branch, stem, and root, *see so far*, and . . . of course, do not forget: can *whisper so far* and *beautifully*!

Do people not see that we lack all the *vices* and *virtues* of times past because we – altogether lack their *firm footing, forces* and *sap, space* and *element*? Indeed no flaw, but why, then, do people also have to *lie* out of this for themselves *praise, absurdities* of *presumption*? Why do they deceive themselves with our *means* of formation [*Bildung*] as though these had *achieved* this? And make every effort in order to deceive themselves concerning the *tinsel of their own weighty importance*? Finally, why, then, do they import the "fiction of *a one-sided mocking lie*" into all *centuries*, ridicule and disfigure with this the ethics of all peoples and time periods, so that a sound, modest, unprejudiced human being really gets to read in almost all the so-called *pragmatic histories of the whole world* nothing more in the end than the disgusting rubbish of the *"praised ideal* [110] *of his own time"*? The whole face of the earth becomes a *dungheap* on which we *seek kernels* and *crow*! *Philosophy of the century*!

"We have no *highwaymen*, no *civil wars*, no *atrocities* any longer." But *where, how*, and *why* should we have them? Our lands are so well *civilly*

[110] Herder probably intends a pun here: *Preisideal* could also mean *price ideal* (in allusion to modernity's excessive devotion to economic and material goals).

administered, cut through with highways, *stopped up* with garrisons, fields are so *wisely* divided up, our *wise* judicial system is so alert – *where* should the poor villain, *even if he* had the courage and force for that rough trade, practice it? But also, *why* practice it? For of course in accordance with the ethics of our century he can in a much *more comfortable*, indeed *honorable* and *glorious*, way become a *robber of houses, chambers, and beds* – get *paid* by the state in these forms of service. Why not rather *have* himself paid? Why that unsafe trade – for which he – and this is what it boils down to – has neither *courage* nor *force* nor *opportunity*? May God have mercy on your *modern, freely willed virtue!*

Have we "no *civil wars*" because we are all such satisfied, fully sated, happy subjects? Or is it not precisely due to causes which often *accompany* precisely the *opposite*? No *vice* because we all have so much *captivating virtue, Greek freedom, Roman patriotism, Oriental piety, knightly honor*, and all in the *greatest measure*? Or is it not exactly because we have *none* of all these and hence unfortunately also cannot have their one-sided, distributed *vices*? *Thin, shaking branches!*

And as such, we admittedly also have the advantage *of being capable* "of precisely *that exhausted, short-sighted, all-despising, solely self-satisfied, nothing-achieving*, and, precisely in its inefficacy, *consoling philosophy*." Orientals, Greeks, and Romans were not capable of it.

As such, we have the advantage *of assessing* and *crediting our means of formation so modestly*. A *class of priests* so that the world has never been as *humanely, theologically* enlightened as now; a *temporal class* so that it has never been as humanely, *uniformly obedient and orderly*; our *justice* so that it has never been as *humane* and *peace-loving*; finally, our *philosophy* so that it has never been as *humane* and *divine*. Through whom? Here each person points to himself! "We are the *doctors*, the *saviors*, the *enlighteners*, the *new creators* – the times of mad fever are past." Now of course, God be praised! – and the consumptive patient lies there so peacefully in his bed, whimpers, and – *gives thanks!* Gives thanks, but does he also *thank?*[111] And if he did, could not precisely this thanks be seen as a mark of his *degeneration, meekness*, and of the *most timid humanity?* What if even the *sensation for something else better* had departed along with the enjoyment? – so that I perhaps expose myself in writing this

---

[111] "Gives thanks" and "thank" both translate the verb *danken* here. I take it that Herder's point turns on the ambiguity between merely expressing thanks and really feeling it.

to the *most poisonous, most mocking distortions?* If only it were already enough for us to *think,* have *manufactures, trade, arts, peace, security,* and *order* . . . Our *governments* with no cause in them any longer for fighting; our *state constitutions* grow up! – such far-reaching vision round about! – playing so far-reachingly round about, so far in advance. What age was able to do that? So!, that is the way our state-, trade-, and art-histories talk. One thinks one is reading satire, but one is reading nothing but people's *true manner of thought.* What is the use of my speaking further? If only it were just illness, and not simultaneously an obstacle that does away with *every means* for countering it! But when in the sweat of death, dream with opium! – why disturb the invalid without helping him?

*

So rather what will also please the invalid more. We are in *this advance admittedly also in our place a purpose and tool of fate.*

Generally, the philosopher is most an *animal* when he would wish to be most reliably a *God* – thus also in the confident calculation of the *perfection* of the world. Of course, if only it were true that everything proceeded prettily *in a straight line* and that every *succeeding human being* and *every succeeding race* got *perfected* according to *his* ideal in a *beautiful progression* for which he alone knew to give the *exponent* of virtue and happiness! Then in that case it always came to him *last of all* – he the last, highest member with which everything *concludes.* "Behold, the world has risen to such enlightenment, virtue, happiness! *I,* high on the swing-bar!, *the golden pointer* of the world-scales – *behold* me!"

And this wise man did not take into account what, really, even the faintest *echo* from heaven to earth would have had to teach him, that probably *human being* always remains *human being, in accordance with the analogy of all things* nothing but *human being!* Angelic and devilish forms in the human being – *fictional forms!* – He nothing but the middle thing in between! – *defiant* and *fainthearted, striving* in *need, tiring* in *inactivity* and *luxury,* without *occasion* and *practice nothing,* gradually *progressing* through them almost everything – *hieroglyph of good and bad,* of which *history is full – human being!* – always only *tool!*

[He] did not take into account that this hidden *double creature* can be modified a *thousandfold,* and, given the structure of our earth, *almost must* be – that there is a creation of *clime,* of *circumstances of an age,* hence

334

national and *generational virtues*, blooms which grow under *that* sky and thrive on almost nothing, die out or miserably *turn yellow* there (a *physics of history, science of the soul*, and *politics* at which our century has of course already fictionalized and pondered so much!) – that there *can* and *must* be all this but that inside beneath the manyfold transformed husk the same *kernel of essential nature* and of *capacity for happiness* can still be preserved, and according to all human expectation almost will be so.

[He] did not take into account that it shows infinitely more solicitude *of the father of all* if this happened, if in humanity *there lies one invisible seed of receptivity for happiness and virtue on the whole earth* and *in all ages* which, *differently* developed, indeed appears in different forms but [is] inwardly only *one measure* and *mixture of forces*.

Finally, [he] did not take into account – all-knowing creature! – that with the human species there can be a *greater plan of God's in the whole* which an individual creature precisely does not survey, precisely because nothing is running towards something merely *individual* as its ultimate *finishing line*, especially not towards the *philosopher* or *throne occupant* of the eighteenth century – because all the scenes only in *each* of which *each* actor has a role in which he can strive and be happy perhaps still . . . *all these scenes* still perhaps can form a *whole*, a *main performance* of which indeed the *individual, selfish player* could *know* and *see* nothing but which the *audience member with the right viewpoint* and *tranquilly awaiting* the *sequence's whole* could well see.

Behold the whole *universe from heaven to earth* – what is means?, what is purpose? Is not everything means for *millions of purposes?* Is not everything the purpose of *millions of means?* The chain of almighty, all-wise goodness is entwined one part *into* and *through* the other a thousandfold – but each member in the chain is in its place a *member* – hangs on the chain and does not see *where in the end the chain hangs*. Each in its delusion feels itself to be the *central point*, in its delusion feels everything *around itself only to the extent* that it pours rays or waves on this point – beautiful delusion! But the great circle of *all* these waves, rays, and seeming central points: *where?, who?, why?*

Would it be otherwise in the history of the *human species?*, even with all *waves* and *periods in the sequence*, otherwise than precisely the "*building-plan of almighty wisdom*"? If the *residential house* reveals "*divine picture*" right down to its smallest fitting – how not the *history of its resident?* The former only decoration!, picture in a *single* act, view! The latter an "*endless drama* of *scenes*!, an *epic* of God's through all *millennia, parts of the world*, and *human races, a thousand-formed fable* full of *a great meaning*!"

That this *meaning*, this *vision of the whole*, must at least lie *beyond the human species* – insect of a lump of earth, look again at heaven and earth! Do you in the whole universe, as it weaves its work dead and alive *all at once*, find *yourself* the exclusive central point towards which everything operates?, or do not *you* yourself cooperate (*where?, how?,* and *when?* – who has asked you about this?) in the service of *higher* purposes *unknown* to you!, of purposes in the service of which the morning star and the little cloud beside it, you and the worm that you are now squashing!, cooperate. Given, now, that this is undeniable and beyond investigation in the great, all-extensive *together-world* of a moment, can you suspect anything less or different in the great, all-extensive *sequential-world*, in all the *events* and *progressive windings* of the human species, in the *drama* full of the inventor's *wisdom* and *knotty plot*? And if the whole were for you a *labyrinth* with a hundred doorways closed, with a hundred open – this labyrinth is a "*palace of God* for *his* all-fulfillment, perhaps for *his* pleasurable viewing, *not* for *yours*!"

The whole world, the vision of God *at one moment*, an abyss. – Abyss in which I stand lost on all sides!, see a great work *without a name* and everywhere *full of names*!, full of *voices* and *forces*! *I* do not feel myself *in that place* where the harmony of all these voices resounds into one ear, but what here in my place I hear by way of abbreviated, confusing sound – this much I know and hear with certainty – also has something harmonious in it!, also resounds as a song of praise in the ear of Him for whom *space* and *time* are nothing. – The human ear stays around for few moments, and only hears few notes, often only a vexatious *tuning* of *false notes*, for this ear came precisely at the time of tuning-up and unfortunately perhaps landed in the whirlwind of one corner. The enlightened *human being of later time* – he wants to be not only a *hearer of all* but himself the final *epitomizing note* of all notes!, *mirror* of *all the past* and *representative* of the *purpose* of the *composition* in *all its scenes*! The precocious child slanders and blasphemes – alas, if it were even only possibly the *after-echo* of the *last left-over death-sound* or a part of the tuning!

Among the great tree *of the father of all*[z] whose peak reaches above all the heavens and whose roots reach beneath worlds and hell, am I an *eagle*

---

[z] A great idea in the Norse *Edda*.

on this tree?, am I the *raven* who on his shoulder daily brings the worlds' *evening greeting* to his ear? What a little *strand of foliage* of the tree I may be!, a small comma or dash in the book of all worlds!

Whatever I may be!, call[112] from heaven to earth that, like everything, similarly I too mean *something* in my place. With *forces set aside for the whole*, and indeed only with the *feeling* of happiness according to the *extent* of these forces too! Which of my brothers had a *privilege before he existed*? And if the purpose and harmony of the household effects required that he became a *golden container* and I an *earthenware* one – I now, precisely an *earthenware container* also in *purpose, sound, duration, feeling*, and *competence*, can I argue with the craftsman? I have not been *passed over*, no one has been *preferred* – the capacity for feeling, activity, and competence of the human species is *distributed*. Here the river current [*Strom*] breaks off, there it begins. He to whom much is given also has much to accomplish. Whoever is enlivened with many senses has to struggle with many senses. – I do not believe that a *single* thought, with what it *expresses* and *keeps quiet*, what it *presents to view* and what it *pulls cloud-cover* over, yields greater sensation [*Empfindung*][113] than this one *in the light of the whole of history*!

*

That the thought should appear therein[114] – that at least is what my wish runs towards, this great *Olympian racecourse*! If our age is nobly useful in any respect at all then it is "its *lateness*, its *height*, its *prospect*!" What all has already been *prepared* for it for millennia!, through what all does it in turn in such a higher sense *prepare* for another age! – the steps *towards* and *from it*. Philosopher, if you want to honor and benefit your century's situation – the *book* of *preceding history* lies before you!, *locked* with seven seals, a *miracle book full of prophecy* – the *end of days* has reached you!, read!

There the *Orient*!, the *cradle* of the human species, of human *inclinations*, and of all *religion*. If religion should be *despised* and burned out in the whole cold world – its word weaving thence, weaving *thence* a spirit of fire and flame.[aa] With *paternal dignity* and *simplicity* which especially still

---

aa That despised book – the bible!

112 Reading *ruf* for *Ruf*.

113 Herder seems to mean this word in a twofold sense here: (1) sensation qua a feeling of wonder, consolation, etc., and also (2) sensation qua interpretative sensitivity in relation to history.

114 I.e. in the aforementioned light.

leads on its way "the heart of the *innocent child*"! The childhood of the *species* will take effect on the childhood *of each individual* – the last *minor* still *born* in the first *Orient*!

The youths of all so-called fine literature and art are the Greeks – what lies further back is perhaps too deep, too childish for the vision of the century, but they in the proper rosy dawn of world events, what an effect they have had on all their *posterity*! The *fairest bloom* of the *human spirit*, of *heroic courage*, of *love of one's fatherland*, of *feeling free*, of *love of art*, of *song*, of the *pitch of poetry*, of the *sound of narration*, of the *thunder* of *oratory*, of the *starting* of all *citizenly wisdom*, as it is now, is theirs. This aside, given to them sky, land, constitution, a fortunate point in time, they formed, invented,[115] named – we still form and name in imitation of them – their century accomplished! But accomplished *only once*! When the human spirit with all its forces wanted to awaken it *for a second time* – the spirit was dust, the shoot remained ashes; Greece did not return.

Romans – the first *collectors* and *distributors* of the fruits which, grown elsewhere beforehand, now fell ripe into their hands. To be sure, they had to leave bloom and sap in its place. But they really did distribute the *fruits – relics* of the *primeval world* in *Roman dress*, in the *Roman manner*, in *Roman language*. What if everything had come immediately *from Greece*? *Greek spirit, Greek culture* [-bildung], *Greek language*? How everything would have been different in Europe! It was not *supposed* to be! Greece still so distant from the north, in its beautiful archipelago of a region of the world; the human spirit in it still so slender and delicate – how was this spirit supposed to *wrestle* with all peoples?, *force upon* them the emulation of itself?, how could the crude northern *husk grasp* the subtle *Greek vapor*? Hence *Italy* was the bridge – Rome the *intermediate period* of the *hardening* of the *kernel* and of its *distribution* – even the *holy language* of the *new Christian world* with everything that adheres to it was for a millennium in all of Europe *Roman*.

Even when Greece was due to have an effect on Europe for a *second time*, it was not able to have an effect *immediately*: *Arabia* became the slime-clogged canal – *Arabia* the subplot in the history of the formation of Europe. If, as is actually the case, *Aristotle* was destined to rule for his centuries alone and to *produce* the *worms* and *decay-moths* of the *scholastic manner of thought* in everything, what if it had been fate that *Plato, Homer*,

---

[115] Or: discovered.

the *poets, historians, orators* had been able to have an effect earlier? How infinitely different everything would have been! It was *not destined*. The circle was due to jump over at that point; the Arab religion and national culture hated these *flowers*; perhaps they would also not yet have *thrived* in Europe in those times, whereas by contrast *Aristotelian hairsplitting* and *Moorish taste* harmonized so well with the spirit of the time – *fate*!

In Europe the *grown harvest* of the ancient *world-centuries* was due only to be *dried* and *pressed* – but *to come from there among the peoples* of the earth. How strange, now, that nations thronged *to the place for the work* without knowing *how* or *why*. Fate summoned them for the labor to the vineyard – gradually, each man at his hour.[116] Everything was already *invented, felt, subtly thought up* that perhaps could be thought up; here everything now got cast into *method*, into *scientific form*. And now, next, there came in addition precisely the new, coldest mechanical *inventions* which writ everything large: *machines of cold northern European abstraction, great tools* for the hand of Him who guides everything! – now the seeds lie there almost *among all nations* of the earth – at least *familiar* to all, *accessible* to all – they will have them when their point in time comes. Europe *dried, strung, eternalized* them. Strange ball![117] What, *you little northern part of the world*, formerly an abyss of *groves* and *isles of ice*, have you *had to become* on this ball! What will you *yet become*!

The so-called *enlightenment* and *civilizing* [Bildung] *of the world* only *touched* and *held* a *thin strip* of the *earth's ball*. Also, we cannot change something in the world's course, situation, and circulation without *everything changing* at the same time. What if, for example, merely the *introduction* of the *sciences*, of *religion*, of the *Reformation*, had been *different?*, the northern peoples had mixed *differently*, followed each other *differently?*, the *papacy* had not had to be *a vehicle for so long?* What ten times more could I not ask in addition? – Dreams! It was not so; and in retrospect we can always penetrate somewhat *why* it was not so. Admittedly, though, a small somewhat!

One can also see why in reality no nation *after another*, even with *all the accoutrements* of the latter, ever *became* what the other *was*. Even if all the *means of their cultures* were the same, *their culture was never the same*

---

[116] Herder is here echoing the parable of the vineyard at Matthew 20:1–16 in which the workers get summoned to work in the vineyard at different times of the day (though all then receive the same pay).

[117] I.e. the earth.

because always all the *influences* of the old, now-*changed* nature needed for that were already missing. *Greek sciences* which the Romans drew to themselves became *Roman*; *Aristotle* became an *Arab* and a *scholastic*; and in the case of the *Greeks* and *Romans of modern times* – what a *miserable affair*! *Marsilius*,[118] thou art *Plato*? *Lipsius*,[119] thou *Zeno*? Where are thy *Stoics?*, thy *heroes* who formerly *did* so much? All you modern *Homers, orators,* and *artists* – where is your *world of miracles?*

Also, into *no land* has civilization [*Bildung*] been able to take a *step back* so as to *become a second time* what it *was* – the path of fate is iron and strict. The scene of *that* time, *that* world, was already over; the *purposes* for which they were destined to exist, past – can today become yesterday? Since *God's course among the nations* proceeds forth with giant steps, will *childish backward paths* be capable of being effected by *human forces?* You *Ptolemies* were unable to re-create *Egypt*! You *Hadrians* unable to re-create *Greece*! Nor was *Julian* able to re-create *Jerusalem*. – *Egypt, Greece,* and thou *land of God*! – how miserably you lie, with naked mountains, without a trace or voice of the *genius* that formerly roamed over you and spoke to the whole world. Why? Because *it has said what it had to say*! Its *impress on the ages has happened* – the *sword is worn out,* and *the shattered, empty sheath lies there*! That would be an answer to so many useless doubts, astonishments, and questions.

*

"*God's course through the nations*! *Spirit* of the *laws*,[120] *ages, ethics,* and *arts* – how they have *followed!, prepared!, developed,* and *displaced!* one another." If only we had such a *mirror* of the *human species* in all faithfulness, fullness, and feeling of *God's revelation*. Enough preliminary works, but everything in husk and disorder! We have crept and rummaged through our *present* epoch of almost all nations and similarly the *history* of almost all earlier times almost without ourselves knowing *why* we have rummaged through them. Historical facts and investigations, discoveries and travel descriptions, lie there – who will separate and sift them?

"*God's course through the nations!*" *Montesquieu's* noble giant work[121] was not able to become through one man's hand what it should have been.

---

[118] I.e. Marsilio Ficino (1433–99), a humanist who taught at the Platonic Academy in Florence.
[119] J. Lipsius (1547–1606), Dutch neo-Stoic philosopher.
[120] Herder is here echoing the title of Montesquieu's work, discussed below.
[121] Montesquieu, *De l'esprit des lois* [*On the Spirit of the Laws*] (1748).

A *Gothic* structure in the *philosophical taste of his century*, esprit!, often nothing more! Torn from its proper place, and *cast as ruins* onto *three or four market-places* under the banner of *three miserable commonplaces – words!* – moreover, *empty, useless, indefinite, all-confusing esprit-words!* Hence through the work a reeling of all ages, nations, and languages, as around the tower of confusion,[122] that each might hang his beggar's load, riches, and satchel on *three weak nails* – the history of all peoples and ages, this great living work of God, *in its sequence too* a heap of ruins with three peaks and covers – but certainly of very noble, worthy materials – *Montesquieu!*[123]

Who is there who might construct for us God's temple throughout all centuries as it is in its *building-forth!* The oldest times of *human childhood* are past, but there are *remains* and *monuments* enough there – the most splendid remains, *the father's own instruction* to this childhood – *revelation.* If you say, human being, that this revelation is *too old* for you in your overly clever, old-man's years – look around you! – the greatest part of the nations of the earth is still *in childhood*, all still speak *that* language, have *those* ethics, provide the paradigms of *that* level of civilization [*Bildung*] – wherever you travel and listen among so-called savages there resound *sounds for the elucidation of scripture!, there waft living commentaries on revelation!*

The idolatry that the *Greeks* and *Romans* enjoyed for so many centuries, the often *fanatical zeal* with which in their case everything got sought out, illuminated, defended, praised – what great *preparatory works* and *contributions!* When the spirit of exaggerated reverence will have been blunted, the factionalism with which each person *cuddles his* people as a Pandora[124] sufficiently brought into balance – you *Greeks* and *Romans*, then we will know you and classify you!

A bypath to the *Arabs* has made its appearance, and a world of monuments lies available from which to know them. Monuments of *medieval*

---

122 I.e. the tower of Babel.
123 Herder's repeated complaint in this paragraph that Montesquieu imposes a simplistic and superficial threefold schema of classification presumably refers to Montesquieu's fourfold distinction in *De l'esprit des lois* between (1) democracy, based on the principle of virtue, (2) aristocracy, based on the principle of moderation, (3) monarchy, based on the principle of honor, and (4) despotism, based on the principle of fear – a fourfold distinction which often seems to collapse into a threefold one when Montesquieu either subsumes both (1) and (2) under the single concept of a republic, or sharply distinguishes (1), (2), and (3) as the only moderate and legitimate forms of government from (4).
124 According to myth, Pandora was chosen by Epimetheus to be his wife for her beauty, but her box proved to be the source of all evils for humankind.

history have been forthcoming, though for quite different purposes, and in part what still lies in the dust will certainly be found soon, perhaps in half a century (if only everything could be hoped for from our enlightened time with such certainty!). Our *travel descriptions* multiply and improve; everyone who has nothing to do in Europe runs *over the earth* with a sort of *philosophical rage* – we collect *"materials from the ends of the whole world"* and will one day find in them what we sought least of all, *treatments of the history of the most important* human *world.*

Our age will soon open a number of eyes, drive us in good enough time to seek at least *ideal springs* for the thirst of a desert. – We will learn to see the value of ages that we now despise – the feeling of *universal humanity* and *bliss* will stir – the result of ruin-filled history will become prospects of a higher than *human this-worldly existence,* will show us *plan* where we formerly found *confusion.* Everything occurs in its proper place – *history of humanity* in the noblest sense – you will come to be! So until then let the great teacher and lawgiver of kings[125] *lead* and *lead astray.* He has given such a beautiful model for measuring everything with two or three words, of *guiding* everything towards two or three *forms of government* in which it is easily visible whence they come and how limited their *extent* and *duration* are. How pleasant to follow after him in the spirit of the laws *of all times and peoples,* and not of his people – that too is fate. One often holds the *tangle of threads* in one's hand for a long time, and takes pleasure in being able to *pluck* at it in a merely individual way in order just to *confound* it the more. A fortunate hand that has the desire to unravel the confused mass gently and slowly in one thread – how far and evenly the thread runs! – *history of the world*!, whither, it now turns out, the smallest and the greatest realms and birds' nests strive.

*

All the events of our age are *at a great height* and *strive far afield* – it seems to me that in these two things lies the *compensation* for the fact that admittedly we are able to have effect *as individuals with less force and feeling of joy.* Hence truly *encouragement* and *strength.*

Socrates of our age!, you can no longer have effect like Socrates – for you lack the small, narrow, strongly active, compressed *stage*!, the *simplicity* of the *times,* of *ethics,* and of *national character*!, the *definedness of*

---

[125] This description refers to Montesquieu again.

your circle! – *A citizen of the earth*, and no longer a citizen at *Athens*, you naturally also lack the *perception* of what you should do in Athens, the *certain feeling* of what you do, the *sensation of joy* at what you have accomplished – your demon![126] But behold!, if you act like Socrates, *strive* with humility *against prejudices*, disseminate *truth* and *virtue* honestly, with love for humankind, self-sacrificingly, how you can... The *scope* of your sphere perhaps compensates for the *less determinate* quality and *lacking* quality of your beginning! A hundred people will read you and not understand you, a hundred read and yawn, a hundred read and despise, a hundred read and slander, a hundred read and prefer to have the dragon-chains of habit and remain who they are. But keep in mind that perhaps a *hundred* still remain left over with whom you bear fruit – when you are long since decayed, still a *world of posterity* which reads you and applies you better. *World* and *world of posterity* is your Athens! *Speak!*

World and *world of posterity!* *An eternal Socrates, having effect*, and not merely the *dead bust* wreathed with poplar foliage which we call *immortality!* Socrates spoke vividly, lively, in a narrow district – and what he said found such a good place. – *Xenophon* and *Plato* fictionalized him into their *memorabilia* and *dialogues* – they were only *manuscripts*, luckily for us better escaped from the stream of time that washes away than a hundred others. What you write should *deserve the world and eternity* word after word because (at least in terms of materials and possibility) you *write for the world and eternity*. Into whose hand your text can come!, how worthy the *men* and *judges* are in whose circle you should speak! Teach virtue in such a light and clarity as Socrates in his age was not yet able to!; encourage to a love of humankind which, if it could exist, would be *truly more* than *love of fatherland and fellow citizens!*; disseminate bliss even in conditions, even in *situations*, in which those people with their thirty *saviors* of the fatherland, who had *their statues* dedicated to them as well, hardly liked to find themselves[127] – *Socrates of humanity!*

Teacher of nature!, how much more you can be than *Aristotle* or *Pliny!* How very much more miracles and works are open to you!, what *aids* that those people did not have to open them for *others' eyes!*, on what a height

---

[126] This is an allusion to Socrates' *daimonion*, or divine sign.
[127] This is an allusion to the Thirty Tyrants who ruled over Athens in 404–3 BC. Herder's point is that the modern author should dare to spread his message even under the prevailing modern conditions of monarchical tyranny.

you stand! Think of *Newton*!, what *Newton* by himself effected for the whole of the human spirit!, what all that has effected, changed, borne as fruit everywhere!, to what a height he has raised his whole species! – You stand on the height!, you strive – instead of confining God's great creation into a small structure belonging to your own head (of *cosmogony, the origins of animals, the shaping of forms*, and that sort of thing)^bb – merely after the *current* of *God's force*, to feel it, and to allow others to feel it, deeply and faithfully in all its forms, shapes, and creations, to serve the Creator and not yourself. – Messenger of glorious majesty through all the realms of beings! Only from *this height in time* were you able to take *this flight to the heavens*, discover, speak with this *fullness* and *nobility* and *wisdom*!, refresh with this innocent, mighty, perfectly beneficent divine vision *human hearts* which could not be refreshed from any other puddle. This you do for the world and the world of posterity! Admittedly, among all discoverers and investigators only *a single person, a single small name*! – but for *the world and the world of posterity*!, and how loftily!, how gloriously – as *Pliny* and *Aristotle* were not able to – angel of God in your age!

What a hundred more *means* the doctor and knower of human nature has now than had *Hippocrates* and *Machaon*!^128 In comparison to these he is certainly a *son of Jupiter, a god*! And what if now he were to become this with all the sensation of those more human times in addition! – god, discoverer, and savior for the sick person in body and soul!, saving here a *youth* who now found a serpent of fire among the first roses of life which he thought he was picking – were to restore him (perhaps he *alone* can do this!) to himself, to his parents, to the posterity that through us awaits an existence full of life or death, to the world, to virtue! Were to support here the man who became a victim of his own merits through labor or sorrow, were to give him the sweetest reward that he could enjoy *now*, though often only as the whole thanks for his life: a *bright old age*! Were to save^129 him – perhaps the *sole pillar* against a hundred calamities of humanity which will attend the last look that his eyes take – from the grave for just *a few years*! The good of these years *his*; the consolation, the brightness, that this man awakened from the dead distributes, his! In times when a single saved man can do so much, and in which even the more innocent part of humanity can so miserably come to grief

---

^bb *Buffon.*

^128 Machaon is a healer in Homer's *Iliad.*   ^129 Reading *rettete* or *rettet'* for *rettet.*

in what a hundred ways – what are you in these times, *doctor with a human heart*!

Why should I go through all ranks and classes of *justice*, of *religion*, of the *sciences*, of individual *arts* – the *higher* each one *is in its kind*, the *further its effects can reach*, then how much *better* and *dearer* it is! Precisely because *you* had to have effect in this way *only of your free will*, because nothing *required* or *forced* you to act so well and greatly and nobly in your rank and class, precisely because nothing even *awakened* you and rather everything pressed to make you into a merely *mechanical servant* of your art, and to put to sleep every *deeper sensation* – and perhaps this unusual case that even planted on your head, instead of laurel, thorns – so much the purer, the quieter, the diviner is your *hidden, more tested* virtue. It is more than that virtue of other ages which, *awakened* by *promptings* and *rewards*, was in the end really only *a citizen's appurtenance* and noble finery of the *body*! – yours is the *life-sap of the heart*.

How I would have to speak if I wanted to describe the merit of those who are really *pillars* or *hinges of our century about whom everything moves*. *Regents!*, *shepherds!*, *guardians* of the peoples! – their force, with the mainsprings of our age, is *semi-omnipotence*! Just their *image*, their *look*, their *wish*, their *silent manner of thought* that simply *lets things happen* – simply their genius tells them that they are there for something nobler than to *play* with a whole flock as a machine for their own – however glorious – purposes;[130] also to *pasture* this flock as a purpose!, and if more, to take care of a *greater whole* of *humanity* – regents, shepherds, guardians of the *peoples!*, with the scepter of omnipotence in their hands!, with *few human forces!*, in years!, to do by means of mere *intention* and *encouragement* how *infinitely much more* than that mogul does on his golden throne or that despot now wants to do on a throne of human heads! Whoever succumbs to merely political intentions is perhaps in the highest rank such a commoner soul as

---

[130] If I understand this sentence correctly, it starts out intending to illustrate the preceding comment that "their force . . . is semi-omnipotence" by referring to the power of "just their image, their look, their wish etc." but before the illustration gets completed the construction and the thought get changed due to "– simply their genius tells them etc." which in effect makes "genius" sum up the list "their image, their look, their wish etc." and hence transforms that list into part of the following construction and thought: "Just their image, their look, their wish, their silent manner of thought that simply lets things happen . . . tells them that they are there for something nobler etc." The sentence is hence another example of Herder using Sophocles' technique of a midstream switch in construction and thought. The net effect is to convey two claims: (1) that "just their image, their look, their wish etc." demonstrate in virtue of their powerful effects these rulers' "semi-omnipotence," and (2) that they – thereby – show that there must be some higher purpose to these rulers' functioning than merely their selfish play.

that lentil-thrower who is only happy to have thrown[131] or that flute-player who merely hits the holes . . .

I prefer to speak with you, shepherd of your flock, father, mother in the poor hut! You too have had taken away from you a thousand *promptings* and *enticements* which formerly made your *fatherly occupation* into a *heaven* for you. You cannot determine the destiny of your child! – you find that it gets marked early, perhaps already in the cradle, with an honorary shackle of freedom[132] – our philosophers' highest ideal! You cannot educate it for the paternal flock, paternal ethics, virtue, and existence – hence you have all along lacked a *circle* and, since everything is and runs confused, your *most facilitating motive* of education, *a clear goal.* You have to worry that as soon as your child is torn out of your hands it will suddenly sink into the century's great ocean of light, abyss! – sunken jewel!, unrecoverable existence of a human soul!, the bloom-rich tree torn too early from its mother-earth, transplanted into a world of storms which even *the hardest stem* often hardly withstands, perhaps even implanted thither with *inverted end,* crown instead of root, and the sad root in the air – it threatens shortly to stand there for you withered, horrible, with its bloom and fruit on the earth. Do not despair in the dregs of the age!, whatever may threaten and impede you – *educate.* Educate all the *better,* the *more surely,* the *more firmly* – for all the *situations* and *miseries* into which he may be thrown!, for *storms which await him!* After all, you cannot be inactive – you have to educate either badly or well – well – and how much *greater the virtue!,* how much *greater the reward* than in every paradise of *easier purposes* and *more uniform formation.* How much more than ever before the world now needs *a single person educated* to simple virtue! Where *all ethics are the same* and all equally *even, right,* and *good* – what need is there of *effort!* Habit educates and virtue gets lost in mere habit. But here! A shining star in the night! A diamond among heaps of earth-stones[133] and limestones! A human being among bands of apes and political ghouls – how much he can form him further through quiet, godlike example!, spread *waves about*

---

[131] Herder is here alluding to a story, ultimately due to Quintilian, according to which a man who possessed the rather trivial skill of throwing lentils through the eye of a needle displayed this skill to Alexander the Great and received from him the "reward" of a large measure of lentils! The story is proverbial for trivial, pointless skill and effort.

[132] According to Suphan, in East Prussia boys destined for military service already early in life received the honor of having a red ribbon placed around their necks.

[133] *Erdsteine* are distinguished – significantly – by having a loose or hollow center (formed of clay or similar matter).

and *after* himself perhaps reaching into the future! – In addition, think how much purer *your virtue* is and how much *nobler!*, how many more and greater the *aids* to education are from certain sides, the more on the other side you and your youth lack external *motives*! – think what a *higher* virtue you are educating him to than *Lycurgus* or *Plato* could or might educate people to! – the fairest age for the virtue that is *quiet, reticent,* mostly *unrecognized*, but so *high*, so *far spreading*!

So this always seems certain to me: the *fewer entirely* and *greatly* good people there may be in our century, the harder the *highest virtue* must *become for us*, and the *quieter*, the *more hidden* it now *can* only become – *where it exists, then that much higher, nobler*, perhaps at some time *infinitely useful* and *consequence-bearing*, [a] virtue [it is]![134] By our for the most part *abandoning* and *renouncing* ourselves, being unable to enjoy a number of *immediate rewards*, strewing the seed out *into the wide world* without seeing where it falls, takes root, whether even there it even eventually bears fruit *for the good*. Nobler to sow into *hiddenness* and the *whole wide world* without oneself expecting a harvest!, and certainly that much greater the harvest in the whole wide world! Entrust the seed to the wafting zephyr – it will carry it that much further; and when at some time there awaken all the germs to which the *nobler part of our century* also quietly and silently made its contribution – in what a blessed age my view loses itself!

*

It is precisely on the tree's *highest twigs* that the *fruits* bloom and bud – behold there the beautiful *prospect* of the *greatest* of *God's works!, enlightenment* – although this does not always benefit *us*, although with the larger surface and scope we lose in the *depth* and *scouring of the river* – certainly precisely in order that we, already ourselves a small sea, might approach a *great ocean. Associated concepts* from the whole world – a *knowledge* of *nature*, of the *heavens*, of the *earth*, of the *human species*, almost as rich as any our universe can offer us – its *essence*, its *substance* and *fruit*, remains for *posterity*. The *century* has been *passed beyond in which* Italy formed its language, ethics, poetry, politics, and arts under confusion, oppression, rebellion, and deception – *what got formed* has *survived* its century – had further effect and became Europe's *first form*. The *misery and woe* under

---

[134] This sentence is another example of Herder's use of brachylogy.

which the century of France's great king[135] groaned is *in part over; the purposes* for which he wanted and needed everything are forgotten, or stand there idle as dolls of vanity and derision; all his brazen seas which he himself bore and the walls where he was himself always present are surrendered to the thought of anyone who does not in the process even want to think *what Louis wanted.*[136] – But the *spirit of the arts* practiced on them has remained. The researches of the *expeditions* for *plants* and *coins* and *gemstones* and *spirit-levels* and *surveying* remain when everyone has perished who *participated* in this and *suffered because of it* and everything for which *it was done*! The future strips us of our *husk* and takes the *kernel.* The *little twig* does not benefit from this at all, but it is from it that the *lovely fruits* hang.

What, then, if at some future time all *the light* which we sow into the world, with which we now blind many eyes, *make* many *miserable* and *gloomy*, were to become everywhere *moderated life-light* and *life-warmth* – the mass of *dead* but *bright cognitions*, the field full of bones that lies *on*, *around*, and *under us*, were to become – *whence?*, *for what?* – *enlivened* – *made fertile?* – what a new world!, what happiness [for a person] to enjoy the work of his hands[137] in it! *Everything* down to *inventions, delights, distress, fate*, and *contingency* strives to raise us above a *certain cruder sensuality of earlier ages*, to *dishabituate* us in the interest of a *higher abstraction* in *thinking, willing, living*, and *acting* – something that is not always pleasant for us, often irritating! The *sensuality* of the Orient, the more beautiful sensuality of Greece, the strength of Rome is passed beyond – and how miserably we are consoled by our *wretched abstract consolations* and *maxims* which often by themselves have to constitute our *reasons to act, motives,* and *blisses* – the child gets cruelly dishabituated even from a last sensuality . . . But behold the *higher age* that *beckons forth.* No fool can deny it – if *the subtle reasons to act*, the *higher, heavenly virtue*, the *more abstracted enjoyment of earthly blisses* are *possible* for human nature, they are most *exalting* and *ennobling*! Maybe therefore *many* now *will perish* on this reef! Maybe, and certainly, infinitely fewer now have this *virtue à la Fénelon*

---

[135] Louis XIV.

[136] The reference to Louis XIV's "brazen seas" and "walls" recalls King Solomon's building project at 1 Kings 7.

[137] The phrase *seiner Hände Werk* echoes Psalm 19, v. 2 (in Luther's bible), where the "his" in question means *God's* rather than a human being's. There is therefore probably an intentional and significant ambiguity of reference in the "his" here: (1) a person's, (2) God's.

than those *Spartans, Romans*, and *knights* had the sensuous bloom of their *world's* and *age's spirit*. – The broad highways become ever *narrower* steps and *steep climbs* on which few can roam – but they are *climbs* and *strive towards the peak*! What a condition at last on the meandering snake's path of Providence when, skin and obstacles left behind, a *rejuvenated* creature bursts forth with life in a new springtime! – a *less sensuous* humanity more *like* itself!, now completely in possession of a *world around it*, of a *life-force* and principle, for which we only *strive* with effort, *within it* – what a creation! And who is there who would have to deny the probability and possibility of this? The *refinement* and the *purifying progress* of *concepts of virtue* from the *sensuous ages of childhood up through all of history is clear*, their *spreading about* and *progress into a wider world clear* – and all this *without a purpose?, without an intention?*

That the *concepts* of *human freedom, sociability, equality*, and *total bliss* are becoming *enlightened* and *widespread* is well known. Not immediately with the best consequences for us – the bad often to begin with outweighing the good at first sight. But! . . .

Sociability and *easy intercourse* between the sexes – has it not *lowered* the honor, decency, and discipline of both parties?, *exploded* all the castles of the great world for rank, money, and polite manners?, how much have [not] *the* first *bloom* of the male sex and the noblest *fruits* of the female sex in marital and maternal love and education *suffered?*, whither has [not] their damage *spread afield?* – abyss of irreparable ills!, since even the sources of improvement and recovery – youth, life-force, and better education – are *stopped up*. – The more slender branches, which hence play about easily, cannot but *wither* in their premature and forceless *life-play* amid the rays of the sun! Irreparable loss! – perhaps *beyond compensation* for all politics!, beyond *sufficient regret* for all love of humankind – but for the hand of Providence still a *tool*. If a hundred poor creatures here sink down, thirst, and languish with a dried-up palate around the first source of life, of sociability, and of joy – the source itself, about which[138] they unhappily deceived themselves, purifies! Behold how in later years they, perhaps *even in an exaggerated way*, now seek *other fruits of delight, idealize new worlds* for themselves, and with their *disaster improve* the *world*! *Aspasias* worn out by life educate [*bilden*] *Socrateses*; *Ignatius*[139] his *Jesuits*; the *Epaminondases* of all time produce for themselves *battles of*

---

[138] Reading *der* for *denen*.   [139] Ignatius of Loyola (1491–1556), founder of the Jesuit order.

Leuktra[140] – *heroes, philosophers, wise men,* and *monks* of such *unsensuous, higher* virtue, *upwards-striving,* and *meritoriousness* – how many merely for *this reason*! Whoever wants to calculate and weigh for the world's benefit, let him do so! He has before him a large sum with, for the most part, a *not uncertain*[141] outcome – the course of Providence proceeds to its goal even over millions of corpses!

Freedom, sociability, and *equality* as they are now *sprouting up* everywhere – they have caused harm and will cause harm in a thousand *misuses. Anabaptists* and *fanatics* wrought havoc on Germany in *Luther's* times; and now, with the general *mixing* of the classes, with the *upwards drive* of the lower people to the place of *withered, proud,* and *useless* high ones in order soon to become still *worse* than these – the strongest, most essential *foundational positions* of humanity become *emptier,* the mass of corrupted *life-sap* flows deep down. Even if a guardianship of this great body *pays attention, praises,* and *promotes* for the sake of a *timely increased appetite* or a *seeming addition* of forces, or even if it were to exercise opposition in the direst way – still, it will never *eliminate* the cause of the "*advancing refinement* and of the *driving* for *rationalization, luxury, freedom,* and *impudence.*" How much the *true, voluntary respect* for the *authorities,* elders, and highest classes in the world has *fallen since* just *one century* ago is inexpressible when one undertakes a small comparison – our great people, both the small and the great ones,[142] continue to contribute to this in a tenfold way: *barriers* and *turnpikes* torn down; *prejudices* – as they are called – of *class,* of *education,* and naturally *of religion* trampled under foot, and even mocked to their harm; we are all becoming – through *one sort of education, philosophy, irreligion, enlightenment, vice,* and finally, as a bonus, through *oppression, bloodthirstiness,* and *insatiable avarice,* which certainly *awakens* minds and *brings* them to self-feeling – we are all becoming – salvation be ours!, and after much disorder and misery, *salvation be ours!* – what our philosophy so praises and strives for – *lord* and *serf, father* and *child, youth* and the most foreign *maiden,* we are all becoming *brothers.* These gentlemen prophesy like

[140] At the Battle of Leuktra in 371 BC Epaminondas, a Theban politician and general, led his Thebans to a surprising decisive victory over the Spartans.
[141] Reading *ungewissem* for *ungewissen.*
[142] This is another example of Herder using a type of deliberate oxymoron (the appearance of contradiction being of course merely superficial rather than fundamental when one keeps in mind the difference between different senses of the great/small distinction).

Caiaphas,[143] though indeed in the first instance about their own heads or the heads of their children!

Even if our *"human government"* had gained nothing more than a *beautiful covering* – *this* good *seeming* and *appearance*, the *language*, the *first principles and dispositions* and *order*, which now every book and every young prince, as though he were a living book, carries on the tongue – *great progress.* Let someone make the experiment of reading *Machiavelli* and *Antimachiavelli*[144] together – the philosopher and friend of humankind will *honor* the latter, will gladly overlook his *untouched* rotten spots *covered over* with flowers and green brush and his *unplumbed wounds* where it has not been desired or liked to get to the bottom of the matter, and say: What a *book!*, what a *prince* he who would think like that book!, would only *confess, acknowledge, know, act* in *accompanying* dispositions – what a prince for the world and the world of posterity! It is true that instead of crude, inhumanly cruel *madness* illnesses could govern which are *just as oppressive* and *more damaging* because they *creep* [*up on one*], get *praised* and not *recognized*, and *eat into the soul* right down to *bone* and *marrow.* The universal dress of *philosophy* and *love of humankind* can hide *oppressions, attacks* on the true, personal *freedom of human beings* and *lands, citizens* and *peoples*, of just the sort that *Cesare Borgia* would wish for.[145] All that *in accordance with* the *accepted first principles* of the *century*, with a *decent appearance* of *virtue, wisdom, love of humankind*, and *care for peoples.* Since it *can* happen that way and almost *must* – I do not like to be a eulogist of these *coverings* as though they were *actions.* Doubtless, even *Machiavelli* would in *our* century *not have written as he wrote* and *Cesare* would in a different context not have *been allowed* to act as he did in his day – at bottom even *with all this* still nothing *but the dress* would be changed. But even just the *changing of this* is a mercy. The fact that in *our century* anyone who *wrote* like *Machiavelli* would get stoned . . . but I take back what I just said . . . He who writes more harmfully for *virtue* than Machiavelli does not get *stoned* – he writes *philosophically, wittily, French*, and of course – without *religion.* Hence *"like one of us"!* And – of course *disavows* his writings!

---

143 John 11:49–52: Caiaphas, high priest of the Pharisees, prophesied that Jesus would die.
144 Frederick the Great, *Antimachiavelli* (1740).
145 Cesare Borgia (1478–1507), son of a pope, and himself a Renaissance prince, provided, through his use of cunning and violence, a model for Machiavelli's *Prince.*

Wildness in thinking, as long as it happens with certain *proprieties of prosperity* (the true prosperity may be all the further off!) – even on this *poisonous, undisciplined* tree there sprout good *fruits*! Do you not believe that this sense and nonsense which is now spoken so uninhibitedly *against religion* will at some future point have excellent effects? Abstracting from *elucidations, justifications*, and *proofs* of religion, which often do not prove much, I do not know what great man would prophesy a next century *of superstition* given that our century exhausted itself into *such stupid unbelief*. – But however this may turn out (and it would be grim if only *superstition* could again take over from *unbelief* and the eternal, miserable circular course yielded no progress!), *religion, reason*, and *virtue* must inevitably one day *profit* through the maddest attacks of their foes! – Wit, *philosophy*, the *freedom to think* were certainly only contrary to their knowledge and volition a *frame* for this new throne – suddenly one day the *cloud parted*, and if they then stand their ground there will emerge in full glory the all–illuminating sun of the world.

Also the *great scope* and the *universality* in which all that proceeds can, we see, clearly become an *unrecognized frame* for this. The more we Europeans invent *means* and *tools* to subjugate, to deceive, and to plunder you other parts of the world . . . Perhaps it will one day be precisely your turn to *triumph*! We affix chains with which *you* will pull *us*; the *inverted pyramids*[cc] of our constitutions will turn *upright* on your ground; *with us you will* . . . Enough, it is evident that everything is tending *to a larger whole*! We embrace the circle of the earth – whatever we may do this with – and what comes next can probably never any longer *narrow* this circle's *foundation*! We are approaching a new act [of the play], even if admittedly only through *decay*!

Precisely the fact that our manner of thought becomes *refined* in good and bad and that precisely thereby our stronger, more sensuous first principles and motives get *worn down*, without the greater mass *having the desire* or *force* to oppose this with anything nor yet to put anything in its place – whither must this bring us? The sensuous, *strong bonds* of the ancient republics and ages are long since (and it is a triumph of our time!) *dissolved; everything gnaws* at the finer bonds of our time: *philosophy, freethinking, luxury*, and an *education* in all this that is from member to member *deeper* and more *widely spread*. – Even *peaceful wisdom* already

---

[cc] The knight [*William*] *Temple* compared a certain form of government with this image!

has to *damn* or *despise* most of our political motives, and what an old reproach and scruple on both sides is the quarrel between Christianity and worldliness! Hence, since *weakness* can end in nothing but *weakness*, and an *overstrenuous resort* to and *misuse* of *the forces' last patient throw* can only hasten that complete *throwing down* . . . But it is not my office *to prophesy*!

Still less to prophesy "what alone *can, will*, and almost *must* be the *substitute* and *source of new life-forces* on a so *broadened stage* – whence *new spirit* can and will bring all the *light* and the *human disposition* that we are working for to *warmth*, to *permanence*, and to *complete bliss*." Without a doubt I am still talking about *distant* times!

Let us, my brothers, work with courageous, happy hearts even *right in the middle of the cloud* [*Wolke*][146] – for we are working for *a great future*.

And let us accept our goal as *pure*, as *bright*, as *free of accretions* as we can – for we run in the light of a *will-o'-the-wisp* and *twilight* and *fog*.

*

When I there see deeds, or rather intuit silent characteristic marks of deeds, proceeding from *a mind* that, *too great* for its age's envelope, and *too quiet* and *shy* for its age's *cry of praise*, goes forth and *sows* in darkness – seeds'which, like *all of God's works* and creations, begin *from a small spore* but in which at the first little shoot one sees and smells, so lovely, that they *will prove to be God's creation in concealment* – and especially if they were dispositions *to the noblest plant of humanity, civilization* [Bildung], *education, strengthening of nature* in its *neediest nerves, love of human beings, sympathy*, and *brotherly bliss* – holy plants, who is there that has roamed among you who would not be gripped by a shudder *of a better future* and would not bless your author – both small and great, *king* and *serf* – in the quietest evening-, morning-, and midnight-offering. All *merely bodily* and *political purposes* fall apart, like shards and corpses – the *soul*!, the *mind*!, *content for the whole of humanity* – this remains – and happy for him who received much there from the pure, uncloudable spring of life!

---

[146] This image of the cloud [*Wolke*] includes, besides (1) its central connotation of a condition of ignorance and uncertainty, also (2) an allusion to the cloud of the Lord that, according to the Old Testament, accompanied the Israelites on their journey through the desert, and (3) an allusion to the modern *tornado* to which Herder referred earlier in this essay, and for which he used the similar word *Ziehwolke*.

353

*

It is almost unavoidable that precisely the higher, widely spread quality of our century must also yield ambiguities of the *best* and *worst* actions which would be absent in narrower, deeper spheres. Precisely that no one any longer knows hardly to what end he operates – the whole is a sea where waves and surges – whither?, but how violently! – roar – do I know whither I am going with my *little surge*? – Not only enemy and slanderer will often be able to cast the beginnings made by the *most effective, best* man in a doubtful light – perhaps there will also appear *fog* and *half-light* even to the warm *admirer* in his *colder hours*. All radii are already *so far* from the center – all run *whither?*, and *when* will they *arrive* there?

It is known what all *reformers* of all ages have been reproached with: that when they took a *new step* they also always left gaps behind them, produced dust and quaking *before them*, and trod what was innocent to pieces *beneath* them. This applies to the reformers of the last centuries more obviously and doubly. *Luther!, Gustavus Adolphus!, Peter the Great! What three* have in modern times changed *more?*, changed *with nobler intentions?* And have their – especially their *unforeseen* – consequences always at the same time been incontrovertible *increases* in the happiness of their posterity? Whoever is familiar with *later* history – will he not sometimes have grave doubts?

A monarch[147] whose name our time carries more and more deserves to carry than the age of Louis[148]

> – whom for us
> his century preserves along with itself![149]

– what a *new creation of Europe* he has effected from his little spot in thirty short years! – In *the art of war* and *of government*, in the *treatment of religion* and *arrangement of the laws*, as *Apollo* of the *Muses*, and as *private man under the crown* – according to the universal impression, the paragon of monarchies – what *good* he has caused! Has spread *enlightenment, philosophical spirit*, and *moderation* all around *from the throne!* Has how terribly *ruined* and *chased off* Oriental, stupid *splendor, revelry*, and *luxury*, which was formerly often the sole golden preserve of the courts! Has everywhere how

---

[147] Frederick the Great.
[148] I.e. Louis XIV. Herder is again using brachylogy here; he means "than the age of Louis carries and deserves to carry the name of Louis."
[149] These lines are taken from Klopstock's ode "An Gleim [To Gleim]."

deeply wounded *fat ignorance, blind zeal,* and *superstition!* Has raised how high *thrift* and *order, regularity* and *industry, fine arts* and a so-called *taste for free thinking!* – The century wears his image as it does his uniform – century without a doubt the greatest eulogy of his name. – However, precisely this coin, with the portrait turned away and the mere result of his creation as a friend of humankind and a philosopher considered, will also without doubt at some point reveal *something more* and *different!* Will reveal perhaps how, through a natural law of the imperfection of human deeds, with the *enlightenment* also just as much luxuriating *exhaustion of the heart* inevitably spread abroad; with *thrift,* its badge and troop *poverty;* with *philosophy,* blind, shortsighted *unbelief;* with *freedom* in *thought,* always *slavery in action, despotism of souls under chains of flowers;* with the great hero, conqueror, and spirit of war, *deadness,* Roman constitution, as armies were everything there, decline, and misery. Will reveal what *love of humankind, justice, moderation, religion, wellbeing of subjects* – all up to a *certain point* treated as *means* to *achievement* – what sort of consequences all this *had to* have on *his age* – on *realms with quite different constitutions* and *orders* – on the *world* and the *world of posterity.* The scales will *hover? Rise – sink –* which pan? How do I know?

"The author *of a hundred years*"[dd] who without quarrel or contradiction has had an effect on his century *like a monarch* – read, learned, admired, and (what is still more) *followed* from *Lisbon* to *Kamchatka,* from *Novaya Zemlya* as far as the *colonies of India* – with his *language,* with his hundredfold talents for *wording,* with his *lightness,* with his *zest in ideas* for sheer metaphors – above all through having been born *at the right point* to *use* the world, to *use* predecessors and competitors, to *use* opportunities, occasions, especially prejudices and pet weaknesses of his age, and of course especially the most useful weaknesses of the fairest brides of his age, the *regents* in all of Europe – this great author, what has he not also without doubt done *for the benefit of the century! Light* spread abroad, so-called *philosophy of humanity, tolerance, facility* in *independent thought, gleam of virtue* in a hundred amiable *shapes, thinned* and *sweetened little human inclinations* – *as an author without doubt on the greatest height* of the century! – But now at the same time with that, what miserable *recklessness, weakness, uncertainty,* and *coldness!,* what *shallowness, planlessness, skepticism* about *virtue, happiness,* and *merit!* – what *laughed off* with his wit, without in part

---

[dd] *Voltaire.*

wanting to laugh it off! – gentle, pleasant, and necessary bonds *dissolved* with a mischievous hand without *giving* us, who do not all reside at the Chateau de Fernay,[150] the least thing *in their place*? And through *what means* and routes has he achieved even *his best*? Into whose hands, then, does he deliver us with all this philosophy and *aestheticism in manner of thought* without *morality* or *firm human sensation*? One is familiar with the great cabals against and for him, knows how differently *Rousseau* preaches – perhaps it is good that *both* preach *far apart from each other* and in many things both *canceling* each other – this is often the end of human beginning!, the lines cancel each other but their final point remains!

To be sure, no great mind through which fate effects *change* can be measured, with everything *that it thinks and feels*, according to the *common rule* of every *mediocre soul*. There are *exceptions of a higher kind* and for the most part everything *deserving of note in the world* happens *through* these exceptions. The straight lines always just carry on straight ahead, would leave everything where it is!, if the deity did not also cast *extraordinary human beings, comets*, into the spheres of the peaceful *orbit around the sun*, did not make them fall and in their deepest fall *rise up* again whither no eye on earth follows them. Also, only God or among human beings a fool puts on the account of the *merit* and the initial intention *of the agent* every *remotest* moral or immoral consequence of an action! – otherwise who would find in everything in the world more *accusers* than the first and sole *agent*, the Creator! – But, my brothers, let us, though, not abandon the poles around which everything turns – *truth, consciousness* of *good intention, happiness of humanity*! Let us, most of all, on the *highest of high seas* on which we are currently floating, in a *light of will-o'-the-wisp* and *fog* that is perhaps worse than *complete night* – let us there look diligently to these stars, the points of all *direction, security*, and *peace*, and then steer our course with *faithfulness* and *industry*.

*

Great must be the whole where already in every individuality there appears such *a whole*!, but in every individuality there also still only reveals itself such an *indeterminate One*, solely for the whole! Where *little* connections already yield great *meaning*, and yet centuries are only *syllables*, nations

---

[150] Voltaire's residence near Geneva, Switzerland.

only *letters* and perhaps *interpunctuations*, which mean nothing in themselves but *so much* for the easier meaning of the whole! What, *O individual human being*, with your inclinations, abilities, and contribution, are you? – And you have pretensions that perfection should *exhaust* itself in you *in all its aspects?*

Precisely the *limitedness* of my point on the earth, the *blinding* of my looks, the *failure* of my purposes, the *riddle* of my inclinations and desires, the *worsting* of my forces only serving the whole *of a day, of a year, of a nation, of a century* – precisely this is a guarantee for me that *I* am nothing but the *whole* is *everything!* What a work to which belong so many shade-groups of *nations* and *ages, colossus-statues* almost without *viewpoint* or *view*!, so many *blind tools*, which all act in *the illusion of freedom* and yet do not know *what* they do or *why*, which have no *overview* and yet *act along* as zealously as if their *antheap* were the *universe* – what *a work this whole is!* In the *tiniest stretch* of it of which we have an overview, so much *order* and so much *confusion, knot,* and *disposition for untying* [*Auflösung*] – both precisely assurance and guarantee for the boundless glorious majesty in the universal. It would have to be miserably *small* if I, *fly* that I am, could have an overview of it! – how little *wisdom* and *manifoldness* if one who *reels* through the world and has so much difficulty in holding firm even *a single thought* were never to find a *complication!* – In a stretch that is nothing and where nevertheless *a thousand thoughts* and *seeds strive simultaneously,* in a *half-measure* of the *musical art* of two beats where, though, perhaps precisely *the heaviest notes* entwine *for the sweetest resolution* [*Auflösung*] – who am *I* to judge, since I precisely only *pass obliquely through* the great hall, and eye a side-corner of the great *covered painting* in the obscurest shimmer? As Socrates said about the writings of a human being who, limited like himself, wrote *in a single measure of forces* with himself[151] – what am I supposed to say about the *great book of God* which *transcends worlds and times!* [A book] of which I am hardly a letter, hardly see three letters around me.

Infinitely *small* for the pride that has pretensions to *be, know, effect, and form everything!* Infinitely *great* for the *meekness* that does not have confidence *to be* anything. Both nothing but *individual tools* in the plan of an *immeasurable Providence!*

---

[151] According to Diogenes Laertius, Euripides gave Socrates the works of Heraclitus to read and then asked him what he thought of them, to which Socrates replied: "What I understood of them is excellent; I believe the same of what I did not understand as well."

And if one day we found a *standpoint* to take an overview of the whole merely of our species! – whither the chain between peoples and regions of the earth which initially advanced *so slowly*, then wound its way through nations *with so much clashing*, and finally, with a gentler but *stricter drawing-together*, was destined to *bind*, and – whither? – to *lead*, these nations – whither this chain reaches – we will see the *ripe harvest* of the seeds which, strewn among the peoples *out of a blind sieve*, we saw sprout so *peculiarly*, bloom *so variously*, yield such *ambiguous* hopes of fruit – we *will ourselves be in a position*[152] to savor what sort of *good taste* the *leaven* that fermented so long, so cloudily, and with such bad taste in the end produced for the *universal formation of humanity*. Fragment of life, what were you?

> – quanta sub nocte iacebat
> Nostra dies![153]

But happy he who even then does not regret his fragment of life!

Blepomen gar arti di' esoptrou en ainigmati, tote de prosôpon pros prosôpon – arti ginôskô ek merous, tote de epignôsomai, kathôs kai epegnôsthên. Nuni de menei pistis, elpis, agapê, ta tria tauta; meizôn de toutôn hê agapê.[154]

---

[152] The futures "we will see . . . we will ourselves be in a position" are in fact present tenses in the German. Herder is exploiting the normal ability of the present tense to bear a future meaning in German, but he is also stretching this, probably in imitation of the ancient Greek use of a *prophetic* present tense.

[153] How deeply beneath the night lay our day! *Or:* How great lay our day beneath the night! (The lines are adapted from Lucan. Herder no doubt intends both the possible meanings.)

[154] 1 Corinthians 13:12–13: "For now we see through a glass, darkly; but then face to face: now I know in part; but then shall I know even as also I am known. And now abideth faith, hope, charity, these three; but the greatest of these is charity" (Authorized Version).

Part V Political Philosophy

Letters concerning the Progress of Humanity (1792) [excerpts on European politics][1]

What *spirit* [*Geist*] is, my friend, cannot be described, drawn, painted – but it can be felt, it expresses itself through thoughts, movements, through striving, force, and effect. In the corporeal world we distinguish spirit from the body and attribute to spirit what ensouls the body down to its elements, what holds life within it and awakens life, what attracts forces and reproduces forces. Hence in the oldest languages *spirit* was the expression for invisible, striving might; on the other hand, flesh, person, body, corpse was the designation of dead inertness or of an organic dwelling, of a tool, which the spirit uses as a powerful occupant and artist.

Time is a thought-formation of successive, mutually linked, conditions – it is a measure of things, the things themselves are its measured content. Hence *spirit of the times* means the sum of thoughts, dispositions, strivings, and living forces which express themselves in a particular progression of things with given causes and effects. We never see the elements of events, but we do see their appearances and in doing so note their form and organization in a perceived connection.

Hence if we want to talk about the spirit *of our* time we must first determine what our time is, what scope we can and like to give it. On our round earth all the hours of the day exist at once, and thus also the spirit of the time in the present moment is not one and the same in Japan and China, in Tatary and Russia, in Africa and Tahiti, in North America and

---

[1] This draft, like the published version which follows, is written in the form of letters between a number of fictional letter writers, not all of whose views represent Herder's own considered positions. The three excerpts included here are all assigned to different writers by Herder. However, they do all seem to reflect his own considered views.

South America. All the modifications take over from each other within it, they have taken over, they will take over, depending on whether the stream of events drives the waves slower or faster.[2]

If we restrict ourselves to Europe, then even within this the spirit of the time is very different depending on lands and situations, for everywhere it is a consequence of preceding conditions modified in accordance with the state of things into a transient Now. This transient Now can certainly be led and guided, just as it for its part also leads and guides. It gets used and misused; it governs and serves.

Hence in order to make this Proteus talk we must bind him and ask him: What sorts of dispositions and first principles have governed since a given time in the part of Europe that is called the richest in thoughts, the fullest in deeds, the governing part? What sorts of common strivings and movements prove visible in it despite the differing characters of the peoples? In which part of these peoples and since when have they stirred? What did they undertake? Did they already bring it about? What do they drive towards, and with what probable success?

The common event which founded Europe was, from the fifth to the tenth or thirteenth century, the *settlement of savage or barbaric peoples in this part of the world, their political organization, and their so-called conversion*. It is on this main event that, with a few modifications brought by the subsequent period, the present arrangement of Europe – the powers' and property-owners' situations of ownership, the various rights and privileges of the human groups – is grounded. The question is therefore: What does the present time think of this attainment, of these privileges and rights? How are these things used and how have they been used for centuries? Is their present condition just, permitted, advantageous for the universal, that is, for the individual in the majority, or not?

History has today – from the eleventh, twelfth, fifteenth, but most of all from the sixteenth, century on – largely decided about one branch of these questions: *religious and church institutions*. The religious community's complaints about the hypocrisy, the emptiness, and the burden of the ceremonies, about the presumptions, the pride, the luxury, and the oppressive rule of the servants of the church, arose in several lands; this was answered with persecution and torture; rivers of blood flowed; but the voice

---

[2] The words "they have taken over, they will take over ... slower or faster" seem to be another example of Herder using chiasmus.

of the community was not suffocated thereby, the spirit of truth not killed. The mass was led by ever more, wiser, more intelligent men; in the end, insightful or selfish princes themselves came over to their side; after many battles the *spirit of the times* was victorious in a large part of Europe. In other lands, it was suppressed for the moment; darkness banded together and reinforced itself. But it is as clear as day that there too it cannot remain suppressed for ever. No fog, no hypocrisy, no order, or rather disorder, of things that is built on illusion can maintain itself eternally; the thickest darkness gives way to light. It is obvious that since the revival of the sciences the spirit of the times now *strives* in this direction in all the lands of Europe. Necessarily from day to day more consequences of the disorder come to light; more oppressions make themselves felt. The Protestant lands have made progress; the lands left behind want to and must follow them; if the advance does not succeed on legal paths, then inevitably it gets attempted on the most violent deviations. The concealed, neglected poison creeps and rages inwardly, for a that much more horrible, more certain death for the troubled body. There is coming, there is coming[3] a time which the clergy, even as it is now, and the parson-regime can as little survive as the much more venerable class of ancient druids could sustain itself in their dark groves. Hence the duty of every person endowed with understanding is to forestall greater evil, and to advance the unhypocritical truth into the world on the gentlest path. For what can a single guild do against the whole pressing number of living and future generations?

If the time has already decided concerning this, the churchly, branch of human arrangements, then its vote concerning the other branch, that of political arrangements, may also no longer seem doubtful to us as soon as the first principles which are in force there also get applied here. Are hypocrisy and oppression, are luxury, mockery, and empty presumption, are injustices and a real status in statu,[4] whether it be called *court* or the guild of *aethelings* (that is what they were called in olden times)[5] – are they less discordant, do they become less harmful, because they are attached to *non-priests?* – since it should be remembered that it was precisely the priestly class that especially and obviously had so many good prejudices in the interest of the human species speaking *for* it, and very usefully proved

[3] This is another example of Herder using anadiplosis.   [4] State within a state.
[5] Like the translation, Herder here uses an antiquated term for aristocrats, *Edelinge*, instead of more modern and civilized-sounding alternatives such as *Adel* or *Edelmänner*.

them through beneficent deeds for which it can never be thanked enough. Now is it likely that a miserable system of conquest and war founded on a horde of barbaric vassals which luckily for the world for the most part no longer exists at all in Europe – is it likely that this would be a firmer rock against the floods of time than a church system which, in appearance and largely also in fact, was founded for the quieting and formation of minds, for the peace of the peoples, hence for the real and most noble purpose of humanity, with inexpressible art and a millennium of labor? That we no longer live in the fifth, ninth, eleventh century is certain; that the vassals who were then powerful are no longer ours is established; that the old system of feudalism and conquest does not suit our times is clear; that the right of blood gives neither competence for the more important tasks nor more faithfulness and uprightness is unfortunately all too proven by history and experience – so why do we want to close our eyes to the midday, along with everything that is and happens around us, in the illusion that we really still lived in the times of warring, of the Hun invasions and the crusades? Everything in humanity that is great, good, and noble works to the end that these times should and can never any longer return – and we would wish to believe that the old frame of these times, newly whitewashed and painted, is eternal in nature? There exists in the state only a single class: the *people* (not the rabble) – to it belongs the king as much as the farmer, each in his place, in the circle destined for him. Nature creates noble, great, wise men, education and occupations form their abilities – these are heads and leaders of the people (aristodemocrats)[6] arranged by God and the state. Any other application or division of this excellent name is and should ever remain a term of abuse.

Now, that these irrefutable concepts are receiving greater and greater expression, are getting articulated ever more clearly and luminously, that insightful princes are themselves acknowledging them and giving them application as far as they are able, that the disadvantaged or even oppressed part of human society is crying out ever louder and louder, "We live at the end of the eighteenth, no longer in the eleventh, century!" – this is indeed the *voice-vote of the time*, of the old and new calendar.[7] And

---

[6] This is probably a neologism of Herder's.

[7] The phrase "of the old and new calendar" is presumably a reference to the last day of the lunar month in the Greek calendar, which bore the name "the old and the new" due to the fact that it marked both the last waning of the old moon and the first waxing of the new one (see especially Aristophanes' *Clouds*). Hence here: the point at which the old political system dies and a new one arises.

I know of no one who could convict this genius of lying or refute the almanac.

But what a prophet of doom you[8] are in taking the barbaric system of war and conquest to be the sole, immovable basis of all the states of Europe! If that is so, then for the peace of humanity may unhappy Europe perish! Has it not caused itself and the world trouble for long enough? Not for long enough conducted senseless wars for the sake of religion or family succession? Do not all parts of the world drip with the blood of those whom it killed, with the sweat of those whom it tortured as slaves? On nature's boards stands written the great law of justice and requital: "*Let it make good the bad that it has done, or let it atone through its own crimes and vices.*" I hope for the first. It will make good the bad that it has done – clear reason, even the law of calculation, the one-times-one, works in that direction, even assuming that we were unwilling to hear the voice of justice. The stupidity of wars, both wars of religion and succession and wars of trade and ministers, will become obvious, and already is so now; innocent, industrious peoples will politely decline the duty and honor of strangling other innocent, peaceful, industrious peoples because the regent or his minister is tempted to receive a new title, a further piece of land in addition to those lands which he already cannot govern. It will seem to Europe horrible to bleed to death or to wither miserably in hospitals and barracks for a few families who regard the government business of the lands as a genealogical leasehold property. Regents will themselves become enlightened enough to acknowledge the stupidity in this, and to prefer to rule over a number of industrious citizens rather than over an army of mutually murdering animals – for if besides the human species which is supposed to govern *itself* there were in nature a kind of animals that cut itself to pieces upon order for the sake not of hunger but of art or fun, what would we think of the author of nature? So let me believe, my friend, that the mad, raging system of conquest is not the basic constitution of Europe, or at least need not[9] be so, and also will not be so for ever. Speremus atque amemus.[10]

The problems which, quietly and in peace, I abstract for myself from the colossal revolution in France, and whose solution or nonsolution I await without partiality or contention but with anxious and happy longing, are:

[8] This refers to the fictional author of a previous letter not included here.
[9] Or: ought not to.   [10] Let us hope and love.

1. Which is the *better constitution* that France gives and is able to give itself? Is it a moderated monarchy (a dubious name!) or must it be brought back, contrary to its will, as fond as it is of the previous name in accordance with its old delusion, to a republic, that is, to *a system common to all?* The earlier this happens the better, it seems to me – for only despotism or common system are the two extremes, the poles, around which the sphere revolves; moderated monarchy is merely the irregular vacillation from the one pole to the other.

2. *Can this common system,* contrary to the usual theory, *also occur in such a large territory of lands and former provinces as France is?* Do mountains and valleys, old habits and privileges, make no difference in this? If this problem gets solved and all parts of the republic find themselves in good shape in the process, then in effect a great step has been taken in speculation about the administration of states; we have a new, higher canon than that which has been acknowledged since Aristotle. And I do not see why it could not exist, since the largest realms have long, albeit unhappily, existed under the most miserable constitution, despotism, or what is still worse, aristocratic despotism.

3. *To what extent can France reach an accommodation about this with other European states,* since, unfortunately!, it is not situated in America nor like Britain bordered by the sea. Will Europe allow it to fall out of its own so-called balance – which is precisely not the balance of justice, but of thirst for conquest and of ancient familial rights – without hostility and bloodshed? To be sure, no one has ever guaranteed the king of France his realm or the usurpations thereof, nor been able or allowed to do so; also, the king was not able or inclined to call on anyone for their sake because he was unaware of any guarantee for them. But all the more is it to be expected that Europe's politics will, in virtue of the fruitful fiction of a balance that never has existed nor ever can or will exist without slavery and crippling, invent something of the sort and disallow France from cleaning out its old, entirely autonomous, throne.

But what may be the result in our times of this strange, extremely tensed, crisis in which without right or authority masters of foreign houses interfere in the administration of a house that is foreign to them, shelter and arm its deserters and traitors?

4. *How, in the case of successful resistance, would France behave according to its first principles which say that it has renounced the system of conquest?* The more generously, firmly, and nobly, the better. It would thereby afford

the first example of a right and just war,[11] for whose running its own constitution has made itself a pledge and watchman.

5. *How will it distribute its legislative, judicial, and executive power?* Inevitably, reason, justice, and order would be bound to receive an evident, enduring predominance if in so large a realm such a distribution could persist without despotism. A mighty step in the ordering of things under the law of a common order! So that this step can be made or attempted, we should wish that no foreign power interfere in the free experiment of an independent nation which undertakes this experiment on itself or disturb this experiment through premature wisdom and interloping.

6. *No nation that constitutes a political whole can be without taxes; how will these be justly distributed, how will they be levied in a way that most spares people?* Will the economistic system,[12] against which many doubts have been raised with the greatest plausibility, persist? Or will it suffer change even in France? Will France thereby sink or rise as a trading state? How and in what respect will it gain by sinking or rising as a trading state? – In Germany we can await the solution to these questions with great tranquillity since extremely few of our lands are real trading states and our taxes, means of livelihood, and products are of a completely different kind than they have been in France. Only the *purest theory* can serve for us – and this neither gets made out through quarreling nor tested in two years.

7. *What will France's attitude be in regard to worship?* And what will be the consequences of this new arrangement of things? We no longer live in the sixteenth century and it is now no longer possible for reformation to take the form that it took under Henry VIII in England. So much the better; the more originally and deeply the thing is done, the more instructive an undertaking it will be for others. It has long been disputed whether unbelief or superstition yields worse consequences; the deity has tolerated shameful idolatries, the wickedest superstition, in so many times and lands; so we can also without worrying leave it to the deity whether it will tolerate a European Chinamen's state, a type of *Confucius-religion*. We Protestants do not want to undertake any crusades for the fallen altars, the secularized nunneries, the oath-breaking priests – or else both the

[11] Due to the rules governing punctuation in German, it is not possible to tell whether the English translation should have a comma here or not. The decision whether to include it or exclude it makes a significant difference to the strength and character of the claim that Herder is making.
[12] I.e. mercantilism.

pope and the high clergy of the French would laugh at us for taking vengeance for that which we have done ourselves and in the possession of which we continue to preserve ourselves. We want to compare in an examining way this reformation with the one that happened two hundred years ago, and to take note of what is best from this one too.

8. Finally, *literature*. Let us not believe that France will become an unliterary ape-land, a Greenland or Siberia, in three or four, in six or seven, years. It has such decided advances ahead of many, indeed most, European lands, despite the fact that they too lay claim to be described as civilly administered; its language is so refined and formed [*gebildet*] even in the mouths of the common people; so many concepts of philosophy, of ethical propriety, and even of delicate taste have since a century ago become such a firm, habitual possession of all classes of the nation – that it is truly an unnecessary fear that all this might be displaced through three or four years. Moreover, the customary use of culture and literature has also of course up to this point anything but ceased; precisely these things are being set in motion among all classes of the people and are now being mightily practiced on the most important objects of human knowledge. Thus in conditions of great misery it is at least the case that a universal school of the art of reasoning and oratory has in effect been opened for the whole nation; whoever can speak speaks, and gets heard by Europe. Children and youths receive this impression, and the second generation will certainly be further advanced than the first was. Book publishing is not in happy shape, and men of decided value in the conducting of the sciences are currently at the head of affairs along with others. In more peaceful times they will return to their Muses after they have made dangerous sacrifices to the gods of their fatherland in stormy times. If they[13] let the old grandiloquence on pulpits and judges' benches, in academies and on the tragic stage, die out – it seems to me that we already have in our hands all the masterpieces of which these genres were capable, and that many a genre had already outlived itself. A new order of things now begins even in these arts; let word become deed, let the deed yield words. What will now stay standing or sink, what rot or be born anew? – the solution to this problem can be nothing but salutary and instructive for us; for of course we Germans do not live solely and exclusively on France's literary products. Only let no foreign umpire interfere in this native quarrel, and

---

[13] Reading *sie* for *Sie*.

let no danger threaten or destroy the old residences and shrines of the French Muse. Among all modern European languages it[14] was the first to lend this primitive part of the world more refined reason, wit, taste, decorum; in this it took precedence even over Italy's language, and in all the sciences, the most difficult and useful as well as the pleasing and easy ones, France has immortal merits. Just as Alexander in conquered Thebes spared Pindar's house, just as all savage barbarians, not excepting the Huns, revered and shrank before the ancient majesty of Rome, likewise let no one, even in the most furious rebellion, be forgetful of the glory of olden times – otherwise his own name would thereby become immortal in a terrible way.

[14] This pronoun could refer to the French Muse or to the French language – or, very likely, to both ambiguously.

Letters for the Advancement of Humanity (1793–7) [excerpts concerning freedom of thought and expression][1]

The more and the more easily messengers reach everywhere here, every-where there, then the more the communication of thoughts is advanced, and no prince, no king will seek to hinder this who understands the infi-nite advantages of the mind–industry, of mind–culture, of the reciprocal communication of inventions, thoughts, suggestions, even of mistakes committed and weaknesses. Every one of these things benefits human nature, and hence also society; the mistake gets discovered, the error gets corrected, thought awakens thought, sensations and decisions stimulate and motivate.[2]

Free investigation of the truth from all sides is the sole antidote against delusion and error of whatever sort they may be. Let the deluded person defend his delusion, the person who thinks differently his thought; that is *their* business. Even if both of them fail to be corrected, for the unbiased person there certainly arises out of every criticized error a new reason, a new view of the truth. Let it only not be believed that truth can ever be captured, or even kept fast in jail for eternity, by means of armed delu-sion! Truth is a spirit and communicates itself to spirits almost without a body. Often its sound may be stirred at a single end of the world, and it resounds in remote lands; but the river current of human cognition always purifies itself through oppositions, through strong contrasts. Here

[1] See for this subject also the excerpt on patriotism which follows, especially section 3.
[2] Excerpt from G7:34.

370

it breaks off, there it starts; and in the end a long- and much-purified delusion is regarded by human beings as truth.[3]

[Through Christianity] the peoples of Europe not only came to know each other better, but also became, through reciprocal needs, with common purposes and strivings, indispensable to each other; their tendency became ever more and more directed at a single point. *Inventions* came in addition, which given these common needs one people borrowed from the other, in which one sought to speed ahead of the other; there arose in their *perfecting* a competition among the nations. Now thoughts, experiments, discoveries, trainings could no longer so easily perish as in the periods of the peoples who were formerly separated from each other; the seed that did not take root here and now was carried by a favorable zephyr to a gentler ground where it perhaps thrived under a new name.[4]

Several teachers in a single faculty, several faculties, several universities facing one another are commonly in competition. With the years this competition inevitably does not decline but grows. The more the restrictions of the trade are weakened (they must necessarily be so), the more the work of the academies becomes a work of the mind and of a free practice, then the more the competition catches fire with a purer flame. Universities are *watchtowers and lighthouses of science*; they spy out what is happening in the distance and abroad, advance it further, and themselves shine a path forward for others. Universities are *gathering- and meeting-places of science*; out of their bringing-together and reciprocal fighting or friendship arise there and then new results. Finally, universities should be the last *sanctuaries and a bulwark of the sciences* if they were to find a sanctuary nowhere [else]. What went unrecognized everywhere, what in daily business raised its voice here and there without protection, should here enjoy an unbiased attention and a support that would be disturbed by no influence. If I am not mistaken, this has happened on several occasions; the counsels of teachers have stopped persecutions which the counsels of the wise men of state could not[5] suppress; and thus for the future too do I see counsels of teachers in universities coming forth which the counsels of stupid wise men can hardly withstand.[6]

[3] Excerpt from G7:251.   [4] Excerpt from G7:319–20.   [5] Or: did not like to.
[6] Excerpt from G7:322.

The public of authors is thus of a distinctive kind: invisible and omnipresent, often deaf, often dumb, and perhaps after years, after centuries, very loud and active. Lost and yet unlost, indeed unlosable, is that which gets deposited in its lap. One can never tally up with it; its book is never closed, the trial before and with it never gets concluded; it is always learning and never arrives at the final result.

People have wanted to appoint guardians for this eternal minor, the *censors* – but as experience has shown, with fruitless effort and for the most part with the most unpleasant outcome. The minor most likes to taste what one denied him; he searches out what one wanted to hide from him; the prohibition of a presentation to this public is precisely the means to afford even a useless word respect, weight, and attention. And what modest man will dare to be a guardian of the entire human understanding, *of the public of all times and lands?* Let each wise man and fool write in his own way *if only he in doubtful cases gives his name and personally insults no one.*

Let me be permitted to explain myself on this point. The wisest censor, even if he represents the voice-vote of a whole, indeed of the most enlightened, state, can hardly want, in what concerns doctrine and opinion, to counterbalance or outweigh the voice-vote of the public, to which an author voluntarily subjects himself. Even if his judgment were the wisdom of Solomon, if it contained the cleverness of all past centuries, and anticipated the tested understanding belonging to a great future, still, though, he is missing one thing: the *legitimation for this.* For neither the past world nor the world of posterity has certified him concerning this. The author will hence always have the ground of objection against him that he is usurping in advance the judgment of the world, that he is without authorization presumptuously taking on himself a decision which only belongs to the public in the broadest sense of the word; he will appeal from this pope of a small state to the *universal concilium* which alone, and indeed only in *ever advancing* voice-votes, can be a judge of the true and the false. Probably many voice-votes will come to his side, and, notwithstanding the highest legal right, the censor will, in form and on account of the consequences, prove in the wrong.[7] I do not have to repeat what has been said so often and so much, where truth is concerned, about freedom of opinions, which may only be refuted, but not suppressed.

---

[7] The oxymoron here, "right ... wrong," is equally present in the German: "Recht ... Unrecht." As usual when Herder uses oxymoron, the superficial contradiction masks a deeper consistency.

If one may therefore rob the public of no opinions, not even the craziest ones, in that the state, when they seem false or dangerous *to it*, may rather occasion their public refutation, so that darkness may be conquered by light for the world's advantage, then, given this unrestrained freedom, given the respect that the state itself shows the public by not withholding from it anything that any author offers it, the state may surely also demand *that every author who sees fit to offer something to the public should give his name.*[8]

[8] Excerpt from G7:324–5.

Letters for the Advancement of Humanity (1793–7) [excerpt on patriotism][1]

To wish oneself back into the times of Greece and Rome would be foolish; this youth of the world,[2] like the iron age of the times under Rome's rule too, is past; even if an exchange were possible, we would hardly win in the exchange in what we actually desire. Sparta's zeal for fatherland oppressed not only the Helots but the citizens themselves and with time other Greeks. Athens was often a burden to its citizens and colonies; it wanted to be deceived with sweet phantoms. Finally, Roman love of fatherland proved destructive not only for Italy but for Rome itself and the whole Roman world. Hence we want to seek out what *we* must respect and love in our fatherland in order to love it worthily and purely.

1. Is it that gods formerly came down from heaven and assigned this land to our fathers? Is it that they have given us a religion and have themselves organized our constitution? Did Minerva receive this city through a contest?[3] Did Egeria inspire our Numa with dreams?[4] – Vain glory – for we are not our fathers. If on Minerva's holy ground we are unworthy of the great goddess, if Numa's dreams no longer accord with our times, then let Egeria rise again from her spring, then let Minerva lower herself from heaven for new inspirations.

---

[1] For this subject, see also in the Tenth Collection that follows the section "Fourth disposition: Purified patriotism."

[2] I.e. ancient Greece.

[3] According to Greek legend, Minerva (Athena) won Athens through a fight with the god Poseidon, after which it bore her name.

[4] According to Roman legend, the spring-nymph Egeria married or consorted with the second king of Rome, Numa Pompilius, and constrained him to wise and just rule.

To speak without images, it is good and laudable for a people to have great ancestors, a great age, famous gods of the fatherland, as long as these awaken it to noble deeds, inspire it to worthy dispositions, as long as the old training and teaching befits the people. If it gets mocked by the people itself, if it has outlived itself, or if it gets misused: "What use to you," (Horace calls to *his* fatherland) "proud Pontic mast, what use to you is your superior descent? What use to you are the painted gods on your walls?"[5] An idly possessed glory lazily inherited from our ancestors soon makes us vain and unworthy of our ancestors. Whoever fancies that he is brave, noble, upright by birth can easily forget to show himself such a person. He fails to struggle for a wreath which he believes himself already to possess from his earliest ancestors on. In such a delusion of fatherland-religion-race-ancestor pride did Judaea, Greece, Rome, indeed almost every ancient mighty or holy state-constitution, perish. It is not what a fatherland was formerly but what it is now that we can respect and love in it.

2. Besides our children, relatives, and friends, this can therefore only be its organization, the good *constitution* in which we readily and most happily care to live with what is dearest to us. Physically, we praise the situation of a place that with healthy air does our body and mind good; morally, we consider ourselves happy in a state in which with a lawful freedom and security we are not ashamed before ourselves, do not waste our effort, do not see ourselves and our families abandoned but may exercise each of our duties as worthy, active sons of the fatherland, and may see these rewarded by our mother's look. Greeks and Romans were right that no other human merit exceeds the merit of having founded such a union, or of reinforcing it, renewing it, purifying it, preserving it. To think, to work, and (great destiny!) to have successful effect for the common cause not only of our own but of posterity and of the entire eternal fatherland of humanity – what, weighed against this, is an individual life, a daily labor of few minutes and hours?

Everyone who is on the ship in the flooding waves of the sea feels himself obliged to aid, to preserve, to save the ship. The word *fatherland* brought the ship afloat at the shore; he can, he may, no longer (unless he casts himself overboard and entrusts himself to the sea's wild waves) stand idly by in the ship and count the waves as though he was on the

5 Horace, *Odes*, bk. 1, no. 14. Here translated from Herder's German.

shore. His duty calls upon him (for all his companions and loved ones are with him in the ship) that if a storm rises up, a danger threatens, the wind changes, or a ship hurtles on threatening to run down his vessel – his duty calls upon him that he should help and call out. Softly or loudly, according to his class – the deckhand, the helmsman, or the skipper – his duty, the collective welfare of the ship, calls upon him. He does not seek security for himself individually; he may not dream his way into the bark of a select shore-society which is not here at his disposal; he puts his hand to the task and becomes, if not the savior of the ship, then at least its loyal fellow traveler and look-out.

What caused it that several formerly very revered classes gradually sank and still sink into contempt, into shame? Because none of them adopted the common cause, because each lived as a favored class of property or honor; they slept in the storm peacefully like Jonah, and destiny struck them like Jonah.[6] Oh, that human beings despite their seeing eyes do not believe in a *Nemesis*! There attaches[7] to every injured or neglected duty a punishment which is precisely not voluntary but the necessary punishment which accumulates from generation to generation. If the fatherland's cause is holy and eternal, then every neglect of this cause of its nature atones for itself, and the revenge accumulates with every more corrupted undertaking or generation. It is not your place to ponder theoretically about your fatherland, for you were not its creator, but you must join others in helping it where and as you can, encourage it, save it, improve it – even if you were the goose of the Capitol.[8]

3. Should not therefore, precisely in the spirit of the ancients, the voice of each citizen, even assuming that it appeared in print, be considered a freedom of the fatherland, a holy court of ostracism? The poor man was perhaps able to do nothing else than write, otherwise he would probably have done something better – do you want to rob the sighing man of his breath that goes forth into desolate emptiness? But still more valuable for the man of understanding are the hints and looks of those who see further. They inspire to activity when everyone is asleep; they sigh perhaps when everyone is dancing. But they do not only sigh; they show higher results in simpler equations by means of a certain art. Do you want to make them be silent because you calculate merely according to the common arithmetic?

---

[6] See Jonah 1.   [7] Reading *hängt* for *hangt*.

[8] According to Livy, when the Gauls attacked Rome in 387 BC the holy geese of the goddess Juno on the Capitol awakened the city's defenders with their cackling so that the city was saved.

They go silent easily and continue to calculate; but the fatherland counted on these quiet calculators. *A single* step of progress that they successfully indicated is worth more than ten thousand ceremonies and eulogies.

Should our fatherland not need this art of calculation? Let it be that Germany is brave and upright – bravely and uprightly did it formerly let itself be led off to Spain and Africa, to Gaul and England, to Italy, Sicily, Crete, Greece, Palestine; our brave and upright ancestors bled there, and are buried. Bravely and uprightly did the Germans let themselves be hired against each other inside and outside their fatherland, as history shows; friend fought against friend, brother against brother; the fatherland got ruined and was left orphaned. Should not, therefore, besides bravery and uprightness something else be necessary for our fatherland in addition? Light, enlightenment, sense of community; noble pride in not letting oneself be organized by others, but organizing oneself, as other nations have done from time immemorial; in being Germans on our own *well-protected* piece of territory.

4. A fatherland's glory can hardly in our time any longer be that savage *spirit of conquest* that stormed through the history of Rome and the barbarians, indeed of several proud monarchies, like an evil demon. What sort of mother would she be who (a second, worse Medea) sacrificed her children in order to capture foreign children as slaves, who sooner or later become a burden for her own children? Unfortunate would be the fatherland's child who, given away or sold, had to run into the sword, lay waste, murder, in order to satisfy a vanity that bears advantage for no one. The glory of a fatherland can in our time and for the even more strictly judging world of posterity be no other than that this noble mother provides for her children security, activity, occasion for every free, beneficent practice, in short, the upbringing that is her own protection and advantage, dignity and glory. All the peoples of Europe (not excluding other parts of the world) are now in a contest of, not physical, but *mental and artistic forces* with each other. When one or two nations accomplish steps of progress in a short time for which formerly centuries were required, then other nations cannot, and may not, want to set themselves back by centuries without thereby doing themselves painful damage. They *must* advance with those others; in our times one can no longer be a barbarian; as a barbarian one gets cheated, trodden on, despised, abused. The epochs of the world form a moving chain which no individual ring can in the end resist even if it wanted to.

A *fatherland's culture* is part of this, and in it also the culture of language. What encouraged the Greeks to their glorious and most difficult works? The voice of duty and glory. Through what did they think themselves to be superior to all the nations of the earth? Through their cultivated language and what was planted amongst them by means of it. The imperious language of the Romans commanded the world – a language of law and deeds. Through what has a neighboring nation[9] won so much influence over all the peoples of Europe since more than a century ago? Besides other causes, especially also through its – in the highest sense of the word – formed [*gebildete*] *national language*. Each person who took delight in its[10] writings thereby entered its[11] realm and sympathetically shared in [*nahm Teil an*][12] them.[13] They formed and deformed, they ordered, they impressed. And the language of the Germans, which our ancestors called a language of tribal stem, pith, and heroes, should pull the victory car of others like a conquered prisoner, and in the process still give itself airs in its clumsy empire- and court-style? Throw it away, this oppressive finery, you matron squeezed in contrary to your will, and be what you can be and formerly were: a language of reason, of force and truth. You fathers of the fatherland, honor her, honor the gifts which – unasked and unrewarded, and yet not without glory – she offered. Should every art and activity through which many a person would like to help his fatherland first hire itself out abroad like that lost son,[14] and entrust the harvest of his industry or his mind to a foreign hand, in order that you might have the honor of receiving it from there? I think that I see a time coming...

However, let us not prophesy, but after everything only observe that every fatherland, already just with its sweet name, has a *moral tendency*. It descends from fathers; with the name *father* it brings to our minds the recollection of our *times of youth* and *games of youth*; it awakens the memory of all the men of merit before us, of all the worthy men after us

[9] I.e. France.
[10] The reference of this "its" could be either to the *nation* or to the nation's *language*. The ambiguity may well be deliberate.
[11] Besides the ambiguity of reference mentioned in the preceding note, this "its" could also mean: their (cf. the "them" that follows). In that case the "their" would mean the writings', or perhaps the writings' and the nation's and/or the language's. Again, the ambiguity may well be deliberate.
[12] The expression *nahm Teil an* could mean either (1) participated in, or (2) had sympathy with. Here both meanings are involved – hence the translation "sympathetically shared in."
[13] The reference of "them" is again ambiguous. The word could refer to the writings only, or to the writings and the nation and/or the language. Again the ambiguity may well be intentional.
[14] This refers to the New Testament story of the prodigal son – Luke 15:11–32.

to whom we will become fathers; it links the human species into a chain of continuing members who are to each other brothers, sisters, betrothed, friends, children, parents. Should we regard ourselves otherwise on the earth? Is it necessary that one fatherland has to rise up against another, indeed against *every* other, fatherland – which of course links its members with the same bonds as well? Does the earth not have space for us all? Does not one land lie peacefully beside the other? Cabinets may deceive each other, political machines may be moved against each other until the one blows the other to pieces. *Fatherlands* do not move against each other in that way; they lie peacefully beside each other, and support each other as families. *Fatherlands against fatherlands* in a combat of blood [*Blutkampf*][15] is the worst barbarism in the human language.

[15] The translation "combat of blood" tries to preserve a significant ambiguity in the German: (1) bloody combat, (2) combat based on blood (i.e. on race).

Letters for the Advancement of Humanity
(1793–7) – tenth collection[1]

[Letter] 114[2]

But why must peoples have effect on peoples in order to disturb each other's peace? It is said that this is for the sake of progressively growing culture; but what a completely different thing the book of history says!

Did those *peoples of the mountains and steppes* from northern Asia,[3] the eternal troublemakers of the world, ever have it as their intention, or were they ever in a position, to spread culture? Did not the *Chaldaeans* precisely put an end to a great part of the ancient majestic glory of western Asia? *Attila*, so many peoples who preceded or followed after him – did they mean to advance the progressive formation [*Fortbildung*] of the human species? Did they advance it?

Indeed, the *Phoenicians*, the *Carthaginians* with their renowned colonies, the *Greeks* themselves with their offshoot cities, the *Romans* with their conquests – did they have this purpose? And if through the friction between peoples there perhaps spread here this art, there that convenience, do these really compensate for the evils which the pressing of the nations

---

[1] Herder intersperses his philosophical argument in this text with long stretches of poetry from various sources. This poetry is omitted here both for reasons of space and because it is in a sense inessential to the philosophical argument (though it is, and is conceived by Herder to be, quite important as an underscoring of his ethical sentiments and an instrument for their communication to the reader – concerning which see my introduction). The poetry's contents are briefly summarized in footnotes instead.

[2] This numbering continues from the previous nine collections of the work. It is retained here for the convenience of readers comparing different editions, etc.

[3] I.e. the Huns and Mongols.

upon one another produced[4] for the victor and the vanquished? Who can depict the misery that the Greek and Roman conquests brought indirectly and directly[5] for the circle of the earth that they encompassed?[a]

Even *Christianity*, as soon as it had effect on foreign peoples in the form of a state machine, oppressed them terribly; in the case of several it so mutilated their own distinctive character that not even one and a half millennia have been able to set it right. Would we not wish, for example, that the spirits of the northern peoples, of the *Germans*, of the *Gaels*,[6] *the Slavs*, and so forth, might have developed without disturbance and purely out of themselves?

And what good did the *crusades* do for the Orient? What happiness have they brought to the coasts of the Baltic Sea?[7] The old *Prussians* are destroyed; *Livonians*, *Estonians*, and *Latvians* in the poorest condition still now curse in their hearts their subjugators, the Germans.

What, finally, is to be said of the culture that has been brought by *Spaniards*, *Portuguese*, *Englishmen*, and *Dutchmen* to the East and West Indies, to Africa among the negroes, into the peaceful islands of the southern world? Do not all these lands, more or less, cry for revenge? All the more for revenge since they have been plunged for an incalculable time into a progressively growing corruption. All these stories lie open to view in travel decriptions; they have also in part received vocal expression in connection with the trade in negroes. About the Spanish cruelties, about the greed of the English, about the cold impudence of the Dutch – of whom in the frenzy of the madness of conquest hero-poems were written – books have been written in our time which bring them so little honor that, rather, if a European collective spirit lived elsewhere than in books, we would have to be ashamed of the *crime of abusing humanity* before almost all peoples of the earth. Let the land be named

---

[a] The French work [by F.-J. de Chastellux] *De la félicité publique ou considérations sur le sort des hommes dans les différentes époques de l'histoire* [*On Public Happiness or Considerations on the Fate of Men in the Different Epochs of History*], Amsterdam, 1772 treats a theme to which enough attention cannot be paid. What is the point of history if it does not show us the image of happy or unhappy, of declining or ascending, humanity?

[4] Reading *gab* for *gaben*.
[5] The phrase "indirectly and directly" is a form of hysteron proteron.
[6] I.e. the Irish and Scottish Celts.
[7] This is an allusion to the Christianizing of the Prussians and the peoples of the Baltic in the thirteenth and fourteenth centuries by German knightly orders.

to which Europeans have come without having sinned against defenseless, trusting humanity, perhaps for all aeons to come, through injurious acts, through unjust wars, greed, deceit, oppression, through diseases and harmful gifts! Our part of the world must be called, not the wise, but the *presumptuous, pushing, tricking* part of the earth; it has not cultivated but has destroyed the shoots of peoples' own cultures wherever and however it could.[b]

What, generally, is a foisted, foreign culture, a formation [*Bildung*] that does not develop out of [a people's] own dispositions and needs? It oppresses and deforms, or else it plunges straight into the abyss. You poor sacrificial victims who were brought from the south sea islands to England in order to receive culture – you are symbols of the good that Europeans communicate to other peoples generally![c] It was therefore no otherwise than justly and wisely that the good *Ch'ien-lung* acted when he had the foreign vice-king rapidly and politely shown the way out of his realm with a thousand fires of celebration.[8] If only every nation had been clever and strong enough to show the Europeans this way!

If, now, we even blasphemously pretend that through these acts of injury to the world is fulfilled the purpose of Providence, which indeed (we assert) has given us power and cunning and tools precisely in order to become the robbers, troublers, agitators, and destroyers of the whole world – who is there who would not shudder at this misanthropic impudence? To be sure, we are, even with our stupidities and deeds of vice, tools in the hands of Providence – however, not to our credit, but perhaps precisely in order that, through a restless and hellish

[b] See, among a hundred others, the humane *Levaillant's* recent journeys into the interior of Africa [original French edition, *Second voyage dans l'intérieur de l'Afrique dans les années 1783–5*], Berlin, 1796, with *Reinhold Forster's* notes: "Not only on the *Cape of Good Hope*, this worthy scholar says (vol. 1, p. 69), but also in *North America*, on the *Hudson Bay*, in *Senegal*, on the *Gambia*, in *India*, in short, everywhere whither Europeans reach, they cheat the poor natives in trade. Especially England, the new Carthage, makes the name of the Europeans detested in all other parts of the world." Thus *Forster*. And if only this cheating alone were the end of it! The yeast from Europe has caused fermentations and preserves fermentations in all parts of the world. (Editor's note.) [Such "editor's notes" are Herder's own, so labeled by him in keeping with the literary fiction of a diversity of letter writers writing the main text.]
[c] Unbiased and unexaggerated remarks about this are to be found in *Reinhold Forster's* notes – as on several, so – on *Hamilton's* Voyage Around the World, Berlin, 1794.
[8] The Chinese troops of the emperor Ch'ien-lung (1736–96) defeated the English who had come to Tibet, expelled them, and pursued them over the Himalayas to Nepal.

activity poor amidst the greatest wealth, tortured by desires, enervated by luxurious sloth, we may die in a nauseating and slow way from the stolen poison.

And if several moderns stain all the sciences with presumptions of such a sort, if they find the whole history of humanity to be aiming at the situation that on no other path than this can the nations experience salvation and solace, should one not here feel most painfully sorry for *our whole species?*

One human being, goes the saying, is for the other a wolf, a god, an angel, a devil. What are the human peoples that affect each other for each other? The negro depicts the devil as white, and the Latvian does not want to enter into heaven as soon as there are Germans there. "Why are you pouring water on my head?" said that dying slave to the missionary. "So that you enter into heaven." "I do not want to enter into any heaven where there are whites" he spoke, turned away his face, and died. Sad history of humanity![9]

[9] At this point in the text there follow several pages of "Negro Idylls" – so titled with bitter irony – based on J. de Crèvecoeur, *Letters of an American Farmer* (London, 1782), and in keeping with the spirit of Herder's preceding critical observations concerning slavery: "The Fruit of the Tree" tells the sorry story of some whites' cruel killing of a negro slave who had dared to defend his fiancée against a white seducer. "The Right Hand" tells the sad story of a noble negro slave verbally intervening to prevent his white master from unjustly killing another slave, receiving in punishment the command that he should perform the execution himself, and cutting off his own right hand rather than do so. The poem is conceived as an example against collaboration. Herder in a footnote likens this noble negro's stance to that of certain Frenchmen who nobly resisted the royal order to kill during the 1572 St. Bartholomew's Day Massacre of Protestants in France. "The Brothers" tells the moving story of a negro slave who was reared with a white man like his brother, and loves him dearly, but who in later years is treated callously by him and attacked by him, and who in the resulting struggle, though winning the upper hand, kills, not the white man, but, in his hurt, himself. A final verse of the poem notes that similar consequences of hurt and even death also result from the imperious treatment of social inferiors by social superiors in Europe. "Zimeo" tells the story of a noble negro slave, Zimeo, who, during a slave revolt against whites in Jamaica plays a bloodless, just, and moderating role. He comes to a plantation owned by whites to whose goodness their negro slaves testify and whom Zimeo therefore warmly praises. He then recounts the pitiful story of having been taken from his home in Africa by slave traders along with his guardian and the latter's daughter, who was by then his own wife and pregnant, and of subsequently being brutally separated from them. However, it turns out that they are on the very plantation in question, and so the poem ends with a joyous and grateful reunion. The poem, told from a white man's standpoint, concludes with his benevolent wish that the reunited family might find their way back home to Africa. "The Birthday" tells of a kindly Quaker who celebrates his birthday by freeing a long-serving negro slave of his on generous terms, and who in the process makes noble remarks about freedom, about God being the father of all men, and against the slave trade. The loyal slave is reluctant to leave his good master, and so the latter proposes that, now free, he should continue to work for him, but now as a well-paid worker and friend – a proposal which the slave gratefully accepts. The poem ends stressing that the Quaker considered his actions to be, not a gift, but simple duty.

[Letter] 115

Certainly a dangerous gift, *power without kindness, inventive slyness without understanding.* The corruptedly cultivated human being wants only *to be able, to have, to rule, to enjoy,* without considering to what end he is able, what he has, and whether what he calls enjoyment does not eventually turn into a killing of all enjoyment. What philosophy will free the nations of Europe from the stone of Sisyphus, from the wheel of Ixion, to which a greedy politics has damned them?

In novels we cry for the butterfly whose wings get wetted by the rain; in conversations we bubble over with great sentimental dispositions – and for this moral corruption of our species, from which all evil arises, we have no eye. We slaughter to greed, to pride, to our slothful boredom a thousand sacrificial victims who do not cost us a single tear. One hears of thirty thousand human beings left dead on the battlefield for nothing as one hears of cockchafers that have been shaken down, of a field of crops ruined by hail, and one will perhaps feel sorrier about the latter disaster than about them. Or one expresses disapproval of what happened in Peru,[10] Ismail,[11] Warsaw,[12] while, as soon as our prejudice, our greed for gain, finds a role in the matter, one wishes something similar and worse with grim anger.

This is indeed how it is. It is a well-known and sad saying that the human species never appears less deserving of love than when it affects one another *by nations.*

But are the machines that affect one another in this way even nations, or does one misuse their name?

Nature begins from *families.* Families combine with each other; they form a tree with twigs, stem, and roots. Each root digs its way into the ground and seeks its nutrition in the earth just as each twig right up to the top seeks it in the air. They do not separate from each other; they do not fall over each other.

Nature has *divided* peoples through language, ethics, customs, often through mountains, seas, rivers, and deserts; it, so to speak, did everything

[10] This refers to the conquest and plunder of Peru by the Spaniards under Pizarro in 1531–3.
[11] Ismail is a port-city on an arm of the Danube that was attacked three times by the Czar's troops during the 1768–74 and 1790–1 Russian-Turkish Wars and destroyed.
[12] During the eighteenth century Warsaw passed from Swedish control to several periods of Russian control, then after a bloody uprising against the Russians in 1794 passed back into Russian control later that same year, before in 1795 becoming a Prussian possession.

Tenth Collection

in order that they should for a long time *remain* separated from each other and become rooted in themselves. Precisely contrary to the world-unifying plan of that *Nimrod*, the languages got confused (as the old legend says); the peoples divided from each other.[13] The diversity of languages, ethics, inclinations, and ways of life was destined to become a bar against the presumptuous *linking together* of the peoples, a dam against foreign inundations – for the steward of the world was concerned that for the security of the whole each people and race preserved *its* impress, *its* character; peoples should live *beside* each other, not mixed up with and on top of each other oppressing each other.

Hence no passions are as mightily effective in everything living as those that aim at *self-defense*. At the risk of her life, with manyfold-multiplied forces, a hen protects her young against vulture and goshawk – she has forgotten herself, has forgotten her weakness, and feels herself only as the mother of her race, of a young people. Thus all nations which get called savages – whether they defend themselves against foreign visitors with cunning or with violence. It is a poor manner of thought that holds this against them, indeed even classifies peoples according to the passivity with which they allow themselves to be deceived and captured.[d] Did their land not belong to them? And is it not the greatest honor that they can accord the European when they consume him at their feast? I do not see why they should believe themselves created in order to stand more precisely recorded in *Büsching's* Geography, in order to delight the idle European in copper engravings, and to enrich the greed of a trading company with the products of their land.

It is hence unfortunately true that a series of works – English, French, Spanish, and German – authored in this presumptuous, covetous conceit, are indeed written in a European manner but certainly not *humanely*. The nation that expresses itself in this without any doubts at all is well known. "Rule, Britannia, rule the waves"[14] – many people believe that with this slogan there is given to them the coasts, the lands, the nations, and the riches of the world. The captain and his sailor are (it is believed) the main wheels of creation by means of which Providence effects its

[d] It seems to me that the letter here takes aim at a passage in [*Henry*] *Home's* history of humanity [i.e. *Sketches on the History of Man* (1774)], which, despite a great wealth of empirical evidence, in several respects may be lacking in firm first principles. In most expeditions of commerce and conquest peoples get ranked in the same way. (Editor's note.)

[13] See Genesis 10–11. [14] Herder writes this in English.

385

eternal work exclusively to the honor of the British nation and for the advantage of the [East] India Company. Such calculations and self-evaluations may serve politically and for the parliament; [but] to the sense and feeling of humanity they are intolerable.ᵉ Absolutely so when we poor, innocent Germans echo the British in this respect – lamentation and misery!

What is a measuring of all peoples *by the measure of us Europeans* supposed to be at all? Where is the means of comparison? That nation which you call savage or barbaric is in essentials much more humane than you – and where it perished under the pressure of its clime, where its senses were unhinged by an organization peculiar to it or by special circumstances in the course of its history, then, however, let each of us beat his own breast and look for the beam in his own brain.¹⁵ All works which nourish the – already in itself intolerable – pride of the Europeans through distorted, unproved, or manifestly unprovable assertions – the genius of humanity throws them back with contempt and says: "An unhuman [*Unmensch*] wrote them!"

You nobler human beings, to whichever people you belong – *Las Casas, Fénelon*, you two good *St. Pierres*, many an honest *Quaker, Montesquieu, Filangieri* – whose first principles aim not at contempt for but at the valuing and happiness of all human nations; you travelers who, like *Pagès*¹⁶ and others, knew how to place yourselves into the ethics and mode of life of several, indeed all, nations, and found it not without value to consider our earth as a sphere on which, along with all the climes and their products, there also must be and will be many kinds of peoples in every condition – representatives and guardian angels of humanity, who is there from your midst, with your beneficent manner of thought, who will give us a *history* of them of the sort that we need?

ᵉ When *Dunbar*, by whom several contributions to the history of humanity are also well known among us [Germans], read the True Basis of Civil Government by D. *Tucker*, a zealous author for the state, he said: "When the benevolence of this writer is exalted into charity, when the spirit of his religion" (he was a priest, Dean of Bristol) "corrects *the rancor of his philosophy*, he will *acknowledge in the most untutored tribes some glimmerings of humanity, and some decisive indications of a moral nature.*" One might wish for many an author this spirit of acknowledging humanity in the human being. (Editor's note.) [Irmischer suggests, plausibly, that the reference here should in fact be to J. Tucker, Dean of Gloucester, *A Treatise of Civil Government* (London, 1781).]

¹⁵ This is of course an echo of Matthew 7:3: "And why beholdest thou the mote that is in thy brother's eye, but considerest not the beam that is in thine own eye?"

¹⁶ P. M. F. de Pagès (1748–93), French explorer. The other men just listed are all discussed by Herder below, and some supplementary information about them will be given in footnotes there.

Editor's[17] *afterword*

Since it might be pleasant for various readers to know something more about the advocates of humanity just mentioned than merely their names, I therefore add this little towards elucidation of the letter.

De Las Casas (Brother Bartolomé),[18] bishop of *Chiapas*, was the noble man who, not only in his short narrative of the destruction of the Indian nation,[19] but also in writings to the highest courts and to the king himself, exposed to light the atrocities that his Spaniards perpetrated against the natives of the Indian nation. People accused him of exaggeration and a heated imagination; but no one convicted him of lying. And why should what gets called heated imagination not rather have been a noble fire of sympathy with the unfortunate, without which he would indeed *not* have written and also not *thus*. Time has justified him and convicted his opponent *Sepulveda* more than himself of untruth. That he did not achieve much with his representations does not reduce his merit; let peace be with his ashes!

*

Fénelon's[20] just and loving manner of thought is universally known. Zealously as he was devoted to his church, and therefore passed harsh judgment on the Protestants[f] because he did not know them, equally did he loathe, even as a missionary for their conversion, their persecution. "Above all," he says to the knight *St. George*, "never force your subjects to change their manner of religious service. A human power is not able to overcome that impenetrable rampart, freedom of the heart. It only produces hypocrites. When kings, instead of protecting it, interfere with commands in the worship of God, then they reduce it to serfdom."

In his *Instruction for Guiding the Conscience of a King*[g] he gives counsels which if they were followed would forestall every revolution. I quote only a few of them, merely as the preceding letter requires them.

[f] This is visible partly in his pastoral writings, partly in the essays of his pupil, the duke of Burgundy.
[g] Directions pour la conscience d'un roi – reprinted in the Hague, 1747. [Originally printed in 1734 with the different title *Examen de la conscience d'un roi*.]

[17] The "editor" here is again Herder himself – this being part of the overall literary fiction of multiple independent letter writers.
[18] Bartolomé de Las Casas (1474–1566), Spanish priest and historian.
[19] De Las Casas, *Brevísima relación de la destrucción de las Indias* [*Short Account of the Destruction of the Indian Nation*] (1552).
[20] F. de Salignac de la Mothe Fénelon (1651–1715).

"Did you thoroughly investigate your state's true need and compare it with the unpleasantness of the levies before you burdened your people with them? Did you not call necessity of the state what only served to flatter your craving for honor? Need of the state what was merely your personal presumption? You must realize personal pretensions only at your own private expense, and at most expect what your people's pure love voluntarily contributes thereto. When Charles VIII went to Naples in order to lay claim to the succession of the house of *Anjou* he undertook the war at his own expense; the state did not believe itself obligated to take this on.

Have you done no injustice to foreign nations? A poor unfortunate comes to the gallows because in deepest desperation he robbed a few talers on the highway; and a conqueror, that is, a man who unjustly takes away lands from his neighbor, gets praised as a hero. To exploit a meadow or a vineyard without permission is seen as an unforgivable sin unless the harm is compensated for; to usurp cities and provinces is assessed as nothing. To take a field away from an individual neighbor is a crime; to take a land away from a nation is an innocent, glory-yielding deed. Where is justice here? Will God judge thus? *Dost thou believe that I will be like thee?* Must one only be just in small things, not in big? Millions of human beings who constitute a nation – are they less our brothers than a single human being? May one do an injustice to millions concerning a province that one might not do to an individual concerning a meadow? If, because you are the stronger, you force a neighbor to sign the peace dictated by you in order to avoid greater evils, then he signs as the traveler reaches his purse to the highwayman because he has the pistol before his chest.

Peace treaties are null and void not only when the dominant power has extorted injustices in them but also when they get cunningly composed in an ambiguous way in order, when the occasion arises, to exploit a favorable ambiguity. Your enemy is your brother – you cannot forget that without renouncing humanity itself. In peace treaties it is no longer a matter of weapons and war but of peace, of justice, humaneness, good faith. To deceive a neighboring people in a peace treaty is more dishonorable and punishable than to cheat a private person in a contract. With ambiguities and insidious expressions in a peace treaty one already prepares the seed for future wars – that is, one brings powder-kegs under houses which one inhabits.

When the question of war arose, did you investigate and have investigated – and this indeed by those with the greatest understanding who least flatter you – what sort of right to war you had? Or did you not have in view in the matter your personal honor – that of finally having undertaken something that would distinguish you from other princes? As though it were an honor for princes to disturb the happiness of peoples whose fathers they are supposed to be! As though a paterfamilias earned respect for himself through actions that make his children unhappy! As though a king should have hopes of glory from any other source but virtue, that is, from justice and from good government of his people!"[21]

These are a few of Fénelon's *thirty-six articles*, which should be a morning and evening lesson for all fathers of a people. His *Conversations*,[22] his *Telemachus*,[23] indeed all his works, are written in the same purpose; the genius of humaneness speaks in them without artificiality or ornamentation. "I love my family," says the noble man, "more than myself; more than my family my fatherland; more than my fatherland humanity."

*

The Abbé *St. Pierre*[24] is, unjustly, known for almost nothing but his project for *eternal peace*[25] – a very goodnatured, indeed noble, weakness, which, though, is not as entirely weakness as people think. In this proposal, as in some others, he was deliberately somewhat pedantic – he repeated himself so that, as he said, if he had gone unheard ten times, he would be listened to the eleventh time; he wrote drily and did not *want* to give pleasure.[h]

There can hardly be a *more decent* manner of thought than that which the Abbé *St. Pierre* expresses in all his writings. Universal reason and justice, virtue and beneficence, were for him the *rule*, the *tendency*, of our species, and its slogan: donner et pardonner, *give* and *forgive*. For this did

---

[h] Generally, he did not think much of mere works of delight; he believed that with our great-grandchildren they would be completely out of fashion. When such a poem was read out to great applause and he was asked what he thought of this work of art, he answered "Eh mais, cela est *encore* fort beau" ["But indeed, that is *still* very fine"] and meant that this *encore* [*still*] would not last for ever. See the Eloge de St. Pierre [Eulogy of St. Pierre] by d'Alembert.

[21] The above title of and quotations from Fénelon's work are here translated from Herder's German, not from the French. The same is true of the quotations from other French authors that follow.
[22] *Dialogues divers entre les Cardinaux Richelieu et Mazarin et autres* (1700).
[23] *Les aventures de Télémaque* (1699).   [24] C.-I. Castel, Abbé de Saint-Pierre (1658–1743).
[25] *Projet pour rendre la paix perpétuelle en Europe* (1713–17).

he read, for this did he look and hear – without presumption. "An inaugural speech on entering the Academy," he said, "deserves to have at most two hours devoted to it; I devoted four to it, and think that is decent enough; our time belongs to the *benefiting* of the state."

Concerning bodily pain, he did not think like a Stoic but considered it a true, indeed perhaps the only, evil, which reason could neither avert nor weaken. Most other evils, he believed, were avertable or merely of an imagined value. To free one's fellow human beings from pain was, in his view, the richest act of beneficence.

"One is not obligated to *amuse* others, but indeed to *deceive* no one" – and thus he strove most strictly for the truth.

Solely occupied with removing what harmed the common good, he was an enemy of wars, of war glory, and of every oppression of the people – but he nevertheless believed that the world had suffered less through the terrible wars of the Romans than through the *Tiberiuses*, the *Neros*. "I do not know," he says, "whether *Caligula, Domitian*, and their kind were gods; only this do I know, that they were not *human beings*. I indeed believe that they may have been sufficiently praised during their lifetimes for the good that they produced; it is only a shame though that their peoples perceived nothing of this good." He often expressed the beautiful maxim of *Francis the First:*[26] "Regents dictate to the peoples; the laws to the regents."

Since he was not permitted to marry, he educated children, without any vanity, solely for usefulness, for benefit. He looked forward to a time when, free of prejudices, the simplest Capuchin monk would know as much as the most skilled Jesuit, and considered this time, however long it might be postponed, to be unpreventable. He accused human beings' sloth and bad habits, but especially despotism, as willful causes of this delay – for even the sciences, he believed, were loved only on the condition that they not benefit the people. Thus did that Carthusian monk, when a stranger praised his Carthusian monastery for its beauty, say, "For passers-by it is certainly beautiful."

St. Pierre saw another cause of the postponement of good in the world in the fact that so few human beings *knew what they wanted*, and among these still fewer had the courage *to know that they know it, to want what they want*. Even concerning the most indifferent things in literature, people, he holds, follow received alien opinions and lack the courage to say what

[26] Francis the First (1515–47), king of France.

they themselves think. To counteract this, he believes, there is only one means: that each man of science should compose *a testament* and at least have the courage to be truthful after his death.

He wrote an essay concerning how "even sermons could become useful," and was especially hostile to the Mohammedan religion because it favors ignorance as a matter of basic principle and makes the peoples animalistic (*abrutiert*).[27]

Christian persecutors, he believed, ought to be brought onto the theatrical stage as fools if people were unwilling to lock them up as lunatics.

At the end of his essays he often put the motto: Paradis aux bienfaisants![28] And it is certain that this man who thought equally [*gleichdenkende*][29] and well [*wohldenkende*][30] right up to his last moment enjoyed this inner paradise. When, in his last breaths, he was asked whether he did not have anything more to say, he said: "A dying man has little to say unless he speaks from vanity or from weakness." During his life he never spoke from these motives – and, oh, might every letter of what he then wrote in a narrow national horizon one day be fulfilled in the widest of scopes! According to his conviction, it will be.[i]

*

His namesake, Bernardin de St. Pierre,[31] a genuine pupil of *Fénelon*, wrote every one of his works right down to the smallest narrative in the spirit of love of humankind and simplicity of heart. He likes to combine nature with the history of human beings, whose goodness he narrates so gladly, and whose badness he everywhere narrates with leniency. "I will think," he says,[j] "that I have benefited the human species if this weak depiction of the condition of the unfortunate blacks can spare them a single crack of the whip, and the Europeans (they who in Europe campaign against tyranny and compose such beautiful moral essays) cease in India to be

---

[i] Oeuvres de morale et de politique de l'Abbé de St. Pierre (Charles Irénée Castel), vols. 1–16, Rotterdam, 1741.

[j] Journey to the Islands France and Bourbon, Altenb[urg], 1774, preface, p. 3. [Original French title: *Voyage à l'isle de France* (1773).]

[27] The German word *abrutiert* comes from French *abrutir*, to make stupid (like a beast, *une brute*).

[28] Paradise for those who do good!

[29] The adjective *gleichdenkend* could mean either (1) thinking the same way, or (2) thinking in an egalitarian way, or (3) (most likely) both.

[30] The word *well* here is meant not only in the sense *properly* but also in the sense *beneficially* (*wohldenkend* in a sense modeled on *wohltuend* = *bienfaisant*).

[31] J. H. Bernardin de St. Pierre (1737–1814), French poet.

the cruellest tyrants." Written in an equally noble spirit are his *Paul and Virginia*, the *Coffeehouse of Surat*, the *Indian Straw Hut*, and the *Studies of Nature*.[k] One lives so gladly with souls of this sort and rejoices that there still exist a few of them.

*

The *Quakers*, whom the letter mentions, bring to mind a series of meritorious men from *Penn* on who have done more for the benefit of our species than a thousand heroes and pompous world improvers. The most active efforts for the abolition of the shameful trade in negroes and slavery are their work – in which connection, still, though, quite generally, Methodists and Presbyterians, all the weak or strong voices from every land when they made some appeal about this to the deafest of ears and the hardest of human hearts, to greedy traders, retain their merit also. A history of the abolition of the trade in negroes and of the discontinuation of slavery in all parts of the world will one day be a beautiful monument in the *courtyard* before the temple of universal humaneness whose construction awaits future times; several names of Quakers will shine on the columns of this courtyard with quiet glory. In our century it seems to be the first duty to banish the spirit of frivolity which destroys everything truly good and great. This the Quakers did.

*

Montesquieu deserved to be named among the advancers of the good of humankind, for his first principles have, beyond fashion, spread good – even given that he may not have attained the level of the *entire* eulogy that *Voltaire* devoted to him.[l] It was not due to the noble man's will; many chapters of his work are, as its motto says, flores sine semine nati, flowers which lacked a ground and genuine seeds; but many of them are salutary flowers and fruits. His *Persian Letters*, his *Treatise on the Greatness and the Decline of the Romans*, indeed even his smallest essays are not lacking

---

[k] Etudes de la nature (Paris, 1776). There is now expected from him a work, Harmonie de la nature pour servir aux éléments de la morale [*The Harmony of Nature as Serving the Elements of Morality*], which can only be written in a good spirit. He behaved wisely during the Revolution.

[l] The eulogy is well known: L'humanité avait perdu ses titres; Montesquieu les a retrouvés. [Humanity had lost its titles; Montesquieu found them again.] Whatever may be said to the contrary, *humanity* owes much to *Voltaire* himself. A series of essays on history, on philosophy and legislation, on the enlightenment of the understanding, etc., sometimes in a mocking and sometimes in a didactic tone, are written *for humanity*. His *Alzire, Zaire*, etc. likewise. (Editor's note.)

in this either. Several chapters of his work *On the Spirit of the Laws* are in everyone's memory. *Montesquieu* had many and great pupils; the good *Filangieri*[32] is among their number too.[m]

Since the preceding letter does not mention the Scots and English, a *Bacon, Harrington, Milton, Sidney, Locke, Ferguson, Smith, Millar,* and others, doubtless because it did not want to repeat a much-praised glory, but by contrast names several Neapolitan authors, let it be permitted to renew the rather forgotten remembrance of a man who in his town before others laid the foundation for a school of *human science* in the true sense of the word: *Giambattista Vico.* An expert on and admirer of the ancients, he followed their footsteps by seeking common first principles in physics, moral theory, law, and international law. *Plato, Tacitus,* and, among moderns, *Bacon* and *Grotius* were, as he says himself, his favorite authors. In his *New Science*[n] he sought the principle of the *humanity of peoples* (dell'umanità delle nazioni) and found this in *foresight* (provvidenza) and *wisdom.* He located all the elements of the science of divine and human things in *cognition, volition, capacity* (nosse, velle, posse), their sole principle being the *understanding,* whose eye is *reason,* illuminated by the light of eternal truth. He founded the chair of these sciences in Naples which was later occupied by *Genovesi, Galanti.*[o] We have received splendid works from this region about the philosophy of humanity, about the economy of the peoples, since the coast of Naples more than any other lands in Italy blesses and values freedom of thought.

[Letter] 116

You wish a *natural history of humanity* written in a purely humane spirit. I wish it too. For we are in agreement that a gathered–together description of peoples according to so-called races [*Rassen*],[33] varieties, modes of play,

[m] System of Legislation, Anspach, 1784. [Original Italian title: *La scienza della legislazione.*]
[n] Prinzipi di una scienza nuova, first published 1725.
[o] Antonio Genovesi, *Political Economy* is familiar in German through a translation; Galanti, *Description of the Two Sicilies* likewise. The former's Storia del commercio della gran Brettagna by Cary, and his textbooks, show just as much knowledge as philosophical and active, citizenly spirit. He also published an edition of Montesquieu with notes. (Editor's note.)

[32] G. Filangieri (1752–88), Italian jurist.
[33] Herder here uses the same word Kant had used in his 1775 essay *Von den verschiedenen Rassen der Menschen,* a founding work in the dubious modern science of racial typology. This is quite striking because when Herder himself talks about "races," as he has sometimes been translated as doing in this volume *faute de mieux,* he virtually always uses the quite different word *Geschlechter*

ways of mating, etc. does not yet deserve this name. Let me pursue the dream of such a history.

1. Above all, let one be *unbiased* like the genius of humanity itself; let one have no pet tribe, no favorite people on the earth. Such a preference often seduces one into ascribing too much good to the favored nation, and too much bad to others. If, in the extreme case, the beloved people were merely a collective name (Celts, Semites, Cushites,[34] etc.) that has perhaps nowhere existed, whose origins and perpetuation cannot be proved, then one would have written at sheer wild random [*ins Blaue des Himmels*].[35]

2. Let one still less contemptuously insult any people that has never insulted us. Even if authors may not hope that the good first principles which they spread will everywhere find quick acceptance, caution against giving rise to dangerous first principles is their greatest duty. People readily draw support from contemptuous judgments about other peoples in order to justify dark deeds, savage inclinations. Pope *Nicholas* the Fifth (already a long time ago) gave away the unknown world; he pontifically gave permission to the white and nobler human beings to turn all unbelievers into slaves. We arrive too late with our papal bulls. Kakistocracy[36] maintains its rights in practice without us having to authorize it to do so theoretically and therefore having to invert the history of humanity. Should, for example, someone express the opinion that "if it *can* be demonstrated that no coffee, sugar, rice, or tobacco plantations *can* survive without negroes, then the *legitimacy* of the trade in negroes is simultaneously proved, in that this trade benefits more than harms the whole human species, that is, the white, *nobler* human beings," then a first principle of this sort would immediately destroy the whole history of humanity. Ad maiorem Dei gloriam[37] it would privilege the most impudent presumptions, the cruellest usurpations. Rather, let one not put into the hands of any people on earth on grounds of "*innate superiority*" the scepter over other peoples – much less the sword and the slave whip.

3. The nature–investigator presupposes no *order of rank* among the creatures that he observes; all are equally dear and valuable to him. Likewise the nature-investigator of humanity. The negro has as much right to

(a word which points to common ancestry and culture rather than to racial type). There is therefore in all probability a critical allusion to Kant's essay here.
[34] For the Cushites, see Genesis 10.   [35] Literally: into the sky's blue.
[36] I.e. rule by the worst. (This is presumably another Herderian neologism.)
[37] For the greater glory of God.

consider the white man a degenerate, a born albino freak, as when the white man considers him a beast, a black animal. Likewise the [native] American, likewise the Mongol. In that period when everything was taking form, nature developed the form of the *human type* as manifoldly as her workshop required and allowed. She developed in form, not various *seeds*P (a word which is empty and which contradicts the formation of humankind), but various *forces* in various proportions, as many of them as lay in her type and as the various climes of the earth could develop in form. The negro, the [native] American, the Mongol has gifts, talents, preformed dispositions that the European does not have. Perhaps the sum is equal – only in different proportions and compensations. We can be certain that what in the *human type* was able to develop on our round earth has developed or will develop – for who could prevent it from doing so? The original form, the *prototype of humanity* hence lies not in a single nation of a single region of the earth; it is the abstracted concept from all exemplars of human nature in both hemispheres. The *Cherokee* and the *Huswana*,[38] the *Mongol* and the *Gonaqua*,[39] are as much letters in the great word of our species as the most civilized [*gebildetste*] Englishman or Frenchman.

4. Each nation must therefore be considered solely *in its place with everything that it is and has* – arbitrary separatings, slingings into a confused jumble, of individual traits and customs yield no history. With such collections one enters into a charnel house, an equipment and clothes closet, of peoples, but not into living creation, into that great garden in which peoples grew up like plants, to which they belong, in which everything – air, earth, water, sun, light, even the caterpillar that creeps[40] upon them and the worm that consumes them – belongs to [*gehört zu*][41] them.q *Living domestic management* [*Haushaltung*] is nature's concept, as

---

P The author of this letter has sketched on this subject a special essay, which does not belong here, however. (Editor's note.) [See *Ideas for the Philosophy of History of Humanity*, bk. 7.]

q That collections of separate peculiarities of the human species can here and there, in this respect and that, be used as inventories, as repertoires, the author of this letter did not mean to deny; only as such they are still no history. (Editor's note.)

38 It is uncertain to whom this word refers, but presumably an African tribe.

39 This is a tribe of Hottentots in south and southwest Africa described by Levaillant.

40 Reading *kriecht* for *kriegt*. (The latter would mean "wages war.")

41 This last occurrence of the expression *gehören zu*, in contrast to the previous one in this sentence, adds to the idea of *participation in* which is present in both cases; also the ideas that everything is *owned by* and *required for* peoples (the expression being able to bear all three of these senses).

in the case of all organizations [*Organisationen*],[42] likewise in the case of
multiform humanity. Suffering and joy, lack and possession, ignorance
and consciousness, stand beside each other in the great domestic man-
ager's [*Haushälterin*][43] book and are calculated to balance each other.

5. Least of all, therefore, can our *European culture* be the measure of
universal human goodness and human value; it is no yardstick or a false
one. European culture is an abstracted concept, a name. "Where does it
exist entirely? With which people? In which times?"[44] Moreover (who
can deny it?), there are so many shortcomings and weaknesses, so many
twistings and horrors, bound up with it that only an unkind being could
make these occasions of higher culture into a collective condition of our
whole species. The culture of humanity is something different; it shoots
forth everywhere *in accordance with place and time*, here more richly and
more luxuriantly, there more poorly and meagerly. The genius of human
natural history lives in and with each people as though this people were
the only one on earth.

6. And it lives in it *in a human way*. All separatings-off and dissections through which the character of our species gets destroyed yield
semi-concepts or delusive ones, speculations. The *Pescherah*[45] is a human
being too; likewise the *Albino*.[46] *Manner of living* (habitus) is what defines
a kind; in our diverse humanity it is extremely various. And yet in the end
everything is linked to a few points; in the greatest variety the simplest
order shows itself. The *negro* reveals himself in his footstep, as does the
Hindu in his finger-tip; likewise both of them in love and hate, in the
smallest and the greatest occupation. A penetratingly perceptive being
who knew every possible alteration of the human type according to situations on our earthly sphere in a genetic manner would easily discover from
a few given characteristic marks *the totality of the entire conformation and
of the entire manner of living* [habitus] *of a people, of a tribe, of an individual*.

Faithful travel descriptions lead to this recognition of the humanity
in the human being much more surely than do systems. I was happy
that your letter[r] named among those who have transposed themselves

[r] Letter 115.

[42] In Herder, as here, this word usually connotes the physical constitution of an organism.
[43] I.e. nature's (hence feminine like *die Natur*).
[44] The closing (emphatic) quotation mark is omitted in Irmischer's text. Its position here is therefore conjectural.
[45] This is a name given to the native tribes of Tierra del Fuego by the French explorer Bougainville.
[46] This name was applied by the Portuguese to white negroes on the coast of Africa.

deeply into the ethics of foreign peoples *Pagès* too.[s] Let one read his depictions of the characters of several nations in America,[t] of the peoples
in the Philippines,[u] and the judgments that he passes here and there on
the behavior of the Europeans towards them, how he sought to, so to
speak, incorporate into himself the manner of thought of the *Hindus*, of
the *Arabs*, of the *Druse*, etc. even through participating in their manner of
living.[v] – Travel descriptions of such a sort – of which (let us be thankful to
humanity!) we have many[w] – expand our horizon and multiply our sensitivity for every situation of our brothers. Without losing a word about this,
they preach sympathy, tolerance, forgiveness, praise, pity, many-sided culture of the mind, satisfaction, wisdom. Certainly, in travel descriptions too,
as on travels, each person seeks his own thing. The base person seeks bad
company, and of course among a hundred nations one will be found there
that favors *his* prejudice, that nourishes *his* delusion. The noble human
being everywhere seeks the better, the best, just as the drawer chooses pic-
turesque regions. This person will notice originally good but misused first
principles even behind the veil of bad habits, and will garner even from the
abyss of the ocean not slime but pearls. – A classification of travel descriptions, not, as might be entertained, only according to noteworthy features
of natural history, but also according to the inner content *of the travel
describers themselves*, to what extent they had a pure eye and in their breast
universal natural and *human sensitivity* – such a work would be very useful
for the distracted flock of readers who do not know right from left.[x][47]

[s] De Pagès, Voyage autour du monde [Journey Around the World], Berne, 1783.
[t] Pp. 17, 18–62.   [u] Pp. 137–48, 155–95.   [v] Vol. 2.
[w] Among many others I name *G. Forster's* and *Levaillant's* – by the latter especially his more
recent travels. The first principles which rule in them concerning how human beings and animals
should be considered and treated provide a *hodopaedia* [education in journeying] which especially
the English seem to lack. Their judgments about foreign nations always betray the *divisum
toto orbe Britannum* [the Briton divided from the whole sphere of the earth] if not indeed the
monarchic merchant; whereas a describer of travels ought actually to have no exclusive fatherland.
(Editor's note.)
[x] Who could provide this work better than *Reinhold Forster?* – even if he only wanted to add his
judgments to an already-printed list of travel descriptions. (Editor's note.)

47 Herder at this point inserts in the main text a longish poem "The Forest Hut [*Die Waldhütte*]"
(explanatorily subtitled: "a mission-narrative from Paraguay"), based on a narrative by the Austrian
missionary M. Dobritzhofer. In the poem a missionary comes upon a remote family of native
Americans – mother, son, and daughter – who are living in idyllic isolation. He persuades them
to come with him. After some initial resistance from the mother, they do so. But they suffer from
the loss of their home. The two women die. The son is then visited at night by visions of his
mother and sister telling him to be baptized because they will fetch him to them soon. To his
delight, the missionary promises to baptize him. On the very day that he is baptized he dies. The
poem concludes with a verse reproaching the missionary for having uprooted the family contrary

[Letter] 117

Certainly, it is not a matter of indifference *according to which first principles* peoples take effect on each other; and yet is there not a history of peoples which lacks *all* first principles about the behavior of the nations towards each other? Is there not another history in which the *most harmful* first principles are set up as just and praiseworthy measures? It is precisely for this reason that some people do not know why they should only condemn the behavior of the Europeans towards the negroes and savages, because after all similar first principles seem to govern in the *whole history of peoples* with more or less modifications.

Most wars and conquests in all parts of the world – on what bases did they rest?, which first principles guided them? Not, as might be assumed, only those rovings of the Asiatic hordes, but also most of the wars of the Greeks and Romans, of the Arabs, of the barbarians. Most definitely the persecutions of heretics and the crusades, the Europeans' behavior towards witches and Jews, their undertakings in both Indias.[48] – How one regrets in all this many a great man who performed almost superhuman deeds as a man deceived, as a madman! With the noblest soul he became a stormer and robber of the world who for the most part also harvested a poor reward for his deeds from courts that were as ungrateful towards him as they were barbaric towards the peoples. One is astonished at the presence of mind that *Vasco da Gama, Albuquerque,*[49] *Cortes, Pizarro,* and many under them displayed in circumstances of the greatest danger; pirates and highwaymen often displayed the same thing. But who that is not a Spaniard or Portuguese will dare to make the deeds of these heroes, of *Cortes,* of *Pizarro,* or of the great *Albuquerque* before *Suez, Ormuz, Calicut, Goa, Malacca,* into the subject of a hero-poem, and to praise still now the first principles that were in force *then?*[y] The eulogists of St. Bartholomew's Night,[50] of the murders of Jews are covered with reproach and shame; it is to be hoped that the robbers and murderers of the peoples too will – despite all their demonstrated heroic deeds, merely

---

[y] One of our poets [i.e. J. F. W. Zachariä] tried it with *Cortes,* but he wisely stopped.

   to the mother's initial resistance, and enjoins, "Oh let, / though, each plant bloom where it blooms!"

[48] I.e. India and America, the land of American Indians.

[49] A. d'Albuquerque (1453–1515), Portuguese navigator and viceroy in India.

[50] On St. Bartholomew's Day in 1572 there occurred in France a government-instigated massacre of Protestants.

and solely in accordance with the first principles of a pure *human history* –
some day stand covered with the same.

The same thing applies to the first principles concerning what one considers permitted to oneself in war. If plundering, mutilating, raping, poi-
soning of wells and of one's weapons are recognized as dishonorable means
of warfare, are not domestic incitements of subjects who do not belong
to the army, Vendée wars,[51] plans for the starvation of nations, faithless
pretenses just as much so? Everyone loathes the plans of *Albuquerque*, who
wanted to turn the whole of *Egypt* into a desert by having it deprived of the
Nile, who wanted to plunder *Mecca* and *Medina*, lands that were involved
in no war with the Portuguese. – Such atrocities against foreign, peaceful peoples, implantings of faithlessness in the hearts of one's enemy,
etc. in the end punish themselves. He who conducts simultaneously both
an open and a secret war usually relies so much on the efficacy of his secret
means that the open ones go awry for him as well. Instigation and betrayal
rarely rewarded their authors otherwise than with loss and shame. He who
pushes aside first principles on which alone still rests what remains of peoples' honor and good name in war poisons the wells of history and of the
international law of peoples right down to the last drop.

It would yield a sad overview if one went through each written history
of peoples in their wars and conquests, in their negotiations, in their plans
for action, *according to the first principles* on which their action and writing
took place. How much more honorable were our ancestors, the ancient
barbarians, who in their duels not only saw to equality of weapons, but also
shared position, light, and sun without bias. How much more honorable
are the savages in their negotiations and peace treaties, in their barter
and trade! Force and arbitrariness may command concerning things over
which they have power, but not concerning *first principles of right and
wrong in human history*.[z52]

---

[z] Concerning the Romans' manner of thinking about this in their best times let one read *Lipsius*
(Doctrina politica [i.e. *Politicorum sive civilis doctrina* (1747)], with its commentary), *Grotius*
(De jure belli et pacis [1625]), or even the good *Montaigne* ([Essais (1580),] bk. 1, chs. 5, 6).
It is very shaming for our times. (Editor's note.)

[51] On 10 March 1793 there erupted in the Vendée region of southwest France a royalist rebellion
against the revolutionary regime in Paris.

[52] Herder at this point inserts in the main text several poems, on themes related to the points just
made, which are omitted here. "The Hun Prince" tells of a prince of the Huns from whom the
Tatars demand his best horse. His captains want to fight, but he says that it is not worth it for a
horse, and gives up the horse. The same thing happens with his fairest woman. Then the Tatars
demand his land, and, while the captains are by now ready to give this up as well, the prince says

[Letter] 118

Since presently during the most accursed war, in which an *early* peace proves so difficult, there is much talk of plans *for eternal peace*, I communicate to you a real attempt made with this purpose in the words of the man who reports it.[53]

On eternal peace (an Iroquois arrangement)

"The Delawares formerly lived in the region of Philadelphia and beyond that towards the sea. Thence did they often conduct attacks on the villages of the Cherokees, mingle unrecognized in their dances at night, and suddenly murder many during these. Still more severe and older were

that this affects not only himself but also the state, and consequently calls for battle. Battle takes place and the prince and his captains not only keep the land but also win back his horse and woman. "The War Prayer" tells of a sheikh and his vizier who go off to fight a war with the former's brother. On the way, they stop and pray at a saint's grave. The sheikh asks the vizier what he prayed for, and the latter says that it was for the sheikh's victory. The sheikh replies that he himself prayed that God should give victory to his brother if He considers the latter more deserving of it than himself. "Kahira" tells of a queen of the Berbers, Kahira, who, intuiting the imminent fall of her realm, laments the failure of her previous generosity to appease the enemy, and tells her people to bury their treasure, which is attracting the enemy, in the ruins of their houses and so achieve peace through poverty. Her people obey, but in vain: The enemy returns, even stronger than before. She sends off their leader, whom she has captured, asking him to treat her sons as well as she has treated him, and then she calls to battle. She and her Berber realm perish – however, not her generosity, in return for which the enemy leader honors her in his good treatment of her sons. "Law in War" tells a story about Mahmud Ghashnawi (the leader of a Turkish-Persian state who conquered and plundered in Iran, Afghanistan, and northern India in the eleventh century). A poor Indian comes to Mahmud complaining that a powerful man from Mahmud's army has come to him demanding his wife and house. Mahmud tells the poor Indian to come back when the man returns – which eventually happens. Mahmud then goes to the poor Indian's house with his bodyguards, and orders that the lights be put out and the man killed. Afterwards he calls for light again, and then falls down in prayer and asks for food. He explains: he had thought that only one of his own sons or favorites would have been bold enough to be so unjust, and it was for this reason that he had had the lights put out, so that they would not blind the judge's eye; but, fortunately, the guilty party was not one of those, and so, having fasted for days out of anxiety, he can now at last eat again. The poem concludes with praise of Mahmud's strict justice, humanity, and piety. "Law at Sea" tells the story of a ship facing disaster in a stormy sea. The ship's captain sails into the enemy's harbor and surrenders in order to save his men's lives. The commander of the harbor says that they have come to him as unfortunate human beings, and that they should repair their ship and leave freely – only if captured at sea would they be his captives. "The Deceived Negotiator" tells the story of an invitation extended by the leader of the French forces in Canada to the chiefs of the Iroquois to attend peace talks. A missionary in good faith urges the chiefs to attend, which they do. But the French leader has them chained and sent to the galleys. The Iroquois nation is outraged. Their elder goes to the missionary and tells him that he knows him to be innocent but that, because others in the nation think otherwise, he should flee to safety. He then gives him an escort to accompany him over the border to safety. The poem concludes with the warm judgment on this elder: "Noble man!"

[53] I.e. G. H. Loskiel (1740–1814), a bishop in Pennsylvania.

the wars of the Delawares with the Iroquois. According to the Delawares' assertions *they* were always the victors over the Iroquois, so that the latter eventually realized that if the war continued longer the inevitable consequence must be their complete destruction.

So they sent representatives to the Delawares with the following message: 'It is not good that all the nations conduct war, for that will eventually lead to the destruction of the Indians. We have therefore thought up a means for preventing this evil – namely, that one nation should be the *woman*. This one we plan to put in the middle; but the other warring nations should be the *men* and live around the woman. No one should touch the *woman* or do her any harm; and if anyone did so then it is our plan to speak to him immediately and say to him: "Why are you hitting the *woman*?" Then all the *men* should attack *him* who has hit the *woman*. The *woman* should not go to war but as far as possible try to preserve peace. Hence if at some time the *men* around her are at blows with each other and the war threatens to become severe, then the *woman* should have the power to address them and say to them: "You men, what are you doing that you belabor each other about with blows in this way? Just remember that your wives and children are bound to die if you do not stop. Do you, then, want to be responsible for your own annihilation from the face of the earth?" And the *men* should then pay heed to the *woman* and obey her.'

The Delawares put up with becoming the *woman*. Now the Iroquois put on a great celebration, invited the Delaware nation to it, and gave an emphatic speech to the Delaware nation's authorized representatives which consisted of three main propositions. In the first proposition they declared the Delaware nation to be the *woman*, which they expressed through the sayings 'We dress you in a long woman's skirt that reaches down to the feet and ornament you with earrings,' and thereby let it be known to them that from now on they should no longer occupy themselves with weapons. The second proposition was formulated as follows: 'We hang a gourd-bottle with oil and medicine on your arm. With the oil you should clean the ears of the remaining nations so that they pay heed to good and not to evil; but the medicine you should use on such peoples as have already entered on foolish paths so that they come to their senses again and turn their hearts to peace.' The third proposition, in which they assigned the Delawares agriculture as their future occupation, was expressed as follows: 'We hereby give into your hand a maize stalk and a hoe.' Each proposition was reinforced by means of a belt of wampum[54] (belt of mussel-shells). Since then these belts have been carefully preserved and their meaning has been repeated from time to time.

Since this strange peace treaty the Delawares have been called *sister-children* by the Iroquois; the three Delaware tribes call each other *fellow female playmates*. But these titles are only used in their councils and when they have something important to say to each other. From the time in question the Delaware nation has been the *woman who preserves peace* into whose care the great belt of peace is given and to whom the chain of friendship is entrusted. It is her duty to watch over this so that it is preserved unharmed. According to the Indians' representation, the middle of the chain rests on her shoulder and is held firm by her; the remaining Indian nations hold onto the one end, and the Europeans onto the other."[aa]

Thus the *Iroquois*. There were times in Europe when *hierarchy* was supposed to play the role of this *woman*.[55] Hierarchy too wore the long dress; oil and medicine were in her hand. People blame her for, instead of administering her office of peace, often herself having stirred up and fanned wars between the men; at least her oil has not yet cleaned the ears of the peoples, her medicine has not yet cured the sick.

Should we, instead of this hierarchy, put women's clothes on a *real* nation in the middle of Europe and bestow on it the office of a judge over peace? Which nation?

But how could this nation administer the office, when world-devastating wars often get waged over a few furs on the Hudson Bay, over a few villages on the Paraguay river (about whose position even those waging the war themselves have sometimes been in error), over a harbor location in the Pacific ocean, over governors' teasings of each other? Indeed, how often did these wars result from a whim of the monarch, from a base cabal of the minister! A history of the *true* origins of the wars in Europe since the crusades would be a sevenfold *Hudibras*,[56] the basest satirical poem that could be written. In a world where dark cabinets initiate and continue wars, all the efforts of the *peace woman* would be lost.

[aa] Loskiel's *Missionsgeschichte in Nordamerika* [*Mission-history in North America*], p. 160. [I.e. *Geschichte der Missionen der evangelischen Brüder unter den Indianern in Nordamerika* (1789).]

[54] Herder writes "belt of wampum" in English.
[55] Herder is referring to the "hierarchy" of the Catholic church in the middle ages.
[56] Herder is alluding to S. Butler's comic epic *Hudibras* (1663–78).

Unfortunately, even with the savages themselves this arrangement did not achieve its purpose for long. When the Europeans pressed closer, at the demand of the men even the *woman* was supposed to participate along with them in the defense. It was their intention, as they expressed it, first of all to shorten her skirt, then to take it away entirely and put the war ax in her hand. A foreign, unforeseen dominant force disturbed the beautiful project of the savages for peace among each other; and this will always be the case as long as the tree of peace does not bloom for the nations with firm, inextirpable roots *from within to outside*.

How many other means human beings have already tried to put a stop to war-thirsty nations and to block their paths. Huge walls were erected between mountain ranges,[57] intervening lands were turned to desert, intimidating fables were thought up and planted in this desert. In Asia a *holy realm* was supposed to set a limit to the rovings of the Mongols;[58] the *great Lama* was supposed to be the peace woman. In Africa obelisks and temples[59] became the *sanctuaries* of trade, the mothers[60] of legislations and colonies. In Greece *oracles*,[61] *Amphiktyonic Councils*,[62] the *Panionium*,[63] the *Panaetolian League*,[64] the *Achaean League*,[65] etc. were supposed to effect, if not an eternal, then at least a long peace – with what success time has taught. It would be best if, as in that well-known trading in the interior of Africa, the nations were *not themselves allowed to see each other at all*. They set down their wares and move off, offer and exchange. Catching sight of each other, deception and quarreling are unavoidable. – My great *peace woman* has a different name. Her medicine takes effect late, but surely. Allow me for this another letter.[66]

[57] Herder is referring to the Great Wall of China.
[58] Irmischer plausibly interprets this as an allusion to the introduction of Lamaism in Tibet and Mongolia in the sixteenth century.
[59] I.e. those of Pharaonic Egypt.   [60] Reading *Mütter* for *Mutter*.
[61] Herder is thinking especially of the oracle of Apollo at Delphi.
[62] The Amphiktyonic Council was a league of Greek tribes and cities responsible for the shrines at Delphi and Delos.
[63] The Panionium was a shrine of Poseidon at Priene, center of the twelve Ionian city-states.
[64] The Panaetolian League was a political league among the Aetolians.
[65] The Achaean League was a league of twelve cities of the Achaeans in the northern Peloponnese.
[66] Herder at this point inserts in the main text a poem based on M. Rauhfrost, *Reden Al Hallils* (1781): "Al Hallil's Address to his Shoe [*Al Hallils Rede an seinen Schuh*]." This is omitted here. In the poem the man Al Hallil goes with his people into a bloody battle. But he has misgivings about killing, which he expresses to God. He treads in a bog and his shoe will not come out again. As the battle rages around him, he addresses his shoe: He recalls how it had avoided with him the paths of violence and wickedness, instead going gentler ways, in particular at night to his beloved. He says that he follows his shoe's present advice to continue now too avoiding the path of violence.

[Letter] 119

My great *peace woman* has only a single name: she is called *universal justice, humaneness, active reason.*

I have read a very ingenious manuscript[67] in which the following propositions formed the basis of human history: 1. Human beings die in order to make room for human beings. 2. And since fewer of them die than are born, nature makes space by violent means. 3. To these belong not only plague, bad harvest, earthquakes, earth revolutions, but also people revolutions, devastations, wars. 4. Just as one animal species reduces the other, so the human species sets itself in proportion and wards off overpopulation. 5. Hence there are in it *preserving* and *destroying* characters. – Terrible system, which instills in us horror and fear at our own species in that according to it we have to look everyone in the face, at his gait, and at his hands to see whether he is a carnivorous or a herbivorous animal, whether he bears in himself a *preserving* or a *destroying* character. Nature has certainly not denuded us of means for securing ourselves against this *destroying* kind of our own species; only she gave us these means not as weapons in our hands but in our heads and hearts. *Universal human reason and justice* is the matron who bears oil and medicine on her arm, a harvest stalk in her hand, not, as might be thought, only as symbols but as the quietly effective means if not for an eternal peace then certainly at least for a gradual diminution of wars. Let us,[68] since we here find our way onto the honorable *St. Pierre's* paths, also not be ashamed of his method, and direct the great *peace woman* (pax sempiterna)[69] to her office with firm first principles. Her function, in accordance with her name and her nature, is to inculcate *dispositions of peace.*

First disposition: Horror of war

War, when it is not forced self-defense but a mad attack on a peaceful, neighboring nation, is an inhuman, worse-than-animal thing to start, in that it not only threatens the nation that it attacks, in its innocence, with murder and devastation, but also sacrifices the nation which conducts it

With bitter irony, he wishes the violent heroes well in their violence – may lions roar in honor of these heroes' victories, may the tiger sharpen his claws, killed armies sing, snakes hiss in ruined homes. But he also asks the quiet moon and the peaceful night, which these heroes disturb, not to shine on them or embrace them.

[67] This has not been identified.

[68] Omitting Herder's redundant and ungrammatical *mich*.   [69] Eternal peace.

just as undeservedly as terribly. Can there be a more horrible sight for a higher being than two armies standing in opposition to each other which without having suffered abuse murder each other? And in the train of war, more terrible than war itself, come diseases, military hospitals, starvation, plague, robbery, violence, desolation of lands, degeneration of minds into savagery, destruction of families, spoiling of ethics for long generations. All noble human beings should spread this disposition with warm human feeling, fathers and mothers should imbue their children with their own experiences on the subject, so that the terrible word 'war' which people articulate with such ease not only becomes hateful to human beings but people, with the same horror as in the case of St. Vitus's Dance, plague, famine, earthquake, the black death, hardly dare to name it or to write it.

Second disposition: Reduced respect for heroic glory

The disposition must spread more and more that the land-conquering *heroic spirit* is not only an angel of death for humanity but also in its talents does not remotely deserve the respect and glory that get paid to it due to tradition, from the Greeks, Romans, and barbarians on down. However much presence of mind, however much comprehensive carefulness and foresight and rapid vision it may require, the noblest hero will before and after battle not only lament the business to which he sacrifices his gifts but also readily confess that in order to be a *father of a people* there are required, if not more, then certainly nobler gifts in *ongoing effort* and a *character* – a *character* that neither owes its battle prize to a single day nor shares it with chance or blind luck. All men of understanding should unite to blow away the false sparkle that dances around a *Marius, Sulla, Attila, Genghis Khan, Tamerlane* until in the end songs to them and to Lips Tullian seem to every educated [*gebildeten*] soul to be equally heroic.[70]

Third disposition: Horror of false statecraft

More and more there must be an unmasking of the *false statecraft* that places a regent's glory and his government's fortune in expansion of borders, in capturing or seizing foreign provinces, in increased income, sly negotiations, in arbitrary power, cunning, and deception. The *Mazarins,*

---

[70] Lips Tullian was the leader of a notorious band of robbers that plagued Germany in the sixteenth and seventeenth centuries. He was executed in 1715.

Louvois's, du Terrai's,[71] and their kind must appear as they are not only in the eyes of the decent people but also in those of the weaklings themselves, so that it becomes as clear as one-times-one that every deception of a false statecraft in the end *deceives itself.* The universal voice-vote must be victorious over the value of mere *state rank* and of its *emblems,* even over the most seductive tricks of vanity, even over early-imbibed prejudices. It seems to me that already now people have advanced far, and perhaps too far, in contempt for some of these things; the crucial thing is that people also properly respect what deserves to be valued in everything that the state imposes on us, and all the more highly so the more it advances the humanity of human beings.

Fourth disposition: Purified patriotism

Patriotism must necessarily more and more clean and purify itself of dross. Every nation must learn to feel that it becomes great, beautiful, noble, rich, well ordered, active, and happy, not in the eyes of others, not in the mouth of posterity, but only in itself, in its own self; and that both foreign and late respect then follows it as the shadow follows the body. With this feeling there is necessarily bound up horror and contempt for every empty invasion of your people into foreign lands, for useless interference in foreign quarrels, for every empty aping and participation that disturbs our business, our duty, our peace and welfare. It must become ridiculous and contemptible when native inhabitants quarrel with each other, hate each other, persecute each other, vilify each other, and slander each other over foreign affairs which they neither know nor understand, in which they can change nothing, and which are none of their business at all. They must appear as foreign bandits and assassins who from mad passion for or against a foreign people undermine the peace of their fellow brothers. People must learn that they can be something only in the place in which they stand, where they *should* be something.

Fifth disposition: Feeling of justice towards other nations

On the other hand, every nation must gradually come to feel it as unpleasant when another nation gets disparaged and abused; there must gradually

---

[71] These were all politicians under French absolutism who were notorious for their unscrupulous exercise of power.

awaken a *common feeling* so that every nation feels itself into the position of every other one. People will hate the impudent transgressor of foreign rights, the destroyer of foreign welfare, the brazen abuser of foreign ethics and opinions, the boastful imposer of his own advantages on peoples who do not want them. Under whatever pretext someone steps over the border in order to cut off the hair of his neighbor as a slave, in order to force his own gods upon him, and in order in return to steal from him his national sacred objects in religion, art, manner of representation, and mode of life – he will find in the heart of *every nation* an enemy who looks into his own breast and says: "What if that happened to me?" – If this feeling grows, then there will arise imperceptibly an *alliance of all civilized* [gebildeten] *nations* against every individual presumptuous power. One can certainly count on this quiet league earlier than on a formal agreement between cabinets and courts in the manner envisaged by *St. Pierre*. One may expect no steps of progress from cabinets and courts; but even they must in the end, without knowing it and against their will, follow the *voice-vote of the nations.*

Sixth disposition: Concerning presumptions in trade

Humane feeling grows loudly indignant against impudent presumptions in trade as soon as innocent, slavish nations get sacrificed to it for a profit which they do not even receive. Trade should, even if not from the noblest motives, *unify* human beings, not divide them; it should teach them to know their common and individual interests at least as children, even if not in the noblest profit. That is why the ocean is there, that is why the winds blow, that is why the rivers flow. As soon as a single nation wants to shut off the sea from all others, take the wind away from them, for the sake of its proud greed, then, the more insight into the *relation of peoples to one another* increases, there must awaken the indignation of all nations against [such] a subjugator of the freest element, against the robber of every highest profit, the presumptuous possessor of *all* the treasures and fruits of the earth.[72] No foreign drop of blood will willingly flow to serve this nation's pride, its greed, the more that an excellent man's true proposition gets acknowledged: "*that the interests of the trading powers do not conflict with each other, and that on the contrary these powers would*

[72] Herder is again using brachylogy here: "there must awaken" is really short for "the more there must awaken."

*have the greatest advantage from a reciprocal universal prosperity and from
the preservation of an uninterrupted peace.*"[bb]

Seventh disposition: Activity

Finally, the *maize stalk* in the *Indian woman's* hand is itself a weapon
against the sword. The more human beings come to know the fruits of a
useful activity and learn to realize that by the war ax nothing is won but
much devastated; the more the shaming prejudices about a caste born for
war with a divine calling, a caste in which from father Cain, Nimrod, and
Og to Bashan[73] and on *hero's blood* is said to flow, become contemptible
and ridiculous – then the more respect will the corn wreath, the apple-
and the palm-twig receive in preference to the sad laurel that grows beside
dark cypresses and, along with nettles and thorns, loves only lizards and
owls[74] among it.

The gentle spreading of these first principles is the *oil* and the *medicine*
of the great peace goddess *Reason* from whose language no one can in the
end escape. Imperceptibly the medicine takes effect, gently the oil flows
down. Reason steps up softly to this people and that and speaks in the
language of the Indians: "Brother, grandson, father, here I bring you a
sign of alliance, and oil and medicine. With this I want to purify your eyes
so that they see clearly; with it I want to clean your ears so that they hear
rightly; I want to smooth your throat so that my words go down fluidly –
for it is not for nothing that I come; I bring words of peace."

[bb] Pinto, *Über die Handelseifersucht* [*On Jealousy in Trade*], translated in the *Sammlung von Aufsätzen,
die größtenteils wichtige Punkte der Staatswissenschaft betreffen*, Liegnitz, 1776. The author of the
aforementioned essay prefaced it with the following passage from *Buffon*: "These times in which
the human being loses his inheritance, these barbaric centuries in which everyone perishes, always
have war as their harbinger, and begin with famine and depopulation. The human being, who
is only able to accomplish anything en masse, who is strong only in unity and combination with
others of his kind, who is happy no otherwise than through peace, is insane enough to arm himself
for his disaster, and to fight for his destruction. Stimulated by an insatiable greed, blinded by a
still more insatiable craving for honor, he renounces the sensations of humaneness, applies all his
forces against himself, strives the one to ruin the other, and in the end causes his actual destruction.
And after these days of blood and murder, when the fog of glory has disappeared, he with a sad
eye sees the earth laid waste, the arts buried, the nations weakened, his own happiness in ruins,
and his true power destroyed."

[73] These are all characters in the first four books of the Old Testament.

[74] The unusual words which Herder employs here, *Lacerten und Bubonen*, are in part chosen in order
to conjure up images of military hospitals (*Lazarette*) and *bubonic* plague.

And the addressee will answer: "Sister, this *string of wampum*[75] is meant to welcome you. I want to extract from your feet the thorns which may possibly have penetrated for your distress. I want to dispel the fatigue that has come upon you on your journey so that your knees become strong and courageous again. The red war ax and the club should be buried in the earth and we mean to plant over them a tree that should grow right up to the heavens. Our friendship should last for as long as sun and moon shine and rise and set, for as long as the stars stand in the heavens and the rivers flow with water."[cc]

If, as I almost believe, an eternal peace will only be *formally* made at the day of judgment, then nonetheless no first principle, no drop of oil, is in vain that prepares for it even if only at the remotest of distances.

[Letter] 120

Every encouragement to good dispositions without taking anxious consideration of the *formality of their execution* is a [mere] sermon of consolation. Often the stupid man says "When will, when can, this happen?" and does nothing at all about it. Often he commits himself too early and too exactly to the definition of the formalities of the outcome, and in the process forgets the essential factor of the means for helping to promote this outcome. Many historical examples show this clearly.

For example, in the old writings of the Hebrew nation beautiful wishes and plans for the future were planted. Hopes of a great light that should shine for all peoples, of a bond of friendship that should encompass all nations, of a religion that would be written into the heart, of a golden peace in which everyone would participate, shone like a rosy dawn. As soon as the spirit of the prophet, his purpose, and the ruling disposition of his speech went unrecognized in these plans and presentiments, when people clung to the letter and defined the fulfillment *formally*, then stupidities came to light – reveries with each one of which people deviated that much further from the meaning of the prophecy the *more formally* they defined.

It was no different in Christianity when people hoped for the visible *coming of the Lord.* In all fanatical sects that wanted to bring about the

---

[cc] Sheer expressions used by the American Indians in their peace treaties and in the consecration of their *peace woman.*

75 Herder uses English for the words italicized.

thousand-year realm it was no different. With many a new philosophy, I fear, it is precisely the same way. How close to the fulfillment people have believed themselves to be with some systems, and how terribly they were deceived! The shining peak that people saw close in front of them moved further and further off. Then in that case the deluded person gives up all hope and lets his hands sink.

Spreaders of good dispositions, do not harm them, do not harm yourselves, through designation of something external that can only be defined by time and by circumstances! Plant the tree; it will grow of itself; earth, air, sun will afford it flourishing. Secure good first principles; they will take effect through their own force – but not otherwise than with modifications which only time and place can give them and will give them.[76]

[Letter] 121

If *human* [menschliche][77] *dispositions* should govern in a single field of science, then it is in the field of *history*. For does this not narrate human actions? And do these not decide the value of the human being? Do these not form our species' happiness and unhappiness?

People say "History narrates *events* [*Begebenheiten*]" and are almost inclined to look upon these as involuntary, indeed as inexplicable, as they in the darkest centuries – did not look upon but – wondered at natural events.[78] A stirred-up war or revolt is for common history like a storm, like an earthquake; those who stirred it up are considered as scourges of the deity, as mighty wizards – and that is enough!

A history of this kind can prove the *cleverest* or the *stupidest* depending on the spirit of the author.

It proves the *stupidest* when it admires everything in a so-called great and divine man, and does not venture to bring any of his undertakings to

---

[76] Herder at this point includes in the main text three poems, again based on material from the book *Reden Al Hallils*, which are omitted here: "The Prince" is a poem in praise of a noble, God-sent prince who seeks the happiness of peoples as a father, not wealth or praise; whom the wicked avoid; and who has only wisdom and love of humankind near his throne influencing him. "Glory and Contempt" is a meditation on the rapid change that befalls people in the valley of human error: fired imagination turns cold, admiration turns into contempt, the lucky conqueror loses his luck and his following, idols engender enthusiasm but then fall into neglect. By contrast, the pious man seeks only *God's unchanging* glory and good. "Al Hallil's Lament" is a lament to a pure, angelic man, Humane (the name is of course significant), who took care of princes and poor alike, but who has now died.

[77] Or: humane.   [78] This sentence is another example of Herder using deliberate anacoluthon.

a measuring-gauge of human reason. Several Oriental histories of *Nadir Shah*,[79] *Tamerlane*,[80] etc. are written in this way – we read a loud eulogistic epic happily woven through with a barren or horrible series of deeds.

Europe has warmly sympathized with this Oriental taste, not, as one might think, only in the times of the crusades, but also in most biographies of individual heroes, in the history of whole sects, dynasties, and *dynastic wars*. One is astonished when one perceives the author's reverence and devotion to his honored subject, and one can only say: "He has drunk from the cup of oblivion; demons' wine has befogged his senses."

The *cleverest* history of this kind is the coldest, as *Machiavelli* practiced and regarded it for example. This too forgets about right and wrong, vice and virtue, in that, cleanly, like a geometer, it measures out the result of given forces and, moving forward, calculates a plan.

That there is much to learn from this *Machiavellian* history when it sees sharply and calculates correctly there is no question. Does it not occupy itself with the most tangled, important problem that our species faces? [That is,] *human forces in relation to their effects and consequences.*

And if only this problem could be cleanly solved! On the stage of the earth, even in its narrowest corners, so much runs confusedly together; opposed forces disturb each other; and circumstances, time, fortune, thousand-armed coincidence interfere in everything. The cleverest got cheated; the coolest head missed his goal. Hence this school of instruction often becomes a *novelistic school* in which people lend the fortunate hero a cleverness that he did not possess and calculate backwards from dazzling successes by a false calculation; or it becomes, when the best forces fail through a coincidence, a depressing lesson, a *school of despair*. Quite generally, though, this whetstone of cleverness easily makes the mind too sharp, too nicked.

Who can read *Machiavelli's Prince* without horror? Even if he were successful in everything, would he be a worthy prince? Would he be happy in his breast? It is terrible to consider humanity only as a *line* that one may bend, cut, lengthen, and shorten to a goal as one wishes so that a plan gets achieved, so that the task just gets solved.

Hence we cannot cut ourselves off from *human feeling* when we write or read history; history's highest *interest*, its *value* rests on this human sensibility, the *rule of right and wrong*. Whoever writes merely for cleverness

[79] Nadir Shah (1688–1747), Shah of Persia.　　[80] Tamerlane (1336–1405), Mongolian conqueror.

easily falls into delusive conceit; whoever writes only for curiosity writes for children.

But what defines this rule of right? Here also there is a history that is too *warm* and one that is too *cold*.

The overheated kind claims to effect everything *for the honor of God* and permits itself wickedness and nonsense in the interest of this supposed goal. Thus did *Tamerlane* subjugate half a world in order to spread the Mohammedan faith, and at the most advanced old age wanted in addition to wage war on peaceful China. Thus did the nations of Europe march to the holy grave; thus did the Spaniards strangle in America; thus did the Inquisition torture and persecute. Terrible passions of human beings covered themselves with the cloak of God and destroyed and tormented.

The cold history calculates under the rule of an alleged positive law *according to reasons of state* – and in its observation of this rule it too often becomes very warm. In it *good of the fatherland, honor of the nation* becomes the battle cry and in deceptive negotiations the state's slogan. The Athenians, the Romans – what did they not include in the *good of their fatherland*, in their *glory*, and hence in their *right*? What did the pope, the clergy, the Christian kings not permit themselves in the interest of the alleged good of their realms? If history narrates all this indifferently, or even trustingly, credulously, then with it one enters into a labyrinth of the most tangled, most loathsome state interests, of personal presumptions, and of state trickeries. A large part of the events of our last two centuries – the so-called memorabilia (mémoires), biographies, political testaments – are written in this cast of mind, in the spirit of *Richelieu*, of *Mazarin*, and still earlier of *Charles V, Philip II, Philip the Fair, Louis XI, XIII, and XIV*, in short, in the spirit of *Spanish-French policy of state*. An awful spirit that considered everything permitted to itself for the good of the state, that is, for the glory and the greater power of kings, for the security and greatness of their ministers! In whatever history this spirit shows through it blackens what is most brilliant with the shadow of vanity, of deceptive cunning, of presumption, of waste. Forgotten in this spirit is humanity, which, according to it, lives merely *for the state*, that is, for kings and ministers.

We have gradually escaped from this fog too – but another dazzling phantom rises in history, namely, the *calculation of undertakings towards a*

future better republic, towards the best form of the state, indeed of all states.[81]
This phantom is uncommonly deceptive in virtue of the fact that it obviously introduces into history a nobler yardstick of merit than the one that
those arbitrary reasons of state contained – indeed even blinds with the
names of 'freedom,' 'enlightenment,' 'highest happiness of the peoples.'
Would God that it never deceived! The *happiness of one single people* cannot be imposed onto, talked onto, loaded onto the other and every other.
The roses for the wreath of *freedom* must be picked by a people's own
hands and grow up happily out of its own needs, out of its own desire
and love. The so-called *best form of government*, which has unfortunately
not yet been discovered, certainly does not suit all peoples, at once, in
the same way; with the yoke of badly imported freedom from abroad a
foreign people would be incommoded in the worst possible way. Hence
a history that calculates everything in the case of every land with a view
to this utopian plan in accordance with unproved first principles is the
most dazzling *deceptive history*. A foreign varnish that robs the forms of
our world and the preceding world of their true stance, even of their outlines. Many works of our time will be read twenty years later as well- or
badly-intentioned fever fantasies; maturer minds already now read them
that way.

Thus history is solely and eternally left with nothing but the spirit
of its oldest author, *Herodotus*, the unstrained, gentle *sense of humanity*.
Without bias he regards all peoples and sketches each one in *its* place,
in accordance with *its* ethics and customs. Without bias he narrates the
events and observes how everywhere only *moderation* makes peoples happy
and every arrogance has its *Nemesis* following behind it. This *measure of
Nemesis*, applied according to subtler or greater conditions, is the sole and
eternal yardstick of all human history.

"What you do not want to have happen to you, do unto no other";
revenge comes, indeed it is present, with every erring, with every wickedness. All bad relations and injustices, every proud presumption, every
hostile incitement, every faithlessness has its punishment with or after it;
the later, the more terrible and strict. The guilt of fathers piles up with
crushing weight on children and grandchildren. God has not permitted
human beings to be vicious except under the hard law of punishment.

[81] As Irmischer suggests, this is probably an allusion to Kant's *Idea for a Universal History from a
Cosmopolitan Point of View* (1784).

On the other hand, in history the smallest good wins its reward too. No reasonable word that a wise man ever spoke, no good example, no ray even in the darkest night was ever lost. Unnoticed it had continuing effect and did good. No blood of the innocent man got spilt in vain; every groan of the oppressed man rose towards heaven and found in its time a helper. Tears too are in time's sowing seeds of the happiest harvest. The human species is *a single whole*; we work and suffer, sow and harvest, for one another.

How compassionate, how gently encouraging, but also how strict and tallying-together [*zusammenhaltend*], this spirit of human history is! It leaves each people right where it is – for each has *its* rule of right, *its* measure of happiness, in itself. It spares all and spoils none. If the peoples sin, then they atone – and atone as long and heavily as it takes until they sin no longer. If they are unwilling to be children, then nature raises them as slaves.

This spirit of history steps destructively in the way of no political constitution. It does not cave in the peaceful man's house over his head before another, better one exists; but with a friendly hand shows the overly secure man mistakes and inadequacies in his house, and with quiet industry delivers materials for supporting the old house or for building a better one.

It does not touch national prejudices – for many good dispositions must grow within them as husks or hard shells. It lets them grow. When the fruit is ripe, then the husk withers, the shell splits open. It is fine by this spirit if the Frenchman and the Englishman depict their humanité and humanity[82] for themselves in English and French;[83] all the less will the foreigner chase after them to his own ruin. From *his* heart must proceed forth a beloved who is appropriate *for him*.

Holiest to the spirit of human history are good-natured fools and dreamers; for they stand under the most special divine protection. Without enthusiasm nothing great or good happened on earth; those whom people considered dreamers have performed the most useful services for the human species. Despite all mockery, despite every persecution and contempt, they made their way ahead – and when they did not reach their goal, still they reached *further* and brought [others] *further*. They were living winds over the stagnant marsh – or they dammed it

[82] Herder gives this word in English.
[83] Note that with the third pairing here Herder once again uses the rhetorical figure of chiasmus.

and made it yield a harvest. The spirit of history never permits itself empty mockery of them; at most it will feel sorry for them, not stigmatize them.

All excessively subtle taxonomies of human beings according to principles from which they are supposed to act exclusively are quite foreign to the spirit of history. It knows that in human nature the principles of *sensuality*, of *imagination*, of *selfishness*, of *honor*, of *sympathy with others*, of *godliness*, of the *moral sense*, of *faith*, etc. do not dwell in separated compartments, but that in a living organization that gets stimulated from several sides many of them, often all, cooperate in a living manner. It allows each of them its value, its rank, its place, its time of development – convinced that all of them, even unconsciously, are operating towards *a single* purpose, the great principle of humaneness [*Menschlichkeit*]. Hence it lets all of them bloom in their time right where they are: *sensuality* and *the arts of the imagination, intellect and sympathy, honor, moral sense and holy worship*. It as little forces the stomach to think as the head to digest, and torments no one with the analysis whether even each bite of bread that he puts in his mouth yields a universal basic moral law of all rational beings in chewing and digesting. Let each person chew as he can – history treats human beings not as word-mongers and critics but as agents of a moral law of nature which speaks in all of them, which initially warns gently, then punishes harder, and richly rewards every good disposition through itself and its consequences. Does this *spirit of human history* not appeal to you?[84]

[Letter] 122

You seem to believe that no history of humanity takes place as long as the *result of things* is not known, or, as people are wont to put it, the day of judgment has not yet been experienced. I am not of this opinion. Whether the human species improves or worsens, whether it some day turns into angels or demons, into sylphs or gnomes – we know what we must do. *We* consider the history of our species in accordance with firm first principles in our conviction about right and wrong – let our species' final act end as it will.

---

[84] This paragraph is of course a critique of Kant's moral philosophy, and in particular its doctrine of the categorical imperative.

For example, *Monboddo* in his history and philosophy of the human being[dd] regards him as a system of living forces in which the elemental aspect, the plant-life, the animal-life, and the life of the understanding are distinct. The animalistic life, he opines, was in its best condition when human beings lived in an animal-like manner. He still finds a similarity to this in the case of children. He considers the ages that the human being passes through as an individual to be also the course taken by the whole species. He therefore traces the species back to its first, naked condition in the open air, in rain, in cold, and shows what effects clothing, living in houses, the use of fire, language have had on the human creature. He shows the abilities that this creature had to swim, to walk upright, to undertake forms of training, and discerns in this condition the basis of that longer life, of that greater form and strength, of which the legend of the primal world tells us. He demonstrates from examples and reports how the human being's body got weakened, shrunk, and his life shortened through change in his way of life, through the eating of meat and the drinking of alcoholic beverages, through his sedentary mode of life in arts, trades, games, through finer foods, pleasures, and pastimes. – On the other hand, he shows how the human being's understanding has increased through society and arts; how the sagacity of a natural human being differs from the cleverness of the civilized man; how all arts arose from imitation and the idea of the beautiful belongs solely to the civilized condition. He finds nations, families, and individuals distinguished in both ages of humanity, but our species overall in the course of a *reduction of animalistic forces*, and he has given reminders about this, which each person should apply as he wishes and can.

If we acquiesce in all this (since in truth *Monboddo's* system certainly does not deserve to be ridiculed on account of a few idiosyncrasies of the author), if we assume – what history teaches us as well – that almost all peoples on earth once lived in a more primitive condition and culture was brought only by a few to others, then what follows from this?

1. *That on our round earth all epochs of humanity still live and function.* There exist there peoples in childhood, youth, manhood, and will probably do so for a long time to come before the seafaring old men of Europe succeed in advancing them to old age through brandy, diseases, and slaves'

[dd] Ancient Metaphysics, vol. 3, London, 1784. This part of the great work would certainly deserve a German epitome for the sake of its collected facts. (Editor's note.)

arts. Now just as every duty of humaneness commands us not to disturb for a child, for a youth, his age in life, the system of his forces and pleasures, likewise it also commands nations such a thing vis-à-vis nations. In this regard several conversations of Europeans, especially missionaries, with foreign peoples, for example, Indians, Americans,[85] please me greatly; the naivest answers full of good heart and sound understanding were almost always on the side of the foreigners. They answered with childish pertinence and correctness, whereas the Europeans, with the imposing of their arts, ethics, and doctrines, for the most part played the role of worn-out old men who had completely forgotten what was appropriate to a child.

2. Since the distinction between elemental, animalistic, vegetative, and understanding's forces is only a thought, in that every human being consists of all these, albeit in different proportions, *let one beware of considering this or that nation to be entirely animalistic* in order to use them as beasts of burden. The pure intellect needs no beast of burden; and hence just as little as even the most intellectual European can do without plant- and animal-forces in his life-system does any nation completely lack understanding. Certainly, the understanding is multiform in regard to the sensuality that stimulates it in accordance with peoples' varying organizations;[86] however, in all forms of humankind it is and remains only *one and the same*. The *law of justice* is foreign to no nation; all nations have atoned for the transgression of this law, each one in its own way.

3. If intellectual forces in greater development are Europeans' advantage, then *they can demonstrate this advantage in no other way than through understanding and goodness* (the two are at bottom but one). If they act impotently, in raging passions, from cold greed, in basely insolent pride, then *they* are the animals, the *demons*, against their fellow human beings. And who guarantees the Europeans that things cannot and will not go for them at several ends of the earth as [they did] in Abyssinia, China, Japan?[87] The more their forces and states in Europe age, the more unhappy Europeans some day leave this part of the world in order to make common cause with the oppressed in this place and that, then

---

[85] I.e. native Americans.

[86] By "organizations" Herder here again means something like *physical constitutions* of human organisms.

[87] Herder is here referring to the persecutions of Christians that occurred in the countries mentioned in the sixteenth century.

intellectual and animalistic forces can unite together in a way that we now hardly suspect.[88] Who has insight into the seed of the future that is perhaps already planted? Cultured states can arise where we hardly believe them possible; cultured states which we considered immortal can wither.

4. If in Europe, on paths that we are unable to identify, reason should at some point gain so much value that it united with human goodness, *what a beautiful season for the members of the society of our whole species!* All nations would participate in this and rejoice in this *autumn of sensibleness.* As soon as in trade and treatment [*Handel und Wandel*][89] the law of justice governs everywhere on earth, all nations are brothers; the younger will gladly serve the older, the child the old man possessed of understanding, with what he has and can.[ee]

5. And is this time unthinkable? It seems to me that *even on the path of necessity and calculation it is bound to appear. Even our excesses and deeds of vice must advance it.* There would have to be no rule governing in the conditions and relations [*Verhältnissen*] of the human species, no nature governing in its nature,[90] if this period were not brought about *through inner laws of this species itself and the antagonism of its forces.* – Certain fevers and stupidities of humanity *must* cease their ferment with the advance of the centuries and the life-ages.[91] Europe *must* give compensation for the debts that it has incurred, make good the crimes that it has committed – not from choice but according to the very nature of things. For reason would be in a bad way if it were not reason everywhere, and the universal good were not also the universally most useful. The magnetic needle of our efforts seeks this pole; after all wanderings and oscillations it will and must find it.

[ee] Among many others, I remind the reader here once again of *Levaillant's* more recent journey. The distinction which he notes between nations that have been corrupted or are mistreated by Europeans and autonomous peoples is sharply incisive. His first principles concerning how one should deal with the latter are applicable on the whole earth.

[88] This sentence is another example of Herder using anacoluthon.

[89] The idiomatic phrase *Handel und Wandel* generally means either *trade* or general *behavior*. Here Herder combines both senses. In addition, though, he seems to be re-etymologizing the phrase to connote a bit more elaborately: (1) trade (*Handel*), (2) behavior (*Wandel*), and (3) travel (*Wandel* again, cf. the verb *wandeln*).

[90] This is another example of Herder using deliberate oxymoron (the superficial inconsistency masking a deeper consistency, as usual).

[91] I.e. the life-ages of humanity (the latter's history being viewed as like a single human life writ large, as in *This Too a Philosophy of History for the Formation of Humanity*).

6. *So let no one augur from the greying of Europe the decline and death of our whole species!* What harm would it do to the latter if a degenerated part of it perished?, if a few withered twigs and leaves of the sap-rich tree fell off? Others take the place of the withered ones and bloom up more freshly. Why should the western corner of our northern hemisphere alone possess culture? And does it alone possess it?

7. *The greatest revolutions in the human species so far depended on inventions or on revolutions of the earth.* Who knows these in the unforeseeable sequence of times? Climates can change; many an inhabited land can become uninhabitable, many a colony can become the motherland, from several causes. A few new inventions can cancel many older ones; and since in general the greatest effort (undeniably the character of almost all European statecraft) must necessarily relax or trip, who can calculate the consequences of this? Our earth is probably an organic being; we creep about on this orange like small, scarcely noticeable insects, torment each other, and settle here and there. The proverb says, "When the sky falls, what happens to the sparrows?" If the orange goes rotten here or there, perhaps another generation makes its appearance – without it therefore being the case that the first one perished precisely due to the intellectual part of its system, due to *understanding*. What was rather able to kill it was excess, vice, misuse of its understanding. Certainly, the periods of nature are calculated with an eye to each other in regard to *all* species, so that when the earth can no longer warm and feed human beings, human beings will also have fulfilled their destiny on it. The bloom withers as soon as it has finished blooming – but it also leaves behind fruit. Thus if our destiny were the highest expression of intellectual force, then precisely this destiny would demand of us that we leave behind a good seed to the future aeon unknown to us, so that we might not die as weakly murderers.

Monboddo regards our earth as an educational institution from which our souls get saved. The individual human being can and may regard it no differently, for he comes and passes. In the place where, without his own volition, he makes his appearance he must cope as well as he can and learn to order the system of *his* elemental and vegetative, *his* animalistic and intellectual, forces. Gradually they die for him until the developed spirit flies off. – Here too *Monboddo's* system is consistent – a system which, incomplete as it is, I prefer to many another *mercantile-political* history of humanity. Mercantile-political considerations belong to a history of our species only as a fragment; this history's spirit is sensus humanitatis,[92] *sense and sympathy for the whole of humanity*.[93]

[Letter] 123

From early years I have tried to put myself into the position of even the most alien hypotheses, and I returned from almost all of them with the gain of a new side of the truth, or of its reinforcement. But I must confess that I can extract nothing good at all from the hypothesis[94] of a *radical wicked basic force in the human mind and will*.[ff] I leave it to everyone who is fond of it; it brings no light to my understanding, no happy stirring to my heart.

The hypothesis of two mutually hostile basic causes of things is usually traced back to the Persians;[95] but its bad application should not be traced back to them. In physics it was obviously the *childhood* of science when night was declared to be bad, day to be good; the laws that produce *both* are good and extremely simple. In morals they are so just as much; and the philosophy of the Persians aimed directly at explaining this. Darkness, it said, is formlessness; light, according to its nature, forms, illuminates, and warms. Despite all his resistances, Ahriman[96] is weak; Ormazd[97] will and must overcome him. Their religion consequently called on people to join this battle for victory, as the real work of human life, in thoughts, words, and deeds. To create and spread forth light, to be effective in every

[ff] It is not here a question of so-called original sin – for this is an illness. (Editor's note.)

[92] Sense of humanity.

[93] Herder at this point includes in the main text three more poems based on the book *Reden Al Hallils* which are omitted here: "The Spirit of Creation" tells the story of a pilgrim suffering in the desert who prays to God for help. An oasis appears; he drinks and eats, and then falls asleep. The spirit of creation comes to him in a dream and tells him to arise so that a doe can now in her turn enjoy the same relief. He arises and sees the doe, a mother, which then happily jumps to feed. The poem ends with the pilgrim praising God for caring for all things, great and small. "The Sequence of Time" reassures the dissatisfied man that God created his creatures to live in bliss. After the creation, the angels wondered at this hopeful scheme. The poem concludes enjoining human beings to have confidence in it and to enjoy the fairest gift of a satisfied heart. "The Antidote" praises God's gifts and the wisdom with which he distributed them. The earth was given to imperfect human beings, not to angels, and so vice thrived. But God provided an antidote: work, industriousness. By contrast, idleness leads to vice and unhappiness.

[94] The hypothesis was Kant's in his *Religion within the Bounds of Reason Alone* (1793).

[95] I.e. to Zoroastrianism in the first instance, and then later Manichaeism. Cf. Herder's *Oldest Document of the Human Species* (1774).

[96] Ahriman is the spirit of evil in Zoroastrianism.

[97] Ormazd is the supreme deity, creator of the world, and spirit of good in Zoroastrianism.

good, to purify, to gladden, is *our* work. Precisely for this reason do we stand between light and dark.

Christianity continued on this path with motives that reached deeper down. According to Christianity, the human species is supposed to be no slavish people that eternally bends beneath the yoke and turns at chains, but a free, happy species which, without fear of a ruling executioner-spirit, does good for the sake of good, from inner desire, from innate character and higher nature, whose law is a *sovereign law of freedom*, indeed to which in fact *no* law is given because the *divine nature* within us, pure humanity, has no need of law.

This is unmistakably the spirit of Christianity, its *native* form and character. Only dark, barbaric times gave back the great feudal lord of evil – of whom we are allegedly the innate inherited people, and from whom customs, atonements, and gifts can allegedly free us, not indeed really, but *superficially* – to stupidity and brutality in an anti-Christian way. Who would want to return into this Miltonian hell of palpable night and solid darkness?

On the surface of the earth we see nothing of this massive primal hell. Where there is evil, the cause of the evil is the *corrupted character* of our species, not its nature and character. Sloth, impudence, pride, error, callousness, carelessness, prejudices, bad education, bad habit – through and through evils that are avoidable or curable if new life, diligence for good, reason, modesty, justice, truth, a better education, better habits from youth on, arrive individually and universally. Humanity calls and groans that this might happen, since clearly every unvirtue and unsuitability punishes itself by granting no true enjoyment and piling a mass of evils on itself and on others. We see clearly that we are here in order to destroy this realm of night in that no one can or should do it for us. Not only do *we* bear the burden of our misfortune, but our nature is *arranged* for this and no other work – it is the *purpose* of our species, the goal of our destiny, to free ourselves of this *corrupted character*. When the fruits of the work do not entice us, the whole universe drives us with nettles and thorns. – So what is the meaning of despair, as though under a yoke that could never be cast off? What use is the dream of a humanity from its very roots beyond restoration?

No hypothesis can be dear to us which moves our species out of its position, which now puts it in the place of the fallen angels, now abases it under their guardianship and sovereignty. We are not acquainted with the fallen angels, but we are acquainted with ourselves and know when and why we fell, fall, and will fall.

The existence of each human being is woven together with his whole species. If our concepts concerning our destiny are not pure, what is the point of this or that small improvement? Do you not see that this sick person lies in infected air? – save him from out of it and he will get better automatically. In the case of radical evil, attack the roots; they bear the tree with its top and twigs.

The work is great, but it should also be continued for as long as humanity lasts; it is the most properly own and sole, the most rewarding and happiest, business of our species.

And how does this business get conducted? Merely through expansion and refinement of the *forces of the understanding*? Intelligence is the human being's noble advantage, the indispensable tool of his destiny. Scientific knowledge of everything that deserves to be known, understanding of everything usable, beautiful, and noble is illuminating sunshine in the dark mist-sphere of the earth; it may and must extend as far as it can extend – from the last hazy star over the whole of nature to the borders of creation in becoming.

Understanding is the common treasure of the human species; we have all received from it, we should all contribute to it our best thoughts and dispositions. We calculate with combinations belonging to earlier times; posterity should calculate with our combinations; and certainly this calculation proceeds forth on a large, broad, and infinite scale. Who would undertake to say whither the human species can reach and perhaps will reach in its continued efforts building on one another? Every newly reached power is the root for a countless series of new powers.

However, understanding alone does not do the job; even to demons do we ascribe a demonic understanding; let ours be *human*, accompanied by active goodness. Look around. How much true and genuine science is unused in the world!, how much understanding lies suppressed and buried!, how much other understanding gets misused! Pseudo-truth, rigid prejudice, hypocritical lying, slothful atmosphere, irrational arbitrariness confuse our species. Hence a *strengthened great and good will*, trainings from youth on, fighting-prizes and habituation, so that what is most difficult becomes easiest for us, and above all that indispensable striving for the *necessary* which our species requires, with neglect of everything dispensable and bad – these things alone can *make* the understanding *telling* for the

good, help it to its feet and advance the work. How long have we [not] occupied ourselves with what is useless? Do not millennia of human history
show us our lack of understanding, our childish triviality and cowardice?

The unity of our forces, therefore, the unification of the forces of several
for the advancement of a single whole in the interest of all – it seems to me
that this is the problem that should be our heart's concern, because each
person's innermost consciousness and need says it to him both quietly
and aloud.

"Legislators, educators, friends of humanity," says a noble man of our
nation,[gg] "let us unite our forces in order to prove to the human being that
he will nowhere find inner happiness in the *infinitely various* situations
of life except in the *effective and active unity of his character*. If he strives
for his own perfection, freely and resolutely observes the ordinances of
a universal and beneficent reason, he will escape errings, crimes, inner
reproaches. As a human being and citizen he will find happiness in the
testimony of his conscience. Thus does the human being bring *the infinite
variety of his sensations, thoughts, and efforts to the unity of a true, pure,
effective, moral character.*"

And if I may develop this noble image further, then there lies in the
human species an infinite variety of sensations, thoughts, and efforts towards the unity of a true, effective, purely moral character *which belongs to
the whole species.* Just as each class of natural creatures constitutes a realm
of its own which builds on other realms and is involved in others, likewise
the human species – with the special and highest distinguishing mark that
the happiness of all depends on the efforts of all and occurs in the human
species, despite the greatest variety, only in this very *exalted unity*. We cannot be happy or entirely worthy and morally good as long as, for example,
a single slave is unhappy through human beings' guilt, for the vices and
bad habits that make him unhappy have effect on us as well or derive from
us. The presumption, the greed, the weakliness that deceive and devastate
all parts of the world reside with and in us; it is *the same* heartlessness that
keeps Europe as well as America under the yoke. Whereas, on the other

[gg] Essai sur la science [Essay on Science], [Erfurt,] 1796, by the gentleman coadjutor *von Dalberg*.
In this sketch, as also in the work *Vom Bewußtsein, als allgemeinem Grunde der Weltweisheit* [*On
Consciousness as the Universal Basis of Philosophy*] (Erfurt, 1793), in the *Betrachtungen über das
Universum* [*Observations on the Universe*] (Erfurt, 1777), and in every smallest essay, the theme
of this work, l'unité composée de l'infini [the composite unity of the infinite], is the content
and symbol, and le caractère vrai, pur, énergique et moral [the true, pure, energetic, and moral
character] is the character.

hand, every good sensation and practice of a human being has effect on all parts of the world as well. The *tendency of human nature* contains within it a *universe* whose inscription is: "No one for himself only, each for all; thus are you all dear to each other and happy." An infinite variety striving for a unity that lies in all, that advances all. Its name is (I wish to repeat this again and again) understanding, justice, goodness, *feeling of humanity*.[98]

[Letter] 124

And why should we conceal a norm of the spread of the moral law of humanity that is so obvious for us? *Christianity commands the purest humanity on the purest path.* Humanly and intelligibly for all, humbly, not with proud autonomy, not even as a *law* but as a gospel of hope [*Evangelium*][99] for the happiness of all, it commands and provides forgiving tolerance, an active love that overcomes bad with good. It does not command this as an object of speculation but provides it as light and life of humanity,[100] through model example and loving deed, through progressively effective *community*. It serves *all* classes and ranks of humanity until in each one of them everything unfavorable withers and falls away in its time of itself. The misuse of Christianity has caused countless evil in the world – a proof of what its proper use can do. Precisely the fact that, as it has thrived, it has so much to make good, to compensate, to indemnify, shows, according to the rule that lies within it, that it must and will do this. The labyrinth of its misuses and errings is not endless; led back to its pure course, it cannot but strive to the goal that its founder already expressed in the name chosen by him, "*son of man* [*Menschensohn*]" (that is, man [*Mensch*]),[101] and in the judgment of the last day. If bad morality is satisfied with the proposition "Each for himself, no one for all!" then the judgment "No one for himself only, each for all!" is Christianity's slogan.[102]

[98] Herder at this point inserts into the main text another poem based on the book *Reden Al Hallils* which is omitted here: In "Joy" the poet enjoins his noble heart to rejoice, since God created the world for joy, his heart is not stained by malice, he has been able to do good to others, and he can look forward to the day of judgment when he will be rewarded for his good deeds.
[99] *Evangelium* means *the gospel*, but etymologically *a good/hopeful message*.
[100] Or possibly: to humanity.
[101] The word *Mensch* has normally in this volume been translated "human being." The switch here to "man" is simply intended to make the biblical quotation recognizable.
[102] Herder concludes with yet another poem based on the book *Reden Al Hallils* which is omitted here: "The Heavenly One" gives praise to Christ, the man who now enjoys heavenly glory; asks for his good will towards doers of good and those in need; notes that it was he who taught humaneness to humankind, and a religion of compassion, gentleness, and forgiveness; and praises him for this.

Index

425

Index

Index

Cambridge texts in the history of philosophy

Titles published in the series thus far

Aristotle *Nicomachean Ethics* (edited by Roger Crisp)

Arnauld and Nicole *Logic or the Art of Thinking* (edited by Jill Vance Buroker)

Bacon *The New Organon* (edited by Lisa Jardine and Michael Silverthorne)

Boyle *A Free Enquiry into the Vulgarly Received Notion of Nature* (edited by Edward B. Davis and Michael Hunter)

Bruno *Cause, Principle and Unity* and *Essays on Magic* (edited by Richard Blackwell and Robert de Lucca with an introduction by Alfonso Ingegno)

Cavendish *Observations upon Experimental Philosophy* (edited by Eileen O'Neill)

Cicero *On Moral Ends* (edited by Julia Annas, translated by Raphael Woolf)

Clarke *A Demonstration of the Being and Attributes of God and Other Writings* (edited by Ezio Vailati)

Condillac *Essay on the Origin of Human Knowledge* (edited by Hans Aarsleff)

Conway *The Principles of the Most Ancient and Modern Philosophy* (edited by Allison P. Coudert and Taylor Corse)

Cudworth *A Treatise Concerning Eternal and Immutable Morality* with *A Treatise of Freewill* (edited by Sarah Hutton)

Descartes *Meditations on First Philosophy*, with selections from the *Objections and Replies* (edited by John Cottingham)

Descartes *The World and Other Writings* (edited by Stephen Gaukroger)

Fichte *Foundations of Natural Right* (edited by Frederick Neuhouser, translated by Michael Baur)

Herder *Philosophical Writings* (edited by Michael N. Forster)

Hobbes and Bramhall on Liberty and Necessity (edited by Vere Chappell)

Humboldt *On Language* (edited by Michael Losonsky, translated by Peter Heath)

Kant *Critique of Practical Reason* (edited by Mary Gregor with an introduction by Andrews Reath)

Kant *Groundwork of the Metaphysics of Morals* (edited by Mary Gregor with an introduction by Christine M. Korsgaard)

Kant *The Metaphysics of Morals* (edited by Mary Gregor with an introduction by Roger Sullivan)

Kant *Prolegomena to any Future Metaphysics* (edited by Gary Hatfield)

Printed in the United States
57158LVS00003B/58-105